Off the
Beaten Path

Off the Beaten Path

A Travel Guide to More Than
1,000 Scenic and Interesting Places
Still Uncrowded and Inviting

Reader's
digest

The Reader's Digest Association, Inc.
New York, NY/Montreal

A READER'S DIGEST BOOK

Copyright © 2009 The Reader's Digest Association, Inc.
Maps © 2009 GeoNova Publishing, Inc.

Project Editor: Siobhan Sullivan
Project Designer: Elizabeth Tunnicliffe
Project Coordinator: Dina Fabry

Contributing Editors: Barbara Booth, Kim Casey, Julienne Marshall, Sharon Fass Yates
Contributing Writers: Peter Benson, Mary Connell, Fred DuBose
Copy Editor: Vicki Fischer
Editorial Assistance: Emily Bigelow, Samuel Chodoff, Fiona Hunt,
      Gesina Phillips, Kathy Triolo
Designers: Patricia A. Halbert, Jill Little, Wayne Morrison
Indexer: Nanette Bendyna

Senior Art Director: George McKeon
Executive Editor, Trade Publishing: Dolores York
Manufacturing Manager: Elizabeth Dinda
Associate Publisher, Trade Publishing: Rosanne McManus
President and Publisher, Trade Publishing: Harold Clarke

The credits and acknowledgments that appear on pages 374-375
are hereby made a part of this copyright page.

Library of Congress Cataloging in Publication Data

Off the beaten path : a travel guide to more than 1,000 scenic and
interesting places still uncrowded and inviting.
      p. cm.
  Newly revised & updated.
  "A Reader's Digest book."
  Includes index.
  ISBN 978-0-7621-0794-0
  1. United States--Guidebooks. I. Reader's Digest Association.
  E158.O33 2009
  917.304--dc22

                              2008037896

A Note to Our Readers

The information for this book was gathered and carefully fact-checked by Reader's Digest
researchers and editors. Since site information is always subject to change, you are urged
to check the facts presented in this book before visiting a destination to avoid any
inconvenience. The Reader's Digest Association, Inc., cannot be responsible for any
changes or for errors or omissions.

We are committed to both the quality of our products and the service we provide
to our customers. We value your comments, so please feel free to contact us.

        The Reader's Digest Association, Inc.
        Adult Trade Publishing
        44 S. Broadway
        White Plains, NY 10601

For more Reader's Digest products and information, visit our website:
www.readersdigest.com

Printed in China

19 18 17 16 15 14 13

Introduction

America's travelers enthusiastically embraced the first and second editions of *Off the Beaten Path*, a unique guide to more than 1,000 of our country's most undervisited, must-see destinations. Now completely revised, meticulously updated, and bigger and better than ever, this exciting new edition is sure to please the guide's legions of fans as well as newcomers to its pages.

As in the first and second editions, we set out to find the most interesting places, coast to coast, that most travelers overlook. Many of the destinations included within these pages are literally off the beaten path. Others are in towns or on main routes but have an unusual appeal: museums featuring old locks, teapots, or antique cars; grand homes with elaborate interiors; historic inns; and much, much more. Well-known places, including national parks, are featured, but the areas highlighted are less frequented by travelers and are interesting in their own right. Each attraction is unusual and compelling, no matter where it is located.

HOW THE BOOK WAS DEVELOPED AND REVISED

In the first and second editions, our editors studied the map and history of every state and made a list of intriguing places that were geographically out of the way or that had subject matter beyond the mainstream. They also chose sites in all parts of each state. For this third edition, we asked tourist boards in each state to confirm that each one of the original sites was still indeed off the beaten path and asked for their suggestions of new, unspoiled gems. With the assistance and recommendation of state travel bureaus throughout the country, we then culled through thousands of brochures, leaflets, and web sites in order to select more than 200 new sites that met the original criteria: appealing and overlooked attractions that travelers shouldn't miss. Once we had settled on the final list of attractions, we sent each of the newly written or revised entries to the sites, where all information was confirmed by a staff member or volunteer.

Every site includes up-to-the-minute tourist information. Every fact has been checked and then rechecked. We have included nearly 400 evocative new photographs and all-new, detailed state maps. For your travel convenience, this new edition also includes phone numbers and web sites, where available, at the end of each entry.

This edition has been scrupulously researched and revised. But careful as we have been, it is possible that you will encounter the unexpected somewhere along the way. Things change: Roads deteriorate or close, opening hours and admission charges are adjusted, services may be curtailed, web site addresses get renamed, places may close down. But if you use this guide in the spirit of adventure (and call ahead to confirm the details of your trip), you are sure to develop a newfound excitement and admiration for this great country of ours.

We are grateful for the help provided by hundreds of people across the country—from travel writers and editors, to state tourist board members, to those at the individual destinations, who offered guidance, photos, and encouragement throughout the project.

—THE EDITORS

Notes on Visitor Information

The icons below are provided at the end of site information, whenever relevant, for easy reference.

Picnicking

Camping/Tenting

Camping/RV Camping

Swimming

Hiking

Bicycling

Canoeing/Rowboating

Fishing

Sight-Seeing/Bird-Watching

Horseback Riding

Skiing/Cross-Country Skiing

Winter Activities

Scuba Diving /Snorkeling

Accessible Facilities

Pet Friendly

Wi-fi Access

Hours of operation, such as Mon.-Fri. Apr.-Oct., are inclusive, meaning Monday through Friday, April through October.

"Twenty years from now you will be more disappointed by the things that you didn't do than by the ones you did do. So throw off the bowlines. Sail away from the safe harbor. ... Explore. Dream. Discover."

—MARK TWAIN

Contents

Alabama

Whether exploring ancient caverns or space travel, visitors have plenty of activities to pick from in Sweet Home Alabama.

Fort Morgan. Re-enactors lock and load at a fort that saw action in the naval Battle of Mobile Bay, fought in the last year of the Civil War (see page 15).

Ancient Native American culture can be explored here in one of the oldest sites of human habitation, a cave discovered by amateur archaeologists just 50 years ago. More geological wonders can be found in Dismals Canyon, complete with its own tiny glowworms.

Inviting hiking trails beckon visitors in a number of parks, including one going over the highest point in the state. Pioneer times are represented by covered bridges, and transportation history abounds in exhibits of cars, planes, and spaceships. Some surprising attractions include a fabulous display of mounted African wildlife and an archaeological site at the state's first capital city.

visit ➡→ offthebeatenpathtrips.com

1 Russell Cave National Monument

3729 CR-98, Bridgeport
Discovered by amateur archaeologists in 1953, this ballroom-size cavern is one of the oldest sites of human habitation in North America. The excavations done here have revealed much about ancient Native American life and culture in the Southeast. A boardwalk allows visitors to experience what it must have been like to enter the cave thousands of years ago.

A small band of nomadic Native Americans discovered the cave about 8,500 years ago and took shelter in it. For about 6,000 years after that it was used almost continuously as a winter refuge by the Native Americans who survived by hunting and foraging. Later, people who had evolved a more complex lifestyle used the cave as a winter hunting camp. From about A.D. 1000, however, when Native Americans had begun to practice agriculture and live in villages, the cave was used only occasionally as a shelter.

A small museum at the visitors center displays weapon points and other tools found at the site.

A short, easily walked trail takes you through the oak-hickory forest. The adjacent cave system has several miles of passageways and caverns, including such attrac-

1 Russell Cave National Monument. This cave sheltered nomadic peoples as early as 6,500 B.C., making it one of the oldest habitation sites in North America.

tions as Waterfall Passage. The park's 310 acres of natural terrain offer trails for hikers. The cavern no longer allows spelunkers.

▶ Open daily except major winter holidays.

www.nps.gov/ruca
(256) 495-2672

2 Madison County Nature Trail

5000 Nature Trail Rd., Huntsville
Set high above the city of Huntsville—atop aptly named Green Mountain—this network of paths in a charming 72-acre park offers the opportunity to observe nature within the southern Appalachians firsthand. On the north side of the 17-acre Sky Lake, along the walking trail, you will come across the original cabin of Charles Green, the homesteader for whom Green Mountain was named.

Overall, about two miles of well-managed trails circle the lake and lead beyond into a woods filled with loblolly pines and hardwoods, like white oak, mockernut hickory, red maple, and black locust. Along the way, some 500 species of trees and shrubs are labeled and identified. You'll also find the state's largest and oldest champion elm tree. One side trail is marked in braille for the blind.

▶ Open year-round except major winter holidays.

www.co.madison.al.us
(256) 883-9501

3 ▶ U.S. Space & Rocket Center

1 Tranquility Base, Huntsville

At this state-of-the-art interactive museum, people of all ages can experience zero gravity, maneuver through space, and travel with astronauts. Out-of-this-world experiences include a step inside the G-Force Accelerator, where bodies actually rise up off their seats, and a genuine blastoff—140 feet straight up in 2.5 seconds—courtesy of the Space Shot. There is even a Mission to Mars, packed with astounding sights, sounds, and physical sensations.

The museum also features dozens of hands-on learning exhibits. Visitors can see inside an authentic *Apollo* Command Module and check out the $200

3 ▶ **U.S. Space & Rocket Center.** The *Pathfinder* space shuttle and Saturn 1B rocket never fail to wow sightseers at Rocket Park.

million *Blackbird,* the sleek U.S. Air Force spy plane that flew coast to coast in less than 68 minutes. Or they can delve into the technology behind the world's first ballistic guided missile and view the latest in high-tech weaponry, including futuristic soldiers armed with particle beam guns. For the youngest aspiring astronauts, a tot-size space station offers rockets for crawling into. And for those who prefer to sit back and be awe-inspired, the Spacedome Theater projects footage of planets, galaxies, and other cosmic amazements, filmed in space by astronauts, onto a 67-foot domed IMAX screen.

Outside the museum, visitors can stroll through what astronaut John Glenn calls the finest rocket collection in the world. Rocket Park boasts more than 1,500 pieces of space hardware, including a Mercury-Redstone rocket, like the one that launched Alan Shepard. The new Davidson Center for Space Exploration is home to NASA's first Saturn V rocket. Next door, Shuttle Park is home to the world's only "full-stack" shuttle.

Alternatively, experience life on Mars in the Olympus Moons Mining Colony. While there, scale a replica of the largest volcanic crater in the solar system, or climb a 25-foot-high wall. (The climb can be strenuous.)

▶ Open year-round except Mon.-Tues. Nov.-Mar. and major winter holidays. Admission charged.

www.spacecamp.com/museum
(256) 837-3400

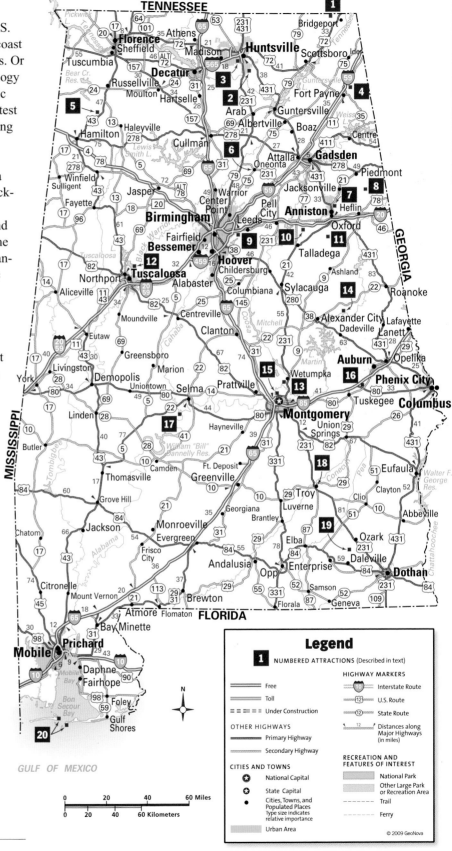

GULF OF MEXICO

Legend

1 NUMBERED ATTRACTIONS (Described in text)

HIGHWAY MARKERS

Free	**10** Interstate Route
Toll	**12** U.S. Route
Under Construction	**12** State Route

OTHER HIGHWAYS
Primary Highway
Secondary Highway

12 Distances along Major Highways (in miles)

CITIES AND TOWNS

⊛ National Capital
⊛ State Capital
• Cities, Towns, and Populated Places Type size indicates relative importance
Urban Area

RECREATION AND FEATURES OF INTEREST

National Park
Other Large Park or Recreation Area
Trail
Ferry

© 2009 GeoNova

0 20 40 60 Miles
0 20 40 60 Kilometers

4 DeSoto State Park Resort

13883 CR-89, Fort Payne

This elaborate complex of recreational and lodging facilities is the nucleus of a 3,000-acre park that stretches for 10 miles along the Little River, the only river in the country to flow its entire course on a mountaintop. The park is named for the Spanish conquistador Hernando de Soto, who in 1540 was the first European to explore the region. Situated on the wooded, undulating terrain of Lookout Mountain, the resort has cabins and camping areas as well as a lodge and an Olympic-size pool.

The area is magnificently scenic. Miles of hiking trails lead to mountain streams, miniature cliffs, mossy glens, and waterfalls. Among the most striking features to be encountered along the paths are huge picturesquely weathered boulders. The park is also noted for its flowering shrubs, and expanses of rhododendron and mountain laurel can be seen at their peak bloom from mid- to late May. A profusion of wild azaleas festoons the Azalea Cascade Trail with delicate clusters of bloom.

Other parts of DeSoto State Park also offer outstanding attractions. At DeSoto Falls, a few miles north of the resort, the Little River takes a 100-foot plunge into a large green lake before continuing its descent through a wide, leafy gorge. At Little River Canyon, the deepest canyon east of the Mississippi, the river makes another spectacular plummet. But the main attraction is the 16-mile-long canyon itself, which, with a depth of some 700 feet, is the deepest chasm east of the Rockies. A two-lane drive hugging the western edge of the rim provides good views. Legend holds that de Soto

4 ▶ DeSoto State Park Resort. The Little River takes a plunge at DeSoto Falls, just one of the natural attractions in a park prized for its wild azaleas and rhododendrons.

searched for gold in the caves along its cliffs.

▶ Open year-round.

www.desotostatepark.com
www.alapark.com
(256) 845-0051

5 Dismals Canyon

901 Hwy. 8, Phil Campbell

Locally, this site is known simply as The Dismals. But visitors should not be put off by the gloomy-sounding name or the unimpressive entry area. In truth the site is a small canyon with an imposing mixture of luxuriant vegetation and intricately eroded cliffs that have won it recognition as a registered natural landmark.

Starting at a waterfall, the 1 1/2-mile-long walking trail follows a boulder-strewn stream and wanders through labyrinthine clefts. Farther on the canyon widens, and its sheer walls are pocked with hollows, marked with striations, and sometimes curiously rippled.

Everywhere, an exuberant, varied growth of trees, shrubs, and vines swarms over weathered, tumbled rocks. Even the stark rock walls of the canyon support pockets of ferns or dizzy ascents of vine.

A possible explanation for the chasm's odd name is that early settlers may have been struck by the subdued quality of the light, which is often blocked by the cliffs and filtered through a canopy of trees. (Among them are some of the country's tallest Canadian hemlocks.)

In any case, it is a place that leads one to observe the ways that the implacable canyon walls check the growth of vegetation. Dismals Canyon also offers a picnic spot and swimming in Dismals Branch, a natural limestone pool.

▶ Open Mar.–Nov. Admission charged.

www.dismalscanyon.com
(205) 993-4559

6 Covered Bridges of Blount County

Oneonta

Lovers of old-fashioned covered bridges can find a trove of these historic spans on the back roads of Alabama, where 10 19th- and early 20th-century examples are still in daily use. Each wooden bridge is unique in style and size, and the oldest predate the Civil War.

A good place to start a tour is Oneonta, the county seat of Blount County and Alabama's Covered Bridge Capital. From Oneonta you can easily drive to three scenic bridge sites. Easley Bridge (1927) is a single-span 95-foot-long tin-roofed bridge over Dub Branch creek in the community of Rosa. Swann Bridge (c. 1933), originally named Joy Bridge, crosses the Black Warrior River; at 324 feet it's the longest of the covered bridges remaining in Alabama. Horton Mill Bridge (1935) also spans the Black Warrior. Rising 70 feet above the river gorge, it's not only the nation's highest covered bridge over water but also the first Southern bridge listed on the *National Register of Historic Places.*

www.blountoneontachamber.com
(800) 252-2262

7 Anniston Museum of Natural History

800 Museum Dr., Anniston

This remarkable museum includes outstanding collections of mounted animal specimens from North

7 ▶ **Anniston Museum of Natural History.** A mounted bull elephant stands next to a baobab tree in the museum.

America and Africa. A bird collection was prepared by the 19th-century ornithologist William Werner, who was a pioneer in the cyclorama style of presentation. The 400-specimen collection, which was assembled between 1865 and 1910, offers a rare opportunity to see now-extinct species, such as the heath hen and the passenger pigeon.

The even more striking African collection is the gift of a local resident who spent years collecting in Africa. Some exhibits concentrate on aspects of animal behavior. Others are panoramic re-creations of the continent's natural environments, such as a Sahara desert landscape complete with oryx, Barbary sheep, and desert snails, and a marshland scene with hippos and egrets. The most outstanding display is a diorama of a grassland showing a giant baobab tree towering over an elephant, a rhino, a giraffe, and many smaller mammals and birds.

The Ancient Egypt exhibit hall features 2,300-year-old Egyptian mummies and mounted specimens of animals representing deities.

▶ Open daily June–Aug. Closed major holidays and Mon. rest of year. Admission charged.

www.annistonmuseum.org
(256) 237-6766 Anniston

8 ▶ Coleman Lake Recreation Area and the Pinhoti Trail

Off Rte. 78, Heflin
Located near the northern tip of the Talladega National Forest, the Coleman Lake Recreation Area lies at the end of a long road that winds through the woodland. A grove of tall pines is dotted with picnic tables set invitingly apart. A section of lakeshore is roped off for swimming, and a bathhouse with showers is on a nearby hill. Bass, shellcrackers, and bluegills are caught in many inlets, and trails circle the lake and lead across wooded hills.

The lake also has an entrance to Alabama's longest hiking route, the Pinhoti Trail. In the Creek language *pinhoti* means "turkey's home," and the hiker does indeed have a chance of seeing wild turkeys. The 135-mile trail, marked with blue blazes that look like turkey tracks, runs mostly along a ridge system in the center of the Talladega National Forest, and it passes through some of the finest wild scenery in the South, skirting the shores of lakes and crossing mountains. Since roads intersect the trail at several points, you can sample it without an overnight outing.

The Pinhoti Trail runs through Georgia and then connects to the Appalachian Trail. These trails are some of the many long paths being connected together to create the Eastern Continental Trail, a continuous footpath that stretches across 16 states, from Florida to Canada.

Spring and fall offer the best weather and are usually less crowded.

▶ Coleman Lake Recreation Area open Mar.–Dec.; Pinhoti Trail open year-round.

www.southernregion.fs.fed.us/alabama
(256) 463-2272

9 ▶ Barber Vintage Motorsports Museum

6030 Barber Motorsports Pkwy., Birmingham
George Barber raced Porsches in the 1960s, picking up more than 60 first-place trophies. That was before he took the helm of his family's business, Barber Dairies, and began building a successful real estate operation. However, the Birmingham businessman's enthusiasm for motorsports never paled, and he became an avid collector of motorcycles.

Today visitors to the 740-acre Barber Motorsports Park can share his passion at one of the country's newest—and, some say, best—motor raceways. The setting itself is exceptional, with trees, gardens, sculpture, wildlife, and rolling hills offering a very different kind of vantage point for car- and bike-racing fans.

Even when no event is scheduled, visitors can tour the museum. Some 650 of Barber's collection of more than 1,100 vintage and new bikes and racing cars, many restored on site, are on show in the spacious five-level facility. Displays are rotated, so returning visitors usually find something new to see. The oldest bike dates to 1902, and the full collection includes bikes from 16 countries and 143 manufacturers.

▶ Open year-round except July 4. Admission charged.

www.barbermuseum.org
(205) 699-7275

9 ▶ **Barber Vintage Motorsports Museum.** A 1956 Maserati 160/T4 Lusso is one of hundreds of motorcycles on display at this tribute to bikes and race cars.

10 International Motorsports Hall of Fame & Museum

3198 Speedway Blvd., Talladega
Established by Bill France, the founder of the National Association for Stock Car Auto Racing (NASCAR), this impressive complex owned by the state is a racing enthusiast's dream.

Adjacent to the museum is the fastest racetrack in the world, Talladega Superspeedway. Home of the NASCAR Sprint Cup Series and the AMP Energy 500 race, this speedway draws shoulder-to-shoulder crowds during race weeks. Enormous showrooms display over 125 racing machines, all in mint condition and valued at more than $15 million.

In addition to record-setting cars raced by legends, the collection features muscle cars, antiques, and classics, as well as assorted motorsports memorabilia dating from 1902. From Sam Packard's 1940 Mercury to Bill Elliott's 1985 Thunderbird, the cars offer a riveting trip through racing history.

A special room honors the men and women behind the wheels, with biographical profiles of more than 100 International Motorsports Hall of Fame inductees—including Henry Ford, Enzo Ferrari, Mario Andretti, Jackie Stewart, and Bobby Unser—as well as the winners of the coveted Driver of the Year Award.

Serious racing devotees will want to take a detour to the McCaig Wellborn Research Library, the most complete motorsports library in existence, housing more than 14,000 books and periodicals, over 10,000 photos, plus a state-of-the-art computer system that is able to retrieve even the most obscure racing facts in a flash.

Beyond cars there's the Cougar Cat Gentry Turbo Eagle, a 54-foot offshore powerboat acclaimed for setting a world-record speed of 148.238 miles per hour in 1987; Bobby Allison's Aerostar, a one-of-a-kind plane powered with Allison turboprop engines; and the Budweiser Rocket Car, a missile on wheels—39 feet long and just 20 inches wide—that broke the sound barrier in 1979 with a record run of 739.666 miles per hour. A combined admission-tour ticket includes a guided van tour of

11 **Cheaha Resort State Park.** Pulpit Rock is a prime place to view (and photograph) the densely wooded slopes of Talladega National Forest.

the world-famous Superspeedway, unless the track is closed for testing or racing events.

▶ Open year-round except major holidays. Admission charged.

www.motorsportshalloffame.com
(256) 362-5002

---

11 Cheaha Resort State Park

19644 Hwy. 281, Delta
This lovely 2,719-acre woodland park occupies the upper slopes of Cheaha Mountain; at 2,407 feet it is the highest point in Alabama. Although you can reach the summit via a short scenic park road off Rte. 49, you can take Rte. 281—Talladega Forest Scenic Hwy.—17 miles to the park.

The narrow blacktop road crosses fields on the valley floor and then immerses you in pine-scented woods, passing small rushing streams. A stone tower at the summit offers a fine view to the distant farmlands, moun-tain ridges, river valleys, and lakes.

Five hiking trails, totaling 7 miles, reveal a diversity of wildlife and panoramic views. There's also a 6-mile mountain-bike trail, and the park is the halfway point in the Cheaha Century Challenge, a 110-mile touring bike race held every May. The Pinhoti Trail covers over 100 miles through the park and surrounding Talladega National Forest, eventually connecting with the Appalachian Trail.

A bronze plaque marks the trail as the end of the Appalachian Mountains. At and near the crest of Cheaha are picnic areas, campsites with hookups and magnificent scenery, a lake with a white sand beach, cabins, chalets, a hotel, a lodge, and several hiking trails, both short and long.

▶ Open year-round. Admission charged.

www.alapark.com
(256) 488-5111; (800) 610-5801

10 **International Motorsports Hall of Fame & Museum.** This 1990 Chevrolet Monte Carlo was driven by none other than racing's perennial champion Dale Earnhardt.

12 Westervelt Warner Museum of American Art

8316 Mountbatten Rd., Tuscaloosa
Perched on a hill overlooking Lake Tuscaloosa, this museum contains a collection of American art that spans three centuries and several different art forms. It is a place to "feel America," according to its founder, Jack Warner, who spent over 40 years collecting the pieces. According to Warner's vision, the collection of more than 400 pieces of artwork encourages viewers—especially young people—to appreciate America's rich history through art.

The museum displays hundreds of paintings and sculptures, in addition to antique handicrafts and artifacts. Exhibits present paintings by artists such as John Singer Sargent, Frederic E. Church, and Mary Cassatt, as well as silver crafted by Paul Revere and furniture made by Duncan Phyfe. Visitors can also see portraits of historical figures such as George Washington, Thomas Jefferson, and Marquis de Lafayette. The museum also regularly hosts events and lectures.

▶ Open Tues.-Sat. Admission charged.

www.warnermuseum.org
(205) 343-4540

---

13 Fort Toulouse–Jackson Park

2521 W. Fort Toulouse Rd., Wetumpka
In 1717, when this region was part of French Louisiana, the French built a fort here near the strategically vital junction where the Tallapoosa and Coosa rivers form the Alabama River. The only serious conflict at this remote outpost came from within, when bored ration-short soldiers mutinied.

The fort was washed away, and in 1751 it was rebuilt and ringed by a palisade of pointed logs.

The French lost the French and Indian War—and the fort—in 1763. It was an overgrown ruin in 1814, when Maj. Gen. Andrew Jackson ordered a larger fort to be built nearby. The Treaty of Fort Jackson, signed here that year, marked the formal end of the Creek War. From the fort, Jackson began his campaign to protect the Gulf Coast from the British—a campaign that ended with their defeat in the battle of New Orleans.

Artifacts found on the site are displayed in the visitors center. The 164-acre park also offers a picnic area, a campground, and a launching ramp. Bass, bream, catfish, and crappies are among the fish that can be caught in the two rivers flanking the park. In a 30-acre arboretum the local shrubs and trees are labeled for identification and benches are placed along the way, offering welcome rest in this humid but lovely subtropical environment. The weather is most comfortable in spring and fall. Fort Toulouse and Jackson Park offer living-history programs, providing insight into the Native American and military history of the site and the lifestyle during the 18th and 19th centuries.

▶ Park and visitors center open year-round; campground open Apr.-Oct. Admission charged.

www.preserveala.org/forttoulousejackson. aspx
(334) 567-3002

---

14 Horseshoe Bend National Military Park

11288 Horseshoe Bend Rd., Daviston
One of the earliest and most crucial clashes between the U.S. government and the Native Americans took place on this site in March 1814. The battle of Horseshoe Bend not only ended the fighting in the nearly two-year Indian Creek War, but it also broke the power of the Native Americans in what is now Alabama, Georgia, and Mississippi.

The battle pitted two strong, shrewd leaders against each other:

14 ▶ **Horseshoe Bend National Military Park.** What's called a "wayside exhibit" enlightens visitors on the final battle of the Creek War, fought here in 1814.

Andrew Jackson, commander of the American forces and future president, and Menawa, a powerful Upper Creek chief. Menawa and his warriors had turned the small peninsula formed by this horse shoe-shaped loop in the Tallapoosa River into a military stronghold.

With the river providing protection on three sides, Menawa and his warriors built a formidable log and earthen barricade across the fourth. In the end, however, Menawa's 1,000 or so warriors, the barricade, and the river could not save the Upper Creek Native Americans from Jackson's army of 3,000 men and 500 Cherokee allies.

The wounded Menawa escaped, but more than 800 of his warriors died in battle; 49 of Jackson's men died, and 154 were wounded.

The small museum in the visitors center contains weapons, historic documents, a diorama showing the storming of the barricade, and an illuminated map tracing troop movements and battle phases. The three-mile drive through the battlefield includes stops at the hill from which Jackson fired 50 cannon rounds at the barricade.

Another stop is the mound on which the Creek prophets (medicine men) performed their prebattle dance to assure Creek warriors that they would be immune to the effects of the army's weapons.

The park has a picnic area by the river, a launching ramp, and several miles of walking trails. The best times to visit are the fall and during the Anniversary of the Battle of Horseshoe Bend in March.

▶ Open daily except major winter holidays.

www.nps.gov/hobe
(256) 234-7111

 Montgomery Zoo. One of the zoo's two white tigers strikes a regal pose.

15 Montgomery Zoo

2301 Coliseum Pkwy., Montgomery

Spanning 40 acres of inviting landscape, this zoo is home to more than 200 distinct species, many of which are endangered. Five realms accommodate more than 500 animals from Africa, Asia, North America, South America, and Australia.

Throughout, natural and hidden man-made barriers replace the iron and concrete of conventional zoos. Lions and cheetahs intently watch their prey (and humans) from rock outcroppings, while tigers take a dip in their own backyard pool.

Visitors can hop aboard a miniature train for a narrated ride, complete with a trip around the zoo's eight-acre Crystal Lake.

Among other highlights, the zoo includes a reptile house, a monkey island, a bald-eagle exhibit, and a North American River Otters exhibit. Volunteers regularly provide live animal demonstrations.

The Montgomery Zoo is also involved in species repopulation programs—one of which has released more than 17 golden eagles—and offers educational and wildlife conservation programs.

Leave time to stop at The Mann Wildlife Learning Museum, where visitors can see more than 270 wildlife displays, hear animal sounds, feel bear fur,

and wonder at fossils of giant prehistoric creatures.

▶ Open year-round except major holidays. Admission charged.

www.montgomeryzoo.com
(334) 240-4900

♿

16 Tuskegee National Forest

East of Tuskegee

In the mid-1770s one of America's first artist-naturalists, William Bartram, passed through here on an epic journey recording the flora and fauna of the Southeast. Today the 8¹/₂-mile Bartram National Recreation Trail is a major feature of this protected woodland.

It is fitting that the pathway was named for a naturalist, since this is terrain that has been beautifully and successfully reclaimed by nature. Most of the path is former farmland, but the only visible signs of this are the nut and fruit trees that sit in the midst of the renewed wilderness.

With only 11,000 acres, this is America's smallest national forest. The Forest Service has deliberately avoided building extensive recreational facilities so that it can be enjoyed primarily as a primitive experience. The Bartram Trail is easily accessible from two trailhead parking areas and at several in-between points where it crosses forest roads. Hikes of various lengths are possible, and the terrain is gentle and rolling. At Tsinia Wildlife Viewing Area a boardwalk and blind allow close-up observation of songbirds, rabbits, turtles, frogs, and waterfowl.

Tuskegee National Forest has a sizable number of deer, turkeys, quail, and other wildlife, and they attract many hunters in season. The Taska Recreation Area, just

off Rte. 29, has picnic tables and grills and the trailhead marker for the Pleasant Hill Trail.

▶ Open year-round.

www.southernregion.fs.fed.us/alabama
(334) 727-2652

⌜ △ 🚶 🚲 🐟 🔬 🐉 📶

17 Old Cahawba

Near Selma

A gift from President James Monroe to the new state of Alabama, Cahawba was built up from the wilderness to become the state's first capital city in 1820. Political power then shifted northward, and Tuscaloosa captured the state capital title. Yet, thanks to its plum location as a distribution point for cotton, the town quickly recovered and thrived. On the eve of the Civil War, more than 3,000 people called Cahawba home.

During the Civil War the Confederate government seized the railroad station and established a prison for captured Union soldiers in the station's cotton warehouse.

Between 1863 and 1865 more than 5,000 prisoners of war were housed there. In 1865 a flood overwhelmed the town, and businesses and families fled. By 1900 most of the buildings had burned or collapsed. Cahawba became a ghost town.

Today Cahawba is an important archaeological site and a place of picturesque ruins. Archaeologists from the Alabama Historical Commission are uncovering the town's historic past. At the welcome center exhibits feature many historical finds, along with vintage photographs of homes and businesses once located in what is now called Old Cahawba. Throughout, interpretive signs bring Old Cahawba's fascinating remnants and forgotten people to life. Columns and chimneys recall distinguished houses. Water still flows through the old ornamental wellheads. Three cemeteries tell the stories of the diverse residents of this Southern antebellum community. Trails, canoe launches, and overlooks provide access to the Cahaba River and

19 **U.S. Army Aviation Museum.** Hanging from the ceiling is a Sopwith Camel, the WWI British biplane that did aerial battle with the single-wing German D-8 (bottom).

the Black Belt Prairie, two of Alabama's greatest natural wonders.

▶ Open daily.

www.cahawba.com
(334) 872-8058

18 The Johnson Center for the Arts

300 E. Walnut St., Troy

Who says art is for big cities only? In communities like Troy—county seat of Pike County and home to Troy University and the Pioneer Museum of Alabama—the arts are thriving, thanks to the efforts of local citizens. Back in 2000 just such a group purchased the town's handsome but vacant U.S. Post Office building, saving the historic neoclassical structure and transforming it into a home for the arts.

The complex currently comprises three facilities: The Holman and Ethel Johnson Center for the Arts (the old post office) includes seven galleries and houses the growing permanent collection and special exhibits. For folk-art aficionados, the museum offers an impressive collection of works by Mose Tolliver, Woodie Long, and many other well-known regional artists. The Cultural Arts Studio, a renovated warehouse across the street from the museum, is a busy venue for exhibitions, concerts, and theatrical performances, as well as workshops and art classes. The Cultural Arts Annex also hosts art classes.

▶ Open Tues.-Sun. year-round.

www.tpcac.org
(334) 670-2287

19 U.S. Army Aviation Museum

Fort Rucker

The entrance to this army base declares it to be "The Heart of Air Assault," and over 160 military aircraft have been put on display here to prove it. The exhibit includes not only attack aircraft but also planes that were used for such key support activities as observing the enemy, taking aerial military photographs, moving troops, delivering supplies, and evacuating the wounded.

The highly technologically sophisticated AH-64 Apache used in Desert Storm in 1991 is displayed here, and the exhibit details various functions, such as refueling the aircraft in a tactical desert environment. In adjacent outdoor areas there are aircraft from many eras, dating back to Piper Cubs used as scout planes in World War II.

The predominant aircraft is the helicopter, first used in Korea in the 1950s and later the workhorse of the U.S. Army in Vietnam. The helicopter used by presidents Eisenhower and Kennedy is also on display, as are a one-man backpack helicopter and a collapsible helicopter that fits in a crate. A driver's license, vehicle registration, and proof of insurance are required for admission.

▶ Open daily except major holidays.

www.armyavnmuseum.org
(334) 598-2508

20 Fort Gaines Historic Site

51 Bienville Blvd., Dauphin Island
Fort Morgan Historic Site
51 Hwy. 180 W. Gulf Shores

"Damn the torpedoes! Full speed ahead!" shouted Adm. David Farragut as his Union fleet ran between the blazing gun batteries of these two forts and across the line of deadly torpedoes (mines).

The twin forts—Fort Gaines on

20 Fort Morgan Historic Site. In 1864 this brick fort played a major role in the Battle of Mobile Bay.

Dauphin Island and Fort Morgan on Mobile Point—guarded the neck of water that leads into Mobile Bay. By entering the bay and seizing control of it in August 1864, Farragut sealed off Mobile, the only remaining Confederate port on the gulf. The forts quickly fell to the Union forces.

Built in the early 1800s, the two thick-walled brick structures are constructed in the classic five-sided design. Visitors can also see the sites of bakeries, blacksmith shops, and officers quarters.

Fort Morgan has a museum that details the history of the site with weapons, uniforms, and other military relics and documents on display.

With more than 350 species sighted, Dauphin Island has been named the "birdiest town in America." Beaches, picnic areas, a fishing pier, and a nature trail are further attractions. A continuous ferry permits both motorists and pedestrians to travel between the forts.

▶ Both sites open year-round.
Admission charged at each.

(251) 861-6992 Fort Gaines
(251) 540-5257 Fort Morgan

seasonal events

MARCH
- Brookside Greenway Festival—Birmingham *(arts and crafts, fishing tournament, 5k run, pageant, food music)*

APRIL
- Art on the Lake—Guntersville *(arts and crafts, games, food vendors, live entertainment)*

MAY
- The Alabama Jubilee—Decatur *(hot-air balloon rally, antique car and tractor shows, art show, kite festival)*
- Limestone Sheriff's Rodeo—Athens *(rodeo, street dance, parade, horseback rides)*

JUNE
- Frontier Days Celebration—Florence *(living-history displays, craft demonstrations, museum tours)*
- Hellen Keller Festival—Tuscumbia *(art exhibits, live entertainment, athletic events)*

AUGUST
- Watermelon Festival—Russellville *(tournaments, beauty pageant, music, antique cars and trucks, arts and crafts)*

SEPTEMBER
- September Skirmish Civil War Re-enactment—Point Mallard Park, Decatur

OCTOBER
- Alabama Renaissance Faire—Florence
- Depot Days Festival—Hartselle *(classic car and truck show, model train display, antique tractor and steam engines, live music, arts and crafts)*

NOVEMBER
- Civil War Re-enactments—Valley Head
- ZooBoo—Montogomery Zoo *(games, treats, costumed characters, haunted hayride)*
- Historic Turkey Trot—Collinsville *(antique car and tractor show, games, cake walk, turkey toss)*

www.touralabama.org

ALABAMA

Alaska

Nature reigns supreme in this glorious rugged wonderland, with its countless rivers and lakes, active volcanoes, majestic mountain peaks, and more than 30,000 miles of tidal shoreline.

Glacier Bay National Park and Preserve. Cruise ship passengers take in the view of Margerie Glacier at Glacier Bay (see page 23).

For most residents of the Lower 48, all of Alaska is off the beaten path. But the relatively few roads and accessible places are in fact quite well known. Facilities are limited, and reservations should be made well in advance.

What people come for is the indescribably magnificent scenery, the abundance and variety of wildlife—on land and sea and in the air—and the near-mystical aura created by such vast reaches of wild, uninhabited space. Hikers can explore many facets of the wilderness—from tide pools to rain forests and glaciers—and observe unparalleled concentrations of the dominant birds and animals.

Excellent museums document the history of the state and feature the totem poles, masks, and other ceremonial objects for which the native peoples are justly famous. Handsome churches reveal the early Russian presence here; gold rush days are recalled; and historic military installations can be visited, as well as a lush valley where 75-pound cabbages are the norm.

visit ➡ offthebeatenpathtrips.com

1 Kotzebue

This city, 33 miles north of the Arctic Circle on Alaska's Western coast, has been home to the Inupiat Eskimos for more than 600 years. Today the population remains over 70 percent Alaska Native.

Kotzebue boasts a colorful waterfront and is surrounded by flowery tundra. It is a natural haven for wildlife, including caribou, oxen, and bears. Birders travel here with binoculars in hand to observe the migratory waterfowl. The native Inupiat Eskimos observe the wildlife here in a traditional way—with a blanket toss. In this tradition a group uses a blanket to toss an observer high into the air to look for walrus, whales, or other game.

The federal lands that surround the Kotzebue Sound protect both wildlife and archaeological sites. These remote wildernesses can be reached by aircraft from Kotzebue. The Kobuk Valley National Park, for example, has archaeological sites that provide evidence of human habitation from over 9,000 years ago, indicating the arrival of humans over the Bering Land Bridge. The nearby Noatak National Preserve has been declared a UNESCO International Biosphere Reserve. At Cape Krusenstern National Monument there are 114 beach ridges laid down successively over the past 5,000 years, each one a repository of artifacts that together

form a chronology of Eskimo culture in Arctic prehistory.

Kotzebue has long winters and cool summers, with ice in the sound from early October through early July. The average ranges from -12°F in January to about 58°F in July.

www.nps.gov/state/ak
(907) 442-3760

1 Kotzebue. An Inupiat couple pose with their sled dogs. The Inupiat (which translates as "real people") rely on hunting, fishing, and whaling for their livelihood.

did you know ❓

Throughout history Kotzebue has been a trading and gathering hot spot. Due to the three rivers that drain into the Kotzebue Sound, people from interior villages and even Russia traveled here to trade furs, seal-oil, rifles, ammunition, and animal skins, as well as other goods and materials.

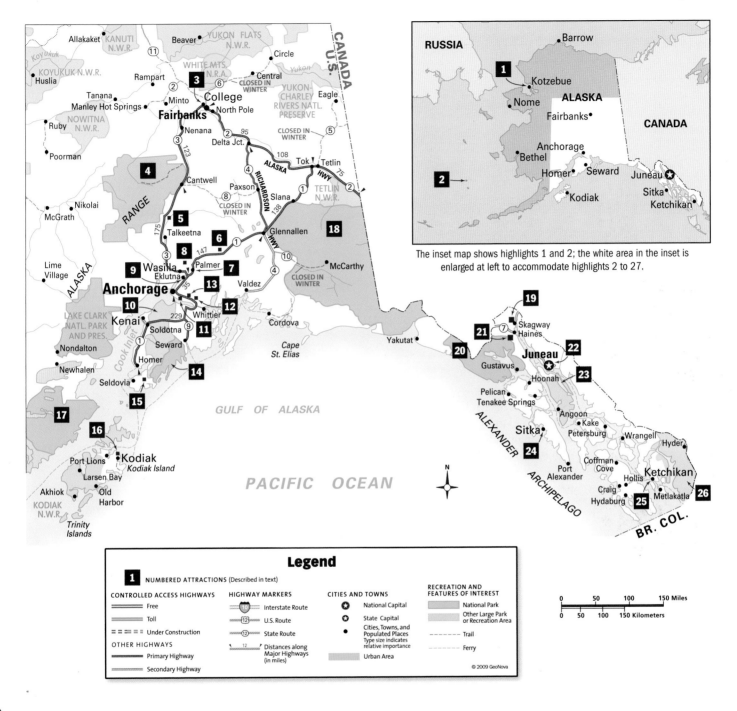

The inset map shows highlights 1 and 2; the white area in the inset is enlarged at left to accommodate highlights 2 to 27.

Legend

1 NUMBERED ATTRACTIONS (Described in text)

CONTROLLED ACCESS HIGHWAYS
Free
Toll
Under Construction

OTHER HIGHWAYS
Primary Highway
Secondary Highway

HIGHWAY MARKERS
⑩ Interstate Route
⑫ U.S. Route
⑫ State Route
12 Distances along Major Highways (in miles)

CITIES AND TOWNS
⊛ National Capital
✪ State Capital
• Cities, Towns, and Populated Places Type size indicates relative importance
Urban Area

RECREATION AND FEATURES OF INTEREST
National Park
Other Large Park or Recreation Area
- - - - Trail
— · — Ferry

© 2009 GeoNova

0   50   100   150 Miles
0   50   100   150 Kilometers

---

2 ▷ **Pribilof Islands**

More than a million fur seals on the beaches and 2.5 million seabirds on easy-to-observe nesting cliffs comprise one of the most wondrous wildlife spectacles in North America. Two of the volcanic Pribilof Islands, St. Paul and St. George, which are situated

270 miles out in the Bering Sea, are inhabited by Aleuts, whose ancestors were brought here by Russians to kill seals for their pelts.

Today the Aleuts provide food and lodging for tourists, who fly in on days when the fog is not too thick for landings. Blinds are available from which to watch the

bull, cow, and pup seals interact, all barking and roaring loudly.

The cliffs also provide an awesome playground. Bird-watchers have close-up views of undaunted black-legged kittiwakes, tufted and horned puffins, red-faced cormorants, common and thick-billed murres, and three species

of auklet. The red-legged kittiwakes, which also nest on the cliffs, are rarely seen away from the Pribilofs.

▶ Accessible early June–late Aug.

www.southwestalaska.com
(907) 562-7380

▶3 University of Alaska

Fairbanks. From Geist Rd. turn into campus on Thompson Dr. Large Animal Research Station is Mile 1 Yankovich Rd., reached by way of Ballaine Rd. from Farmer's Loop.
Modern sculpture, a Russian blockhouse, a totem pole, and hard-rock mining equipment surround the University of Alaska Museum of the North. Most impressive is the museum's stunning cutting-edge design, which has won major architectural awards. Inside, superb exhibits explain aspects of Alaska's wildlife, geology, and history, as well as the culture and crafts of the native peoples.

A unique display is an Ice Age bison that was well preserved in permanently frozen ground for 36,000 years before it was unearthed by gold miners. The museum also houses a large collection of gold and has 30-minute auditorium shows in summer.

Other Ice Age creatures still very much alive—musk oxen, moose, caribou, and reindeer—are pastured at the university's Large Animal Research Station. These animals can be watched from an elevated platform that offers an unobstructed view of the area. Binoculars are recommended.

The subarctic agricultural research gardens of the university experimental farm demonstrate the productivity possible when there are 20 hours of summer daylight. Sandhill cranes can be seen feeding in the experimental fields.

▶ University open year-round. Museum open daily except Sun. in fall/winter and major holidays. Admission charged.

www.uaf.edu/uaf/community/visiting.html
(907) 474-7505

▶4 **Denali National Park and Preserve.** In this spectacularly scenic preserve, caribou share space with Dall sheep, moose, grizzly bears, wolves, and numerous species of birds.

▶4 Denali National Park and Preserve

George Parks Hwy. (Hwy. 3), Milepost 237
Alaska's best-known attraction, this park was created as Mount McKinley National Park in 1917, primarily to protect the Dall sheep and other wild animals. Mount McKinley, the highest peak in North America (20,320 feet), is usually wreathed in clouds, but this remains one of the nation's most magnificent parks. Wildlife can be seen almost anywhere along the road, but there are no guarantees.

To avoid undue disturbance of the animals, private vehicle access is limited. The best way to see the park is via an inexpensive shuttle bus from the park entrance. Visitors are encouraged to stop first at the visitors center. Along the 90-mile park road, which traverses a glorious natural tapestry of stunningly colorful tundra wildflowers and offers marvelous scenery, visitors may spot Dall sheep on Igloo Mountain, grizzlies (brown bears) at Sable Pass and many other sites, moose along the eastern section of the road, and caribou. A visitor may also spy Alaska's state bird, the willow ptarmigan, or a golden eagle. It is a rare privilege to see wolves, but other canines—the park's sled dogs, used for winter patrols—demonstrate their work three times daily from Memorial Day to Labor Day.

▶ Open year-round. Park road passable only mid-May–mid-Sept.

www.nps.gov/dena
(907) 683-2294

▶5 Denali State Park

George Parks Hwy. (Hwy. 3)
The Athabascan word for Mount McKinley is *Denali,* "the high one." The peak itself was named in 1896 for the presidential nominee William McKinley, but this 325,420-acre park—almost one-half the size of Rhode Island—is called by its Native American name.

From the highway bisecting the park, particularly from the Denali View overlooks, you can see the snow-mantled upper slopes of the great mountain and its companion peaks and the multitude of glaciers flowing from them. But in the summer, clouds veil Mount McKinley's soaring summit most of the time.

Nonetheless, with the perpetual snow line at just 8,000 feet, the other white-topped peaks of the Alaska Range create magnificent views along the highway and park hiking trails. Byers Lake is the center of most recreation in the park. A five-mile trail circles the lake and provides hiking access to another scenic trail to K'esugi Ridge. Black bears and grizzlies inhabit the park, together with moose, wolves, and smaller mammals, such as foxes, lynx, and beavers. Bears can be troublesome along Troublesome Creek Trail when they gather here for the salmon that spawn in July and August. All posted precautions regarding bears should be carefully followed.

▶ Open year-round except mid-July–Aug. due to bears in the area.

www.dnr.state.ak.us/parks/units/denali1
(907) 745-3975

▶6 Sheep Mountain

Glenn Hwy. Mileposts 107 to 123
Dall sheep, cousins of the Rocky Mountain bighorn, are easy to spot here, for in spring and summer

their white coats stand out sharply against the green vegetation or rust and yellow rocks of this highly mineralized mountain.

The sheep are most numerous in early and late summer. Early summer is also the best time to see migrating birds, such as raptors. If you don't have good binoculars, use the viewing telescope at Sheep Mountain Lodge (Milepost 113.5).

From Caribou Creek (Milepost 107) a hiking trail winds up the 6,300-foot mountain, and you can look down on the valley from the sheep's perspective. Road passable year-round.

www.wildlife.alaska.gov
(907) 822-3461

7 Matanuska Valley

Palmer

Nineteen hours of summer sun and loamy soil promised rich harvests when the federal government established the Matanuska Valley Colony in 1935. In May of that year, some 200 families who had lost their farms in the economic turmoil of the Great Depression were selected to go north to build new lives. Most of them came from Minnesota, Michigan, and Wisconsin, where farming in very cold climates was common. Even so, only some of the colonists were successful. Many of their offspring still live in the Matanuska Valley, and a few are still on their original farms. Some of the original structures including a church and a barn, have been moved to Colony Village on the Alaska State Fairgrounds at Palmer.

More significant as a memorial are the lush crops flanking the country roads backed by rugged mountains. If you attend the state fair in August, you'll see Matanuska Valley cabbages weighing in at 75 pounds or more. The Matanuska Glacier, one of Alaska's largest, can be viewed from Mile 103 on the Glenn Hwy., 58 miles east of Palmer.

▶ Accessible by road year-round.

www.palmerchamber.org
(907) 745-2880

8 Independence Mine State Historical Park

Palmer, 17½ miles along Fishhook-Willow Rd. from Glenn Hwy.
Hard-rock mining—in this case wresting ore from the heart of a mountain—is a difficult operation, as evidenced by these gold mine buildings, ruined and reconstructed, perched above the tree line in the Talkeetna Mountains.

The first lode claim in the Willow Creek Valley was staked in 1906 on the west side of Fishhook Creek, and it became the Alaska Free Gold (Martin) Mine; nearby claims, which were staked on the east side of Granite Mountain in 1908, became the Independence Mine.

By 1938 both mines were controlled by the Alaska-Pacific Consolidated Mining Company. In 1941, its biggest year, the 200-man camp produced gold worth $1,686,790 (in today's dollars worth $17 million). Second only to Juneau's AJ Mine in producing hard-rock Alaskan gold, Independence brought forth a total of 10,300 pounds before closing in 1951.

In 1980 new gold mining nearby stimulated the creation of the state historical park here and the renovation of the existing buildings. The red-roofed mine manager's house has old photos, artifacts, a simulated gold mine tunnel, and displays showing how the gold was extracted, milled, and shipped. Other buildings include mess halls, bunkhouses, the sheet-metal shop, and the old assay office, now a hard-rock mining museum. You can camp, bike, snowmobile, and dog sled nearby.

▶ Park open year-round. Visitors center open only during the summer.

www.dnr.state.ak.us/parks/units/
indmine.htm
(907) 745-3975

9 Eklutna Historical Park and Heritage Center

Eklutna Village Rd., Eklutna
The name of this small Dena'ina Athabascan village means "mouth of river between two hills," but today it is tucked away beside the active Glenn Highway. Here is the St. Nicholas Russian Orthodox Church, the second oldest in Alaska, built in Anchorage in the 1830s and later moved to its present location. What makes this place especially distinctive are the brightly painted "spirit houses" that mark the graves in the churchyard. Some of the little structures are multistoried and some have glass windows; they contain a variety of objects that belonged to the deceased but have no letters or dates to identify the dead person. Rather, each spirit house follows a particular family's design, and this is how parishioners know who is buried where. A tiny, hand-hewn log prayer chapel also stands in the churchyard.

▶ Admission charged. Open daily mid-May–mid-Sept.

www.eklutna-nsn.gov
(907) 688-6020

▶ **Matanuska Valley.** The Matanuska Glacier is the largest Alaskan glacier accessible by automobile—but you'll have to take a 15- to 20-minute hike to reach the ice.

10 Kenai National Wildlife Refuge

Soldotna

This refuge used to be called Kenai National Moose Range. Although the name has changed, there are still thousands of these fascinating animals (the largest of which can weigh 1,400 pounds) roaming the area. They are most commonly seen along the Swanson River and Skilak Loop roads (both gravel), and smaller roads that branch from the Sterling Highway.

Thousands of lakes spangle amid this wilderness of nearly 2 million acres. Many, such as Bottenintnin Lake, reflect the Kenai Mountains, glacier-accented peaks on the refuge's boundary with Kenai Fjords National Park. Graceful trumpeter swans glide across the lakes, and the haunting call of the loon can be heard.

It is common to see Dall sheep and mountain goats above a marked observation point near Kenai Lake, on the Sterling Highway east of the refuge boundary. Beluga whales are often spotted from Fort Kenay Overlook, above the mouth of the Kenai River in the town of Kenai.

Wearing waterproof boots is suggested for hikers, since many of the 200 miles of trails can be wet. Berry picking is popular in late summer and fall. Canoe routes can be found in the Swan Lake and Swanson River canoe systems, and chartered floatplanes provide access to some of the lovely remote lakes.

▶ Open year-round. Visitors center open year-round also.

http://kenai.fws.gov
(907) 262-7021

13 ▶ **Chugach State Park.** Mushers and their dog teams travel more than 1,150 miles in the incomparable Iditarod Dogsled Race—a 10- to 17-day journey to Nome.

11 Anchorage Coastal Wildlife Refuge with Potter Marsh

New Seward Hwy. (Hwy. 1). 12 miles south of downtown Anchorage

This bird-watching area within Alaska's largest city is host to trumpeter swans, bald eagles, Canada geese, ducks, gulls, terns, and shorebirds, as well as mink, bear, moose, beaver, muskrats, and salmon. Migrating birds make spring the best time to visit, but wildlife enthusiasts with cameras and binoculars will likely be rewarded at any time of the year.

The refuge attracts its 130 species of birds primarily because there are four distinct habitats within the 32,000 acres. Geese are drawn to the salt marsh along Turnagain Arm (an inlet of spectacular beauty). Ducks and other water birds flock to Potter Marsh, a freshwater marsh created in 1917, when the Alaska Railroad was constructed and its roadbed became a dike. Muskegs, in the transition area between marsh and dryland, house snipe, grouse, and sandpipers. Such deciduous trees

as birch, alder, willow, and cottonwood support warblers, thrushes, and other songbirds in the wooded areas. And of course these habitats each support a distinctive community of plants. The refuge is served by Anchorage's bus system, paved bike trails, and there are turnouts overlooking Potter Marsh.

▶ Open year-round.

www.wildlife.alaska.gov
(907) 267-2182

12 Crow Creek Mine

Along Crow Creek Rd., which branches off the Alyeska ski area road 1.9 miles from its junction with Seward Hwy. (Hwy. 1)

Placer gold mining began in Crow Creek around 1895; at its peak the area produced more than 700 ounces per month. According to the mine's managers, there is still more gold available than ever was removed. Large-scale mining is limited because hydraulic mining is not permitted in the national forest. But visitors from around the world can still pan for "color"

here, and half-ounce nuggets may still be found glittering in the gravel. All the necessary gold-panning equipment can be rented at the mine, which is only a 40-minute drive from Anchorage.

Listed on the *National Register of Historic Places,* the mine preserves its original equipment and buildings, which were the first non–American Indian structures in the Anchorage area. Today the rugged authenticity of the site is softened somewhat by the mine's beautiful flower gardens. They splash bright color against the dark greens of the surrounding spruce and hemlock rain forest—a welcome function today, but one the old-timers, feverishly panning for color of another kind, would probably have found incomprehensible.

▶ Open daily., mid-May-mid-Sept. Admission charged.

www.crowcreekgoldmine.com
(907) 229-3105

13 Chugach State Park

This awesome wilderness, accessible from Anchorage in the Chugach Mountains, has almost half a million acres of jagged peaks, alpine meadows, lakes, glaciers, and marshy tidal flats and shelters an abundant variety of wildlife. More than 20 outstanding trails found in this park include part of the Old Iditarod Trail, used by dogsled teams to speed diphtheria serum to Nome in 1925. The segment of the trail outside the park is part of the course for the grueling Iditarod Dogsled Race, which is held annually in commemoration. Although the trails are easily accessible from heavily populated Anchorage, they are sufficiently numerous to remain peaceful even in summer.

Wildlife here includes beluga whales seeking fish in Turnagain Arm and mountain goats scaling the nearby precipices. Telescopes at the Eagle River Nature Center (reached from Glenn Hwy.) focus on surrounding steep slopes where Dall sheep and black bears are normal sightings. Moose are plentiful, and there is a salmon-viewing deck a short way down a fine nature trail that begins at the attractive log visitors center.

The altitude in the park ranges from sea level to 8,000 feet, and the annual rainfall is from 70 inches in the east to 15 inches in the west. The resulting climatic zones nurture an astonishing and beautiful variety of trees, shrubs, wildflowers, lichens, and mosses.

▶ Open year-round.

www.dnr.state.ak.us
(907) 345-5014

14 Kenai Fjords National Park

The gateway to the almost 670,000 acres of glaciers, mountains, ice fields, and some of the world's most spectacular coastline is the town of Seward. The park offers easy access to the groaning spires and ice-blue tongues of Exit Glacier, as well as to Bear Glacier, the largest of the more than 36 named glaciers flowing from the broad Harding Ice Field, and a popular destination for kayakers.

But the main attractions here are the deep, narrow fjords, which can be viewed on boat trips from Seward. From scenic Resurrection Bay the boats pass tide-carved Three Hole Arch and enter Aialik Bay, where bald eagles dive for fish. At Chiswell Islands, in

the Alaska Maritime National Wildlife Refuge, as many as 50,000 seabirds may nest, including black-legged kittiwakes, tufted and horned puffins, and black oystercatchers with carrotlike bills. Sea mammals often seen in the fjords include harbor seals and Steller's sea lions, killer and humpback whales, porpoises, and sea otters.

▶ Park open year-round. Boats run mid-May–mid-Sept.; fare charged.

www.nps.gov/kefj
(907) 224-7500

15 Kachemak Bay State Park and State Wilderness Park

Homer
Wild and undeveloped, this 370,000-acre park offers majestic peaks, glaciers, and forests, and a rugged coastline with tides among the highest in the world. Access is by boat or floatplane from the fishing community of Homer, across the bay.

Perhaps the best introduction to the park's ecology is on a boat tour conducted by the China Poot

Bay Society to its Center for Alaskan Coastal Studies. Twice daily a tour boat leaves Homer for a 45-minute ride to Gull Island, nesting site for thousands of puffins, murres, gulls, and cormorants. On the way, sightings of sea mammals (sea otters, seals, porpoises, whales) are common. The tour pauses near such sights as a bald-eagle nest in a spruce tree atop a wave-battered cliff.

At the center in Peterson Bay, a naturalist leads an exploration of pools teeming with life—giant sunflower starfish, bright sea anemones, sea urchins, and moon snails—all revealed by a 15- to 28-foot drop of the tide. At high tide the tour ascends to trails in the rain forest and archaeological sites of ancient Tanaina tribe. The boat back to Homer may pause while the crew pulls up crab pots to harvest some of the bounty of Kachemak Bay.

▶ Park open year-round. Boat runs summer only; fare charged.

www.dnr.state.ak.us
(907) 235-7024

14 Kenai Fjords National Park. For many visitors to Alaska, a boat tour of the waters of Kenai Fjords National Park is one of the highlights of their trip.

16 Fort Abercrombie State Historical Park

Kodiak, off Rezanoff Dr. E.
Over the centuries, Alaska's largest island has attracted a variety of invaders. The Alutiiq people were subjugated by Russian fur traders in 1784. In 1867 America bought the island from Russia, along with the rest of Alaska. Another invasion threatened when the Japanese attacked Pearl Harbor on December 7, 1941. As a result, the buildup of a new naval base, started in 1939, moved at a faster pace. Fort Abercrombie became one of the three main coastal defense installations on Kodiak Island.

Concrete bunkers, gun pits, and a massive eight-inch gun barrel, occasionally shrouded in Kodiak's ghostly fogs, are all that remain of this installation. The restored Ready Ammunition bunker houses the Kodiak Military Museum, which is open weekdays in the summer. Although the site had little charm for the 8,000 soldiers stationed in Kodiak, the Sitka spruce rain forest, a small meadow vibrant in summer with wildflowers, the crash of waves, and the cries of seabirds appeal to visitors today.

A Russian Orthodox church on a hill overlooking the Baranof House Museum, built around 1793 near Kodiak's harbor, preserves the Russian heritage here. A drive south of town along the island's only road reveals a lovely stretch of rugged coast.

▶ Open year-round.

www.dnr.state.ak.us/parks/units/kodiak/ftaber.htm
(907) 486-6339

17 Katmai National Park and Preserve

Fly from Anchorage to King Salmon, then hop a floatplane to Brooks Lodge on Naknek Lake. On June 6, 1912, Novarupta Volcano exploded from the flank of Mount Katmai, scattering seven cubic miles of ash and pumice around the Northern Hemisphere and filling the nearby Ukak River valley 700 feet deep with ash; the summit of Mount Katmai collapsed, forming a caldera that now holds the blue waters of Crater Lake.

This was the second largest eruption in recorded history, but because of its remote location, there were no known casualties. Expeditions over the next few years explored the region, including the steaming Ukak River valley, which was named Valley of Ten Thousand Smokes. The area, made a national monument in 1918, has been enlarged into a national park and preserve. The ash has cooled

17 Katmai National Park and Preserve.
In the rushing whitewater at Brooks Falls, grizzly bears fish for a dietary staple—salmon.

now, the fumaroles are depleted of their water vapor, and the valley no longer smokes.

Beyond the sheer vast beauty of the wilderness, the major attraction here is perhaps the great number of grizzly bears that come in the summer to feast on the abundant salmon. On their protein-rich diet these magnificent, dangerous animals can attain a weight of 900 pounds; they are common around Brooks Lodge and the nearby Park Service campground during the July and late August salmon runs. Visitors should pay careful attention to the advice available in Park Service leaflets about how to behave in bear country.

The park offers ranger-guided activities, including various educational programs and a cultural walk exploring human history in the surrounding area.

▶ Open daily June–early Sept.
 Fees for van and plane tours.

www.nps.gov/katm
(907) 246-3305

18 Wrangell–St. Elias National Park & Preserve

This is our largest national park, overwhelming in its size (its 13.2 million acres stretch north for 170 miles from the Gulf of Alaska) and in the wild, astonishing grandeur of its scenery.

Wrangell–St. Elias, Kluane National Park in Canada, Glacier Bay National Park, and Tatshenshini-Alsek Park in British Columbia are together a United Nations World Heritage area. Among them they include 10 of the continent's highest peaks and the greatest wealth of mountains, canyons, and glaciers in North America. The park's highest peak

19 Klondike Gold Rush National Historical Park.
One can only imagine what prospectors thought when they saw the breathtaking views surrounding the Chilkoot Pass for the first time.

is the towering 18,008-foot Mount St. Elias, the second highest peak in the United States.

Road access to the wilderness is from Slana in the north and from Chitina in the west. From Slana the normally well-maintained gravel road crosses the tundra to Nabesna, a small mining settlement. Inquire at the Slana Ranger Station about conditions on this lovely 45-mile trip, which requires some stream fording.

About 10 miles off Nabesna Road is Tanada Lake, where the fishing, especially for grayling, is as rewarding as the scenery and the views of wildlife. The hiking trail to the lake may be muddy and difficult, and the easiest access is by charter floatplane. A lodge and cabins are available in summer.

From Chitina the dirt road toward McCarthy runs for 60 miles (three hours) through superb scenery along an old railroad route. Vehicles with high clearance should have no trouble in summer, though flat tires can be a problem

on such back roads. Good highways follow the western and northern borders of the park and offer spectacular views of shield and strato volcanoes: Mount Drum, more than 12,000 feet high, and Mount Wrangell, more than 14,000 feet.

Summers are cool and can be rainy and foggy. July is the warmest month, but the mosquitoes can be out in force. August has fewer bugs but may be more rainy.

▶ Open year-round.

www.nps.gov/wrst
(907) 822-5234

19 Klondike Gold Rush National Historical Park

Skagway
When gold fever struck in 1897–98, some 20,000 to 30,000 adventurers came through Skagway to brave the Chilkoot and White Pass trails on their way to the Klondike gold fields. They suffered immense hardship, many died, and only a

very few got rich. But Skagway prospered, as did nearby Dyea at the head of the trail that crosses the Chilkoot Pass into Canada.

The park commemorating the gold rush includes the Skagway Historic District, Dyea (now in ruins), and the American portion of the Chilkoot Trail, as well as Pioneer Square in Seattle, where so many dreamers made plans for the trip north. For many the dreams ended here in Skagway, where some 80 saloons and gambling halls and the notorious "Soapy" Smith and his cronies were all willing and able to relieve the unwary of their grubstakes.

The aura of those days pervades the Skagway Historic District, with its boardwalks and old false-fronted buildings. A walking tour includes the restored railroad depot (home of the park visitors center), the Mascot Saloon, Goldberg's Cigar Store, and the Arctic Brotherhood Hall, whose Victorian façade is uniquely embellished with thousands of bits of driftwood.

The Skagway Museum in city hall houses relics of pioneer days and the gold stampede. The native cultures in Alaska are represented by the arts and crafts of the Eskimos, Aleuts, Athapaskans, and the coastal Tlingit and Haida Indians.

did you know ?

The father of Glacier Bay National Park was William Skinner Cooper. He studied plants that grew in the soil the retreating glaciers uncovered. The Ecological Society of America was impressed, and helped convince President Coolidge to proclaim Glacier Bay a national monument.

The Chilkoot Trail, open when weather permits, is an extremely strenuous 33-mile hike that takes from three to five days and is recommended only for the most experienced backpackers. There are, however, several other hiking trails into the hills outside of Skagway.

▶ Historic district open year-round.

www.nps.gov/klgo
(907) 983-2921

---

20 ▶ Glacier Bay National Park and Preserve

Gustavus
This primeval wilderness of more than 3 million acres is accessible from Juneau or Haines. It is a short flight from Juneau to Gustavus and a 10-minute drive to the park visitors center, lodge, and park headquarters at Bartlett Cove.

From Haines it takes about 45 minutes by air.

Eleven glaciers feed into park marine waters, and there are daily boat trips to several glacier "snouts," precipitous ice cliffs that "calve" 200-foot-high bergs into the tidal inlets.

To explain how glaciers form and how they advance and retreat, park naturalists show films and give guided walks at Bartlett Cove. In this area most of the ice is now retreating (200 years ago it was up to 4,000 feet thick and the bay was entirely buried), and in its wake have come many marine and terrestrial species such as whale, porpoise, sea lion, sea otter, salmon, brown and black bear, moose, wolf, mountain goat, and over 200 species of birds. Whales, sea lions, seabirds, and bears are most readily observed on the daily

---

boat cruise from the lodge. Local air-taxi operators offer "flightseeing" trips over the park. Also near the lodge are short trails leading through the moss-draped rain forest down to rocky beaches; be sure to bring waterproof footwear and rain gear. Wildlife that favors the forest include grouse, thrush, ruby and golden-crowned kinglet, black bear, and porcupine.

Bartlett Cove tides range up to 25 feet, and when the tide is out, the shorelines reveal a fascinating variety of starfish, sea urchins, shellfish, and other tide-pool creatures.

▶ Open year-round. Glacier Bay Lodge open late May–early Sept. For reservations visit www.visitglacierbay.com.

www.nps.gov/glba
(888) BAY-TOUR

20 ▶ Glacier Bay National Park and Preserve. Within the boundaries of this national park is the world's largest collection of tidewater glaciers, most named for colleges in the eastern United States. Here the Johns Hopkins Glacier looms in the distance.

21 Fort William H. Seward

Haines

In 1903 the U.S. Army began construction of a fort at Haines on land that was deeded to the government by the Presbyterian Board of National Missions. It was dedicated the following year as Fort William H. Seward, honoring the Secretary of State whose folly it had been to purchase Alaska from the Russian government in 1867.

The first contingent of soldiers arrived in September, and the fort then became the regimental headquarters for all of Alaska. In 1922 it was renamed Chilkoot Barracks to avoid confusion with the town of Seward.

World War II saw new military installations in Alaska, and Chilkoot consequently became an induction center and rest camp. Years later it was deactivated in favor of newer installations.

Now on the *National Register of Historic Places,* its stately white buildings backed by the towering peaks of the Chilkat Range still form an imposing sight. Several buildings have been put to new uses, such as an artist's studio and crafts workshop. Totem Village, with its totem poles and a Tlingit tribal house, is the home of the well-known Chilkat Dancers, who perform traditional dances of the Northwest Coastal Native Americans.

The Haines area is noted for its eagles. At the 48,000-acre preserve, about 20 miles up the Haines Hwy., as many as 3,500 bald eagles, the largest gathering in the world, feed on the spawning salmon. Although the best time to see them is from October through January, they are also numerous in spring and early summer.

▶ Fort open year-round.

www.haines.ak.us
(800) 458-3579

22 Juneau

Juneau, whose history goes back long before Joe Juneau struck gold in 1880, offers a unique mix of cultural and wilderness attractions.

The Alaska State Museum reflects the area's diversity with displays on wildlife, the region's Indian and Russian heritage, and the gold rush of the 1880s and 1890s. At the octagonal St. Nicholas Russian Orthodox Church, built in 1894, you can see handsome icons and other church relics. The U.S. Forest Service desk at Centennial Hall gives information about hiking, camping, and other outdoor recreational opportunities and has logging, fishing, and mining displays.

Tour buses run to Mendenhall Glacier, making it one of the continent's most accessible ice fields. Its cold blue face rises some 100 feet above the waters of Mendenhall Lake. Telescopes at the nearby visitors center enable you to get a detailed look at the glacier. Hiking trails lead back into the woods. Arctic terns perform aerial acrobatics during the spring nesting period, and in autumn bald eagles fish for salmon in nearby Steep Creek.

For information about "salmon bakes," scenic plane rides, charter fishing, Glacier Bay tours, and other area activities, check with the visitors center in Centennial Hall, 101 Egan Dr.

www.traveljuneau.com
(888) 581-2201

24 Sitka. A Tlingit dance company is one of the city's cultural gems.

23 Admiralty Island National Monument

Juneau

Almost 100 miles long and 30 wide, this island is indeed a unique place of thick forest, lakes, streams, inlets, estuaries, bogs, alpine meadows, and snowcapped peaks rising above the tree line. Few trails penetrate its nearly 1 million acres, and there are no roads of significant length. Most travel is by boat.

The island's dominant residents are some 1,500 huge Alaskan brown bears. Frequently bears can be observed fishing near a viewing stand at the mouth of Pack Creek. Some 500 to 600 bald eagles are hatched here annually, more than in the entire lower 48 states. Deer, seals, sea lions, and river otters are often seen. The waterways yield an abundance of fish, crabs, and shrimp.

The jumping-off spot for visiting the bear viewing area is Juneau, where visitors can charter floatplanes for the journey to Pack Creek. Visitors who are traveling with outfitter guides can also go by kayak or in outfitters' boats. A permit from the Forest Service is required for visitors.

Because the island is a remote and vast wilderness, careful preparations should be made. Forest cabins on Admiralty can be reserved at the National Recreation Reservation Service at (877) 444-6777.

▶ Open year-round.

www.fs.fed.us/r10/tongass/districts/admiralty
(907) 586-8800

24 Sitka

In 1804 Alexander Baranof, the manager of a Russian fur-trading company, burned the Tlingit Native American fort here and reestablished the Russian colony the Tlingits had destroyed two years earlier. Sitka became the foremost city on the North American Pacific Coast. Eventually, however, overhunting ruined the fur trade, and in 1867 the Russians sold Alaska to the United States for $7.2 million in gold. The official transfer took place on Castle Hill, overlooking Sitka's harbor, on October 18—Alaska Day, celebrated annually in Sitka with five days of pageant and ceremony.

Today Sitka retains much of its czarist and Tlingit heritage. Russian cannon face the harbor from atop the Castle Hill National Historic Site, and the colorfully costumed New Archangel Dancers perform Russian folk dances at the Harrigan Centennial Hall. St. Michael's Russian Orthodox Cathedral dominates the downtown area, and the Bishop's House, built in 1842 for Alaska's first Russian Orthodox bishop, is maintained by Sitka National Historical Park. Within the park is the site of the Tlingit fort and a lovely two-mile forest trail lined with magnificent totem poles. Crafts and artifacts of the Tlingits and other regional tribes are displayed at the park's Southeast Alaska Indian Cultural Centers. The park's visitors center features exhibits on Sitka's history, and a world-famous collection of tribal masks is found at the nearby Sheldon Jackson Museum.

▶ Park open year-round except major holidays.

www.sitka.org
(907) 747-5940

25 ▶ Tongass Historical Museum and Totem Heritage Center

Ketchikan. Museum at 629 Dock St.; Heritage Center at 601 Deermount St.
The material in the Tongass Historical Museum is largely from three highly creative peoples: the Haidas, Tlingits, and Tsimshians. The totems, tools, baskets, and ceremonial objects displayed here are among the best of their kind. Also shown are exhibits related to the history of the town of Ketchikan.

In the Totem Heritage Center some 30 totem poles, house posts, and fragments from Tlingit and Haida villages can be seen in their unrestored state. These great totems, carved from red cedar trees, indicate personal status and clan relationships and serve as memorials. They are unique to the Pacific Northwest and are widely celebrated for their emotional power and strength of design.

The center conducts workshops where established native artists teach the traditional skills of carving, basketry, and engraving.

▶ Museum open daily May–Sept.; Wed.–Sun., Oct.–Apr. except major winter holdays. Heritage Center open daily mid-May–Sept.; Mon.–Fri., Oct.–mid-May.

www.city.ketchikan.ak.us/departments/
museums/tongass.html
(907) 225-5900

26 ▶ Misty Fiords National Monument

Ketchikan
Nearly 156 inches of precipitation drench Misty Fiords annually, adding to the abundant water provided by melting glaciers and ice fields. The fiords are narrow ocean inlets carved by glaciers from the Ice Age. The nearly vertical granite cliffs lining their shores tower to a height of 3,000 feet. Cloud-wreathed waterfalls spangle amid the soaring precipices.

All but the steepest slopes are covered by an evergreen rain forest composed of Sitka spruce, firs, cedar, and western hemlock, broken only by glacially excavated lakes and muskegs. Even above the tree line, the land is covered with shrubs and grasses that provide summer pasture for Sitka black-tailed deer. Other wildlife that may be seen includes bears, bald eagles, and mountain goats; the waters abound with sea lions, salmon, porpoises, and whales.

Most visitors arrive by boat or floatplane from Ketchikan, about 30 air miles away. There are no roads, but seven short hiking trails penetrate the rugged terrain of this 2.3-million-acre wilderness. A number of campgrounds are scattered throughout the monument, as well as 14 rustic cabins with basic facilities that are maintained by the U.S. Forest Service.

▶ Monument accessible year-round but lakes not accessible in winter.

www.fs.fed.us/r10/tongass/forest_facts/
resources/wilderness/misty.shtml
(877) 444-6777
(907) 228-6220

26 ▶ **Misty Fiords National Monument.** Rising above the fiords, known as a kayaker's paradise, is a lure for hikers and birders: a dense evergreen rain forest.

seasonal events

FEBRUARY
- Iditarod Days Festival—Wasilla *(ski races, snowshoe softball, ice fishing, arts and crafts)*
- Winterfest—Denali National Park *(snowshoeing, skiing, food, music)*
- State Winter Carnival—Willow *(fireworks, dogsled races, fishing, arts and crafts)*

MARCH
- World Ice Carving Championship—Fairbanks

APRIL
- Alaska Folk Festival—Juneau
- Whalefest— Kodiak *(view migrating whales)*

MAY
- Juneau Jazz & Classics—Juneau *(live jazz, education programs)*
- Kodiak Crab Festival—Kodiak *(food, raffle, music, entertainment, kid's games, contests)*
- Kachemak Bay Kayak Festival—Homer *(kayaking, seminars, demonstrations, workshops)*

JUNE
- Summer Solstice—statewide festivals
- Midnight Sun Baseball Game—Fairbanks

JULY
- Golden Days—Fairbanks *(parade, arts, music, food)*

AUGUST
- Alaska State Fair—Palmer

OCTOBER
- Alaska Day Celebration—Sitka *(parade, entertainment, music, dancing)*
- Spirit Days—Anchorage *(storytelling, drumming, arts and crafts, speeches)*

NOVEMBER
- Alaska Bald Eagle Festival—Haines *(speakers, presentations, eagle viewing)*

www.travelalaska.com

Arizona

The ghost towns and prehistoric ruins of the Grand Canyon State are juxtaposed with forests of cacti, Joshua trees, and petrified logs.

Hubbell Trading Post. The country's oldest continuously operating trading post stocks a wealth of Navajo, Hopi, and Zuni arts and crafts (see page 27).

Arizona was once home to a thriving semi-nomadic agrarian people who built cliff dwellings. The ruins they left in canyons and on mesas still evoke a sense of wonder. The architectural heritage of the early white settlers is evident in towns born of the rough-and-ready mining industry.

The Hualapai Valley and Sonoran Desert reveal botany's bold designs with sizable tracts of the towering saguaro cactus, the organ-pipe cactus, and the Joshua tree, while an arboretum in the town of Superior offers one-stop viewing of these and other dramatic desert species.

Additional delights await you at a national park filled with the petrified logs of a prehistoric forest, a cave with an endless array of amazing formations, and a restored 19th-century trading post and farm.

visit ➡ **offthebeatenpathtrips.com**

1 Navajo National Monument

Rte. 564, Kayenta

Although the Navajos became one of the most powerful tribes in the Southwest, they are relative newcomers, migrating south from their Canadian homeland in the 1400s. Sometime later they discovered the ruins of villages built by the ancient Puebloans and settled in the area.

A half-mile trail (open year-round) leads to an overlook with a fine view of Betatakin ("ledge house" in Navajo). Nestled in a great alcove in the face of a sheer sandstone cliff, it looks like a fairy-tale setting. You can visit the ruin itself only on guided tours. Tours given from May–Sept. include talks on the prehistoric occupants of the area, and the present-day Navajo dwellers, as well as geology, flora, and other topics. The outing requires a strenuous four-hour round-trip hike; keep in mind that the elevation here is 7,300 feet.

The ruins of Keet Seel ("broken pieces of pottery" in Navajo) are even more remote and are open only from Memorial Day–Labor Day. The trail is an arduous 17-mile round-trip hike. You can go and return in a day or camp near the ruins in the canyon. Only 20 people per day are allowed to visit the site, and permits and reservations are required.

1 **Navajo National Monument.** A fish-eye camera lens gives a new perspective to the Keet Seel Ruins left behind by the ancient Puebloans some seven centuries ago.

▶ Park and visitors center open daily except winter holidays.

www.nps.gov/nava
(928) 672-2700

2 Canyon de Chelly National Monument

Headquarters 3 miles east of Chinle on Rte. 7

Of all the spectacular canyons in Arizona, Canyon de Chelly is, in the eyes of many, the most breathtakingly beautiful. Two scenic roadways lead to overlooks offering magnificent views of deep vertical-walled canyons, towering sandstone spires, the Rio de Chelly flowing through the valley floor, and the dwellings of the ancient Puebloans snugly sheltered along the face of the cliffs.

Since Navajos live within the monument, visitors are allowed in some areas only when accompanied by an authorized guide. An exception is the White House Trail, which zigzags down the cliff to the canyon floor 600 feet below. Impossible though it seems from above, the path is perfectly safe, provided you are wearing appropriate shoes.

For a close-up view of the ancient cliff dwellings, wade across the Rio de Chelly and follow a path along the river. You'll find some ruins at the base of the cliff. Overhead you'll see the White House ruins, perched on a deep ledge in the towering wall of sandstone. The climb back up the cliff is a little arduous, but the entire adventure is memorable. Check at the visitors center for flash-flood warnings beforehand. Additional hiking trips and four-wheel-drive excursions can be arranged, but advance reservations are needed.

▶ Open daily year-round.

www.nps.gov/cach
(928) 674-5500

3 Hubbell Trading Post National Historic Site

Rte. 264, Ganado

A visit to the trading post on this 160-acre homestead evokes its heyday, when the post was the social center for Navajos.

Established in the late 1870s by John Lorenzo Hubbell, it is the oldest continuously active trading post in the Navajo Nation. Now owned by the National Park Service, it sells groceries and Navajo, Zuni, and Hopi crafts—turquoise and silver jewelry, rugs, blankets, and baskets. English and Navajo are spoken.

Guided tours are given of the Hubbell home, which looks much as it did 100 years ago. It has rough-hewn timbered ceilings and is filled with excellent Native American craftwork. Then stroll around the farm, which the park is restoring with a vegatable garden, terraced fields, Navajo-Churro sheep, angora goats, and other animals.

▶ Admission charged. Open daily except winter holidays.

www.nps.gov/hutr
(928) 755-3475

4 Hopi Cultural Center

Second Mesa

The Hopis are believed to be descendants of a farming people who first settled in the Southwest some 1,500 to 1,600 years ago. Today the Hopi villages, a fascinating mixture of modern technology and ancient architecture, are centered on three towering desert mesas.

The Hopi Cultural Center at Second Mesa has a museum that also serves as an informal visitors center for the entire reservation. The displays recount the tribe's long history, from the earliest times through the Navajo, Spanish, and American invasions of its homeland.

One of the most popular exhibits concerns the kachinas, deities central to the Hopi religion. Exquisite craft displays include examples of Hopi bridal clothes and finely wrought jewelry pieces, pottery, and basketry. Both the museum and the nearby Hopi Arts and Crafts Guild offer opportunities to observe various craftsmen at work.

▶ Museum open daily, but schedule may be erratic from Nov.–Jan. Admission charged.

www.hopiculturalcenter.com
(928) 734-2401

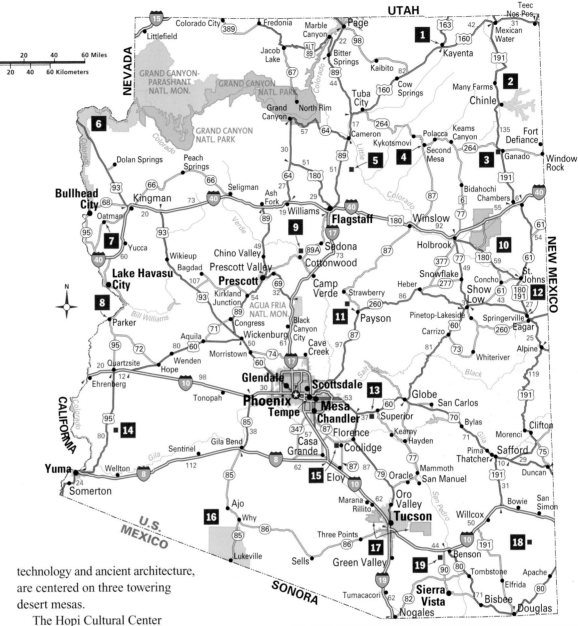

Legend

1 NUMBERED ATTRACTIONS (Described in text)

CONTROLLED ACCESS HIGHWAYS
— Free
— Toll
= = = = = Under Construction

OTHER HIGHWAYS
— Primary Highway
— Secondary Highway

HIGHWAY MARKERS
🛡 Interstate Route
⬭ U.S. Route
⬭ State Route
↳ 12 Distances along Major Highways (in miles)

CITIES AND TOWNS
⊛ National Capital
✪ State Capital
• Cities, Towns, and Populated Places Type size indicates relative importance
Urban Area

RECREATION AND FEATURES OF INTEREST
National Park
Other Large Park or Recreation Area
- - - - Trail
- - - - Ferry

© 2009 GeoNova

5 ➤ Wupatki National Monument
Flagstaff

Sometime between 1040 and 1100 the eruption of Sunset Crater Volcano sent clouds of ash and cinders into the sky, causing the local Sinagua people to flee. The ash settled over 800 square miles, and when the Sinaguas returned, they found that the ash retained moisture, improved the soil, and made their crops more productive. The area attracted Native Americans from neighboring regions and became a cultural melting pot. Wupatki grew to be a major pueblo, eventually rising to four stories in some places and containing more than 100 rooms. But less than 100 years later the residents were forced to leave again, possibly because of severe drought. By 1225 Wupatki and the surrounding villages stood vacant.

At the 56-square-mile Wupatki National Monument, you may tour pueblo ruins. A scenic loop road leads to other archaeological sites, among them fortified pueblos, and continues 18 miles to Sunset Crater Volcano National Monument, the site of the 11th-century eruption. Mineral deposits around the crater's rim give the upper slopes of the mountain a glowing coloration.

Although no hiking is allowed on the volcano's cone, a one-mile loop trail leads through the lava beds. Bonito campground, maintained by the U.S. Forest Service, is near the visitors center.

➤ Monuments open year-round; visitors
   centers open daily except Christmas.
   Campground open late May-mid-Oct.

www.nps.gov/wupa
(928) 679-2365 Wupatki

www.nps.gov/sucr
(928) 526-0502 Sunset Crater

5 ➤ **Wupatki National Monument.** Prehistoric farmers who settled in small groups close to the San Francisco Peaks built the once-flourishing Wupatki pueblo.

6 ➤ Hualapai Valley Joshua Trees
Turn east off Rte. 93 onto Pearce Ferry Rd. for Dolan Springs

Believe it or not, these odd-looking prickly trees here in the desert are members of the lily family. They can grow to 40 feet, and they bear beautiful greenish yellow or cream-colored flowers in spring. According to legend, the Mormons gave the tree its biblical name because its form, with upraised branches, suggested the prophet Joshua at prayer.

You'll spot the first Joshua trees slightly beyond Dolan Springs. As you continue, the trees become larger and more frequent until finally, some 20 miles down the road, you'll find yourself in a forest.

The strangeness of the scene is enhanced by the spectacular backdrop of the Grand Wash Cliffs. There are facilities here, but otherwise you are on your own amid the desert's solitude. The elevation is about 4,000 feet, so the heat is not oppressive.

➤ Available year-round.

**www.americansouthwest.net/arizona/
   pearce_ferry**
(928) 767-4473

7 ➤ Oatman
I-40, Exit 44

Founded in 1906 on the western slopes of the Black Mountains, Oatman was an important mining town and served as the business center for several surrounding communities. By 1931 the area is said to have had 15,000 inhabitants, to have produced 1.8 million ounces of gold, and even to have engendered its own stock exchange. In 1942 the mines were closed for good.

The town is now something of a tourist center, with cafés, artists' studios, and craft shops. Along Main St. there are boarded-up entrances to the old mines, and burros roam the street looking for handouts. Gunfights are staged on the weekends. Film companies have produced movies here, including *How the West Was Won*.

From the main highway the 28-mile drive to Oatman includes 8 miles of rough mountain road with sharp switchbacks that can be treacherous if one is distracted by the scenery.

➤ Open year-round.

www.legendsofamerica.com/az-oatman.html
(928) 768-6222

8 ➤ Colorado River Indian Tribes Museum
Second Ave. and Mojave Rd., Parker

Four different tribes live on the Colorado River Indian Reservation, which spreads into California. The Mojaves, Navajos, Hopis, and the southern Paiutes, known here as Chemehuevis, share a tract of nearly 300,000 acres. The purpose of the museum is to depict the characteristic lifestyles, histories, and cultural attributes that distinguish the varied heritages of these four tribes.

Costumes and models of the traditional homes of each tribe are shown, along with historic artifacts. The nearby ghost town of La Paz has contributed some pieces from long ago. Among the outstanding crafts displayed are Mojave beadwork, Hopi kachina dolls, Navajo rugs, and Chemehuevi baskets. Many crafts are for sale.

➤ Open Mon.-Fri. except holidays.
   Admission free but donations encouraged.

www.critonline.com
(928) 669-7037

9 ➤ Tuzigoot National Monument
Tuzigoot Rd., Clarkdale

Atop a barren ridge 120 feet above the Verde River are the ruins of a town constructed by the people known today as the Sinagua—farmers and artisans who moved into the valley about A.D. 900. Around 1000 they began building the pueblo at Tuzigoot (an anglicized Apache name meaning "crooked water") using stone and clay. Originally it housed about 50 people, but by 1300 it had grown to 110 rooms and accommodated a population of 270. Even at this point there were few doorways; the rooms were entered by ladders through hatchways in the ceilings. The village flourished for another 100 years before the Sinaguas abandoned the valley; their descendants were probably absorbed by pueblos to the north.

The small visitors center displays an extensive collection of artifacts recovered from the site. A furnished reconstruction of a typical pueblo room vividly portrays Sinagua daily life. An easy quarter-mile loop trail leads from the visitors center to the ruins, where the interior of the pueblo may be viewed.

▶ Open year-round except Christmas. Admission charged.

www.nps.gov/tuzi
(928) 634-5564

10 Petrified Forest National Park

I-40, Exit 311, Petrified Forest
The park's geological story began over 200 million years ago, when pinelike trees were carried by waterways here and buried in the silt of a huge floodplain. The silica-rich waters slowly penetrated the logs' tissue. Eventually the silica crystallized, turning the logs into a stone aglow with a rainbow of colors. Millions of years of erosion created the area's magnificent mesas, badlands, and buttes and exposed the logs.

Rainbow Forest Museum, at the southern end of the 28-mile road traversing the park, has exhibits explaining the area's paleontology. Extraordinary specimens of petrified logs may be seen along the half-mile Giant Logs Trail, just behind the museum. Trails lead to Agate House, the colorful ruins of a pueblo built from petrified wood, and Long Logs, where the ancient timbers have remained intact.

One of the most beautiful areas is Blue Mesa, 10 miles north of Rainbow Forest on the park road. Here erosion has left the petrified logs resting on stone pedestals. A mile-long trail leads from the mesa top to the badlands below.

▶ Open daily except Christmas. Admission charged.

www.nps.gov/pefo
(928) 524-6228

11 Tonto Natural Bridge State Park

Off Hwy. 87, on NF-583A, 10 miles north of Payson
A fluke of nature created by millennia of rock melting, shifting, settling, and finally eroding away, Tonto Natural Bridge is a 400-foot-long tunnel cut through by burbling Pine Creek. It is the world's largest bridge formed of travertine (calcareous rock deposited by mineral springs), measuring 183 feet tall and up to 150 feet wide and looming over a picturesque canyon.

On the River Trail—one of three trails to the canyon floor—you'll see stalactite-like formations hanging from the bridge and along the canyon wall. The Waterfall Trail leads you to a grotto with greenery hanging from the ceiling.

The canyon and its star attraction were discovered in 1877 by a Scottish prospector named David Gowan, who hid in one of the area's many caves while on the run from Apaches; he later moved his family here. Today visitors take in the canyon and bridge from lookouts as well as the trails.

▶ Open year-round. Entrance fee.

www.azstateparks.com/Parks/TONA
(928) 476-4202

10 ▶ Petrified Forest National Park. Colorful petrified wood is scattered throughout the park, including Rainbow Forest, where you can also see the badlands of the Chinle Formation.

12 Casa Malpais Archaeological Park

418 Main St., Springerville
On a terraced height in the country's third largest volcanic lava field, overlooking the Little Colorado River, lie the stone ruins of a mystery-shrouded culture. More than seven centuries ago Casa Malpais ("House of the Badlands") was home to the Mogollon, one of the earliest native peoples of the Southwest. The Mogollon lived here for less than 200 years, abandoning the location sometime before 1450.

Built into fissures in a fallen basalt cliff, the pueblo includes archaeological remains of the Great Kiva, believed to be a ceremonial building, and the Solar Calendar, a round structure where Mogollon farmers and hunters tracked the seasonal equinoxes. The top of the mesa, reached by a steep, natural rock stairway, offers a stunning panoramic view of the Round Valley and the mountains beyond.

The site is open to guided tours only, weather permitting (wear good hiking shoes). Tours begin at the Casa Malpais Visitor Center and Museum in Springerville, where artifacts from the site are displayed.

▶ Open daily except major winter holidays. Admission charged for tour.

www.springerville-eagarchamber.com
(928) 333-5375

did you know

The petrified wood found in the Petrified Forest National Park is almost entirely made of quartz. The bright, varied colors come from impurities such as iron.

13 Boyce Thompson Arboretum State Park

Hwy. 60, west of Superior

This collection of cacti and other hot-climate plants was started in the 1920s by William Boyce Thompson, a mining magnate. The 323-acre living museum has become an outstanding botanical garden and research center with over 3,000 species of plants from around the world. It is Arizona's oldest and largest botanical garden.

More than two miles of intersecting paths, most of them level and easy, wind through the gardens, and the scenery changes dramatically as you walk. Desert plants, including yuccas, palo-verdes, chollas, and a towering 200-year-old saguaro cactus, seem almost out of place when you encounter the lush vegetation around tiny Ayer Lake or the pomegranate, olive, and Chinese pistachio trees clustered along a stream.

The plants are delightfully fragrant, and at practically any time of year, some of them are in bloom. The best time to visit, however, is from Oct.–May. In summer the temperature here can reach a sizzling 110°F.

▶ Open daily except Christmas. Admission charged.

http://arboretum.ag.arizona.edu
(520) 689-2811

14 Castle Dome Mines Museum

Castle Dome Rd., Castle Dome City

The ghost town—forlorn buildings and dusty streets once teeming with people who lived hard and dreamed of striking it rich—is intrinsic to Wild West history and legend. Allen and Stephanie Armstrong have devoted themselves to bringing one ghost town back to life.

In the 1870s Castle Dome City was bigger than Yuma and a key part of the Castle Dome silver and lead mining region, but by 1990, when mining ceased, the town was a tumbledown ghost of its former self. The Armstrongs purchased what remained and have rescued or re-created more than two dozen buildings, including a hotel, church, blacksmith shop, saloon, dentist's office, and assay office. Each is stocked with period furnishings, artifacts, and equipment mostly recovered onsite and in the mines. The result is a colorful history of mining life in its heyday. One modern touch has been added: solar power.

▶ Open Tues.–Sun., mid-May–Sept. Admission charged.

(928) 920-3062

15 Casa Grande Ruins National Monument

Coolidge

One of the most mysterious of the Southwest's Native American ruins, Casa Grande was built around 1350. The three-story earthen structure sits like a crown on a high foundation at the center of a walled village, and the placement of openings in the upper stories suggests that it may have been used in part as an astronomical observatory. But beyond that its function is lost in the past.

The building was constructed by the Hohokam, proficient desert farmers who built hundreds of miles of canals to irrigate their crops. They lived in earthen village complexes and were known for their earth-colored pottery and their skill in carving stones and shells. About a century after Casa Grande was built, they abandoned their Gila River Valley villages for reasons that are not fully understood.

On display at the visitors center are ceramics, implements, jewelry, and other artifacts. A self-guiding hiking trail leads through the ruins of Casa Grande and the surrounding village.

▶ Open year-round except winter holidays. Admission charged.

www.nps.gov/cagr
(520) 723-3172

17 Saguaro National Park, Rincon Mountain District. The saguaro cactus at left sports a so-called cristate crown—a deformity that occurs in about one in 50,000 plants.

16 Organ Pipe Cactus National Monument

Ajo

Organ pipe is an apt name for a cactus whose slender stems curve upward in clusters to an average height of 15 feet. During May and June the creamy white flowers at the ends of the branches bloom at night and attract the bats required for pollination. The red egg-shaped fruit matures in July, splitting open as it ripens to disclose the black seeds that are consumed by many of the hundreds of species of birds observed here. Fruit that drops to the ground provides food for many types of animals. The park, 500 square miles of Sonoran Desert, is this rare plant's northernmost habitat.

Ajo Mountain Dr., a 21-mile loop, winds through the monument, offering scenic views and picnic areas. The park has several hiking trails, some through the desert and others into the Ajo Mountains.

▶ Open year-round except Christmas.

www.nps.gov/orpi
(520) 387-6849

17 Saguaro National Park, Rincon Mountain District

3693 S. Old Spanish Trail, Tucson

The giant saguaro cactus, with its huge upright arms extending from a sturdy trunk, may after some 200 years reach a height of 50 feet. Literally thousands of these giant saguaro cacti fill the Sonoran Desert here in the eastern section of the national park's two units.

The saguaros are a great boon to desert birds. Woodpeckers drill holes in the fleshy arms for nests, which are often used later by screech owls, purple martins, and sparrow hawks.

The plants and creatures of the desert can be studied closely on an 8-mile drive that loops through the saguaro forest and also on a 1-mile nature trail near a sheltered picnic area. Over 50 miles of hiking and horseback-riding trails traverse a 58,000-acre wilderness and ascend to the summits of the fir-forested Rincon Mountains at an altitude of 8,700 feet.

▶ Open year-round. Admission charged.

www.nps.gov/sagu
(520) 733-5153

18 Chiricahua National Monument

13063 E. Bonita Canyon Rd., Willcox

Strangely beautiful pinnacles, towers, spindle-thin columns, spires, and balanced boulders are so huddled together here that they seem almost surreal. For centuries this area was part of the Chiricahua Apache homeland. The range in altitude here, from about 5,000 to more than 7,000 feet, helps to create a hospitable environment for a wide assortment of plants.

The monument has 17 miles of hiking trails, a 24-site campground, and picnic areas. Of historic interest is the Faraway Ranch, a pioneer homestead that was a working cattle and guest ranch. From here a paved 6-mile scenic drive leads through a maze of canyons to Massai Point, which offers views of the surrounding valleys and has an exhibit building with displays describing the region's dramatic geology.

▶ Park open year-round. Admission charged.

www.nps.gov/chir
(520) 824-3560, Ext. 302

18 **Chiricahua National Monument.** In the Chiricahua Mountains, boulders balance precariously in a section the Apaches called the "land of standing-up rocks."

19 Kartchner Caverns State Park

State Hwy. 90, Exit 302, Benson

In 1974 two young cavers exploring the abundant limestone hills at the base of the Whetstone Mountains followed the trail of a narrow crack. To their amazement they uncovered an extraordinary "living" cave—with formations in a dazzling array of sizes, shapes, and colors, dropping down thousands of feet and still growing.

Visitors can walk through this amazing underworld and revel at its impressive speleothems. Kartchner Caverns is home to many unique formations, from the tiny and delicate to the massive. Within its walls explorers will glimpse the first cave sighting of the "bird's nest" needle quartz formation, the tallest and widest column in the state of Arizona, and the longest soda-straw formation in the United States, measuring 21 feet, 2 inches. In addition to pointing out the cave's distinctive features, tour guides share highlights from its prehistoric past and active present. Paleontologists have declared the cave a treasure trove of local fossil history, thanks to finds including the skeletons of an 80,000-year-old Shasta ground sloth, a 14,000-year-old horse, and an 11,000-year-old bear. Today the cave serves as a nursery roost for over 1,000 female cave myotis bats.

Once outside the cave, visitors can stretch their legs on a scenic trail. The park also offers food vendors, picnic areas, and camping sites.

▶ Open year-round. Admission charged.

www.azstateparks.com/Parks/KACA
(520) 586-2283

did you know ?

Each summer night mother bats leave Kartchner Cave to forage the countryside for insects to feed their young. In one season the colony consumes half a ton of insects, including flying ants, beetles, mosquitoes, and termites.

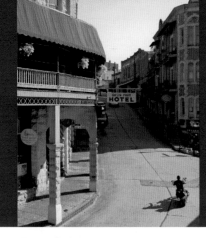

Arkansas

Bordered by the Mississippi River, Arkansas is steeped in history and mountain culture and boasts some of the nation's most eye-popping scenery.

Eureka Springs. Architecture is among the draws in this venerable spa town.

Attractions in Arkansas's historic towns include antebellum houses, antique shops, and even vintage motorcar and motorcycle museums. A battleground, a scenic wilderness river, and the relics of prairie culture are here to be appreciated as well.

Most surprising is a state park where you can dig for diamonds and keep what you find. Oil is another treasure drawn from Arkansan earth, as a natural resources museum reveals.

visit ➤➤  offthebeatenpathtrips.com

1 Pea Ridge National Military Park

15930 Hwy. 62, Garfield

In the early phase of the Civil War, the Union forces in Missouri, intent on controlling that state, drove the pro-Confederate troops into neighboring Arkansas. Inevitably, when the Southern forces attempted to move back into Missouri to capture the vital crossroads city of St. Louis, the two armies clashed. After a raging battle at Pea Ridge, the Confederate soldiers, low on ammunition, were forced to retreat, and Missouri was saved for the Union.

A seven-mile self-guiding automobile tour on an excellent paved road takes you to the scenes of that struggle, including Pea Ridge, which overlooks the battlefield, and the restored Elkhorn Tavern, a focal point of much of the fighting. A seven-mile hiking trail also makes a loop of the region. A 28-minute film depicting the famous battle is presented at the visitors center.

▶ Open year-round except major winter holidays. Admission charged.

www.nps.gov/peri
(479) 451-8122

2 Eureka Springs

This little town in the Ozarks has been renowned for its legendary waters, which were once believed to have healing properties. The town was built up during the Victorian era and still boasts incredible original architecture from the period. Health-seekers have flocked to the town over the last 200 years, making it a popular retreat. The town has numerous art and antiques shops; offers garden, cave, and ghost tours; and puts on the annual New Great Passion Play, which draws crowds in the summer that swell its population beyond the usual 2,500. Day spas, adorable Victorian bed-and-breakfasts, and quirky festivals all preserve the town's legendary charm.

Eureka Springs is surrounded by miles of trails, rivers, and streams, and there are several places in town to rent boats and fishing equipment. Nearby resorts offer golf, horseback riding, and winter activities.

▶ Open year-round.

www.eurekasprings.com
(866) 566-9387

Buffalo National River. Roark Bluff rises above Steel Creek, a tributary of the Buffalo— the first waterway to be named a national river by the National Park Service.

3 Buffalo National River

Harrison

One of the most scenic rivers in the United States, the Buffalo has miraculously escaped alteration or impairment by civilization. To keep it that way, it has been designated a national river for 135 miles of its 150-mile length. It is protected by the National Park Service, which also administers a 95,000-acre strip of wilderness bordering its serpentine course.

The Buffalo is especially popular with canoeists and kayakers, who can enjoy a half-day trip or a 10-day, 120-mile expedition. Canoes and kayaks can be rented, with transportation provided to and from any of the 20 access points. Picnic areas and campsites are scattered along the river. Some 74 kinds of fish have been found in the Buffalo; the most popular are smallmouth bass, goggle-eye, perch, bream, and catfish.

Several hiking trails and old abandoned roads give access to the surrounding Ozark wilderness, which has changed little in character in the last century.

In this richly varied environment over 1,500 different plant species come into flower between late January and late autumn. The Lost Valley Nature Trail, which follows Clark Creek as it skirts waterfalls, towering fern-clad cliffs, a natural bridge, and a 200-foot cave, is especially rewarding. The dense forests are home to deer, beavers, red foxes, coyotes, and a great variety of native birds.
▶ Open year-round.

www.nps.gov/buff
(870) 429-2502

4 ▶ Withrow Springs State Park

Rte. 23, north of Huntsville
Bordered by towering bluffs along the War Eagle River, this secluded 786-acre retreat contains everything associated with the Ozark mountain region: a magnificent wilderness of ridges and valleys, wildlife, woodlands, and a small creek fed by clear springs.

The sparkling waters of War Eagle Creek nourish the life of the park, providing an excellent canoe run and fine fishing. Hikers have three scenic trails to explore. The three-quarter-mile Dogwood Trail, named for the area's most prevalent tree, makes a loop along ravines and ridges in colorful wooded terrain. The moderately difficult War Eagle Trail begins at a bridge, climbs up a 150-foot hill to a bluff that lets you look down to the river 200 feet below, and then continues on to a large cave with an underground stream. The trail is about a mile long and requires backtracking. The Forest Trail follows an old roadway through a hardwood forest and connects with a paved highway that leads back to the campground, a trip of about 2 1/2 miles.
▶ Open year-round.

www.arkansasstateparks.com
(479) 559-2593

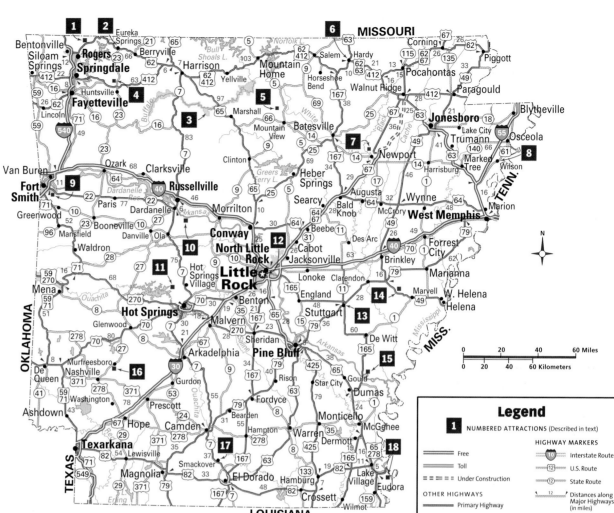

4 ▶ Withrow Springs State Park. Campers who pitch tents at certain campgrounds in this secluded wilderness can avail themselves of electrical outlets and a water spigot.

5 Blanchard Springs Caverns

Off Ark. 14, 15 miles northwest of Mountain View

Because some of the more enchanting caves here were not discovered until the 1960s, this magnificent underworld system isn't yet as well known as New Mexico's Carlsbad Caverns, though it is in many ways just as spectacular.

Visitors to this subterranean marvel have a choice of three tours. Along the easier Dripstone Trail found in 1963, you pass through the aptly named Cathedral Room, an enormous chamber whose size is accentuated by a play of light on a number of dazzling cave formations, and the stunning Coral Room.

The Discovery Trail is a taxing 90-minute walk, including 700 steps, and is open only from Memorial Day through Labor Day. Commensurate rewards include seeing the underground stream that creates Blanchard Springs and the haunting Ghost Room. The Wild Tour, available only by reservation, is a very strenuous three- to four-hour tour of the deeper reaches of the caves.

The caverns are located in an unspoiled area of the Ozark National Forest near Sylamore Creek, a pristine stream claiming one of the few old-fashioned swimming holes left in this part of the country. A recreation area at the cavern site offers camping.

▶ Open year-round. Admission charged.

www.blanchardcavetours.com
(888) 757-2246

6 Historic Hardy

At the juncture of U.S. Rtes. 63/62 and 412

Listed on the *National Register of Historic Places,* this charming small town looks much as it did during the Model-T days. Centered on Main St., the town's business district consists of three square blocks. Among its 43 buildings are three churches and dozens of vintage craft nooks and antiques shops. In fact, Historic Hardy prides itself as the Antique and Craft Capital of the Arkansas Ozarks. Quaint shops feature the work of local artisans, including

handmade musical instruments, like wooden flutes and mountain dulcimers. Local musicians often gather at the Main St. Gazebo to play time-honored favorites from the Ozarks region.

Formally established in 1883, Hardy got its start in a heavily timbered, sparsely populated area. The town gained prestige as the county seat in 1894 but remained tiny. By 1900 its residents numbered just about 600. During the next couple of decades, thanks to an economic boom and the expanding railroad, Hardy built up a small but thriving downtown business district, including general stores, two cafés, two livery stables, and a livestock sale barn. In 1982 a devastating flood severely damaged most of the downtown buildings. After the flood the nostalgic townspeople made a pledge to restore Hardy to its old-town glory.

The Vintage Motorcar Museum boasts a private collection of more than 50 classic vehicles, from a 1908 Sears Runabout to a 1981 DeLorean. Just one block off Main St. the cool, clear waters of Spring River beckon with the promise of excellent fishing, as well as canoeing and swimming.

7 Jacksonport State Park. The *Mary Woods No. 2* steamboat plied the Mississippi, White, and Cache rivers to transport lumber for the Woods Lumber Company.

www.oldhardytown.net
(870) 856-3811 City Hall

7 Jacksonport State Park

Avenue St., Newport

The romance of the Old South and the boisterous steamboat days lives on in this small, pretty park along a sweeping bend of the White River. Jacksonport began as a shipping point in the early 1800s and later became a busy steamboat port. Its glory days came to an end in 1891, when a new railroad line made nearby Newport the center of commerce and the county seat. From that time Jacksonport steadily declined. All of its buildings have vanished, many destroyed by floodwaters, except for the old Jacksonport Courthouse, which was refurbished following a 1997 tornado.

The stately courthouse, built in 1872 on a high, sturdy foundation of Arkansas limestone, has been restored and included on the *National Register of Historic Places.* It is now the focal point of the park, housing a museum of memorabilia and relics that trace the history of the community through the steamboat era. Other

5 Blanchard Springs Caverns. Visitors wend their way through the caverns' magnificent Cathedral Room. The hanging formation on the left is called a drapery.

exhibits show local architecture and a 19th-century courthouse and clerk's office. Moored at the steamboat landing across the levee from the courthouse—and maintained as though ready for a week's cruise—is the *Mary Woods No. 2*, a white double-deck paddle boat.

Campsites and picnic tables are pleasingly situated on an open, grassy expanse along the river beneath a scattering of shade trees. The 154-acre park also boasts a sandy swimming beach, a boat ramp, a small woodland, and a lovely pecan grove.

▶ Park open year-round. Courthouse open Tues.-Sun.; paddle boat open Tues.-Sun., Apr.-Oct. Admission charged.

www.arkansasstateparks.com
(870) 523-2143

8 ▶ Hampson Archaeological Museum State Park

2 Lake Dr., Wilson
Persons interested in America's past, in particular Native American history, will find the Hampson Archeological Museum an especially rewarding one. Its enormous collection of artifacts—some 41,000 items, including remarkably beautiful ceramics, stone tools, weapons, human and animal effigies, and skeletal remains—serves to portray the culture of the farming and mound-building people who lived in this area from about 1400 to 1650 and who then seemed to disappear.

There are usually 300 exhibits on display at any one time, and many of them were excavated by Dr. James K. Hampson in the 1920s and '30s on his family plantation, Nodena (five miles from Wilson), where a palisaded village with two pyramid mounds once existed.

The small park, which is right in the village of Wilson, also offers a pleasant picnic area and a playground.

▶ Open Tues.-Sun. year-round except major holidays. Admission charged for museum.

www.arkansasstateparks.com
(870) 655-8622

9 ▶ Janet Huckabee Arkansas River Valley Nature Center

8300 Wells Lake Rd., Barling
Situated on 170 acres dense with hickory and oak trees, this nature center is dedicated to the appreciation of the landscape and the preservation of its wildlife. Its main building houses several fun and informative exhibits, including a 1,200-gallon aquarium filled with native Arkansas fish and a life-size oak tree exhibit with animal displays. Signs highlight interesting features along the various short trails that explore the surroundings. The Wells Lake Trail, a half-mile wheelchair-accessible paved path, follows the edge of Wells Lake, where Canada Geese live year-round and blue herons can be seen fishing.

▶ Open Tues.-Sun. year-round except major holidays.

www.rivervalleynaturecenter.com
(479) 452-3993

10 ▶ Holla Bend National Wildlife Refuge

From Dardanelle take Rte. 7S and turn left on Cty. Rte. 155
This 7,050-acre sanctuary is actually an island that was formed in 1954 when the U.S. Army Corps of Engineers cut a new channel for the Arkansas River across a deep bend in the old channel.

Located on a main flyway of migrating birds, the refuge, with its ponds and lakes, is a wintering home for some 5,000 Canada geese and at least 35,000 ducks. Up to 40 bald eagles can be seen sojourning here from Nov. to Mar. Permanent residents include herons, egrets, gulls, and terns. More than a quarter of the refuge is farmed, and a portion of each year's crop of corn and wheat is left in the fields for the birds.

10 ▶ Holla Bend National Wildlife Refuge. Snow geese take flight at this quiet sanctuary, most of which can be seen on an eight-mile self-guiding drive.

You can observe most of the refuge by following the eight-mile self-guiding all-weather drive. Fishing is good, and boat ramps are located on Lodge Lake, Long Lake, and Old River Channel.

▶ Open year-round. Fee charged.

www.fws.gov/southeast/HollaBend
(479) 229-4300

---

did you know ?

The Holla Bend National Wildlife Refuge marks the northern extreme of the American alligator's habitat.

11 ▶ Lake Ouachita State Park

5451 Mountain Pine Rd., Mountain Pine
The park is nestled in the pine-covered hills bordering the eastern end of Lake Ouachita (pronounced Wash-i-taw), the state's largest man-made lake. This site offers camping, boating, waterskiing, swimming, and fishing along the lake's 975 miles of shoreline.

Boaters taking the Geo-Float Trail can examine the area's unusual geologic features, including mini caves and earthquake remains. Landlubbers can walk two hiking trails that wander through the lush woodlands of the 365-acre park.

Since the late 1800s, vacationers have been lured by the Three Sisters natural springs, which are said to have curative powers. The springs are no longer used as the park's water supply but are still open as a historical display. Note: No pets allowed on beaches.

▶ Open year-round.

www.arkansasstateparks.com
(501) 767-9366

12 Arkansas Museum of Discovery

500 President Clinton Ave., Suite 150, Little Rock

Little Rock's oldest museum is located right in the heart of the River Market District, making it an easy stop on a tour of the state capital. Over 25,000 square feet of hands-on, interactive exhibits entertain adults and children alike with the wonders of science, technology, and mathematics. Room to Grow, a 3,000-foot permanent

13 **Museum of the Arkansas Grand Prairie.** In 1976 this wagon represented Arkansas in the Bicentennial Wagon Train that traveled from California to Washington, D. C.

exhibit for kids six years old and under, includes the Construction Zone, which introduces children to the mechanics of construction while they build and play. A climbable lighthouse and friendly Mimi the Dragon captivates even the most active children. More educational exhibits include the Bug Zoo, the Health Hall, World of the Forest, and Arkansas Indians, which introduce kids to environmental and cultural history.

▶ Open daily year-round except major holidays. Admission charged.

www.amod.org
(501) 396-7050

13 Museum of the Arkansas Grand Prairie

921 E. Fourth St., Stuttgart

This fascinating museum complex preserves the farm equipment, household antiques, and other relics of the prairie farm culture that developed here in the years after the Civil War.

Funds to build the museum were donated by local farm families, who also contributed all the items on display, among them some impressive 19th-century steam-

powered farm machinery. Local craftsmen have also built replicas of a 1914 schoolhouse, the old community firehouse, complete with the refurbished 1926 fire engine, a fully furnished 1880 prairie home, a scaled-down model of an 1896 Lutheran church, and the façades of stores that once existed here.

Among the charming and unexpected exhibits is a collection of musical instruments and music boxes that entertained the great-grandparents of the women who run the museum today, and one of the largest game-call collections in the United States.

▶ Open Tues.-Sat. year-round except major holidays.

www.arkansas.com/attractions
(870) 673-7001

14 Louisiana Purchase State Park

Off U.S. Rte. 49, south of Brinkley

In 1815, 12 years after the Louisiana Purchase, a team of government surveyors blazed two big sweet gum trees in a trackless swamp in eastern Arkansas. Those marks were the starting point for the monumental task of determining the bounds of that addition to the United States.

Though the blazed trees are gone, 37½ acres of the headwater swamp have been preserved as a state park. A 950-foot-long boardwalk leads through the area to a marker designating the initial point for the entire survey. A stroll offers a close-up view of this environment, where you can find the uncommon swamp cottonwood tree, the golden prothonotary warbler, and the little brown-and-green tree frog.

▶ Open year-round.

www.arkansasstateparks.com
(888) 287-2757

15 Arkansas Post National Memorial

1741 Old Post Rd., Gillett

Called the birthplace of Arkansas, the small settlement of Arkansas Post was established in 1686 by Henri de Tonti on a grant given to him four years earlier by his chief, the great French explorer La Salle. The trading post was probably abandoned a few years later, but in the early 1700s profitable trade with the Native Americans revived

interest in the region, and Arkansas Post was rebuilt.

After becoming an American village in 1803, Arkansas Post grew into a bustling frontier town, and in 1819 it was made the first territorial capital of Arkansas. But it faded away when the government moved to Little Rock in 1821.

During the 1700s and 1800s Arkansas Post was relocated many times because of the river's instability. Several of these sites are within today's 747-acre memorial park. Spring and fall are the best seasons for viewing alligators. Self-guiding trails through this setting of quiet beauty help re-create the past.

The park is also a wildlife preserve and a magnificent spot for bird-watching. Park Lake yields large bass and catfish. A launching ramp for small boats just beyond the park gives access to the Arkansas River, Moore, and Post bayous, and Post Bend Lake. The visitors center has first-rate archaeological, historical, and wildlife exhibits.

▶ Park open year-round.

www.nps.gov/arpo
(870) 548-2207

15 **Arkansas Post.** Exhibitions in the visitors center trace the history of the state's first settlement.

16 Crater of Diamonds State Park

Rte. 301, south of Murfreesboro

Here's a unique chance to combine fun and profit by prospecting in the only significant diamond deposit in North America. Plus, you get to keep any stones you find.

Best known for diamonds, the area also yields amethyst, agate, jasper, quartz, and other semi-precious stones. A 37-acre field is deep-plowed regularly to expose new earth.

Many of the diamonds are of an industrial quality, but every year visitors turn up hundreds of gems of significant quality and value, and some lucky prospectors carry away diamonds ranging from 2 to 5 carats.

The first diamond from this area was found in 1906, but for various reasons commercial mining has never been successful here, and in 1972 the field was made part of an 911-acre park along the piney banks of the Little Missouri River. Some tips: Wear a hat because there's little shade. Bring boots or overshoes because the plowed earth is usually muddy. The park visitors center has digging equipment available to rent, or visitors can bring their own. The staff will identify and certify any diamonds you unearth.

▶ Park open year-round.

Admission charged for diamond field.

www.craterofdiamondsstatepark.com
(870) 285-3113

17 Arkansas Museum of Natural Resources

3853 Smackover Hwy., Smackover

The French called the area *sumac couvert*—"covered with sumac." To American ears those words sounded like "Smackover," though its history has less to do with sumac than petroleum. Smackover was the scene of a wild and woolly oil boom during the 1920s. After that it faded to a kind of uneventful small-town respectability. You'll see no evidence of the old shoot-em-up, strike-it-rich excitement, and though just about every cow pasture and vacant lot in this area has one of those woodpecker-looking oil rigs silently pumping away, few local residents know much about the colorful history of the petroleum industry or the nuts and bolts of how it works.

This museum gives visitors a historical and practical understanding of the oil business. Giant antique derricks and a working well are among the outdoor exhibits tucked into a pretty section of pinewoods along scenic Rte. 7, just north of town.

▶ Open daily year-round except major holidays.

www.amnr.org
(870) 725-2877

18 Lakeport Plantation

On AR-142, off Hwy. 82, near Lake Village

This historic plantation which once covered more than 4,000 acres evokes a time when cotton was the leading crop in the South. One of the few plantations that survived the Civil War, it resourcefully adapted farming methods in the absence of slavery. The house, built in the late 1850s, is the only remaining Mississippi River plantation home in Arkansas and was added to the *National Register of Historic Places* in 1974.

The extensive history of cotton production here provides a fascinating glimpse into the evolution of Southern culture and the African-American experience. The area was restored by Arkansas State University as a museum and educational center, with the house as the primary exhibit. Through special exhibits and programming, visitors relive the glory days of the South and follow the effects of changing technology and agricultural techniques on the plantations of the Mississippi River Delta.

▶ Open Mon.-Fri. year-round, except major holidays. Admission charged.

http://lakeport.astate.edu
(870) 265-6031

California

For all its popularity as a travel destination, the Golden State still has plenty of wonderful out-of-the-way places to explore.

San Francisco Maritime National Historical Park and Museum.
A square-rigger and a tugboat berthed at Hyde Street Pier are a part of a historic fleet that transports visitors into maritime history (see page 41).

Pinnacles and Lava Beds national monuments and some other intriguing California landscapes owe their existence to volcanism, while fanciful shapes in sandstone and tufa were sculpted by erosion or calcium compounds. Must-see man-made points of interest here include a San Francisco maritime museum offering cruises on vintage vessels, the charming Catalina Island town of Avalon, and an incredible underground residence and gardens carved out of the San Joaquin Valley hardpan by an enterprising immigrant.

Migrating waterfowl by the millions descend on inviting marshes and ponds in the desert, and Monarch butterflies flit among the eucalyptus trees at Natural Bridges State Beach. At seashores elsewhere, travelers spy seals and sea lions in rocky coves and keep an eye on the blue Pacific should a pod of dolphins or a breaching whale come into view.

visit ➡ (offthebeatenpathtrips.com)

1 Prairie Creek Redwoods State Park

127011 Newton B. Drury Pkwy., Orick
Driving north on Rte. 101, travelers are almost certain to notice the sudden appearance of the majestic Roosevelt elk in Boyes Prairie near the park headquarters and visitors center. A display at the center features a month-by-month account of the life cycle of this magnificent tree—the largest in California. Another entire room is devoted to the ecology of the mighty redwoods, for instance.

The 14,000-acre park is a preserve for these trees *(Sequoia sempervirens),* the tallest species on Earth. Some specimens here soar 300 feet. They and their companion plants can be seen close up on more than 30 trails that range from easy to strenuous and from one-tenth of a mile to seven miles long. Some lead down to Gold Bluffs Beach. The James Irvine Trail, for example, is a four-mile hike through redwoods and a lush undergrowth of hemlock, laurel, and alder. It connects with the Fern Canyon Trail, where eight species of ferns cling to the steplike ledges of the canyon wall. A herd of elk roams the beach and should be given a wide berth. They are wild and unpredictable. You can camp at the beach or near park headquarters at Elk Prairie.

1 Prairie Creek Redwoods State Park. Four Roosevelt elk cows pause as they graze at Boyes Prairie. To the north the prairie gives way to old-growth coast redwoods.

▶ Open year-round. Admission charged.
www.parks.ca.gov
(707) 465-7347

2 Lava Beds National Monument

1 Indian Well Headquarters (off Rtes. 139 and 161), Tulelake
A vast, majestic stretch of high desert ringed with purple mountains, the monument preserves the special beauty and strangeness of land marked by volcanic activity. From the northeast entrance the park road winds through scrubby sagebrush and rolling hills dotted with juniper and, finally, stands of yellow pine. Jagged lava rocks, deep orange in color, lie precariously amid the wispy sage.

At the visitors center near the southeast entrance, information is available on the area's turbulent volcanic origins and its plant and animal life, and a rock display illustrates the variety of minerals found here. An interpretive trail in the adjacent, illuminated Mushpot Cave explains lavacicles, spatter cones, balconies, and other formations found in the monument's 811 lava-tube caves. More than 15 of these are accessible from Cave Loop Rd., which begins at the visitors center. If you want to explore them, the center will lend you portable lights.

The terrain once provided

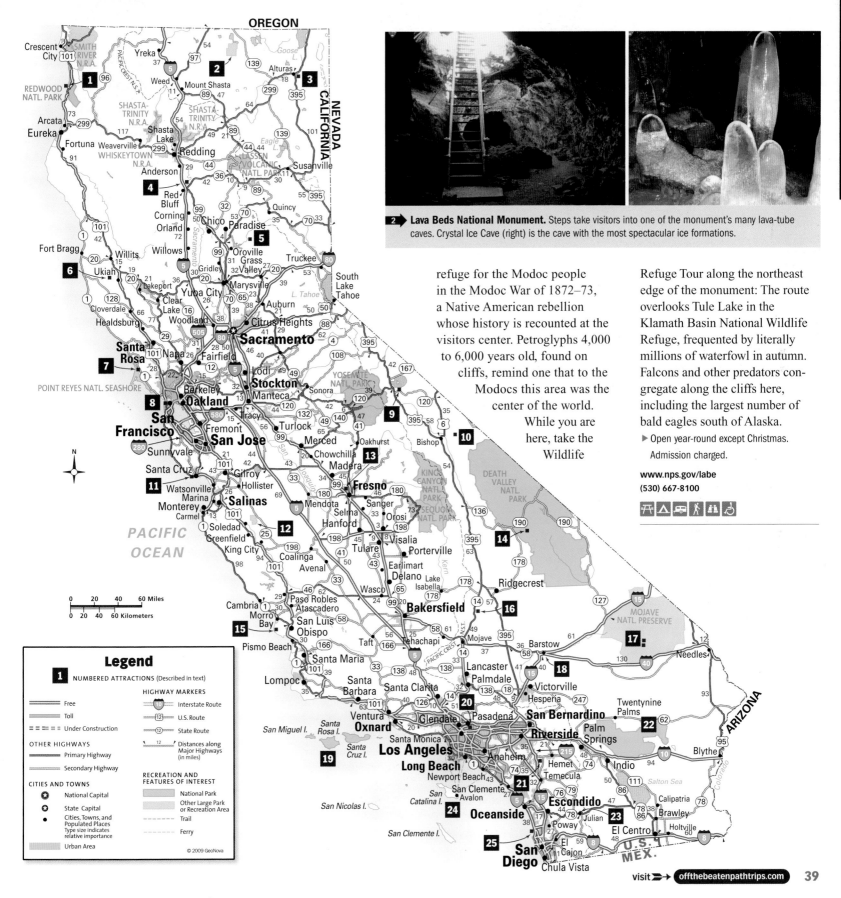

2 **Lava Beds National Monument.** Steps take visitors into one of the monument's many lava-tube caves. Crystal Ice Cave (right) is the cave with the most spectacular ice formations.

refuge for the Modoc people in the Modoc War of 1872–73, a Native American rebellion whose history is recounted at the visitors center. Petroglyphs 4,000 to 6,000 years old, found on cliffs, remind one that to the Modocs this area was the center of the world.

While you are here, take the Wildlife Refuge Tour along the northeast edge of the monument: The route overlooks Tule Lake in the Klamath Basin National Wildlife Refuge, frequented by literally millions of waterfowl in autumn. Falcons and other predators congregate along the cliffs here, including the largest number of bald eagles south of Alaska.

▶ Open year-round except Christmas. Admission charged.

www.nps.gov/labe
(530) 667-8100

Legend

1 NUMBERED ATTRACTIONS (Described in text)

OTHER HIGHWAYS
Free
Toll
Under Construction
Primary Highway
Secondary Highway

HIGHWAY MARKERS
Interstate Route
U.S. Route
State Route
Distances along Major Highways (in miles)

CITIES AND TOWNS
⊛ National Capital
⊛ State Capital
• Cities, Towns, and Populated Places Type size indicates relative importance
Urban Area

RECREATION AND FEATURES OF INTEREST
National Park
Other Large Park or Recreation Area
Trail
Ferry

© 2009 GeoNova

3 Modoc National Wildlife Refuge

Alturas

An expanse of golden desert with a managed system of marshes, lakes, and ponds, this 7,000-acre refuge on the Pacific Flyway is specifically designed for migratory birds, and it's a bird-watcher's delight.

While geese, hawks, ducks, egrets, and a variety of shorebirds and warblers are most frequently seen here, some 220 species have been recorded. A drive around Teal Pond is a good way to see them at close range. Grassy, tufted islets dot the pond, and herons and egrets often stand motionless along their shores. Great numbers of tundra swans may also be seen gliding on the placid blue waters.

The refuge is the summer home for the largest population of sandhill cranes in California. This wading bird with blue-gray body and bright red patch on the head grows to about four feet tall and is easy to spot. If birding is your special interest, April and September are the best times to see the greatest number of species.

Among the mammals seen here year-round are rabbits, muskrats, minks, raccoons, coyotes, and mule deer. Fishing is allowed in Dorris Reservoir, and part of the refuge is set aside for seasonal hunting.

▶ Open daily year-round.

http://modoc.fws.gov
(530) 233-3572

4 William B. Ide Adobe State Historic Park

21659 Adobe Rd., Red Bluff
This 1850s home is a focus for year-round programs aimed at giv-ing visitors a firsthand feel for pioneer life. William Brown Ide, fresh from Illinois, served as the leader of the short-lived Republic of California from June 14, 1846, when a small band of American settlers revolted against Mexican rule. His term ended abruptly on July 10, when the republic was declared a U.S. protectorate.

The state acquired the compound in 1951, embarking on extensive restoration of the low-roofed main house, carriage house, well, and smokehouse.

Throughout the summer months visitors can view various craft demonstrations, such as brick-making, candle-making, blacksmithing, quilting, and wood-working.

▶ Open year-round. Parking fee.

www.parks.ca.gov
(530) 529-8599

5 Feather Falls Scenic Area

Feather Falls Trailhead Rd., Oroville
Gleaming like a glass skyscraper, the three tiers of Feather Falls plunge 640 feet into a valley cut into the Sierra foothills.

Hikers can take a moderate-level well-marked trail leading through sparse manzanita and pine chaparral to an observation deck with a spectacular top-to-bottom view of the falls. Hikers should plan on an afternoon to make the seven-mile round-trip and be sure to carry plenty of water. The best seasons to visit are in the spring, when wildflowers provide a painter's palette of colors, and in autumn when the trees are adorned with reds and golds.

The scenic area, which encompasses 15,000 acres in the Plumas National Forest, includes a number of other hiking trails, scenic spots, and campgrounds. The three branches of the Feather River (whose middle fork is fed by the falls) afford some of the most challenging whitewater rafting in the state. Downstream are calmer stretches of water for canoeing or kayaking.

▶ Open year-round.

www.r5.fs.fed.us/plumas
(530) 534-6500

5 Feather Falls Scenic Area. The observation deck, set on a rocky promontory, affords views of the entire falls from across a gorge. Feather Falls is the sixth longest waterfall in the lower 48 states and the fourth longest in California.

6 Montgomery Woods State Reserve

Orr Springs Rd., Ukiah
Montgomery Woods is a fine place to see giant redwoods in their primeval state. A clearing ringed with the largest trees—10 to 15 feet in diameter—opens about four-fifths of a mile along the steep loop of Memorial Grove Trail, which begins at the reserve pullout. From a carpet of their red-brown needles, redwoods rise like temple columns, and any stage designer would envy the hazy amber light and vivid green of the ferns in this setting. Silence is deep, civilization distant. Camping is prohibited in the 2,743-acre reserve, but there are picnic tables near the creek that border the trail.

An added aspect of the woods' appeal is the pleasure of getting there. Orr Springs Rd. winds through barren, rocky areas with views of rolling hills and pasture-lands and glimpses of the Napa and Mendocino valleys. Narrow, steep, and full of hairpin turns, the road is an exciting experience, but one should not attempt it with a trailer or mobile home in tow.

▶ Open year-round.

www.parks.ca.gov
(707) 937-5804

7 ▶ **Tomales Bay State Park**

1208 Pierce Pt. Rd., Inverness
From clearings in the dense, aromatic undergrowth above the sandy crescent of Heart's Desire Beach, there are endless views beyond the circling gulls and hawks to the golden hills across the bay. If you don't mind chilly water, you can swim here at the surf-free beaches, then warm up with a hike along the Johnstone Trail at the south end of the beach: a corridor lined with huckleberry, oak, giant fern, and braids of green lichen. Or take the Indian Nature Trail at the north end to Indian Beach, where with a California

fishing license you can dig for littleneck clams and the occasional giant four-pound horseneck.

Off Rte. 1 on the way into the park, stop at the Bear Valley Visitors Center for a wealth of information on the history, plants, and wildlife of Tomales Bay. A word about the weather: Vital for sustaining the park's abundant vegetation through the Mar.– Sept. dry season are the picturesque but chilly fogs that roll in the rest of the year.

▶ Open year-round. Admission charged.

www.parks.ca.gov
(415) 669-1140

8 ▶ **San Francisco Maritime National Historical Park and Museum**

*Hyde St. Pier,
San Francisco's Fisherman's Wharf*
For avid sailors and vicarious seafaring adventurers the Hyde Street Pier offers a fascinating sail back through time. On the Hyde Street Pier landlubbers can tour an impressive fleet of historic vessels, including the 1886 square-rigger *Balclutha*, the 1890 steam ferry

7 ▶ **Tomales Bay State Park.** Tomales Bay offers more than just a beach. In winter migrating whales and elephant seals may be spotted.

8 ▶ **San Francisco Maritime National Historical Park and Museum.** The graceful curve of the Municipal Pier defines the outer edge of the Aquatic Park Historic Landmark District.

Eureka, the 1907 steam tugboat *Hercules*, and the 1895 lumber schooner *CA Thayer.*

Visitors can also experience what life was like for submariners during World War II when they step aboard the USS *Pampanito,* a fully restored floating exhibit, now a national landmark, at Pier 45.

Continuing the journey, the park's collection of small craft, both traditional and trailblazing, provide a lively introduction to boat building and the maritime trades.

Built as a project of the New Deal's Works Progress Administration, the Aquatic Park Bathhouse is a work of art in itself. The museum inside includes mast sections, jutting spars, and authentic ship figureheads are arranged among the colorful fish and gleaming tiles of renowned muralist Hilaire Hiler's expressionist vision of Atlantis. Also, *Mermaid,* the one-man sailboat that transported a daring solo adventurer across the Pacific Ocean from Japan in 94 days, is displayed on the balcony.

Along with detailed ship models, intricate works of scrimshaw, and whaling guns, the museum features video presentations and interactive exhibits.

In addition, the park offers frequent historical re-creations, interpretive programs, and a visitors center with exhibits, including a "First Order" fresnel lighthouse lens. Visitors might catch a demonstration of rigging, a class in navigation or woodworking, or a rousing concert of sea chanteys. There are also activities designed especially for kids. The voyage culminates at the Maritime Store, managed by the non-profit San Francisco Maritime National Park Association, offering a range of maritime-related books, games, and videos, ship plans and models, and a selection of maritime folk music.

▶ Open year-round. Entrance fee for historic vessels.

www.nps.gov/safr
(415) 447-5000

9 Mono Lake Tufa State Reserve

Hwy. 395, Lee Vining

Author Mark Twain called the fantasy landscape of Mono Lake a "sullen, silent, sail-less sea," and indeed the 1,000,000-year-old lake is three times saltier than the ocean and has a forbidding mien.

It is fed by melting snow and underwater springs and is dotted with dramatic and intricately fili-greed white limestone towers, knobs, and spires, produced when calcium-laden fresh water wells up through alkaline lake water, precipitating calcium carbonate, or tufa.

As the lake level drops (through natural evaporation) and as freshwater sources are diverted to provide drinking water for the city of Los Angeles, the lake bed's tufa formations are exposed.

No fish can live in the concentrated minerals and salts of Mono Lake, but brine shrimp and alkali flies thrive in the trillions. They provide food for the thousands of gulls and other migratory birds that flock here in spring and summer.

The lake's South Tufa area features a one-mile nature trail that clearly explains the lake and its peculiarities. Other attractions in this immense reserve (17,000 acres) include exceptionally buoyant swimming at nearby Navy Beach, boating, and if you arrive at the right time—dusk, say—a glimpse of the awesome alpen glow, the strange phenomenon of reflected light that bathes the High Sierra with rose and gold.

▶ Open year-round.

www.parks.ca.gov
(760) 647-6331

10 Ancient Bristlecone Pine Forest

White Mountain Rd., Big Pine

Suspended eerily on the rugged slopes of the White Mountains, at an altitude of 10,000 or more feet, is a stand of one of the planet's oldest living trees: the Great Basin bristlecone pine *(Pinus longaeva)*. The most ancient specimen is the 4,700-year-old Methuselah, which stands in a grove of pines that has been growing here for 4,000 years

10 ▶ Ancient Bristlecone Pine Forest. In the United States ancient bristlecone pine trees are found only in California and Nevada.

or more. The exact location of the tree is kept confidential in order to protect it.

Twelve miles farther along the road that crosses the forest is the world's largest bristlecone pine. Here in the Patriarch Grove, at 11,000 feet, is the Old Patriarch itself, which measures more than 36 feet in circumference.

The bristlecones' tortured shapes reflect the barren, wind-swept conditions amid which they persevere, jutting out from the mountainside like bleached bones or driftwood. Many branches appear dead, while others are thickly furred with green needles. Drippings of clear, bluish sap perfume the air. For all the seeming aridity of the land, there are lovely stands of wildflowers in the Patriarch area in August.

In most weather conditions the steep road to the forest provides breathtaking views across Owens Valley to the sheer white face of the Sierra Nevada. But after big snowfalls cars must turn back at the Sierra Vista lookout, which is at an elevation of 10,000 feet. In good weather take advantage of miles of trails and picnic grounds beautifully sited in and around this great forest.

▶ Open daily mid-May-Oct.

www.fs.fed.us/r5/inyo
(760) 873-2500

11 Natural Bridges State Beach

2531 W. Cliff Dr., Santa Cruz

The Monarch butterflies come from somewhere west of the Rockies (no one is sure just where), but every September they return to the same spot—a eucalyptus grove at the Natural Bridges State Beach, where milkweed, the only food the Monarch caterpillar eats, abounds. When the magnificent Monarchs move on, usually in late December, plenty of marvels remain: shore birds diving and soaring, whales plying migratory passages, and seals and sea otters amusing themselves just offshore.

Visitors can view Monarch eggs, caterpillars, and chrysalides close up at a demonstration milkweed patch maintained at Natural Bridges. In the spring native wildflowers bloom in the coastal scrub meadows along Moore Creek as it winds its way toward the sea. Low tides reveal sea stars, crabs, and sea anemones.

The one thing nature lovers won't find here, however, is a

did you know ?

The Monarch Grove at Natural Bridges State Beach protects over 100,000 butterflies each winter.

9 ▶ Mono Lake Tufa State Reserve. Strange calcium carbonate formations called tufas give the lake, with its exceedingly salty water, an otherworldly feel.

 **Natural Bridges State Beach.** The formations that explain this beach's name once numbered three, but only one has stood up to time and tides.

bridge. Over many years the hollowed-out sandstone cliffs that gave the park its name were turned into islands by the powerful waves of the Pacific, and today only one natural bridge survives.

▶ Open year-round. Fee for parking.

www.santacruzstateparks.org/parks
    /natbridges

(831) 423-4609

12 Pinnacles National Monument

5000 Hwy. 146, Paicines
It's a surprise, driving through the gentle coastal hills of Monterey and San Benito counties, to suddenly come upon the jagged red spires and rugged canyons of Pinnacles National Monument. The rich soil here, on the weathered remains of an ancient volcano, helps support a variety of plant and animal life, and the Pinnacles' high, open terrain is well suited to hiking. There are over 30 miles of tended trails against a backdrop of the endlessly changing hues and textures of

eroded volcanic rock. "Wilderness treks" are for experienced hikers, cave trails for would-be spelunkers (don't forget a flashlight). Scaling the Pinnacles' sheer pink cliffs, however, demands experience and specialized equipment.

Several trailheads are accessible from Bear Gulch Visitor Center. The Moses Spring Self-Guiding Trail, for instance, climaxes with a visit to the Bear Gulch Reservoir. Hikers who want even more of a challenge can take High Peaks Trail, a two-mile ramble along the higher reaches.

▶ Open year-round. Admission charged.

www.nps.gov/pinn
(831) 389-4486

13 Forestiere Underground Gardens

5021 W. Shaw Ave., Fresno
Sicilian immigrant Baldassare Forestiere made a big mistake in the early 1900s. Dreaming of growing fruit trees and vines in the San Joaquin Valley, he bought land that turned out to be hardpan rock, useless for agriculture. But Forestiere found a way to beat the barrenness of the property and the blistering heat: He began to dig.

Working only from a vision in his mind, Forestiere patterned his designs from what he remembered from seeing the catacombs of Rome. He labored alone to build 10 acres of space for living and for crop cultivation on three levels: at 10 feet, 22 feet, and 25 feet underground.

Today visitors can tour the underground home Forestiere created for himself—a naturally air-conditioned refuge made airy and bright with the strategic placement of skylights. They also marvel at Forestiere's underground farm, complete with fruit trees and grape vines still thriving today, all in a subterranean labyrinth designed to let in just enough sunlight and rain and to keep out the heat and frost.

▶ Open year-round. Admission charged.

www.forestiere-historicalcenter.com
(559) 271-0734

 **Pinnacles National Monument.** While the rocky terrain may look foreboding, it is laced with 30 miles of trails. Lucky hikers may spot a rare California condor: In 2003 Pinnacles was designated as a national release site for the California Condor Recovery Program.

14 Wildrose Charcoal Kilns and Mahogany Flat, Death Valley National Park

Hwy. 190, Death Valley

From Wildrose campground a narrow and sometimes difficult gravel track climbs through Wildrose Canyon to Thorndike Campground at 7,400 feet, near which looms a strange colony of what look like giant beehives or prehistoric dwellings. These are the Wildrose Charcoal Kilns, 10 perfectly aligned stone-and-mortar structures some 30 feet in diameter at the base and rising to a height of about 25 feet. They were built in the 1870s to turn local juniper and pinyon pine into charcoal for the lead-and-silver-ore smelters near the Modoc and Minnietta mines.

Nobody has used the kilns for at least a century, but their sooty, conical interiors remain architecturally and acoustically fascinating. When you speak inside one, the echo seems to come from many places at once, and you can still smell the odor of burned wood.

A mile beyond the kilns lies Mahogany Flat (with campground), the site of a forest of sinewy mountain mahogany, and the trailhead for the strenuous seven-mile hike to Death Valley's highest point, Telescope Peak (11,049 feet).

▶ Open year-round, weather conditions permitting; check with park ranger. High-clearance vehicles recommended. Admission fee.

www.nps.gov/deva
(760) 786-3200

15 Montana de Oro State Park

Pecho Rd., Los Osos

This stretch of seaside marine terrace is known as the Mountain of Gold for the blaze of orange and yellow California poppies and monkey flowers that grace its slopes when spring arrives (in mid-April).

At water's edge the land crumbles into cliffs that plunge into an abundance of rocky inlets and tide pools along the four miles of shoreline in this 8,000-plus-acre park. At one point the shoreline

15 Montana de Oro State Park. Tidal pools merge with a pebble beach in a park named for the masses of yellow wildflowers growing on its slopes in spring.

16 Red Rock Canyon State Park. Even in the arid isolation of the Mojave Desert, the White House Cliffs at Red Rock canyon are a world apart.

edges inward to form a crescent pebble beach, a good place to set off on an investigation of the rocks and pools, but the water is usually too cold and rough for swimming.

The beach itself is littered with treasures: driftwood, colored pebbles, bull kelp (a seaweed whose air-bubbled stems explode with a loud crack when stepped on). The tide pools teem with snails, limpets, sea anemones, and hermit crabs. Whale spotting is a favorite pastime from Nov.-Mar., and the area is a wintertime stop for migrating monarch butterflies, which can turn entire trees into fluttering fantasies.

To all this add some year-round good weather, good picnic and camping facilities, a network of easy and challenging trails—and tonic sea air mingled with the restorative scents of coastal sage scrub.

▶ Open year-round.

www.parks.ca.gov
(805) 528-0513

16 Red Rock Canyon State Park

Hwy. 14, Cantil

The smoothly sculpted clay, sandstone, lava, and cliff formations in the canyon form a natural divide between the Sierra Nevada and the Mojave Desert. At Red Cliffs Preserve (on the eastern side of Rte. 14, which runs for about seven miles through the park), erosion has carved the stone into corrugated ripples whose shades range from pristine white to peppermint-candy reds. The colorful rock formations in the park served as landmarks during the early 1870s for freight wagons that stopped for water. The entire area is a geological treasure house, but rock hounds may be happiest in Opal Canyon (first right after Red Cliffs Preserve). Many movies have been filmed here, including *Jurassic Park*.

At Red Cliffs, where the bluffs crumble into dunes, Joshua trees offer shelter to the ubiquitous jackrabbits. Much rarer and well worth looking for are desert tortoises, the official state reptile. You can catch a glimpse of them here from Mar.–June, when they venture out of their burrows morning and evening.

On the opposite side of the highway from Red Cliffs loom the appropriately named and colonnaded White House Cliffs. A campground nestles beneath their white walls, and Hagen Canyon Preserve Trail—for hikers only—commences at the nearby ranger station. There are, however, many other sandy tracks suitable for horses, and a few are open to cars.

Despite such easy accessibility, the park's reaches are usually so invitingly empty that it's hard to believe Los Angeles's teeming millions are only a few hours away from you.

▶ Open year-round. Admission charged.

www.parks.ca.gov
(661) 942-0662

17 Providence Mountains State Recreation Area and Mitchell Caverns Natural Preserve

Mojave Desert, Essex
For 16 miles leading north from Rte. 40, on Essex Rd., a glistening blacktop is the sole evidence of human intrusion into this windswept desert vista, rimmed by the jagged Providence Mountains. The views as you climb have a calm, eerie quality and a rare dimension of spaciousness and mystery. At 4,330 feet the road ends, and there you'll find a campground and visitors center.

From here tours of the Mitchell Caverns are conducted by a ranger who points out interesting features along the three-quarter-mile trail, which is steep but offers fantastic scenery. Steel gates in the mountainside, designed to let bats in and

out but to restrict people to the tours, admit visitors to two of the caverns, illuminated to set off the calcite formations.

Most of the park's 5,250 acres are open for hiking, and in this clear atmosphere many amateur astronomers set up their telescopes for days at a time. But remember that water is scarce and the nights are cold. Wildflowers are a major attraction in March and April, but the desert blooms in September, too. Checklists of the area's plants, birds, amphibians, and reptiles are available. Rattlesnakes are common, so be on the lookout.

▶ Open year-round. Cave tours daily, except winter holidays. Admission fee.

www.parks.ca.gov
(760) 928-2586

18 Mojave River Valley Museum

270 E. Virginia Way, Barstow
Situated at the heart of the Mojave region, the museum is packed with a miscellany of objects related to valley history and geology. There's a large section devoted to the Calico Early Man Archaeological Site discoveries, including 200,000-year-old chipped stone tools. Dr. Louis Leakey, among others, believed that the Mojave may be one of the earliest sites of human habitation in the New World, and until his death in 1972, he supervised the Calico dig.

Material from other archaeological sites is on display, including the 15-million-year-old bones of a three-toed horse at the Barstowian fossil beds and the teeth of a 15-million-year-old camel. There are also objects from the Chemehuevi culture, as well as a gruesomely fascinating case containing the remains of a myste-

rious "headless horseman" and the rusting weapons that apparently belonged to him. Collections of precious and semiprecious stones provide milder excitement for rock lovers (the mineralogy exhibits also include borax miners' tools and artifacts).

A block from the museum is the Barstow Way Station, an information center where tours of the Calico Early Man Site can be arranged.

▶ Open year-round.

www.mojaverivervalleymuseum.org
(760) 256-5452

The islands, rarely crowded, offer an unrivaled opportunity to observe the overwhelming diversity of marine, bird, animal, and plant life sustained in the park and the surrounding National Marine Sanctuary. Any list of what to look for would be encyclopedic, but most people come to see the seals and sea lions, pelicans, and foxes, as well as the porpoises and dolphins. Most whales may be seen offshore from Dec.–Mar.; humpbacks and blues can be seen in the summer.

Anacapa is only a 95-minute boat ride from the coast; Santa

19 Channel Islands National Park.
The only crowds found on the islands off the coast of the Los Angeles metropolitan area are the hosts of animal and bird species.

19 Channel Islands National Park

1901 Spinnaker Dr., Ventura
The park's mainland visitors center—which is in Ventura—provides an enticing view of what to expect here, and it's well worth a visit. It adjoins a dock from which commercial boats depart regularly for Anacapa and Santa Cruz islands and occasionally for Santa Rosa, San Miguel, and Santa Barbara islands.

Cruz island lies 20 miles south. Visitors can hike, kayak, camp, dive, or fish. When snorkeling in the coves, visitors can see spiny sea urchins, bright sea stars, and brilliant orange garibaldi.

▶ Boats go to all islands (weather permitting) year-round. Fare charged.

www.nps.gov/chis
(805) 658-5730

20 Huntington Library, Art Collections, and Botanical Gardens

1151 Oxford Rd., San Marino
As they walk the paths and pavilions, visitors to the Garden of Flowing Fragrance at the Huntington might imagine that they are walking into a Chinese scroll painting of exquisitely arranged scenes. The scroll slowly unrolls to reveal one new vista after another. On 3 1/2 acres of what's to be a 12-acre site, the garden, opened in 2008, is said to be as large and authentic a private Chinese garden as any found outside China itself.

More than a dozen gardens, each one a botanical wonder, can be toured on the 207-acre estate that railroad baron Henry E. Huntington bought in 1903 and filled with plants, books, and art. Among the precious volumes in the library are a Gutenberg Bible on vellum and early editions of the works of William Shakespeare. Included in the sterling collection of 18th-century British art at the main gallery is *Blue Boy* by Thomas Goldsborough, which faces Thomas Lawrence's *Pinkie*.

▶ Open daily except Tues. Closed major holidays. Admission charged.

www.huntington.org
(626) 405-2100

21 March Field Air Museum

22550 Van Buren Blvd., Riverside
From several angles the Lockheed SR-71 Blackbird looks like a UFO. Named for its flat black paint job, the aircraft in its day made manned covert flights nearly 17 miles high on reconnaissance missions for the U.S. Air Force. Satellite surveillance hastened the Blackbird's retirement,

20 ▶ **Huntington Library, Art Collections, and Botanical Gardens.** The grand estate house contrasts with a structure in the Japanese Garden (right), one of two Asian-style havens in the beautiful botanical gardens.

but the mysterious high-flyer continues to intrigue museum visitors.

The Blackbird sits alongside more than 60 historic aircrafts on some 27,000 square feet. Among the others: the Boeing B-17G, the so-called *Flying Fortress*, which did so much to help bring the Allies victory in World War II. You'll also see the P-59, the first jet put into service by the air force.

The place is hard to miss. You'll see the museum's orange-and-white checkerboard roof from I-215 as you near the Van Buren exit.

▶ Open Tues.–Sun. Closed major holidays. Admission charged.

www.marchfield.org
(951) 697-6600

did you know ?

The oldest Joshua tree in Joshua Tree National Park is said to be over 900 years old.

22 Joshua Tree National Park

7448 National Park Blvd., Twentynine Palms
Here is the very essence of the desert: clear skies; crisp, clean, sparkling air; and some half-million acres of fascinating landforms, plants, and animals. The area is in fact the conjunction of two deserts—the Colorado to the east and the higher, cooler, and moister Mojave in the western part of the park, where the Joshua trees grow.

These strange trees—with their shaggy bark resembling a pelt of rough fur and their contorted branches resembling outstretched arms—could hardly be imagined, but once seen, they can never be forgotten. Great jumbled mounds of gigantic rounded boulders appear randomly among the trees, adding to the surreal character of the landscape.

At the park's northeast entrance is the Oasis Visitor Center, where there is indeed an oasis—The Oasis

Mara. From the center a road heads south through the Colorado Desert, where cholla cactus and scarlet-flowering ocotillo thrust their thorny limbs above patches of creosote bushes, the prevailing form of plant life here. Near the south entrance a 7 1/2-mile trail to Cottonwood Spring (a man-made oasis that bird-watchers will find rewarding) leads to Lost Palms, the largest of the park's five oases.

There are nine campgrounds, mainly in the central section of the park, and a variety of hiking trails. Water is scarce, so bring your own.

▶ Open year-round.

www.nps.gov/jotr
(760) 367-5500

23 Julian

Junction of State Hwys. 76, 78, and 79
Historians say Confederate veterans and former slaves alike converged on this mountaintop haven after the Civil War and that in 1869 ex-slave Frederick Coleman spied a piece of gold shimmering in the water as he bent down to take a drink from a creek. He panned and turned up more, setting off a gold rush that would last nearly a decade.

After the gold was gone, pioneers stayed on in the town of

Julian, discovering rich land especially suited for growing apples. Visitors now stand in line at the bakeries along historic Main St. for a slice of the justly famous Julian apple pie.

A short trip takes you from leafy Julian down into the desert. In just six miles you'll travel from 4,235 feet above sea level to vast Anza-Borrego Desert State Park, with an elevation of 15 feet.

Another tip: Say hello to Julian's North American gray wolf pups and adults at the California Wolf Center, a non-profit education, conservation, and science center.

www.julianca.com
(760) 765-1857 Julian Chamber of Commerce

24 ▶ Avalon on Catalina Island

1202 Avalon Canyon Center, Avalon; 22 miles off the coast from Los Angeles
This island is a magical getaway that can be reached from Los

Angeles in less than an hour by boat or 15 minutes by helicopter. Your first stop should be Santa Catalina Island Interpretive Center, an interactive museum nestled in a large canyon at an elevation of about 500 feet. Visitors can learn about the ocean, marine life, history of the island, and its flora and fauna while listening to recordings of whales and dolphins. Hiking trails begin next to the center.

Remote, seldom-seen parts of the island's rugged interior can also be explored. An off-road guided tour in a large four-wheel-drive vehicle takes you along mountain ridges and through a canyon, with views of isolated coves, 2,000-foot peaks, and the Pacific Ocean.

You can check out the American bald eagle habitat at Middle Ranch, where restoration projects and conservation efforts around the island are on display. On the way, stop at the Catalina nature center, with its native plant garden, and at the Airport-in-the-Sky, which sits on two leveled mountain

peaks at an elevation of 1,600 feet. During the tour, passengers are likely to spot wild buffalo, introduced to the island by a film production company in 1924.

▶ Museum open daily.

www.catalina.com
(310) 510-2000 Tours
(310) 510-2514 Interpretive Center

25 ▶ Torrey Pines State Reserve and State Beach

12600 N. Torrey Pines Rd., San Diego
Torrey pines, which grow only here and on Santa Rosa Island, far to the north, cover the reserve's rocky headland like dense green jade set against golden sandstone. They extract moisture from fog and mist through exceptionally long needles and have an extensive system that holds them firm against the fierce Pacific winds. Mojave yucca and mission manzanita also thrive here. The sandy track of Razor Point Trail, which begins near the handsome old adobe visitors center, winds its fragrant way seaward among a profusion of trees and other plants.

From the smooth red stone of Razor Point itself, there are spacious views of the pines, Los Penasquitos Marsh, and the graceful sweep of the beach—protected and warm year-round. Another path descends rugged yellow cliffs to Flat Rock. Dolphins can often be seen from the beach, and, in season (Dec.–Mar.), gray whales.

▶ Open year-round for daytime use only. Parking fee.

www.torreypine.org
(858) 755-2063

22 ▶ **Joshua Tree National Park.** Snowy cholla cacti in the park are much shorter than the Joshua trees, with the tallest tree being 40 feet high.

seasonal events

JANUARY
• Morro Bay Winter Bird Festival—Morro Bay

FEBRUARY
• Cloverdale Citrus Fair—Cloverdale

MARCH
• Mendocino Whale Festival—Mendocino (whale-watching, wine and chowder tasting)

APRIL
• Red Bluff Round-Up—Red Bluff (rodeo events)

California Poppy Festival—Lancaster

MAY
• Whole Earth Festival—Davis (Gold Rush car show, chili cook-off, crafts)
• Backyard Bird and Butterfly Festival—Fremont (wildflower walks, garden tours, Monarch butterfly release)

JUNE
• North Beach Festival—San Francisco (arts and crafts, entertainment)
• The Isleton Crawdad Festival—Isleton (spicy food, Cajun music)

JULY
• Mammoth Lakes Jazz Jubilee—Mammoth Lakes

AUGUST
• Monterey Bay Strawberry Festival—Watsonville

SEPTEMBER
• Gold Rush Days—Sacramento (costumed re-enactors, Wild West gunfights)

OCTOBER
• San Carlos Fine Arts & Crafts Festival—San Carlos

NOVEMBER
• California Indian Storytelling Festival—San Leandro
• San Diego Dixieland Jazz Festival—San Diego

www.visitcalifornia.com

CALIFORNIA

Colorado

The vast sand dunes, ancient Native American ruins, and the splendor of the Rockies blend with memories of mining camps, pioneers, and the Santa Fe Trail.

Colorado Railroad Museum. Locomotive 346 chugs along a narrow gauge railroad in the country west of Denver (see page 50).

In one grand wilderness, straddling the Continental Divide and studded with magnificent peaks, there are over 150 miles of hiking and horseback trails. In other areas trails traverse foothills and prairies, canyons and mesas.

Watery settings include a reservoir and spectacular falls. The Great Sand Dunes, in their unlikely inland location, are the tallest in America.

Native American culture is recalled by some 11th-century dwellings and a museum devoted to the Utes, the last Native Americans to roam freely here. Other museums document the lives of the soldiers, miners, farmers, and ranchers who settled this rugged land.

visit ➤ **offthebeatenpathtrips.com**

 **Trail Ridge Road—Rocky Mountain National Park.** The sweeping views from the nation's highest mountain road show the Colorado Rockies in all their splendor. Completed in 1938, this spectacular section of U.S. Hwy. 34 crosses the Continental Divide.

1 Mount Zirkel Wilderness, Routt National Forest

At Steamboat Springs take Cty. Rte. 129 north 19 miles to Clark, then follow Seedhouse Rd.
Visitors to this 160,000-acre wilderness will find nature's splendor and solitude in its most primeval magnificence. Spreading along the Continental Divide, the area contains dozens of peaks around 12,000 feet high, more than 65 small lakes, and countless cascading streams.

However, in 1997 an unusually strong windstorm blew down some 4 million trees, triggering a spruce beetle epidemic, which is killing many trees. Because of this, the fire danger here is high, so be sure to check with the U.S. Forest Service about restrictions before hiking or riding on some of the 150 miles of trails.

Elk and deer graze in the meadows during summer. Anglers will take brook, rainbow, and cutthroat trout. Two campgrounds are maintained by the Forest Service.
▶ Open year-round but often inaccessible in winter; campgrounds open June–Sept.

www.wilderness.net
(307) 745-2300

2 Trail Ridge Road–Rocky Mountain National Park

Estes Park
With more than eight miles lying above 11,000 feet and a maximum elevation of 12,183 feet, this scenic route, which crosses the U.S. Continental Divide, is the highest continuous paved road in the nation.

Cutting through Rocky Mountain National Park, it pro-vides a spectacular view of majestic mountain peaks, deep gorges, and rocky cliffs. In spring and summer fields of alpine wildflowers appear on the tundra above the timber line; vibrant fall colors contrast with pine trees bordering rocky outcroppings and dark-shadowed lakes. Wildlife abounds throughout the year. There is always a chance sighting of moose or bighorn sheep, or spotting smaller denizens of the forests in river valleys near the highway. Clean air and quiet stillness are bonus attractions, along with the park's excellent recreational facilities.
▶ Open Memorial Day–mid-Oct.; park open year-round. Admission charged.

www.nps.gov/romo
(970) 586-1206

3 ▶ Overland Trail Museum

2105 CR 26, Sterling

In the 1860s the Overland Trail was one of the most heavily used routes in the nation. Long lines of covered wagons and frequent runs by the coaches of the Overland Stage Line carried settlers and adventurers westward by the thousands. The starting segment of the trail along the South Platte River here was notable as an easy-to-follow natural highway with a sure supply of water and game.

The stone structure that houses the museum is a replica of an old fort, a stronghold established for protection from Native Americans. The "village" behind the main structure is composed of several buildings from pre-1915, including a one-room schoolhouse, general store, blacksmith shop, country church, barn, and barbershop. The cattle business that later flourished on the vast surrounding plains is recalled with displays of branding irons and an array of early farm implements.

The area's earliest history is represented by cases of mastodon and mammoth bones and Native American arrowheads.

▶ **Rifle Falls State Park.** Each of the park's three cascades drops about 90 feet.

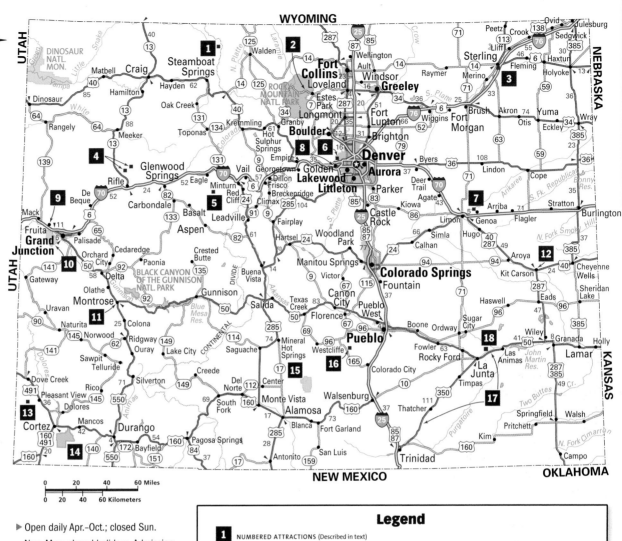

▶ Open daily Apr.–Oct.; closed Sun. Nov.–Mar.; closed holidays. Admission free but donations encouraged.

www.sterlingcolo.com/pages/dept/plr/museum.php

(970) 522-3895

Legend

| 1 | NUMBERED ATTRACTIONS (Described in text) |

CONTROLLED ACCESS HIGHWAYS
- Free
- Toll
- Under Construction

OTHER HIGHWAYS
- Primary Highway
- Secondary Highway

HIGHWAY MARKERS
- 10 Interstate Route
- 12 U.S. Route
- 12 State Route
- 12 Distances along Major Highways (in miles)

CITIES AND TOWNS
- ⊛ National Capital
- ⊛ State Capital
- • Cities, Towns, and Populated Places Type size indicates relative importance
- Urban Area

RECREATION AND FEATURES OF INTEREST
- National Park
- Other Large Park or Recreation Area
- Trail
- Ferry

© 2009 GeoNova

4 ▶ Rifle Gap and Rifle Falls State Park

Hwy. 325, Rifle

This remote mountain area has two state parks, and—surprisingly in this dry region—the most notable feature of each is water. The reservoir in Rifle Gap is a 350-acre lake created by the damming of East and Middle Rifle creeks in 1965. The other part is Rifle Falls, where East Rifle Creek takes a spectacular plunge.

Filled with mountain runoff, the reservoir has clear turquoise water that makes it an inviting place to swim, boat, sail, and water-ski. Anglers are likely to catch walleyes, bass, pike, perch, and trout. The trout come from a hatchery that is open to visitors.

About four miles north of the reservoir, Rifle Falls State Park not only has an impressive trio of 90-foot cascades side by side, but

its limestone cliff has a number of small caves, the largest about 90 feet long and 25 feet high. The caves' walls and ceilings are covered with an amazing pattern of small crisscrossing stalactites.

▶ Open year-round. Admission charged.

http://parks.state.co.us
(970) 625-1607

5 Sylvan Lake State Park

1500 Brush Creek Rd., off
Hwy. 6W, Eagle

For anyone craving an authentic taste of Colorado's rugged natural beauty, this incredibly scenic park is the perfect stop. Not only is it nestled in the heart of the Rocky Mountains at an elevation of 8,500 feet, it's also surrounded by the White River National Forest. This unspoiled alpine retreat boasts miles of fir, spruce, aspen, and

5 ► **Sylvan Lake State Park.** "Peace and quiet" is the rule in this placid park. No motorized watercraft are allowed on the lake, and the campsites are intentionally rustic.

juniper amid giant formations of glacial rock and sandstone. Migratory and resident birds include the raven, golden eagle, and mountain bluebird.

Ideal for hiking, picnicking, or simply relaxing, the park also contains a shimmering 40-acre lake. Anglers will revel in the bounty of trout. And for winter enthusiasts there's ice fishing as well as cross-country skiing, snowshoeing, and snowmobiling.

► Open year-round. Entrance fee.

http://parks.state.co.us
(970) 328-2021

6 Colorado Railroad Museum

17155 W. 44th Ave., Golden

Railroad buffs can experience a nostalgic trip back in time at the Colorado Railroad Museum. Established in 1959 to preserve Colorado's pioneering mountain railroads, this museum has the largest collection of narrow-gauge rolling stock in the Rocky Mountain West, with more than 100 locomotives and railcars.

On the museum's 15 acres are the Museum Depot, a replica of an 1880s railroad depot, with exhibits about Colorado's colorful railroad history; tracks with historic railcars; and the circular Cornelius Hauck Roundhouse, a modern facility that restores locomotives but is designed to look like a 1900s roundhouse. Outside there is a working Armstrong turntable, enabling one man to rotate a locomotive by pushing a pole. You can climb aboard locomotives, passenger cars, and cabooses.

► Open daily year-round except holidays. Admission charged.

www.crrm.org
(800) 365-6263; (303) 279-4591

7 Tower Museum

30121 Frontage Rd., Genoa

One of the first things a visitor to this offbeat 22-room museum encounters is a puzzling array of some 20,000 artifacts. Anyone who can identify 10 in a row gets an admission refund. Few people today, however, can recognize such items as a buggy-whip holder, a buffalo cud, and a magician's knife. But it is fun to try, and it is a good introduction to the truly eccentric nature of the collection.

The 75-foot wooden tower and the sprawling complex of rock rooms at its base are the brainchild of C. W. Gregory, sometimes known as Colorado's P. T. Barnum. He put up the tall structure to attract visitors and dubbed it the World's Wonder View Tower. It offers a spectacular view extending into six states on a clear day.

The museum's chief attractions, however, are its collections of archaeological materials, antique items, and oddities. These include 75,000-year-old mammoth bones, 8,500-year-old Native American buffalo bones, 20,000 Native American arrowheads, 1,000 paintings by the Native American princess Ravenwing, and collections of old firearms.

► Open year-round. Admission charged.

(719) 763-2309

8 Bradford Washburn American Mountaineering Museum

710 10th St., Golden

Newly opened in February 2008, the American Mountaineering Museum in Golden is the first and only museum in the country dedicated to the heroism, technology, culture, and spirit of mountaineering.

Whether you are a novice, an experienced climber, or just an admirer of those who dare to ascend perilous heights, this is the perfect place to explore mountaineering lore and appreciate the climbers' skill and passion for their sport.

Nestled at the base of the Rocky Mountains, the museum has amassed a collection of breathtaking photography and has one of the world's largest libraries on mountaineering. It also features educational displays and interactive exhibits. Visitors can try a virtual climb of Mount Everest, thanks to a very realistic 135-square-foot scale model of this famous mountain slope, or climb into an imaginative base camp on a mountain face, as intrepid climbers do.

► Open year-round Tues.–Sat. Admission charged.

www.bwamm.org
(303) 996-2755

8 ► **Bradford Washburn American Mountaineering Museum.** This museum is a shrine to mountain climbing and notable climbers.

9 ▶ Dinosaur Journey

550 Jurassic Ct., Fruita

More than 140 million years ago, colossal creatures thrived on the warm, humid plains of what is now the American West. Over time, however, these humongous beasts were trapped and buried under many layers of sedimentary rock, but their bones have survived as fossils.

Today Fruita, a glowing carat in the "Dinosaur Diamond" of western Colorado and northeastern Utah, is world famous for its wealth of dinosaur excavation sites.

Just 30 miles northwest of downtown Grand Junction, off I-70, explorers can find their way to Dinosaur Journey. Visitors can view the genuine bones of a stegosaurus, allosaurus, and other long-extinct species and tour a working paleontology laboratory where scientists are restoring fossils.

The adventure continues out on the nearby dinosaur trails. Riggs Hill, a mile-long trail, marks the site of the world's first brachiosaurus. Dinosaur Hill, a half-mile trail, boasts the quarry of the 70-foot-long apatosaurus. The Trail Through Time, about 17 miles outside of Fruita within Rabbit Valley Research Natural Area, features a camarasaurus skeleton and a glimpse of a quarry in action. For those who are dinosaur enthusiasts or for those who are simply more curious (and adventuresome), there is a five-day expedition, providing a crash course in geology and hands-on excavation experience. You can sign-up at the museum or call (888) 488-DINO.

▶ Open year-round. Admission charged.

www.dinosaurjourney.org
(970) 858-7282

10 ▶ Colorado National Monument. Overlooks along Rim Rock Drive provide stunning views down into steep-wall canyons and out across the Grand Valley.

10 ▶ Colorado National Monument

Rim Rock Dr., Fruita

The wild vastness and beauty of this series of canyons and mesas have been preserved, thanks to local Grand Valley residents led by John Otto, a turn-of-the-century maverick who campaigned tirelessly for a national park.

Sculpted by flash floods, freezing and thawing, rainwater and wind over millions of years, the magnificent formations of orange, yellow, and red sandstone can be enjoyed not only by campers and backpackers but also by day visitors. The 23-mile Rim Rock Drive that snakes through the park can be covered on a short outing. The historic road offers excellent vantage points for motorists and bicyclists.

Forty-three miles of long and shorter trails proceed across mesas and zigzag up and down the canyon walls. Golden eagles, turkey vultures, and several hawk species are among the birds that swoop overhead. Spring and fall are the best times for hiking. In the summer heat a hat and a supply of water are essential. Overnight backpackers are required to register at the visitors center.

▶ Open year-round. Admission charged.

www.nps.gov/colm
(970) 858-3617

11 ▶ Ute Indian Museum

17253 Chipeta Rd., Montrose

The Utes were a diverse, widely scattered people who lived throughout the Rockies, in Colorado as well as Utah, the state named for them. They are believed to be the only tribe native to Colorado; the Cheyennes and other Plains tribes were pushed westward into the state by white settlements.

In the late 1800s and early 1900s Thomas McKee, a photographer, lived among the Utes, documenting their lives in pictures and acquiring artifacts. His collection is effectively displayed in this small but fascinating museum run by the Colorado Historical Society.

In one of the two galleries, you'll find traditional and ceremonial items used by the various bands of the tribe. An interactive computer kiosk interprets the Bear Dance, the oldest of the Ute ceremonies, and you can see a Ute wickiup dwelling.

The second gallery features famous Utes, most notably the great chief Ouray, who led the tribe in signing a treaty with the United States in the 1860s. Ouray's wicked-looking horn-handled knife and a beaded buckskin shirt are on display.

▶ Open daily mid-May–mid-Oct.; Mon.–Sat. Nov.–Dec. Tues.–Sat. Jan.–mid-May. Admission charged.

www.coloradohistory.org
(970) 249-3098

12 ▶ Kit Carson Museum

302 Park St., Kit Carson

This museum's name is somewhat misleading. It is not dedicated to the legendary Western hero but rather to the town here that was named after him. In its glory days more than a century ago, Kit Carson was a thriving railhead, a town of Western legend. But little survives from that town, which burned to the ground, and the museum's collection concentrates on the farming and grazing center that replaced it.

The museum is housed in a 1904 Union Pacific depot and stationmaster's house, still furnished with an old-fashioned telephone, a telegraph key, and signal levers. Several displays re-create late-19th-century rooms. There is a small doll collection and another of farm implements. Among the other diverse items that outline the community's history are arrowheads and grindstones, a bear trap, branding irons, and a caboose stove.

▶ Open daily Memorial Day–Labor Day.

www.ourjourney.info
(719) 962-3306

13 Lowry Pueblo

27 miles northwest of Cortez

For centuries the ancestral Puebloan Native Americans dominated the Four Corners region (the meeting place of Utah, Colorado, Arizona, and New Mexico), where they built pueblos and cliff dwellings. But long before the time of Columbus, they migrated, leaving their homes behind. One of these habitats is Lowry Pueblo, part of the Canyons of the Ancients National Monument, a complex of three dozen rooms and nine kivas, or ceremonial chambers, built on a mesa around the end of the 11th century. It probably accommodated a farming community of about 100 people, but it was abandoned after 50 years or so, and its stone walls were not discovered until the 20th century.

Now a national historic landmark, the pueblo is open to visitors. The unique feature at Lowry is the painted kiva, now protected with a roof. Its plastered walls are neatly painted with a cloud motif. A good place to start is the Anasazi Heritage Center with photo exhibits and a virtual-reality tour of village life.

▶ Open year-round.

www.co.blm.gov/ahc/lowry.htm
(970) 882-4811

14 Mesa Verde National Park

Cortez

Mesa Verde Country has been home to Native American Puebloans for thousands of years. Come marvel at the lasting marks of their heritage, the dwellings of their ancestors, who for more than 700 years made the canyons, cliffs, and mesa tops of Mesa Verde their thriving and populous home until they moved

 **Mesa Verde National Park.** The Cliff Palace site is the centerpiece of Mesa Verde (green table), named by Spanish explorers for the flatness of its forested terrain.

away in the early 14th century.

With more than 4,800 known archaeological sites and 600 of the best-preserved, multistoried cliff dwellings in the United States, the park is an archaeologist's treasure trove. Cliff Palace, a 150-room living space that once housed about 100 people, awaits visitors to scale up the cliff walls and enter it. Hike along self-guiding tours, climb ladders to go in and out of cliff dwellings, drive by, or take a bus tour through this marvel.

▶ Open year-round, but many sites closed in winter months.

www.nps.gov/MEVE
(970) 529-4465

15 Great Sand Dunes National Park and Preserve

Hwy. 150, Mosca

The "Great" in the name of this fascinating natural phenomenon is more than appropriate. Not only are these ever-changing dunes ranked as the tallest in North America, but the dune field stretches

over 30 square miles of high mountain-valley floor. The vast expanse of sand was formed over thousands of years as sand blew off a prehistoric lake bed on the valley floor and piled up against the Sangre de Cristo mountains.

The park also includes six peaks more than 13,000 feet high, alpine tundra, forests, grasslands, and wetlands. Most popular is the natural mountain beach created by Medano Creek, which flows across the sand in waves in spring and early summer and attracts many swimmers.

Not surprisingly, this unusual park appeals to sand skiers as well as to hikers, backpackers, and campers, who stay in a campground in an area of junipers and pines at the dunes' edge. Some visitors venture onto the dunes at night with flashlights in hopes of spotting kangaroo rats and giant sand-treader camel crickets that manage to survive in this arid environment.

The best weather is generally spring and fall. In summer, even

though the air temperature is moderate, the sand can get uncomfortably hot.

▶ Park and campground open year-round.

www.nps.gov/grsa
(719) 378-6300

16 Bishop Castle

12705 CO-165, Rye

On a mountainside in central Colorado, a Gothic castle rises unexpectedly into the sky. Its window-pierced walls and tall tower are supported by authentic flying buttresses, like a medieval monument. A dragon's head, its modern "gargoyle," puffs smoke from a chimney fire, more to greet today's visitors with cheery warmth than to ward off evil spirits.

For almost 40 years, Jim Bishop has single-handedly gathered and set over 1,000 tons of stones and steel to create his castle, and he's not finished yet. According to Jim, this one-person construction project, the largest in the nation, is his tribute to the hardworking American Everyman, whose home is their castle. Visitors can explore, an adventure in some places, because the tour continues through wrought-iron platforms high in the rafters.

▶ Open year-round.

www.eagleriverpewter.com/bishop.html
(719) 485-3040

17 Santa Fe Trail

Closely parallels 1-25, CO-350, and US-50

The historic Santa Fe Trail was the main 19th-century route connecting Independence, Missouri, at the eastern end with Santa Fe, New Mexico, at its western terminus. The modern Santa Fe Trail National Scenic Byway roughly follows the old trail's path. The section of the trail that traverses Colorado is known as the Mountain Branch.

Pioneer William Becknell first cut the trail in 1821. This 184-mile corridor through Colorado and northern New Mexico saw merchants, cattlemen, railroad workers, miners, and eventually settlers ply their goods and work their trades along its way.

Wagon trains carried manufactured goods westward and freshly mined silver and trapped furs eastward. U.S. troops traveled over it as they invaded New Mexico in 1846. Traffic along the trail shifted to railway cars when the Santa Fe Railroad opened in 1880. Economic development and settlement in the area then progressed even more rapidly.

Today travelers can retrace the journeys of Old West celebrities like Kit Carson along the historic route and view Pike's Peak from the same vantage point as did explorer Zebulon Pike. Wide bands of wagon ruts across the prairie are still visible.

▶ Open year-round.

www.santafetrail.org
www.santafetrailscenicandhistoricbyway.org
(719) 846-7217

18 Bent's Old Fort National Historic Site

35110 Hwy. 194, La Junta
Hard on the heels of the first American explorers, trappers and traders eagerly extended their range into the high plains and mountains of the Southwest. Among the trading posts that sprang up in their wake, the most important was this one, which was built in the early 1830s by two Missouri brothers, William and Charles Bent, in partnership with a reputed French nobleman, Ceran St. Vrain.

Located on the Mountain Branch of the Sante Fe Trail, a fairly safe route following the Arkansas River, the adobe fort soon became a major hub for trade radiating south to Santa Fe and Mexico, as well as west to the Pacific and north into Wyoming.

For years the three men controlled a huge commercial empire. But a sequence of events—the Mexican War, the decline in trade, the death of Charles Bent, the departure of St. Vrain, and a cholera epidemic—led William Bent to abandon the fort in 1849. Tradition holds that Bent was so irked by the army's refusal to buy the fort that he blew it up.

This national historic site is a reconstruction of the post as it appeared in its heyday in 1846. Within thick, high walls an open plaza is ringed by furnished living quarters, warehouses, workshops, and even a billiard room.

Inside the fort, you can view the 20-minute documentary film *Traders, Tribes, and Travelers.* Self-guiding tours are also available. Staff members dressed as trappers, traders, and craftsmen demonstrate frontier activities.

▶ Open year-round. Admission charged. Call for updated schedule of events.

www.nps.gov/beol
(719) 383-5010

15 ▶ **Great Sand Dunes National Park and Preserve.** America's tallest dunes gained national park status in 2004. The Sangre de Cristo Mountains rise in the background.

Connecticut

Gracefully spanning the centuries, the Constitution State is a pleasure to explore, from charming small towns to centers of technology.

Lockwood-Mathews Mansion Museum.
The oil-on-canvas ceiling painting in the mansion's drawing room is titled *Venus at Play with Her Cupids* (see page 55).

The Audubon Center here is one of the best of its kind, as is the collection of early-day tools at the Sloane-Stanley Museum. Connecticut's contribution to Yankee ingenuity is acknowledged in the American Clock & Watch Museum. A colonial copper mine, which also served as a prison, is now open for visitors. Further examples of the variety available here include a castle, dinosaur tracks, a museum of contemporary art, an opulent mansion, and some appealing historic houses.

visit ➡ offthebeatenpathtrips.com

1 Sharon Audubon Center

325 Cornwall Bridge Rd. (Rte. 4), Sharon

Here on 1,150 acres of woodlands, ponds, open fields, and marshes is a microcosm of 19th-century Connecticut. Habitats for the great variety of plants and wildlife found here are fast disappearing.

The property, donated by Clement and Keyo Ford, includes the Ford home, which now houses the center's offices, library, nature store, and display areas.

Among the indoor exhibits are live turtles, insects, and birds. The center has over 11 miles of scenic hiking trails, gardens, and aviaries housing birds of prey.

At the Children's Adventure Center a coral reef aquarium invites inspection of a tropical underworld habitat, while silhouettes of birds suspended from the ceiling show their various sizes and shapes.

Workshops, nature classes, films, guided field trips, training programs and internships, and seasonal bird counts are all part of the center's program. And in early spring visitors can watch the making of maple syrup with sap collected from local trees.

▶ Open year-round. Trail fee for nonmembers.

www.audubon.org/local/sanctuary/sharon
(860) 364-0520

3 The Aldrich Museum of Contemporary Art. The quaint 18th-century exterior of the museum belies the collection of avant-garde art within its walls.

2 Sloane-Stanley Museum and Kent Furnace

31 Kent-Cornwall Rd. (Rte. 7), Kent

Eric Sloane, the late Connecticut artist and writer, started this museum as a tribute to the ingenuity and craftsmanship of the early settlers in New England. It houses his extensive collection of tools made by these inventive Yankees for the seemingly countless outdoor chores, as well as household equipment. The objects range from pots and baskets to axes and wheelbarrows. Several of Sloane's still lifes are also on display.

The property and the barn that houses the museum were donated by the Stanley Works of New Britain to celebrate its 125 years as a maker of hand tools, then turned over to the state of Connecticut's Historical Commission.

Next to the museum, Sloane built a small cabin using only old tools, local lumber, and stones—referring to an 1805 farmboy's diary as a guide. The cabin has an unusual chink-log chimney, a dirt floor, bottle-glass windows, and a small herb garden in the dooryard.

During the 19th century this was the site of the Kent Iron Furnace. Down a slight slope from the museum are the ruins of the sturdy granite structure, with its Gothic arch.

The museum is set on a wooded hillside overlooking the Housatonic River. Although the foliage in summer is so dense that the river is lost to view, the shady rise is an ideal setting for the picnic tables scattered there.

Open Wed.–Sun., mid-May–Oct.
Admission charged.

www.chc.state.ct.us
(860) 927-3849

3 ▶ The Aldrich Museum of Contemporary Art

258 Main St., Ridgefield
A recently completed expansion doubles the size of this museum and provides a nice architectural contrast to the original 18th-century building. The museum, founded about 40 years ago by Larry Aldrich, a collector of contemporary art, is known for its exhibits focusing mainly on major trends in today's art world and the works of undiscovered artists.

Behind the museum, on a sloping lawn surrounded by flowering trees and shrubs, are sculptures. The terrace overlooking the garden is a pleasant place to sit and view the collection.

The museum presents three major exhibitions and six or seven smaller ones every year. Widely respected educational and cultural programming complements the exhibition schedule.

▶ Open Tues.–Sun. year-round except winter holidays. Admission charged.

www.aldrichart.org
(203) 438-4519

4 ▶ Lockwood-Mathews Mansion Museum

295 West Ave., Norwalk
LeGrand Lockwood, who grew up in Norwalk and left home at an early age, returned as a millionaire in 1864 and built the grandest house in town, a magnificent 62-room mansion on a hill overlooking the Norwalk River.

With towers, turrets, arches, and iron grillwork on the rooftop, the granite building resembles a European castle overlaid with Victorian elegance. The interior is decorated with exceptionally fine frescoes, marble carvings, etched glass panels, marquetry, parquetry, and has a skylighted rotunda 42 feet high. Many of the rooms open onto a balcony and sweeping up from the rotunda to the balcony is the main stairway, whose carved walnut banister has an elegant inlay of boxwood. A peacock of blue stones decorates one of the mansion's 25 fireplaces.

Shortly after the house was completed, the Lockwoods lost their fortune, and the Charles D. Mathews family of New York bought the estate and occupied it for more than 60 years.

▶ Open Wed.–Sun. or by appointment, mid-Mar.–Dec. Admission charged.

www.lockwoodmathewsmansion.com
(203) 838-9799

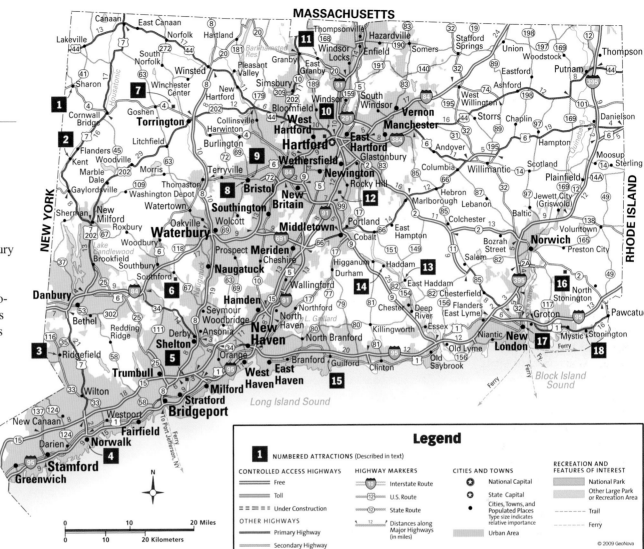

4 ▶ **Lockwood-Mathews Mansion.**
The architectural style of the ornate country house is Second Empire.

5 ▶ Boothe Memorial Park and Museum

5774 Main St. Putney, Stratford
On a hill overlooking the Housatonic River, this park is maintained as a memorial to two eccentric bachelor brothers, David and Stephen Boothe, who willed the property to the town of Stratford.

Within the 32 acres of their estate is an amazing collection of 20 buildings. Included is a Dutch windmill, a blacksmith shop, a miniature lighthouse, and a pagoda-like redwood cathedral.

A 77-foot clock tower and belfry, known as the Anniversary Tower, houses family heirlooms gathered from cousins far and near, along with the family genealogy. Boothe Homestead Museum gives tours Tuesday through Friday and weekend afternoons.

Walking trails wind through the park to the various exhibits and to a rose garden and sundial set in a circle of stones. Picnic tables under the trees overlook the river.

▶ Park open year-round.
   Museum open daily June–Sept.

www.townofstratford.com
(203) 381-2046

6 ▶ Southford Falls State Park

175 Quaker Farms Rd., Southbury
The waterfall that gives the park its name is on Eight Mile Brook, which flows eight miles from Lake Quassapaug to the Housatonic River. The plunging and cascading falls once drove a waterwheel that powered a sawmill, a gristmill, and a fulling mill for finishing wool cloth. Almost all that remains of these 19th-century industries is a grindstone, a part of the sluiceway, and a few foundation walls.

8 ▶ New England Carousel Museum.
Carousel horses are painstakingly restored by hand at the museum.

Several trails loop through the woods, along the stream, and above the falls to Papermill Pond, formed by a dam across the brook. Here a quiet, woodsy expanse has picnic tables and barbecue pits. The pond, stocked with trout, is popular with fishermen. A mile-long loop trail leads to a lookout tower, which can be climbed for an overview of the park.

▶ Open year-round.

www.ct.gov/dep
(203) 264-5169

7 ▶ Action Wildlife Foundation

Two miles east of Goshen on Hwy. 4
How did llamas, yaks, and water buffalo come to graze the lush pastures of Litchfield County? They're among the 30-plus species of exotic animals and large birds (think emus and ostriches) residing at Action Wildlife, an animal preserve established on a former dairy farm in 2000.

The vision of Connecticut businessman Jim Mazzarelli, the nonprofit Action Wildlife Foundation provides loving care to the animals, many of which are viewed on a driving safari through

50 acres of pastureland shaded with maples, oaks, and pines. The petting zoo is a resounding hit with children. Mazzarelli is a hands-on administrator, sometimes even driving the wagon-pulling tractor on the popular hayrides.

Taxidermy is on display in the museum gallery, housing mounted animals that include a rhino, lion, leopard, antelope, zebra, moose, coyote, and a once-fierce grizzly bear from Siberia.

▶ Open daily late Apr.–Oct. Open weekends in Nov. Admission charged.

www.actionwildlife.org
(860) 482-4465

8 ▶ New England Carousel Museum

95 Riverside Ave., Rte. 72, Bristol
What Americans of today know and adore as the merry-go-round was not created for child's play. In its earliest incarnation the carousel helped noblemen train for jousting and even for war, providing rounds of target practice in "lancing" the brass ring. Many years later carousels became a favorite with elite, wealthy grown-ups.

This delightful museum is filled with fascinating facts about the ride's history and folklore, as well as its unique craftsmanship and art. Situated in a beautifully restored 33,000-square-foot brick building, it's also home to the country's largest collection of antique carousels. Inside, carousel fans can wander among the pretty painted horses (and the occasional pigs, cows, ducks, lions, tigers, and giraffes) at their leisure or take a wonderfully informative guided tour.

In addition to carousels and their animals, the museum showcases an antique Wurlitzer carousel

organ, an exhibit on how wooden carousel horses were traditionally created, and an array of carousel art. Children can sign up to create a carousel-themed craft. The museum's showroom sells full-sized resin reproduction horses.

In the center of nearby Hartford, the museum manages an antique beauty—the Bushnell Park Carousel. Created in 1914, the artistic merry-go-round was rescued from an Ohio amusement park 60 years later and painstakingly restored. The huge three-row carousel sports 36 jumper horses, 12 stander horses, two chariots, and a Wurlitzer 153 bend organ. Visitors to the lovely, revitalized downtown area can take a memorable spin for a mere dollar.

▶ Open daily Apr.–Nov.; Thurs.–Sun. Dec.–Mar. Closed major holidays. Admission charged. The Bushnell Park Carousel is open Tues.–Sun. May–Oct.

www.thecarouselmuseum.org
(860) 585-5411

9 ▶ American Clock & Watch Museum

100 Maple St., Bristol
Here you will see an exceptional collection of American timepieces, including jeweled watches, alarm clocks, and wall clocks—many still running.

The museum is housed in an 1801 building called the Miles Lewis House. The addition of the Ebenezer Barnes Wing, which has paneling that comes from a 1728 house of that name, extends the museum into an authentic early American sundial garden. The collection includes examples from early American clockmakers, many of whom lived nearby, as well as timepieces of the 20th century.

Among the exhibits are comic character watches displayed in glass cases, papier-mâché shelf clocks in the kitchen of the old house, Hickory Dickory Dock clocks, and dozens of tall grandfather clocks that strike and chime on the hour.

The Edward Ingraham Memorial Wing is dedicated to Bristol's clockmaking history.

▶ Open Apr.–Nov. Closed Thanksgiving. Admission charged.

www.clockandwatchmuseum.org
(860) 583-6070

10 Harriet Beecher Stowe Center

77 Forest St., Hartford
Nook Farm, a shady enclave west of downtown Hartford, was once home to a spirited community of writers and political thinkers. One such was Harriet Beecher Stowe, the author of *Uncle Tom's Cabin,* the 1852 anti-slavery novel that profoundly affected the nation in the years leading up to the Civil War. The "cottage" Stowe purchased in 1873 has 17 rooms and halls but was considered modest

for the neighborhood at the time. After touring the furnished, art-filled rooms, visitors can stroll through Stowe's Victorian gardens—the pastime of her twilight years.

The visitors center and museum are housed in the carriage house. On view here are fascinating collections related to women's suffrage, abolition, and other pressing issues of the 19th century.

Next door to Stowe's home is the Mark Twain House, a whimsical Victorian fantasy open for tours; the adjacent museum has rotating exhibitions. It was here that Twain penned two American classics: *The Adventures of Tom Sawyer* and *Adventures of Huckleberry Finn.*

▶ Open year-round except major winter holidays. Admission charged.

www.harrietbeecherstowecenter.org
(860) 522-9258

11 Old New-Gate Prison and Copper Mine

115 Newgate Rd., East Granby
The mine, one of the earliest in the American colonies, was opened in about 1706 by a group of Simsbury

citizens, and it continued in operation for more than 40 years. At the height of its productivity, more than 20 miners worked here.

Although there had been several attempts to smelt copper ore in America, a new British law prohibited it, and the ore from this mine was shipped to England for processing. After two valuable consignments of copper were lost at sea, it was decided that shipping was uneconomical, and the mine was closed in the 1750s.

In 1773 the Connecticut colony designated the mine as a prison, the state's first, naming it after the infamous Newgate Prison in London. The prison held criminals as well as political prisoners during the Revolutionary War. Some prisoners managed to escape; one escaped three times. New-Gate was closed in 1827. In 1976 it was declared a National Historic Landmark. Visitors enter into the prison yard, surrounded by 12-foot-high stone walls, and can tour the underground tunnels where prisoners were kept. The one original building still standing is the guardhouse, which has exhibits and a 15-minute video.

▶ Open Wed.–Sun., mid-May–Oct. Admission charged.

www.cultureandtourism.org
(860) 653-3563

did you know ?

The city of Bristol has had several nicknames. It was once known as the Bell City, because of its history with manufacturing innovative spring-driven doorbells. It is now also referred to as the Mum City because it was once a leader in chrysanthemum production and still holds an annual mum festival every fall.

12 Dinosaur State Park

400 West St., off Rocky Hill
In the late 1960s, during a routine excavation for a new building, workers accidentally uncovered 2,000 early Jurassic Period fossil tracks. Fifteen hundred of the ancient foot-

12 Dinosaur State Park. A bony crest is one of the defining features of the Dilophosaurus.

prints have been buried for preservation. The remaining 500 have been enclosed beneath a geodesic dome for family viewing.

Under the dome visitors will also find formidable life-size Jurassic and Triassic dioramas, a reconstruction of a geologic formation, and interactive displays.

Outside the dome 21st-century explorers can walk the grounds once strolled by prehistoric giants. In addition to ample spots for picnicking, the park features more than two miles of nature trails and an arboretum.

An added attraction for visitors is the ability to make actual casts of dinosaur tracks (from May 1–Oct. 30). You must bring your own supplies, however.

▶ Open year-round except Mon. and winter holidays. Admission charged.

www.dinosaurstatepark.org
(860) 529-8423

American Clock & Watch Museum. On display in this 1801 house is an extraordinary collection of timepieces, many made before the age of mass production.

13 Gillette Castle

67 River Rd., East Haddam
Towering atop a bluff overlooking the Connecticut River, this majestic castle rivals the famed medieval abodes of Europe. Recently restored to its original glory, the 24-room stone dwelling was meticulously designed by William Gillette, the actor renowned for his stage portrayal of Sherlock Holmes.

Until his death in 1937, Gillette called the colossal structure, complete with an authentic stone parapet, home. In fact, he spent most of his last 20 years here, living alone as a near recluse. Today the castle and its surrounding 184 acres comprise the state's most scenically impressive and tranquil public park, welcoming all romantic travelers.

Inside the castle visitors will find a treasure trove of distinctive details. Each of the 47 intricately carved wooden doors features a unique mechanical locking device, including a lock shaped like an owl whose wings spread when the key turns. Twisting passages wind in and out of rooms reflecting Gillette's imaginative personality. In addition to four bedrooms, four baths, and an expansive third-floor suite, the castle houses a library, an art gallery, and a collection of Sherlock Holmes memorabilia.

After strolling through the interior, visitors can explore the exterior architecture or see a restored example of one of Gillette's personal electric train engines.

▸ Open Memorial Day–Columbus Day.
Camping available May–Sept.
Admission charged.

www.ct.gov/dep
(860) 526-2336

13 ▸ **Gillette Castle.** Stage actor William Gillette brought theatricality to the design of his 24-room house, set on a hill with a commanding view of the Connecticut River.

14 The Thankful Arnold House

On the corner of Hayden Hill and Walkley Hill Rds., Haddam
Built in 1794–95, the house had only two rooms and a loft, all stacked against the chimney wall. It was bought four years later by Joseph Arnold, a descendant of one of the founders of this community on the Connecticut River, after his marriage to Thankful Clark.

In their 15 years of marriage before Joseph died at age 49, the Arnolds had 12 children, and the house, as can be imagined, had to be expanded. The additions, made in two stages about 1798 and 1810, brought the structure to its present size.

Thankful lived here for 26 years after the death of her husband, and the house was known locally as hers. All told, it was occupied by members of the family for more than 150 years.

The pumpkin-colored dwelling, which New Englanders call a bank or hillside house, has three stories in front and two on the slope at the back. Its restoration in the 1960s was sponsored by Isaac Arnold, a direct descendant, who turned it over to the Haddam Historical Society. The house, furnished with period pieces, is the society's headquarters and museum.

▸ Open year-round Wed.–Fri. and Sun.
Admission charged. Call ahead for guided tours.

www.haddamhistory.org/arnold_house.htm
(860) 345-2400

15 Thomas Griswold House

171 Boston St., Guilford
The white clapboard saltbox, built about 1774 by Thomas Griswold III for his two sons, stands on a gentle rise called the Griswold Ledge above the Old Post Road. It started as a double house of the classic saltbox design and for almost 200 years was lived in by the Griswold family. In 1958 Robert Griswold DeForest sold the property to the Guilford Keeping Society, an organization dedicated to the preservation of the town's historic beginnings, and the Griswold House became the society's headquarters.

Through the years many changes had been made, with an ell, dormer windows, a shed, and a porch added. The society undertook a complete restoration in 1974, returning the saltbox to its original design.

During the restoration the 10-foot-wide kitchen fireplace was opened and was found to have two beehive ovens as well as a warming oven. Other features include a round-back Guilford cupboard, and a few pieces of the original Griswold furniture, among them a 1760 cherry lowboy and a ladder-back "Pilgrim" chair.

The surrounding gardens contain plants available only before 1820.

▸ Open weekends May and June; Tues.–Sun., July and Aug; Fri.–Sun. Sept. and Oct.

www.guilfordkeepingsociety.com
(203) 453-3176

16 Mashantucket Pequot Museum & Research Center

110 Pequot Trail, off Rte. 214, Mashantucket
By the 17th century the Pequot tribe numbered some 8,000 strong and inhabited 250 square miles of prime land in southeastern Connecticut. By 1638, however, the tribe's fortune drastically changed when a brutal war with English colonists slaughtered many of its members and sentenced survivors to a life of either slavery or exile.

More than 300 years later, in the 1970s, many tribal members began moving back to Mashantucket to reclaim their homeland and restore their native culture to its former pride. Tribally owned and operated, this state-of-the-art 308,000-square-foot complex

did you know ❓

The Pequot Museum has collected more than 2,000 Native American objects, most of which come from the tribes that were native to present-day New England.

dramatically brings to life the tragedies and triumphs of the Pequots and other native people of the Northeast.

The museum's best exhibit is a re-creation of a 16th-century Pequot coastal village. Visitors will step back in time and experience the everyday life of tribal members, circa 1550. The village includes 12 wigwams, a sweat lodge, dugout canoes, stone tools and weapons, hand-woven cattail sleeping mats, and food-storage pits.

Throughout the village 51 life-size, perfectly lifelike figures, handcrafted from casts of American Indians, show Pequot men, women, and children partaking in daily activities.

▶ Open year-round Tues.-Sat. except winter holidays. Admission charged.

www.pequotmuseum.org
(800) 411-9671

---

17 ▶ Lyman Allyn Art Museum

625 Williams St., New London
The museum, founded in 1932, was built in memory of Lyman Allyn, a New London whaling captain, by his daughter, Harriet U. Allyn. The original building, a large granite structure with a pillared entrance, has been enlarged several times and now has 10 galleries for the permanent collection and four for changing exhibits.

Its primary focus is on paintings by Connecticut artists such as Willard Metcalf and William Chadwick, other American artists, and antique Connecticut furniture. The museum also has 17th- and 18th-century regionally crafted silver and pewter.

The Allyn home, an 1826 Federal stone building now called the Deshon-Allyn House, is on the museum grounds and has been renovated and furnished with outstanding 19th-century furniture.

▶ Museum open year-round Tues.-Sun. except major holidays; house open by appointment. Admission charged.

www.lymanallyn.org
(860) 443-2545

---

18 ▶ Stonington Lighthouse Museum

7 Water St., Stonington Borough
Salt air and storms took their toll on this lighthouse which was built

18 ▶ Stonington Lighthouse Museum. What was once a dwelling is now a showcase for local artifacts.

in Stonington in 1823, and once it was dismantled, its stones were used to build the present dwelling and tower—from 1840 to 1889 the beacon for vessels sailing into the harbor. Today the quaint building houses the Stonington Historical Society's museum.

Visitors view fascinating relics from Stonington's days as a shipbuilding and whaling center (some handmade tools date to the early 1600s) and can climb to the top of the lighthouse on the original iron stairs.

Also here are artifacts from a War of 1812 encounter: the Battle of Stonington. The British Navy fired more than 50 tons of shells, missiles, and cannonballs at a local militia holed up in a makeshift fort in the summer of 1814, yet the men fought off the Redcoat's ships. Stoningtonians still celebrate the triumph every August 10.

▶ Open daily May-Nov. Admission charged.

www.stoningtonhistory.org
(860) 535-1440

16 ▶ Mashantucket Pequot Museum & Research Center. A diorama of a caribou hunt 11,000 years ago is enhanced by a 21st-century touch-screen display.

seasonal events

APRIL
• Connecticut Storytelling Festival— New London

MAY
• May Day Parade & Bed Race— Mystic *(also features traditional dances)*

JUNE
• International Festival of Arts & Ideas—New Haven *(live music and dance, panel discussions, film and performances, walking tours)*
• Strawberry Festival—Cheshire *(pony rides, petting zoo, children's activities)*

JULY
• Riverfest—Hartford/East Hartford *(family-friendly Independence Day celebration)*
• Annual Antique Fire Apparatus Show & Muster—Milford *(parade, competitions and contests, flea market, exhibitions and demonstrations)*
• Museum Powwow Festival— Pequot Museum, Mashantucket *(native celebration with traditional music, dances, stories, and foods)*

AUGUST
• Italian Festival—Ansonia *(Italian food, live music, games, Italian marketplace)*
• Hamburg Fair—Lyme *(living-history demonstrations, contests, live entertainment, children's activities)*

SEPTEMBER
• Norwalk Seaport Association Oyster Festival—Norwalk *(live music, arts and crafts, children's activities, exhibits, harbor cruises)*
• Litchfield Hills Harvest Festival— Litchfield *(grape harvest, pony rides, hay rides, grape stomping)*
• Bethlehem Fair—Bethlehem *(green fair featuring live entertainment, car show, demonstrations, midway rides)*

DECEMBER
• Light Parade—East Lyme *(holiday parade of festive lighted floats)*

www.ctvisit.com

Delaware

This small state, bounded by water and crisscrossed by an excellent network of roads, offers visitors a wealth of places to explore.

Fort Delaware State Park. Two re-enactors at historic Fort Delaware cook catfish in the manner of the 19th-century soldiers who manned the fort (see page 62).

Although about half of the perimeter of this long, narrow state is bounded by water—the Delaware River, Delaware Bay, and the Atlantic Ocean—strikingly diverse attractions await your pleasure in Delaware. Forested hills, beaches, meadows, and a mansion patterned after a Louis XVI chateau compete for attention with a plantation owned by one of America's founding fathers and a 16,000-acre wildlife preserve where more than 300 species of birds dwell.

visit ➤➤ **offthebeatenpathtrips.com**

1. Nemours Mansion and Gardens

Rockland Rd. between Children's Dr. and Rte. 202, Wilmington
Designed to emulate a Louis XVI chateau and named after the king's ancestral home in France, Nemours is the former residence of renowned philanthropist Alfred I. DuPont. Built between 1909–10, the mansion is exquisitely furnished and beautifully preserved. Its 102 rooms feature fine period antiques, rare Oriental rugs, and tapestries and paintings dating back as far as the 15th century.

Surrounding the striking villa, the 300-acre estate boasts extensive and truly magnificent formal French gardens, which have been assiduously cultivated to express old-world elegance. In addition, the grounds offer expertly planted conservatories, fountains, natural woodlands, and an old-time water tower.

Guided tours are the only way to see the estate. Taking a minimum of two hours, tours include a series of rooms on three floors of the mansion, followed by a bus tour of the gardens—with stops at DuPont's personal billiard room and bowling alley. Visitors will leave with a vivid sense of what it was like to live on a grand scale at the beginning of the 20th century.

▶ Open May–Oct. Admission charged.
No children under 12 admitted.
Reservations recommended.

1. Nemours Mansion and Gardens. The Nemours estate underwent a major renovation in 2008. The statue *Achievement*, regilded with 23-karat gold leaf, was placed in the center of the estate and gazes out over the Maze Garden.

www.nemours.org/mansion.html
(302) 651-6912

2. Brandywine Creek State Park

41 Adams Dam Rd., Wilmington
Named after the small river that almost bisects its 933 acres, this park has open meadows, hills, wooded trails, a floodplain, marshland, and a majestic stand of tulip poplars, some of them 190 years old, in an area known as Tulip Tree Woods.

The park also contains Delaware's first two nature preserves. For dedicated birders, one hilltop offers a superb vantage point for viewing migrating hawks in late autumn as they follow the course of the Delaware River southward.

Guided walks are led by members of the park's nature center, which also features films and displays. One can also hike independently along 14 miles of nature trails, play some Frisbee, have a picnic, or fly kites.

The river is open to canoeists, and fishermen can angle for crappies, bluegills, rock bass, and—in spring—trout. Several bridle paths through groves of tulip, beech, and oak trees invite riders, and in winter the park attracts sledders and cross-country skiers.

▶ Open year-round. Admission charged.

www.destateparks.com
(302) 577-3534

3 ▶ White Clay Creek State Park

425 Wedgewood Rd., Newark
You can look into Pennsylvania and Maryland from this pleasant park nestled in the northwestern corner of Delaware, where the three states come together. Their meeting point, known as The Wedge, was once popular with bandits, who could quickly escape the law of one state by crossing the boundary into another. The park has a spacious 3,384 acres, rising to about 300 feet—which is high for Delaware—and offering long views of the surrounding countryside.

Hikers can explore valleys and impressive rock outcrops on 37 miles of trails. The Millstone Trail shows where grindstones were once quarried from the exposed boulders. In the spring fishermen like to cast for trout from the banks of a creek that runs alongside the

park. And in winter the slopes provide fine tobogganing.

▶ Open year-round.
Admission charged.

www.destateparks.com
(302) 368-6900

4 ▶ Read House and Gardens

42 The Strand, New Castle
This handsome redbrick mansion, one of the finest examples of Federal architecture in the United States, was built in 1804 by George Read II, a prominent Delaware lawyer whose father was a signer of the Declaration of Independence. George Read married his cousin, Mary Thompson, and they brought up their seven children in this house.

Situated on the banks of the Delaware River, the 22-room, 14,000-square-foot mansion is known for its elaborately carved woodwork, handsome relief plasterwork, and delicate fanlights. Its second owner, William Couper, who bought the property in the 1840s, added the garden, which encompasses 1.5 acres. The garden

3 ▶ White Clay Creek State Park. A pedestrian bridge spans a stream in a park where hikers and mountain bikers find 37 miles of serene and scenic trails.

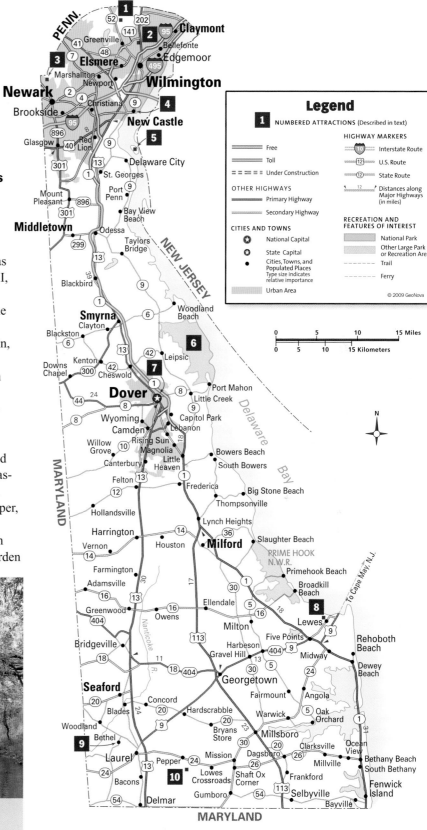

Legend

1 NUMBERED ATTRACTIONS (Described in text)

HIGHWAY MARKERS

Free
Toll
Under Construction

10 Interstate Route
12 U.S. Route
12 State Route
12 Distances along Major Highways (in miles)

OTHER HIGHWAYS

Primary Highway
Secondary Highway

CITIES AND TOWNS

National Capital
State Capital
Cities, Towns, and Populated Places Type size indicates relative importance
Urban Area

RECREATION AND FEATURES OF INTEREST

National Park
Other Large Park or Recreation Area
Trail
Ferry

© 2009 GeoNova

is divided into three sections: a formal parterre flower garden, a specimen garden, and a kitchen garden.

The property was bought in 1920 by Mr. and Mrs. Philip D. Laird, who refurbished the house and furnished it in Colonial Revival style. They extended their taste for Colonial Revival to the garden as well.

When Mrs. Laird died in 1975, the estate was donated to the Historical Society of Delaware, and the house has since been restored to its original Federal-style elegance.

Guided tours of the mansion are conducted by the historical society. Also available are guided walking tours of New Castle, including visits to three of the town's 18th-century buildings.

▶ Open Tues.-Sun. except holidays, Mar.-Dec.; Jan.-Feb. weekends only, with weekday tours by appointment. Admission charged.

www.hsd.org/read.htm
(302) 322-8411

---

5 Fort Delaware State Park

Pea Patch Island, ½ mile offshore from Delaware City
Accessible only by ferry, this distinctive state park—one of Delaware's oldest—offers a journey back in time. The park's impressive Union fortress dates back to 1859. Inside the massive granite-and-brick structure, visitors will discover an authentic military city, going about the business of everyday life in 1864.

Hands-on demonstrations and interactive programs abound. Highlights include a crash course in the blacksmith trade, an eye-opening look at the workload of a laundress, a stop at the officers kitchen for a whiff of delicious,

freshly baked bread, and a lesson in the lost art of loading and firing a giant seacoast cannon. In addition, kids can get in line for an infantry drill, and the whole family can sign on for a personal tour of the fortress.

Conducted by tradesmen, craftswomen, business proprietors, socialites, activists, and generals of the day, tours include a boxed lunch and souvenir Civil War paperwork. When the sun goes down, fearless history buffs can cap off their visit with a ghost tour.

Beyond the fortress, Pea Patch Island offers many national treasures. Marked by remote marshes, it is the largest Atlantic Coast nesting ground north of Florida for wading birds and is the summer home to nine different species of herons, egrets, and ibises. A hiking trail and observation tower offer opportunities to see these beautiful birds in flight. Visitors can bring lunch to enjoy on the spacious, grassy picnic area. Tables and grills are provided, and water and snacks are available from the fortress.

5 Fort Delaware State Park.
The sally port of the granite pentagon-shaped fort, completed on Pea Patch Island in 1859, glows in the setting sun.

▶ Open Sat.-Sun. and holidays late Apr.-late Sept.; Wed.-Fri. mid-June-Aug. Confirm in advance. Admission charged.

www.destateparks.com
(302) 834-7941

---

6 Bombay Hook National Wildlife Refuge

2591 Whitehall Neck Rd., Smyrna
The Kahanasinks were the first known occupants of this appealing sprawl of marshland, tidal stream, freshwater ponds, and timbered swamps. In 1679 the Native Americans sold part of the area to Dutch settlers from New York, who hunted birds, trapped muskrats, and cut salt hay from the marshes.

Bombay Hook now encompasses 15,978 acres and is one link in a chain of waterfowl refuges established in the 1930s along major migratory routes. Some 300 species have been observed since the refuge opened. Waterfowl abound, especially in March and November; shorebirds, wading birds, and songbirds are most evident during May,

August, and September. Others for whom this is a haven include owls, woodpeckers, and hawks.

Short walking trails and a long, winding automobile trail lead through the area, which is a habitat for foxes, river otters, beavers, and varieties of turtles, snakes, salamanders, and frogs. An information center is open on weekdays during spring and fall.

▶ Refuge open year-round.

http://bombayhook.fws.gov
(302) 653-6872

---

7 John Dickinson Plantation

340 Kitts Hummock Rd., Dover
One of America's founding fathers, John Dickinson grew up in this spacious brick home that looks across cultivated fields to the St. Jones River. Dickinson was often called the "Penman of the Revolution" for the many pamphlets and articles he wrote about American independence. After the Revolution he served in the legislatures of both Delaware and Pennsylvania and was among the framers of the Constitution.

The house, built in 1740 by Dickinson's father, Samuel, provides insight into the lifestyle of a prosperous colonial landowner.

In 1804, when much of the interior of the building was destroyed by fire, a document

10 ▶ **Trap Pond State Park.** Anglers and bird-watchers are drawn to the placid lake in this park, flush with loblolly pines, dogwoods, and many species of birds.

In 1869 a shipyard was constructed in Lewisville, as the town was called, and five years later the first vessel was built.

In 1880 the town's name was changed to Bethel—"the sailor's retreat" (according to the Bible)—and in 1889, when the flat-bottomed Chesapeake Bay sailing ram was designed here, Bethel's reputation as a shipbuilding town was assured.

Although the shipyard was dismantled in the 1940s, the historic town remains a colorful place to visit. A small museum displays local maritime artifacts.

▶ Museum open year-round Tues.-Fri.; weekends also July, Aug., and Dec.

(302) 875-5314

---

listing the contents of the house was found. Several of the original pieces are on display today in the rooms. Members of the staff give presentations in costume as characters from that era and provide tours of the reconstructed outbuildings and a slave/tenant house.

▶ Open daily except Mon. and holidays. Closed Sun. in Jan. and Feb. Donations encouraged.

http://history.delaware.gov/museums
(302) 739-3277

---

8 ▶ Overfalls Maritime Museum Foundation

Front Rd., off Rte. 9, Lewes
Built in 1938, the *Overfalls* was the last lightship built by the U.S. Lighthouse Service. Upon being decommissioned in 1972, the Coast Guard donated the ship to the Lewes Historical Society, and it fell into disrepair despite preservation attempts by community groups. Although listed on the *National Register of Historic Places* in 1988, the ship languished until a dedicated group of volunteers restored it in 2001.

Today the ship is almost fully restored. Members of the Dirty Hands Gang, as the volunteers call themselves, have dedicated thousands of hours to the restoration and upkeep of this piece of maritime history. Visitors can tour its three decks and imagine living on the vessel for two weeks at a time—the original Coast Guard shift.

▶ Open Thurs.-Mon. mid-May-mid-Oct. Admission charged.

www.overfalls.org
(302) 644-8050

---

9 ▶ Historic Bethel on Broad Creek

Rd. 493, West of US-13
The history of this picturesque little town and its role in early American shipping began in 1795, when Capt. Kendall M. Lewis built a small dock here on Broad Creek, a tributary of the Nanticoke River.

The dock became the busy center of the town, whose primary industry was transferring cargoes from large ships to shallow-draft scows that could reach the towns that were farther upstream on Broad Creek.

---

10 ▶ Trap Pond State Park

33587 Baldcypress Ln., Laurel
This wooded park surrounds a small, attractive lake where fishermen angle for perch, catfish, bass, pickerel, and sunfish. Rowboats, canoes, kayaks, and paddleboats are available for rent, and boat owners can launch their own.

Circle the entire park on the self-guiding five-mile Loblolly Trail, or hike along pine-forested trails. Many species of birds make their home here, including the great blue heron, the bald eagle, and the pileated woodpecker.

The Cypress Point Trail takes you to the nation's most northern stand of cypress; a sandy beach and shaded lakeside picnic grove are popular spots, especially on summer weekends.

▶ Park open year-round; facilities available Apr.-Oct. Admission charged.

www.destateparks.com
(302) 875-5153

Florida

The beaches and amusement parks of Florida are well known. But the state is also full of surprises, some even dating from prehistoric times.

Grayton Beach State Park. The pristine white sands and clear waters of the Gulf of Mexico beckon visitors to take a stroll and soak up the salt air (see page 65).

The Sunshine State seems an unlikely place for the re-establishment of the buffalo—a prototypical symbol of the Western plains—but at Paynes Prairie the living evidence can be seen on the hoof. Near Tampa, exotic animals are sheltered at Big Cat Rescue, the world's largest accredited sanctuary of its kind. Among other highlights are fine parks, a Civil War battlefield, a botanical garden devoted to orchids, and a memorial to a much-loved writer.

visit ➤ offthebeatenpathtrips.com

1 Blackwater River State Park

7720 Deaton Bridge Rd., Holt
This 590-acre preserve is a good example of Florida's enlightened policy of public-land management. The objective of the Florida Park Service is to maintain—and re-create where necessary—the plant communities and ecological systems that prevailed in the area before the first Europeans arrived in the early 16th century.

The Blackwater is one of the few remaining sand-bottom rivers in the Southeast, and despite the darkish color of the tannin-stained water, it is one of the cleanest. The water contrasts dramatically with the pristine white of the ever-changing sandbars deposited on the curves and oxbows of the meandering river.

The Blackwater, understandably, is a great favorite for both canoeing and swimming, with its fine sand beaches. Other features are the nature trails and a board-walk across a swamp to a picnic area, where you find the state's champion Atlantic white cedar, a noble tree indeed.

The ecological systems here include the river floodplain, with swamps, sandbars, and oxbow lakes; the pine flatwoods, dominated by slash pine with an understory of blackberry vines, blueberry bushes, and gallberry; and the high pinelands that support longleaf

Blackwater River State Park. A boardwalk typical of those found at other Florida nature sites takes visitors across a swamp to a pleasant picnic area.

pines, turkey oaks, and sweetleaf. White-tailed deer and gray fox may be seen in the woods, and the river otter roams the floodplain.

▶ Open year-round. Admission charged.

www.floridastateparks.org
(850) 983-5363

2 Indian Temple Mound Museum

139 Miracle Strip Pkwy. SE, Fort Walton Beach
Beginning with a Smithsonian dig in 1888, excavations of the Fort Walton Temple Mound, a monumental earthen structure that was

constructed sometime between A.D. 800 and 1400 have yielded thousands of relics of the pre-Columbian peoples who once inhabited this coastal area. Today the ceremonial mound—18 feet high with an expanse of more than 200 feet—is the highlight of the Fort Walton Heritage Park and Cultural Center.

The extensive collection of prehistoric items, including superb ceramic, is housed in the museum, along with artifacts from the eras of European exploration, settlement, and the Civil War. The interactive educational exhibits are especially popular with young visi-

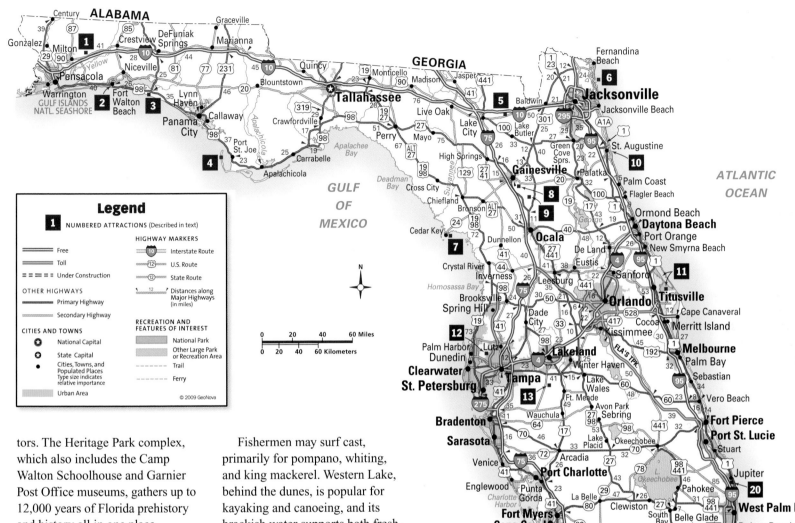

Legend

 NUMBERED ATTRACTIONS (Described in text)

HIGHWAY MARKERS

Free — Interstate Route

Toll — U.S. Route

Under Construction — State Route

OTHER HIGHWAYS — Distances along Major Highways (in miles)

Primary Highway

Secondary Highway

CITIES AND TOWNS

RECREATION AND FEATURES OF INTEREST

National Capital — National Park

State Capital — Other Large Park or Recreation Area

Cities, Towns, and Populated Places Type size indicates relative importance — Trail

— Ferry

Urban Area

© 2009 GeoNova

---

tors. The Heritage Park complex, which also includes the Camp Walton Schoolhouse and Garnier Post Office museums, gathers up to 12,000 years of Florida prehistory and history all in one place.

▶ Open Mon.–Sat. except major holidays.
Admission charged.

www.fwb.org/museum
(850) 833-9595

▶ Grayton Beach State Park

County Rte. 30A, Grayton Beach
A superb mile-long beach of brilliant white sand awaits visitors to this interesting park. Behind the beach, high barrier dunes stabilized by sea oats and scrub overlook the clear green and azure waters where dolphins are sometimes seen. The appeal it has for swimmers is obvious.

Fishermen may surf cast, primarily for pompano, whiting, and king mackerel. Western Lake, behind the dunes, is popular for kayaking and canoeing, and its brackish water supports both fresh- and saltwater species.

For those interested in wildlife, there is the 40-minute Barrier Dune Nature Trail. It provides markers keyed to entries in a trail guide explaining the many phenomena of the shoreline ecosystem, such as shifting sands, dune building, plant pruning by wind and salt spray, and decomposition and recycling.

Raccoons and alligators are common sights throughout this 2,228-acre expanse of salt marshes, slash pines, and palmettos. In the summer loggerhead turtle nests may be found on the beach. The park has five sheltered picnic

areas, cabins, and a campground. Although the sites are close together, dense scrub separates them and offers privacy.

▶ Open year-round.
Admission charged.

www.floridastateparks.org
(850) 231-4210
(800) 326-3521 Reservations

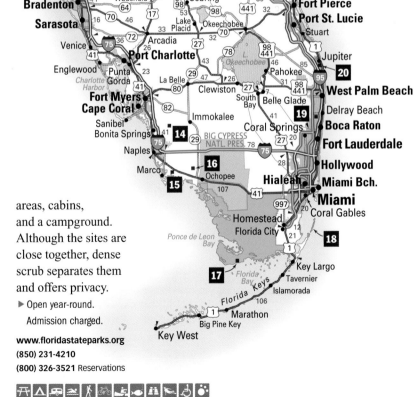

4 ▶ T. H. Stone Memorial St. Joseph Peninsula State Park

8899 Cape San Blas Rd., Port St. Joe

A long barrier extending north between St. Joseph Bay and the Gulf of Mexico, this 2,516-acre park will appeal to a wide range of interests. Its miles of fine natural beach are good for swimming and fishing.

Three walkovers placed among the high palmetto-dotted dunes provide panoramic views of pristine terrain similar to that encountered by the first Spanish settlers to arrive in this area.

These vantage points are popular with birders interested in the vast array of resident and transient species found here. Besides the many brown pelicans, willets, and great blue herons, more rarely seen species include white pelicans,

5 ▶ **Olustee Battlefield Historic State Park.** A Confederate monument stands tall at the site of the only Civil War battle fought in the young state of Florida.

green herons, magnificent frigate birds, American golden plovers, and Acadian flycatchers, according to the season. In autumn this park is one of the best places in the country to observe monarch butterflies and migrating hawks, including the rare peregrine falcon.

On the bay side salt marshes nurture populations of fiddler and blue crabs, horse conchs, green turtles, diamondback terrapins, and the inevitable alligators.

Near the Gulf beaches are two separate camping sites. On the bay side is a boat basin. The park also offers two nature trails.

▶ Open year-round.

www.floridastateparks.org
(850) 227-1327

5 ▶ Olustee Battlefield Historic State Park

Off US-90, east of Olustee

This site commemorates Florida's major Civil War battle. In February 1864 a Union force of 5,500 men, who were charged with severing enemy communications and food supplies between east and west Florida, clashed here in an open pine forest with nine Confederate regiments. The Southern soldiers, although slightly outnumbered, forced their foes to retreat after a five-hour fight. The events of the day and other aspects of Florida's role in the Civil War are explained in a small interpretive center. A short trail through the battlefield is dotted with interpretive signs that further explore the course of the battle.

▶ Open year-round.

www.floridastateparks.org
(386) 758-0400

6 ▶ **Amelia Island.** Dunes beyond the island's beaches support sea oats and other coastal dune species.

6 ▶ Amelia Island

Northeast of Jacksonville

Graced with 13 miles of beautiful beaches, lush forests, and a unique, colorful history, Amelia Island is the perfect spot for collecting seashells, riding mountain bikes, or taking a quick trip back in time. In spite of its turbulent past and the waves of industrialization and modernization surrounding it, the island remains a quaint and authentic Victorian seaport village. It's also productive: Nearly 80 percent of Florida's Atlantic white shrimp are harvested here.

Discovered by a Frenchman in 1562, the island was soon claimed by the Spaniards. Its only town, Fernandina Beach, was named for King Ferdinand VII. Later, when Spain swapped Florida for Havana with England, British loyalists took control and christened the island Amelia. In the mid-1930s the founders of Afro-American Life Insurance bought 200 acres on the

island's southern end. Known as American Beach, this property became an oceanfront haven for African Americans during the Jim Crow era. Today American Beach is the first stop on Florida's Black Heritage Trail.

While basking in the island's distinctive past and character, visitors can swim, sail, kayak, or even go horseback riding on the beach—one of only a handful of places in the United States where this exhilarating activity is permitted. Kelly Seahorse Ranch provides horses and expert guidance. Sightseers can also take a river cruise through the Intracoastal Waterway past Cumberland Island, where wild horses play. Along the way, amid the salty marshes, guests just might get to meet an Atlantic bottlenose dolphin.

www.ameliaisland.com
(800) 226-3542

7 ▶ Cedar Key Museum State Park

Cedar Key

Many small museums owe their existence to the energy and enthusiasm of just one individual, and this one is such an example. Much of the material here was assembled by the late Saint Clair Whitman, a dedicated naturalist, collector, and former resident of Cedar Key. Along with artifacts dating from 6000 B.C. to the Colonial period, the museum houses a display of late 19th-century glassware, old bottles, exhibits that chart local history, and Whitman's extensive collection of seashells.

The town of Cedar Key has had its ups and downs. It was a bustling community in the 19th century and an important Confederate port during the Civil War. The lumbering industry boomed for a brief period, as did shipbuilding and associated activities. Today Cedar Key is a quiet town but one worthy of exploring.

The museum documents the lumbering era in particular with an excellent collection of photographs and tools. Also on view: mementos of the fishing, oystering, and sponge industries, and the brushes and brooms of a palm fiber industry. The latter enterprise was swept away by the advent of plastics.

▶ Open year-round. Closed Tues. and Wed. Admission charged.

www.floridastateparks.org
(352) 543-5350

8 ▶ Marjorie Kinnan Rawlings Historic State Park

18700 S. CR-325, Cross Creek
Readers familiar with author Marjorie Rawlings will recognize this setting as having pervaded much of her work. An unknown writer when she moved here in 1928, Mrs. Rawlings committed herself to this small, remote community. Three years passed before

she sold her first story. But as the people and environs of Cross Creek fueled her creative fire, she eventually penned her most famous work, *The Yearling,* which won her a Pulitzer Prize.

A typical Cracker homestead, designed for optimum cross-ventilation, the house consists of three board-and-batten units connected by porches and shaded by wide overhangs and the surrounding orange and magnolia trees. A 45-minute tour takes you through the farmyard and into the house. The park has two loop walking trails through the woods and farmyard.

▶ Open year-round. House closed Aug.-Sept. Admission charged.

www.floridastateparks.org
(352) 466-3672

9 ▶ Paynes Prairie Preserve State Park

100 Savannah Blvd., Micanopy
If King Payne, chief of the Seminoles, (who was killed in a battle with American settlers near the Georgia border in 1812) could have imagined that the white man would name a prairie in his honor,

8 ▶ Marjorie Kinnan Rawlings Historic State Park. The author of the famous novel *The Yearling* lived simply at her farm near Cross Creek. The house at left was her home.

9 ▶ Paynes Prairie Preserve State Park. Over the centuries this area of north-central Florida changed from a huge lake to savanna. Today buffalo graze in the grasslands.

he would have been doubly surprised—because in his time this basin was a vast lake.

It was also a lake when explorer Hernando de Soto saw it in about 1540, and there was water here when naturalist William Bartram visited the site in 1774. But the water has had a way of coming and going in this huge saucerlike basin because of a sinkhole in one corner.

From time to time the sinkhole would fill with debris, and the water would rise and remain. Years later the sinkhole would become "unplugged"; that is, the water would drain away, and the area would revert to savanna. In 1892 a small steamer plying the lake was stranded when the water disappeared. Since that time the basin has been a treeless prairie.

In 1970 some 18,000 acres here were purchased by the state, and preservation of the prairie and its historic function as a habitat for wildlife was thus assured. A program is now in operation to perpetuate the ecosystem that Bartram once observed and recorded. American buffalo have been reintroduced, and efforts are

being made to breed native scrub cattle similar to the Andalusian stock first brought to Florida by Spanish settlers.

A fine panoramic view of the prairie can be enjoyed from a 50-foot observation tower. The birding is superb. A list of 241 species seen here is available at the visitors center. Also listed are 27 mammals, 41 reptiles, and 20 amphibians native to the area. An audiovisual program explains the purpose and scope of the activity here, and Indian artifacts are on display. The region was inhabited as early as 10,000 B.C.

A recreation area at Lake Wauberg and Sawgrass Pond is popular among visitors for picnicking, kayaking, boating, and fishing. In addition, the preserve has several miles of riding trails. On Saturdays from November through April, buffalo and other wildlife are best seen during guided observation walks.

▶ Open year-round.

www.floridastateparks.org
(352) 466-3397

10 **Florida Lighthouse Tour.** The Ponce de Leon Inlet Lighthouse rises near the town of Daytona.

10 Florida Lighthouse Tour

Follow the coastline from St. Augustine to Pensacola

With more than 1,200 miles of coastline, Florida has long been a natural beacon for lighthouses. The state's impressive collection—30 still standing proud—includes some of the nation's oldest and tallest. Many invite visitors to step inside and climb their spiraling staircases to the top for the reward of a dazzling panoramic view. Others, conveniently located in public parks, encourage appreciation from a short distance.

The best way to see all of Florida's lighthouses is to hit the road. Spanning the coastal highway from St. Augustine to Pensacola, the complete tour takes about five days. The first stop is the famous St. Augustine Lighthouse. Built in 1874, this 165-foot lighthouse is the state's oldest and most recognizable, recently restored to its early glory. Next, near Daytona Beach, comes the 175-foot Ponce de Leon

Inlet Lighthouse, the second-tallest lighthouse in the nation and one of the few still busily working.

Farther on down, just south of downtown Miami on Key Biscayne, stands the Cape Florida lighthouse. This cheerful lighthouse is famous for surviving a slew of assaults, from hostile Seminoles to a fierce hurricane. Near the end of the trail, on Florida's West Coast, St. Mark's Lighthouse beckons from a 65,000-acre national wildlife sanctuary for alligators, birds, and deer.

Last but certainly not least is the Pensacola Lighthouse. Built in 1858 on the grounds of the Pensacola Naval Air Station, this structure has braved lightning strikes, a tornado, and an earthquake but continues to operate.

www.floridalighthouses.org

11 Merritt Island National Wildlife Refuge and Canaveral National Seashore

Titusville

The history of Merritt Island extends from prehistoric times to the space age. Inhabited by Native Americans since about 7000 B.C., the island in recent years has rocketed to renown as the site of the John F. Kennedy Space Center, with which the refuge and seashore share a border.

The unspoiled seashore spans 24 miles between Apollo and Palyalinda beaches. You may hike this distance, stopping to swim and beachcomb. Other possibilities are shellfishing, crabbing, and surf casting for pompano, bluefish, and other species. Boating, canoeing, and fishing are also enjoyed at the adjacent Mosquito Lagoon. (Bring insect repellent.)

The refuge can be explored by car along two nature drives or by

foot via five hiking trails. Either way, the range of wildlife is stunning. Many of the 310 bird species that have been observed here make their nests on the refuge, including great blue and green herons, snowy egrets, anhingas and black skimmers, and pie-billed grebes.

The refuge is also home to 19 endangered species, most notably the Southern bald eagle and manatee. Porpoises and whales are occasionally glimpsed offshore, and large tracks of sea turtles are frequently seen on the sands.

The Canaveral information center offers a slide show on the history of this tidal area and the wildlife it supports.

▶ Open year-round.

www.fws.gov/merrittisland
(321) 861-0667

www.nps.gov/cana
(321) 267-1110

12 Big Cat Rescue

12802 Easy St., Tampa

What happens to a magnificent tiger or leopard that has been abused or abandoned or even retired from a career in showbiz? If it is very lucky, it will find a home at Tampa's Big Cat Rescue, the largest accredited sanctuary of its kind in the world. The 45-acre site provides safe shelter for almost 150 lions, tigers, cougars, bobcats, lynx, snow leopards, ocelots, and other varieties of exotic cats to recover and heal in a natural environment.

A nonprofit organization, Big Cat Rescue makes it clear that it's not a zoo; the welfare of the animals is paramount, so visits are by guided tour only (no pets allowed). On the tour you can watch tigers swimming in the lake and bobcats draped in the trees overhead. Short of going on an African safari, there's no better way to see, photo-

12 **Big Cat Rescue.** Some snow leopards, an extremely endangered species, live here in large habitats complete with air-conditioned dens and rocky ledges.

graph, and learn about these endangered animals, now living out their lives as nature intended.

▶ Open Mon.–Sat. Call for tour times.

www.bigcatrescue.org
(813) 920-4130

13 Mulberry Phosphate Museum

101 S.E. 1st St., Mulberry
Housed in an authentic 1899 train depot, the history of the local phosphate industry is on display here. When the Ice Age began, the

 Big Cat Rescue. A regal lion pads his way through the preserve.

animals that had found plentiful food and warm weather died away. Their remains petrified and left a fossil record of prehistoric Florida, along with an abundant supply of a mineral called phosphate.

In the museum, visitors will see an outstanding display of fossils and bones that have been excavated from the phosphate pits in Florida's Bone Valley. Both animal and plant life are represented.

A mastodon, a woolly mam-

moth, a saber-toothed cat, and a giant ground sloth are included, as well as an 18-foot baleen whale skeleton, thought to be 10 million years old.

▶ Open year-round Tue.–Sat.

www.mulberrychamber.org/attractions.htm
(863) 425-2823

14 Corkscrew Swamp Sanctuary

375 Sanctuary Rd. W, Naples
Extending over an 11,000-acre wilderness of pine flatwoods, wet prairie, swampland, and typical hardwood hammocks, this haven for wildlife and native plants may be enjoyed on foot by means of an incredibly beautiful 2¹/₄-mile-long boardwalk overhung by Spanish moss.

Among the many sights to be savored are lettuce lakes, cypress knees, floating tussocks, water hemlock, strangler fig, ferns and lilies, brilliant hibiscus, royal palms, and various epiphytes (plants such as the tree-growing butterfly, cigar, and clamshell orchids that grow on other plants).

Cardinals, red-shouldered hawks, and rare birds known as limpkins make their homes here, and the country's largest colony of wood storks also take up residence. In addition, there are the familiar alligators, Florida water snakes, mosquito fish, and turtles.

A 34-page field guide describing

did you know ?

The Corkscrew Swamp Sanctuary is the home of the nation's largest surviving stand of virgin bald cypress trees, many of which are now over 700 years old.

what you'll see on the self-guiding boardwalk tour can be purchased. A 14-minute audio-visual introduction to the sights and sounds of Corkscrew is held at Swamp Theater in the new Blair Center. The sanctuary is managed by the National Audubon Society.

▶ Open year-round. Admission charged.

www.corkscrew.audubon.org
(239) 348-9151

 **Collier-Seminole State Park.** Visitors can rent canoes for freshwater and saltwater fishing or simply relish the tranquillity of the mangrove-lined Blackwater River.

15 Collier-Seminole State Park

20200 Tamiami Trail E, Naples
This 7,280-acre park is named for Barron Collier, an entrepreneur who financed the Tamiami highway across the Everglades, and for the local Seminole Native Americans, whose ancestors fought removal in the Seminole wars.

Self-guiding and conducted walks on the nature trail (nearly a mile long) reveal an interesting environment common to the coastal wilderness of Yucatan and the West Indies.

Here, too, is the rare Florida royal palm, with its distinctive lime-green upper trunk. The mangrove and cypress swamps, pine flatwoods, tidal creeks, and

salt marshes shelter a broad range of wildlife.

An observation platform permits an elevated view of ospreys, spoonbills, bald eagles, wood storks, and other colorful birds. With patience and luck, elsewhere in the park you might even glimpse the rare Florida panther, the Florida black bear, or the manatee, which are observed a few times a year.

Visitors may also explore the park on a 13¹/₂-mile round-trip canoe trail to the northernmost tip of the Ten Thousand Islands. The rivers and bays provide chances to fish for snook, mangrove snapper, and redfish.

A replica of an 1840s blockhouse serves as an interpretive center, with photo exhibits of native plants and animals and a review of Collier's achievements as a pioneering developer in the area. In the winter campfire slide shows outline park activities. Canoes may be brought in or rented. A reminder: Insects can be a problem in summer, so bring bug repellent.

▶ Open year-round. Admission charged.

www.floridastateparks.org
(239) 394-3397

16 Fakahatchee Strand Preserve State Park

Janes Memorial Scenic Dr., Copeland

A strand is a regional name for the long, narrow drainage channels, or sloughs, that develop in Florida's limestone rock. The Fakahatchee is the largest of many such strands in the Big Cyprus Swamp region of the Everglades.

This tract in southwest Florida, about 20 miles long and 3 to 5 miles wide, harbors some 44 species of orchids, the greatest such concentration in North America. One, the Ghost Orchid, is found only here and in Cuba. The preserve also contains the largest number of rare Florida royal palm trees and the only known mix of bald cypresses and royal palms in the world.

In addition to bald eagles and American alligators, the strand is a home for mangrove fox squirrels, eastern indigo snakes, Everglades minks, black bears, and bobcats.

The preserve maintains a 2,000-foot boardwalk, seven miles west of SR-29 on US-41 (Tamiami Trail). Booklets describe the highlights along the walkway, which is wide enough for wheelchairs.

Reservations are available for a

17 **Flamingo Area, Everglades National Park.** The open jaws of a Cuban crocodile, a small species, signal his readiness to attack.

18 **Biscayne National Park.** Two snorkelers head toward Elkhorn Reef at the park, 96 percent of which lies underwater. The less adventurous can choose boat tours.

three-hour guided wade through the swamp to see tropical plants.

▶ Open year-round.

www.floridastateparks.org
(239) 695-4593
For reservations:
www.friendsoffkahatchee.org

17 Flamingo Area, Everglades National Park

Flamingo, on the shore of Florida Bay, is the center for sightseeing in the southern sector of the primeval Everglades. Visitors have their choice of foot trails, canoe trails, and privately operated cruises to take in the beauty of this area.

Of the trails suitable for families and children, Snake Bight Trail (four miles round-trip) is the most popular. You can walk it or bike it. The trail unwinds beneath the umbrella of a hardwood forest inhabited by hundreds of species of birds and butterflies, from white-crowned pigeons to zebra longwings.

The park is host to a diverse array of wildlife, including manatees and turtles. It is the only place in the world where alligators and crocodiles exist side by side. On the Rowdy Bend, Bear Lake, and Christian Point trails, you can see other facets of this unique ecological system.

In winter two cruises ply the local waterways, one of them into scenic Florida Bay, where at low tide you can expect to see brown pelicans, egrets, herons, and other large birds scouting the shoreline for food. (The flamingo, however, is rarely seen.) For those more intrigued by the inland waterways and plant life, a pontoon boat makes sorties into the Everglades wilderness.

Canoeists can take any of five different trails. If time is no problem, you can tackle the 100-mile Wilderness Waterway, which takes you through the backcountry between Everglades City and Flamingo. Canoes, skiffs, kayaks, bicycles, and fishing gear may all be rented. Ranger-guided canoe tours are available during the winter.

▶ Open late Dec.-Mar. Admission charged.

www.nps.gov/ever/
planyourvisitflamdirections.htm
(239) 695-2945 For ranger-led tours

18 Biscayne National Park

9700 S.W. 228th St., Homestead

This oceanic expanse of 173,000 acres encompasses most of Biscayne Bay, the Keys, and living coral reefs south of Miami. It's one of the largest marine preserves in the United States. The waters are turquoise and crystal clear, making it ideal for fishing, boating, snorkeling, scuba diving, and marine gazing in general.

The most obvious way to explore this watery paradise is by boat. Visitors can launch their own at one of the adjacent county marinas or take one of the tours available from the visitors center. A three-hour excursion in a glass-bottomed boat gives you a marvelously colorful view of the reefs and grassy meadows, as well as lobsters, turtles, sponges, and exotic tropical fish lurking there. For an even better view, you may wish to try snorkeling.

To savor the special appeal of a

subtropical island, you can take an excursion boat to one of the park's islands seven miles offshore. Elliott Key offers an opportunity to stroll through a tropical hardwood forest and along the rocky shoreline, while Boca Chita Key harkens back to a time when the area was millionaire Mark Honeywell's personal retreat. His private lighthouse affords one of the park's best views.

At the Dante Fascell Visitor Center several videos and exhibits familiarize visitors with local wildlife and history. Picnic tables with grills are located along the shore beside sea grape and mahogany trees. Here you can watch brown pelicans, double-crested cormorants, herons, terns, and gulls seeking food offshore.

▶ Open year-round.

www.nps.gov/bisc
(305) 230-7275

19 American Orchid Society Visitors Center & Botanical Garden

16700 AOS Ln., Delray Beach
What do you associate with the word "orchid"? If "purple" and "prom night" are about all that come to mind, then you're in for something amazing at the national headquarters of the American Orchid Society. Wander through 3½ acres of outdoor gardens filled with orchids growing as they do in the wild. Explore every corner of a 4,000-square-foot exhibit greenhouse that has its own waterfall. No one knows exactly how many orchid species grow worldwide (estimates range up to 35,000), but there are thousands of unexpected variations in size, shape, fragrance, and color included in the Society's lush collection and special displays. Just one visit and you'll see these exotic beauties with new eyes.

▶ Gardens open daily. Admission charged.

www.aos.org
(561) 404-2000

20 Loggerhead Marinelife Center

14200 US-1, Juno Beach
The loggerhead sea turtle, the most common nesting turtle on the Florida coast, is the namesake of this nonprofit venture in the West Palm Beach area. Loggerhead Center is housed in a new state-of-the-art certified "green" facility on the beach. Its busy marine veterinary hospital is devoted to the rescue, treatment, and rehabilitation of wounded and ill sea turtles—loggerheads, leatherbacks, greens, as well as even rarer types. Exhibits, including saltwater aquaria and the Sea Turtle Yard (habitat for the center's recovering "patients")—focus on the lives of sea turtles and other sea creatures, their role in the ecosystem, and the natural and man-made dangers they face. Here lies an altogether fun and fascinating learning experience for every age!

▶ Open daily except major holidays. Admission free but donations appreciated.

www.marinelife.org
(561) 627-8280

19 American Orchid Society Visitors Center & Botanical Garden. Tropical plants are intermixed with orchid species, such as *Dendrobium farmeri* (inset), native to the Himalayas, Myanmar, Thailand, and Malaysia.

seasonal events

JANUARY
- Kumquat Festival—Dade City *(harvest festival, farmer's market, wagon rides, live music, car show, crafts)*

FEBRUARY
- Ybor City Fiesta Day—Tampa Bay *(multiethnic festival, parade, children's activities, arts and crafts, local food)*
- Garlic Fest—Delray Beach *(demonstrations, live music, competitions, children's activities)*

MARCH
- Azalea Festival—Palatka *(car show, parade, arts and crafts, live music)*
- Florida Strawberry Festival—Plant City *(carnival, live music, local food, agricultural exhibits)*
- Olustee Battle Re-enactment—Olustee *(educational programs, parade, live music)*

APRIL
- Black Bear Festival—Umatilla *(presentations, field trips, live animals, live music, educational events)*

MAY
- Florida Folk Festival—White Springs *(live music, demonstrations, historical exhibits, local food)*
- Isle of Eight Flags Shrimp Festival—Amelia Island *(local food, fine arts show, antiques, live entertainment, children's activities)*

JUNE
- Silver Spurs Rodeo—Kissimmee

SEPTEMBER
- Latin Festival—Hollywood Beach *(live music, children's activities, arts and crafts, local food)*

OCTOBER
- Bayou Bogy Mullet Festival—Niceville *(regional food, live music, arts and crafts, children's activities)*
- Old Florida Festival—Naples *(historical festival, re-enactments, arts and crafts, period food)*

www.visitflorida.com

Georgia

The history of the Empire State of the South is a tapestry of colorful threads—some of which lead back to prehistoric times.

Cloudland Canyon State Park. This park is among the most scenic in the state.

The mysterious earthen mounds left behind thousands of years ago by the Native Americans who resided here and—not surprisingly—the war that weighed so heavily on the South is tellingly memorialized. Remarkable, however, is the variety of other highlights here. These include state parks with great scenery, fishing, birding, and museums that recall the demands and pleasures of 19th-century life.

The "trembling earth" of the Okefenokee Swamp is another world, as are the barrier islands that helped protect the Georgian colony from the fury of the Atlantic.

visit ➔ offthebeatenpathtrips.com

1 Cloudland Canyon State Park

Off Rte. 136, 122 Cloudland State Park, Rising Fawn

Over millions of years Sitton Gulch Creek has carved a large gorge through the western edge of Lookout Mountain, so that today the difference in elevation between the highest and lowest point is more than 1,000 feet. Spectacular scenic views of rugged rock faces, ridges, valleys, and two waterfalls—including one that spills for almost 100 feet—await outdoor enthusiasts who visit this 3,485-acre area.

The forest is lush with hemlock, dogwood, holly, mountain laurel, and rhododendron. Hikers and nature lovers will enjoy the Rim and Waterfall trails through thickly wooded mountain terrain frequented by cardinals, red-tailed hawks, barred owls, and pileated woodpeckers. Gray foxes and white-tailed deer are often seen, and occasionally a bobcat is spotted.

The park offers picnic areas, a playground, and accommodations that range from cabins with fireplaces and screened porches to family camping areas and more remote primitive sites accessible only by foot.
▶ Open year-round.
www.gastateparks.org
(706) 657-4050

2 Tallulah Gorge State Park. In Georgia's mountainous northeast, Tallulah Gorge rewards hikers, campers, bikers, and whitewater paddlers with spectacular natural beauty.

2 Tallulah Gorge State Park

338 Jane Hurt Yarn Dr., Tallulah Falls

Originally a tourist town in the late 1880s, Tallulah Falls is now a 2,694-acre state park. Running through the park is the Tallulah River, the force that created this two-mile-long, 1,000-foot-deep Tallulah Gorge. A suspension bridge 80 feet above the bottom of the gorge offers breathtaking views of the waterfalls below. Several hiking and mountain-biking trails traverse the interior of the gorge and the surrounding area. A free permit, available at the interpretive center, allows access to the gorge floor. Trails entering and exiting the gorge and on the gorge floor are very difficult and should not be attempted by visitors with health problems. Also available are trails that offer scenic views of the waterfalls cascading into the gorge.

In addition to the hiking opportunities at the park, visitors can visit Tallulah Lake, play tennis, or go whitewater rafting on the first two weekends in April and the first three weekends in November.
▶ Fee charged for parking. Open daily.
www.gastateparks.org
(706) 754-7970

3 Kangaroo Conservation Center

222 Bailey-Waters Rd., Dawsonville

Home to over 300 kangaroos of nine different species, the Center boasts the largest collection of kangaroos outside of Australia. The founders and staff of this 87-acre facility are dedicated to preserving these amazing marsupials through captive breeding and public awareness. In addition to kangaroos, the Center also exhibits several other species of birds and reptiles native to Australasia (the region containing Australia and the southeastern portion of Asia), including blue-winged kookaburras and ridge-tailed monitor lizards.

There are several different ways to experience the offerings of the Conservation Center, including the KangaRanger guided truck tour, the Wild Australia show, and the basic Wander Down Under tour, which allows visitors to explore the grounds and exhibits at their leisure. Tours are conducted no matter the weather, so dress appropriately. Also at the facility are nature trails to hike or walk and a butterfly picnic garden.

▶ Admission charged (advance ticket purchase highly recommended; children under 6 not admitted). Open Mar.–Nov.

www.kangaroocenter.com
(706) 265-6100

4 The Len Foote Hike Inn at Amicalola Falls State Park

240 Amicalola Falls State Park Rd., Dawsonville

A cozy alternative to camping, the Hike Inn lies at the end of a five-mile wilderness trail of easy-to-moderate difficulty. It takes about two to four hours to hike to the Inn from the trail's start at the top of Amicalola Falls. Along the trail distance markers and highlights of important aspects, such as descriptions of the flora, are provided. With soft beds, hot showers, and family-style dining awaiting them at the end of the trail, guests need only carry personal items on the hike. Other aspects of the Inn include the Star Base, where rocks mark the seasonal positions of the sun, and the community Sunrise Room with a wood-burning stove, library, and porch overlooking the Blue Ridge Mountains. Also in the vicinity of the inn are short hiking trails, as well as access to the southern terminus of the Appalachian Trail.

▶ Fee charged. Open year-round.

www.hike-inn.com
(800) 581-8032

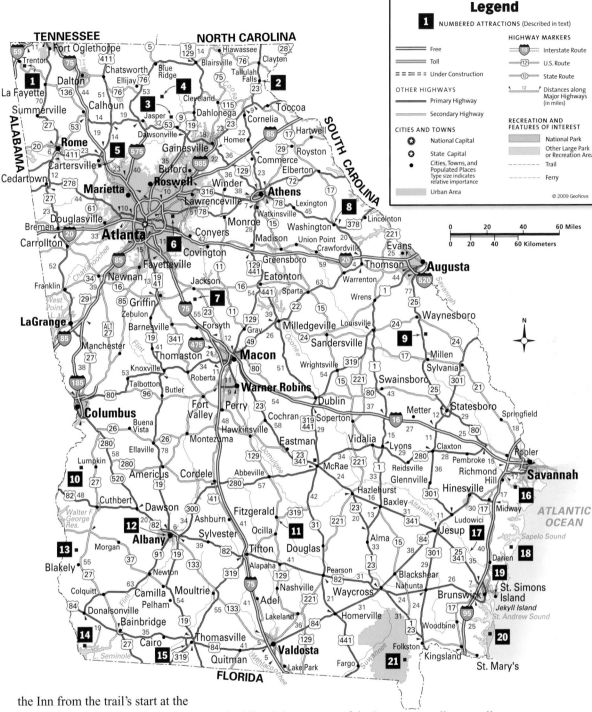

Legend

1 NUMBERED ATTRACTIONS (Described in text)

HIGHWAY MARKERS

Free	**10** Interstate Route
Toll	**12** U.S. Route
Under Construction	**12** State Route

OTHER HIGHWAYS
Primary Highway
Secondary Highway

12 Distances along Major Highways (in miles)

CITIES AND TOWNS
⭐ National Capital
✪ State Capital
● Cities, Towns, and Populated Places Type size indicates relative importance

Urban Area

RECREATION AND FEATURES OF INTEREST
National Park
Other Large Park or Recreation Area
Trail
Ferry

© 2009 GeoNova

5 Etowah Indian Mounds Historic Site

813 Indian Mounds Rd. SW, Cartersville. Off Rte. 113
For 500 years, from A.D. 1000 to 1500, the Etowah tribe flourished here. Along the river that now carries their name, they built a village with two plazas, dominated by three great earthen mounds with flat platform tops.

As many as several thousand Etowah people may have lived here. The plazas, made of packed red clay, were gathering places for the villagers and other Native Americans from the valley, who came for commerce, festivals, and burial ceremonies conducted by the priest-ruler. The largest of the platform mounds (63 feet high, with a platform one-half acre in extent) is believed to have supported a temple that may also have been the priest-ruler's residence. Excavations of one of the smaller platform mounds have revealed the burials of more than 500 of the tribal elite.

Today the great mounds loom in eerie silence above a plaza overgrown with field grasses.

Traces of the moat and the borrow pits from which earth was taken for mound construction can still be seen. If you climb the steps to the top of the highest mound, you will see on the eastern horizon a deep notch in the Allatoona mountain range. At the time of the summer solstice (about June 22), the sun rises through this notch, a phenomenon that may have figured into Etowah rituals.

Near the entrance to the 54-acre site is the Etowah Archaeological Museum, which has artifacts, slides, and a diorama showing the lifestyle of the Etowah, who were part of the widespread Mississippian culture.

▶ Open Tues.–Sun. except major holidays. Admission charged.

www.gastateparks.org/historic
(770) 387-3747

6 Stone Mountain Park

US-78 E, Exit 8, Stone Mountain
This 3,200-acre park is home to the South's greatest natural wonder and answer to Mount Rushmore.

6 Stone Mountain Park. The 825-foot-tall granite dome is the backdrop for a five-mile ride on the Stone Mountain Railroad, powered by vintage engines.

Visitors will stand in awe of the world's largest mass of exposed granite with the world's largest relief carving.

The Memorial Carving immortalizes three of the Confederate's most distinguished Civil War heroes: Jefferson Davis, Robert E. Lee, and Thomas "Stonewall" Jackson. Towering 1,683 feet above sea level, Stone Mountain covers 583 acres.

At the Summit Skyride, visitors can hop aboard a Swiss cable car for an 825-foot ride up to the mountain's top. Upon arriving, they'll be greeted by breathtaking views of Atlanta and the Appalachian Mountains. Back down at the mountain's base, visitors can hop aboard a diesel-engine locomotive for a scenic five-mile excursion, departing from a scale replica of Atlanta's Main Train Depot, circa 1870. Visitors can also take a detour back in time to a place called Crossroads, which recaptures a small Georgia town from the 1870s, featuring hands-on demonstrations in candy making, blacksmithing, and glassblowing. Hungry tourists can sample the best of down-home Southern cooking at Miss Katie's Sideboard Restaurant.

Visitors can also explore woodlands, lakes, streams, and miles of nature trails. In addition, the park offers golf and fishing. Picnicking is available in two public areas. Camping is welcome, and there are guest rooms available at the Stone Mountain Inn.

▶ Open year-round except Christmas. Entrance fee.

www.stonemountainpark.com
(800) 401-2407; (770) 498-5690

7 Dauset Trails

360 Mt. Vernon Rd., Jackson
Perfect for nature lovers of any age, Dauset Trails offers a variety of fun outdoor activities. Founded in 1977 by Hampton Daughtry and David Settle—the word "Dauset" is a combination of their last names—Dauset Trails is committed to promoting environmental education in a family setting.

The Animal Trail is a home to animals that were injured or orphaned and now cannot be returned to the wild. Native animals such as coyotes, bobcats, bison, and great horned owls can be found in this exhibit. Other main exhibits include the Woodland Garden, Farm Animals, and the Wonder Room, which is filled with reptiles, amphibians, and fish. Visitors can also bring a lunch to the scenic picnic grounds, situated near a lake, or observe aquatic plants and wildlife at the quiet Lotus Pond.

Aside from the exhibits, Dauset Trails' 1,200 acres of forests, fields, streams, and lakes offer numerous recreational opportunities. There are 17 miles of trails for hiking or mountain biking, chances to observe wild animals in their natural habitats, and 10 miles of trails for horseback riding.

▶ Open year-round except major holidays.

www.dausettrails.com
(770) 775-6798

8 Washington Historical Museum

308 E. Robert Toombs Ave., US-78, Washington
The antebellum house that serves as the Washington Historical Museum was built in 1835 or 1836 and acquired 20 years later by

Samuel Barnett, Georgia's first railroad commissioner, who added the front rooms, hallways, and the staircase. Now owned by the city of Washington, the house has been restored to its mid-1800s condition. Elegant in its simplicity, this "upcountry" two-story white frame dwelling mainly reflects local events and customs from the cotton plantation era through the advent of the railroads in the period 1835–55. Many rare and unusual articles can be seen here, including a 1790s cotton gin and a number of 19th-century South Carolina pottery jars, some of which were made and signed by Dave the Slave. Also in the collection are earthenware dishes that were carried by ships from England.

Many of the period furnishings in the museum were donated by residents of the town of Washington; among the choice pieces are an 1855 Weber piano and Belter furniture of carved rosewood.

The second-floor Civil War collection displays wartime memorabilia, including original newspapers, Native American relics, an 1861 Ballard breech-loading carbine, and Jefferson Davis's camp chest, sent to him by English sympathizers in 1865.

▶ Open Tues.–Sun. except major holidays. Virtual tour available on site. Admission charged.

http://museum.washingtongeorgia.net
(706) 678-2105

---

9 **Magnolia Springs State Park and Aquarium**

Off Hwy. 25, 1053 Magnolia Spring Dr., Millen

This delightful spring might not be so well-known had it not been for one of the horrors of the Civil

10 ▶ **Providence Canyon State Park.** The chasms, plateaus, cliffs, and pinnacles of this canyon were created by water runoff from early 19th-century farms.

War. The notorious conditions at Andersonville Prison led to the construction of Camp Lawton, a 42-acre stockade, where good water and plentiful timber were available. More than 10,000 captured Union soldiers were held in the camp in 1864, and vestiges of the fortifications can still be seen on a hill by the main entrance to Magnolia Springs State Park, a 1,071-acre recreation area that now includes the site.

The park is named for a spring with a prodigious flow of ice-cold water bubbling up to form a 15-foot-deep pool so clear that aquatic plants on the bottom are plainly visible. A large picnic area, with shelters, tables, and grills, is set among loblolly pines near the spring, overlooked by a boardwalk and observation deck.

A 28-acre lake can be fished for bass, crappies, catfish, and bream, and a launching ramp and boat

dock are provided. The park also offers a supervised swimming pool, hiking and biking trails, rental cottages, and many tent and trailer sites with water and hookups.

On the Woodpecker Woods Nature Trail seven different species of woodpeckers may be observed. Highlights on the trail are identified in a free booklet.

A freshwater aquarium displays various fish, turtles, and alligators.

▶ Open year-round. Fees charged for boat rentals and use of swimming pool.

www.gastateparks.org
(478) 982-1660

---

10 ▶ **Providence Canyon State Park**

Hwy. 39C, Lumpkin

The farmers who scratched a hard living out of the soil here in the 1800s didn't know about contour plowing, cover crops, and crop rotation and would be astounded

at the erosion they started with their mule-driven plows.

Under the grass and sod lies a deep layer of red clay called the Clayton Formation. Underneath it is the Providence Formation, whose susceptibility to erosion is dramatically demonstrated by the gullies, some 150 feet deep, which began to form generations ago in the white, pink, and purple strata.

This scenic area, which contains 16 canyons, dominates the 1,003-acre park. It serves as a colorful backdrop for wild plants and shrubs, including the rare plumleaf azalea, whose flowers, ranging in color from orange to various shades of red, bloom from July to September. Other indigenous plants include verbena, maypop, wild ginger, and prickly pear.

The three-mile Canyon Rim Trail, with 20 overlooks, winds past clumps of sumac and stands of hickories and slash pines, where raccoons and opossums might be seen and hawks circle overhead. Visitors are amazed at the 43 breathtaking colors of Georgia's "Little Grand Canyon."

The park also has primitive campsites, a group shelter, and two picnic shelters. The interpretive center offers two dioramas, a live beehive, and exhibits showing the park's history.

Geologists say that because of the claylike erosion-resistant soil underlying the Providence Formation, the canyons will not get deeper, but the sides of the canyons will continue to erode. Visitors are warned not to cross any barriers at the canyons' rims.

▶ Open daily.

www.gastateparks.org
(229) 838-6202

11 Blue and Gray Museum

116 N. Johnston St., Fitzgerald
With a collection that includes both Northern and Southern mementos of the Civil War period, this museum reflects the strange beginnings of the town of Fitzgerald.

In the early 1890s, when hostility between Yankees and Southerners was still deeply felt, P. H. Fitzgerald, an Indiana newspaperman and former Civil War drummer boy, became concerned about aging Civil War veterans, who found the cold Northern winters difficult. Fitzgerald dreamed of a settlement in a milder climate for these retired Union soldiers. In newspaper editorials he told of his hopes, and the response was so great that he began a campaign for funds.

In 1895 Fitzgerald used the money he had raised to purchase 100,000 acres of pineland in the heart of Georgia. People began to arrive by wagon, train, steamboat, and on horseback; Confederate veterans also joined the colony. The town that quickly developed was named Fitzgerald. Some Southern antipathy toward the project was diminished when streets were named in equal numbers for Confederate and Union generals.

In the ensuing years the families of the Blue and the Gray have donated many reminders of the Civil War period to the museum, which occupies a turn-of-the-century railroad depot. Among the items are a drum from a New York State regiment, a muzzle-loading rifle of the 4th Illinois Cavalry, an 1863 land grant signed by President Lincoln, a key to Andersonville Prison, a Confederate flag, and the mortar and pestle used by Jefferson Davis's physician.

13 Kolomoki Mounds Historic Park. The burial mounds near the town of Blakely were built by the Swift Creek and Weeden Island tribes. Shown here is the Temple Mound.

▶ Open Tues.-Sun. year-round.
  Admission charged.

www.museumsusa.org/museums/info/1164720
(800) 386-4642

12 Thronateeska Heritage Center

100 W. Roosevelt Ave., Albany
The museum, which takes its name from a Creek word meaning "the place where flint is picked up," is devoted to artifacts that reveal a great deal about the history and natural environment of southwest Georgia, in addition to showcasing aspects of the entire United States. The museum is housed in a 1913 railroad station that is now on the *National Register of Historic Places.*

Exhibits change frequently at the museum, so be sure to call in advance to find out what will be displayed during your visit.

On permanent display is the Model Railroad Exhibit, the only collection of its type in southwest Georgia. Housed in a real railroad baggage car, the exhibit details a trip from city to country.

Also on the grounds are the Weatherbee Planetarium and the

13 Kolomoki Mounds Historic Park

205 Indian Mounds Rd., Blakely
This 1,300-acre park is both a recreational area and a mystery-shrouded archaeological site where seven mounds dating from A.D. 250 to 950 have been preserved. Kolomoki, with its mounds, plaza, and outlying villages, was an important population center for perhaps as many as 2,000 people.

The largest of the mounds, known as the Temple Mound, rises from a base 325 feet by 200 feet to a height of 56 feet. It is believed to have had two distinct platforms at the top, each with a structure, which may have been a temple. Two smaller mounds proved on excavation to be burial mounds. One excavated mound is now housed by the museum; from a platform you can look down into the archaeological dig. The museum

Science Discovery Center, truly making a trip here one that will please the entire family.

▶ Open Thurs.-Sat. year-round.

www.heritagecenter.org
(229) 432-6955

interprets events that took place at Kolomoki via a short film, dioramas, and exhibits of artifacts.

The two lakes in the park, together with Kolomoki Creek, offer fishermen ample opportunities for catching bass, crappies, bream, and catfish. Rowboats may be rented, and there is a boat-launching ramp, but motors are limited to 10 horsepower.

Hikers on the two short nature trails may see white-tailed deer, foxes, cardinals, hawks, and possibly an alligator. The park also has a swimming pool, two picnic areas, and a 24-site campground.

▶ Park open year-round; museum open year-round except major holidays. Admission charged for museum. Fee charged for use of pool.

www.gastateparks.org/historic
(229) 724-2150

14 Seminole State Park

7870 State Park Dr., Donalsonville, off Hwy. 253
Named for the Native Americans who lived in this region before white settlers came, this 604-acre park is best known for water sports—boating, waterskiing, canoeing, and swimming.

Seminole Lake, the main feature here, is a favorite with fishermen. Its shallow waters with beds of stumps and grass contain more species of fish than any other lake in Georgia. The lake is also reputed to have the best large-mouth bass fishing in the United States. Experienced anglers who come here maintain that live bait is the best for bass.

Picnic tables, some beneath shelters, are located along the lake-front. Rental cottages and tent and trailer campgrounds, shaded by longleaf pines, poplars, sweet gums, and cedars, also give a view of the lake. Pioneer camping is available in the more remote sections of the park. Be alert: Signs leading to the park can be confused with signs for the Lake Seminole launching ramp, which is not on park property.

▶ Open year-round.

www.gastateparks.org
(229) 861-3137

15 Thomasville

The effect of the Civil War on this small town in southern Georgia was unpredictably beneficial. In 1861 the Atlantic and Gulf Railroad, with its terminus at Thomasville, was built to move men and supplies north to support the Confederate Army. The railroad's major contribution to the South, however, was the postwar transportation of wealthy Yankees, who came here to escape the rigors of Northern winters. A number of luxurious resort hotels were established, and wealthy families from Chicago, Cleveland, Philadelphia, and New York built winter cottages here. Thus, the town became a fashionable social center.

The Northerners bestowed upon Thomasville a heritage of eclectic architecture that the local citizens have managed to preserve. The houses are a charming mélange of plantation, Greek Revival, Neoclassical, Georgian, Victorian, Queen Anne, and bungalow styles. A walking tour includes 35 interesting homes, a number of which are on the *National Register of Historic Places,* and some are open to the public.

In the heyday of the large resort hotels, a popular wooded area by the railroad tracks was called Yankee Paradise. Today the 26-acre area is more circumspectly called Paradise Park. A stately symbol of preservation here is the 300-year-old "Big Oak," some 70 feet high—the largest live oak tree east of the Mississippi. Thomasville is also an agricultural center, and the farmers' market is the largest in the state. Open all year, it features a variety of fruits and vegetables, as well as an auction.

▶ Open Mon.-Sat.; closed last week in Sept. and major holidays. Admission charged.

www.thomasvillega.com
(866) 577-3600 Welcome Center

16 **Fort McAllister Historic Park.** A Civil War cannon is aimed at the Great Ogeechee River as if to defend the port of Savannah. The city would escape Sherman's torch.

16 Fort McAllister Historic Park

3894 Fort McAllister Rd., Richmond Hill (Spur 144, I-95, exit 90)

An interesting blend of history and recreation is combined in the park's 1,724 acres of high ground salt marsh, forest, and riverfront. The focal point, Fort McAllister, was built here at the mouth of the Great Ogeechee River in 1861 to protect Savannah during the Civil War.

The earthen fort withstood eight battles with Union gunboats from June 1861 to March 1863. It was finally taken from the landward side in hand-to-hand fighting by the troops of General Sherman at the end of their epic march to the sea. A walking tour with interpretive plaques encompasses the fortification, with its central parade ground, reconstructed magazine, and reproduction cannons. A printed tour guide describing 21 locations helps bring to life the drama and intensity of the action here.

A new museum displays dioramas of the final battle, early photographs of the fort, and Confederate uniforms. Machine parts and artifacts recovered from the wreck of a Confederate blockade runner contribute to an interesting collection. On summer weekends Civil War lectures and demonstrations in firing small arms are given by staff members.

A picnic area with tables, shelters, and a playground is located along the riverfront beneath tall slash pines.

Nearby Savage Island, which is accessible by a causeway, offers a myriad of accommodations: camping area for tents and trailers, rental cottages, and a nature trail among palmettos, water oaks, magnolias, and other native trees, some festooned with Spanish moss. A boat ramp is provided, and fishermen try for whiting, flounder, mullet, shrimp, and crabs. Care should be taken in the wooded areas to avoid poisonous snakes.

▶ Open daily except major winter holidays.

www.gastateparks.org
(912) 727-2339

14 ▶ **Seminole State Park.** Anglers flock to Lake Seminole to fish for large-mouth bass and myriad other catches, while swimmers can take a dip off a sandy beach.

18 **Sapelo Island Reserve.** Among the rooms in the Reynolds mansion is this soaring conservatory.

17 Altamaha River

One of the "Last Great Places" in the world (designated by The Nature Conservancy), the Altamaha River is a 100-mile-long opportunity to discover southeastern Georgia. The river begins at the confluence of the Ocmulgee and Oconee rivers and eventually empties into the Atlantic Ocean. Along the way, however, are many opportunities to explore the river and its surrounding areas. Using the boat ramps and landing facilities available in each county, visitors can explore the river for themselves or take a fishing trip. Those preferring to admire the river from the shore can utilize the picnic areas and hiking trails that often appear nearby.

Nature lovers will enjoy the river as well. The river and surrounding watershed are home to a wide variety of wildlife, including over 100 threatened and near-threatened species, such as the gopher tortoise, Atlantic sturgeon, and red-cockaded woodpecker.

▶ Open year-round.
www.altamahariver.org

18 Sapelo Island Reserve

Reached only by ferry from Meridian. Tickets must be purchased at the Sapelo Ferry and Visitor Center, 8 miles northeast of Darien, off Ga. Hwy. 99.
This small barrier island, with its uplands, wetlands, marshes, and combination of fresh and salt water, harbors an impressive array of birds, mammals, and fish. In the many marsh areas—carpeted with smooth cordgrass and black needlerush—green herons, clapper rails, and ruddy turnstones may be seen, as well as minks and raccoons. Purple marsh and fiddler crabs, oysters, white shrimp, mullet, and anchovies also find sanctuary here.

Native Americans had occupied the island for some 4,500 years before English colonists began to arrive in the 1700s. During the next few centuries the island changed hands repeatedly as the French, Spanish, and British fought for control. In 1934 R. J. Reynolds, Jr., purchased most of the island and assisted in establishing the University of Georgia Marine Institute. After Reynolds's death the state acquired some 8,000 acres from his widow and created the Reynolds Wildlife Refuge. You can also visit the Reynolds mansion and see the restored working lighthouse.

A 30-minute ferry ride takes visitors to the island, where buses tour the marshland, dunes, and wildlife management areas. It is advisable to take insect repellent. Half-day trips are offered two or three times a week year-round.

All-day tours, which include a nature walk, are scheduled once a month from Mar. to Oct. Tour reservations should be made two to four weeks in advance.
▶ Fee charged.

www.gastateparks.org
(912) 437-3224

19 Little St. Simons Island

The secluded nature of this small island off the coast of Georgia makes it an enticing retreat. Accessible only by boat and with accommodations for only 30 visitors at a time, this is the perfect island getaway. Here visitors find 10,000 acres of preserved land and seven miles of beautiful shell-covered beaches. Located on the Atlantic Flyway and designated an Important Bird Area by the Audubon Society, the island is a great spot for bird-watchers to observe over 280 different species of birds. Island naturalists have observed piping plover, painted buntings, and nesting bald eagles, in addition to the many varieties of shorebirds and wading birds that frequent the island. Loggerhead sea turtles also visit the island, crawling onto the beach during the summer months to lay their eggs.

The Lodge on Little St. Simons Island consists of 15 rooms in five charming cottages, dating back to 1917. Guests can enjoy 20 miles of bicycle trails, chef-prepared Southern cuisine, fishing with complimentary gear and bait, boating on rivers and creeks or on the ocean, and guided tours conducted by naturalists. Day trips to the island are also offered.
▶ Fee charged for lodging and transportation to island. Open daily.

www.littlestsimonsisland.com
(888) 733-5774

20 Cumberland Island National Seashore

From Rte. 40 in St. Marys, turn right at waterfront to visitors center.
This historic sandspit, the southernmost of Georgia's sea islands, has been inhabited for some 4,000 years. In the 16th century the Spanish built a fort here to protect their Florida holdings. Their religious faith was buttressed also—by the establishment of a Franciscan mission

19 **Little St. Simons Island.** Secluded beaches are part of the charm at Little St. Simons, one of the four Georgia barrier islands known as the Golden Isles.

20 ▶ **Cumberland Island National Seashore.** Cumberland Island is one of the country's last unspoiled barrier islands, a treasure trove of pristine beaches, maritime flora and fauna, and ghostly ruins glimpsed through gnarled live oaks.

and the conversion of many Timucan people. The Spanish called the island San Pedro.

In the 18th century the island's present name was proposed by a Native American who had visited the Duke of Cumberland in England. Gen. James Oglethorpe, the founder of England's Georgia colony, accepted the suggestion.

There were no further significant developments until after the Revolutionary War, when Gen. Nathanael Greene bought a large tract of land on which his widow built an imposing mansion. After the Civil War, Andrew Carnegie's brother, Thomas, built a handsome home, which still stands. Plum Orchard, a mansion built for Lucy and Thomas Carnegie's son in 1898, can be toured on the second and fourth Sundays of the month.

This small island, about 17½ miles long and 3 miles across at its widest point, supports a fascinating range of ecological zones, each with its own population of plants, birds, and animals. The

beach is spangled with shells and frequented by shorebirds that follow the tides. Where the soil is deepest, a maritime forest of oaks, magnolias, red bay, and various pines is established.

The sloughs and ponds are home to alligators, otters, and minks; feral horses, left behind by residents, may also be seen.

▶ Ferry runs daily Mar.–Nov.; Ferry does not run Tues. and Wed., Dec.–Feb. For ferry schedule and reservations (suggested), call (877) 860-6787.

www.nps.gov/cuis
(912) 882-4336

---

21 ▶ **Okefenokee National Wildlife Refuge, Suwannee Canal Recreation Area**

7 miles south of Folkston, on Hwy. 121
Although a foothold has been established on the edge of this mysterious land, mankind comes as a stranger. This is the rightful realm of the alligator, black bear, bobcat, opossum, muskrat, and

otter. It is also home to lizards, turtles, toads, and snakes. Some 40 kinds of fish and 230 species of birds are native to this region.

The area contains numerous islands and lakes, and prairies cover about 400,000 acres. A variety of wading birds, such as herons, ibises, and cranes, can be seen here.

This fascinating environment can be enjoyed from a variety of perspectives: on the hiking trails; the boardwalk over the bogs; guided after-dark tours; and from the observation towers. A restored homestead suggests the character of early-day life in the swamp.

To explore the 11-mile Suwannee Canal, one can rent a boat with an outboard motor. For a wilderness canoe trip lasting up to five days, reservations must be made two months in advance.

▶ Wildlife refuge open year-round except Thanksgiving and Christmas; recreation area open year-round. Admission charged.

www.fws.gov/okefenokee
(912) 496-7836

GEORGIA

Hawaii

For all the similarity of their volcanic origin and tropical climate, each of the five main islands has a character all its own.

Ke'e Beach. Its protective coral reef and abundance of colorful fish make Ke'e Beach the most popular snorkeling beach on Kauai's north shore.

A tourist haven it may be, but Hawaii still has plenty of out-of-the-way enticements. On each island are lesser known beaches, scenic waterfalls, hiking trails, and cultural attractions. Remote lookouts offer panoramas ranging from the merely spectacular to the breathtaking.

On four of the islands, you can view a mind-boggling array of plants and birdlife in botanical gardens, while museums focus on native Polynesian culture and natural history. Petroglyphs, heiaus (temples), a lava tube you can walk through, and a modern-day lavender farm highlight the rich variety of islands known for their incomparable beauty.

visit ➡ **offthebeatenpathtrips.com**

KAUAI—The Garden Isle

1 Ke'e Beach and Kalalau Trail

End of Rte. 560

Ke'e Beach is protected by an offshore reef and, unlike other beaches in the vicinity, provides safe wading, swimming, snorkeling, and scuba diving even in winter.

Ke'e is part of Ha'ena State Park, a scenic wildland that includes the Waikapalae and Waikanaloa wet caves, which contain pools of glowing green water. Hawaiian legend says that chiefs of old used to gather here.

There's much to see, and you can camp nearby, at Hanakoa, and Kalalau, but the real attraction is Kalalau Trail, used since prehistoric times to reach Kalalau Valley, 11 miles away. Beginning at Ke'e Beach, the trail follows the spectacular Na Pali Coast. You can backpack and make an overnight stop at Kalalau or make a day trip to Hanakapi'ai Beach.

Side trails lead to waterfalls and lush valleys, and hikers won't go hungry. The way is lined with delicious wild yellow guavas. Swimming is not recommended, and in wet weather hiking the entire trail calls for caution.

▶ Open year-round during daylight hours.

www.hawaiistateparks.org/parks/
Kauai/index.cfm?park_id=8

(808) 274-3444

1 ➤ **Kalalau Valley.** From Kalalau Lookout in Kokè State Park, the Na Pali Coast gives hikers views of some of the most spectacular scenery on the planet. The mountains rise up to 4,000 feet, sheltering the valley below.

HAWAIIAN ISLANDS

PACIFIC OCEAN

Kauai
Lehua
Lihu'e
Oahu
Wahiawa
Ho'olehua
Honolulu
Molokai
Kalaupapa
Lāna'i Lāna'i City
Wailuku
Maui
Kahului
Lahaina
Hāna
HALEAKALĀ N.P.
Kaho'olawe
Hawaii
Hāwī
Waimea
Hilo
Kailua
Kona
HAWAII VOLCANOES NATL. PARK

Kauaiakahi Channel
Kaua'i Channel
Kaiwi Channel
Alenuihaha Channel

0   25   50 Miles
0   25   50 Kilometers

© 2009 GeoNova

Legend

1 NUMBERED ATTRACTIONS (Described in text)

HIGHWAY MARKERS

Free
Toll
Under Construction

10 Interstate Route
12 U.S. Route
12 State Route

OTHER HIGHWAYS

Primary Highway
Secondary Highway

12 Distances along Major Highways (in miles)

CITIES AND TOWNS

⊛ National Capital
⊛ State Capital
• Cities, Towns, and Populated Places
Type size indicates relative importance

Urban Area

RECREATION AND FEATURES OF INTEREST

National Park
Other Large Park or Recreation Area
Trail
Ferry

© 2009 GeoNova

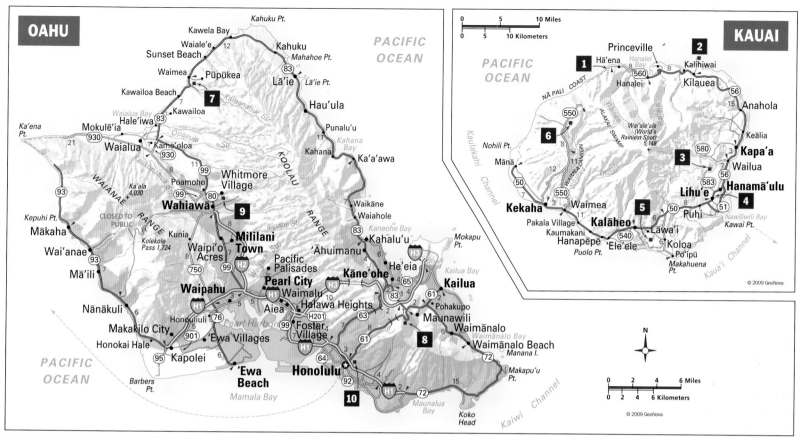
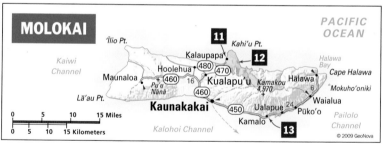
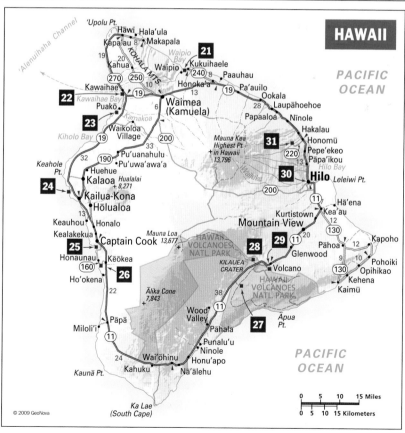
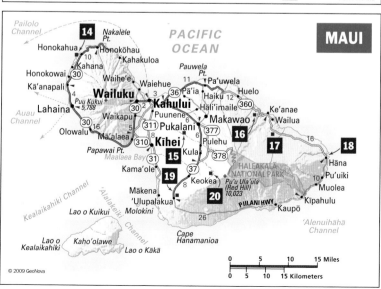

2 Kilauea Point National Wildlife Refuge and Lighthouse

Hwy. 56 to the town of Kilauea; turn right on Kolo Rd., then left on Kilauea Rd. to reach the entrance
Blanketing one of the most spectacular sections of coastline on the main islands, this 203-acre stretch is on the forefront of Hawaii's efforts to protect its wildlife. Working with volunteers, the U.S. Fish and Wildlife Service has restored coastal habitats to provide the state's indigenous seabirds with a safe and beautiful home. Not only does this refuge welcome the official state bird, the nene (Hawaiian goose), but it offers a haven to two of the most distinctive endangered endemic mammals: the Hawaiian monk seal and the Hawaiian hoary bat.

Kilauea Lighthouse, built in 1913 and named to the *National Register of Historic Places,* stands as a monument to Hawaii's colorful past and natural splendor.

From the shore, visitors might catch spinner dolphins at play or experience the majestic grace of the humpback whale. Each December through April these magnificent animals migrate from Alaska to Hawaii to mate, give birth, and rear their huge babies.

▶ Open year-round except federal holidays. Admission charged.

www.fws.gov/kilaueapoint
(808) 828-1413

3 Wailua Falls

At the end of Hwy. 583, Kapaia
Even if you knew there was a natural wonder on the scale of Wailua Falls in the vicinity, you'd never dream this prosaic little road past a Buddhist cemetery and through four miles of waving sugarcane would be

 Wailua Falls. Like frangipani blooms and cloud-brushed green peaks, waterfalls like Wailua are part of the romance of Polynesian paradises such as Kauai.

the way to reach it. The double torrent that feeds the falls (*wai* means "fresh water," *lua,* "two") drops 80 feet to a flower-ringed pool. The plunge is especially dramatic after heavy mountain rains—a comparatively frequent occurrence, since 5,000-foot Mount Waialeale, which dominates the center of Kauai, is considered one of the wettest spots in the world, with a yearly rainfall of almost 400 inches.

Unfortunately, there's no safe way to climb down to the base of the falls, so your view is limited to what can be seen from just one spot.

▶ Open year-round.

www.hawaiiweb.com/kauai

4 Kauai Museum

4428 Rice St., Lihu'e
This history museum focuses on the preservation, interpretation, and exhibition of artifacts and documents relevant to the history of both Kauai, the "garden island," and the nearby "forbidden isle" of Nihau. You'll find almost everything worth knowing about the islands' natural history and Hawaiian culture before Westerners came. The displays range from poi-pounding tools to weapons. Recorded history begins with Captain Cook's landing on Kauai at Waimea in 1778, moving through the little-known Russian attempt to dominate the island, and finally to the impact of Protestant missionaries.

Other periods covered include the islands' plantation heyday (when labor was imported from Japan and elsewhere), the Hawaiian monarchy, and contemporary times. There is one unexpected exhibit worth a detour: a collection of bowls made from the calabash gourd.

Along with rotating exhibits and a permanent collection, the museum offers a variety of informational workshops and programs for all ages. Call ahead for an updated schedule.

▶ Open Mon.–Sat. Admission charged except first Sat. of month.

www.kauaimuseum.org
(808) 245-6931

5 McBryde Garden, National Tropical Botanical Garden

Lawa'i Rd., off Rte. 520, Lawa'i
Your tour begins when you board a tram at the visitors center to begin your descent into the Lawa'i Valley. Entering the gardens on what was once a sugarcane train railbed, visitors are treated to panoramic views of the valley and adjacent bay.

The 252-acre McBryde Garden is home to the world's largest collection of native Hawaiian plants, the most endangered group of plants in the 50 states. The spectacular specimens include Brighamia species, which were nearing extinction on the extremely steep and inaccessible cliffs of the islands until botanists suspended themselves by ropes nearly 3,000 feet above the ocean and became human pollinators in order to save these plants.

Also in the Lawa'i Valley and adjacent to McBryde Garden is Allerton Garden. Guided walking tours of this enchanting estate are offered by reservation.

The National Tropical Botanical Garden is a nonprofit institution, with active programs in tropical plant research, conservation, and education. Now maintaining four gardens and three preserves in the Hawaiian islands, the organization is supported by donations and grants.

▶ Open daily. Admission charged.

www.ntbg.org
(808) 742-2623

---

6 ▶ Koke'e State Park & Koke'e Natural History Museum

Off Rte. 550 or 552
At nearly 4,000 feet, the park's 4,345 acres are considerably cooler than lower elevations, which accounts for the different character of the scenery here. Pines and other temperate plant life replace palms and tropical vegetation. Along the road there are views from Koke'e's luxuriant green surroundings into red-walled Waimea Canyon, and at the northernmost point of the park, Kalalau Lookout affords a sweeping overview of Kalalau Valley.

The park contains several trails, some leading into the 30 square miles of Alakai Swamp. Bird-watching is excellent, and in August and September you can catch trout. From June to August delicious Koke'e plums are here for the picking, and all year long there are lilikoi (passion fruit) and guavas.

The Koke'e Natural History Museum, in addition to offering visitor information, contains several exhibits about Kauai history and wildlife. Permits are required for trout fishing and fruit picking.

▶ Open year-round.

www.hawaiistateparks.org/parks/kauai/index.cfm?park_id=7
(808) 335-9975

---

did you know ?

The birds that congregate around the Koke'e Museum, Polynesian jungle fowl, are descended from birds that Polynesians brought from Tahiti. They now survive only on Kauai.

5 ▶ McBryde Garden, National Tropical Botanical Garden. A bamboo bridge is one of the pathways to the world's largest collection of Hawaiian native plants.

8 ▶ Nu'uanu Pali State Wayside. In the 1795 battle that unified the Hawaiian islands, Kamehameha I's army drove hundreds of enemy warriors over the *pali* (cliffs).

OAHU—The Gathering Place

7 ▶ Pu'u O Mahuka Heiau State Historic Site

Exit Hwy. 83 at Pupukea Homestead Rd.; temple on unmarked road on right
This *heiau* (temple) from the 1600s is the largest on Oahu and provides a commanding view of the north shore of the island, from Ka'ena Point to Waimea Bay.

The wooden images of the old gods may have been destroyed here in 1819, when the old religion was abolished, but ancient customs survive—people still leave offerings of fruits, vegetables, and flowers.

Constructed during a time of political turmoil, it is likely that this heiau was used as a *heiau luakini,* or sacrificial temple. After it was abandoned, it was probably adapted for other uses, such as agriculture. Visitors are asked to observe the site from outside the walls to prevent further damage.

www.hawaiistateparks.org/parks/oahu
(808) 587-0300

---

8 ▶ Nu'uanu Pali State Wayside

Off Pali Hwy. 61; follow signs at Nu'uanu Pali Summit
Although this dramatic view over the mountains, hills, and bays of windward Oahu is at its magnificent best in the morning, you might want to time your visit for lunch or later to avoid the crowds and tour buses. The viewing platform, enlarged to accommodate the crowds, also detracts from the area's original wilderness atmosphere, so descend to the ledge just below it (about 1,000 feet above sea level).

Because the lookout is at a low point in the Koolau Range crest, trade winds drive so forcefully through the gap that you can virtually lean into them. There are stories of would-be suicides blown right back onto the top of the *pali* (cliffs). But watch out, because when the wind is blowing in the opposite direction, it can be dangerous. When the battle of Nu'uanu was fought here in 1795, pitting Kamehameha I against Kalanikupule, king of Oahu, warriors were said to have been driven—or blown—over the *pali.*

▶ Open year-round.

www.hawaiistateparks.org/parks/oahu
(808) 587-0300

9 Wahiawa Botanical Garden

1396 California Ave., Wahiawa
This verdant, secluded—and educational—haven is missed by the many tourists who go as quickly as possible through Wahiawa, an "army town" near the famous Schofield Barracks, which, it must be admitted, is not one of the island's most attractive settlements. It is worthwhile, however, to stop and see the splendid collection of plants in the botanic garden.

In the 1920s the wooded gulch in which the garden is situated was used by the Hawaii Sugar Planters' Association as a nursery and for forestry experiments. In 1950 the 27-acre plot was turned over to the city and county of Honolulu, and although the area is still being developed, it's a charming and informative place to visit. Following the self-guiding tour folder, you enter past Australian tree ferns 40 feet tall and native tree ferns *(hapu`u)* whose stalks are covered with a wool-like substance *(pulu)* once exported for pillow and mattress stuffing. Other native plants in the Hawaiian Garden range from hibiscus (the state flower) to loulu palms. The last of the indicated stops (No. 23) is given over to a collection of small plants and vines of the aroid family, ranging from the decorative anthurium to the edible taro. As you might imagine, birds abound in this garden environment.

▶ Open daily except major winter holidays.

www.co.honolulu.hi.us/parks
(808) 522-7060

10 Pu`u Ualaka`a State Wayside

Round Top Dr., Honolulu
Many *malihini* (newcomers) miss this glorious view because it's not easy to find. But look for Makiki St. on a detailed map and you'll see that it connects from a scenic drive to this mountaintop wayside. A second, longer route—Tantalus Dr.—begins farther west, off Puowaina Dr. Honolulu residents usually ascend by one drive and descend by the other. The heights tend to be much cooler than the lowlands, and the wayside is an ideal spot to visit on a hot summer day.

When you get here, the expected facilities make it seem like just another park: trees, grass, picnic tables, and a comfort station. But then there's the view: No other area open to the public boasts anything like it. The city is spread out before you, from Pearl Harbor and the airport in one direction to Diamond Head and Koko Head in the other.

Pu`u `Ualaka`a (known locally as Round Top) means "hill of the rolling sweet potatoes." It got its name, according to the story, because Kamehameha I ordered sweet potatoes to be planted here—and when they were dug up, they rolled down the hill.

▶ Open dawn to dusk year-round.

www.hawaiistate parks.org/parks/oahu
(808) 587-0300

MOLOKAI—
The Friendly Isle

11 Molokai Museum & Cultural Center

Kalae Hwy. (Hwy. 470), northeast of Kualapu`u
In 1848 Rudolph Wilhelm Meyer, a German immigrant, came to the lush, idyllic island of Molokai to work as a surveyor. Before long he married Molokai's high chieftess, Kalama, and took charge of managing the island's largest ranch settlement. In 1878 he built the R. W. Meyer Sugar Mill, now considered the oldest sugar mill in Hawaii and listed on the *National Register of Historic Places.*

Although sugarcane is no longer widely grown or harvested on the island, the R. W. Meyer Sugar Mill invites anyone with a taste for homegrown history to learn all about the process—up close and in action. The mill has been fully restored, complete with an operational steam engine. On a tour of the plant, knowledgeable guides explain, step by step, how the cane was transformed into sugar and molasses.

Next door to the mill at the museum complex, visitors can take a self-guiding tour through a treasure trove of local history, industry, and culture. Along with personal memorabilia from the Meyer family, exhibits offer a vivid sense of the everyday life of a 19th-century plantation worker. In addition, changing displays and artifacts range from authentic hula instruments to 18th-century fishing-net weights, from antique stone weapons to vintage hand-crafted toys and games.

▶ Open year-round Mon.–Sat. except major winter holidays. Admission charged.

www.hawaiiweb.com/molokai/html/sites/
rw_meyer_sugar_mill_museum.html

(808) 567-6436

12 Kalaupapa National Historical Park

This settlement on Molokai's north shore lies some 2,000 feet below the towering sea cliffs that line the back of the park's peninsula which is what residents call the rest of Molokai. The difficulty of reaching it was one reason why the leprosy patients, who were treated by the Belgian priest Father Damien, were exiled here in the 19th century. Today only a few former patients remain, living amid touching reminders of Father Damien and his mission. To visit this settlement, one needs permission from the state of Hawaii Department of Health and must

12 Kalaupapa National Historical Park. Beginning in 1866, thousands of leprosy patients were treated in the colony established on Molokai's remote Kalaupapa Peninsula.

13 **St. Joseph's Church.** Built in 1876 by Father Damien, the Belgian priest who ministered to victims of leprosy, the church is now used only for special occasions.

be 16 or older. Tour sponsors can make the necessary arrangements.

A steep trail leads down the 1,700-foot cliff from Pala'au State Park, which can be navigated by foot or by mule ride. But there's reliable air-taxi service from Molokai Airport, and charter flights are available from Oahu and Maui.

Once you've reached this remote but beautiful spot, a guided bus tour is the only way to see the historic sites in the village where the remaining residents now live, along with the care facility and buildings from the days when thousands were treated here. The affliction, now called Hansen's disease, can be controlled by modern drugs, which finally ended the practice of forced isolation.

On the eastern side of the peninsula, you'll find Father Damien's church, St. Philomena's, and the gravesite of the heroic priest who, in his service to the patients, contracted the disease and died here. This is Kalawao, the original site of the colony, and the park is an ideal place to lunch (bring your own) as you contemplate the dramatic cliffs here.

▶ Park access by permit only. Guided tours offered Mon.–Sat. Damien Tours: (808) 567-6171. For mule rides, call (800) 567-7550

www.nps.gov/kala; www.muleride.com
(808) 567-6802

13 St. Joseph's Church
Kamalo

Father Damien ministered to needs beyond those of the Kalaupapa leprosy colony. He also built four churches for his parishioners on Molokai's uplands, or "topside," and made his ecclesiastical rounds by horseback. St. Joseph's, built in 1876, is a white one-room building with a churchyard that contains several graves. One small but poignant stone is incised partly in Hawaiian: "Margarita Kameekua, *hanau* Honolulu March 1, 1914, *make* Kamalo February 27, 1915." *Hanau* means "born," and *make* means "died."

A lifesize black metal statue of Father Damien stands just outside the tiny church, which, like St. Philomena's at Kalawao, is kept in good repair but used only for special occasions. Farther east along Rte. 450, near Mapulehu Stream, is Our Lady of Sorrows (1874), another of Father Damien's topside churches.

▶ Open year-round.

www.gohawaii.about.com/library/gallery/
bleast_molokai_65.htm
(808) 553-5220

MAUI—The Valley Isle

14 D. T. Fleming Beach Park
Kapalua

Nearby Kapalua Beach used to be called Fleming Beach (in honor of a local ranch manager, David T. Fleming) until the name was reassigned to this county beach that is located farther north along Rte. 30. Although confusion about the names has kept the park off the beaten path, it has long been a favorite with locals. Fleming is one of the most convenient of the rugged area's picturesque beaches, with showers, barbecue grills, and picnic tables—at least one of which always seems to be available (on weekdays, anyway).

Winds ruffle the ironwood and palms at the top of a sandy crescent, which slopes down to meet usually gentle ocean swells for some good swimming. When the waves pick

15 **Surfing Goat Dairy.** At this goat dairy farm, children enjoy helping with the evening chores, including bringing in the herd, feeding, and hand milking the goats.

up, body and board surfers turn out in force. Stay on the beach, though; when heavy winter waves roll in, there are strong rip currents and undertows. And when you stroll the beach, wear rubber sandals *(zoris)*: Fallen ironwood cones can be rough on bare feet.

▶ Open year-round.

www.co.maui.hi.us
(808) 661-4685

15 Surfing Goat Dairy
3651 Omaopio Rd., Kula

The Surfing Goat Dairy, which is set on the slopes of the Haleakala Crater and operational since 2002, has become one of Maui's top agritourism destinations. This dairy is as proficient at entertaining visitors as it is at making cheese. The fun-filled spirit of the dairy is reflected not only in its name but also in its slogan: "Da' Feta Mo' Betta!"

As adults taste their choice of more than two dozen goat cheeses, 16 of which have won national awards, children can pet the goats ("kids petting kids," as the owners like to say). Tours of the dairy are offered daily, and anyone who wants to be part of the action can book an Evening Chore and Milking Tour, which is held every Tuesday, Thursday, and Saturday afternoons.

▶ Open daily. Admission fee for tours.

www.surfinggoatdairy.com
(808) 878-2870

16 ▶ Puohokamoa Falls and Kaumahina State Wayside

Falls parking area is at an unmarked pull-off along Hwy. 360, 2 miles west of Kaumahina State Wayside. Look for a green picnic table and low stone wall.

Visitors tend to drive right by this site, unaware of the lovely falls, which cannot be seen from the road. Park and follow the some-times muddy path. You can eat yellow guavas that may be seen along the way, but avoid the oily *kukui* (candlenuts), which the ancient Hawaiians used for light—and as a strong laxative.

There's another table and a barbecue pit at the falls, but no drinking water. If you decide to refresh yourself in the pool at the base of the falls, be prepared to find yourself a target of tourists' cameras. If picnicking is a must and the tables at the falls are taken, drive a little farther to Kaumahina, where there are plenty of facilities and good views of the ocean and the northeast Maui coastline. Watch for the *hala* (pandanus) tree and several types of eucalyptus (including the shaggy paperbark).

▶ Open year-round.

www.hawaiiweb.com/maui
(808) 984-8109

17 ▶ Pua`a Ka`a State Wayside

On Hwy. 360, 0.6 miles past mile marker 22

Pua`a Ka`a is a delightfully inti-mate park with two modest 25-foot waterfalls. A paved path-way takes you across the top of the first falls, then leads along a stream to the second. Both tum-ble into pools that are bordered by picnic tables, and conveniently situated a little farther along the

road, near a second parking lot, are restrooms. The road crosses a small bridge, and if you walk across, you can see still more falls and pools, though they're not really a part of Pua`a Ka`a Wayside. *Pua`a ka`a* is an ancient Hawaiian name meaning "rolling pig."

Tropical foliage is abundant here: banana palms, guava trees (often bearing ripe, ready-to-eat fruit), heliconia flowers, ferns, African tulip trees, red and green varieties of *ti* plants, and the giant-leaved *ape-ape*.

▶ Open year-round.

www.hawaiistateparks.org/parks/maui/
index.cfm?park_id=40
(808) 984-8109

18 ▶ Helani Farm

Off Rte. 360 about a mile west of Hana

The beneficence of the Hawaiian climate is beautifully demon-strated here. H. F. Cooper established these gardens as a wholesale nursery in 1975; now he has opened them to visitors, who are free to wander the five-acre

lower gardens along paths called Main Drag or Six Bridges to Heaven.

The specimens, tropical and subtropical plants and trees from throughout the world, are generally well marked. But Cooper has added his own twist to the expected common, genus, and species names. Here you will find aphorisms, Bible and poetry quotations, or anony-mous quotes he feels ought to be passed onto visitors. Near a bed of spider lilies, for instance, we learn that "Knowledge is power only when it is translated into direct and positive action."

In addition to the plants and flowers, there's a pond of Japanese carp *(koi),* whose churnings and gulpings are in noisy contrast to the peace that reigns in the rest of this quiet place, where the only other sound is likely to be the rhythmic clatter of bamboo blow-ing in the wind.

Picnic facilities and restrooms are located in the lower gardens.

▶ Open year-round. Admission charged.

www.helanitropicalflowers.com
(808) 248-8274

20 **Ali`i Kula Lavender Farm.** A pretty gazebo set next to a lavender field is one of the places guests can stop and enjoy tea and scones at their leisure.

19 ▶ Tedeschi Vineyards

Off Rte. 37, Ulupalakua

Few tourists heading for Haleakala National Park think of stopping off in the cool, bucolic up-country region that is Hawaii's only true wine country.

Tedeschi Vineyards lies at the end of a drive so spectacularly scenic that for many the journey itself is reason enough to come. All who stop are invited to try a glass of Maui Blanc, a "light, dry pineapple wine," which was the first Tedeschi product in 1977.

When Emil and Joanne Tedeschi moved here from California's Napa Valley in 1974, they and their part-ner Erdman entertained high hopes of reviving the island's wine indus-try. These have been fulfilled. An award-winning sparkling wine they produced was served at President Reagan's inauguration.

Visitors can tour the property, where Hawaiian royalty threw lavish parties when it was used as a cattle ranch and sugar mill. You can sam-ple still and sparkling wines in a cottage that was built for Hawaii's last king or tour the winery, where the wines are available for purchase.

▶ Open year-round except major holidays.

www.mauiwine.com
(877) 878-6058

20 ▶ Ali`i Kula Lavender Farm

1100 Waipoli Rd., Kula

Gazing out over the blue Pacific from the foot of a lavender meadow is nothing less than heavenly. At Ali`i Kula Lavender Farm, a self-guiding tour on winding paths takes you through gardens filled with lavender, protea, hydrangea, and other ornamentals. On the hill-side above are the commercial lavender fields, a fragrant sea of silvery mounds.

The farm also offers five walking tours daily. A tradition at the farm is "tea at leisure." Visitors buy tea and scones at the gift shop and enjoy them at a private nook or grassy spot of their choice. Lavender is a known relaxant. So where better than a lavender farm to enjoy a cup of tea?

▶ Open daily except major winter holidays. Fee for guided tours.

www.aklmaui.com
(808) 878-3004

HAWAII—The Big Island

21 Waipi`o Valley Lookout

In a state whose islands seem to provide panoramic vistas at every turn, here on the Big Island it is easy to miss the spectacular view across Waipi`o Valley. It is, however, worthwhile to take the nine-mile Rte. 240 to Waipi`o Valley Lookout.

From this vantage point you can see the island's largest valley, some 2,000 feet below. This was once home to the ancient Hawaiian kings—and to as many as 50,000 Hawaiians, who gradually abandoned the valley settlements for fear of tidal waves. Many kings were buried here. Because of their "divine power," it was believed that no harm would come to those who lived in the valley.

The narrow road down to the valley, which is private land, is accessible by guided tour, guided horseback ride, or an hourly shuttle from Kukuihaele. Farther down you can walk along the black sand beach.

▶ Open year-round; charge for shuttle tour.

www.bigisland.org
(808) 961-5797

 **Waipi`o Valley Lookout.** The sweeping view from this lookout takes in Waipi`o Beach, one of the Big Island's most secluded black sand beaches.

22 Pu`ukohola Heiau National Historic Site

Kawaihae

This enormous rock *heiau* (temple), the last such religious structure built by pre-Christian Hawaiians, rose in early 1790 at the order of King Kamehameha I. The smooth lava rocks used to build it were passed from man to man, and it was finished in one year. Today visitors can view the structure, which was made a National Historic Site in 1972, either from the visitors center below or a walking trail that affords a closer look.

The *heiau's* three platforms were the scene of religious observances that included human sacrifice—a practice that Kamehameha put an end to just before he died (1819). On the beachfront is a smaller *heiau,* named Mailikini. The beachfront is also the site of the Hawaiian

Cultural Festival, held every August as a celebration of Hawaiian crafts, dance, and music.

▶ Open daily.

www.nps.gov/puhe
(808) 882-7218

23 Puako Petroglyph Archaeological District

Mauna Lani Resort, off Hwy. 19

Nobody is quite sure why this lava field on the northwest coast was significant to the original Hawaiians, but there can be no doubt that it was. Over the course of centuries, they carved thousands of petroglyphs into the stone, representing individuals, families, and animals. The meaning of these petroglyphs—the reason for their existence—is one of Hawaii's most enduring archaeological mysteries.

A short trail to the carvings

begins at an informational kiosk north of the Mauna Lani Resort. Morning and evening are the best times to visit, when the shadows help define the shallow grooves. Wind and rain have taken a toll; visitors are asked not to add to the erosive forces already at work.

▶ Open year-round.

www.bigisland.org/beaches/243/holohokai-beach-park
(808) 886-1655

24 Kaloko-Honokohau National Historical Park

Ocean side of Queen Ka`ahumanu Hwy. 19, 3 miles north of Kailua-Kona, 3 miles south of Kona International Airport

Until the early 20th century this national park was a thriving Hawaiian community, created to preserve, interpret, and perpetuate traditional Hawaiian culture.

Among the many archaeological sites and features within the park are petroglyphs, *heiaus* (temples), a one-mile restored section of the ancient mamalahoa trail, house sites, fishing shrines, canoe landings, and fishponds.

The park is restoring the massive wall of Kaloko fishpond and the fish traps at Ai`opio. Sea turtles regularly bask on the beaches of Honokohau Bay, and the park is home to three endangered water birds. You can hike, fish, and picnic (no fires or glass) in the park, and swimming and snorkeling are safe in the waters of Honokohau Bay.

▶ Open year-round.

www.nps.gov/kaho
(808) 329-9057

25 Kealakekua Bay State Historical Park

Napo`opo`o Rd., or Pu`uhonoa Rd., off Mamalahoa Hwy.

Today Kealakekua Bay, on the Kona Coast, is a Marine Life Conservation District: a popular place for snorkeling and scuba diving, with boat tours for the less athletic.

But in 1779, when the bay was an important anchorage, it achieved undying notoriety as the place where Capt. James Cook was killed. It is ironic that the great navigator who discovered Hawaii for the Western world and who was honored as a god by the Hawaiians should die at their hands in a skirmish over a stolen boat.

The Captain Cook Monument, an obelisk on the northwest side of the bay, marks the spot where he fell. It can be reached by hiking down to Ka`awaloa, on the north side of the bay. On the bay's south shore you may drive almost up to the beach, then walk to the ruins of Hikiau Heiau. It was at this temple that Cook conducted (for a member of his crew) the first Christian burial service on the islands.

▶ Accessible year-round.

www.hawaiistateparks.org/parks/hawaii
(808) 974-6200

26 Pu`uhonua o Honaunau National Historical Park

Off Hwy. 160, Honaunau

Spanning 180 acres of idyllic oceanfront land, this heavenly park preserves a revered place of refuge and profound significance in ancient Hawaiian culture. According to island natives, a visit to a pu`uhonua had the power to shelter those fleeing from battle, as well as absolve those who broke a

26 **Pu`uhonua o Honaunau National Historic Park.** God images stand guard at Pu`uhonua o Honaunau, the fully restored city of refuge on the Big Island.

kapu—one of the sacred laws that governed everything. To break a *kapu* was to incur the wrath of the gods, with potential consequences from lava flows to tsunamis, not to mention certain death. Upon reaching this sanctuary, *kapu* breakers were purified by a priest and spared further punishment.

Meticulously restored, the royal compound includes exquisitely carved wooden images, a mausoleum for the Kamehameha dynasty, and the impressive wall built stone by stone without mortar.

Beyond its sublime natural beauty and mana, or spiritual power, the park offers abundant interactive cultural opportunities. On a 30-minute self-guiding trail, you will see many archaeological sites, including reconstructed burial temples and canoe sheds. Watch your head—the ceiling is low—and flashlights are recommended. Ask at the visitors center for a back-country trail guide.

▶ Open year-round. Admission charged.

www.nps.gov/puho
(808) 328-2326

27 Kīlauea Iki Trail

Hawai`i Volcanoes National Park

Once a forested crater, Kīluaea Iki erupted in 1959, with lava fountains reaching 1,900 feet high. Explore the hardened but still steaming crater floor and the deep pit where lava once emerged.

The four-mile loop trail begins at the Kīlauea Iki Trailhead on Crater Rim Dr. and then it winds through lush rain forest with native birds in its canopy before descending 400 feet into the crater. Hike across the crater floor and then up the switchback trail on the other side. Self-guiding brochures are available at the trailhead and Kīlauea Visitor Center. If you are starting from the visitors center, take the Earthquake trail and then add two miles round-trip to the hike. Be prepared for hot, windy, or rainy weather and bring water.

▶ Open year-round. Park entrance fee.

www.nps.gov/havo
(808) 985-6000

28 Kipukauaulu

Mauna Loa Rd. NW, off Hwy. 11

Part of Hawai`i Volcanoes National Park, this quiet 100-acre oasis provides a habitat for a number of unusual plants and birds. This haven was created when a lava flow parted and came together again, sparing a 100-acre island of forest in between (*ki puka* is the Hawaiian name for this phenomenon).

On a mile-long self-guiding loop trail you'll see the giant koa, papala kepau, mamani, and thickets of pilo trees. The birds flitting through the treetops include exotics like the melodious laughing thrush and such natives as the wrenlike `*elepaio* and the `*amaki-hi,* `*i`iwi,* and `*apapane.* You may not see all of them, but you will certainly hear their chatter.

▶ Open year-round.

www.nps.gov/havo
(808) 985-6000

29 Thurston Lava Tube

Hawai`i Volcanoes National Park

When lava flows like a stream or river, the sides begin to harden and build up until they meet in the center, crusting over the flow and creating a tube for lava to travel through. As volcanic activity changes, the underground river of molten lava can drain away, leaving a long cylindrical tunnel called a lava tube. In Hawaii Volcanoes National Park you can walk through one of these geological curiosities.

The Thurston Lava Tube (Hawaiian name, Nāhuku) is on the easternmost point of Crater Rim Dr., which loops around Kīlauea, one of the world's most active volcanoes. A walk through the dimly lit 450-foot-long tube, set in a bird-filled tropical rain forest, requires ducking when the ceiling gets low. The formation was named for its discoverer, local newspaper publisher Lorrin Thurston, who came upon it in 1913.

▶ Open year-round. Park entrance fee.

www.nps.gov/havo
(808) 985-6000

30 Lyman Museum and Mission House

276 Haili St., Hilo

In 1832 David and Sarah Lyman, devout Protestant missionaries, traveled by boat from New England to the Sandwich Islands, now called Hawaii. They had been married for all of 24 days before leaving on the six-month voyage. In 1839 they built a house in Hilo, with a school for young Hawaiian men nearby. It would remain their home for life.

Over the years, the house became a center of culture and communication, hosting members of Hawaiian royalty and notables such as author Mark Twain. Nearly

100 years later, in 1931, descendants of David and Sarah established a museum to honor their pioneering work.

The oldest wooden structure on the Island of Hawaii, listed on both the *State* and *National Register of Historic Places,* the Lyman Mission House has been fully restored. The house features furniture, tools, and everyday items used by the Lymans and other early missionary families. Its isolated location inspires visitors to reflect on what it meant to live 5,000 miles from home, with no running water or electricity, in a place with a foreign language and local customs, guided by a fervent commitment to a sacred duty.

Next door the Lyman Museum houses a superb collection of fine art, artifacts, and seashells and minerals showcasing the natural and cultural history of Hawaii. The Island Heritage Gallery celebrates the spirit and traditions of native Hawaiians, as well as vital immigrant groups, including Japanese, Chinese, Korean, and Filipino people. The Earth Heritage

Gallery focuses on the island's flora and fauna, ecosystems, and geological formations.

▶ Open Mon.–Sat. except major holidays. Admission charged.

www.lymanmuseum.org
(808) 935-5021

31 `Akaka Falls State Park

Rte. 220, 3.6 miles southwest of Honomu

You reach this park after a six-mile drive west, passing through the former sugarcane plantation town of Honomu. Here in a setting of tropical foliage and flowers is `Akaka Falls, which plunges a sheer 442 feet down black volcanic rock, and its neighbor, Kahuna Falls, which cascades 300 feet to the stream below. The falls are visible from a sometimes steep but paved pathway that loops nearly a half mile through deep forest greenery. Flora such as ginger, orchids, heliconias, azaleas, and birds-of-paradise grow along the path.

Where the path begins, there are giant monkeypods sheltering a picnic table, but the spectacular drop of `Akaka Falls is the big attraction here. No swimming is allowed, and it would be difficult indeed to make your way to the base of either falls.

▶ Open year-round.

www.hawaiistateparks.org/parks/hawaii
(808) 974-6200

did you know ?

Hawai`i Volcanoes National Park has been honored as an International Biosphere Reserve and is the only World Heritage Site in Hawaii.

29 **Thurston Lava Tube.** Walk where molten rock once flowed at the 450-foot-long Thurston Lava Tube, a geological anomaly in Hawaii Volcanoes National Park.

HAWAII

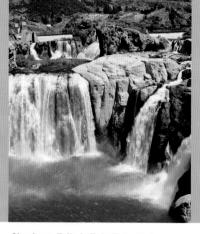

Idaho

This mountainous state offers recollections of its vigorous past, a wondrous variety of places to visit, and a chance to dig for garnets and opals.

Shoshone Falls in Twin Falls. Visitors to Thousand Springs (see page 95) may also want to stop at nearby Twin Falls to view Shoshone Falls (above), plunging as far as 212 feet.

Ghost towns stand today as poignant reminders of the hopes, hard labor, and broken dreams of those who came to Idaho to make their fortune, and one such town has survived those days and returned to vibrant life. The oldest structure in the state was built to serve God, not Mammon, and is beautifully preserved.

Some of the wonders in these parts seem to have been touched by the supernatural: sand dunes in an unlikely place, waterfalls that spring from a canyon wall, and a surreal "city" of huge megaliths. Not so surprising, but with great appeal, is the wealth of rivers, mountain lakes, canyons, wildflower meadows, and wildlife in this amazingly scenic state.

visit ➡ **offthebeatenpathtrips.com**

1 Priest Lake State Park

314 Indian Creek Park Rd., Coolin
The park's three campgrounds give access to an aqueous jewel: a 19-mile-long sapphire-blue mountain lake. Priest Lake takes its name from the indefatigable Jesuit missionary Pierre Jean De Smet, who in 1846, according to legend, became the first white man to see it.

Fishing is excellent, with mackinaw among the likely catches. Just north of Priest Lake is Upper Priest Lake, a wilderness area accessible only by boat or foot trail. The two lakes are connected by a meandering two-mile stream known locally as the Thoroughfare, which provides an enjoyable and picturesque route for a day trip by powerboat or canoe from the Lionhead Campground at the northeastern end of Priest Lake.

A three-quarter-mile hiking trail beginning at the Indian Creek Campground, located near the center of Priest Lake's eastern shore, leads through a cedar forest to a promontory from which there are magnificent views. There are

did you know ?

The forest surrounding Priest Lake is so thick that until logging roads were put through during the 1950s, the main mode of travel through here was by boat.

Old Mission State Park. Dating from the early 1850s, this European-style Jesuit mission is Idaho's oldest building. Its framework is made of rough-hewn logs.

also longer backpacking trails into the Selkirk Mountains. The area is accessible in the winter and offers miles of snowmobile and cross-country ski trails.

▶ Indian Creek Campground open year-round; day-use fee charged. Lionhead and Dickensheet campgrounds open May–Oct.

www.parksandrecreation.idaho.gov
(208) 443-2200

2 Old Mission State Park

S. Mission Rd., Cataldo
The former Jesuit mission that is the focal point of this park is the oldest building in Idaho. It was built between 1850 and 1853 by members of the Coeur d'Alene Indian tribe under the direction of Father Anthony Ravalli, and its design reflects a pragmatic blend of Old World ideals and the building materials available in the Idaho wilderness.

The walls of the mission are rough-hewn logs covered with a wattle and daub lattice. In 1865, after a sawmill was built on the mission's grounds, siding and interior paneling were added, which made the walls 18 inches thick. European-style chandeliers were fashioned from tin cans, and wooden altars and crosses were painted to imitate gilt and marble. Many of the wall hangings were made of cloth from the Hudson Bay Trading Post, and others were made by painting newspapers. A thriving Coeur d'Alene farming village was established at the mission, and many Native Americans lived here until the tribe was forced onto a reservation in 1877.

▶ Open year-round. Admission charged.

www.parksandrecreation.idaho.gov
(208) 682-3814

3 Wallace

To visit this remarkably preserved town is to step back into the turn of the century. Indeed, the entire downtown district, a virtual compendium of architectural styles, is listed on the *National Register of Historic Places.*

One can take a self-guiding walking tour of 38 historic buildings constructed between 1890 and 1930, including Victorian commercial, neoclassical, Renaissance revival, and art deco styles. The tour can be done in about 45 minutes, but there is a wealth of finely crafted detail, and many of the interiors are as fascinating as the exteriors.

Visitors should not miss the Wallace District Mining Museum, with its collection of old mining tools, rock samples, and memorabilia, or the Sierra Silver Mine Tour, where visitors can explore the underground world of the area's prominent silver mines.

The Wallace region is a haven for hikers and bicyclists. It provides access to the Trail of the Coeur d'Alenes and the Route of the Hiawatha, which run along historic railway lines converted for recreational use, allowing visitors to enjoy the area's scenic splendor.

▶ Museum open daily most of the year. Admission charged.

www.wallaceidahochamber.com
(208) 753-7151

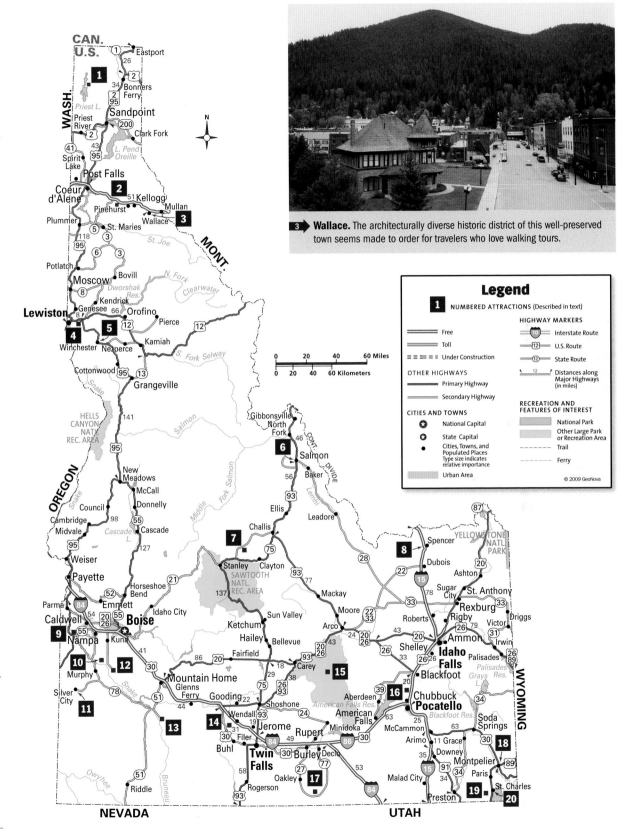

3 **Wallace.** The architecturally diverse historic district of this well-preserved town seems made to order for travelers who love walking tours.

Legend

1 NUMBERED ATTRACTIONS (Described in text)

HIGHWAY MARKERS

Free — 10 Interstate Route
Toll — 12 U.S. Route
Under Construction — 12 State Route
— 12 Distances along Major Highways (in miles)

OTHER HIGHWAYS
Primary Highway
Secondary Highway

CITIES AND TOWNS
⊛ National Capital
⊙ State Capital
• Cities, Towns, and Populated Places Type size indicates relative importance
Urban Area

RECREATION AND FEATURES OF INTEREST
National Park
Other Large Park or Recreation Area
Trail
Ferry

© 2009 GeoNova

IDAHO

4 Nez Perce National Historical Park

39063 Hwy. 95, Spalding

For centuries the Nez Perce Native Americans have lived in the valleys of the Snake and Clearwater rivers. In 1805 they welcomed the explorers Lewis and Clark and told them of the great water route to the Pacific along the Snake and Columbia rivers.

The tribe lived in relative peace with the influx of American settlers until gold was discovered on tribal lands in the 1860s, and the U.S. government proposed to limit the Native Americans to a reservation one-tenth the size of the territory they had been guaranteed.

The war of 1877 eventually led to the defeat of the Nez Perce people. Chief Joseph is one of the Nez Perce leaders, famous for the lucid eloquence with which he expressed the finality of his people's tragic surrender: "From where the sun now stands, I will fight no more forever."

The park comprises 38 separate historically significant sites that are scattered over four states, most of them within the Nez Perce reservation. These sites commemorate not only the Nez Perce people but also explorers, missionaries, traders, and gold miners.

The park headquarters at Spalding has a visitors center that offers films and interpretive talks and includes a museum portraying the Nez Perce culture with beautiful examples of Native American dress, beadwork, and other artifacts.

Within a short drive of Spalding, you can see the various sites of the 1836 mission, a gristmill, the early Indian Agency, and Fort Lapwai. In the surrounding area camping, boating, swimming, hiking, and fishing are available.

4 Nez Perce National Historical Park. The design of the park's visitors center and museum echoes the low-lying mountains on the horizon.

▶ Visitors center closed major winter holidays.

www.nps.gov/nepe
(208) 843-7001

5 Wolf Education and Research Center

518 Joseph Ave., Winchester

Spanning 300 acres of pristine, protected tribal land at the juncture of three national forest systems, the Nez Perce Reservation is one of the largest homes to a single wolf pack in the United States. Within a 20-acre enclosure of rolling timberland with meadows and streams, the Sawtooth Pack lives in as natural an environment as possible within a captive world.

Visitors get the rare opportunity to observe and learn about wolves in their natural habitat from two observation decks or between two fences on guided walking tours. By educating people about their kind, these gray wolves serve as ambassadors for their wild cousins.

Committed to enhancing the public's awareness of wolves as a distinctive and threatened species, the nonprofit center conducts extensive research on the characteristics and habits of wolves and on how they interact with their environment.

At the center visitors also get a chance to see the all-but-vanished wilds of Idaho. Amid vast woodlands and shimmering streams, wild turkeys, hawks, owls, elk, and deer roam the land.

Nearby, situated on the edge of a former millpond, Winchester Lake State Park offers a chance to learn more about the wolves. The Wolf Education and Research Center sponsors programs at the park's amphitheater, including videos, movies, and slide shows about wolf reintroduction programs, as well as a "wolf box," where visitors can learn more about the biology of the wolf.

▶ Open daily Memorial Day–Labor Day and weekends May and Sept. Guided tours year-round by reservation only, with fee charged.

www.wolfcenter.org
(888) 422-1110

6 Sacajawea Interpretive, Cultural & Educational Center

200 Main St., Salmon

When Meriwether Lewis and William Clark conducted their famous expedition to the West, they were accompanied by a Lemhi-Shoshone woman named Sacajawea.

Using her cultural awareness and familiarity with the terrain, she guided Lewis and Clark. The center celebrates this remarkable woman, exploring both her contribution to the expedition and the parts of her life before and after the expedition that are not as well documented.

The facilities here include a visitors center, outdoor amphitheater, the Meriwether Theater, and a monument to Sacajawea. The School of Discovery teaches skills and knowledge useful to pioneers and the Shoshone people of Sacajawea's time. Outside, visitors find a low-ropes course, the Community Heritage Gardens, and the Sacajawea Gateway Grove, a one-mile interpretive trail with several exhibits. The nearby park provides picnic areas, fishing access, and nature trails.

▶ Visitors center open daily mid-May–Sept. Trails and park open year-round. Admission charged.

www.sacajaweacenter.org
(208) 756-1188

6 Sacajawea Center. A statue of the guide Sacajawea and her child welcomes visitors.

7 ▶ Custer

Yankee Fork Rd., north of Sunbeam

The remains of mines and mining camps are scattered throughout the land of the Yankee Fork in the Challis National Forest, where gold and silver were found during the last quarter of the 19th century. By the 1890s Custer was the region's central town, with a peak population of 600 to 700 and a mill that crushed some $12 million worth of ore.

Today not many of the abandoned town's structures still stand, but the ruins of several other buildings are all labeled and still evoke their spirited past. The schoolhouse and the Empire Saloon now serve as a museum, whose displays tell the story of various Yankee Fork mines.

The ghost town of Bonanza, just to the south, is also of interest. On the way, you'll pass the Yankee Fork gold dredge, which was used to extract the last of the area's retrievable gold in the 1940s and early 1950s. Former workers give tours of the dredge and explain its operation. Nearby the U.S. Forest Service runs four campgrounds along the road leading from Sunbeam to Custer.

▶ Custer Museum and Gold Dredge open Memorial Day–Labor Day. Fee charged for gold dredge tour.

www.fs.fed.us/r4/sc/yankeefork
(208) 879-4100; (208) 879-5244

8 ▶ Spencer Opal Mines

Headquarters: 27 Opal Ave., Spencer

Unlike most gems, opals have no crystal structure; rather, they are a solidified silica jelly. A regular array of holes between the microscopic globules of silica creates a diffraction grating, which breaks white light into the rainbow of color that plays upon the stone's surface.

Here in Spencer is a different kind of mine, run by the Stetler family since 1964, where rock hounds can collect material for their jewelry making.

Visitors are charged $10 per person ($5 for children) to dig through a stockpile of opal-bearing material. The ore is hauled to the site from the mine, which is eight miles away. Anyone can join in, and although visitors are encouraged to bring their own hammers, chisels, and safety glasses, they can also be rented there.

For the serious rock hound, the mine is open on holiday weekends for digging at a daily rate of $40. Contact the mine for specific dates.

▶ Open daily May–Sept.

www.spenceropalmines.com
(208) 374-5476; (928) 859-3752

9 ▶ Snake River Valley Wine Country

In the 1860s French and German immigrants began producing fine wines in the Snake River Valley, making Idaho nationally renowned for its award-winning wines. Unfortunately, Prohibition caused the wineries to shut down. Today 16 of Idaho's 32 wineries are located in the Snake River Valley, which provides the perfect climate for growing wine grapes. The cold winters, high elevation, consequent

temperature fluctuations, and relative lack of rainfall help produce grapes with the proper sugar and acid balance.

While touring Idaho's wine country, you'll discover wineries and vineyards ranging from small by-appointment-only cellars to larger facilities, offering year-round tours, tasting rooms, and restaurants. In their relatively short history Idaho wineries are already

9 ▶ Snake River Valley Wine Country. At the Sawtooth Winery near Nampa, what was once pastureland now grows Pinot Noir, Cabernet Sauvignon, Merlot, and other wine grapes.

winning awards for their excellent Merlot, Syrah, Chardonnay, and Cabernet Sauvignon, in addition to their world-class Reisling.

www.idahowines.org
(888) 223-9463; (208) 455-8354

10 ▶ Celebration Park

5000 Victory Ln., Melba

At Idaho's only archaeological park, visitors get a chance to bask in the area's unspoiled beauty while learning about its fascinating natural and cultural history.

A short hiking trail leads the way past petroglyphs carved on massive boulders. Other trails link to scenic sites, such as Halverson Lake, a small pond nestled along a canyon wall, and eventually converge at Swan Falls Dam. A onetime railroad bridge built in 1897 and restored for bikes and feet provides only one of the few crossings over the Snake River.

As the park's interpretive center reveals, Idahoan archaeology is a treasure trove of diversity. Thousands of years ago Idaho was home to people who traversed the landscape in search of wild game and edible plants. About 160 years ago hundreds of immigrants traveled through Idaho on their way out West. In the 1880s Idaho attracted Chinese people to work on its railroads and Basque people to raise sheep in its vast deserts.

▶ Open year-round. Admission charged.

www.canyonco.org
(208) 495-2745

11 ▶ Silver City

25 miles southwest of Murphy

In 1863 Michael Jordan discovered gold along the creek that today bears his name, starting a rush of prospectors into the Owyhee Mountains. Besides gold, the miners found rich slabs of silver.

Silver City boomed and quickly became the county seat. According to conservative estimates, over $40 million in silver was taken from the area. By the early 1900s those glory days were over.

Today approximately 75 stark and weathered buildings of this historic mining town still stand on the rugged hillsides. The once colorful streets were the scenes of several gunfights. In the former drugstore one can still inspect old pharmaceutical equipment.

Silver City's centerpiece now, just as it was in the 1860s, is the five-story Idaho Hotel. With advance reservations you can spend the night here in a room with original furnishings. Family-style meals are served. Woodstoves provide heat in some rooms.

Dominated by the 8,000-foot War Eagle Mountain to the south, the countryside offers ample opportunity for recreation. Abandoned mills, mine shafts, old town sites, and historic cemeteries are spread throughout the area. Snowmobiling and cross-country skiing are popular in the winter.

Visitors should note that few supplies are available in Silver City. Gasoline, food, water, and other necessities should be purchased before driving in. Also, the dirt road from Rte. 78 is rather rough, and trailers are not recommended. Allow an hour or more to complete the 23-mile journey. Heavy snow can fall as early as October, and the road may be impassable as late as Memorial Day. Check with the Owyhee County sheriff for road conditions early or late in the season.

▶ Generally open June–mid-Oct. and by special arrangement in the winter. Admission charged for some buildings.

www.historicsilvercityidaho.com
(208) 896-5912 Bureau of Land Management
(208) 583-4104 Idaho Hotel
(208) 495-1154 Road conditions

12 ▶ **Snake River Birds of Prey National Conservation Area.** Hawks are among the 16 species of raptors that come in pairs to nest at Snake River Canyon.

13 ▶ **Bruneau Dunes State Park.** On the largest single structured sand dune in North America, a five-mile nature trail with markers explains the area's geology.

12 ▶ Snake River Birds of Prey National Conservation Area

Take Swan Falls Rd. south from Kuna to Swan Falls Dam

Nearly half a million acres along a remote 80-mile section of the Snake River have been declared a protected habitat for one of the densest populations of nesting birds of prey anywhere in the world.

Over 700 pairs of raptors, as birds of prey are called, nest here annually—16 different species in all, including prairie falcons, golden eagles, and even a few turkey vultures and Swainson's hawks. In addition, bald eagles, peregrine falcons, and several other species stop here during migration.

Binoculars are a must for viewing the birds, which can be seen most easily during the courting and nesting period from mid-March through June. After that, high summer temperatures and the scarcity of food drive many birds to other areas. With advance reservations local wilderness outfitters offer canoe and raft trips along the Snake River, providing visitors with a vivid sense of the raptors' wild domain.

▶ Open year-round.

www.birdsofprey.blm.gov
(208) 384-3300

13 ▶ Bruneau Dunes State Park

Bruneau Dunes Rd., Mountain Home

The two enormous mountains of sand that form this park's centerpiece are in striking contrast to the high, flat plateaus that dominate the landscape here. Covering some 600 acres of the 4,800-acre park, the picturesque dunes give way at their base to lakes and marshland, creating an ecological anomaly.

Eagle Cove, where the dunes stand, was formed by the meandering Snake River about 15,000 years ago. The sand was blown in from the surrounding plateau and trapped by opposing winds, which still keep the dunes from moving far or dramatically changing their shape. The lakes and marsh began to form in 1950, when a nearby reservoir caused the underground water table to rise.

Climbing the dunes is the park's chief attraction. At first

glimpse the tallest dune, which is 470 feet high, does not seem particularly challenging. But the hike through shifting sand with no firm footholds and no well-trod trail is surprisingly strenuous, but the crest offers rewarding views. Sand skiers will find the dunes especially inviting. In summer the sand can be extremely hot, and it's best to climb in the early morning or late afternoon. The climb can be predictably gritty, so be sure to pack cameras and food in well-sealed plastic bags.

The park also offers a public observatory, featuring the Obsession telescope, a custom-made 25-inch reflector that allows the viewer to see the rings of Saturn or the Owl Nebula.

▶ Open year-round. Observatory presentations given at dusk Fri. and Sat., mid-Mar.–mid-Oct. Admission charged.

www.parksandrecreation.idaho.gov
(208) 366-7919

14 Thousand Springs

Best viewed from Rte. 30, between Buhl and Hagerman

The dozen or more waterfalls that spout suddenly from the wall of the Snake River Canyon here were long a puzzle to geologists as well as laymen. Now scientists believe that their source lies 150 miles to the northeast, where the Big and Little Lost rivers vanish into the lava beds that cover much of the region. Increased greatly in volume by melting snow and seepage, the underground streams course through the porous lava until they reach this canyon and plunge into the Snake River.

The springs assume a dramatic variety of forms—wispy curtains; slender columns; foamy, rushing cascades; and raging torrents. Binoculars are helpful—as is a telephoto lens for photographers—since the viewing area is across the river at a commercial resort. The viewing area, however, is open and free to the public, and visitors are welcome to use the picnic tables without charge.

Trout thrive in the cool, aerated water pouring from the springs, making this the state's prime area for trout fishing. Facilities for boaters and campers are available all along this beautiful stretch of U.S. 30, justly known as the Thousand Springs Scenic Byway. The area has other spectacular cascades, at Twin Falls and Shoshone Falls, the picturesque gorge of the Malad River and the remarkable Balanced Rock.

▶ Open year-round.

www.hagermanchamber.com
(208) 837-9131

15 Craters of the Moon National Monument and Preserve

Hwy. 20/26/93 between Arco and Carey

At first glance this 1,100-square-mile park appears to be a stark and forbidding wasteland of black rock as desolate as the moon itself. But it is actually a fascinating geological wonder—a barren area complete with spatter cones, fissure vents, cinder gardens, and lava flows, with tunnels, caves, and the molds of trees that were once encased in molten lava. Sixty lava flows lie within the crater's lava field, ranging in age from 15,000 to just 2,000 years old. All of this is the result of eight major eruptions from more than two dozen lava vents.

Many of the most intriguing features can be seen along a seven-mile loop drive. In addition, a hiking trail runs south for six miles to the Great Rift, the ultimate source of the volcanic events that created this landscape.

The trail passes near Echo Crater, where many backpackers camp for protection from the area's often harsh winds. Overnighters should

15 Crater of the Moon National Monument. Astronauts used this lunar landscape for moonwalking practice in the 1960s.

obtain a free permit at the visitors center. Throughout the park use care when going off the trail. Carry water on hikes and a flashlight to explore the caves.

The park also has a surprising diversity of plant and animal life. The best time to visit is mid-June, when the wildflowers bloom. Later in the summer the heat-absorbing black lava can become uncomfortably hot.

▶ Open year-round. Admission charged.

www.nps.gov/crmo
(208) 527-1300

did you know ?

In 1924 President Coolidge signed a proclamation declaring the black wavy rock lava field found in central Idaho to be the Craters of the Moon National Monument. At the time, people imagined the surface of the moon might resemble this terrain.

14 Thousand Springs. Multitudes of waterfalls springing from a wall at Snake Creek Canyon bring a softer note to a world of barren rock.

16 Fort Hall Replica

Upper Ross Park, Pocatello

Fort Hall was once a fur-trading center and a rest stop for pioneers making the journey west. The fort was built in 1834, on the Snake River along the Oregon Trail, by Nathaniel Wyeth, an explorer and fur trader. The ruins of the fort were destroyed by floods in the 1860s, and this full-scale replica was completed in 1966, 13 miles from the original site, in Ross Park.

Enter Fort Hall through its huge wooden gates, where you will find yourself transported back in time to the 1800s. Experience the flavor of that bygone era in the reconstructed buildings, including a blacksmith's shop, carpenter's shop, trading post, company mess hall, and living quarters.

Just outside the fort walls the Bannock County Historical Museum highlights the history of Pocatello and Fort Hall. Pocatello, first known as Pocatello Junction, is a replica of a small 1893 railroad town. At Ross Park Zoo, a short walk from the fort, buffalo and elk still roam.

The original Fort Hall is located at the Fort Hall Indian Reservation, which is home to the Shoshone-Bannock tribes. Each year on the second weekend in August, the reservation hosts a traditional Native American festival, complete with rodeo, games, stunning craft work, and dramatic dance competitions.

▶ Open Tues.-Sun. Memorial Day-
  Labor Day; Tues.-Sat. Apr. and Sept.

www.forthall.net
(208) 234-1795 Fort Hall
(208) 478-3700 Reservation

17 **City of Rocks National Reserve.** Massive granite outcroppings as tall as 60 stories are a dramatic sight on an otherwise featureless branch of the Oregon Trail.

17 City of Rocks National Reserve

4 miles west of Almo

These huge natural megaliths, silently dominating the plain like a procession of brooding and forgotten prehistoric gods, are as breathtakingly startling to visitors today as they were to pioneers traveling to California in the middle 1800s.

Numerous pioneer diaries comment on the "wild and romantic scenery . . . all manner of fantastic shapes" that held the visitors "spellbound with the beauty and strangeness of it all." Many immigrants, their individual fates now lost to history, were moved to leave their names marked with axle grease on these ancient stones. Perhaps, confronting the frailty of their own lives on the difficult way west, they sought to connect themselves with something timeless.

Among the hundreds of rocks found here—some formations are 2.5 billion years old—30 are so strikingly evocative that they have been given colorful names, such as Squaw and Papoose, Giant Toadstool, King on the Throne, Kaiser's Helmet, and Devil's Bedstead. A descriptive pamphlet and map, giving the names of many of the formations and the best angles from which to view them, is available at the visitors center in Almo.

The area is remote and undeveloped, and the access road has a rough, unpaved surface that may be inaccessible in inclement weather or during the winter months.

www.nps.gov/ciro
(208) 824-5519

18 National Oregon/California Trail Center

320 N. 4th St., Montpelier

Sitting on the very spot where travelers would camp to rest their animals, stock their larders, and prepare for the next leg of their journey west, this center celebrates Idaho's part in the pioneer trails of 150 years ago and lets visitors step back into history.

On its way through Idaho, the Oregon/California Trail crossed deserts, mountains, and rivers. The trail was winding, arduous, and treacherous. If a valley was 10 miles wide, so was the trail. If a ford was less than a foot in diameter, so was the trail.

This living-history museum captures the trailblazing experience with a main-floor exhibit area that dramatically re-creates the historic Clover Creek Encampment, where real pioneers come alive as wagon-train captains, mountain men and their women, traders, and scoundrels. Complete with the feel of prairie dust and the smell of meat, dumplings, and beans boiling for dinner, visitors can learn how the pioneers dealt with their epic trek and its everyday challenges.

The main floor houses an authentic mercantile and gun shop, an art gallery, and a gift shop boasting the best in period Western souvenirs.

The downstairs floor is home to the Rails and Trails Museum, whose three main exhibits explore the influence of the railroad, the history of the town of Montpelier and the surrounding valley, and the lives of the courageous women who traveled in the wagon trains.

▶ Call for scheduled operating hours.
  Admission charged.

www.oregontrailcenter.org
(866) 847-3800

19 Minnetonka Cave

*Minnetonka Cave Rd.,
St. Charles*

More than a half-mile of well-lighted paths and stairways (448 steps) leads through nine subterranean rooms, the largest more than 300 feet long and 90 feet high. In the cave giant limestone stalactites and stalagmites glisten like melting wax.

Despite this ephemeral appearance, the cave's formation took thousands of years. Water absorbed carbon dioxide as it slowly filtered through the ground, forming carbonic acid, a solution that dissolves limestone into calcite. As this solution dripped through cracks and fissures in the stone, large caverns were gradually hollowed out and filled with calcite deposits—the bizarre formations you see today.

Tours are approximately 90 minutes. The pathway, damp in some places, is gently graded; however, there are spots where you'll need to climb fairly steep stairs. Warm clothing should be worn, since the temperature inside stays at 40°F. Picnic and camping areas are a few minutes' drive away.

▶ Open daily Memorial Day–Labor Day, weather dependent. Admission charged.

www.bearlake.org/cavexplore.html
(800) 448-BEAR

20 ▶ Bear Lake State Park

5637 E. Shore Rd., St. Charles
Bear Lake is legendary for its sparkling turquoise waters and luxurious beaches. Located at an altitude of 5,900 feet in the southeastern corner of Idaho, straddling the border with Utah, it is a watersports paradise: Throughout its 120 miles it offers unparalleled swimming, powerboating, waterskiing, sailing, and fishing. Its gradually sloping floor creates enormous, safe swimming areas at two long beaches. The lake is packed with trout, as well as four other species that are totally unique to Bear Lake.

The 966-acre park is scattered with hundreds of miles of trails connecting Idaho and Utah. The possibilities for enjoying this park are virtually endless; bring an all-terrain vehicle or mountain bike and take the Bloomington Lake Trail to a small glacial lake set within a spectacular setting of waterfalls and cliffs, or hike some of the 55-mile Highline Trail to see some of the park's impressive canyons.

August brings the raspberry

20 ▶ **Bear Lake State Park.** Tents for campers are located on the east side of mountain-high Bear Lake.

harvest, which is accompanied by entertainment and fireworks. In the winter the park keeps almost 300 miles of snow groomed for snowmobiling and skiing. Ice-fishing for Bonneville cisco, a species of fish unique to the area, is also a popular winter activity.

▶ Open year-round. Vehicle entrance fee.

www.parksandrecreation.idaho.gov
(208) 847-1045

seasonal events

FEBRUARY

- Chocolate Walk—Coeur d'Alene *(Valentine chocolate festival, chocolate-related arts and crafts, food, and activities)*

MAY

- Challis Mountain Lilac Festival—Challis *(lilac arts and crafts, golf, photography contest, barrel race, horse show, cowboy poetry, lilac parade)*

JUNE

- Jazz in the Canyon—Twin Falls *(3-day festival featuring live music, food, entertainment)*

JULY

- Annual Lavender Festival—Buhl *(craft fair, music and entertainment, lavender feast)*

- Butch Cassidy Days—Montpelier *(weekend of outlaw-themed entertainment and games: log-cutting contest, hatchet throw, parade, afternoon shoot-out re-enactment, dancing, fireworks)*

AUGUST

- Annual Soul Food Extravaganza—Boise *(fried catfish, collard greens, jambalaya, sweet-potato pie, and barbecued meats; live music, African storytelling, children's activities)*

- Raspberry Days—Bear Lake *(craft fair, Miss Berry Princess contest, raspberry recipe cook-off, rodeo, dancing, fireworks)*

SEPTEMBER

- Ernest Hemingway Festival—Sun Valley *(lectures, panel discussions, short-story contest, living-history vignettes, art gallery, special functions at select Hemingway historical sites)*

- Idaho Botanical Garden's Mad Hatters Tea Party—Boise *(games, entertainment, shopping, special guests, including Alice, the Mad Hatter, and the White Rabbit)*

- Spud Day—Shelley *(parade, music, demolition derby, free baked-potato lunch at noon, Dutch oven cook-off, World Championship potato picking)*

www.visitidaho.org

18 ▶ **National Oregon/California Trail Center.** Inside the museum, visitors can climb aboard a covered wagon and experience what it was like to be part of a wagon train heading west on the Oregon Trail.

Chautauqua National Wildlife Refuge. In the shallows at this refuge in west-central Illinois, a young blue heron waits to nab a passing fish (see page 102).

Illinois

The attractions in this influential Midwestern state embody the spirit of the prairie and the heart of America.

The tiny town where Abraham Lincoln cut his teeth on politics and the law has been reconstructed in Illinois, as has the blacksmith shop where John Deere invented the steel plow that changed the face of agriculture. Centuries before, native peoples built the largest city in what would become the United States on the banks of the Father of Waters—the Mississippi.

The Land of Lincoln boasts a wealth of other attractions as well—among them tranquil wildlife sanctuaries and wetlands, inviting state parks, a wilderness with enormous rock formations rivaling those of the West, and an exquisite Japanese garden in the city of Rockford.

visit ➤ **offthebeatenpathtrips.com**

1 ▶ Apple River Canyon State Park

8763 E. Canyon Rd., Apple River
The cool, clear waters of Apple River flow through the center of this lovely park, gently but steadily cutting through masses of limestone, dolomite, and shale as they have done for thousands of years. In the canyon, vertical cliffs now rise 150 feet above the small stream. Flowering plants, shrubs, and some 14 different kinds of ferns grow in the crevices of the rock face, transforming it into a hanging garden.

For nature lovers and amateur geologists the 297-acre park has special interest. It is in a small region that was untouched by glaciation, and it apparently served as a refuge for many plants that did not survive the glacial period in most parts of Illinois. As a result, several exquisite relict plants are found here, including the bird's-eye primrose, the flower-of-an-hour, and the jeweled shooting star.

In more recent times the region was prized for its deposits of lead. Native Americans dug it out for exchange with French traders 300 years ago, and in the 19th century, settlers established profitable mines here.

Five hiking trails wind among the wooded hills, providing an opportunity to enjoy lush vegetation; a chance to amble alongside

1 ▶ Apple River Canyon State Park. Serenity, wildlife, and rare plant life that survived the last Ice Age attract travelers to a park on the Illinois-Wisconsin border.

streams and springs; and possibilities to spot deer, small mammals, hawks, pileated woodpeckers, and the occasional bald eagle.

Wildflowers splash the park roadsides from spring into fall. The river is stocked with rainbow trout in early April.

▶ Open year-round except Christmas.

http://dnr.state.il.us
(815) 745-3302

2 ▶ Anderson Japanese Gardens

318 Spring Creek Rd., Rockford
Long in love with Japan and its culture, businessman John Anderson was inspired to express his affection botanically after tour-ing a Japanese garden in Portland, Oregon. So he and wife, Linda, hired its director of landscaping, Hochi Kurisu, to create a place in Rockford where visitors can find peace, tranquillity, and inspiration.

A formal Japanese garden complete with teahouse shares space with the Garden of Reflection, a contemporary international garden with a strong Japanese influence. In the shadow of a five-story-high waterfall, visitors watch colorful koi ply the plant-lined streams. When birds flock into Rockford during migration season, birdsong fills the air as the winged arrivals settle at the 12 acres for an extended stay.

▶ Open year-round except major winter holidays. Admission charged.

www.andersongardens.org

(815) 229-9390

3 ▶ Illinois Railway Museum

7000 Olson Rd., Union

At this museum railroad buffs can steam into the past along some four miles of track aboard old coaches pulled by locomotives. Vintage streetcars also make a loop, stopping at the car barns that house elevated trains, mail and baggage cars, and a wide range of antique trolleys.

More than 200 engines and cars recall the charm and excitement of railroading in days gone by. Much of the equipment has been restored and is fully operational. Of special interest is the 1889 Nevada Northern private car Ely, with paneled and mirrored bedrooms and a plush sitting room. An elevated railroad car from Chicago still displays 1907 advertisements for chewing gum, while another veteran of Chicago's busy

traffic—a Green Hornet streetcar—harks back to the 1940s, when there was a popular radio program of the same name.

Frequent departures from an authentic depot are announced by stationmasters, and the trains are staffed by uniformed engineers, conductors, and trainmen. One of the interpretive charts translates the intriguing code of "whistle talk," while another explains why the expansion of the railroads had

created a need by 1883 to divide the country into standardized time zones. Special events include a Fourth of July Trolley Pageant.

▶ Open daily Memorial Day–Labor Day, Sun. Apr.–Oct., weekends in Sept. and May. Trains run only on weekends and holidays. Admission charged.

www.irm.org

(800) 244-7245

Legend

1 NUMBERED ATTRACTIONS (Described in text)

HIGHWAY MARKERS

Free

Toll

Under Construction

OTHER HIGHWAYS

Primary Highway

Secondary Highway

HIGHWAY MARKERS

Interstate Route

U.S. Route

State Route

Distances along
Major Highways
(in miles)

CITIES AND TOWNS

☆ National Capital

★ State Capital

• Cities, Towns, and
Populated Places
Type size indicates
relative importance

Urban Area

**RECREATION AND
FEATURES OF INTEREST**

National Park

Other Large Park
or Recreation Area

Trail

Ferry

© 2009 GeoNova

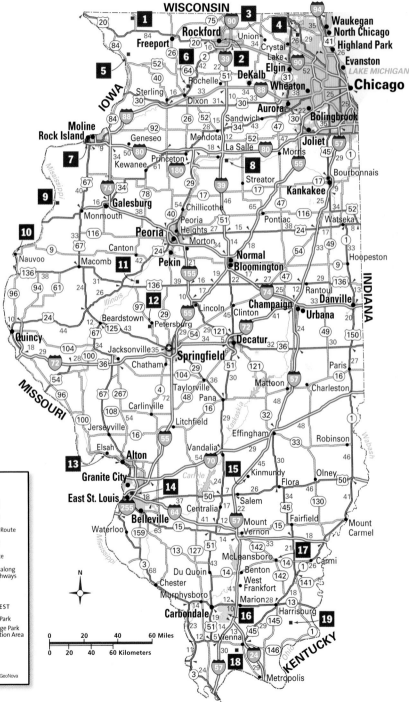

4 Volo Bog State Natural Area

28478 W. Brandenburg Rd., Ingleside

Visitors to this 1,200-acre wilderness area can find themselves on shaky ground: The main attraction here is a so-called quaking bog about 50 acres in extent, designated a National Natural Landmark. In places the bog is a deep, spongy mat of vegetation and roots floating atop the water, and if you were to tread directly on it, the sensation would be similar to that of walking on a water bed. To preserve the bogs, visitors are required to stay on the half-mile loop trail, which starts at the visitors center. The wetland areas are crossed by a floating boardwalk.

Fourteen stops along the trail permit close-up inspection of an unusually rich plant life, which changes from area to area because of the changing light, soil, and water conditions. In the tamarack forest you'll find blueberry, yellow birch, bog birch, winterberry, and several types of fern. As for the poison sumac, look but don't touch. It is illustrated in the seasonal trail brochures.

Rose pogonias are all that remain of the six kinds of wild orchids that were once found here, along with marsh cinquefoils, starflowers, Indian pipes, and other wildlings. Nearly 200 species of birds may be seen, including sandhill cranes, great blue herons, veery, and white-winged crossbills.

Summer programs include guided bird and wildflower excursions and a "Bats in Your Belfry" visit to an old barn, where hundreds of these mosquito-eaters literally hang out.

▶ Park open year-round. Visitors center open Wed.–Sun. except major holidays.

http://dnr.state.il.us
(815) 344-1294

5 Mississippi Palisades State Park

16327 IL-84, Savanna

This hilly 2,500-acre park was named for the Hudson River Palisades, and the resemblance is striking, with a dramatic limestone bluff dominating the region and overlooking the Mississippi.

The recreation area offers 15 miles of hiking trails, some with steep climbs from river level to overlooks that reward you with sweeping views, especially magnificent at sunset. There are also less demanding trails, and if you don't want to hike, you can drive to Lookout Point to enjoy the scenery.

Thick growths of oak, ash, and hickory provide a fertile haven for wild turkeys, deer, and many kinds of songbirds. In spring and summer violets, lobelias, and other wildflowers carpet the valleys and slopes, and many kinds of ferns grow rampant in the ravines.

Of particular note among the unusual rock formations are Indian Head, etched by ages of erosion, and the two rock columns called the Twin Sisters. In all, this majestic setting encourages climbers to challenge the many limestone walls, seamed by centuries of wind and rain.

At the base of the cliffs, there is river access for boating and fishing. In winter the slopes and trails are used for cross-country skiing and sledding.

▶ Open year-round.

http://dnr.state.il.us
(815) 273-2731

6 John Deere Historic Site

8334 S. Clinton St., Grand Detour

Without the highly polished, contoured steel plow John Deere fashioned in a blacksmith shop just like the one replicated at this site, farmers might still be getting stalled in the rich, sticky soil of the Midwest. Today visitors watch a blacksmith demonstrate the skills that Deere employed when—from a discarded saw blade—he forged the plow that opened the prairie to agriculture.

Many of Deere's actual tools are on display, unearthed in 1962 by an archaeological team that discovered the exact location of the inventor's shop. You can get another authentic glimpse of pio-

6 John Deere Historic Site. A replica of the blacksmith shop where Deere made history features demonstrations of the skills employed by the inventor of the steel plow.

4 Volo Bog State Natural Area. A half-mile loop trail surrounds this famous quaking bog. Visitors tread on boardwalks in other wet areas at the site.

neer life at the house Deere built for his family in 1836, complete with furnishings true to the era.

▶ Open Wed.–Sun. May-Oct.
  Admission charged.

www.JohnDeereAttractions.com
(815) 652-4551

7 ▶ Black Hawk State Historic Site

1510 Blackhawk Rd., Rock Island
Those who fish the creeks and hike the trails of this 207-acre park follow the footsteps of the Sauk and Mesquakie Native Americans, to whom this region was once home. The park is named for one of the Sauks' greatest leaders.

You'll find an activities center in the limestone lodge, one of those many built-to-last structures erected by the Civilian Conservation Corps during the Great Depression. The park itself occupies the site of a former recreation and amusement area. Highly popular at the turn of the century, it boasted the first figure-eight roller-coaster west of Chicago.

The essence of that era is captured by a photo display in the Hauberg Museum, a part of the lodge. The museum is otherwise devoted to portraying the lifestyle of the Sauk and Mesquakie people. Among the objects on view are a bark house, containing articles of everyday use, and a bust of Black Hawk copied from a life mask.

About half the park is a nature preserve where hackberry, hickory, and oak trees provide a canopy for rue anemone, wild orchids, trilliums, and some 30 other kinds of wildflowers. More than 100 bird species have been identified, and migrations fill the sky in spring and autumn.

8 ▶ **Starved Rock State Park.** The picturesque Upper LaSalle Waterfall spills gracefully over rock terraces into one of the state park's numerous canyons.

▶ Open daily except major winter holidays.

www.blackhawkpark.org
(309) 788-0177

8 ▶ Starved Rock State Park

IL-178, Utica
According to a legend from the 1760s, the Illiniwek Native Americans, one of whom had murdered the Ottawa chief, Pontiac, sought safety from the avenging Ottawas atop a high sandstone butte. Surrounded by their opponents, they eventually starved to death.

The appeal of this 2,630-acre park, which stretches along the southern edge of the Illinois River, is primarily in the 18 canyons cut in the sandstone bluffs by feeder streams and in the enormous variety of plant life found here, all of which can be enjoyed from the 13 miles of well-marked hiking trails.

The Interior Canyon trails penetrate the cool, damp canyon recesses, with their rugged rock formations, impressive waterfalls, and a lush growth of ferns, mosses, and delicate flowering plants. The Bluff Trail takes you along the many slopes where oaks and sugar maples shade witch hazel, wild hydrangeas, and trilliums, and the bluff tops are crowned by oaks, cedars, white pines, and shrubs preferring a drier soil.

Along the River Trail one walks beneath a light canopy of cottonwoods and black willows and enters the forested floodplain, where the deeper soil nurtures hickories and bur oaks, blueberries, jack-in-the-pulpits, and many other nut-, fruit-, and flower-bearing plants. The River Trail also leads to Starved Rock.

Fishermen may be lured to the park's streams by white bass, bull-heads, channel catfish, and walleye. Playgrounds, picnic sites, and campgrounds further the wide appeal. Cross-country skiing is also popular in winter.

▶ Open year-round.

http://dnr.state.il.us
(815) 667-4726

9 ▶ Delabar State Park

1½ miles north of Oquawka
Stretching along the Mississippi River, these 89 acres constitute a well-planned recreation area with two nature trails, a campground, and several inviting picnic areas. The park is named for the brothers who donated the land.

Most of the park is densely shaded by tall blackjack oaks, but birch trees and the stately shagbark hickory also cast their shadows. Within this limited space, deer as well as smaller woodland mammals are sometimes seen, and more than 50 bird species have been counted—among them are wild canaries and white-tailed hawks.

Fishermen may launch boats at the river ramp or use the two boat docks to try for channel catfish, buffalo, walleye, and crappies, as well as bass. In the Mississippi backwaters ice fishing and ice skating are winter possibilities.

▶ Open daily year-round.

http://dnr.state.il.us
(309) 374-2496

ILLINOIS

did you know ❓

Starved Rock State Park is famous for its rock formations, such as St. Peter's sandstone, formed 425 million years ago under an inland sea.

10 Nauvoo Restoration

Off Rte. 96, Nauvoo

Joseph Smith, the Mormon leader, gathered his people here after they had been driven from Missouri in 1839. Buying land that was then partly swamp, he named it Nauvoo, the Hebrew word for "beautiful place." His followers were quick to make it so, building a community with stately brick homes, a school, shops, farms, and orchards and commencing a holy temple. But in June 1844 Joseph Smith and his brother were murdered in Carthage, 24 miles away. Two years later, shortly after completion of their temple, the Mormons were again forced to move, this time under the leadership of Brigham Young.

Today many of the original buildings have been restored to illustrate what life was like for settlers in the 1840s.

Attractions include the magnificent home of Heber Kimball, a Vermont blacksmith, with its delicate hand-carved porch railings, and the elegant Federal-style house of Wilford Woodruff. A memorial to the pioneers called "Exodus to Greatness" honors those who lost their lives trekking across the continent to the Rocky Mountains.

Displays in the large visitors center include paintings of many of the key episodes in Smith's life and a model of the Nauvoo Temple, which was partially destroyed by fire.

The Nauvoo Temple was reconstructed in 2002 and now stands on the original site at the corner of Mulholland and Wells streets.

▶ Open year-round.

www.beautifulnauvoo.com
(800) 453-0022

11 Chautauqua National Wildlife Refuge

19031 E. CR-2110N, Havana

In the fall and winter enormous concentrations of migrating waterfowl settle down for rest and replenishment at this 4,500-acre refuge. A major stop along the Mississippi Flyway, the refuge comprises Lake Chautauqua and a narrow rim of timber, sandy bluffs, and marsh. More than 100,000 mallards, northern pintails, wood

10 ▶ **Nauvoo Restoration.** The Temple, shown in the distance, was built of limestone quarried in Alabama and is a faithful reproduction of the original, which was lost to a fire in 1848.

ducks, and other duck species stop here, and some 40,000 geese can also be expected to pay a call.

In all, nearly 300 kinds of birds frequent this area. Bald eagles claim it as a winter home. In the summer visiting herons can be seen along the shores as they patiently wait for unsuspecting fish to come within striking range.

In addition to birding, wildlife enthusiasts are likely to observe deer and a wide assortment of small mammals. Since the refuge includes several distinct environments, a great variety of trees,

grasses, and wildflowers grow here. Along the short interpretive trail near the refuge headquarters, you may find showy lady's slippers, prairie dandelions, and other rare plants.

Boats may be launched at the recreation area. Fishing is permitted. To their delight visitors are also permitted to gather nuts and mushrooms and pick the wild raspberries and blackberries. Chautauqua has been designated as a Globally Important Bird Area and a Western Hemisphere Shorebird Reserve Network Site.

▶ Refuge open year-round, but some areas close seasonally to protect migrating birds.

www.fws.gov/midwest/Chautauqua
(309) 535-2290

12 Lincoln's New Salem State Historic Site

15588 History Ln., Petersburg

A replica of the town where Abraham Lincoln first ran for office—after a failed first attempt

he was elected to the state assembly—is chock-full of period-style buildings and the stuff of 19th-century life. Costumed interpreters welcome visitors to authentic reproductions of New Salem's log cabins, stores, mills, workshops, and the schoolhouse where church services were held. The one original building is the Henry Onstot Cooper Shop (1830), the source of the villagers' buckets and barrels. Other buildings contain the likes of cord beds, candle molds, wheat cradles, and wool cards (combs).

Here, too, is the Berry-Lincoln Store, half owned by the young future president, and a reproduction of the Rutledge Tavern, whose door the teetotaling Abe may never have darkened.

The village is on the Sangamon River, and the 21-year-old Lincoln first visited New Salem when the flatboat on which he worked got stuck on the town's milldam. When his family moved from Indiana to Illinois in 1830, Lincoln homesteaded in the 25-family village he had discovered by accident. Today the 700-acre historic site offers canoeing and camping, along with a look back in time.

▶ Open daily except major holidays.
Admission free but donations encouraged.

www.lincolnsnewsalem.com
(217) 632-4000

11 **Chautauqua National Wildlife Refuge.** Close to 300 species of birds either nest in this sanctuary permanently or pass through on their yearly migration.

13 Elsah and the Vadalabene Bike Trail

Elsah is a town that time forgot, leaving visitors all the richer. It courted prominence in 1883, when it was thought that railroad magnate Jay Gould might build a bridge there. He did not, and by the 1890s Elsah had settled into its role as a sleepy Mississippi port.

The town, a small community with two parallel main streets, has changed little since the 1850s. As a charming result, limestone, frame, and brick buildings peer modestly through leafy branches and picket fences. The houses, privately owned, cannot be visited. No matter. A sidewalk stroll transports you back to mid-Victorian times with flower gardens, decorative porch railings and pillars, and the pervading sense that tomorrow here will be much like today.

Among the many places to see are the Bates-Mack house, with its carved gingerbread eaves, the 1850s brick Bradley house, and the Riverview House, a rambling clapboard that was once a hotel.

The town school, circa 1857, is now the civic center. The Village Hall (1887) houses the museum with displays of local history and artists. Little wonder that the entire town of Elsah has been entered on the *National Register of Historic Places.*

A restaurant on La Salle Street has two walls lined with folk art, pottery, and homemade bread. This is a good stopping point when biking the Vadalabene Bike Trail, a 20-mile macadam artery that runs from Alton to Pere Marquette State Park and offers fine views of the Mississippi.

www.elsah.org
(618) 374-1568

www.greatriverroad.com/vandalabcne.htm
(217) 782-7454 Biking information

14 Cahokia Mounds State Historic Site

30 Ramey Dr., Collinsville Rd., Collinsville

One of the first—and largest—of the hundreds of towns built by Native Americans of the remarkable Mississippian culture, Cahokia once covered nearly six square miles on the now extinct meander channel of the Mississippi River. Like St. Louis today, it was at the crossroads of America, well located for trade as well as farming. At its peak Cahokia may have had a population of 10,000 to 20,000. It was the largest prehistoric center north of Mexico, with a "central city," suburbs, and outlying farm communities.

Of the hundred or so earthen mounds constructed here between 900 and 1250, the centerpiece is Monks Mound. Covering 14 acres of land and rising in terraces 100 feet above the plain, it dominated several plazas and avenues. On its uppermost platform loomed a stockaded building about 104 by 48 feet—the "White House"—where the ruler was ensconced.

For reasons that may never be known, Cahokia eventually went into a decline, and by 1400 it was nothing but a ghost town.

Advancing civilization has destroyed many of the mounds, but 70 are still found at this UNESCO World Heritage site. Of particular interest is Mound 72. Its excavation has disclosed the grave of a chief (buried with a rich hoard of ornaments) and the remains of some 300 sacrificial victims, more than half of them young women.

Other excavations have revealed several circular arrangements of wooden posts. The most precise of these has been dubbed Woodhenge because of its similarity to England's Stonehenge; it may possibly have been a horizon calendar.

Exhibits in the museum portray life at Cahokia, including a life-size diorama. An orientation show highlights the accomplishments of the people who built the mounds. Self-guiding and seasonal guided tours are available.

▶ Open Wed.–Sun. except major holidays. Donations encouraged.

www.cahokiamounds.com
(618) 346-5160

14 **Cahokia Mounds State Historic Site.** Covering 14 acres and rising 10 feet high, Monks Mound is the largest pre-Columbian earthwork in the Americas.

15 Ingram's Pioneer Log Cabin Village

6100 Gesell Rd., Kinmundy
If you are curious about frontier life, you'll find some answers here. A meal could set you back a nickel, while the price of a night's lodging at Jacob's Well Inn was six cents (if you had to share your bed with a stranger, the cost was shared).

Jacob's Well was formerly a stagecoach stop on the old Egyptian Trail between Terre Haute, Indiana, and St. Louis, hosting such guests as Abraham Lincoln and Jesse James.

Today the building is one of 16 log structures in this replication of a pre–Civil War frontier village. The log cabins are furnished with period pieces. The rarest item is the immigrant's chest at the inn. Such chests were often used as coffins, and few of them have survived their owners.

During weekends in late September and mid-October, craftspeople demonstrate weaving, leather tooling, basket-making, and other old-time skills. The sounds of a country fiddler are often heard.

▶ Open daily mid-Apr.–mid-Nov. Admission charged.

www.iplcv.com
(618) 547-7123

---

16 Crab Orchard National Wildlife Refuge

8588 State Rte. 148, Marion
At this extensive watery refuge (43,890 acres), a stopping place for migratory waterfowl on the Mississippi Flyway, sharecropping arrangements with local farmers specify that certain amounts of milo, corn, soybeans, and clover be left in the fields for the vast flights of Canada geese and ducks alighting here.

Common loons, green herons, turkey vultures, and yellow-crowned night herons can usually be found here as well, and the refuge is a nesting site for bald eagles and many kinds of songbirds. Two observation towers on Crab Orchard Lake offer excellent views of waterfowl and occasionally of other wildlife.

Two of the three lakes have swimming beaches, boat docks, and boat-launching sites. The refuge has nine hiking trails—don't miss the Rocky Bluff Trail with its steep bluffs, waterfalls, and numerous wildflowers. The refuge also has three campgrounds with 400 campsites.

In the southern sector of the refuge, a 4,050-acre wilderness area has been established. Dramatic sandstone outcroppings and woodland creeks make this an exhilarating place for hiking, but fires and camping are not permitted.

▶ Open daily year-round.

www.fws.gov/midwest/craborchard
(618) 997-3344, Ext. 334

---

17 McCoy Memorial Library

118 Washington St., McLeansboro
An elegant mansion built in 1884 as the residence of a local merchant now serves as the home of the McCoy Memorial Library and the Hamilton County Historical Society Museum. The original furnishings attest to the first owner's taste for gracious living. Visitors may admire, among other things, a handsome fireplace of African mahogany, a French *vernis Martin* cabinet, a Steinway piano, various art objects, examples of finely crafted woodwork, and a stairway of carved walnut.

A special genealogy library occupies the second floor in rooms that still preserve their original paneling of carved walnut, chestnut, and cherry, along with some handsome pieces of furniture. Objects in the museum, including photographs of street scenes and shop interiors, trace the development of this typically Midwestern county. Also featured are Native American stone artifacts and several of the celebrated plaster groups executed by John Rogers in the 1870s. Of

17 **McCoy Memorial Library.** Displays in the museum include a lady's sidesaddle and other period items.

special interest is a huge wooden desk with hinged sides revealing mailboxes and a letter slot.

▶ Library open Mon.–Sat. except holidays; genealogy library open Mon.–Fri.

www.mcleansboro.net/community/mccoy.php
(618) 643-2125

---

18 Cache River State Natural Area

930 Sunflower Ln., Belknap
In a setting of natural wetlands, forests, and bluffs along the Cache River, this picturesque preserve provides a variety of habitats for many plants and animals not usually found this far north. The large pileated woodpecker is common, along with a host of songbirds. Occasionally river otters and bobcats are seen, as well as poisonous cottonmouth snakes that must be watched for and avoided.

Hiking trails have been marked in parts of the area's 14,489 acres, and a floating boardwalk provides visitors with an intimate view of the swamp environment. The northern edge of the preserve is bordered by steep slopes and sheer rock cliffs more than 50 feet high. From the high bluffs visitors are

16 **Crab Orchard National Wildlife Refuge.** This lake and two others in the refuge are a welcome way station for migratory waterfowl on the Mississippi Flyway.

rewarded with an inspiring view across almost five miles of the forest-swamp mosaic below.

▶ Open year-round.

http://dnr.state.il.us/lands/landmgt/
parks/r5/cachervr.htm

(618) 634-9678

19 Garden of the Gods Wilderness Area

SR-34, Herod

Illinois' most celebrated natural landmark, this truly awesome collection of rock formations was carved by ancient forces of nature. Over hundreds of millions of years, fierce wind and freezing water eroded huge slabs of limestone and sandstone to create impressive ridges and canyons. Once home to prehistoric peoples, the area now attracts photographers, bird-watchers (who hope for a peek at the resident raptors), and avid climbers.

Particularly interesting and aptly named formations include Camel Rock, Anvil Rock, Devil's Smokestack, and Old Stone Face. Made of natural flagstone and just one-quarter-mile long, the popular

19 Garden of the Gods Wilderness Area. The colors of autumn make the massive limestone and sandstone rocks in this wilderness all the more striking.

Observation Trail leads to areas immediately above the cliffs for outstanding views of the surrounding Shawnee Hills mountain range and nearly 3,300 acres of forest. Five additional trails lead into more of the expansive, unspoiled wilderness.

In fall the terrain turns into a tapestry of brilliant color. To maximize the view, both hikers and equestrians alike can follow the River-to-River Trail, which winds across the center of the wilderness in a spacious S for nearly 10 miles, stretching from Battery Rock on the Ohio River to Grand Tower on the Mississippi. Along the trek spectacular sights include Burden Falls, the tallest waterfall in Illinois; Bell Smith Springs, boasting a mighty rock bridge and the Devil's Backbone, jutting from its clear water; and Sand Cave, the largest sandstone cave in North America. From the area hikers can also opt for a detour on the famous American Discovery Trail.

For those eager to dine or sleep with the gods, picnic sites, complete with tables and fire grills, as well as ample space for camping and overnight parking are available. Motorized vehicles, however, are strictly forbidden from entering the wilderness.

▶ Open year-round.

www.fs.fed.us/r9/forests/shawnee/
recreation/

(618) 287-2201

18 Cache River State Natural Area. A winter sunset casts a rosy glow on the frozen floor of the swamp forest, an intriguing destination come rain, shine, or snow.

seasonal events

APRIL

• Birding Fest of Southernmost Illinois—Belknap *(guided tours, birding competition, demonstrations, wildlife exhibits)*

MAY

• Southwestern Illinois Spring Festival—Wamac *(barbecue competition, live music, sporting events, motorcycle show)*

JUNE

• Chicago Blues Festival—Chicago *(huge four-day music festival in downtown Chicago)*

• Route 66 Festival—Edwardsville *(car show, live entertainment, guided tours, children's activities, arts and crafts)*

• Long Grove Strawberry Festival—Long Grove *(local food, live entertainment, classic car show)*

AUGUST

• On the Waterfront—Rockford *(popular music festival, carnival, fireworks, sporting events)*

• Air and Water Show—Chicago *(navy and air force aviation show, parachute performances, live music, fireworks)*

SEPTEMBER

• Cedarhurst Craft Fair—Mt. Vernon *(crafts and artisans, demonstrations, live entertainment, children's activities)*

• Victorian Festival—Jerseyville *(re-enactments, mansion tours, historical displays and demonstrations, arts and crafts, antiques)*

• Italian Fest—Collinsville *(ethnic food, live entertainment, cooking contest, grape stomp, parade, sporting events)*

OCTOBER

• Scarecrow Festival—St. Charles *(arts and crafts, live music and entertainment, children's activities, carnival)*

DECEMBER

• Festival of Lights—East Peoria *(Christmas-light extravaganza, carnival, live theater)*

www.enjoyillinois.com

Indiana

Enhancing the gentle beauty of the land are reminders of this state's early settlement and the hard labor and creative energy of its pioneers.

Falls of the Ohio State Park. Dioramas in this fossil-rich park's interpretive center depict some of the prehistoric wildlife that once roamed the region (see page 112).

Early frontier life in Indiana is re-created at a prairie village built around a historic mansion, while a second historical park pays tribute to a heroic frontiersman whose achievements were not given their due in his lifetime. The diversity of the countryside is revealed in forests and fossil beds and at Abraham Lincoln's boyhood home.

Restorations throw light on the life of the Amish and other pioneers who farmed here. American ingenuity is recalled in gristmills, canals, and other inventions. Car fanciers will savor the collection of Cords, Auburns, and Duesenbergs, all built in Indiana and ranked among the finest automobiles ever made.

visit ➤ (**offthebeatenpathtrips.com**)

1 Amish Acres

1600 W. Market St., Nappanee

In 1874 Christian Stahly, the first Amish settler in this area, built a farmhouse here for his son. Today the 80-acre restored farm provides not only a fascinating look at the old-fashioned ways of the German-speaking Plains people, but it also gives an overview of 19th-century American farm life.

The main house, its smoke-house and other outbuildings, and the nearby Grossdaadi Haus (Grandfather House) are visited in a group tour, which originates near the farm's main gate. The 12-room white-frame farmhouse, which was greatly expanded in the 1890s, is outfitted with period furniture, cookware, woodstoves, and equipment, such as a sausage stuffer, spinning wheel, and rocker-action churn. After the tour, visitors can take a hayride and are free to roam the grounds and look at the other buildings, many of which were brought here from town and from other farms.

The sweet smell of hay fills a large barn containing threshing equipment and a hay wagon. Stables and milking stalls adjoin a barnyard and pasture. A horse-drawn school bus and an Amish church-bench wagon are among the old carriages in the wagon shed.

Other buildings include a smithy, an icehouse, a sawmill, a

1 Amish Acres. Amish quilts air out on a split-rail fence at this restored farm. The Amish community in northern Indiana is the third largest in the United States.

windmill, and a small 1870s town house. The farm has a sorghum press, a mint still where aromatic oil was distilled from mint plants, and a shop where brooms are still made from broom corn. The kitchen garden includes herbs and flowers, while mulberries and other old-time favorite fruit trees grow in the orchard. The Acres are least crowded in spring and fall.

▶ Open daily May–Nov.; Fri.–Sun. in Mar.; Tues.–Sat. in Apr.; Wed.–Sun. in Dec. Admission charged.

www.amishacres.com
(800) 800-4942; (574) 773-4188

2 ⟩ Bonneyville Mill

53373 CR-131, Bristol

In 1837 Edward Bonney, a local tavern keeper and entrepreneur, constructed a mill on the wooded shores of Little Elkhart River. Now known as Bonneyville Mill, it is the oldest continuously operating gristmill with a horizontal water-wheel in the state of Indiana, and as it probably has from the beginning, it produces both flour and meal. In 1976 the mill was listed on the *National Register of Historic Places.*

Rather than standing upright, the waterwheel here is installed lying on its side and is enclosed in a steel case submerged in about seven feet of water. When the 12 doors on the sides of the case are opened, water flows through and drains out the bottom. The whirlpool that is created spins the wheel, which then turns the gears that drive the mill. Visitors enter the mill through the basement, where the gear system is visible, along with a display of old milling equipment.

The main floor contains the milling area with two sets of grind-stones. On this floor the flour that is produced—corn, wheat, rye, and buckwheat—is for sale.

On the second floor visitors can see a buckwheat flour sifter used to separate the flour from the hulls after it is ground. The third floor houses a grain cleaner composed of a series of screens for sifting, a fan for winnowing the grain before it is milled, as well as the gears and heavy equipment that operate the mill's elevator.

▶ Open daily May–Oct.

www.elkhartcountyparks.org
(574) 535-6458

3 ⟩ Chain O' Lakes State Park

2355 E. 75 S, Albion

The predominant feature in this 2,700-acre park is a series of 11 small lakes, all but three of which are strung together by natural channels of water.

The lakes, called kettle lakes, were formed at the end of the last Ice Age. The weight of enormous blocks of ice that were left in the ground by a retreating glacier created the basins for the lakes. The subsequent meltwater filled the lakes and thereby carved the connecting channels.

Not surprisingly, the principal activities here are swimming, fishing, and boating. Swimming is permitted only in summer, and the only motorized crafts allowed on the lakes are low-powered electric troll boats.

Rowboats and canoes can be rented by the day, and paddleboats can be rented by the hour. Anglers try for bluegills and bass. Wintertime activities include ice fishing, skating on the lakes, sledding, and cross-country skiing. The park also has some interesting trails circling the lakes and meandering through woodlands and meadows. In addition to more than 400 campsites, there is a small village of housekeeping cottages.

▶ Open year-round; facilities turned off Nov.–Mar. Admission charged.

www.in.gov/dnr/parklake/11086.htm
(260) 636-2654

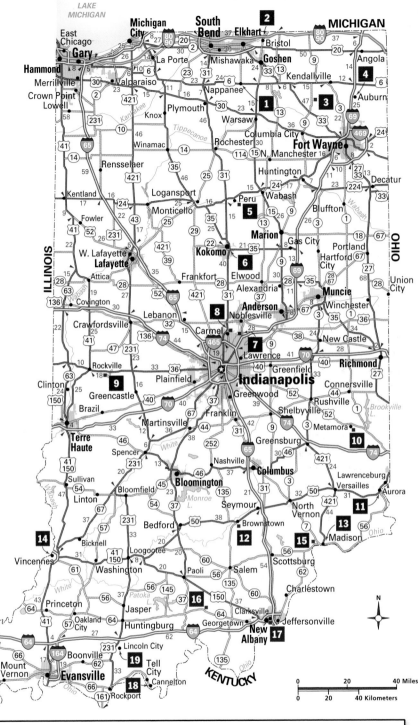

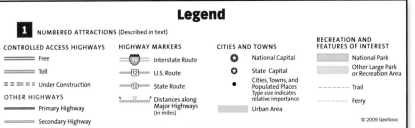

Legend

1 NUMBERED ATTRACTIONS (Described in text)

CONTROLLED ACCESS HIGHWAYS
- Free
- Toll
- Under Construction

OTHER HIGHWAYS
- Primary Highway
- Secondary Highway

HIGHWAY MARKERS
- **10** Interstate Route
- (12) U.S. Route
- (12) State Route
- 12 Distances along Major Highways (in miles)

CITIES AND TOWNS
- ✪ National Capital
- ⊛ State Capital
- • Cities, Towns, and Populated Places Type size indicates relative importance
- Urban Area

RECREATION AND FEATURES OF INTEREST
- National Park
- Other Large Park or Recreation Area
- Trail
- Ferry

© 2009 GeoNova

4 Auburn Cord Duesenberg Automobile Museum

1600 S. Wayne St., Auburn

Named for the three legendary marques produced by the Auburn Automobile Company, this museum is both a showcase for automobiles and a celebration of the era between World War I and World War II, when the luxury car was in its hey-

4 **Auburn Cord Duesenberg Automobile Museum.** A 1935 Auburn 851 Speedster is one of the roadsters on display in the Gordon Buehrig Gallery of Design, named for a renowned Auburn designer. Auburns were manufactured from 1903 to 1936.

day. The building, now a National Historic Landmark, was the Auburn Automobile Company's headquarters, a spacious structure that has been restored to its 1930 art-deco splendor. The floor is geometrically patterned in marble, and the high ceiling friezes are enriched with complementary designs.

The ground-floor exhibit contains some of the best engineered and most luxuriously appointed cars ever built, including a 265-horsepower 1932 Duesenberg coupe that oil tycoon J. Paul Getty paid $15,000 for, and a stunning 1935 Auburn Boattail Speedster that sold for $2,245. (Today it's valued at $150,000.)

The most striking automobiles here are Auburns, Cords, and Duesenbergs from the 1920s and 1930s. But other makes, such as Stutz, Rolls-Royce, and Packard, are also represented, as well as a 1952 Crosley once owned by architect Frank Lloyd Wright.

The cars exhibited on the second floor provide an overview of automotive history. Thematic galleries are devoted to early Auburns (1903–1924); rare cars built in the city of Auburn (McIntyre, Kiblinger, Zimmerman); uncommon makes built in Indiana (Lexington, Cole, Marmon); and cars of special interest, such as a 1933 Checker taxicab, a 1936 Auburn hearse, and pioneer-era electric cars.

▶ Open daily year-round except major holidays. Admission charged.

www.acdmuseum.org
(260) 925-1444

5 International Circus Hall of Fame & Museum

3076 E. Circus Ln., Peru

Peru, also known as Circus City, is the former winter home of America's three largest traveling circuses. There is enough circus memorabilia here to keep you happy for hours, along with some fascinating history. One exhibit, for example, explains how a red-coat from the Revolutionary War got credit for launching the circus in America after the war ended: After being given a horse in lieu of retirement pay, he taught the steed to prance in a circle and charged people money to watch it.

Peru's Circus City Festival Inc., which also runs a museum, sponsors a professional circus that wows crowds under the Big Top every July. Another circus, the "greatest amateur show on earth," also takes place in July, featuring young people ages 7 to 21.

▶ Open Mon.–Fri. May–Oct. and weekends in July. Admission charged.

www.circushof.com
(800) 771-0241

6 Elwood Haynes Museum

1915 S. Webster St., Kokomo

Kokomo prides itself on being the City of Firsts, and the most outstanding of those firsts were the inventions of Elwood Haynes. In 1894 Haynes tested the prototype for a horseless carriage with an engine fueled by gasoline, a substance then considered of little commercial value. Four years later he put it into production, and if it was not America's first commercially successful automobile, as Haynes advocates claim, it was certainly one of the earliest. Haynes also developed several

metal alloys, most notably tungsten stainless steel and stellite, an extra-hard blend of chromium, cobalt, and tungsten.

The museum, which is in Haynes's home, has four of his cars—the 1905 Haynes Model L, the Haynes roadster, a touring car from the early 1920s, and a 1916 Haynes. It also contains photographs and documents relating to Haynes's life and inventions.

Upstairs local manufacturers have mounted exhibits of historic and contemporary products made in Kokomo. Haynes's alloys are well represented. Products using them include not just rollers, bearings, and valves but also turbine blades, machine-gun barrels, and surgical instruments.

▶ Open Tues.–Sun. except holidays.

www.visitkokomo.org/attractions.htm
(765) 456-7500

7 Conner Prairie

13400 Allisonville Rd., Fishers

William Conner settled in this area in 1800. He lived as a trader and then as a farmer and became prominent in state politics. His Federal-style mansion of mellow redbrick, built in 1823, still stands, having been restored, and an entire village duplicating a typical prairie settlement of the 1830s is also on the premises.

The village has more than five historic areas with 45 buildings. Included among them are an inn, a schoolhouse, a loom house, and a barn with bins of sweet-smelling grain. The houses include those of a doctor and a weaver, and homes and shops for a carpenter, a blacksmith, a potter, and a storekeeper. The furnishings throughout include period pieces or accurate reproductions.

7 ▶ **Conner Prairie.** Visiting children keep pace with a shepherd at the re-created village. In the Animal Encounters area kids can pet or hold lambs and other baby animals.

The buildings also have occupants in period attire, and they take their roles to heart. The carpenter, for example, hews wood and constructs items using authentic tools and materials. The doctor discourses on a then popular medical notion of the four cardinal humors that affect one's health. And a talkative widower regales visitors with tales about his exploits as riverboatman and soldier.

The Conner house itself has been furnished simply but elegantly in the manner of the period. There are built-in cupboards and bookcases in the dining and drawing rooms; in the kitchen is a beehive oven that held 15 loaves of bread; on the stairs are rag-strip loomed carpets; and the main bedroom includes a four-poster bed with an 1858 patchwork quilt.

For youngsters and the young at heart, there is also the Discovery Station. Here visitors can build a log cabin, play with toy trains, dress up in period costumes, or put on a puppet show, all in the spirit of prairie life.

▶ Hours change seasonally. Admission charged.

www.connerprairie.org
(800) 966-1836; (317) 776-6006

---

8 ▶ **The Museum of Miniature Houses and Other Collections**
111 E. Main St., Carmel
Don't be surprised if you find yourself humming "It's a Small World" at this museum, where the actual, the historical, and the fantastic are replicated on a scale of 1 inch to 1 foot.

When you peer at, inside, and around a classic San Francisco house—complete with handsome contemporary furniture and a thriving backyard garden—you may not hear the cable cars clanging, but you'll be transported from Carmel, Indiana, to the City by the Bay. And yes, a

person is tending to scale-model flowers in the garden. Elsewhere in the museum a breadbox houses a fully equipped vintage kitchen: sink, table and chair, utensils, and even a toddler on the floor.

Special exhibitions are held each season of the year, introducing visitors to painstakingly crafted works like those of famous miniaturist Robert Olszewski—pieces showing how some miniatures can rise to the level of fine art.

▶ Open Wed.–Sun. except major holidays. Admission charged.

www.museumofminiatures.org
(317) 575-9466

---

9 ▶ **Raccoon State Recreation Area**
160 S. Raccoon Pkwy., Rockville
Located in the heart of Parke County, Cecil M. Harden Lake, often referred to as Raccoon Lake, was created by a dam on Big Raccoon Creek, a branch of the Wabash River. It provides an area for water sports, as well as habitats for fish and wildlife.

Parke County, once the home of the Delaware, Shawnee, and Miami tribes, is known for its wealth of sugar maples, the source of a sweetener that was enjoyed by both the American Indians and the pioneers who followed them. Maple sugaring is carried on today at several local sugar camps in Parke County.

The county is also known as the Covered Bridge Capital of America. Thirty-one such structures, built between 1856 and 1921, still remain. Two of them span Big Raccoon Creek.

The lake's sandy beach is surrounded by grassy bluffs set with picnic tables. The roped-off swimming area has a bathhouse. From the beach a road leads past several more picnic grounds to a campground. And just beyond this area visitors will find a boat-launching ramp and a small marina for fishermen.

▶ Open year-round; water provided summer only. Admission charged.

www.in.gov/dnr/parklake/6731.htm
(765) 344-1412

8 ▶ **The Museum of Miniature Houses.** The exterior of a miniature house (inset) is impressive enough, but the painstakingly crafted dishes and cooking equipment in the kitchen of another miniature (a Georgian colonial) is nothing less than amazing.

10 Whitewater Canal Historic Site

19083 Clayborn St., Metamora
So popular was the Whitewater Valley as a thoroughfare for pioneers making their way from Ohio to Indiana that by 1830 it was the most heavily populated area in the state. In 1836, seeking a means of shipping produce from the valley to distant markets, the Indiana legislature voted to build a 76-mile canal from Lawrenceburg to Hagerstown.

By 1847 the four-foot-deep Whitewater Canal was completed. It was fed by the west fork of the Whitewater River, and soon several mills, using tub wheels powered by water diverted through flumes, sprang up along its banks. The cost of maintenance and competition from the expanding railroad system led to its demise after less than 15 years of service.

Fourteen miles of the canal have now been restored as the Whitewater Canal State Memorial, a project that includes the restoration of the Metamora Grist Mill. Built in the 1800s on the bank of the canal, this two-story redbrick mill, with a porch across the front and a museum on the second floor, has a waterwheel set in the spillway of one of the canal's locks.

Today the mill grinds white cornmeal and grits, both for sale here. On the lower level one can see the elaborate system of slow-turning wheels and belts that power the grinding stones and sifters. A half mile away is the restored wooden Duck Creek Aqueduct, which was built in 1848 to carry the canal 16 feet above the small stream. The *Ben Franklin,* a barge pulled by two draft horses, offers half-hour canal rides that include crossing the aqueduct.

Just below the mill a bridge crosses the canal to a picnic area with shade trees and a small bandstand. A stroll around the town of Metamora reveals some handsome old buildings.

▶ Gristmill open Wed.–Sun. Apr.–Nov.; Canal boat open Wed.–Sun. May–Oct. Admission charged for boat rides.

www.in.gov/ism
(765) 647-6512

11 Hillforest Victorian House Museum

213 Fifth St., Aurora
The Victorian mansion known as Hillforest was named Forest Hill by its builder, Thomas Gaff, a Scotsman who reached America at the age of three. Gaff grew up in the East, and in 1837, when that area was experiencing an economic decline, he and his brothers journeyed west, finally settling in Aurora in the 1840s. There they found water that was especially well suited to the production of whiskey and began to manufacture their own brand, Thistle Dew. Over time the Gaffs owned other businesses, including a fleet of steamboats that transported their products.

Thomas Gaff set his home, where he lived with his family from 1855–1891, into a hill overlooking the Ohio River. Hillforest's architectural design, greatly influenced by the riverboat industry of

 Historic Madison. The streets of this port are chockablock with impressive houses born of the wealth generated by transportation and commerce. The Lanier Mansion (above), which dates from 1844, was the home of James Franklin Doughty Lanier, a successful banker who had a stake in real estate and the railroads.

the 1850s, features decorative balconies, symmetrical front facades, and a round belvedere reminiscent of a riverboat pilothouse. The interior central hall has a flying staircase, with mahogany banisters and tiger maple spindles, similar to those found in majestic riverboats of the time.

The mansion also reflects the influence of Italian Renaissance architecture so popular during that era. The main doorway, paneled with Venetian glass, opens onto an entrance hall with grain-painted Circassian walnut woodwork and parquet flooring in the Greek key design. The walls are decorated with *trompe l'oeil* painting of wood paneling and stylized lotus blossoms. Italian molds were used for the decorative plasterwork.

Arched walk-through windows open onto the porches, and a doorway leads from a stairway to the pilothouse, the gentlemen's retreat.

Now restored, the mansion, whose name was changed by a subsequent owner, is filled with handsome antiques—including a collection of rare blue milk glass, Meissen china, bohemian glass candleholders, and a Pennsylvania Dutch weight-driven clock. Hillforest became a National Historic Landmark in 1990.

▶ Open Tues.–Sun. Apr.–Dec. Admission charged.

www.hillforest.org
(812) 926-0087

12 Jackson-Washington State Forest

1278 E. State Rd. 250, Brownstown
One of the most spectacular features of this primitive forest area is Skyline Drive, a five-mile auto loop running along the crest of a

wooded ridge. Observation areas just off the road offer vistas of the surrounding woodlands and fertile plain, checkered with farm fields and the roofs of silos and barns. Visitors are encouraged to stop at Skyline Shelter for a picnic or climb to the top of the firetower, both along Skyline Drive.

In addition, the forest is a key access point to the 60-mile Knobstone Trail for backpackers. There are also ten hiking trails of varying difficulty within the forest's boundaries, including an 8-mile loop. Two trails are available for horseback riding, although horses cannot be rented. Fishing and boat-launching facilities are provided on Knob Lake and Spurgeon Hollow Lake, where likely catches include catfish and bass. Swimming is available at nearby Starve Hollow State Recreation Area. Picnic areas and campgrounds make this a great place for travelers.

▶ Open year-round.

www.in.gov/dnr/forestry
(812) 358-2160

13 Historic Madison

Located on the Ohio River
Hailed as the most beautiful small town in the Midwest, Madison is known for its historic 19th-century architecture, antiques, specialty shops, distinctive restaurants, and wineries. In the mid-1800s this charming river port was a thriving center of transportation, commerce, and culture. Much of what was unique about Madison then remains the same. Boats and barges still pass on the Ohio River. Many of the grand homes and stately buildings remain in mint condition and active use.

In addition to admiring and

14 **George Rogers Clark National Historical Park.** The park commemorates Clark's history-changing capture of Fort Sackville in Vincennes, Indiana's oldest city.

touring the historic houses, visitors can catch a demonstration in traditional saddle-making at the Ben Schroeder Saddletree Factory, which opened for business in 1878; take a detour through the Madison Railroad Station, constructed in 1895; or get a glimpse of the life and work of a frontier physician at Dr. William Hutchings's office, preserved precisely as he operated it until his death in 1903.

For outdoor enthusiasts the scenic Riverfront Park sports a gazebo, plenty of benches, and a lighted brick walkway. At its docks visitors can launch their own boat. Nearby, landlubbers can head down the Heritage Trail, a paved pathway with ample space for strolling, biking, and skating.

▶ Open year-round.

www.visitmadison.org
(812) 265-2956; (800) 599-2956

14 George Rogers Clark National Historical Park

401 S. 2nd St., Vincennes
The park commemorates a soldier who in his lifetime was one of our most neglected heroes. In the early 1770s a young Virginian moved to

the Kentucky wilderness. A born leader, he soon turned a small group of frontiersmen into a remarkably effective group of soldiers. On February 5, 1779, George Rogers Clark and some 170 of his troops began crossing 157 miles of cold and flooded terrain to launch a surprise attack on the British contingent at Fort Sackville. He had previously neutralized the British strongholds at Kaskaskia and Cahokia without firing a shot.

Clark's victories broke England's hold on the Old Northwest and helped secure it for the United States. The area now includes Ohio, Indiana, Illinois, Michigan, Wisconsin, and parts of Minnesota. This courageous leader, however, spent most of his later life plagued by political rivals, falsely accused of malfeasance, and on the verge of poverty. His great contributions to our nationhood were not recognized until shortly before his death in 1818.

Today Clark is honored by an imposing granite memorial built in the classical Greek style, with 16 massive columns and a skylight in the domed roof. In its limestone and marble interior are a bronze statue of Clark and seven murals

depicting key episodes in his campaign. The memorial is the centerpiece of a small, graceful park built on the site of Fort Sackville, with formal lawns, steps, and a walk overlooking the Wabash River.

Other historic places in Vincennes include the Basilica of St. Francis Xavier, the Indiana Territory Capitol, and Grouseland—the home of William Henry Harrison, the Indiana Territory's first governor and the ninth president of the United States. Nearby, a prehistoric Native American mound recalls the area's most ancient civilization. Note: At time of publication, the memorial was closed for renovation. The park and visitors center remain open. Please check for current information.

▶ Open daily year-round. Closed major holidays. Admission charged.

www.nps.gov/gero
(812) 882-1776—Ext. 210

14 **George Rogers Clark National Historical Park.** Hermon Atkins MacNeil scuplted the classical statue of Clark.

15 Clifty Falls State Park

2221 Clifty Dr., Madison
The highlight of this varied woodland park is a two-mile-long gorge, cut by Clifty Creek through layers of shale and limestone 450 million years old—some of the oldest exposed bedrock in the state.

Clifty Falls, located at the upper end of the gorge, cascades over a series of wide, shallow steps of rock jutting from the cliff before tumbling more than 70 feet into the pool below. Even in midsummer, when the flow of water is diminished, the falls are a dramatic sight. The strata of the cliff disappear into the woods on the other side of the falls like a bony shelf with a cargo of bonsai.

Ten hiking trails of varying lengths and difficulty run along the gorge and through surrounding woodlands. Other recreational facilities include a swimming pool, picnic areas, tennis courts, and a nature center, containing exhibits of fossils from the gorge and a bird-watching room where a one-way window enables onlookers to view the winged visitors, leaving them undisturbed. An observation tower, just a short walk from the nature center, offers a panoramic view of the Ohio River half a mile to the south.

▶ Open year-round. Admission charged.

www.in.gov/dnr/parklake/6719.htm
(812) 273-8885

16 Marengo Cave

400 E. State Rd. 64, Marengo
A spelunker's garden of delights greets visitors to the cave at Marengo, where nature shows off its artistry in the form of intricate crystal formations—stalactites and stalagmites—that grow from the ceiling and floor. The formations grew over a million years.

did you know

Four major waterfalls, ranging in height from 60 to 82 feet, give Clifty Falls State Park a rugged grandeur reminiscent of Alpine regions.

16 **Marengo Cave.** Thanks to its excellent acoustics, the huge "naturally air-conditioned" room known as the Music Hall is a popular venue for concerts and dances.

17 **Falls of the Ohio State Park.** The fossil beds of what was once an ocean yield fossils of sea plants and animals that lived hundreds of millions of years ago.

Rainwater dissolved limestone rocks as it seeped into the ground, and as it evaporated, it left behind minuscule mineral deposits that grew and grew and grew.

Marengo reaches as deep as 350 feet below ground, and the temperature in the cave stays a constant 52°F. The cave itself is some 4.6 miles long, while the park above covers 122 scenic acres of hills and valleys.

▶ Open daily year-round except Thanksgiving and Christmas. Admission charged.

www.marengocave.com
(888) 702-2837

17 Falls of the Ohio State Park

201 W. Riverside Dr., Clarksville
Today no one visits Indiana for its ocean, yet 220 acres of fossilized coral provide living (or once living) proof that an ocean, indeed, flourished in the state—some 200 million years before dinosaurs existed. At this scenic site on the banks of the Ohio River, visitors can marvel over the prehistoric evidence.

Scientists and curious explorers have flocked here since the 1790s. Experts date its active ocean life back to the Devonian Period, between 400 and 360 million years ago. More than 600 species of plants and animals once lived on its coral reefs—two-thirds of them "type" specimens, recorded here for the first time anywhere in the world. And five distinct fossil layers lie exposed at the park. In total the site has the world's largest known exposure of Devonian fossils.

From Aug.–Oct., when the river is at its lowest level, visitors can find the best accessibility to the fossil beds. While fossil collecting is strictly prohibited, the park staff encourages visitors to discover fossils galore from the primeval sea bottom.

Any time of year, visitors can learn all about the ancient history and wonders of the park at its state-of-the-art 16,000-square-foot interpretive center.

In the lobby a re-creation of the prehistoric Indiana island dazzles with a huge mammoth and a giant 18-foot-long Devonian fish floating overhead. Beyond the entrance 78 exhibits take visitors back through time. The center's spacious, enclosed observation room, graced with 18-foot-tall windows, beckons with breathtaking views of the fossils and water. A wildlife viewing area lets kids of all ages not only see songbirds feeding or raccoons bathing but also listen in on their tunes and chatter.

Beyond its fossils the park offers hiking trails, grassy spots for picnicking, a boat launch ramp, and excellent opportunities for birdwatching and fishing. Biologists have recorded 280 species of birds flying through the park, including the occasional bald eagle.

As its name suggests, the park also features the falls—the Ohio River's famous cascading rapids, which cause the river to drop 26 feet in elevation over a 2½-mile stretch.

▶ Open daily year-round. Admission charged.

www.fallsoftheohio.org
(812) 280-9970

18 Cannelton Locks and Dam
Rte. 66, Cannelton
Congress authorized the Corps of Engineers to start improving the navigability of the lower Ohio River in 1824. Since then improvements have constantly been made, and today shipping moves easily along this great waterway by virtue of a series of dams and locks along its length. Each dam backs up the water behind it, creating a long navigable "lake" that reaches upstream to the next dam and lock.

The whole structure cost nearly $100 million to build in the 1960s, and ample provisions have been made for the taxpayer to get a good view of the operation from a lockside walkway and an observation tower. From the tower the viewer sees not just the locks in operation but also the sandy banks on the Kentucky side of the river and the boiling water at the foot of

the dam's massive gates. It is especially fascinating to watch a tug push a colorful thousand-foot-long convoy of barges through the main lock chamber. The whole process takes about a half hour.

▶ Observation deck open daily.

www.perrycountyindiana.org/attractions/
cannelton locks.cfm
(812) 547-2962

19 ▶ **Lincoln Boyhood National Memorial.** Relics of pioneer life are on view in the visitors center, and a reconstruction of the Lincoln family cabin stands outside.

19 Lincoln Boyhood National Memorial
Rte. 162, Lincoln City
Thomas Lincoln, the president's father, had moved three times in Kentucky because of land-claim disputes. When he took his family across the Ohio River into Indiana in December 1816, he was searching for a more permanent homestead site. He found it near Little Pigeon Creek on a quarter section (160 acres) of government-surveyed land, a plot he had laid claim to earlier. Here the family finally settled down and remained for 14 years.

Today the site of the Lincoln cabin is marked by bronze castings of sill logs and a stone hearth. Just beyond this, behind a split-rail

fence, is a cabin reconstruction. It contains not only the homely and convincing clutter of a log table and benches but also a trundle bed, spinning wheels, a fireplace with iron pots, a broom, and bunches of dried herbs. In a shed behind the cabin, there is a smokehouse for preserving meat.

A few horses, sheep, and chickens complete the pleasant pioneer farm scene. Interpreters in period dress are at hand to answer one's questions.

Five bas-relief panels depicting scenes from Abraham Lincoln's life decorate the visitors center, an impressive white building that contains the Abraham Lincoln and the Nancy Hanks Lincoln halls, which are used for meetings, lectures, and conferences, and a small museum of pioneer life. A walkway leads from the center to the small hill where the president's mother is buried.

▶ Open daily year-round.

www.nps.gov/libo
(812) 937-4541

seasonal events

MAY
• Spirit of Vincennes Rendezvous—Vincennes *(battle re-enactment, live music, grand ball, food, children's activities)*

JUNE
• Vintage Indiana—Indianapolis *(wine tastings, local food, live music, arts and crafts)*
• Fishers Freedom Festival—Fishers *(parade, live music, fireworks, arts and crafts, sports events, food)*
• Indiana University Summer Music Festival—Bloomington *(orchestra, opera, chamber, jazz)*

JULY
• Indiana Microbrewer's Festival—Indianapolis *(beer tasting, live music, food, games and activities)*

AUGUST
• Little Italy Festival—Clinton *(parade, carnival rides, live entertainment, regional food, children's activities)*

SEPTEMBER
• Indiana Wizard of Oz Festival—Valparaiso *(costume contests, arts and crafts, children's events)*
• Johnny Appleseed Festival—Fort Wayne *(live entertainment, re-enactments, children's activities, regional food, arts and crafts)*

OCTOBER
• Parke County Covered Bridge Festival—Rockville *(guided tours, shopping, regional food, antiques, live entertainment)*
• Southern Indiana FiberArts Festival—Corydon *(crafts, demonstrations, workshops, vendors, activities, live music)*

NOVEMBER
• Contemporary Music Festival—Terre Haute *(orchestral performances, chamber music, educational activities)*

DECEMBER
• Dickens of a Christmas—Lafayette *("A Christmas Carol" performances, carolers, vendors, crafts, carriage rides)*

www.visitindiana.com

Iowa

Natural wonders, inviting historic sites, and scenic places provide another perspective on the state where the tall corn grows.

Seed Savers Exchange/Heritage Farm. A cornucopia of open-pollinated (non-hybrid) gourd vegetables attests to the mission of this nonprofit organization (below right).

Beyond Iowa's cornfields and tallgrass prairie are bluffs and caves and a rich history that runs from burial mounds dating from 500 B.C. to the pioneer settlements of the 1800s. The Corn State is also full of surprises: a windmill transported from Denmark, a craftsman who has revived 19th-century furniture-making methods, a Frank Lloyd Wright house where even the furnishings were designed by the iconic architect—plus a serving of Midwestern whimsy at an old-time soda fountain and a marvelous museum of matchstick miniatures.

visit ➤ **offthebeatenpathtrips.com**

1 Ice Cream Capital of the World Visitors Center

Hwy. 75, Exit 118, Le Mars
If you are near Le Mars, the Ice Cream Capital of the World according to the Iowa State Legislature, head for the Wells' Dairy, maker of Blue Bunny Ice Cream. The Wells family has been churning ice cream and other frozen dairy products since 1913 when the founder, Fred Wells, started out with just a horse, a delivery wagon, some cans and jars—and a steady supply of milk from a local farmer.

In the family-friendly museum you can view the history of the dairy, watch a simulated factory-production line, and then stop at the old-fashioned ice-cream parlor, complete with vintage equipment, décor, and comfortable booths. Try a malt shake or smoothie, or go for the ultimate challenge: the six-scoop, multi-topped Goliath. Early morning visitors can enjoy cinnamon rolls topped with melted-ice-cream icing.

Little tykes can work off extra calories in an indoor playground or the Play Scoop history room.

▶ Open daily May–Sept.; Tues.–Sat. Oct.–Apr. Call for holiday hours. Admission charged.

www.wellsdairy.com
(712) 546-4090; (800) 942-3800 Ext. 4090

1 ➤ **Ice Cream Capital of the World Visitors Center.** A giant sundae greets travelers to the town deemed the world's ice cream capital by the Iowa legislature.

2 Seed Savers Exchange/Heritage Farm

3074 Winn Rd., Decorah
Are you looking for red-, ochre-, and yellow-colored ears of corn for a harvest centerpiece? Would you like to grow everlasting sweet peas like the ones in your grandmother's garden?

Now you can hunt down hundreds of heirloom vegetables, herbs, fruit trees, and flowers at the Heritage Farm or obtain them from the online store. Headquarters of the Seed Savers Exchange, the 890-acre farm is a living museum where professional gardeners grow thousands of heirloom varieties.

Thanks to their efforts and those of thousands of gardeners who save and trade precious seeds, many great heirloom plants and trees are being saved from extinction. The farm also fosters organic growing methods.

The Lillian Goldman Visitors Center includes a gift shop and a garden center. It offers seeds, garden furniture, and gardening tools, as well as unique and whimsical items such as hot chili-pepper characters cavorting on flour-sack towels.

▶ Open daily Apr.–Dec. Admission charged.

www.seedsavers.org
(563) 382-5990

3 Montauk Historic Site

26223 Harding Rd., Clermont

It is odd to find a house in Iowa named for a lighthouse far away on New York's Long Island. But William Larrabee was an Easterner for whom Montauk Lighthouse was a symbol of safety, steering ships through perilous waters, and he felt that his home should serve the same function for his family. Larrabee, a wealthy miller and landowner who later became Iowa's governor, built this fine Italianate home in 1874.

The Larrabees, with their four daughters and three sons, were the only people ever to live in the house, and when daughter Anna died in 1965 at age 96, the house and everything in it was left to the state. All the furnishings, silver, china, toys, musical instruments, books, paintings, statuettes, photographs, and bric-a-brac belonged to the Larrabees.

Seldom does a house-museum so accurately reveal the taste and activities of one specific household. In any of the nine rooms on display, one almost expects a family member to come walking in.

The outbuildings on the 80-acre estate include a laundry, creamery, well house, windmill, and workshop.

▶ Open daily Memorial Day weekend–Oct.; other times by arrangement for group tours.

www.iowahistory.org/sites
(563) 423-7173

4 Effigy Mounds National Monument

3 miles north of Marquette on Hwy. 76

Dart points found locally attest to the presence of a primitive hunting people that inhabited these lands as far back as 12,000 years ago. But the fascination with this 2,526-acre national monument dates from more recent times.

Found here are 195 mounds of several types—linear, compound, conical, and effigy—and from several periods. The mounds shed light on a succession of cultures in this area from around 500 B.C. to almost historic times. The oldest (which include both linear and conical mounds) were created by Native Americans of the Red Ocher culture, so called because they put their burials on a floor first sprinkled with red ochre (iron-ore dust).

Excavations of other mounds have revealed an assortment of elaborate grave goods fashioned from seashells, obsidian, and other unexpected materials obtained by far-reaching trade. The artifacts show the influence of the Hopewell culture, which was centered in Ohio around 100 B.C. to about A.D. 400.

The most intriguing formations to see, however, are the 33 effigy mounds in the shapes of bears and birds in flight which had been built by Native Americans who farmed this land until about 1250. The Great Bear Mound is especially impressive, being 137 feet long, 70 feet wide from shoulder to foreleg, and more than 3 feet high.

A network of hiking trails connects the mound sites with scenic river overlooks. A brief orientation film is shown in the visitors center, where displays illustrate mound-building techniques. Ranger-guided tours of the mounds leave the visitors center on a regular schedule each day.

▶ Open daily year-round.

www.nps.gov/efmo
(563) 873-3491

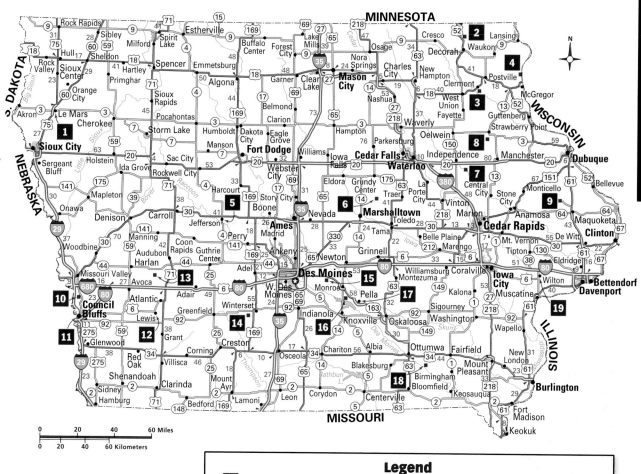

Legend

1 NUMBERED ATTRACTIONS (Described in text)

CONTROLLED ACCESS HIGHWAYS
— Free
— Toll
===== Under Construction

OTHER HIGHWAYS
— Primary Highway
— Secondary Highway

HIGHWAY MARKERS
10 Interstate Route
12 U.S. Route
12 State Route
12 Distances along Major Highways (in miles)

CITIES AND TOWNS
★ National Capital
★ State Capital
• Cities, Towns, and Populated Places Type size indicates relative importance
Urban Area

RECREATION AND FEATURES OF INTEREST
National Park
Other Large Park or Recreation Area
--- Trail
--- Ferry

© 2009 GeoNova

IOWA

5 ▶ **RVP~1875.** Visitors flock to see master craftsman Robby Pedersen create furniture using tools and techniques from centuries past.

5 ▶ RVP ~ 1875

115 S. Wilson Ave., Jefferson

A wide-planked harvest table with matching sturdy benches, a panel bed, a chimney cupboard—these and other pieces of furniture reminiscent of yesteryear are yours to buy—or build yourself—in this unique furniture shop.

For more than 15 years, master furniture maker Robby Pedersen has been crafting furniture pieces in 1800s style using only the types of tools, woodworking techniques, and natural-product finishes that were available at that time.

Come browse the selection of timeless treasures, such as immigrants' trunks, sideboards, trestle tables, hutches, and writing desks, which are among the many items in his signature line. Or sign up for beginning or advanced woodworking classes and learn how to use handheld wood-shaving planes, a hand-cranked rip saw, and a foot-powered lathe.

▶ Open year-round Tues.-Sat. or by appointment.

www.rvp1875.com
(515) 975-3083

6 ▶ Matchstick Marvels

319 Second St., Gladbrook

For over 30 years artist Patrick Acton has constructed scale models of world-famous buildings, historic ships and aircrafts, and even a very lifelike gun-slinging cowboy. Using more than 3 million matchsticks, he glued over 60 models together, made entirely with matchsticks. The Matchstick Marvels Museum in the Gladbrook City Centre displays some of his world-renowned collection. Compare his Capitol Building to the real one in Washington!

For fantasy lovers of all ages, there is a fantastic model that envisions a trip to Middle Earth and its Great White City, Minas Tirith, that spreads over Pelennor Fields in the Land of Gondor. This is Acton's re-creation of scenes from J. R. R. Tolkien's City of Kings in the *Lord of the Rings* trilogy.

▶ Open daily Apr.-Nov. and by appointment. Closed national holidays. Admission charged.

www.matchstickmarvels.com/
matchstickmain.html
(641) 473-2410; (888) 473-3456

7 ▶ Cedar Rock

2611 Quasqueton Diagonal Blvd., Doris

Iowa businessman Lowell Walter and his wife, Agnes, commissioned Frank Lloyd Wright to build their dream home on a limestone bluff overlooking the Wapsipinicon River.

The Walters were ardent admirers of Wright's uncluttered architectural designs, and they gave him free rein to design the building—plus all the furniture, carpets, draperies, and even the accessories. When completed in 1950, he "signed" Cedar Rock with one of his red signature tiles.

One story high and measuring 150 feet in length, Cedar Rock was built "green" and blends in with its natural surroundings. The roof and floors are concrete; the walls are brick, glass, and natural walnut. Daylight floods the interior. Spectacular floor-to-ceiling windows enclose the Garden Room on three sides and frame a breathtaking view of the river and wooded valley below.

The home is now open to the public in Cedar Rock State Park,

7 ▶ **Cedar Rock.** The eminent architect Frank Lloyd Wright designed this one-story private house and all of its furnishings. Shown here is the light-flooded Garden Room.

a gift of the Walter family to the Iowa State Conservation Commission, along with a trust fund to assure its preservation.

▶ Open Tues.-Sun. May-Oct. Admission charged.

www.exploreiowaparks.com
(319) 934- 3572

8 ▶ Backbone State Park

1347 129th St., Dundee

A high quarter-mile "spine" of rock runs through the center of this scenic 2,000-acre state park, where some 20 miles of hiking trails offer excellent opportunities to explore caverns, climb natural rock stairways, and admire the tall white pines overhanging the cliffs. Deer, wild turkeys, raccoons, and an occasional coyote roam the land, and songbirds, including bluebirds, flit through the woods.

A lake offers swimming, and Richmond Spring at the north end of the park is stocked with trout. Paddleboats, canoes, and kayaks may be rented. Cabins are available to rent year-round.

In winter the roads are not plowed out, and campers must either backpack in or use a snowmobile.

▶ Open year-round.

www.iowadnr.com/parks
(563) 924-2527

9 ▶ Maquoketa Caves State Park

10970 98th St., Maquoketa

A network of 13 caves runs beneath this park, and as early as 1835, explorers cut their names into the limestone walls. Chambers range from 30 feet to more than 800 feet in length. Some are lighted and have walkways, but experienced

spelunkers using flashlights may enjoy the challenge of several unlighted caves. The temperature stays at about 50°F.

For visitors who are more interested in aboveground activities, there are birds, wildflowers, shady forests, and scenic views to enjoy. Great horned and barred owls, red-tailed hawks, and hummingbirds can be found in the stands of oak, ash, hickory, and maple. Columbines, bloodroot, may apples, hepaticas, and the endangered monkshood share ground space with morels.

Hikers in all seasons can enjoy some six miles of trails in the park, leading to overlooks with views of the steep ravine that is a dominant feature here, and to a natural bridge, which stands almost 50 feet above Raccoon Creek. A trail in the western area of the park takes hikers past a restored prairie, a wildlife food plot, and an experimental savanna restoration.

▶ Open daily year-round. Admission charged.

www.iowadnr.com/parks
(563) 652-5833

10 Hitchcock Nature Center

27792 Ski Hill Loop, Honey Creek
As new homes and even whole towns continue to encroach upon existing prairies, grasslands in our nation's heartland are slowly disappearing. The Pottawattamie County Conservation group has acted to stem the tide. On more than 1,000 acres, members set up the Hitchcock Nature Center and Loess Hills landform. The area preserves some of the largest remaining natural prairie areas in Iowa and provides refuge for plants and animals found nowhere else in the state.

Visitors who enter the Loess Hills Lodge at the Center are more likely to come away with a conservation mind-set. A 3D tour of the preserve is shown in the mini-theater. Exhibits show raptors in flight, and children love Curiosity Cove, where they can build habitat scenes on a magnetic mural or investigate (yucky!) insects at a discovery table. Ongoing renovations of the lodge serve an additional purpose: They teach environmental practices such as sustainable building construction, water savings, energy efficiency, materials selection, and indoor environmental quality.

Stay for a while and enjoy the camping, picnicking, hiking, snow sledding, and low-impact recreation facilities, some of the best in Pottawattamie County.

▶ Open daily year-round. Admission charged.

www.pottcoconservation.com/html/
hitchcock.html
(712) 545-3283

11 Historic General Dodge House

605 Third St., Council Bluffs
General Grenville M. Dodge, a Civil War commander of Union troops, was later influential in political, financial, and military affairs. His most lasting claim to fame, however, comes from his railroad-building efforts at a time in history when Americans were moving westward.

Ever since he had laid tracks for the Eastern Railroad at age 14, he dreamed of building a railroad clear across the country. He went on to become an engineer for the Illinois Central Railroad and after that surveyed the route of the Rock Island Line across Iowa. Finally, as chief construction engineer of the Union Pacific Railroad, he supervised the completion of the section of the nation's first transcontinental railroad that passed through Iowa.

In 1869 he finally settled down in a lavish Victorian mansion on 1.8 acres. He and his wife, Ruth, raised their family in this 14-room, three-story mansion overlooking the Missouri Valley, which had a number of "modern" conveniences.

Considered one of the finest residences in Iowa at the time, it has since been dedicated as a National Historic Landmark.

▶ Open daily Feb.-Dec. Closed national holidays and Mother's Day. Admission charged.

www.dodgehouse.org
(712) 322-2406

12 Hitchcock House

One mile west of Lewis
The Rev. George B. Hitchcock built his sandstone house with a definite purpose in mind for the secret room he had tucked away in its basement. It was to be a stopping place along the Underground Railroad, a safe haven he offered runaway slaves as they made their way to the "Promised Land" of Canada.

The house was designated a National Historic Landmark in 2006 due to its importance as a site in the national network organized by persons who were sympathetic to the slaves' plight and helped them escape to freedom before the Civil War.

▶ Open Tues.-Sun., May–Sept. Admission charged.

www.hitchcockhouse.org
(712) 769-2323

13 Danish Windmill Museum

4038 Main St., Elk Horn
Velkommen to the Danish Windmill, the only authentic and fully operable Danish windmill in North America.

You don't have to be a Dane to marvel at the ingenuity of how the mill grinds the grain that is fed to its huge revolving stones. Built in 1848 in Norre Snede, Denmark, and later transported to Elk Horn, it processed grain for local farmers before falling into disuse when automated methods replaced it during the Industrial Revolution.

Now it is back in operation again. The visitors center gives tours and shows a video of how it was reconstructed in its current location. With painstaking care and old-world craftsmanship, a Danish carpenter disassembled the 60-foot-tall structure, numbering every piece of timber and simultaneously building a 6-foot small scale model so American carpenters wouldn't be puzzled when putting it back together.

The largest Danish import gift shop in the United States on site displays old-world souvenirs and cookware, including collector plates and authentic replicas of King Haraldsson and other Norse heroes and their terror-striking Viking longboats.

▶ Open daily except national holidays. Admission charged.

www.danishwindmill.com
(712) 764-7472; (800) 451-7960

14 Pammel State Park

IA-322, 4 miles southwest of Winterset
The main features of this tranquil park are a long limestone ridge called Devil's Backbone and the

13 **Danish Windmill Museum.** This windmill was reassembled from pieces numbered in Denmark.

Middle River, which flows north along one side of the ridge, makes a sharp turn, and re-enters the park on the ridge's other side, flowing southeast. One of three picnic areas sits atop the ridge and affords views of this natural phenomenon. Burrowing through Devil's Backbone is a rustic highway tunnel that once carried water to a nearby gristmill.

Hikers on trails shaded by hickories, walnuts, and centuries-old burr oaks may spy wild turkeys, hawks, deer, and foxes. (Camera-toters can snap shots of the two largest black walnut trees in Iowa.) Park-goers can also pick mushrooms and fish in the river.

The park is in Madison County, of covered bridge fame. To drive through the Cedar Covered Bridge—of the original 19 county bridges, the only one still open to traffic—take IA-322 north to US-92 N, then turn left on Cedar Bridge Road. The bridge is actually a replica of the 1883 original—sadly, destroyed by fire in 2002.

▶ Open year-round.

www.madisoncountyparks.org/parks/ pammel.htm

(515) 462-3536

15 Neal Smith National Wildlife Refuge and Prairie Learning Center

9981 Pacific St., Prairie City
Drive your car along the auto tour or hike on foot through the wide-open expanse of over 5,000 acres. There you will find stretches of tallgrass prairie, where herds of buffalo and elk graze with their calves and where pheasants, badgers, and white-tailed dear roam at will. In this wildlife refuge the meadows are carpeted with more than 200 species of multi-colored native prairie flowers and grasses.

The Learning Center, with its 13,000 square-foot exhibit hall, has state-of-the-art educational facilities that offer native prairie-grass and prairie flowers exhibits, a model of the tallgrass prairie ecosystem, and exhibits that tell the history of the buffalo and elk herds. There is even a special tallgrass prairie maze for kids.

▶ Open daily year-round.

www.tallgrass.org
(515) 994-3400

16 Cordova Park Observation Tower

Cordova Park, 1378 Hwy. G28, Pella
Two million visitors a year climb to the top of the Cordova Park Observation Tower. Completed in 1998, the current tower, with its winding staircase, is an imaginative use of a 106-foot-high, 15-foot-round converted water tower. No elevators here. The climb is the prime thing to do. Hardy visitors ascend 170 steps in a continuously flowing spiral from the ground to a windswept observation deck where they have an over-the-treetops 360-degree bird's-eye view of the surroundings and the sweep of the Des Moines River Valley where it widens out into Lake Red Rock, Iowa's largest lake.

Apart from the tower, Cordova Park has a nature trail, a butterfly garden, picnic areas, and a boat ramp. A planned Environmental Learning Center will house exhibits on the ecology of watersheds and art exhibits that will feature local environmental

15 **Neal Smith National Wildlife Refuge and Prairie Learning Center.** The exhibit hall at this preserve opens a window to the ecology of the tallgrass prairie.

projects. A café and gift shop will also be housed in the center.

▶ Open daily, weather permitting. Admission charged.

www.redrockarea.com
(641) 627-5935

17 Pella Historical Village/Vermeer Mill

Located one block east of downtown Pella

Within the town of Pella, this charming and authentic area offers travelers a chance to visit the Netherlands without having to cross the Atlantic. In 1847 Dominie Scholte led a group of immigrants out of Holland in search of religious freedom. They landed in Iowa and named their town Pella, or "refuge." Nestled in a courtyard laced with red brick walkways and beautiful gardens, 21 buildings, some more than 140 years old, preserve Pella's history and Dutch traditions.

Highlights include a traditional *werkplaats* (wooden shoe shop), a working gristmill, a Dutch bakery, a Dutch street organ, and the boyhood home of U.S. lawman Wyatt Earp. There's also a Dutch windmill, America's tallest working mill, built to celebrate Pella's Dutch heritage. An elevator takes visitors to the mill's working floor and a spectacular view of Pella.

▶ Open Mon.-Sat. Mar.-Dec. Admission charged.

www.pellatuliptime.com/historical-village
(641) 628-4311

18 American Gothic House and Center

300 American Gothic St., Eldon
You know the image of an elderly farmer and his wife standing side by side in front of their Gothic home, pitchfork at the ready? That image is from the 1930s painting *American Gothic,* illustrating a farm couple from America's heartland idealized by Iowan painter Grant Wood.

The real-life 125-year-old house with its Gothic window still stands in Eldon and serves as a backdrop for couples who strike their own Gothic pose in front of it. It is listed on the *National Register of Historic Places,* and the painting has become an American icon.

The interior of the house is not open to the public. The Visitors Center has a gift shop with prints and exhibits that interpret Grant Wood's influence upon Midwest regional art. An American Gothic Parodies Exhibit showcases amusing spin-offs of the original painting.

Gothic Day is the second Saturday in June every year. For added photo authenticity, costumes and pitchforks are available from the visitors center.

Outdoor enthusiasts can find hiking, fishing, and hunting opportunities nearby.

▶ Open daily except major holidays.

www.iowahistory.org/sites
(641) 652-3352; (515) 281-4221

19 Wilton Candy Kitchen

310 Cedar St., Wilton
If you are driving past Wilton, make a quick hop off I-80 and treat yourself to an old-fashioned lunch or dessert at the Candy Kitchen.

Built in 1856, it is considered to be the oldest soda fountain/ice-cream parlor in the nation. The "updated" establishment dates from 1910, when immigrant Gus Nopoulos began churning ice cream and making chocolate candies. Today shaded by a red- and white-striped awning, the shop is run by one of his descendants, the charming George Nopoulos. This shop is an example of Genuine Americana, a small-town soda fountain where ice cream is king.

Slide into an old-fashioned booth or sit at the counter to watch George push levers as he smothers first-rate ice cream with fresh syrup flavors. Vats of ice cream, carbonated soda waters, and waffle cones are all "homemade" at the shop, a rarity these days. Butter brickle and

19 Wilton Candy Kitchen. The past lives on in a soda fountain that first opened its doors in 1856.

cherry pecan are just two of the unique flavor combinations for ice creams here, and a specialty of the house is the "dipsy doodle" soda, a concoction made with six flavors.

▶ Open daily year-round.

www.roadfood.com
(563) 732-2278

did you know ?

The Wilton Candy Kitchen has recently been listed in the *National Register of Historic Places.*

IOWA

seasonal events

JANUARY
• Bald Eagle Appreciation Days—Keokuk *(view eagles over the Mississippi River)*

FEBRUARY
• Color the Wind Kite Festival—Clear Lake *(team kite flying and displays)*

MARCH
• Maple Tree Tapping—Hancock

MAY
• Tulip Time Festival—Pella *(parades, Dutch dancing, flower shows, theatrical shows, crafts, quilting, Dutch food)*
• Iowa Book Festival—Adel *(readings, presentations, workshops, book sale, children's storytelling)*

JUNE
• Ice Cream Days—Le Mars *(family fun in the ice cream capital of the world)*
• Schaller Popcorn Days—Schaller *(parade, craft show, carnival)*

SEPTEMBER
• Coca-Cola Days—Atlantic *(one of the largest Coca-Cola conventions)*
• Ham Jam—Hampton *(blues music and barbecue event highlighted by the "running of the hogs")*
• Log Cabin Days—Indianola *(antiques, flea market, historical building tours)*

OCTOBER
• Madison County Covered Bridge Festival—Winterset *(cross-county tours of the bridges, arts and crafts)*
• Harvest Fest—Emmetsburg *(scarecrow contest and retail specials)*
• Cruise to the Woods—Fort Dodge *(Iowa's largest cruise and car show)*

NOVEMBER
• Rivers and Bluffs Fall Birding Festival—Lansing *(boat tours, lectures, vendor sales, silent auction)*

DECEMBER
• Victorian Stroll—Albia *(lights, live window displays)*

www.traveliowa.com

Kansas

Among the wooded hills and rolling plains are memories of Spanish adventurers, Native Americans, pioneers, and those who stayed to work the land.

Sandsage Bison Range and Wildlife Area. American bison roam this 3,670-acre range and wildlife area, which has pleased visitors since 1924 (see page 124).

The first Europeans in what would become Kansas were the Spaniards who came seeking gold—unsuccessfully—in 1541; their meeting with the peaceful Quivara Sioux is commemorated in a museum. Other museums and two army posts recall the conflict between the Native Americans and the pioneers who traveled through or settled here. An original Pony Express station, remnants of the Santa Fe Trail, and a vast expanse of unplowed prairie color in the outlines of the state's early days.

Geology, wildlife, and the unexpected can be found in parks with oddly shaped standing rocks. Bison ranges, a museum devoted to barbed wire, and the hideout of a gang of famous outlaws are also to be found.

visit ➤→ (offthebeatenpathtrips.com)

1 Last Indian Raid Museum

258 S. Penn Ave., Oberlin

The "last Indian raid" in Kansas refers to the tale of some 300 displaced Northern Cheyenne Native Americans who wanted to return to their ancestral home.

Forcibly removed to a camp in what is now Oklahoma, they were sick, hungry, and despondent. In September 1878 some 100 warriors with their wives and children escaped and headed north through Kansas with the U.S. Army in pursuit. As they approached Sappa Creek, they recalled that three years before, 27 of their people had been slaughtered there. Between Sept. 30 and Oct. 1 the Cheyennes raided the area, killed 30 people, and moved on. A number of the Cheyennes were later killed, and the survivors were sent to a reservation in Montana.

The 14-building museum contains a few relics from the raid, such as war clubs, arrowheads, and a settler's revolver. The museum also displays rooms with typical period furnishings, a doctor's office, a barbershop, and a music room with a player piano. A sod house pays tribute to pioneer life.

▶ Open Tues.–Sat. Apr.–Nov. except holidays. Admission charged.

www.rootsweb.ancestry.com/~ksdclirm/
(785) 475-2712

4 ▶ **Pawnee Indian Museum State Historic Site.** The nucleus of this six-acre site is a museum built around the excavated floor of an 1820s two-family dwelling.

2 "They Also Ran" Gallery

Mezzanine of the First State Bank
105 W. Main St., Norton

Founded in 1965, this memorial hall was established by a local banker with a passion for Americana—with a twist. Inside a working bank, trivia buffs will find photographs and colorful capsule biographies of unsuccessful candidates for president—as in President of the United States.

Spanning election history from Thomas Jefferson to John Kerry, losers like Horatio Seymour and Rufus King share the walls with famous men, like eventual winner Andrew Jackson (who lost to John Quincy Adams in 1824) and *New York Times* publisher Horace Greeley. In addition to his run for president, Greeley earned local notoriety for once spending the night at a bustling stagecoach station just outside Norton. A replica of this very station, Station 15, appointed with period furnishings, stands in a roadside park beside Highway 36. Local legend has it that Station 15 was also a resting stop for two other famous people, Buffalo Bill and Billy the Kid.

▶ Open year-round during banking hours.

www.firstatebank.com
(785) 877-3341

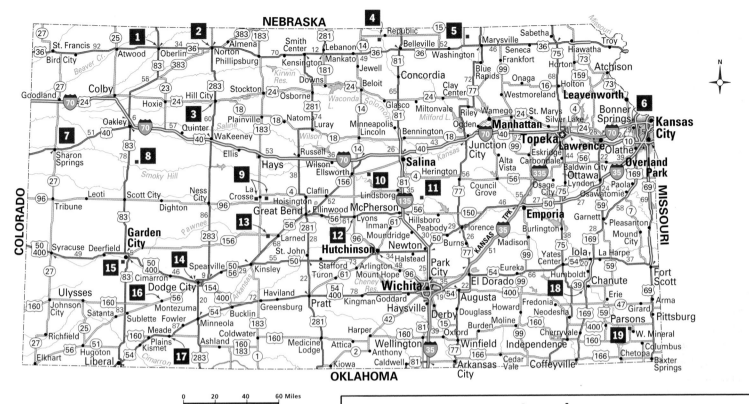

Legend

1	NUMBERED ATTRACTIONS (Described in text)			

CONTROLLED ACCESS HIGHWAYS
Free
Toll
═ ═ ═ ═ Under Construction

OTHER HIGHWAYS
Primary Highway
Secondary Highway

HIGHWAY MARKERS
Interstate Route
U.S. Route
State Route
Distances along Major Highways (in miles)

CITIES AND TOWNS
⊛ National Capital
⊛ State Capital
• Cities, Towns, and Populated Places Type size indicates relative importance
Urban Area

RECREATION AND FEATURES OF INTEREST
National Park
Other Large Park or Recreation Area
- - - Trail
- - - Ferry

© 2009 GeoNova

---

3 ▶ Hill City Oil Museum

Hwy. 24W, Hill City

This museum, featuring items devoted to the petroleum industry, lies in the heart of the oil-producing area of Graham County, which boomed in the late 1930s and 1940s. The look of the "oil patch" is evident in the yard, where cable-tool equipment and a pumping jack are installed.

Inside, a replica of a cable-tool derrick, along with other 1892 vintage equipment from Neodesha, Kansas, contrasts dramatically with the working-scale model of a modern rig. Early boom days are depicted by photos of the Spindletop Field (Beaumont, Texas) and pen-and-ink drawings of other notable fields.

There are several exhibits that should not be missed: One display of a geological cross section gives an in-depth example of how wells were cored from the different rock formations, and another is a diorama of geological history portraying oil and gas formations from the Paleozoic to the Cenozoic eras, illustrating the different procedures in oil exploration.

▶ Open daily year-round by appointment.

www.discoverhillcity.com
(785) 421-5621

---

4 ▶ Pawnee Indian Museum State Historic Site

480 Pawnee Trail, Republic

Built on a grassy knoll overlooking the tree-lined Republican River, this fascinating museum encloses the site of an excavated Pawnee two-family dwelling. Of the 30 to 40 houses in a village of some 1,000 people, this was one of the largest, with nearly 2,000 square feet of floor space.

The village was probably abandoned in 1830 when its inhabitants decided to join other Pawnees in what is now Nebraska. Ashes from the residents' last fire still remain in the hearth, and tools, weapons, and corn lie exactly as found during the excavation; in the fire-hardened earth floor, you can see the 218 holes for the posts that supported a framework of willow poles and a covering of earth and grass.

Exhibits representing various aspects of Native American life include artwork, bone and metal tools, and weapons and pipes. One diorama depicts a buffalo hunt—in summer and winter the Pawnees rode southwest to the High Plains in quest of these animals. Yet another describes Pawnee astronomy.

In the six-acre fenced area behind the museum, you can see 22 other lodge sites and the remains of a sod-and-timber wall that had surrounded the village.

▶ Open Mar.-Nov. Wed.-Sun.; Dec.-Feb. Thurs.-Sat. except holidays.

www.kshs.org
(785) 361-2255

Monument Rocks. These towering, free-standing rock sculptures on an otherwise barren Kansas plain are sometimes called the Chalk Pyramids.

5 Hollenberg Pony Express Station State Historic Site

2889 23rd Rd., Hanover

During the days of the Pony Express (April 1860–October 1861), its riders galloped into the history and folklore of America.

The Pony Express feat of delivering mail from St. Joseph, Missouri, to Sacramento, California, in 10 days (less than half the previous best time) required 120 riders, 400 horses, and a relay station every 10 to 15 miles. The operation ended when the transcontinental telegraph line was completed.

This national historic landmark is the only unaltered relay station still standing in its original location. Built in 1858 by rancher Gerat Hollenberg, the sturdy weather-beaten structure served as home, general store, post office, hotel, and stagecoach stop on the Oregon-California Trail. It was also the westernmost Pony Express station in Kansas.

Here you can get the feel of the Pony Express and stagecoach businesses and see the general store with its ox shoes, bows and arrows, powder horns, kitchen utensils, and branding irons. Climbing the steep steps to the rough-planked attic, you follow the bootsteps of the Pony Express riders and stagecoach passengers who slept there. There are picnic tables and a small playground in a wooded eight-acre setting.

▶ Open Wed.-Sun. Mar.-Nov.; Thurs.-Sat. Dec.-Feb. Closed major holidays. Admission charged.

www.kshs.org
(785) 337-2635

6 National Agricultural Center and Hall of Fame

630 Hall of Fame Dr., Bonner Springs

The center pays homage to the skillful, hardworking farmers, and the exhibits are housed in two main buildings set on 172 acres of beautiful rolling countryside.

In the Museum of Farming, which has one of the greatest collections of agricultural equipment in the country, visitors are able to see Harry Truman's plow, a 307-piece set of antique woodworking tools, and hand-operated milk-processing machines.

Thirty-eight people have been inducted into the Hall of Fame, including George Washington, Thomas Jefferson, Cyrus McCormick, George Washington Carver, and Eli Whitney.

You can also visit Farm Town, an early 1900s farming community with farmstead, one-room school, smithy, country store, train depot, and hatchery.

For a change of pace, you can climb aboard the narrow-gauge railroad that circles Farm Town or amble down a mile-long wooded nature trail.

▶ Open daily Tues.-Sun. Jan.-mid-Dec.; Closed major holidays. Admission charged.

www.aghalloffame.com
(913) 721-1075

7 Fort Wallace Museum

Hwy. 40, Wallace

Fort Wallace was one of a string of army posts established to control the Plains Native Americans and protect travelers along the Smoky Hill Trail. Active from 1865 to 1881, it was built for about 500 soldiers and was the busiest bastion in Kansas. Nothing remains of the old fort except the cemetery.

The museum, located about one and a half miles from the fort site, is a treasury of locally found artifacts, plus old military equipment and a painted Native American buffalo robe. It also houses a collection of animal scenes made entirely from barbed wire. Also on view is a Union Pacific depot from Weskan, complete with telegraph, switch equipment, and signal tower.

▶ Open daily May-Sept. Admission free but donations encouraged.

www.ftwallace.com
(785) 891-3564

8 Monument Rocks

From Oakley, 20 miles south on US-83, 7.5 miles south and east on Jayhawk Rd.

Rising abruptly above the treeless plain of the Smoky Hill River, the 70-foot-high "monuments" look like lonely sentinels. Sculpted by wind and water erosion, many sport crenellated tops, like castle battlements.

The rocks graduate in color from pale gray at the bottom to gold at their peaks. They are composed of soft cretaceous chalk from the sediment of an ancient sea, and their layered formations abound with fossils.

Fort Wallace Museum. A buffalo sculpted from the barbed wire that transformed the prairie stands at an army post dubbed "the Fightin'est Fort in the West."

Numbering fewer than a dozen, the towers are found in an area about a quarter-mile long and 200 yards wide. These distinctive formations served as landmarks for early wagon trains and military parties as they trekked the arduous journey westward from Kansas to Colorado along the Smoky Hill Trail. The area has now been designated as a National Natural Monument and has been selected as one of the Eight Wonders of Kansas.

This area also once contained fossils of shark's teeth, vertebrae, and oyster shells. These unique and eclectic items can be viewed at the nearby Fick Fossil and History Museum.

▶ Museum open Sept.–May Mon.–Sat.; June–Aug. daily

www.kansastravel.org/monumentrocks.htm
(785) 671-4839

 Kansas Barbed Wire Museum
120 W. 1st St., La Crosse
Post Rock Museum
202 W. 1st St., La Crosse
When Joseph F. Glidden patented a barbed wire "lighter than air, stronger than whiskey, and cheaper than dirt," the fate of the Great Plains was sealed. The open range was transformed into fenced farmland, and the sod-busting farmer was now able to confine his livestock and protect his homestead and crops from free-ranging cattle.

Glidden's success spurred innovative competition to create new patterns—eventually over 500 separate barbed wire patents were issued. The museum presents this history, together with more than 2,000 varieties of the wire. One of the most unusual exhibits in the museum's collection is an authentic raven's nest built primarily of barbed wire.

Of equal importance to frontier life were the posts used to support the wire. Wood was too scarce in 19th-century Kansas to use for fence posts. Creative settlers found a solution by making posts of soft limestone, which hardens in the sun.

Slabs of the limestone, which is abundant in Kansas, were quarried and split into stone posts averaging five to six feet long. About 40,000 miles of post-rock fence cross this section of Kansas, bestowing upon the region a distinctive character.

In the Post Rock Museum you'll see tools used to make the posts, as well as a miniature quarry showing how the limestone was stripped and cut to size.

▶ Both museums open daily May–mid-Sept.

www.rushcounty.org
(785) 222-9900

---

10 **Mushroom Rock State Park**
200 Horsethief Rd., Marquette
The effects of wind erosion are widespread in the Great Plains but nowhere more apparent than at this five-acre site.

These persistent and sometimes violently swirling winds have gradually shaved away the ground of soft sandstone, leaving small islands of resistant sandstone and gradually sculpting them into huge, dramatic mushroom shapes.

The two largest are approximately 25 feet tall, with caps about 15 feet wide. These rocks once served as meeting places and landmarks for Native Americans and early pioneers, such as Kit Carson and John C. Fremont.

A gentle brook meanders through the area, shaded by trees. North of the brook you'll find some man-made art—a rock carv-

ing of a U.S. flag with 15 stripes—done by a child as he stopped on his daily walk home. The small park has picnic tables. A few miles to the south are the two areas of the popular Kanopolis State Park. The extensive recreational facilities in its more than 22,000 acres include swimming, boating, and fishing on Kanopolis Lake, as well as many land-based activities, such as hiking and horseback riding.

10 ▶ **Mushroom Rock State Park.** Wind-sculpted sandstone rocks that look like mushrooms once served as guideposts for Native Americans and early pioneers.

▶ Both parks open year-round. Admission charged for Kanopolis.

www.kdwp.state.ks.us
(785) 546-2565

---

11 **Maxwell Wildlife Refuge and McPherson State Lake**
From Canton go 6 miles north on McPherson CR-304, then left 1.2 miles to refuge headquarters.
Located on the Prairie Trail Scenic Byway in the southeastern tip of the Smoky Hills, this wildlife refuge preserves a precious remnant of the original American prairie, with 2,560 acres of native

grassland, rolling hills, wildflowers, creeks, and springs. Some 200 buffalo and 50 elk graze and roam here. A gravel road and an observation tower provide excellent views of the majestic mammals and the prairie. (The elk can be seen only from mid-Sept. to mid-Apr.) More than 100 species of birds have been recorded, and there is a bluebird trail with 25 boxes.

The adjacent McPherson State Lake has a handicap-accessible boat ramp and fishing pier. Anglers are rewarded with largemouth bass, channel catfish, crappie, and bluegill. A campground is on the lake's western shore and offers a nature trail.

Guided tours of the refuge are available aboard a tram, but reservations are needed. Check ahead for special seasonal events.

▶ Open year-round; tours are offered by reservation only. Admission free.

www.cyberkraft.com/maxwell
(620) 628-4455

Coronado-Quivira Museum

105 W. Lyon, Lyons

This museum commemorates Francisco Vasquez de Coronado's expedition into Kansas to find gold with exhibits of Quivira pottery, arrowheads, stone tools, and beads, as well as original chain mail, replicas of helmets, spurs, and other items left behind by Coronado's soldiers. Also shown is a model of a Quivira-Wichita Native American grass hut and paintings depicting the time.

Additional exhibit areas feature daily life in rural Kansas around 1902 and the history of the Santa Fe Trail, which runs through the county, with Native American and pioneer artifacts.

▶ Open Tues.-Sat. year-round except major holidays. Admission charged.

http://skyways.lib.ks.us
(620) 257-3941

Fort Larned National Historic Site

Six miles west of Larned on KS–156

As a principal guardian of the Santa Fe Trail, Fort Larned provided military escort for wagon trains, stagecoaches, and travelers from 1859 to 1878. The original sod and adobe structures were replaced by 1868 with nine durable sandstone-and-timber buildings enclosing the traditional parade ground. Still standing much in their original condition, they offer an authentic glimpse into military life on the Western frontier. As such, it is the best-preserved Indian Wars military post on the Santa Fe Trail.

One of the barracks, converted into a visitors center, features an audiovisual program, exhibits, numerous relics, infantry and cavalry uniforms, a life-size model of a 10th Cavalry soldier leading his mount with full equipment and regalia, and some excellent Native American artifacts and photographs of prominent chiefs.

▶ Open daily except major winter holidays.

www.nps.gov/fols
(620) 285-6911

The Santa Fe Trail at Dodge City

Nine miles west of Dodge City on Hwy. 50

The best preserved section of the fabled Santa Fe Trail remains carved in the windswept grass-covered prairie nine miles west of Dodge City. Despite a century's erosion, the trail is still clearly marked. In some places here the grooves are as much as three feet deep. It is apparent that the trail was not one single lane but numerous parallel tracks, so that several ranks of traffic—freight wagons, stagecoaches, horses, soldiers, and cattle—could travel side by side for protection. Also contained on the site are remnants of the Eureka Irrigating Canal, known as the Soule Ditch, which was begun in 1883 by Asa T. Soule.

Now listed on the *National Register of Historic Sites,* this area has never been plowed and probably looks much as it did when the trail was at its busiest. Boot Hill Museum, nine miles east on Front St., pays homage to the Wild West from the 1870s–1900.

▶ Accessible year-round, weather permitting.

www.visitdodgecity.org
(620) 227-8188

Sandsage Bison Range and Wildlife Area

785 S. Hwy. 83, Garden City

In what was once the heart of the great American bison range, these 3,670 acres provide shelter for a herd of approximately 75 buffalo.

These monarchs of the plains, officially designated the Kansas state animal, once numbered some 60 to 70 million. Their wanton slaughter during the 19th century reduced them to only a few hundred. This herd was established in 1924 with one bull and two cows.

This herd usually grazes at some distance from the headquarters, on the south bank of the Arkansas River, but visitors can get a close look and take photos on a 60-minute tour.

▶ Viewing by tour only. Accessible daily by appointment except major holidays.

www.gcnet.com/fofgr
(620) 276-9400

Stauth Memorial Museum

111 N. Aztec St., Montezuma

Claude Stauth, a wealthy farmer, and his wife, Donalda, were ideal tourists. They traveled the world, covering more than 95 countries over a 40-year span. They looked, listened, and learned. And they brought back "souvenirs," collected with what a radio commentator termed "an enviable sophistication." The Stauths left behind their treasures—including Donalda's extensive photographic record—together with funds to build the Memorial Museum, opened in their hometown in 1996. It also houses the North American big-game collection of hunter and conservationist Ralph Fry; an excellent exhibit of works by celebrated painter/sculptor Frederic Remington and other Western artists; and top-flight traveling exhibitions throughout the year.

Fort Larned National Historic Site. This fort protected the fabled Santa Fe Trail, which ran from Franklin, Missouri, to Santa Fe by way of Kansas and Colorado.

---

did you know ❓

In the mid-1800s the Santa Fe Trail, stretching 780 miles from Franklin, Missouri, to Santa Fe, New Mexico, was the most important artery of commerce in the development of the Southwest.

17 ▶ **Dalton Gang Hideout.** The barn on the property of the Dalton brothers' sister hid the entrance and exit of a tunnel that served as an escape route for the outlaws.

If you are in the Montezuma area during the Christmas season in an even-numbered year, check out the biannual "Christmas in Southwest Kansas" display of holiday traditions and customs staged at the museum.

▶ Open Tues.-Sun. except major holidays.

www.stauthmemorialmuseum.org
(620) 846-2527

17 ▶ Dalton Gang Hideout

502 S. Pearlette St., Meade
The Dalton Gang, named for the Dalton brothers who were its godfathers, was among the most feared, if not so successful, criminal bands that terrorized the Midwest in the 1890s. One of the notorious gang's hideouts was this pretty wood-frame house, the home of the Dalton boys' sister Eva and her husband. Restored in the 1940s, the house and barn (now including a small museum and a gift shop) are connected by a 95-foot underground tunnel, thought to be the gang's escape route when the law was in hot pursuit of them. Walking through the tunnel today gives visitors an eerie sense of the perils of being a bad guy in the wild and woolly Old West days.

The gang fell apart in 1892, when two Dalton brothers were killed and a third was captured in a gun battle following a failed bank robbery in Coffeyville, Kansas.

▶ Open year-round except major holidays. Admission charged.

www.oldmeadecounty.com
(800) 354-2743

18 ▶ Martin and Osa Johnson Safari Museum

111 N. Lincoln Ave., Chanute
In the first half of the 20th century, Martin and Osa Johnson, an intrepid young couple from Kansas, captured the nation's imagination through their films and books of adventure in exotic, faraway lands. From 1917 through 1936, they traveled to Africa, Borneo, and the South Pacific islands documenting their experiences.

Located in Osa's hometown of Chanute, the Safari Museum was established in 1961 with a core collection of the couple's photographs, manuscripts, and personal belongings. In 1993 the museum relocated to Chanute's renovated Santa Fe train depot as part of a $2 million project. Within its main touring areas visitors will find a gallery

about the Johnsons, an African gallery featuring masks and headdresses, a theater, a library, and a gallery for special events.

▶ Open year-round except major holidays. Admission charged.

www.safarimuseum.com
(620) 431-2730

19 ▶ Big Brutus

6509 N.W. 60th St., West Mineral
In the heart of the Mined Land Wildlife Area, Big Brutus looks like a creature designed for a science-fiction movie. The largest electric shovel in the world, the Bucyrus Erie model 1850B stands 16 stories tall (160 feet) and weighs a whopping 11 million pounds. Visitors can climb five stories to the operator's compartment to get a great view. This mining monster was built in 1962 at a cost of $6.5 million and was retired in 1974 when it was no longer economically feasible to mine high-sulfur coal. Yet Big Brutus lives on through a nonprofit corporation dedicated to the mining heritage of southeast Kansas.

In addition to Big Brutus itself, visitors to the museum can see a 1920 Page dragline used by the Wilkinson Coal Company. And you can't forget Little Giant, the world's smallest working replica of an early day electric mining shovel. For those eager to stay a while, the Big Brutus visitors center offers picnic tables and comfort facilities—complete with hot showers.

▶ Open year-round except major winter holidays. Admission charged.

www.bigbrutus.org
(620) 827-6177

KANSAS

Kentucky

The state where Daniel Boone blazed a trail to the West was also the birthplace of Abraham Lincoln.

Fort Boonesborough. Wooden bucket-making is one of the crafts demonstrated at this living-history state park (see page 134).

The prehistory of this area is recalled by Mississippian Native American mounds and the bones of beasts, now extinct, that came to the salt licks, became mired in the bog, and perished there.

In the days of the pioneers, Daniel Boone explored the Appalachian Range, and evidence of his personal courage and wilderness skills still remains.

In Kentucky you can see where Abraham Lincoln was born, a historic log meeting-house, the world's largest cave system, and some lovely parks. A gristmill is a reminder of early industry, and a tiny remote community still stands in tribute to a hardy breed of Kentuckians.

visit ➤ offthebeatenpathtrips.com

1 ▶ William Clark Market House Museum

121 S. 2nd St., Market House Square, Paducah

In 1827, more than 20 years after returning from his westward journey with Meriwether Lewis, Gen. William Clark came to western Kentucky and purchased 37,000 acres of land for five dollars. The tract included a small village called Pekin. Clark renamed it Paducah and set aside an area near the river-front for a marketplace. The present Market House, built in 1905, is the third to exist here and is now a cultural center featuring the William Clark Market House Museum, with more than 4,800 square feet of exhibits.

One of the most intriguing is the reconstructed interior of the 1877 List Drugstore, with its oak gingerbread woodwork, stained-glass windows, and patent medicine displays. Other treasures are a life-size carving of U.S. statesman Henry Clay, which was created by a 12-year-old boy; Paducah's first motorized fire truck (1913 vintage); and the rudder wheel and brass fog bell of the USS *Paducah,* which served in the two World Wars.

In the Civil War exhibit are a quilt made by Mrs. Robert E. Lee, furniture used by the Lincolns in the White House, and a parlor set

1 ▶ William Clark Market House Museum. An old dentist's chair is typical of the displays in this jam-packed museum.

used by Gen. Ulysses S. Grant when he occupied Paducah.

The block-long building also houses the Yeiser Art Center and the Market House Theatre.

▶ Open Mon.-Sat. Closed major holidays. Admission charged.

www.markethousemuseum.com
(270) 443-7759

2 ▶ Wickliffe Mounds State Historic Site

94 Green St., Wickliffe

Atop a bluff above the mighty Mississippi River lie two platform mounds with eight smaller, round mounds placed unevenly around them—remnants of a Native American civilization that thrived here between A.D. 1100 and A.D. 1350. These ancient Mississippians built a complex settlement composed of houses and earthen mounds surrounding a central plaza that was most likely used for meetings and ceremonies. They farmed, hunted, fished, and traded with other communities. They also made pottery by crushing the shells of mussels and mixing them with clay. They buried their dead with respectful ceremonies.

Today the site, about three miles downstream from where the Mississippi River meets the Ohio River, is an archaeological museum, offering visitors an intriguing glimpse into the way these ancient people lived. There are three exhibit buildings, each sheltering an excavation site. One

did you know ?

The Wickliffe Mounds were built by Native Americans of the Mississippian culture about 900 years ago.

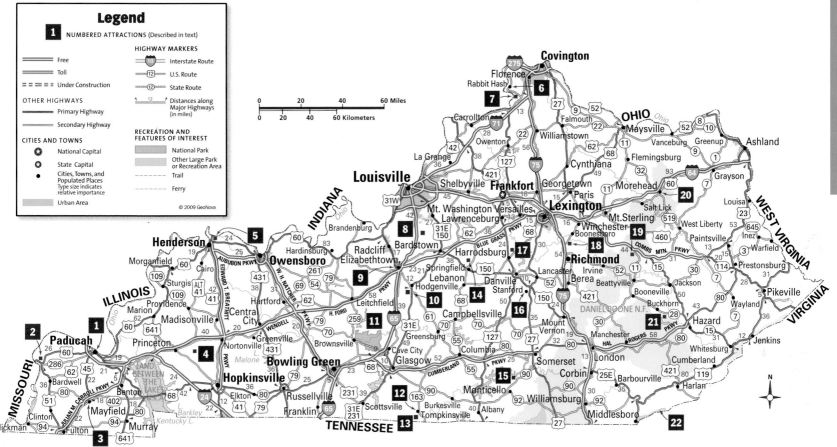

Legend

1 NUMBERED ATTRACTIONS (Described in text)

HIGHWAY MARKERS

Free
Toll
Under Construction

10 Interstate Route
12 U.S. Route
12 State Route
12 Distances along Major Highways (in miles)

OTHER HIGHWAYS
Primary Highway
Secondary Highway

CITIES AND TOWNS
⊗ National Capital
⊗ State Capital
• Cities, Towns, and Populated Places Type size indicates relative importance
Urban Area

RECREATION AND FEATURES OF INTEREST
National Park
Other Large Park or Recreation Area
Trail
Ferry

© 2009 GeoNova

showcases replications of the ancient burials that took place here. Placards and other displays explain the history of the mounds and the story of their excavation. Also on display is an extensive collection of the Mississippian pottery and stone tools. Both everyday utensils and formal and ceremonial ware, including animal effigy vessels, are exhibited.

The ceremonial mound, which is still intact, gives a view of the village site overlooking the Mississippi River. Special events and workshops are held throughout the year.

▶ Open year-round except Mon. and some Sun.; Wed.-Fri. Dec.-Feb. Closed major holidays. Admission charged.

www.parks.ky.gov
(270) 335-3681

2 ▶ **Wickliffe Mounds State Historic Site.** A canvas mural in the Lifeways building depicts the inhabitants of a 12th-century Mississippian village.

3 ▶ **Wooldridge Monuments**
Lockridge St., Mayfield
This curious example of 19th-century eccentricity—a collection of 18 marble and sandstone figures—depicts the nearest and dearest of well-known horse trader

Henry G. Wooldridge, who moved to Kentucky in 1840 at age 21.

For the last 19 years of his life, Wooldridge lived in Mayfield and, shortly before his death in 1899, began assembling a statuary entourage—dubbed a "strange pro-

cession which never moves"—that now surrounds his tomb.

According to Mayfield lore, Wooldridge lost his only true love in a riding accident and never married. His widowed mother, seven brothers and sisters, and two young nieces are represented, as well as two effigies of himself. The life-size figures surround his tomb, although only Henry G. Wooldridge himself is buried here.

The sandstone figures have now begun to erode, giving the faces of Wooldridge's entourage a bland look in contrast to the more enduring details of his marble statue. The figures thus appear to distinguish between the man and his memories.

▶ Cemetery open daily.

www.cityofmayfield.org/cemetery/tour.html
(270) 247-6101

4 Pennyrile Forest State Resort Park

Dawson Springs

Despite its many provisions for outdoor activities, this is a quiet, secluded resort pleasantly situated on a slope overlooking a small lake and beach. Its name comes from pennyroyal, an aromatic wildflower. The grounds of Pennyrile Lodge, which is built of native stone, are landscaped with flowering shrubs, including the delicately scented fringe tree.

With a sandy beach and a beach pavilion, the 56-acre lake attracts many swimmers. Rowboats, canoes, and pedal boats are available for rent. Lake Beshear, four miles from the lodge, is popular with fishermen, who try for crappies, largemouth bass, channel catfish, and bluegills.

Several trails wander through the park and the adjacent 15,000-acre forest, where white-tailed deer and wild turkeys are often seen. Bobcats also live here but rarely appear. Cardinals, wrens, and mourning doves fill the woods with their songs, particularly in spring.

The park offers an 18-hole golf course, a tennis court, a basketball court, and three playgrounds. The picnic area, overlooking the lake, is equipped with tables and grills. The park also has a campground open seasonally. The park's lodge, cottages, and restaurant are open year-round.

▶ Campground open daily Mar.–Nov.; lodge and park open year-round.

www.parks.ky.gov
(270) 797-3421

5 John James Audubon State Park

3100 U.S. Hwy. 41N, Henderson

This is a relatively small park of some 800 acres, but it contains a full range of camping and cottage facilities, a nine-hole golf course,

4 Pennyrile Forest State Resort Park. The lakeside cottages available for rent in this secluded resort are much in demand, especially in summer and fall.

5 John James Audubon State Park. The park's Museum and Nature Center offers nature and art programs for school children and other groups throughout the year.

several miles of hiking trails, a 325-acre nature preserve, and a lake with a boat-launching area. In addition, it is situated on one of the main migratory flyways and offers fine opportunities for observing many species of birds, especially the warblers that stop off here in the spring and fall.

The showpiece of the park is the John James Audubon Museum and Nature Center. The great painter of wildlife made his home in this area of Kentucky during the early 19th century, and it was here that he did much of the work from which his world-famous prints were made. The museum's superb collection of original Audubon paintings, prints, and memorabilia is remarkably comprehensive. It includes not only the familiar pictures of birds and animals but also family portraits.

The building itself, financed by the Works Progress Administration (WPA), was completed in 1938. The masonry structure, with its steep roofs and tower, suggests a French château. The Nature Center has a wildlife observatory and conducts environmental and art programs.

▶ Park and museum open year-round except major holidays and Christmas week. Admission charged for museum.

www.parks.ky.gov
(270) 826-2247; Museum: **(270) 827-1893**

6 Rabbit Hash General Store

10021 Lower River Rd., Rabbit Hash

Since 1831 this working general store has been doing business as usual, untouched by time or fate, in the heart of Rabbit Hash, Kentucky—a little river town whose fortunes have literally risen and fallen with the waters of the Ohio. (In fact, the town's very name is said to have originated during a flood when the abundant local rabbit population became a culinary staple.)

Over the years the store has survived many changing tides—including complete submersion during a flood in 1937 that crested at an incredible 79.9 feet. Though the store remained anchored securely to the ground, thanks to a series of iron rods running throughout the entire structure, mud continues to linger in its attic crawl space.

Rabbit Hash General Store boasts an expansive front porch and a large painted sign welcoming visitors. To meet the needs of local residents, it still sells groceries and other necessities.

Many of its eclectic wares, however, cater to tourists. It stocks an ample selection of antiques, collectible potteries, hand-woven towels and brooms, handmade soaps, wooden kitchen utensils, and the required souvenir hats, shirts, and postcards. While visitors won't find any "rabbit hash" simmering on a stove, the store also serves up lots of old-fashioned goodies, including homemade jams and cream pull candy.

Rabbit Hash also features a local history museum and small shops specializing in local Appalachian crafts and quilts.

▶ Open daily.

www.rabbithash.com
(859) 586-7744

---

7 **Big Bone Lick State Park**
3380 Beaver Rd., Union
Tens of thousands of years ago, when the glaciers of the last Ice Age blanketed northern Kentucky, this 525-acre park was a marshland with a sulfur spring. Prehistoric mammals, including giant mammoths, mastodons, ground sloths, tapirs, and arctic bears, driven south from their natural habitats, were attracted to the salt licks around the spring. Many of these

7 **Big Bone Lick State Park.** At this intriguing park, woolly mammoths and other lifelike models of prehistoric mammals are seen at various points along the mile-long Discovery Trail. These animals roamed southern Kentucky at the end of the last Ice Age.

6 **Rabbit Hash General Store.** During Old Timers Days, a local festival held annually, this store has been known to serve up rabbit hash and other old-fashioned treats.

very big animals became mired in the bog and perished, thus converting it into the vast prehistoric graveyard from which the park today takes its descriptive name.

A mile-long self-guiding Discovery Trail winds through the swamp area, leading to a "bog" diorama. Visitors approach the diorama on a boardwalk that rises above the floor of the marsh, enabling them to "look history in the eye." The final portion of the trail, the Bison Trace, brings a live buffalo herd into view.

A small museum offers further educational displays about the history of the giant mammals.

Other enjoyable features include a 62-site campground with electrical and water hookups; a swimming pool (for campers only); a small man-made lake stocked with bluegills, bass, and catfish for anglers; a playground; and a recreation area with facilities for tennis, volleyball, and basketball. A pleasant footpath meanders around the lake.

▶ Park open year-round; campsite closed mid-Nov.–mid-Mar. Museum open daily Apr.–Dec. Admission charged.

www.parks.ky.gov
(859) 384-3522

did you know ?

Eighteenth-century explorers found the prehistoric bones from which Big Bone Lick State Park derives its name, but they were much more interested in the discovery of salt at the site, which supported a thriving salt industry for several years.

8 ▶ Bernheim Arboretum and Research Forest

Hwy. 245, Clermont

In 1928 Isaac W. Bernheim, a German immigrant who made his fortune distilling bourbon whiskey, purchased a 14,000-acre tract "for the people of Kentucky" to be used as an arboretum and wildlife sanctuary. He also created a nonprofit institution to connect people and nature.

Today Bernheim is divided into two sections—an extensive wilderness home and a parklike arboretum with 6,000 varieties of trees and shrubs.

The entrance road takes you along the edge of a restored native grassland to a unique visitors center. The center overlooks two ponds that attract hundreds of waterfowl in the spring and fall, including the elusive snow goose. From the center you can walk or drive to the Arboretum Center, with its formal gardens, which include azaleas, junipers, and witch hazels.

Nearly 35 miles of trails loop through the wilderness, including

8 ▶ Bernheim Arboretum and Research Forest. This tribute to trees is two parks in one: a well-designed botanical garden and a wilderness area attractive to wildlife.

one that circles a 47-foot fire tower, which offers a superb view of the surrounding forested countryside. A self-guiding nature trail leads past a corral containing several deer and wild turkeys, and biking is also a popular activity.

The several picnic groves include tables and grills. A map of the forest is available at the visitors center.

▶ Open year-round except major winter holidays. Admission charged weekends and holidays.

www.bernheim.org
(502) 955-8512

9 ▶ Schmidt Museum of Coca-Cola Memorabilia

109 Buffalo Creek Dr., Elizabethtown

For more than 100 years the Coca-Cola Company has been quenching the thirst of America—and that of the whole world—and furnishing us with a barrage of brilliantly colored signs, coasters, dishes, glasses, ashtrays, and posters that have become as much a part of Americana as apple pie.

For most of those years the Schmidt family has been bottling Coca-Cola in Elizabethtown and collecting an astonishing assortment of Coca-Cola memorabilia. This assemblage—the private collection of Mr. and Mrs. W. B. Schmidt—which is said to be the largest in the world, is now on display at the Schmidt Museum.

Arranged chronologically, the

exhibits illustrate the company's ingenious approach to advertising—from the turn-of-the-century trays picturing Victorian ladies dressed as for a garden party to cigar bands, hand axes, children's toys, and the convenient packaging of the present-day six-pack. The range of items emblazoned with the familiar logo is nothing less than overwhelming. On the case of a clock, Coca-Cola is heralded as a brain tonic and a way to relieve headaches and exhaustion.

Special exhibits throughout the year assure visitors there is always something new to see, from the 1931 Ford Coca-Cola delivery van to the Coca-Cola R2D2 robot.

▶ Open daily except major holidays. Admission charged.

www.schmidtmuseum.com
(270) 234-1100

10 ▶ Abraham Lincoln Birthplace National Historic Site

2995 Lincoln Farm Rd., Hodgenville

Kentucky abounds with log cabins, but none so enshrined as this. On a hill at the site of Sinking Spring Farm, a 348-acre tract bought by Nancy Hanks and Thomas Lincoln in 1808, stands a Doric-columned marble-and-granite memorial building with an impressive flight of 56 steps—one for each year of Abraham Lincoln's life. The memorial contains a simple one-room symbolic log cabin in which the 16th president of the United States was born, on February 12, 1809.

Built of stout, squared white-oak beams, with a wattle-and-clay chimney at one end, the cabin, unlike most dwellings of that day, has no half-loft and only one small

9 ▶ Schmidt Museum of Coca-Cola Memorabilia. The history of the soft drink is traced here, from its Georgia origins to its status as one of the world's most famous brands.

square window, which perhaps was covered with oiled paper or an animal skin to keep out the winter cold.

Since the 1860s, as the Sinking Springs property changed hands, the cabin has been removed and later returned to the farm several times. This gave rise to a controversy over its authenticity.

In 1905 the Lincoln Farm Association was formed by several prominent Americans, including Mark Twain and William Jennings Bryan, to preserve Lincoln's birthplace. Four years later President Theodore Roosevelt laid the cornerstone of the memorial building, and soon the cabin—if not the actual one, at least a fine facsimile—came to a permanent resting place. Original or not, it clearly captures the spirit of the time. And the contrast between the stark simplicity of the cabin and the grandeur of its protective covering seems both poignant and ironic.

The spring for which the farm was named is still there, rising from a grottolike cave at the foot of the hillside. A hiking trail winds through the fields and forests of the park, and picnic facilities are available.

▶ Open daily.

www.nps.gov/abli

(270) 358-3138

11 Mammoth Cave National Park

1 Mammoth Cave Pkwy., Mammoth Cave

The main attraction at this 52,000-acre park is the extensive network of passageways and caverns in the cave itself. Grand chambers and spectacular stone formations create a jaw-dropping underground experience not soon forgotten. It is the world's longest cave system, and tours range from 1 1/2 hours to a strenuous 6-hour Wild Cave tour, which are all available by reservation.

Meanwhile, back on the surface, the hills and valleys along both sides of the Green River offer a wide range of opportunities for outdoor activities, including hiking, bicycling, backpacking, camping, and horseback riding.

11 **Mammoth Cave National Park.** Visitors can take a 90-minute tour of the world's longest cave system or reserve a six-hour tour in advance. Aboveground, activities at this national park include hiking, bird-watching, horseback riding, and camping.

Eighty-five miles of trails and backpacking routes, some through the primitive backcountry, wind through the countryside. Camping is permitted on designated sites. Permits, available at park headquarters, are required for camping in the backcountry.

The forest is home to the Virginia white-tailed deer, raccoons, and other small mammals, as well as owls, warblers, wild turkey, pileated woodpeckers, and cardinals. Fishing and boating are permitted in the park.

▶ Open year-round. Fee charged for tours.

www.nps.gov/maca

(270) 758-2180

12 Monroe County Marble Club Super Dome

Armory Rd., Tompkinsville

The exterior of this building gives little hint of the history of the game played within, a local game passed down from generation to generation.

Pioneers brought the game to Kentucky using marbles made of rocks. The Super Dome, built in 1988, contains a 20- by 40-foot marble yard of carefully sifted dirt. The yard has the three evenly spaced holes necessary for the local game of Rolley-Hole. This game made its way to England in 1992, when the players from Kentucky competed in the British and World Marbles Championship in Tinsley Green, England, and taught their competitors the local variation. The team, who had just learned the circle-style game of marbles played at the tournament, cleaned up with a score of 10–0. Returning home, they were greeted by headlines in the *Louisville Courier-Journal* declaring them "simply marbleous."

Today one wall of the building displays a scoreboard, and lining the sides of the room are chairs, cedar shavings, and a woodstove, evidence of some members' habit of whittling while waiting for a turn. Local men, still using homemade marbles of flint or granite, usually gather at about 5:00 P.M. to enjoy an evening of their favorite game.

▶ Open daily.

(270) 487-1314

10 **Abraham Lincoln Birthplace National Historic Site.** The humble one-room log cabin where the 16th president was born on February 12, 1809, now sits within the walls of an imposing memorial building built of marble and granite.

13 Old Mulkey Meetinghouse State Historic Site

38 Old Mulkey Park Rd., Tompkinsville

Situated in woodland near an ancient cemetery, this simple and austere log structure was built in 1804 by the Mill Creek Baptist Congregation, whose leader was John Mulkey, the son and grandson of Baptist preachers. Several years after the meetinghouse was completed, John Mulkey rejected the Baptist doctrine of the time and the congregation became divided. Mulkey was followed by a majority of the members, and he became a significant force in the religious "awakening" of the time in Kentucky and Tennessee.

Mulkey delivered approximately 10,000 sermons and encouraged four of his six sons to become preachers. The log building in which Mulkey had preached his sermons, having withstood the forces of both a civil war and of Mother Nature, had come to be known as "Old Mulkey's Meeting-house." The 30- by 50-foot building has a puncheon floor, pegleg seats, chinked walls, and clapboard shutters. It is designed with two shallow transepts, creating 12 corners to represent either the 12 apostles of Christ or the 12 tribes of Israel; its three doors represent the Trinity. Instead of glass, the windows and doors have been fitted with rough wooden shutters. Visitors can view pictures of John Mulkey and his wife, which are hanging on the wall beside the preacher's stall.

On its 60 acres there are picnic tables and grills, a playground for children, and a shelter located under trees, reminding visitors of the tradition of serving dinner on the meetinghouse grounds.

▶ Open year-round.

www.parks.ky.gov
(270) 487-8481

---

14 Lincoln Homestead State Park

5079 Lincoln Park Rd., Springfield

This is Lincoln country, and three buildings that were important in the life of Thomas Lincoln, the president's father, have been brought together in this 275-acre park: his boyhood home, the girlhood home of his bride, Nancy Hanks, and the blacksmith and carpenter shop where he learned his trade. Of the three, only the Berry House, where Abraham's mother lived when she was courted by Thomas Lincoln, is original.

Although the 16- by 18-foot Lincoln homestead is a replica, it is constructed of 115-year-old logs and stands on the same spot as the one built by the president's grandfather (for whom he was named), who was the first of the family to settle in Kentucky. Behind the cabin is the creek that became known as Lincoln's Run shortly after the family settled here. Several of the cabin's furnishings were made by Thomas, the president's father.

The Berry House, a two-story structure built of massive yellow poplar beams and furnished in pioneer style, was moved to the park from its original site about a mile away. On display in the house is a copy of the marriage bond of Thomas Lincoln and Nancy Hanks.

15 Mill Springs Mill. A stream fed by 13 springs powers the giant iron mill wheel, which has ground corn for over a century.

A small covered bridge has been built across the creek, leading to a replica of the shop that belonged to the master craftsmen who are said to have taught Thomas Lincoln his woodworking skill.

Something of an anomaly is the 18-hole golf course in the park.

▶ Open daily May–Sept. Admission charged.

www.parks.ky.gov
(859) 336-7461

---

15 Mill Springs Mill

Hwy. 1275, Mill Springs

Since the early 1800s this steep, wooded hillside has been a mill site. The present mill, which dates from 1877, has a 40-foot iron overshot waterwheel that was added in 1908 and believed to be one of the largest in the world. Power for the mill comes from 13 springs, which form a stream that cascades down the hillside into a large pipe leading to the waterwheel.

The building, a large white clapboard structure with a stone foundation, overlooks Lake Cumberland. A walkway takes you under the mill for a view of the wheel and the main drive shaft. Belts run from the shaft to the upper floor, where the corn is ground, usually on Saturday and Sunday afternoons.

The opening battle of the Kentucky-Tennessee campaign in the Civil War was fought at Mill Springs on January 19, 1862, a conflict that resulted in a victory for the Union forces. Still standing on the hillside above the mill is Lanier House; once the home of an early mill owner, it served as the Confederate headquarters. A fortification also remains at Mill Springs.

From the mill a path leads to Mill Spring Park on Lake Cumberland, where picnic areas and a boat dock are located. Several scenic hiking trails wind through the park.

▶ Park open Memorial Day–Oct.; mill and gift shop open Memorial Day–Labor Day.

www.lrn.usace.army.mil/history/
mill_springs_park.htm
(606) 679-6337

16 **William Whitley House.** The first brick house in Kentucky was built by war hero William Whitley in the late 18th century. On view inside are period artifacts and weapons.

16 William Whitley House State Historic Site

625 William Whitley Rd., Stanford

William Whitley, who was one of Kentucky's early pioneer settlers and hero of both the American Revolution and the War of 1812, completed his sturdy three-story brick dwelling in 1792. The first brick house in Kentucky, it sits on a low eminence enhanced with stately shade trees. The walls are 18.5 inches thick, and the windows are set higher than usual to give protection against attack by Native Americans. A secret stairway leads from the kitchen to the second floor, providing an escape route and a hiding place.

Among the period pieces on view are Whitley's rifle and powder horn, which he engraved with his own encouraging verse: "... fill me with the best of power I'le make your rifle crack the lowder." These possessions were

returned to Mrs. Whitley after her husband's death in 1813 at the battle of Thames in Ontario. A soldier later claimed it was Whitley who killed the great Shawnee chief Tecumseh in that encounter.

But there was more to Whitley's life here than worry about Native Americans. Nearby he built a horse-racing track, one of the first in a long Kentucky tradition. Whitley's pride in his home is perhaps most evident on the exterior walls, where glazed bricks prominently form his initials in front and those of his wife in back. A costumed guide interprets the house and its history for visitors. Two picnic shelters are on the grounds.

▶ Open Tues.–Sun. Apr.–Oct.; Tues.–Fri. Nov.–Mar. Closed major winter holidays. Admission charged.

www.parks.ky.gov
(606) 355-2881

did you know ❓

The William Whitley House was one of the first houses built west of the Allegheny Mountains.

17 Shaker Village of Pleasant Hill

3501 Lexington Rd., Harrodsburg

The American Shaker Movement began in 1774, when members of a religious sect with a conviction in Christ's second coming and simple living left Liverpool, England, and arrived in New York City. By 1776 the group settled in Niskeyuna, New York, near Albany. At first the group's missionaries, who spread through New England, met with persecution, brought on by their unorthodox theology and ways of worship.

Eventually, however, the Shakers attracted many followers within and beyond New England. In 1805 believers in Kentucky began moving to a community taking shape. Pleasant Hill came into being when 44 members signed the first family covenant and purchased land on a nearby hilltop. By 1823, 491 Shakers called Pleasant Hill home.

Today Pleasant Hill claims the nation's largest and most completely restored Shaker community and living museum. A National Historic Landmark, the village offers visitors the chance to discover sim-

plicity—in architecture, furniture, and daily activities—as intended by its founders. Thirty-four of the 270 original buildings erected by the Shakers remain. Along a self-guiding tour, visitors can meet interpreters in authentic Shaker garb.

Within the community skilled artisans work at 19th-century trades and old-style farming. Daily demonstrations include broom making, spinning, weaving, coopering, woodworking, gardening, and domestic and farm labor.

In the village two craft stores feature Shaker reproductions, furniture, and miscellaneous items, including hand-sewn brooms. Visitors can also board the *Dixie Belle* stern-wheeler to take a trip back in time on a beautiful stretch of the historic Kentucky River.

▶ Open year-round except Christmas Eve and Christmas Day. Fee charged for riverboat tour.

www.shakervillageky.org
(800) 734-5611

17 **Shaker Village of Pleasant Hill.** Interpreters guide visitors at the nation's largest Shaker community, set on 3,000 pastoral acres of Kentucky Bluegrass Country.

18 Fort Boonesborough State Park

4375 Boonesborough Rd., Richmond

The fort that stands here today, evoking the period of Kentucky's early pioneer settlement, is a detailed reconstruction of one built nearby on the banks of the Kentucky River by Daniel Boone and about 30 fellow frontiersmen in 1775. These were the first settlers sent out by Col. Richard Henderson of North Carolina to establish a colony west of the Appalachians. Despite the fact that Henderson had purchased a vast tract of land from the Cherokees for the colony, the settlers immediately found themselves at odds with the Shawnees and other local people who were being encouraged by the British to attack American settlers during the Revolutionary War. Boone's daughter and two other girls were kidnapped by Native Americans. Boone and nine of his companions tracked the captors and rescued the three girls.

About two years later Boone and a group of companions were captured by the Shawnees. Boone escaped, made his way to Boonesborough, and urged improvement in its defenses. The precautions were taken, and late in the summer of 1778, the little fort withstood a 10-day siege by the Native Americans, thus securing the survival and growth of the Kentucky settlements.

Upon entering the fort today, a visitor is taken back to the settlers' world. Several of the cabins display furnishings typical of the period and the Spartan circumstances, and in others frontier crafts are demonstrated. A small museum is devoted to Boone and the life of the pioneers.

The park also offers a large campground with hookups as well as primitive tenting sites, a recreation area with facilities for various activities, an inviting sandy beach along the river for swimming, and a boat-launching ramp. Fishermen usually catch bass, perch, bream, and catfish. The park's Kentucky River Museum traces the development of commerce on the river. The park is heavily visited on holidays and summer weekends.

▶ Campground open year-round.
   Admission charged to view fort.

www.parks.ky.gov
(859) 527-3131

19 Natural Bridge State Resort Park

2135 Natural Bridge Rd., Slade

The work of millennia, the natural sandstone arch for which the park is known, is a wonder at 78 feet in length. The park itself, located in the Daniel Boone National Forest, contains 2,500 acres, 1,188 of which have been set aside as a nature preserve. The magnificent arch and other stone formations give the park a distinctive character.

To get to the Natural Bridge, visitors can either hike a portion of the park's 20 miles of trails or pay a fee to take the sky lift to its terminus, within 600 feet of the bridge. Other attractions include Hoedown Island, the site of weekly square dances, and an 18-hole miniature golf course. Fishing on Mill Creek Lake is also popular because the lake contains a good supply of bass, bream, catfish, crappie, and rainbow trout. A pool complex is available, and visitors' options for overnight stays include the park lodge, cottages, and campgrounds.

▶ Open year-round. Campground closed
   mid-Nov.–mid-Mar.
   Admission charged.

www.parks.ky.gov
(606) 663-2214; (800) 325-1710

18 Fort Boonesborough State Park. Daniel Boone was one of 30-odd frontiersmen who built the fort. The buildings seen today are authentic reconstructions.

20 Kentucky Folk Art Center

102 W. First St., Morehead

Housed in the restored historic Union Grocery building, the Folk Art Center is a service of Morehead State University that presents the work of Kentucky's self-taught visual artists. By displaying the art of Kentucky, the center also exhibits the unique culture of the region.

The first floor is a riot of color and captivating themes, presenting pieces from the center's growing collection of more than 1,300 works by Kentucky artists. The Garland and Minnie Adkins Gallery, located on the second floor, is the site of five or more new exhibits each year. These special shows deal with a wide variety of subjects, ranging from folk art to world cultures.

The center also designs exhibitions that travel to sites across the United States. In addition to visual art, the center presents programs relating to other aspects of regional culture, including music, dance, literature, and cultural traditions. Collaboration with the Kentucky Center for traditional music and community groups leads to educational programs and an annual traditional music festival.

Each June the center hosts a popular "A Day in the Country" folk-art show, where more than 60 artists from 12 states present and sell their work to the public. The center also hosts a large regional crafts fair, which is held in December.

▶ Open year-round. Closed Sun. Jan.–Mar.
   Admission charged.

www.morehead-st.edu/kfac
(606) 783-2204

21 Buckhorn Lake State Resort Park

4441 Rte. 1833, Buckhorn

This quiet mountain park takes excellent advantage of the lake that was created in 1961 by a 162-foot dam built several miles downstream on the middle fork of the Kentucky River. Primarily designed for secluded family holidays devoted to water sports, the park offers a sandy beach, a boat-launching ramp, and a marina with 95 slips for water enthusiasts. In addition, the park has a picnic area, a playground, tennis courts, and a self-guiding nature trail that winds through the woodlands. Anglers, either in boats or on the spacious fishing pier, are likely to catch largemouth and smallmouth bass, crappies, bluegills, channel catfish, and muskies. Rental boats are available.

The quiet park roads invite cyclists. A modern 36-room lodge and three cottages are operated by the park, and a publicly operated campground is located nearby. Musical shows, square dancing, and other entertainment is offered occasionally in the lodge.

www.parks.ky.gov
(800) 325-0058

22 Cumberland Gap National Historical Park

Hwy. 25E, Middlesboro

It was the creek flowing north toward the Cumberland River that first showed the way through this section of the Appalachian Range. Herds of buffalo wandered along Yellow Creek; then the Native Americans followed, creating the so-called Warriors Path, linking the Cherokees of the East with the Shawnees to the Northwest.

22 **Cumberland Gap National Historical Park.** The discovery of Cumberland Gap allowed explorers and settlers to make their way west for the first time.

Fur traders, hunters, and pioneer farmers traveled the route. In 1775 Daniel Boone and a crew of axmen blazed the Wilderness Road for some 200 miles and opened a corridor that started the first migration to the West.

In the early 1800s faster and easier westward routes were developed, and the importance of Cumberland Gap declined. Today it is primarily known for its colorful history and scenery.

A road (closed to trailers and vehicles more than 20 feet long) from the park's visitors center winds precipitously up to the 2,500-foot pinnacle. A short footpath bordered with wild phlox and mountain laurel leads from the parking lot to an overlook with an astounding view of the gap and the valleys and peaks of three states.

Within the park is the Hensley Settlement, a wilderness community of 12 farmsteads established on Brush Mountain in the early 1900s by the Hensley and Gibbons families. It flourished for almost

50 years before it was abandoned in the 1950s. Visitors can hike to the area on a four-hour guided tour that leaves from the visitors center several times a day.

Now being restored, the community can be reached only by shuttle or a hike over rough terrain. Those who make the trip will gain some insight into the self-sufficient way of life that these stouthearted people chose to pursue.

Four primitive campsites, accessible only by foot, are located on the Ridge Trail, a route along the Kentucky-Virginia border. Picnic areas and hiking trails are scattered throughout the park. Maps and information are available at the visitors center in Middlesboro. Tour times change throughout the year depending on staff and weather.

▶ Park open year-round; visitors center open daily except Christmas.

www.nps.gov/cuga
(606) 248-2817

seasonal events

APRIL
- Kentucky Derby Festival—Louisville *(Great Balloon Race, Great Steamboat Race, Pegasus Parade)*
- Chocolate Festival—Maysville *(homemade chocolate, fudge contest, candy hunts, carriage rides, tours)*

MAY
- Strawberry Festival—Beaver Dam *(live music, dancing, parade, car and motorcycle shows)*

JUNE
- Ben E. Clement Gem and Mineral Show—Marion *(mineral digs, tours)*
- Kentucky Blueberry Festival—Edmonton *(live entertainment, games, cook-off, children's activities)*
- Chaney's Dairy Barn, Barnfest!—Bowling Green *(antique tractor show, celebrity milk-off)*

AUGUST
- Flemington County Covered Bridge Festival—Flemingsburg *(guided tours, arts-and-crafts show, live music)*

SEPTEMBER
- Great Outhouse Blowout at Penn's Store—Danville *(outhouse racing, live music, car and motorcycle show)*
- Rolling Fork Iron Horse Festival—New Haven *(train rides, live entertainment, parade, displays, car show, arts and crafts)*

OCTOBER
- Buffalo Daze—Stamping Ground *(mechanical bull rides, live entertainment, arts and crafts)*
- Jerusalem Ridge Bluegrass Celebration—Rosine *(some of the biggest names in bluegrass)*
- Hunter Moon Festival—Grand Rivers *(live music, parade, crafts, children's activities)*
- Salt Festival—Union, Big Bone Lick State Park *(hands-on demonstrations of pioneer activities, atlatl [spear throwing] contest, crafts)*

www.kentuckytourism.com

KENTUCKY

Louisiana

Bayous, dazzling camellias and azaleas, stately plantation houses, and some unexpected pleasures await travelers to this culturally rich state.

Sam Houston Jones State Park. Fishing and boating lure kids of all ages to this park near Lake Charles (see page 139).

One of the richest archaeological sites in North America is Poverty Point, in northeastern Louisiana, where prehistoric hunters built vast earthworks. Another site was once a fortress and capital of the Spanish province of Texas. The 19th-century Greenwood Plantation boasts the prototypical antebellum mansion, while Melrose Plantation—developed by a former slave—is now a popular center for local writers, artists, and craftspeople.

Travelers can stop and smell the flowers for which the South is famous at an arboretum, a state park, and a botanical garden. On the natural history side is a New Orleans museum dedicated to bugs. Reptiles and birds and mammals are the stars of the much-lauded Creole Nature Trail, which passes by the area where the pirate Jean Lafitte hid his treasure.

visit ➤ offthebeatenpathtrips.com

1 Cypress Black Bayou Recreation Area

135 Cypress Park Dr., Benton
This 340-acre piney park is perched at the junction of two large bayou-fed reservoirs. Here one can fish from several of the piers, launch a boat, swim at a sandy beach (at your own risk), along wood chip–paved nature trails, rent a cabin, pitch a tent, or enjoy a picnic.

The park's nature center has facilities for the study of plants, and there is a zoo for animals native to these woods.

The park is popular with birders, who often come to observe the many kinds of songbirds and waterfowl that inhabit the towering pine forest and the quiet waterways. The park is usually crowded from April to Labor Day.

▶ Open daily except Christmas.
Admission charged.

www.cypressblackbayou.com
(318) 965-0007

2 Poverty Point State Historic Site

6859 Hwy. 577, Pioneer
Despite its name, Poverty Point is one of the richest archaeological sites in America. The lower Mississippi Valley was inhabited from 3,500 to 2,500 years ago by Native American tribes who developed a culture sufficiently organized and enduring to construct massive earthworks here on a bluff along Bayou Macon.

It is estimated that 5 million man-hours were required to build the complex, which consists of six semicircular rows of long, low ridges (divided into sections by aisles) and four mounds, the largest of which is bird-shaped and rises to a height of 70 feet.

These ridges and mounds were assumed to be part of the natural landscape, but when they were viewed from an airplane, it became obvious from the striking symmetry of their design that they were the work of man.

 **Los Adaes State Historic Site.** The excavation site of a former capital of the Spanish province of Texas lies in quiet countryside west of Natchitoches.

Scholars still ponder the purpose for which the Poverty Point complex was built. Although one of the mounds was located over a crematory, archaeologists do not interpret the place as an ancient burial site. Conjectures about the use of the concentric ridges range from building foundations to an astronomical observatory.

A guided tram tour loops through the 400-acre site. The museum in the information center displays effigies, jewelry, tools, weapons, and other artifacts from the site.

The ingenuity of the residents of this rock-free terrain can be seen in their production of fire-hardened clay balls to use as cooking stones.

▶ Open daily except major winter holidays. Admission charged.

www.lastateparks.com
(888) 926-5492

3 R. S. Barnwell Memorial Garden & Art Center

601 Clyde Fant Pkwy., Shreveport

The peaceful, domed indoor botanical garden, filled with tropical flora like the seven-foot powder-puff tree and the cardboard plant, draws people to visit here. The fragrance garden outside is an unexpected bonus. Designed as a sensory garden for the visually impaired, it is inviting for all guests—with its rare scented geraniums, rosemary, and mint, and intimate picnicking area nearby. Named for a northwest Louisiana oil pioneer, this refuge on the Red River offers views of the skylines of the twin cities of Shreveport and Bossier, and the Texas Street Neon Bridge—a public art project completed in 1993.

The art center features exhibits by local, regional, and national artists representing all genre, while the store is known for its one-of-a-kind contemporary handmade works by skilled artisans from the Louisiana Crafts Guild.

▶ Open year-round Tues.–Sun. Closed Mon. and major holidays.

www.barnwellcenter.com
(318) 673-7703

4 Los Adaes State Historic Site

6354 Hwy. 85, Robeline

The fortress and mission known as

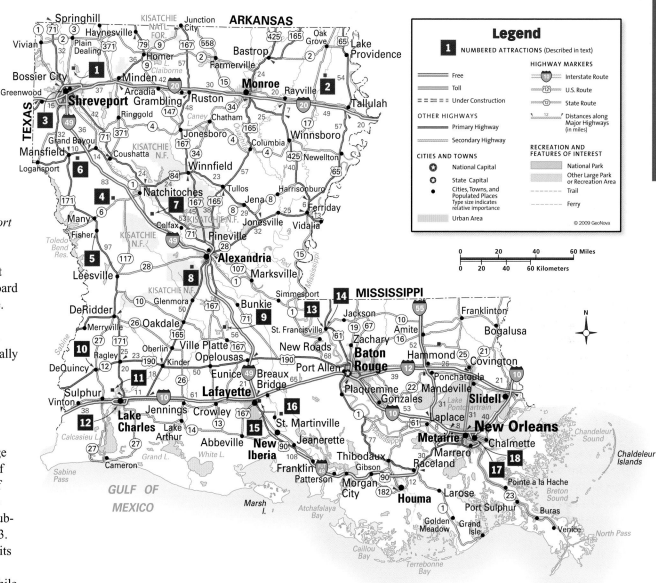

Los Adaes, which under Spanish rule served as the capital of the province of Texas, was built in 1719 as a stronghold against the French. Its reign as the center of the Texas government ended a half century later, when France gave the unprofitable Louisiana colony to Spain, and the fort was closed down and deemed unnecessary.

In the 18th century, when Los Adaes flourished, the town was inhabited by Spanish soldiers and Adaes Native Americans. It included a blacksmith's shop, a small chapel, and soldiers barracks. The buildings have long disappeared, but the 58-acre site has a historic hiking trail, earthenworks, a timber outline of the fort, and part of the original El Camino Real de los Tejas, the major roadway to Mexico City.

The visitors center displays a collection of tools, weapons, and other artifacts found on the grounds, and the staff offers programs on the day-to-day lives of the Spanish

Colonial settlers of the area. The site of the fort itself is marked by a flag.

▶ Grounds open daily except major winter holidays.

www.lastateparks.com
(318) 472-9449

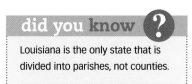

did you know ?

Louisiana is the only state that is divided into parishes, not counties.

5 ▶ Fisher: Historic Sawmill Town

Sabine Parish

Shaded by the longleaf pines that once brought wealth to its citizens, this almost completely deserted turn-of-the-century sawmill town lies at the end of a quiet road a half-mile downhill from the First Baptist Church.

As you approach the town, the long, low, white commissary faces you across a square, its porch stretching the entire width of the building. Off to one side, with a white picket fence in front, stands the old opera house, a hall that served as the center of the town's activities. Its ticket window, with a little rounded shelf, opens onto the front porch. Alongside the old railroad tracks is the railroad station, with its paneling, benches, and ticket office still intact. The interiors can be visited by appointment.

The town comes to life once a year during the third weekend in May, when the annual Sawmill Days festival is held.

www.sabineparish.com
(318) 256-2001; (318) 256-2623

6 ▶ Mansfield State Historic Site

15149 Hwy. 175

Fought on April 8, 1864, the battle of Mansfield was one of the largest Civil War conflicts west of the Mississippi River and one of the last major Confederate victories of the Civil War. The defeat of Union forces thwarted Union Gen. Nathaniel Banks's invasion of Northwest Louisiana and Texas. Banks, who commanded 35,000 troops, was soundly defeated by the Confederate Gen. Richard Taylor, son of former president Zachary Taylor.

The state historic site encompasses 178 acres of the original battlefield, and it also features markers, monuments, and cannon displays, as well as a battlefield trail.

The park's interpretive center and museum feature weapon and uniform displays, battlefield artifacts, dioramas, and an introductory audiovisual program.

Monthly interpretive programs include musket and cannon firing, soldier encampments, lectures, and battlefield tours.

Some of the heaviest fighting occurred in Mansfield during the Civil War, but one would never guess that today when walking down its tranquil tree-lined streets adorned with antebellum mansions.

▶ Open daily except major holidays. Admission charged.

www.lastateparks.com
(888) 677-6267; (318) 872-1474

7 ▶ Melrose Plantation

3533 Hwy. 119, Melrose

Two remarkable women held sway here a century apart. The first was a determined and enterprising slave named Marie Therese Coincoin, who in 1778 was freed along with several of her 14 children. She obtained a land grant on the Cane River from the Spanish colonial authorities and, aided by her sons, cleared the land and established a successful tobacco and indigo farm that eventually became known as Melrose Plantation.

The other woman was Mrs. Cammie Garrett Henry, known simply as Miss Cammie, who came into possession of the plantation about 1898. She carefully restored the original four-room cypress-timbered house called Yucca that Marie Therese built in 1796, as well as the imposing white clapboard Big House that Marie Therese's grandson completed in 1833, and turned Melrose into a

9 ▶ Louisiana State Arboretum. The rustic wooden gate is a fitting introduction to this pleasant, no-frills nature site in the hills of south-central Louisiana.

center for local arts, crafts, history, and folklore.

Miss Cammie invited artists and writers to come and work in Yucca House, and the little structure probably housed more notable writers than any other in the South. One writer came for a six-week visit and stayed for 32 years.

Yet another remarkable woman came out of Melrose. In the 1940s the plantation's onetime cook, Clementine Hunter, began to paint and became known as the black Grandma Moses. Some of her colorful murals can be seen upstairs in Yucca House.

Other buildings on the grounds include the African House, the Weaving House, and the Bindery, which serves as a visitors center.

▶ Open year-round Tues.–Sun. except major holidays. Admission charged.

www.natchitoches.net/melrose
(318) 379-0055

8 ▶ Wild Azalea Trail

Hwy. 28 W, Boyce

The 31-mile trail (27 miles in the woods), named for the wild azaleas that bloom in the forest in early spring, winds through great stands of hardwoods and pines, skirts a bog, and crosses open meadows and several creeks as it makes its way from Valentine Lake, west of Alexandria, to Rte. 165, south of the city.

Well marked with yellow blazes, the trail takes hikers through the Castor Creek Scenic Area, a part of the forest that has remained untouched for years.

At several places the trail crosses U.S. Forest Service roads, where hikers who want to walk only partway can park cars or arrange to be picked up. Tent camping is permitted adjacent to the trail, and RV parks can be found four miles north of the trail's western end.

▶ Open year-round.

www.fs.fed.us/r8/kisatchie
(318) 793-9427

9 Louisiana State Arboretum

4213 Chicot Park Rd., Ville Platte
In this unexpectedly hilly region of Louisiana, a little more than three miles of good, well-marked trails traverse woodlands and wander down into a ravine, with plants identified along the way.

Because of the variations in topography and microclimates, almost every kind of Louisiana plant life can be found in this arboretum. Among the trees in the forest are American beech and the unusual big-leaf magnolia. The animal life that flourishes here includes white-tailed deer and great barred owls.

The interpretive center contains exhibits on the life of Caroline Dorman, a premier naturalist in Louisiana. For birders a checklist of both migratory and native species is available at the center.

Walking and looking are the only activities that are allowed here but the adjoining Chicot State Park has full facilities, including another arboretum site within the park; its entrance is 1½ miles to the south on Hwy. 3042.

▶ Open year-round except major winter holidays.

www.lastateparks.com
(888) 677-6100

10 DeQuincy Railroad Museum

400 Lake Charles Ave., DeQuincy
DeQuincy was settled in 1895 at the juncture of the Kansas City Southern and the old Missouri Pacific railroads. The imposing tile-roofed Spanish Colonial Kansas City Southern depot, which houses the museum, is listed on the *National Register of Historic Places.*

On display at the museum are the tickets and timetables of the early 1900s, the old-fashioned mail pouch that the engineer of a passing express train had to catch with a hook, and memorabilia of the town's railroad men. The mannequin of a ticket agent, sitting in his office with his back to the door, is so real that visitors sometimes whisper for fear of disturbing him as he works at his desk.

A 1913 steam locomotive with coal car and vintage caboose is also on display. An annual railroad festival is held here the second weekend of April.

▶ Open daily except major holidays.
Admission free but donations encouraged.

www.visitlakecharles.org
(337) 786-2823

11 Sam Houston Jones State Park

107 Sutherland Rd., Lake Charles
Named originally for the hero of the Alamo, who according to legend often stayed in this area, the 1,087-acre park now carries the name of the 1940s Louisiana governor who was responsible for preserving these grounds. Here you will find some of the loveliest landscape in Louisiana—towering pines, dense woodlands, lakes, and cypress-bordered lagoons.

The quiet, scenic waters are ideal for boating, and boats are available for rent. A launch ramp and two docks are provided for those who bring their own. Fishing from a boat or along the banks can produce a catch of white perch, bream, or bass. The park has several campsites, picnic grounds, and nature trails.

During the migrating season birders come here for a tally of the species that stop to rest and feed on their way across the state.

▶ Open year-round. Admission charged.

www.lastateparks.com
(888) 677-7264; (337) 855-2665

12 Creole Nature Trail

*Exit 36 off I-10, Lake Charles;
exit 20 off I-10, Sulphur*
Just beyond the interstate lies Louisiana's Outback—a world of natural beauty and bustling activity. This 180-mile stretch is the Gulf South's only official National Scenic Byway and All-American Road—coveted designations awarded by the Federal Highway Administration that ensures a rewarding driving experience. It's in this area that the notorious pirate Jean Lafitte hid his treasure and where Louisiana's Cajun culture took root.

From the car this vast expanse of prairie and marshland appears peaceful and tranquil. Yet it's teeming with life, boasting 16 species of mammals. With thousands of alligators, it's now supported by a major alligator research center.

The Creole Nature Trail is also considered one of the nation's top birding destinations. Sightings of some 250 species of birds have been recorded. Butterflies of all colors also flock here by the millions.

To better view the abundance of lovely winged creatures, drivers can stop at the Sabine National Wildlife Refuge, the Cameron Prairie National Wildlife Refuge, or the Peveto Woods Birds and Butterfly Sanctuary. And there are downloadable MP3 audio tours available for every leg of the trail.

▶ Open year-round.

www.creolenaturetrail.org
(800) 456-7952; (337) 436-9588

Creole Nature Trail. Bird-watchers at the four wildlife refuges on the 180-mile nature trail spy waterfowl of many species. This area is also home to thousands of American alligators.

13 St. Francisville Historic District

Ferdinand St.

Set on a narrow bluff rising above the junction of the Bayou Sara and the Mississippi River, the small town of St. Francisville is a charming example of the value of architectural preservation. The historic district includes almost 130 well-kept residences, churches, and public and mercantile buildings that date from the early 19th to early 20th centuries. The diversity of building styles—neoclassical manor to cozy bungalow—amounts to a trip through history. Start your visit by picking up a walking-tour map at the West Feliciana Parish Historical Society Museum.

After exploring the town, you can stop by the Greenwood Plantation (see site #14). Also nearby is the Audubon State Historic Site, named for naturalist and painter John James Audubon, who lived and worked at the on-site Oakley Plantation early in his remarkable career.

www.stfrancisville.net
(800) 307-8241

14 Greenwood Plantation

6838 Highland Rd., St. Francisville

Colonnaded on all four sides, this Greek Revival structure stands on a rise overlooking a reflecting pool edged with azaleas, willows, and moss-draped live oaks. Lavishly furnished with Victorian antiques, it is such a perfect-looking antebellum Southern mansion that it has been used as the setting for five movies and two TV miniseries.

Surprisingly, however, the building is a reconstruction, though some of the furniture and paintings are original. The home, built by cotton and sugarcane planter Ruffin Barrow in 1830, was completely destroyed by fire in 1960 except for the 28 columns surrounding it. The rebuilding was the dedicated undertaking of Carolyn and Richard Barnes, who also farm the plantation, now reduced in size from 12,000 acres to 278.

▶ Open year-round except major holidays. Admission charged.

www.greenwoodplantation.com
(800) 259-4475; (225) 655-4475

Audubon Insectarium. This unique museum pays homage to bugs, including the Thai sagra beetle shown at right.

15 Vermilionville

300 Fisher Rd., Lafayette

Vermilionville is now a living-history museum and folk life and heritage park, but it was originally a colony of Cajuns (Acadians—French settlers expelled from eastern Canada) and Creoles (possibly of French, Spanish, Native American, and/or African mixed racial heritage). The name comes from the red clay banks of the Bayou Vermilion in southwest Louisiana. Interpreters demonstrate music and traditional crafts, reflecting life in the colony, from its founding in 1765 through 1890. Structures include a blacksmith shop, a forge, and a schoolhouse. Zydeco, Creole, or Cajun dance bands perform their joyful music on weekends, and boat tours snake down the bayou in the fall and spring.

In the period just before Ash Wednesday, the Basil Mardi Gras Krewe revives colorful old country traditions, going house to house, begging, dancing, and singing for gumbo ingredients in an exuberant atmosphere of costumed merry-making and music.

▶ Open year-round Tues.–Sun. Closed major holidays. Admission charged.

www.vermilionville.org
(866) 992-2968; (337) 233-4077

16 Longfellow-Evangeline State Historic Site

1200 N. Main St., St. Martinsville

This 120-acre park commemorates the original French Acadian settlers who came to the area in the mid-1700s after being expelled from Canada by the British.

It is named for Henry Wadsworth Longfellow and his beloved epic poem *Evangeline,* about star-crossed lovers separated by the expulsion. Tradition holds that the poem, although it ends differently, was inspired by the story of Emmeline Labiche, who died brokenhearted after discovering her long-lost beau had married someone else. A mile

did you know ?

Longfellow was inspired to write *Evangeline* after hearing a story at a dinner party with his friend Nathaniel Hawthorne.

Greenwood Plantation. All but the columns of this grand house, built in 1830, was destroyed by fire in 1960. The present-day house is an exact replica.

down the road a statue of Evangeline, sculpted in 1927, rests over the grave thought to be Emmeline's in the yard of nearby St. Martin's Church.

Along with the new visitors center, which focuses on early Louisiana history, including Acadian and Creole, the main attraction in the park is the plantation house Maison Olivier. Built of bousillage (a mixture of clay and Spanish moss in a cypress framework) and brick in 1815, the structure is typical of French plantation architecture. It has been carefully restored and is filled with early Louisiana pieces.

The park backs onto Bayou Teche, and by a little lagoon you will find an exceptionally inviting picnic area filled with trees curtained with Spanish moss.

▶ Open year-round except major winter holidays. Admission charged.

www.lastateparks.com
(888) 677-2900; (337) 394-3754

---

17 Audubon Insectarium

U.S. Custom House, 423 Canal St., New Orleans

If sharing a table with a silkworm or a tarantula in a vivarium and chowing down a burger with a side of Crunchy Cajun Roasted Crickets is your idea of a satisfying meal, then come to the Bug Appétit section of the Tiny Termite Café at this attraction, the largest museum in America devoted to the insect world.

Of course, you don't have to eat insects; you and your children can simply enter the Life Underground exhibit and experience life *as* an insect! It's a cavelike space, where everything is enlarged, so you feel like a tiny bug crawling along the ground.

Entomologists are stationed throughout the museum to help you get up close and personal with velvet ants, beetles, and the odd praying mantis. See the damage Formosan termites can do via a balsa wood silhouette of New Orleans, or leave time behind in the serenity of the Japanese Butterfly Garden.

▶ Open year-round Tues.-Sun. Closed major holidays. Admission charged.

www.auduboninstitute.org
(800) 774-7394; (504) 581-4629

---

18 The National World War II Museum

945 Magazine St., New Orleans (Entrance on Andrew Higgins Dr.) Opened June 6, 2000, to commemorate the 56th anniversary of the Normandy invasion that liberated Europe, this one-of-a-kind museum—designated by Congress as the country's official World War II Museum—celebrates the spirit of the men and women who sacrificed and persevered to win World War II in Europe and the Pacific. Founded

by the late author Stephen Ambrose, who taught history at the University of New Orleans, it is the only museum in the United States to cover all of the amphibious invasions of World War II. It is located in New Orleans because it was here that Andrew Higgins designed and built more than 20,000 landing crafts used by the Allies that helped win the war.

Located in the city's growing downtown arts district, the multi-story museum tells the story of *The War That Changed the World*—why it was fought, how it was won, and what it means today. The gallery showcases powerful oral histories, never-before-seen film footage, frontline artifacts, and photographs of the home front and battlefront. Within the complex the Malcolm Forbes Theater features two films: *D-Day Remembered* and *Price for Peace*.

▶ Open daily Oct.-June; closed Mon., major winter holidays. Admission charged.

www.nationalww2museum.org
(504) 527-6012

18 ▶ The National World War II Museum. Boats known as LCVPs (Landing Craft, Vehicle, Personnel) were used for the Normandy D-Day landings of June 1944.

---

seasonal events

FEBRUARY
- Mardi Gras—Statewide

MARCH
- Audubon Pilgrimage—St. Francisville (*entertainment, period dress in honor of ornithologist John James Audubon*)

APRIL
- Holiday in Dixie—Shreveport (*celebration of Louisiana Purchase*)

MAY
- Breaux Bridge Crawfish Festival— (*Cajun, Zydeco, and Swamp pop music, Cajun food and culture*)
- Mudbug Madness—Shreveport (*four-day crawfish Cajun festival*)

JUNE
- Peach Festival—Ruston (*cooking contests, pageants, family activities*)

JULY
- Essence Music Festival—New Orleans (*celebration of African-American culture and music*)

AUGUST
- Satchmo Summerfest—New Orleans (*four-day French Quarter tribute to trumpeter Louis Armstrong*)

SEPTEMBER
- Southwest Louisiana Zydeco Festival—Plaisance Community, Opelousas

OCTOBER
- Natchitoches Pilgrimage—(*historic homes and candlelight tours*)
- Festivals Acadiens et Créoles—Lafayette (*salute to Cajun and Creole cultures with dancing and crafts*)

NOVEMBER
- Three Rivers Arts Festival—Covington

DECEMBER
- Bonfires on the Levee—between Lutcher and Gramercy (*Christmas Eve bonfires along the Mississippi*)

www.louisianatravel.com

LOUISIANA

Maine

Man-made attractions hold their own in a state best known for its wild and beautiful forests, offshore islands, and rockbound coasts.

Lily Bay State Park. Like all moose, those seen in the woods of this rugged park often roam singly until they band together in preparation for winter (see page 144).

Whether by the sea or in Maine's remaining wilderness, the parks and recreation areas in the first state to greet the sunrise enchant travelers with their beauty. From Moosehead Lake to fog-shrouded Roque Bluffs, Maine is a picture postcard come to life.

Also in these pages are glimpses of the people's life and work—a logger's museum, a preserved blacksmith shop, and a farm where visitors can experience life as it was in 19th-century Maine. You'll also visit an island whose inhabitants exemplify the rugged individualism on which Mainers rightly pride themselves.

visit ➤ **offthebeatenpathtrips.com**

1 Fort Kent State Historic Site

Blockhouse Rd., Fort Kent

This area was first settled in the early 1800s by French colonists who were forced from their Canadian homes in Acadia (now the Maritime Provinces) when they refused to pledge allegiance to the conquering British.

The great stands of timber attracted lumbermen from Canada and the United States, and border disputes developed. Concerned about its interests, the state of Maine dispatched troops to the area and built a fort at a strategic juncture of the Fish and St. John rivers. Completed in 1839, the fort was named for Gov. Edward Kent. It was armed and manned, but the boundary disputes were settled in 1842, and no shots were ever fired.

The Blockhouse, which housed officers in the mid-1800s, was restored by the Boy Scouts and is maintained by the Maine Bureau of Parks and Lands and a local troop. A collection of antique hand tools is displayed inside.

Parking spaces, water taps, picnic tables, and fireplaces are available on the bank of the Fish River. True to its name, the river yields salmon and trout.

▶ Open Memorial Day–Labor Day.

www.maine.gov/doc/parks
(207) 941-4014

1 Fort Kent State Historic Site. The Blockhouse, built of square-hewn cedar logs in 1842, is the anchor of a fort that was named Maine's first historic site in 1891.

2 The Nylander Museum

657 Main St., Caribou

This museum is a tribute to one man's lifelong curiosity about the world around him. At the young age of 10, Olof Nylander, the son of a shoemaker in a small Swedish town, sold his collection of local Stone Age and Bronze Age implements to a museum in the nearby city of Ystad.

Nylander came to America in his teens and developed a consuming interest in geology. Before his death in 1943 at age 79, he had established a reputation as a tireless and innovative fieldworker and had published many articles

in scientific journals. His wide-ranging personal collection of geological and freshwater and marine-life specimens, as well as Native American and other arti-facts, is housed in the museum.

The tidy white clapboard structure was built in 1938 by the Works Progress Administration, a federally funded organization established to provide much needed employment during the Depression.

In addition to the extensive Nylander collections and archives, the museum houses permanent displays of butterflies, artifacts made by the local Micmac and Malecite people, large taxidermy specimens from northern Maine, and local Devonian and Silurian fossils. Special exhibits are mounted during the summer season.

▶ Open Tues.–Sat. Memorial Day–Labor Day.

www.nylandermuseum.org

(207) 493-4209

---

did you know ?

Under a charter issued by King William and Queen Mary in 1691, the province of Maine was part of the Massachusetts Bay Colony until its separation in 1820.

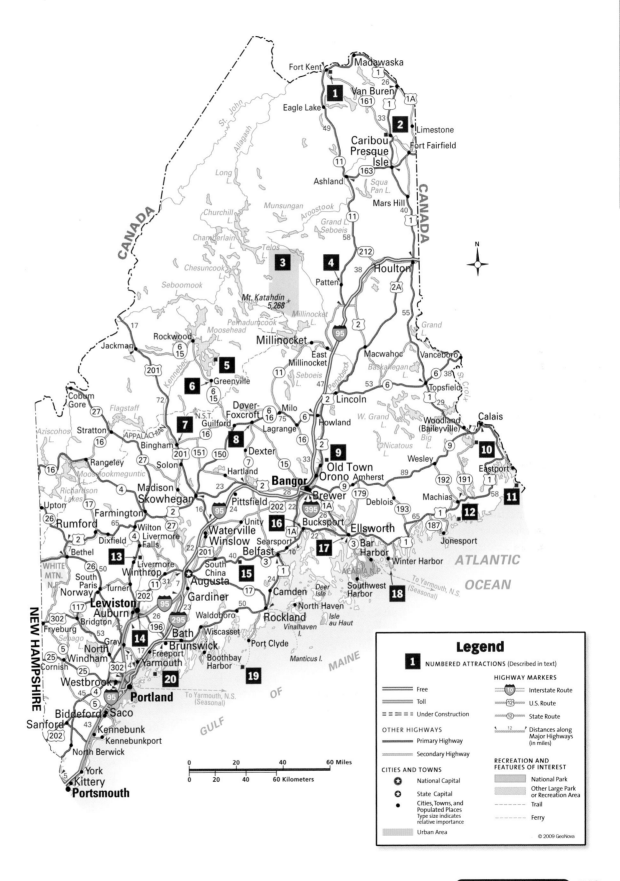

3 Baxter State Park

Millinocket

Few governors have been more generous to their constituents than Percival P. Baxter. Between 1930 and 1962 he bought and gave to the people of the state of Maine some 200,000 acres of wilderness and set up trust funds to defray the costs of development and maintenance.

The state has kept faith with the intent of the gift, and it strictly enforces the rules that sustain the spirit of wilderness here. No pets or other domestic animals are allowed, and no motorcycles, trail bikes, or other all-terrain vehicles are permitted in the park. Snowmobiles are strictly limited to specific areas. Hunting, trapping, and the use of weapons are prohibited except in certain areas during the hunting season. For anyone seeking the peace and quiet that the wilderness can offer, these are all welcome regulations.

Vehicles more than 9 feet high, 7 feet wide, and 22 feet long are not allowed in the park. Maximum length for a car and trailer is 44 feet.

At South Branch Pond, in a tranquil woodland setting, you can rent a canoe, enjoy one of the inviting picnic spots that offer fireplaces, or spend the night in a lean-to shelter or tent site (available by reservation) in a grove of white birches. Hiking trails range from less than half a mile to almost 10 miles. Tours about forestry are offered.

▶ Park open for daytime use year-round; camping mid-May–mid-Oct. and Dec.–Mar. Admission charged. Reservations suggested.

www.baxterstateparkauthority.com
(207) 723-5140

 Baxter State Park. Sandy Stream Pond mirrors the autumn-tinged forest of the North Basin. In the background is Mount Katahdin, the highest mountain in Maine.

4 Patten Lumbermen's Museum

61 Shin Pond Rd., Patten

Before the Revolution, when Britannia ruled the waves, the great stands of pine along the coastline were reserved by the Crown for masts on their mighty ships.

The product has changed in size, from 75-foot masts to the toothpicks now made here by the billions, but the material is the same: pine from the Pine Tree State. It is fitting that the history of lumbering is commemorated here in Patten, where the industry still survives and logging trucks continue to roar by.

Of the 4,500 artifacts on display, a goodly percentage are from the collection of the late Dr. Lore Rogers. They include tools and equipment for every imaginable lumber-camp chore.

One of the 10 buildings on the site is a reconstructed 1820 logging camp, where crew members once slept on rows of evergreen boughs.

Photographs, dioramas, and working models illustrate how standing timber was felled and converted to lumber in the early days. A featured display is the old and rare Lombard Steam Log Hauler. As the predecessor of the continuous-tread bulldozer and the military tank, it has been declared a national historic mechanical engineering landmark.

▶ Open Fri.–Sun. Memorial Day–June; Tues.–Sun. July–Columbus Day. Admission charged.

www.lumbermensmuseum.org
(207) 528-2650

5 Lily Bay State Park

13 Myrle's Way, Greenville

This is a pleasant place to sample the appealing character of the rugged Maine woods, and with 925 acres in the park, crowding is not a problem. The moose in the area frequently favor Lazy Tom Bog. Although any moose in the wild is a memorable sight, they are at their most impressive here when autumn nights foreshadow the coming of winter and the animals begin to group together.

Also unforgettable is the haunting cry of the loon, a beautiful diving bird with a distinctive white necklace in sharp contrast to its black plumage.

The views of Moosehead Lake and Big Moose Mountain to the southwest are magnificent. The park offers a pebbled swimming beach and a small field for Frisbee, volleyball, and other games.

▶ Open mid-May–mid-Oct.

www.maine.gov/doc/parks
(207) 695-2700 Park season
(207) 941-4014 Off season

6 Moosehead Marine Museum

17 Lily Bay Rd., Greenville

The museum houses a small onshore collection of marine memorabilia, but the centerpiece here is a 110-foot lake steamer. The steel-hulled *Katahdin* was built in 1914 to take tourists to the luxurious Mount Kineo Resort and other destinations on Moosehead Lake. The lavishly appointed ship, with fixtures and furnishings of brass, mahogany, leather, and velvet, was queen of the Maine lake steamers for more than 20 years. When the resort failed after World War I, the *Katahdin* was reduced to the hard service of towing log rafts on the lake. Then environmental considerations put a stop to the rafting of logs, and it seemed that this historic ship (the oldest-surviving steel hull built by the Bath Iron Works) was headed for the scrap heap.

She was saved, however, by a group of local enthusiasts who preserved the ship as a floating museum and put her back in service on the lake. The newly refurbished *Katahdin* is now available for short cruises and group charters.

From the deck of the original passenger carrier here, one can see the sleek seaplanes that now serve the lakeshore and the wilderness beyond.

▶ Open late June–Columbus Day weekend. Admission charged.

www.katahdincruises.com
(207) 695-2716

---

7 Wyman Lake

Rte. 201, Moscow
Few hydroelectric projects relate so well to their surroundings as does this one. For 16 miles along its high eastern shore, superb panoramic views of Wyman Lake and its somber background of timbered mountains await the visitor. History is remembered here; at a scenic outlook about four miles south of Caratunk, a tablet marks the place where Benedict Arnold and more than 1,000 men

left the Kennebec River on an expedition to Canada in 1775. Their mission was to participate in an assault on Quebec.

Today there is excellent access to the lake to the north at the Caratunk boat landing and to the south at the Moscow boat landing.

The views are less spectacular along the road that follows the west shore, but other attractions are found, including bathing beaches and, seven miles north of the dam, a picnic area. Of interest to birders are the bald eagles, osprey, and loons seen here.

www.byways.org/explore/byways/11510
(207) 672-4100

---

8 The Blacksmith Shop Museum

100 Dawes Rd., Dover-Foxcroft
Before the days of mass production, mail-order parts, paved highways, and automobiles, every small community had to be largely self-sufficient, and the skills of the

6 **Moosehead Marine Museum.** Visitors to the museum cruise Moosehead Lake—seen here from Mount Kineo—on the *Katahdin*, a lavishly appointed vintage steamer.

ironworker were much in demand. The village smithy in earlier times was as essential to the community as the general store.

Here in a small shingled barn, where the fires of the forge went out in 1905, the tools of this demanding and disappearing craft are displayed along with some of the handmade iron objects that were used for farming, transportation, recreation, and everyday living.

A harness-repair bench, a cheese press, an ox lifter, and other old-time implements remind the visitor of a less complex time— when horsepower was provided by horses instead of machines.

▶ Building is open daily Memorial Day weekend–Oct.

www.rootsweb.ancestry.com/~medfhs
(207) 564-8618

---

9 Sunkhaze Meadows National Wildlife Refuge

Milford
Established in 1988 to protect the

fragile ecosystem of the state's second largest peat land, this wildlife refuge boasts a tremendous variety of vegetation—from an expanse of trees and shrubs to an array of fungi. This gorgeous habitat is home to an abundance of diverse wildlife. Butterflies and damselflies are often seen flitting around, as are more than 200 different species of birds. You may even encounter a lone bear, bobcat, or moose on occasion.

There are a few short trails for hiking or skiing around the perimeter of the meadow, but perhaps the best way to enjoy the ecological diversity of the watery refuge is by canoeing or kayaking up or down the Sunkhaze Stream and its tributaries exploring the variety of landscape that the bogs offer. Insect repellent is strongly recommended during the warmer months.

▶ Open daily year-round.

www.sunkhaze.org
(207) 236-6970

9 **Sunkhaze Meadows National Wildlife Refuge.** The grasses, trees, and wetlands of this peat-rich refuge draw birds, butterflies, reptiles, amphibians, and mammals.

10 ▶ Moosehorn National Wildlife Refuge

Rte. 1, Baring

Anyone who is interested in seeing Northeastern wildlife in its natural habitat would be well advised to spend some time here.

The refuge, one of more than 400 across the nation, is on the Atlantic Flyway and provides feeding and resting grounds for flights of migratory birds.

More than 200 species have been observed here, and most of these, including the osprey and bald eagle, are commonly seen. There are two observation decks from which birders can view the many different varieties that flock here. Visitors can even accompany wildlife biologists on certain bird-tagging expeditions. The refuge puts a major emphasis on determining and providing for the ecological needs of the American woodcock. This interesting bird has been steadily declining in number because its woodland habitat has been encroached upon.

The various tracts in the refuge total about 25,000 acres and support some 40 kinds of mammals year-round. At the Edmunds Unit, 20 miles to the south, harbor seals and Atlantic porpoises are seen offshore. The bear, moose,

10 ▶ Moosehorn National Wildlife Refuge. Once on the brink of extinction, the American bald eagle is easy to spot at this refuge.

11 ▶ Quoddy Head State Park. The West Quoddy Head Light, the easternmost lighthouse in the United States, was one of the first to use fog bells and steam-powered foghorns.

fox, bobcat, deer, and beaver are to be expected inhabitants in this environment, but that supposed Westerner, the coyote, is something of a surprise.

▶ Open year-round.

http://moosehorn.fws.gov
(207) 454-7161

11 ▶ Quoddy Head State Park

Quoddy Head Rd., Lubec

A bit of the Maine wilderness can be sampled in this 532-acre park, which includes the easternmost point of land in the United States. Here in the spruce woodlands deer and an occasional moose may be seen, but predatory bobcats and coyotes are said to be reducing their number. Porcupines and rabbits range through the park, and the usual birds of the Northeastern woods and meadows are abundant.

One of the inland trails includes a section of boardwalk beside a peat bog, with signs to identify the wildflowers that grow here in profusion. The main trail that runs for about 2½ miles around the head offers good views of nearby West Quoddy Head Light, where a beacon has served

mariners since 1808. The sunrise can be spectacular here and often has an interesting greenish cast. In summer this is a favorite place for whale-watching.

▶ Open mid-May–mid-Oct.
  Admission charged.

www.maine.gov/doc/parks
(207) 733-0911

12 ▶ Roque Bluffs State Park

145 Schoppee Point Rd., Roque Bluffs

The 274 acres that make up this relatively new coastal park were acquired in 1968 and converted for recreational use a decade later. Roque Bluffs is still quiet and infrequently visited, partly because it is often enshrouded by fog. July is the best month to enjoy its half-mile crescent beach, but even then the waters of Englishman's Bay are chilly. The shore affords pleasing views of several wooded islands, one of which is Roque Island.

The park includes the 33-acre Simpson's Pond, where swimming and fishing are permitted. Among the park's many species of winged residents is the bald eagle.

At several spots there are well-equipped picnic sites, one of which has a playground. The park has boardwalks but no camping facilities.

▶ Open mid-May–Sept.
  Admission charged.

www.maine.gov/doc/parks
(207) 255-3475; (207) 941-4014

13 ▶ Washburn-Norlands Living History Center

Norlands Rd., Livermore

This impressive complex was built for the Washburns, a remarkable family of 19th-century political, military, and business leaders.

The Washburn house is a fine example of the Italianate style. Pure New England, however, are the farmer's cottage and the large barn attached to the house in deference to the hard winters here.

The library, built in 1883 to serve the family and the community, is a handsome granite building in the High Victorian Gothic style. Architecture of an earlier day is also exemplified by the old-time schoolhouse and the white clapboard church with tall, narrow arched windows, ornate latticed bell tower, and a steeple crowned with an old-fashioned weathervane.

Today Norlands is a multifaceted museum offering in-depth experiences in 18th- and 19th-century rural life. Here, the visitor becomes an active participant in daily and seasonal farming and housework, taking part in the social, political, and educational activities of the times. Norland's stated mission is to be a site where visitors can experience opportunities for hands-on involvement in the activities and skills of sustainable and independent rural living in both historical and contemporary times.

The museum offers a number of programs for tour groups, including families and individuals, but visitors are encouraged to make advance reservations.

▶ Open July–Oct. for tours and year-round by appointment. Admission charged.

www.norlands.org
(207) 897-4366

14 Thorncrag Nature Sanctuary

Montello St., Lewiston
Surrounded on three sides by the city of Lewiston, this 357-acre sanctuary is the highest point in the city at 510 feet. It is a small natural oasis amidst the bustling town. It boasts six different wildlife habitats, from wetland to forest, which host a variety of flora and fauna,

including dozens of species of birds.

Owned in the 19th century by a local family, the land had been used for a variety of purposes before it was turned over to the Stanton Bird Club, which created and maintains the sanctuary, and evidence of previous tenants can be found along the trails that crisscross the grounds. Hiking and picnicking and, in the winter, skiing, snowshoeing, and skating are all encouraged.

▶ Open daily year-round.

www.stantonbirdclub.org/thorncrg.htm
(207) 782-5238

15 Lake St. George State Park

278 Belfast Augusta Rd., Liberty
This attractive lakeside park is a pleasant place for picnicking, swimming, and fishing. Its handsome administration buildings are

reminiscent of the 19th-century architecture prevalent in the area.

Of the three main picnic areas, one is adjacent to the lake. It has bathhouses for swimmers and a camper parking area that accommodates small- to average-size vans and trailers.

About 100 yards of the pebbly shoreline serve as a swimming beach. Wood steps provide easy access to the water, and a string of buoys outlines the safe area.

Fishermen here catch mostly bass and landlocked salmon. Boat launching is permitted, and canoes and rowboats are available for rent. In addition, the park offers trails for hiking and snowmobiling.

▶ Open daily mid-May–Sept.

www.campwithme.com
(207) 589-4255

16 Penobscot Narrows Bridge.
The bridge over the Penobscot River stands next to the aging original. The lookout atop it is the world's tallest bridge observatory open to the public.

16 Penobscot Narrows Bridge and Observation Deck

740 Fort Knox Rd., Prospect
In 2003 engineers discovered severe corrosion in the cables of the old Waldo-Hancock Bridge across the Penobscot River and determined that the bridge would have to be replaced. In just three short years a new bridge was designed and built right next to the old one, its two granite towers soaring 420 feet above the river. To take advantage of this height, an observation deck was constructed at the pinnacle of one of the towers, providing spectacular views of the river and its surroundings.

Next door Fort Knox State Historic Site showcases a well-preserved example of a 19th-century stone fort, and the nearby town of Bucksport has shops and restaurants as well as a good view of the bridge spanning the river.

▶ Open May–Oct. Admission charged.

www.fortknox.maineguide.com
(207) 469-6553 Friends of Fort Knox

12 **Roque Bluffs State Park.** Swimming aficionados who visit this park, named for the village on its edge, can choose from saltwater swimming off the pebble beach on the ocean shore or freshwater swimming in 33-acre Simpson's Pond. Fishing is also permitted.

17 Stanwood Wildlife Sanctuary and Homestead

289 High St., Ellsworth

This property was owned and cared for by one family for more than 100 years, and one member of that family devoted her lifetime to the careful study of nature. It is not surprising, therefore, to find here a delightful aura of tranquillity. Capt. Roswell Stanwood built his simple white-frame cottage in 1850. Fifteen years later a daughter, Cordelia, the first of five children, was born in that house.

The surrounding woods, the spring, the stream, and the ponds were affectionately called Birdsacre by Cordelia Stanwood. It is here where she developed a deep appreciation of the ways of nature— especially of birds. Her inquiring mind and compelling interest in the subject led her to become an accomplished amateur ornithologist and wildlife photographer.

She lived and worked here for more than 50 years. It is fortunate that others can now visit the rooms and walk the paths and thus share a legacy of peace and quiet in a place where nature was studied, respected, and preserved.

The complex includes the unpretentious house, with its comfortable lived-in quality, the nature trails and bird sanctuary, and the Richmond Nature Center, which includes egg and nest collections and bird mounts, an art

---

did you know ?

Maine is known as the nation's lobster breadbasket, with fishermen hauling in more than 60 million pounds a year.

---

gallery featuring the work of local wildlife artists, and a gift shop.

▶ Sanctuary open daily year-round. Homestead open daily June–Sept.

www.birdsacre.com
(207) 667-8460

---

18 Schoodic Peninsula

The only part of Acadia National Park on the mainland, Schoodic Peninsula has fewer tourists than the larger, more diverse, and better-known Mount Desert Island.

But something of the special character of Acadia is perhaps more beguiling here, where headlands of weathered rock reach down to the water, and farther out, at Schoodic Point, the ocean is tumultuous and spectacular. The heavy seas thunder headlong into great shelves of pink granite and spray high into the air.

John G. Moore acquired the peninsula to use as a wild park adjacent to a resort he was planning to build. But he died in 1899, and the property went to his heirs.

 **Schoodic Peninsula.** At this mainland portion of Acadia National Park, the dizzying view of a cove takes in the North Atlantic surf and the rugged cliffs along the shoreline.

They offered it as an addition to the existing Lafayette National Park on Mount Desert Island, with the stipulation that the name of the park be changed. By an act of Congress in 1929, the peninsula was added, and the name of the park was changed to Acadia.

From Rte. 186 the entire rugged shoreline is paralleled by a six-mile-long stretch of well-maintained one-way road that drivers share with cyclists. At frequent turnouts splendid seascapes break through the forest wall and offer views of bogs, coves where shorebirds feed, bays dotted with lobster boats, and wooded islands in the distance. A mile-long gravel road climbs to Schoodic Head, where on clear days the coastal view is magnificent.

The Blueberry Hill parking area is the departure point for hiking trails ascending inland through stands of spruce and across open hillsides dotted with low-bush blueberries. One steep trail ascends 180 feet to a promontory called the Anvil. One can also walk down toward the water to view marine flora and fauna.

▶ Open year-round.

www.acadiamagic.com/schoodic
(207) 288-3338

---

19 Monhegan Island

Situated 10 miles out in the Atlantic, this 650-acre isle epitomizes the beauty of wind-swept Maine, with its rocky coasts, rugged headlands, moors, and forests of spruce and balsam. The surrounding ocean surf is calm enough for fishing or an invigorating dip on some beaches, but it can be turbulent and unpredictable on the seaward sides. Here, also, the traditional Maine industry of

Monhegan Island. This unspoiled island's scenery has long inspired watercolorists and painters.

lobster fishing has been refined to a science with an enforced shortened season to sustain the size and quality of the catch.

In its remoteness Monhegan has resisted one of the pervasive features of modern life: automobiles, which cannot be brought to the island. The attractions are to be enjoyed on foot. Of the 17 miles of trails, some are quite rough, marked only by stacked rocks.

In the village, as dusk descends, most of the residents light up their gas or kerosene lamps to accompany the stars and moonlight. For several generations artists have summered on the island and contributed to a prodigious output of coastal landscapes and seascapes. Beginning in July, many of these works are on display in the Monhegan Museum (open limited hours June–Sept.), the Lupine Gallery, and artists' studios.

Inns, guesthouses, and cottages offer accommodations, and there are a few restaurants. There are no bars, and hard liquor is not

sold. Camping and backpacking are not permitted. Boats make daily round-trips from mid-May through mid-October, for which advance reservations are strongly advised.

▶ Three ferry lines go to Monhegan:
Monhegan Boat Line (207) 372-8848
Hardy Boat Cruises (207) 677-2026
Balmy Days Cruises (207) 633-2284

www.monheganwelcome.com

20 ▶ Eagle Island State Historic Site

Eagle Island, about two miles offshore, was the lifelong retreat of Adm. Robert E. Peary, who discovered the North Pole on April 6, 1909. The celebration Peary expected on his return did not take place, because another explorer claimed to have been there first.

Scientific evidence and a congressional inquiry later confirmed, however, that Peary's expedition was the first to raise a flag at the

top of the world. Peary built the house on Eagle Island and spent most of his summers here. He left the place to his daughter and son, who donated it to the state of Maine for use as a historic museum.

The large house, with a three-sided fireplace in the living room and a big restaurant-style stove in the kitchen, has an aura of hospitality that belies the admiral's reputation as a stern authoritarian.

A small ocean beach is open to swimmers who are willing to brave the chill waters, and the woods offer a pleasant choice of short nature trails.

If you plan to stop over, bring food and refreshments, because none are sold on the island. Contact the Bureau of Parks and Lands for boat information to the island.

▶ Open daily mid-June–Labor Day. Admission charged.

www.maine.gov/doc/parks
(207) 624-6080

20 ▶ **Eagle Island State Historic Site.** Eagle Island, in Casco Bay, is a private island known for the imposing summer home of North Pole explorer Adm. Robert E. Peary.

MAINE

seasonal events

FEBRUARY
• Winter Carnival—Caribou *(festival, sports, live entertainment)*

APRIL
• Bangor Garden Show—Bangor *(garden festival, flower show, lectures)*

JUNE
• Acadian Festival—Madawaska *(live entertainment, local food, sports, parade)*

JULY
• Annual Heritage Days—Bath *(land and boat parade, carnival, arts and crafts, regional food, live entertainment)*
• Maine International Film Festival—Waterville *(film shows, along with question-and-answer sessions)*
• Yarmouth Clam Festival—Yarmouth *(culinary festival, carnival, live entertainment, parade, arts and crafts, sports)*

AUGUST
• Maine Lobster Festival—Rockland *(parade, carnival, arts and crafts)*
• Maine Antiques Festival—Union *(dealers, arts and crafts)*
• American Folk Festival—Bangor *(music, regional food)*

SEPTEMBER
• Country Road Artists and Artisans Tour—Rockport
• Harvest Fest & Chowdah Cook-Off—Bethel *(live entertainment, wagon rides, pie contest, arts and crafts)*

OCTOBER
• Fryeburg Fair—Fryeburg *(agricultural festival, livestock contests, sports, live entertainment, flower show)*
• Leonard's Mill Living History Days—Bradley *(period food, live entertainment)*

NOVEMBER
• Maine Literary Festival—Camden *(lectures, readings, signings, workshops)*

DECEMBER
• Shaker Christmas Fair—New Gloucester *(arts and crafts)*

www.visitmaine.com

Maryland

From the coastal plain to the Appalachian Mountains, all the natural regions that typify the eastern United States are found within this state's borders.

Historic St. Mary's City. A model sailboat is one of the many artifacts found at a town that relives its 17th-century past day by day (see page 154).

Maryland offers spectacular mountain scenery, lakes, streams, beaches, and a seaside cliff studded with Ice Age fossils. The state is also the home of an important refuge for waterfowl. Here on the Atlantic Flyway it isn't surprising that the art of decoy carving was highly developed, and a museum is dedicated to the subject. Other attractions include Historic St. Mary's (the state's first capital), an elegant mansion whose owner played host to the Washingtons and the Adamses, and a small town that has laid claim to being the seafood capital of the world.

visit ➤ offthebeatenpathtrips.com

1 ▶ Swallow Falls State Park

2700 Maple Glade Rd., Oakland
This peaceful woodland park on the rocky banks of the swift-running Youghiogheny River has been a longtime favorite with campers. A plaque marks the site where naturalist John Burroughs and inventors Thomas Edison, Harvey Firestone, and Henry Ford camped in 1918.

Hiking trails, which cut through a stand of 300-year-old virgin hemlocks towering above verdant expanses of ferns, mountain laurel, and rhododendrons connect to a system of paths and old logging roads in adjoining Garrett State Forest.

The Canyon Trail, considered to be one of the most beautiful in the state, leads from Swallow Falls to Muddy Creek Falls. Along the rocky ledges are many plant fossils. The highest vertical waterfall in Maryland, with a plunge of over 50 feet, is seen to best advantage from its base or from a popular overlook. In these deep, quiet woodlands the visitor is likely to observe deer, wild turkeys, beavers, black bears, and an occasional fox.

The Youghiogheny River is stocked with trout several times a year.

▶ Open year-round; camping mid.-Apr.–mid-Dec.

www.dnr.md.gov
(301) 334-9180

1 ▶ Swallow Falls State Park. Rapids on the Youghiogheny are just one of the attractions in this park. "Youghiogheny" is a Native American word for "river in a roundabout course."

2 ▶ Boonsborough Museum of History & Crystal Grottoes Caverns

Museum: 113 N. Main St.
Caverns: 19821 Shepherdstown Pike Boonsboro
Founded in 1792 by brothers George and William Boone, relatives of Daniel, Boonsboro prospered during the early 1800s as it became a stopping place for pioneers traveling westward by wagon.

This museum houses a unique collection of Civil War relics from the battlefields of South Mountain, Antietam, and Harper's Ferry and boasts a formidable collection of firearms, from tiny watch fob pistols to cannons weighing several tons, as well as more than 500 weapons from around the world.

Here are rare books, including an original copy of *Martyr's Mirror,* the largest book printed in Colonial America; a fossil collection that includes dinosaur bones and mammoth and mastodon teeth; Russian icons and "relics" of famous saints; mummified birds; objects from the Spanish galleon that sank off the Florida coast in 1733; and reconstructions of a cabinetmaker's shop of 1860 and a turn-of-the-century country store.

Boonsboro is also home to Crystal Grottoes Caverns, one of the largest caves of its kind in the country. Winding through illuminated walkways, visitors will revel

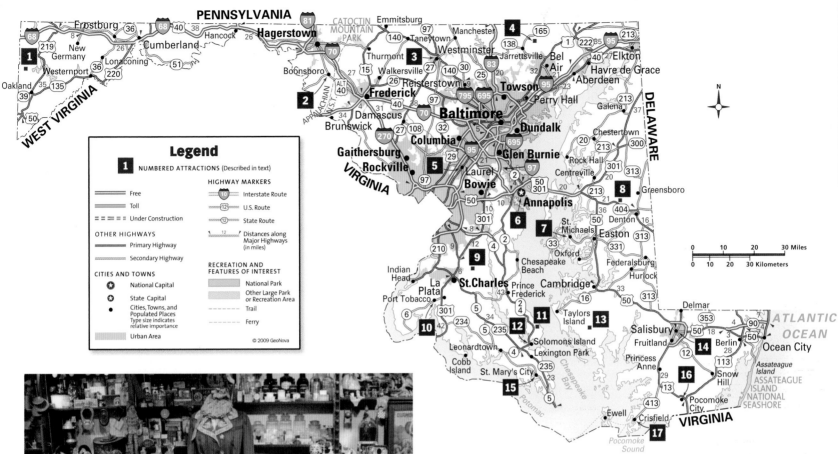

Boonsborough Museum of History. One of the exhibitions is the reconstruction of a country store stocked with dry goods and other items sold in the mid-1890s.

3 Historical Society of Carroll County's Sherman-Fisher-Shellman House

206 E. Main St., Westminster

One of Westminster's finest buildings is on Main St. at No. 206. The handsome Georgian town house was built in 1807 by Jacob Sherman, a German settler from Pennsylvania, as a wedding gift for his daughter.

Now called the Sherman-Fisher-Shellman House after a series of owners, the 2½-story brick mansion is a house museum depicting life in Carroll County in the early 1800s.

Next door, in the Kimmey House (circa 1800), is the Shriver-Weybright Exhibition Gallery, which has rotating exhibits on topics relating to Carroll County

Sherman-Fisher-Shellman House. The house, now a museum, has been restored to its original appearance.

history. The Willis-Boyle house, known as Cockey's and down the street, is home to the museum shop.

▶ Open year-round except major holidays. Admission charged.

http://hscc.carr.org

(410) 848-6494

at natural sculptures made of pure-white stalactites and stalagmites. Guides demystify the rare formations on a 35-minute tour.

▶ Museum open Sun., May–Sept. and by appointment. Caverns open daily Apr.–Oct.; weekends in winter. Admission charged.

www.boonsboromd.govoffice2.com
(under History)

(301) 432-6969 Museum

www.goodearthgraphics.com/showcave/md/crystal.htm

(301) 432-6336 Caverns

 **Rocks State Park.** Few formations are odder than those found here.

4 Rocks State Park

3318 Rocks Chrome Hill Rd., Jarrettsville

Atop a 190-foot cliff overlooking the rolling hills of Deer Creek valley looms an enormous thronelike rock formation known as the King and Queen Seat—so named, it is said, for the ceremonial meetings held here by the Susquehannock Native Americans.

Trails of varying length and steepness lead up the cliff. The park is also home to Kilgore Falls, Maryland's second highest free-falling waterfall.

Delightful picnic sites are set along the banks of Deer Creek, a mountain stream that winds among steep-sided hills clad with mixed evergreens and hardwoods. Bring your own kayak or tube.

▶ Open year-round except major winter holidays. Picnic areas open Mar.–Oct. Admission charged.

www.dnr.md.gov
(410) 557-7994

5 Montpelier Mansion

9650 Muirkirk Rd., Laurel

This beautifully proportioned Georgian house was built for Maj. Thomas Snowden and his wife, Anne, just after the American Revolutionary War. Elegant and situated on a high knoll, its English boxwood gardens are considered to be among the loveliest in the United States. Many of the rooms have been furnished as they would have appeared from the end of the 18th century. The staff offers tours, re-enactments, teas, and lectures.

Major Snowden's marriage in 1774 to Ann Ridgely, a rich heiress, gave the vast plantation a name—Montpelier—in honor of his bride's birthplace in Anne Arundel County.

George and Martha Washington occasionally visited Montpelier, as did Abigail Adams, who praised the "large, handsome, elegant House" and the Snowdens' "true English hospitality."

▶ Tour hours: Sun.–Thu., Mar.–Nov.; Sun. only Dec.–Feb. Gardens open year-round. Admission charged for house tours.

www.pgparks.com
(301) 953-1376

 **Montpelier Mansion.** A planting bed and terraced grounds complement the Georgian contour of this house. The construction of Montpelier began in 1781.

6 Annapolis Maritime Museum and Thomas Point Shoal Lighthouse

723 Second St., Annapolis

Set on the shores of Back Creek, with panoramic views of the Chesapeake Bay and Annapolis Harbor, the Annapolis Maritime Museum revels in the richness of Chesapeake lore. Its Bay Experience Center offers an unrivaled interactive facility. Family-oriented outdoor activities include sailboat race watching and "chicken-neckin'," the time-honored way to catch Atlantic Blue Crabs.

In 2004 the museum joined a consortium that took over ownership of the beautiful Thomas Point Shoal Lighthouse. Built in 1875 and on the *National Register of Historic Places*, the hexagonal 1½-story wooden cottage lighthouse is the Bay's most recognizable symbol. It is the last screwpile lighthouse left in its original location, 1½ miles offshore in the Chesapeake Bay. Hardy, adventurous souls can take a tour beginning at the Annapolis Maritime Museum's Barge House and continuing on a 30-minute boat ride, on possibly heavy seas, to the lighthouse. Once there, a rigorous climb up a steep ladder and through a trapdoor allows access into the lighthouse.

▶ Open daily except major holidays. Lighthouse tours weekends; reservations required. Admission charged for tour.

www.amaritime.org
(410) 295-0104

 **Montpelier Mansion.** An 1820 canopy bed is draped with toile.

7 St. Michaels

This delightful little Colonial town on the Miles River, an inlet from Eastern Bay, is centered at St. Mary's Square, the original "green" around which the town was built. Here you will find some of the best-preserved and most picturesque 18th- and 19th-century houses on the Eastern Shore.

Along the harbor nine waterfront buildings have been incorporated into the Chesapeake Bay Maritime Museum. Exhibits focused on Tidelands include the boatbuilder's shop; the historic

Colchester Beach bandstand; an 18th-century corncrib, which houses small gunning boats; and the (circa 1879) Hooper Strait Lighthouse, moved from its original site on Hooper Island.

The waterfowl building contains a splendid collection of decoys, hunting guns, and the sneakbox and sinkbox boats once used by commercial duck hunters.

▶ Museum open daily Apr.–Dec. except major holidays. Call for additional hours.

www.cbmm.org
(410) 745-2916

8 ▶ Tuckahoe State Park

13070 Crouse Mill Rd., Queen Anne

Rolling, wooded hills and open meadows are traversed by quiet, lovely Tuckahoe Creek.

Trails of varying difficulty are in this 3,800-acre park, from the Tuckahoe Valley Trail to the Lake Trail. For an even more vigorous workout, try the two-mile, 20-station exercise course and two playgrounds, which are provided. Other popular pastimes at the park include kayaking and fishing. And if you have your own canoe, you can try the 5½-mile trail on Tuckahoe Creek, or take a guided trip with a park naturalist, available in season. And for nature lovers the 500-acre Adkins Arboretum (the first to be built in Maryland) contains all the trees, shrubs, and plants indigenous to the Delmarva Peninsula. A dam across Tuckahoe Creek forms Crouse Mill Lake, at the end of which is a flooded forest. Bald eagles may be seen here perched on the spectral white trunks rising from the water.

▶ Park open year-round; camping late Mar.–late Oct. Camping fee.

 Thomas Point Shoal Lighthouse. Screwpile lighthouses such as this one were built by threading piles through steel disks on the sea bottom and then bolstering the piles.

www.dnr.md.gov
(410) 820-1668

9 ▶ Cedarville State Forest

10201 Bee Oak Rd., Brandywine

A scant 25 miles southeast of the nation's capital, this extensive forested area, once the favored winter hunting grounds of the Piscataways, provides a welcome contrast to the fast pace and clamorous noise of the city. Within the 3,510 acres are 19.5 miles of marked trails for hiking, biking, and horseback riding (but no rentals), as well as picnic sites and a 4-acre fishing pond. Self-guiding tours lead you through pine plantations established in the 1930s by the Civilian Conservation Corps, and past a historic kiln once used to make charcoal.

Cedarville is also the site of the headwaters of the mile-wide, 20-mile-long Zekiah Swamp, home to many plant, bird, and wildlife species. A few drainage ditches are the only remaining

evidence of backbreaking efforts in Colonial times to drain the swamp for cultivation. The labor was in vain, and the wooded bottomland remains largely as it was hundreds of years ago.

▶ Park open year-round; camping mid-Apr.–Oct. Admission charged per car.

www.dnr.md.gov
(301) 888-1410

10 ▶ Port Tobacco

Chapel Point Rd., off Rte. 6W, Port Tobacco

As early as 1608, a Native American settlement called Potopaco was noted here on a map drawn by Capt. John Smith. In the 1630s an English community was established, and about a hundred years later the town of Port Tobacco became the seat of Colonial government in Charles County. The burgeoning tobacco trade brought the planters modest prosperity, and a few handsome homes were built. Some have been restored and can be seen today around the village.

The reconstructed courthouse,

an unusual blend of late medieval and classic Georgian styles of architecture, now includes a 19th-century courtroom and a museum of Native American artifacts, Civil War relics, and local memorabilia. Port Tobacco has an ongoing archaeology program with occasional public digs.

▶ Courthouse and museum open weekends, Apr.–Sept. Admission charged. Schoolhouse open by appointment, Apr.–Sept.

www.thenationsbackyard.com
(800) 766-3386

11 ▶ Calvert Cliffs State Park

9500 H. G. Truman Pkwy., Lusby

These steep-sided 60- to 75-foot-high cliffs, which dominate the western shoreline of Chesapeake Bay for over 30 miles, are dramatic reminders that a warm, shallow sea covered this area some 15 million years ago. During the subsequent Ice Ages the sediments were compressed. As the ice finally receded, the land was uplifted, the sea level lowered, and the ancient seafloor was exposed to the forces of wind and water, which created the massive, precipitous cliffs.

More than 600 species of fossils have been identified here, but because of erosion, climbing on the cliffs and digging for these relics is prohibited. Fossils can, however, be found on the beach. Sharks' teeth are the most abundant, but various kinds of fossil shells are also found. An easy two-mile trail leads to the beach.

▶ Open daily year-round. Donations encouraged.

www.dnr.md.gov
(301) 743-7613

12 Solomons Island

At the confluence of the Patuxent River and Chesapeake Bay at the southern tip of Calvert County. Museum: State Rte. 2 on the Chesapeake's western shores

Barely a mile long and fittingly fishhook-shaped, Solomons Island was named in 1870 for Isaac Solomon, the Baltimore businessman who established its first oyster plant. At one time the island was separated from the mainland, but a 23-foot causeway now links the two.

This charming seaside town also offers about 20 casual restaurants; dozens of antiques, craft, and gift shops; several lovely inns and guesthouses; unique attractions.

One of them is Calvert Marine Museum, which reflects the area's rich maritime heritage, natural marine environments, and prehistoric past. Inside, visitors can see a giant Megalodon shark; touch 20-million-year-old fossils; see live marine life, including skates and rays; watch otters at play; and explore how human history has shaped this part of the Chesapeake region since Colonial times.

Outdoors, exhibits include a boat basin and a re-created salt marsh. From the museum's dock seafaring spirits can sign on for a one-hour harbor cruise aboard the *Wm. B. Tennison,* the oldest Coast Guard–licensed passenger-carrying vessel on the Chesapeake, built in 1899.

For more scenic views the adventurous can climb through the hatch of the Drum Point Lighthouse, constructed in 1883 to mark the entrance to the Patuxent River. It is beautifully restored and appointed with period furnishings.

Also restored and also listed on the *National Register of Historic Places,* the Joseph C. Lore & Sons Oyster House offers a taste of sea-

12 **Solomons Island.** Built in 1899, the *Wm. B. Tennison* is an example of a so-called bug-eye, a sailboat designed for oyster dredging in Chesapeake Bay.

food packing, circa 1934, featuring the tools and gear used by local watermen to harvest fish, softshell clams, eels, crabs, and oysters.

For landlubbers the peninsula offers the idyllic Annmarie Garden on St. John's Creek, which combines sculpture with cultivated flora. Throughout the year the garden hosts cultural programs and seasonal festivities, including the Garden of Lights each holiday season.

▶ Museum open year-round except major holidays. Garden also closed July 4. Admission charged for both.

www.sba.solomons.md.us
(410) 326-6027

13 Blackwater National Wildlife Refuge

2145 Key Wallace Dr., Cambridge

This 27,000-acre preserve consists mostly of salt marsh and saltwater ponds interspersed with stands of pine and mixed woodland. It is on the Atlantic Flyway and attracts

vast numbers of migratory waterfowl that winter here, including tundra swans, geese, and some 20 kinds of ducks. The refuge is one of the best spots on the East Coast to view bald eagles year-round. Found here, too, are great blue herons, peregrine falcons, and the fish-eating ospreys, for which nesting platforms are built. At the visitors center there is live video of two nests. All told, more than 241 species have been identified on the refuge.

A five-mile auto drive traverses the best of the area, and there are many walking and canoe trails.

Mammals here include the otter, opossum, deer, and red fox. The habitat of the endangered Delmarva fox squirrel, a large light gray species is being expanded.

▶ Open year-round. Wildlife drive charge per vehicle. Federal passes accepted.

www.fws.gov/blackwater
(410) 228-2677

14 Ward Museum of Wildfowl Art, Salisbury University

909 S. Schumaker Dr., Salisbury

The Ward Foundation, named for the late Steve and Lem Ward, is an unusual museum dedicated to the craft and art of decoy carving. The brothers, who began carving and painting decoys in 1918, were acknowledged masters. The museum features a replica of the Wards' workshop at Crisfield in southern Maryland (see also site #17).

The Wards fashioned both classic working decoys and remarkably lifelike decorative models. Fine examples of both styles—and the work of many others—are on display.

Using decoys to attract live ducks and geese is a practice of long standing. There are specimens made of rushes by Native Americans about 1,000 years ago. Here, too, are boats and blinds, firearms, carver's tools, a nature trail, and a video presentation of waterfowl migrations.

The museum sponsors competitions and workshops on the art of decoy carving and painting; examples are available in the gift shop.

▶ Open daily except major holidays. Admission charged.

www.wardmuseum.org
(410) 742-4988

15 Historic St. Mary's City

Take a turn off Rte. 5 in southern Maryland, and you could chance upon vibrant tableaux straight out of the 17th century. Listed on the *National Register of Historic Places*, St. Mary's comes to life via historical interpreters, archaeological excavations, and re-created village buildings.

While at St. Mary's be sure to visit St. John's Museum, which preserves the remains of the home of the first Provincial Secretary of Maryland. Experience life in the early colony through its interactive exhibits, such as its Print House or its Godiah Spray Tobacco Plantation with livestock. Learn about how this colony was the first to have all freemen in its government, and see where a woman first asked for the right to vote in British America.

▶ Open year-round except major winter holidays. Exhibits open mid-Mar.–Nov. Admission charged.

www.stmaryscity.org
(800) 762-1634; (240) 895-4990

16 Delmarva Discovery Center

2 Market St., Pocomoke City
It's all about the river—the Pocomoke River—at the Delmarva Discovery Center. Its exhibits pull you into the over 400 years of life on the river, from the Native Americans portrayed in a full-size diorama of their camp along the riverbank, to the 1870s steamers and the products they carried. You can hear lapping water and smell the docks.

The scenes immerse you in their depictions of life in the early days of settlement, and docents invite you to hoist sails and try basket making. Fishing, ecology, and environmental stewardship are all dealt with in its fascinating

did you know ?

Historic St. Mary's City was the fourth permanent English settlement in North America and the first state capital of Maryland.

displays. The cypress tree canopy seems alive as it changes in density while you follow the river's banks. And since the center is by the Pocomoke River, you can also enjoy its beauty outside while strolling on the Discovery Nature Trail (in Cypress Park across the street).

▶ Open year-round except major winter holidays. Admission charged.

www.delmarvadiscoverycenter.org
(410) 957-9933

17 Crisfield

Marina: 715 Broadway
The large marina, public boat landing, wholesale and retail fish markets, and numerous crab houses and restaurants support the town's claim to be the seafood capital of the world.

The Gov. J. Millard Tawes Historical Museum lets you trace the history of the Chesapeake Bay and offers exhibits on seafood

harvesting and processing. One can also take the Ward Brothers Heritage Tour and visit the workshop where the Ward brothers, famous decoy carvers, lived and worked.

For good tidewater swimming, crabbing, and fishing the Janes Island State Park beach is accessible only by boat. You can rent canoes and kayaks or use your own watercraft. Family camping is open late Apr.–Oct. on the mainland. Three primitive campsites are on the island itself.

Crisfield is also the point of departure for boat trips to nearby islands. Smith Island has three quaint fishing villages and a bus service. Tangier Island has a number of restaurants, craft shops, and guesthouses.

www.crisfield.com
(410) 968-1565 Janes Island State Park
(800) 782-3913 Chamber of Commerce
(410) 425-2771 Smith Island Cruises
(800) 863-2338 Tangier Island Cruises

15 ▶ Historic St. Mary's City. Children help a costumed interpreter with gardening chores at St. Mary's, the fourth oldest permanent settlement in British North America.

MARYLAND

MASSACHUSETTS

Massachusetts

Beyond Boston lie the forested Berkshires, Cape Cod, nature preserves, and the homes of some of America's most historic figures.

Moore State Park. A sawmill built in 1749 was powered by the waters of burbling Turkey Hill Brook (see page 159).

Known as the Bay State, Massachusetts maintains many superb parks, preserves, and wildlife sanctuaries. It also recognizes its historic and literary figures. Here you'll find the estate of the family that produced two presidents—the Adamses—and the homes of poets Emily Dickinson and John Greenleaf Whittier.

Early industry is represented by the Saugus Iron Works and Lowell Historical Park, while state-of-the-art oceanographic research is conducted in the waters off a picturesque town on Cape Cod.

visit ➤➤ offthebeatenpathtrips.com

1 ▶ Mount Greylock State Reservation

Accessible from Rte. 2 near North Adams or from Rte. 7 near Lanesborough

As you drive the steep, winding road up the mountain, the lush hardwood forests at the lower levels give way to the low-growing, wind-sculpted evergreens at the summit, the only subalpine habitat in Massachusetts.

Greylock, at 3,491 feet, is the highest peak in Massachusetts. On the summit is the Massachusetts Veterans War Memorial Tower, a stone tower erected here in 1933. Weather permitting, the top of the tower offers an incomparable panorama of the lovely green-clad mountains and valleys of Massachusetts, New Hampshire, Vermont, Connecticut, and New York. At the peak of Greylock is Bascom Lodge, which was built by the Civilian Conservation Corps in the late 1930s and offers food and accommodations.

Among the hiking paths in the reservation is an 11 1/2-mile section of the Appalachian Trail, on which you might meet some of the hardy backpackers going the full distance between Mount Katahdin in Maine and Georgia's Springer Mountain.

The weather at the summit may be quite different from that at the lower levels. Even in summer it is a good idea to take a sweater or

1 ▶ Mount Greylock State Reservation. Hikers who climb this trail to the top of Mount Greylock, in the Berkshire Mountains, are rewarded with 360-degree views.

windbreaker. The roads to the summit are open from mid-May to mid-Oct.

▶ Reservation open year-round.

www.mass.gov/dcr
(413) 499-4262

⛩🏕🚶🚴🔭⛴🎿❄♿🎣

2 ▶ Mohawk Trail State Forest

175 Mohawk Trail/Rte. 2, Charlemont

One of the most scenic woodland areas in Massachusetts, the state forest covers more than 6,000 acres of mountain ridges and deep gorges. Here you will walk on paths that connect the Connecticut and Hudson River valleys, where

Native Americans walked, following the course of the river. The pioneers heading west through this opening named it Pioneer Valley, and they aptly called the water the Cold River.

Flowing past the picnic area and campsites, the Cold River here is swift and boulder-strewn except for a pool for swimming. To the north rises the pine-covered bulk of Mount Todd. Many paths are available to the hiker. You can take a trail to the summit, follow the Indian Trail, which branches off to the left to a high viewpoint, or choose the one-mile trail to the south, leading you to the Totem Lookout.

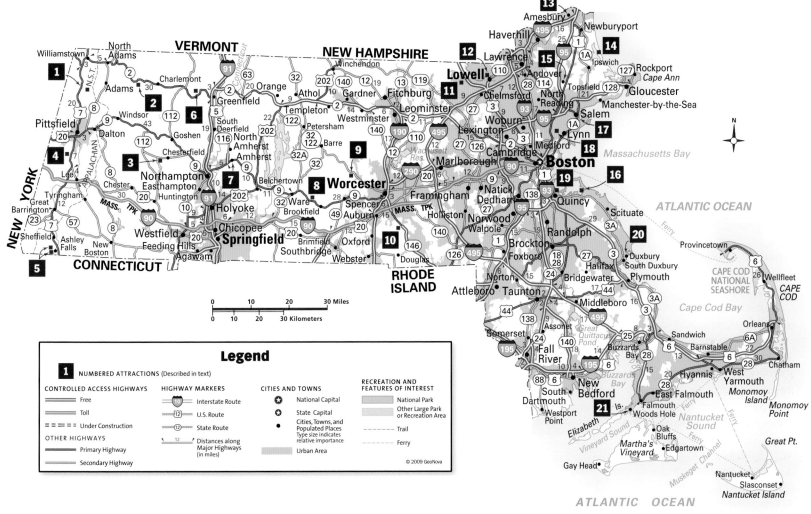

Legend

1 NUMBERED ATTRACTIONS (Described in text)

CONTROLLED ACCESS HIGHWAYS	HIGHWAY MARKERS	CITIES AND TOWNS	RECREATION AND FEATURES OF INTEREST
Free	**10** Interstate Route	★ National Capital	National Park
Toll	**12** U.S. Route	☆ State Capital	Other Large Park or Recreation Area
Under Construction	**12** State Route	• Cities, Towns, and Populated Places Type size indicates relative importance	
OTHER HIGHWAYS	**12** Distances along Major Highways (in miles)		Trail
Primary Highway			Ferry
Secondary Highway			Urban Area

© 2009 GeoNova

▶ Open year-round.

www.mass.gov/dcr

(413) 339-5504

3 ▶ Chesterfield Gorge

River Rd., off Rte. 143, Chesterfield
The dramatic power of nature is demonstrated here, where the action of ancient glaciers and the erosive force of the Westfield River have cut a gorge about 100 feet deep through solid granite. The river today cascades between vertical cliffs into a deep green pool.

The gorge lies hardly 50 yards from a road running through farmland that offers no hint as to the powerful natural forces that

Chesterfield Gorge. Glacier meltwater originally cut this chasm through metamorphic rock. Today the east branch of the Westfield River courses through the gorge.

created it. The ample parking and picnic facilities are a further invitation to stop off here.

▶ Accessible year-round. Admission charged.

www.thetrustees.org

(413) 684-0148

did you know ?

During the Revolutionary War the redcoats marched toward Boston, following their defeat in Saratoga, New York, over a bridge that once spanned the Chesterfield Gorge. Its stone abutments still remain.

4 Pleasant Valley Wildlife Sanctuary and Canoe Meadows Wildlife Sanctuary

Off Rte. 7/20, Pleasant Valley is located at 472 W. Mountain Rd., Lenox; Canoe Meadows is located on Holmes Rd., Pittsfield

The lifestyle of that busy builder and hydraulic engineer, the beaver, is available for all to see at Pleasant Valley, where you will get a close-up look at the gnawed stumps of the beavers' building material and the complex dams they make to control the water level in their mounded lodges.

Beavers were introduced here along Yokun Brook in 1932, and their dams have made ponds that now provide habitats for migrant waterfowl and other birds. Because the sanctuary is at a relatively high elevation, such birds as the hermit thrush, winter wren, and slate-colored junco, normally rare to this area, stay here in spring and summer instead of pushing on farther north to their usual nesting grounds.

The 1,314-acre area is laced with some seven miles of trails winding past ponds and waterways and through meadows and woods. The Trail of the Ledges, which leads to a fire tower and a fine view, is steep in places and should probably not be tried by those unaccustomed to uphill hiking.

A hummingbird garden attracts numbers of these jewel-like flyers from June–Aug.

And if the trails and sites at Pleasant Valley have got you yearning for more, visit Canoe Meadows, located just four miles away. Established in 1975, the sanctuary consists of 264 acres of wetlands, fields, and forests along the Housatonic River, with three miles of trails and a "hidden" wildlife observation building.

▶ Sanctuaries open year-round. Admission charged.

www.massaudubon.org
(413) 637-0320

5 ▶ **Bartholomew's Cobble.** Hurlburt's Hill at this historic site affords great views of the Housatonic River Valley scenery, here with the first brushstrokes of autumn color.

5 Bartholomew's Cobble and John Ashley House

Off Rte. 7-A; Bartholomew's Cobble: Weatogue Rd.
Ashley House: Cooper Hill Rd.

7 ▶ **Emily Dickinson Museum.** The poet was born in the comfortable house known as The Homestead, now a museum and research center owned by Amherst College.

This site is best known for the remarkable diversity of its ferns, wildflowers, trees, and shrubs and the many species of birds they attract. One need not be a naturalist to appreciate the topography here, with its steep cliffs and spines of marble and quartzite.

Cobble is the New Englander's word for rocky outcrops that rise steeply, like islands of stone, from adjacent bottomlands. This one, named for George Bartholomew, who farmed the surrounding fields in the 1800s, is a natural rock garden of grand proportions.

At the small museum of natural history, you can learn more about almost everything you will see here. Walking the self-guiding Ledges Trail takes 40 minutes and provides a delightful experience of small-scale craggy grandeur. Another trail leads down to the Housatonic River and a classic oxbow lake.

At the nearby Ashley House, built in 1735, learn how members of the household, both free and enslaved, fought for freedom in 18th-century Massachusetts. Col. John Ashley was a member of the committee that in 1773 drafted resolutions against British tyranny. In 1781 an enslaved member of the household, Elizabeth Freeman, also known as Mum Bett, successfully sued for her freedom, basing her case on the new Massachusetts constitution. Her case was instrumental in ending slavery in the state. The Ashley House is an anchor site on the Upper Housatonic Valley African American Heritage Trail.

▶ Cobble open year-round. Natural history museum closed Sun. and Mon. Dec.-Mar. Ashley House open weekends Memorial Day-Columbus Day. Admission charged.

www.thetrustees.org
(413) 229-8600

---

did you know ❓

The Ashley House is believed to be the oldest standing house in Berkshire County. Col. Ashley acquired over 3,000 acres.

6 High Ledges Wildlife Sanctuary

Off Patten Rd., Shelburne

Stone ledges at this wildlife sanctuary offer spectacular views of Mount Greylock and the entire Deerfield River Valley. In addition to the ledges for which the sanctuary is named, an extensive network of trails wanders the 616-acre site. While exploring the trails, visitors can find a large variety of plants, including pink and yellow lady's slippers and numerous species of ferns and uncommon wildflowers. The best time to view the beautiful wildflower displays is between May and September.

The sanctuary also offers trails for hiking and snowshoeing. Visitors are reminded to remain on the trails in order to avoid ticks and poison ivy. The parking area is located on the sanctuary road, about a mile's walk from the ledges.

▶ Open daily. Admission charged.

www.massaudubon.org
(978) 464-2712

7 Emily Dickinson Museum

280 Main St., Amherst
Two historic houses, The Homestead and The Evergreens, stand preserved as a monument to the life and works of the poet Emily Dickinson. Though only 10 of her poems are known to have been published during her lifetime, Dickinson gained posthumous recognition for her works, including letters and almost 1,800 poems.

Dickinson was born at The Homestead in December of 1830 and lived all but 15 years of her life there. The gardens and natural surroundings of the house and The Evergreens, home of her brother and sister-in-law, most likely inspired many of her poems. Despite her reclusive nature, Dickinson had a strong relationship with her brother, Austin, and his wife, Susan, who were probably members of her limited audience during her lifetime.

The museum, owned by Amherst College, seeks to educate visitors about the life, works, and legacy of Emily Dickinson, in addition to preserving the houses as historical

resources. The museum offers guided tours of the houses and grounds, exhibits, and numerous events and programs.

▶ Open Wed.-Sun., Mar.-Dec.

www.emilydickinsonmuseum.org
(413) 542-8161

8 Rock House Reservation

Rte. 9, West Brookfield
More than 10,000 years ago glaciers created the mammoth, cavelike rock shelter that inspired this reservation's name. Thanks to its southern exposure, as well as the enormity of its size, the Rock House served as an ideal winter camp for centuries of Native Americans. Following the arrival of colonists from England, the surrounding forests were cleared for farming. By 1866 the Rock House was no longer a rustic haven but part of a bustling 281-acre farm owned by William Adams, whose family would tend the land for more than 125 years. In the early 20th century the Rock House was reborn as a popular tourist stop on the local electric trolley.

Today explorers from around the country can marvel at the Rock House in its glory as the centerpiece of a 135-acre nature preserve. Two miles of trails wind around the massive structure and through a young forest rich in red pine and spruce. Along the way, hikers can pass a butterfly garden and catch a glimpse of a passing blue heron, wild turkey, white-tailed deer, or even a coyote. Local reptiles, as well as lovely wildflowers, ferns, and mosses, congregate around the Carter Pond, created when a descendant of William Adams dammed the small spring-fed stream that runs through the property. A trailside

museum overlooks the lovely pond.

▶ Open daily year-round. Donations accepted.

www.thetrustees.org
(978) 840-4446

9 Moore State Park

Sawmill Rd., Paxton
Long forgotten in this peaceful setting are the strident sounds of the sawmill, corn mill, and triphammer shop for which the waterways here were originally built. Turkey Hill Brook, the source of power for the mills, flows into the 25-acre Eames Pond,

 Rock House Reservation. Farmer F. A. Carter's cottage, now a trailside museum, is perched on the rocks above spring-fed Carter Pond.

then down a succession of three cascades and on through the park.

A walking trail follows the edge of the pond, where fishermen try for pickerel, perch, and bass.

The exterior of the sawmill that was first operated in 1747 by Jaazaniah Newton has been restored with siding of weathered wood, and the remains of the old

water-driven turbines can still be seen. An old schoolhouse is also being restored in the park.

In the well-tended naturalized gardens are great drifts of azalea and mountain laurel, but the star performers are the rhododendrons. The many species and hybrids produce a profusion of flowers from mid-May–mid-June.

Among the birds to be seen here are chickadees, goldfinches, nuthatches, bluebirds, cardinals, mourning doves, and scarlet tanagers. The park staff proudly calls this a botanical garden in a mill-village setting. It is certainly a serene and pleasant place to

break a journey. The park is named for Maj. Willard Moore, a Paxton patriot who led the local farmers to fight the British at Bunker Hill.

▶ Open year-round.

www.mass.gov/dcr
(508) 792-3969

10 Purgatory Chasm State Reservation

198 Purgatory Rd., Sutton

On venturing into Purgatory Chasm, one is likely to agree that it is well named. Although it is only about 50 feet wide, it reaches a depth of 70 feet or so between precipitous walls accentuated by tall Eastern hemlocks growing from seemingly solid rock. The chasm is believed to have been formed by dammed-up glacial meltwater near the end of the last Ice Age.

The entrance to the chasm is across the street from the visitors center. The boulder-strewn trail descends gradually for a quarter-mile. On reaching the bottom, one has the awesome feeling of having plunged suddenly into the Earth's rocky body. From the bottom, trails lead along the edge of the chasm and circle back to the parking lot. The site also has a recreation area with picnic tables.

▶ Open year-round except major winter holidays. Chasm Trail closed in snowy conditions.

www.mass.gov/dcr
(508) 234-3733

11 The Butterfly Place

120 Tyngsboro Rd., Westford

Enter the 27-foot-high glass atrium at the Butterfly Place and see hundreds of butterflies up close in a warm and sunny imitation of their natural environment. Up to 500 butterflies live in the atrium at one time, representing up to 50 species, some native and some exotic. A variety of different plants line the winding walkway, providing nectar for butterflies as well as decoration. Although other areas of the facility are air-conditioned, the atrium is kept at approximately 80

10 Purgatory Chasm State Reservation. A trail descends a quarter-mile into the narrow, aptly named chasm.

degrees to provide a comfortable habitat for its delicate inhabitants.

Those who do not wish to enter the atrium may view the butterflies from the observation room, where there are also educational displays about the life cycle of butterflies and moths. A short video presentation offers further information, and knowledgeable staff members are always available to answer questions.

▶ Open daily mid-Feb.–mid-Nov. except major holidays. Admission charged.

www.butterflyplace-ma.com
(978) 392-0955

12 Lowell

For anyone concerned with America's heritage and with community revitalization, Lowell is a place of special interest. Sometimes referred to as the Birthplace of the American Industrial Revolution, the town has a proud past as a model industrial community of the early 1800s.

In the 1920s, as New England's

textile industry declined, the town began its downward trend. Efforts to reverse that trend now include the establishment of the Lowell Heritage State Park and the Lowell National Historical Park, a cooperative undertaking of the city, the state, and the National Park Service.

At the park's visitors center, located at Market Mills, a restored mill complex, you can arrange to take a tour by trolley, barge, or on foot that reveals the city's past. You can also visit the Boott Cotton Mills Museum, which has a re-created operating weaving room with 88 power looms. The old mill buildings, immaculate with their spanking-new paint and clean brickwork, stand out against the rest of the urban architecture and give the curious impression of two contrasting cities—one resuscitated by a tranfusion of galleries, shops, offices, and fresh paint, the other a timeworn city.

▶ Open year-round. Admission charged for some attractions.

www.nps.gov/lowe
(978) 970-5000

13 Whittier Home

86 Friend St., Amesbury

For 56 years this was the home of John Greenleaf Whittier, an active abolitionist, a founder of the Republican Party, and one of America's best-known poets. The house was simply a four-room cottage when Whittier bought it in 1836. Over the years he added the portico, the upper stories, and the summer kitchen.

By the time of his death in 1892, Whittier was quite famous. Only four years later his niece (to whom he had bequeathed the property) opened his home as a museum. This continuity ensured that the Whittier memorabilia remained largely intact. It is the completeness of the personal belongings and furnishings (hats, boots, shaving brush, books, manuscripts, portraits, letters, even the original wallpaper) that gives the place its particular intimate charm. On the walls there is ample evidence of Whittier's work as a writer and abolitionist. He wrote most of his poetry in the Garden Room, including his classic *Snow Bound.*

11 The Butterfly Place. Visitors can watch butterflies in the atrium (above) or in an adjacent observation room. Shown in the inset is a Blue Wave butterfly.

The house is now a registered National Historic Landmark. Just up the street is the Friends Meetinghouse, which Whittier, a Quaker, attended, and which served as a station of the Underground Railroad.

▶ Open Fri. and Sat., May–Oct. Admission charged.

www.whittierhome.org
(978) 388-1337

14 Parker River National Wildlife Refuge

Sunset Dr., Plum Island
This 4,662-acre refuge, which lies on the Atlantic Flyway, is a magnificent place to visit, especially during the spring and fall migrations. Most of the refuge is on Plum Island, which is eight miles long and one mile wide. A road runs its entire length. On the left, going south, are sand dunes. On the right there are fresh- and saltwater marshes, and beyond are the waters of Broad Sound, a long, narrow inlet. The beach, one of the finest on the Eastern Seaboard, is reached by boardwalks tightly controlled to preserve the delicate ecology of the dunes, which act as a barrier to the sea. The beach is closed Apr. 1 each year to provide a nesting habitat for the piping plover. It reopens mid- to late Aug.

Self-guiding nature trails lead to various ecological niches. The longest is a boardwalk trail that wanders for two miles through Hellcat Swamp, where a freshwater swamp and cranberry bogs are pocketed among the dunes. At the end of the trail is an observation area for bird-watchers. More than 300 species rest and feed here. Among the mammals are deer, foxes, muskrats, minks, and weasels, but they are rarely seen

 **World's End.** The famous park designer Frederick Law Olmsted put his stamp on a wild peninsula that became part of the Boston Harbor Islands National Recreation Area.

during the day. In winter harbor seals sun themselves on offshore rocks.

The best seasons to visit are in the early spring and in fall. Fishing permits are available at the refuge gatehouse. Be sure to check out the interactive exhibits at the visitors center, located on the mainland side of the bridge to the island.

▶ Open year-round. Admission charged.

www.fws.gov/northeast/parkerriver
(978) 465-5753

15 Ipswich River Wildlife Sanctuary

87 Perkins Row, Topsfield
Occupying 2,265 acres, this is the largest of the 41 sanctuaries supervised by the Massachusetts Audubon Society. It is also the most varied, not only because of the number of wildlife habitats but also because of its extensive landscaping.

In the early 1900s the land was bought by Thomas Proctor, a wealthy Bostonian who applied himself with zeal and open-handedness to the creation of a private arboretum with an enormous rock garden—called the

Rockery—as its centerpiece. In effect, the Rockery, set by a small lake, is a man-made mountain, complete with little gorges, caves, and paths and profusely planted with exotic trees and shrubs. Among the trees Proctor imported for his arboretum, the most notable are cork, magnolia, Korean pine, and Sawara cypress. A fine grove of pine trees stands on the hill above the Rockery.

There are 10 miles of trails on the sanctuary and a causeway crossing a large pond to an island covered with beech trees. The woodlands are carpeted with partridge berries, starflowers, and wintergreen, while masses of blue irises grow in the marshy areas and a wildflower garden offers its special beauty. The sanctuary, which is a major courting and breeding ground for the American woodcock, has wildfowl impoundments, a special area for bird-watching, and an observation tower overlooking a freshwater marsh.

▶ Open Tues.–Sun. year-round. Admission charged.

www.massaudubon.org
(978) 887-9264

16 World's End

250 Martin's Ln., Hingham
Spanning 250 acres and more than five miles of shoreline, this peerless peninsula has long been prized for its scenic vistas and dramatic topography. According to prehistoric evidence, it was a popular campsite among Native Americans. The famous landscape architect Frederick Law Olmsted in the late 19th century saw it as the perfect place for developing a residential community. Although his plan never came to fruition, the terrain still reflects his influence. True to Olmsted's philosophy of working with nature to design places of pastoral beauty, the peninsula features lush hedgerows, meandering gravel paths, and formal plantings of 900 trees.

One of the 30 islands of the Boston Harbor Islands National Recreation Area, World's End boasts four hills affording 360-degree views of the Boston skyline and Atlantic Ocean. Open grassy meadows lead to steep cliffs covered with red cedar and blueberry thickets, attracting birds and a tremendous variety of butterflies.

In addition to picnicking and gazing at the natural splendors, the peninsula offers seven miles of trails—for hiking, biking, and horseback riding—plus opportunities for fishing and cross-country skiing or snowshoeing. Trail maps are available at the ranger station, which also offers natural-history kayak tours from June–mid-Sept. and educational walks year-round.

▶ Open daily year-round. Admission charged.

www.thetrustees.org
(781) 740-6665

17 Misery Islands

Salem Bay, between Marblehead and Manchester harbors, just off West Beach in Beverly Farms

Just how the scenically delightful Great and Little Misery islands got their names is a mystery. Legend attributes the pair's christening to a shipwrecked man who spent three brutally cold December days stranded alone on the islands in the 1600s. By the early 1900s Great Misery had overcome its unfortunate appellation to emerge as a posh summer retreat, with a nine-hole golf course and a colony of 26 cottages. But in 1926 a fire destroyed most of the buildings, and for more than 50 years the islands were abandoned. Finally, in 1997, after prolonged battles over proposals to make Great Misery the site of oil storage and sewage-treatment operations, all 87 acres comprising both islands came under the ownership and protection of the Trustees for Reservations.

Today the sister islands, separated by a narrow, shallow channel, are easy to reach via your own rowboat, canoe, or kayak. From Great Misery's meadow hilltop, island tourists can see the bordering harbors of Marblehead and Manchester, not to mention the expanse of the Atlantic Ocean. While following three miles of woodland trails, explorers will find remnants of the island's summer resort heyday, including the stone pillars of a water tower that once served vacationers.

From Little Misery's beach it's impossible to miss the wooden remains of *City of Rockland,* a steamship that ran aground in 1923, poking above the waterline. Great and Little Misery also offer numerous coves for exploring and perfectly pleasant spots for picnick-

 Saugus Iron Works. Iron-making at this 17th-century plant relied on water power from the Saugus River. The reconstruction of the iron works opened to the public in 2008.

ing, hiking, bird-watching, and general relaxing.

▶ Open daily year-round.

www.thetrustees.org
(978) 526-8687

18 Saugus Iron Works

244 Central St., Saugus

This national historic site is a full-scale working replica of the original ironworks founded here in the early 1640s by John Winthrop, Jr., son of the governor of Massachusetts Bay Colony. Since the 1630s the small colony had been in an economic slump, suffering from a sharp decline in immigration. With fewer ships arriving from England, there was a serious scarcity of iron products—tools, nails, hinges, pots, and kettles—all of which had been imported.

To meet that need, young Winthrop sailed to England to obtain capital and a team of skilled ironworkers. Securing both, he returned home, chose a site where waterpower, wood for charcoal, and iron ore were available, and built an up-to-date plant and company houses for the workers. The commu-

nity was known as Hammersmith.

In the 1650s the ironworks failed because of production costs and an insufficient market for its products. But its employees trained others in their skills and thus helped to establish an iron industry in America.

The whole complex has been recreated with wonderful precision and thoroughness. A small museum showcases the history of the area with a short slide show and exhibits. From the museum a path leads to the smelting furnace and from there to the "finery." Draft for the furnace was provided by huge bellows driven by water power from the Saugus River. Water power also drove a huge hammer, used to pound the brittleness out of the cast pig iron and turn it into wrought iron. The machinery in the rolling and slitting mill, where sheets and rods of iron were made, also depended upon waterpower. Worth visiting, too, is the blacksmith's shop. Three rooms have been restored in a "high 17th-century" style with elaborate furnishings.

In addition to the remarkable authenticity of the site, Saugus Iron Works is rewarding to visit

because the processes displayed are easily understood, unlike modern high technology, and that maybe with a little application and ingenuity one might have been credited with inventing the whole operation oneself.

▶ Open daily Apr.–Oct.

www.nps.gov/sair
(781) 233-0050

19 Adams National Historical Park

Visitors center, 1250 Hancock St., Quincy

Throughout four generations one of America's most distinguished families lived on the land here, building and rebuilding to suit the changing needs of their remarkably active lives.

The family saga begins, however, about a mile south on Franklin St. (ask at the visitors center for directions), where two 18th-century houses stand side by side. John Adams, second president of the United States, was born in one house, and his son, John Quincy Adams, the sixth president, was born in the other.

The Old House, on Adams St., was built as a country villa in the 1730s and bought by John Adams in 1787, when he and his wife, Abigail, returned from diplomatic service abroad. It is interesting to consider the contrast between the grandeur of public life enjoyed by the great and powerful in 18th-century America and the modesty of their domestic arrangements, especially compared to the estates of their counterparts in Europe. This contrast, in fact, was duly noted by Abigail Adams upon her return from the Court of St. James in London.

Among the members of the family based here were a remarkable number of accomplished statesmen, educators, historians, lawyers, and authors dedicated to demanding intellectual pursuits and compassionate service to their fellow men.

The furnishings in the Old House reflect the tastes and interests of a widely traveled family over a period of 140 years. No other house in America offers a personal historic record of such impressive scope. The park provides a trolley bus that offers transportation between the sites. Trees planted by John Quincy Adams in the garden have grown strong, as has the country that he and his family served so well.

▶ Open daily mid-Apr.–mid-Nov.

www.nps.gov/adam
(617) 770-1175

---

20 ▶ **Alden House Historic Site**
105 Alden St., off 3A, Duxbury
Recently declared a National Historic Landmark, this shingled colonial is a direct link with the first colonization of America. John Alden, voyager on the *Mayflower*, was a signer of the Mayflower Compact and a leader of the Plymouth Colony. Like many of the colonists, including Captain Standish, the Aldens secured a farm plot in Duxbury and became

did you know ❓

John Alden courted Priscilla Mullins, and the story of their romance is recounted in Henry Wadsworth Longfellow's poem "The Courtship of Miles Standish." The poem's account may or may not be true, but the couple did indeed marry, and they settled first in Plymouth.

one of the founding settlers of that town in the 1630s.

The present dwelling, which was built in the second half of the 17th century, was the second home built on the Alden property. John and Priscilla's third son, Jonathan Alden, had inherited the homestead, and his descendants lived in the house until the early 20th century.

Now owned by the Alden Kindred of America, which has held annual meetings at the homestead for more than 100 years, the house contains some handsome Early American fixtures and furnishings.

▶ Open mid-May–Columbus Day and by appointment. Admission charged.

www.alden.org
(781) 934-9092

---

21 ▶ **Woods Hole Oceanographic Institution**
Woods Hole
A research center with a rich history, the mission of the Woods Hole Oceanographic Institution is to study the oceans and promote awareness of their importance. Instrumental in

the discovery of the wreck of the *Titanic* in 1985 and of hydrothermal vents brimming with life on the floor of the Pacific Ocean, the facility has been a significant force in ocean research for many years.

Visitors may choose to begin their exploration at the WHOI information office, which offers walking tours in July and August. The tours detail the institution's research and history and end at the exhibit center, where visitors can see examples of the tools used in the institution's research. Step into a full-sized model of the interior of the deep-ocean research submersible, *Alvin*, and watch footage taken at the bottom of the ocean. Several short videos and an interactive exhibit offer further information about the institution's research. Public talks are also offered in July and August by WHOI experts.

▶ Exhibit center open Mon.–Sat. May–Oct. and Tues.–Fri. Nov.–Dec. Donations encouraged.

www.whoi.edu
(508) 289-2252

21 ▶ **Woods Hole Oceanographic Institution.** This aerial photograph shows all three deep-sea vessels operated by the institution docked at the port in Woods Hole: the *Knorr* (foreground), the *Oceanus* (left), and the *Atlantis* (rear).

seasonal events

FEBRUARY
• Winterfest Celebration—Lowell *(National Human Dogsled Championships, live entertainment, fireworks)*

APRIL
• Battle of Concord and Lexington Reenactment—Lexington *(followed by parade and activities)*

JUNE
• African Festival—Lowell *(traditional dance and music, speakers, arts and crafts)*
• Summer Solstice Celebration—World's End, Hingham *(music, food, tractor-drawn hayride)*

JULY
• Barnstable County Fair—Barnstable *(animal shows, live music, petting zoo)*

AUGUST
• Buskers Festival—Newburyport *(street performers from all over the world)*
• Great New England Feast of the Holy Ghost—Fall River *(Portuguese festival, live entertainment, fireworks, a classic car show, parade)*

SEPTEMBER
• Bread and Roses Festival—Lawrence *(music, dance, historical tours, petting zoo)*

OCTOBER
• Eastern European Festival—Deerfield *(music, demonstrations, traditional Polish food)*

NOVEMBER
• Cider Days—Franklin County *(events throughout Franklin County celebrating apples and cider)*

DECEMBER
• Boston Tea Party Reenactment—Boston *(theatrical storytelling, interactive debate, free to those dressed in Colonial attire)*
• Holidays By-The-Sea—Falmouth *(caroling at Nobska Lighthouse, parade, lighting of the village green)*

www.massvacation.com

MASSACHUSETTS

Michigan

Steeped in the history of mining and lumbering, the Great Lakes State is also shaped by the lakes bordering it on three sides.

Oktoberfest. This annual festival celebrating German culture draws thousands to the Bavarian outpost of Frankenmuth (see Seasonal Events, page 171).

An abundance of beaches and lighthouses reminds visitors that the waters of four of the five Great Lakes wash Michigan's shores. The early iron and copper mines and the lumber camps present themselves in museums and historic towns. The wise use of old buildings is exemplified in a historical museum in a former church in the Upper Peninsula's Menominee County, while Henry Ford's Dearborn estate has been turned into an intriguing, multifaceted destination.

Nature lovers will welcome the hiking trails, rivers and waterfalls, a unique spring, and a beautifully landscaped garden filled with world-class art.

visit ➤ **offthebeatenpathtrips.com**

1 ▶ Little Girls Point County Park

17 miles north of Ironwood
The point is named in memory of a Chippewa girl who drowned here in the 1800s. The sandy beach is very pebbly at the waterline, and the crystal-clear water is too cold for swimming until August.

But swimming is not this park's main attraction. The beach is celebrated for the agates that can easily be found among the waterline pebbles. Look for those that have a translucent quality. They are most often white but can be other colors as well. A visit to the nearby agate shop will give beginning agate hunters a good idea of their prey.

Besides agates, there are attractive pebbles of all kinds and colors here, most smoothed and symmetrically shaped by Lake Superior's constantly churning waters.

There is also great fishing here and a large campground. And be sure to take some time to scan the skies: Bald eagles are regular residents, and you may even spot them nesting in trees near the shore.

▶ Open May–Sept. Admission charged.

www.gogebic.org/forestry.htm
(906) 663-4428

2 ▶ Agate Falls

Rte. 28, south of Paynesville
The short trail to the falls begins in

2 ▶ Agate Falls. Steelhead trout and dramatic cascades compete for the attention of anglers at Agate Falls, on the Upper Peninsula's Ontonagon River.

the Joseph F. Oravec Roadside Park just south of Rte. 28, passes under the highway, and then continues through woods above the broad middle branch of the Ontonagon River.

At a point opposite a flat-topped rock above the falls, you can either rest on the massive roots of a white pine or, with a little care and agility, climb onto the rock for a much better view of the tumbling spate of lacy water.

But the best view of the falls is attained only by way of a daring

scramble down an earthen bank with crumbling rock "steps," slippery roots, and a few necessary handholds. This route, which is dangerous in wet weather, leads to a ledge from which one has a view of the first and second plunges of the falls. Only those in excellent physical shape are encouraged to try this part of the trail.

▶ Open year-round but not staffed.

www.michigan.gov/dnr
(906) 353-6588

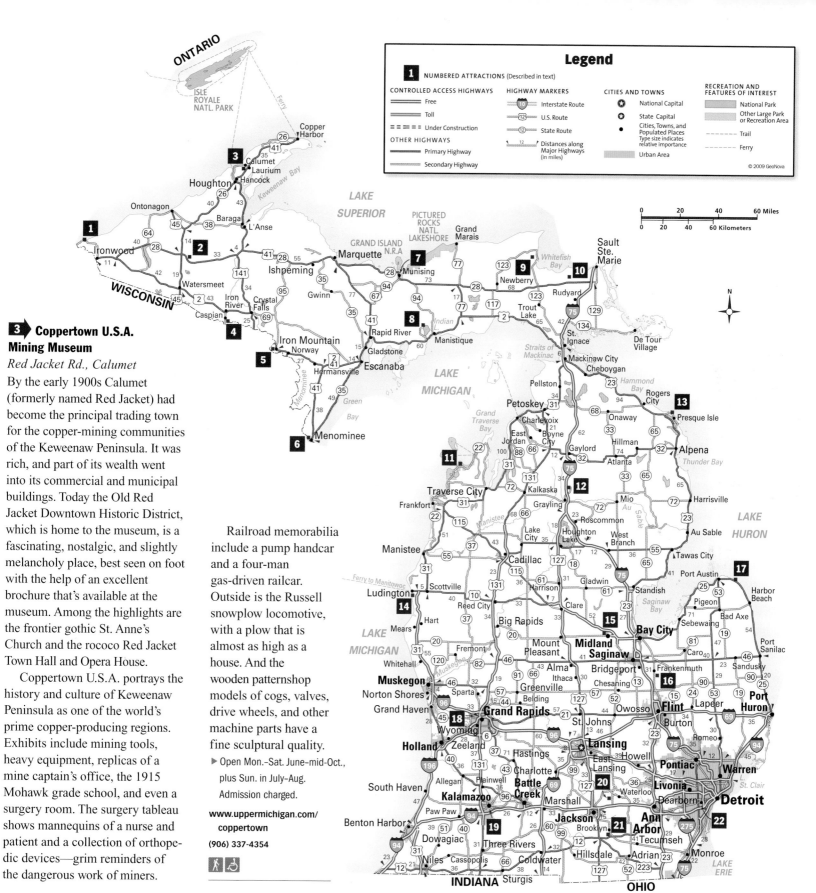

3 ▶ Coppertown U.S.A. Mining Museum

Red Jacket Rd., Calumet

By the early 1900s Calumet (formerly named Red Jacket) had become the principal trading town for the copper-mining communities of the Keweenaw Peninsula. It was rich, and part of its wealth went into its commercial and municipal buildings. Today the Old Red Jacket Downtown Historic District, which is home to the museum, is a fascinating, nostalgic, and slightly melancholy place, best seen on foot with the help of an excellent brochure that's available at the museum. Among the highlights are the frontier gothic St. Anne's Church and the rococo Red Jacket Town Hall and Opera House.

Coppertown U.S.A. portrays the history and culture of Keweenaw Peninsula as one of the world's prime copper-producing regions. Exhibits include mining tools, heavy equipment, replicas of a mine captain's office, the 1915 Mohawk grade school, and even a surgery room. The surgery tableau shows mannequins of a nurse and patient and a collection of orthopedic devices—grim reminders of the dangerous work of miners.

Railroad memorabilia include a pump handcar and a four-man gas-driven railcar. Outside is the Russell snowplow locomotive, with a plow that is almost as high as a house. And the wooden patternshop models of cogs, valves, drive wheels, and other machine parts have a fine sculptural quality.

▶ Open Mon.–Sat. June–mid-Oct., plus Sun. in July–Aug. Admission charged.

www.uppermichigan.com/coppertown

(906) 337-4354

4 Iron County Historical Museum. Exhibitions on the site of the now-closed Caspian Mine cast light on the mining, lumbering, and everyday life of Iron County.

4 Iron County Historical Museum

Museum Rd., Caspian

This is an exemplary museum of mining, lumbering, and everyday life in Iron County. It occupies the former site of the Caspian Mine, whose gaunt old head frame presides over the site like a somber guardian of times gone by.

In the onetime engine house is the Mining Hall, where intricate glass dioramas indicate different levels and convey the immense labor and skill of the old miners.

In the Lumbering Hall is the Monigal Miniature Lumber Camp, which contains more than 2,000 items, hand carved from cedar telegraph poles by William Monigal. It's an astonishing piece of work, full of vigor, color, and information. Among other exhibits are fine photographs, including one of a 20-sled logging train carrying a 900-ton load.

The main exhibition area houses numerous other exhibits, among them the Pioneer Hall (with oil-paper maps and surveying instruments), the Athletics Hall (note the photograph of the 1911 girls basketball team), and the Pioneer Home.

The Village Green, an extensive section of the exhibition hall, contains authentic re-creations of local craft and trade shops. MacDonell's Blacksmith's Shop, for instance, has been rebuilt with the original timbers, bricks, and tools—even the furnace ashes.

On the grounds of the museum are the Transportation, Mining, and Farm complexes and the Logging Camp, all showing relevant tools and equipment.

▶ Open daily mid-May–Oct.
  Admission charged.

www.ironcountymuseum.com
(906) 265-2617

5 Menominee Range Historical Museum

300 E. Ludington St., Iron Mountain

The museum is housed in the old Carnegie Public Library, a distinguished neoclassical stone structure with a massive porch and second-floor balcony. At the entrance is a reproduction of an old general store packed with goods of the late 19th century.

There are exhibits of pioneer settlers, a diorama of the Menominee tribe, and replicas of a trapper's cabin and a trading post. The cabin looks authentically uncomfortable; the trading post has whiskey and rum, bear grease, knives, snowshoes, and bolts of cloth. Among the other displays are a saddle shop and detailed exhibits of period office, banking, and brewing environments.

A watchmaker's shop is complete with workbench and tools, and the optician has an eye chart. The barbershop is endowed with a chair that looks as if it might easily be converted for electrocutions. And the Morely Folding Bath Tub (1885) provided a convenience for cramped quarters at home.

▶ Open daily June–Labor Day;
  call for occasional off-season hours.

www.menomineemuseum.com
(906) 774-4276

6 Menominee County Historical Museum

904 11th Ave., Menominee

The museum celebrates the spectrum of life in Menominee County, from the earliest periods of Native American settlement to World War II, with emphasis on the mid-19th and early 20th centuries. The collections are housed in a former church, rebuilt in 1921 on the site of the original place of worship and notable for its stained-glass windows.

Menominee is named for a tribe of Native Americans whose name means "wild rice," and whose heritage is displayed in stone and copper weapons, bead-work, and two dugout canoes believed to be more than 800 years old. There is also a fine collection of arrowheads among the many other artifacts.

Menominee is in lumber country, and the museum has good photographs of logging camps, river drives, and timber trains, as well as a variety of lumbering tools. There are also re-creations of a law office, photographer's studio, cobbler's workshop, music store, railroad ticket office, and dentist's office. Law and order are represented by leg irons, handcuffs, a ball and chain, and early types of police radar.

The church's bell tower still holds the original bell, which dates

7 Pictured Rocks National Lakeshore. Wind, waves, and ice carved the multicolored sandstone cliffs on the Lake Superior shoreline into myriad shapes.

to 1871. The church itself is a piece of history: It's on the *National Register of Historic Places*.

▶ Mon.-Sat. Memorial Day-Labor Day.

www.menomineehistoricalsociety.org/
   museum.htm

(906) 863-9000

 Pictured Rocks National Lakeshore

Munising

The park is 42 spectacular miles long and no more than 5 miles at its widest. The entire length is traversed by the North Country National Scenic Trail.

Miners Castle Overlook, reached via Miners Castle Rd., gives stunning views of a smoothly curved inlet of white cliffs above a submarine outcrop of yellow sandstone; the offshore water of Lake Superior is intensely blue, but above the yellow lake bed it becomes a rim of vivid green.

At the northern tip of the inlet is Miners Castle, a crag of cliff carved by erosion into the semblance of a medieval castle. A side road from Miners Castle Rd. goes to Miners Falls, a high and narrow plummet between two massive cliffs; at their base are swirl holes, and the face of the nearer wall has been scooped out by erosion.

The park is a camper's delight. Three campgrounds in the park are accessible by car: Little Beaver Lake, Twelvemile Beach, and Hurricane River.

From Little Beaver Lake it's a short walk to Beaver Lake and the North Country Trail. The campground at Twelvemile Beach provides access to an unbroken stretch of white sand.

From Hurricane River one can walk 1¹/₂ miles to the 1874 lighthouse at Au Sable Point and

beyond that to a 500-foot wooden log slide and the Grand Sable Banks and Dunes area.

There are also 13 backcountry campgrounds along the Lakeshore Trail. Scuba divers are catered to along the shore by the Alger Underwater Diving Preserve. Late summer provides magnificent weather, but the park is also beautiful in winter, when visitors flock there for snowshoeing.

▶ Open year-round. Fees for camping.

www.nps.gov/piro
(906) 387-3700

---

8 The Big Spring at Palms Book State Park

Rte. 149, 10 miles north of Thompson, Manistique

Here is a wide pool of eerily clear green water, 40 feet deep, fed by a cluster of springs flowing at a rate of 10,000 gallons per minute. The flow is such that the water never has time to freeze in winter or warm up in summer—it's always a steady 45°F.

To view the Big Spring, visitors climb into rafts that run round-trip along a cable. The sides of the pool are steep and white, delicately streaked with drifts of darker clay and sand. Bleached logs lie under the water like massive bones, and the springs belch plumes of white silt resembling miniature volcanoes.

Large, slow lake trout cruise the pond, which is surrounded by hemlock and arborvitae; ducks and seagulls paddle its periphery. The outflow of the mighty spring is a shallow, bubbling river.

The spring is open year-round for viewing, but the road and parking lot are not plowed. However, the park offers hearty cross-country skiers some excellent trails.

9 **Tahquamenon Falls State Park.** The Lower Falls drop 22 feet in some places. When the Chippewa camped at Tahquamenon, they fished for walleye and hunted deer.

▶ Open year-round. Admission charged.

www.michigandnr.com
(906) 341-2355

---

9 Tahquamenon Falls State Park

Paradise

This nearly 50,000-acre park has three developed sections: the Upper Falls, the Lower Falls, and the Tahquamenon Rivermouth.

The Upper Falls are among the largest east of the Mississippi and are most easily approached by way of the Brink stairs, an elaborate series of observation decks that wind down to river level.

The 200-foot-wide lip of the falls, about 50 feet high, is a shallow S-curve of ancient sandstone over which the soft brown water, stained by its passage through cedar and hemlock swamps, pours at a rate of up to 50,000 gallons per second. The Gorge stairs downstream are steeper and longer but allow more complete views.

The Lower Falls, actually a series of falls, lie on either side of an island (reached by renting a rowboat) and can be seen from several viewing points. A half-mile boardwalk path through the forest leads to an observation platform offering close-up views of the water churning over the falls. Visitors can camp here or at Rivermouth, which also has swimming, a new picnic area, and a boat launch.

▶ Open year-round. Admission charged.

www.michigandnr.com
(906) 492-3415

---

10 Wheels of History Museum

Depot St., Brimley

This tiny museum in the tiny village of Brimley offers a peek back in time to when this area was a busy and bustling industrial center. Housed in a bright red train car refurbished to its original 1905 condition, exhibits focus on the history of the railroad, the logging and fishing industries, and daily life in Brimley. Its once vibrant but now nearly abandoned neighbor, Bay Mills, whose sawmill once employed 800 people and turned out 160,000 feet of lumber a day, is also featured. The nearby Iroquois Point Lighthouse, built in 1870, offers testament to the early importance of the shipping lanes, which continue to be some of the world's busiest. On the shore of Lake Superior, Brimley State Park offers a picnic area where boat watchers can see freighters heading to and from the Soo Locks into the lower lakes, as well as campsites and a beach for those eager to brave the northern waters.

▶ Open Wed.–Sun. late June–Labor Day; weekends mid-May–late June and Labor Day–mid-Oct. Admission free but donations appreciated.

www.baymillsbrimleyhistory.org
(906) 248-3665

11 Sleeping Bear Dunes National Lakeshore

9922 Front St., Empire

The most spectacular feature of this beautiful 71,000-acre park on the Lake Michigan shoreline is the Sleeping Bear Dunes area, readily seen from the 7.6-mile Pierce Stocking Scenic Dr., which overlooks South and North Manitou islands. The lake views from here

at sunset can be surreal, and the inland views to the east of ridges, valleys, and lakes are no less beautiful.

A nine-mile trail also crosses the dunes; it's easy to get lost here, and no drinking water is available. At Glen Lake, just west of the dunes, there is a lovely picnic area. The nearby village of Glen Haven hosts the Coast Guard Station/ Maritime Museum.

The park also includes the Platte Bay and Pyramid Point sections to the north and south and North and South Manitou islands. Canoe rentals are available at the

Platte and Crystal rivers, and there are hiking trails throughout.

In the Pyramid Point section there is a hiking trail, beach access, and picnicking at Good Harbor Bay. Both South Manitou Island and the primitive wilderness of North Manitou Island can be reached mid-spring to mid-fall by a ferry from Leland.

▶ Park open year-round. Pierce Stocking Scenic Dr. open May–Nov., road conditions permitting.

www.nps.gov/slbe
(231) 326-5134

11 **Sleeping Bear Dunes National Lakeshore.** The rippling sand dunes on the Lake Michigan shoreline are among the largest (and most visited) in the world.

12 Hartwick Pines State Park

4216 Ranger Rd., Grayling

When the first loggers came to Michigan, they found white pines of amazing size in the virgin woods. Legend has it that there were trees more than twice as high as those you'll see in Hartwick Pines State Park now.

But the present-day giants are remarkable in their own right. They tower more than 150 feet above the forest floor, each green pinnacle seeming to sway to its own rhythm. It's cool, shady, and easy to walk the forest, as the canopy of foliage shields the sun and limits the undergrowth.

On the north end of the park is the Hartwick Pines Logging Museum. Nineteenth-century logging life is reflected here in exhibits that tell the story of the fast-paced and freewheeling industry that carved up much of the surrounding white pine forest.

The state of Michigan's Forest Visitor Center is also here. It, too, features exhibits on the colorful history of logging and forestry, but its focus is on preserving the forest. The stunning 49-acre Old Growth Pines area is strong testament to that effort.

▶ Park and visitors center open daily year-round. Museum open daily May–Oct. Admission charged.

www.michigandnr.com
(989) 348-7068

13 Old Presque Isle Lighthouse and Museum

5295 E. Grand Lake Rd., Presque Isle

About 150 years ago Presque Isle had the finest harbor in the Great Lakes, a cove protected from Lake Huron's fierce weather by headlands to the north and south. A busy port grew up there, and $5,000 was appropriated in 1838 from federal funds to build a lighthouse. In 1840 the light was lit, and for the next 30 years it served as a beacon to mariners up and down the coast.

In 1870 a taller lighthouse began service just a mile north, and the old light was left to weather the storms of time as best it might. Its four-foot-thick walls of hand-cut stone proved durable, and so did the keeper's small cottage. In the early 1900s the property passed into private hands and was steadily restored by a series of owners. In 1995 the property passed to the local township, which continues its upkeep.

Today the cottage houses a museum crammed with curios, as a place on a trade route should be: a wine cabinet with hand-blown bottles, a crab-shaped incense burner, and a saucy Native American statuette. Best of all, one is urged to handle things, whether it's the torpedo-boat binnacle or the elephant trainer's hooked stick.

At the foot of the lighthouse is a bronze bell from Lansing city hall's old clock tower. It weighs 3,425 pounds, more than 1½ times that of the Liberty Bell, and visitors can make it ring out over the bay by pulling the bell hammer.

▶ Open daily mid-May–mid-Oct. Admission charged.

www.keepershouse.org
(989) 595-6979

13 ▶ **Old Presque Isle Lighthouse.** The museum in this lighthouse, once a beacon in a busy Lake Huron harbor, houses an eclectic collection of curios and artifacts.

14 ▶ **Historic White Pine Village**

1687 S. Lakeshore Dr., Ludington
An extensive reconstruction of a small Michigan town in the late 1800s, this village's buildings are set in carefully tended grounds and are all authentically furnished.

The Abe Nelson Blacksmith Shop, for example, has a working smithy, and Cole's General Store has an intriguing stock of goods, a countertop extended to accommodate hoopskirts, and an exotic green pagoda-like tea chest.

Dwellings include the Quevillon trapper's cabin, built before 1850, where a hand-colored photograph of a severe-looking Catherine Quevillon presides over a single bed strewn with animal skins. The Burns farmhouse, built around 1880, is one of the most detailed reconstructions. In the kitchen is an elaborate flour and spice cabinet, in the dining room a portable home altar, and in the drawing room a 100-year-old Regina Music Machine that plays perforated metal discs and still produces a tuneful mellow sound.

In the Abe Nelson Lumbering Museum are mementos of the old lumber camps, including excellent models of ox- and horse-drawn lumber wagons and good collections of lumbering tools, cowbells, and railroad lamps.

The Mason County Courthouse was built in 1849 from loose lumber pulled from the lake and still sits on its original site.

▶ Open Tues.–Sat. mid-Apr.–mid-Oct.; Tues.–Sun. Memorial Day–Labor Day. Admission charged.

www.historicwhitepinevillage.org
(231) 843-4808

15 ▶ **Dow Gardens**

1809 Eastman Ave., Midland
The Dow Gardens were developed in 1899 by Herbert Dow, founder of the Dow Chemical Company. They include beautiful massed plantings of annuals and perennials, a necklace of ponds, and collections of flowering crab-apples, roses, viburnums, and rhododendrons.

Famed architect Alden B. Dow, son of Herbert, added many architectural elements to the gardens.

He believed, as did his father, that the entire beauty of the garden should never be revealed in a single glance. A walk down streamside reveals a curving pathway bordered by lush annuals and a stream, leading to a historic red bridge, that takes you to a conservatory.

Additional attractions include the Children's Garden, a maze, and a rockery of dwarf evergreens near the entrance. Special events include concerts in the gardens, butterflies in the conservatory, and tours of the estate home.

▶ Open year-round except holidays. Admission charged.

www.dowgardens.org
(800) 362-4874

16 ▶ **Grandpa Tiny's Farm**

7775 Weiss St., Frankenmuth
Children and adults alike will delight in the sights and sounds at this historical farm, which re-creates a turn-of-the-century agricultural experience. Between the horse-drawn wagon ride over an early iron trestle bridge, the 150-year-old one-room schoolhouse that has been restored to working condition, and the seasonal demonstrations of plowing, planting, and harvesting using period equipment, everything here is a lesson about life in a previous era. Animals abound: There is a petting farm in the old barn, while chickens, turkeys, and other farm animals live out in the yard. Outside the farmhouse, which has itself been painstakingly furnished in period style, is an authentic outdoor stove used for baking bread on special occasions, like the annual farm fest.

▶ Open daily Apr.–Oct. Admission charged.

www.grandpatinysfarm.com
(989) 652-5437

17 Huron City Museums

7995 Pioneer Dr., Port Austin

Huron City was founded in the 1850s by lumberman Langdon Hubbard. It prospered, suffered two major fires, and finally declined when its wells went dry. Today it's a museum town that reconstructs life here in the latter part of the 19th century.

Dogcarts, sleighs, and coaches are displayed in the carriage house. In Hubbard's barn is a collection of farm equipment that includes a forerunner of the forklift.

The ground floor of the Community House Inn (1877) is furnished in the busy style of the Victorian period, and the general store is provisioned with goods from toys to tea chests.

One of the most interesting buildings is the Point Aux Barques Life Saving Station, built in 1876 and moved here from its original site. Its lifeboat, which once saved 200 lives in a single mission, is on display in the Wreck Room.

Also worth seeing is the large, airy Huron City Church, where as many as 1,000 used to gather to hear the sermons of William Lyon Phelps, a Yale professor and one of the notable literary figures of his day. The Phelps family's House of Seven Gables contains his desk (made from a grand piano), Staffordshire pottery, and other memorabilia.

▶ Open daily July–Labor Day, weekends June and Sept. Admission charged.

www.huroncitymuseums.org
(989) 428-4123

18 Frederik Meijer Gardens and Sculpture Park

1000 E. Beltline Ave. NE, Grand Rapids

This unique botanical garden features colorful flowers, exquisite

18 Frederik Meijer Gardens and Sculpture Park.
Among the park's sculptures is *The American Horse*. The sculptor, Nina Akamu, is an Oklahoma-born artist known for massive bronzes that pay homage to Renaissance master Leonardo da Vinci.

topiary, and world-class works of art. Thirty of the gardens, 125 acres, comprise an open-air museum showcasing the work of more than 25 renowned sculptors in a variety of natural settings. Complementing the sculpture park is an indoor gallery that also highlights celebrated pieces from the late 19th century to the present. The impressive collection features works by Degas and Rodin, as well as more contemporary artists such as Roy Lichtenstein and Henry Moore, intelligently and artfully integrated into the park's landscapes and garden displays.

Trails wind through about one mile of Michigan woodlands and wetlands. Visitors are able to see a variety of both native and indigenous plants, as well as many types of birds and other wildlife. Inside, conservatories and greenhouses highlight plants galore. A popular stop with kids, "Little Greenhouse of Horrors" presents an up-close and riveting look at bug-devouring plants.

The gardens specialize in seasonal events, so there is something going on here nearly every day.

▶ Open year-round. Closed New Year's Day and Christmas. Admission charged.

www.meijergardens.org
(888) 957-1580

19 Kalamazoo Nature Center

7000 N. Westnedge Ave., Kalamazoo

This imaginative, attractive site includes an interpretive center, an arboretum and botanical garden, a farm, a period homestead, and nature trails. It's a wonderful family destination, and children will love the diversity of the activities.

The Tropical Sun–Rain Room in the interpretive center stretches from the basement to the glass roof and re-creates the environment of many exotic plants, with 600 tons of rock serving as the thermal mass in the naturalistic landscape. A walkway spirals past this jungle to the basement, where there are fascinating displays of living snakes, fish, turtles, toads, a crow, and a screech owl.

The Glen Vista Room has a picture window on a tract of woodlands, with microphones bringing in the sounds of the wild. Outside

the center are cages for predatory birds and access to the 11 different hiking trails.

The young trees in the 11-acre arboretum are spaciously set in a large meadow, which also includes the botanical garden, featuring rhododendrons, junipers, and plants adapted to arid conditions. Nearby is the Family Farm, with pettable horses, cows, pigs, goats, and sheep.

▶ Open year-round except holidays. Admission charged.

www.naturecenter.org
(269) 381-1574

20 Waterloo Farm Museum

9998 Waterloo Munith Rd., Waterloo

This is a small but attractive and well-maintained mid-19th-century farm outside the peaceful village of Waterloo. The brick farmhouse was built in 1846-47 with decorative panels of fieldstone in the fashion then popular with German-American builders.

The kitchen pantry has an ingenious cabinet that forms a dividing wall with drawers accessible from the dining room. The dining room itself has an aura of period charm with rag rugs, woodstove, and tea leaf–pattern china.

Upstairs are a children's toy room with clothing and toys of the period, a bedroom with a trundle bed, and a device for tightening the ropes supporting the mattress so that one can "sleep tight."

The outbuildings include a granary, blacksmith's shop, barn, log cabin, windmill, and bakehouse. The blacksmith's shop has a full complement of tools. On Pioneer Day (the second Sunday in October) cookies are baked in a brick oven, and old-time crafts like blacksmithing are practiced.

▶ Open Fri.-Sun. June-Sept.; call for occasional off-season hours. Admission charged.

www.waterloofarmmuseum.org
(517) 596-2254

21 Walker Tavern

13220 Rte. 50, Brooklyn
In the mid-1800s taking a trip from Detroit to Chicago meant that a traveler had to endure an arduous five-day trek by horse-drawn stagecoach, which is why this tavern became a favorite stopover. Located near a major junction and two premier ports, it was also a popular venue for local gatherings.

No longer serving ale or offering rooms for rent, and scrupulously run by the state, the tavern now stands as the centerpiece of a historic site devoted to Michigan's frontier settlement and stagecoach heyday. Along with a vintage barroom, the tavern includes a kitchen, fully equipped with the tools of its day, and a dining room and parlor decked out in 1840s style.

After a tour of the tavern, anyone thirsty for a taste of local history can head next door to the visitors center. Exhibits celebrate pioneering people who traveled these historic crossroads, as well as Sylvester Walker, the man who owned and ran the popular tavern at its peak. He was also an accomplished farmer. On display are his tools of that trade, from a scythe for harvesting buckwheat to a flail to separate the grain from the chaff.

In addition, the tavern complex features a reproduction of a New England–style barn similar to the one the Walkers actually used. The barn was an essential building for both the farm and the tavern. It housed animals, feed for livestock, and—when the tavern was full— even the extra visitors.

▶ Open Tues.-Sun. Memorial Day-Sept. Closed holidays and during race weekends at speedway next door. Admission charged.

www.michigan.gov/walkertavern
(517) 467-4401

22 Fair Lane—Henry Ford Estate. On display in the museum is a still-working touring car—a 1916 Model T Ford, the assembly-line car that put America on wheels.

22 Fair Lane–Henry Ford Estate

4901 Evergreen Rd., Dearborn
In 1914, flush with the success of the groundbreaking Model T, Henry Ford and his wife, Clara, commissioned a new home to be built on a 1,300-acre plot in Dearborn, near Henry's birthplace. This elegant mansion was the Ford family residence until Henry's death in 1947.

Guided tours take visitors through the two major sections of the estate: the mansion proper with its 31,000 square feet divided into 56 rooms—including a library, billiard room, and an indoor pool that now hosts a restaurant. The other part of the tour covers the powerhouse—which includes generators, pumps, and other equipment that made the estate self-sufficient and still provide electricity today— the experimental laboratory where Henry Ford and his engineers

22 Fair Lane–Henry Ford Estate. The estate was named after the area in Ireland where Ford's ancestors had lived.

worked on new projects, and the garage where many of the cars that the Fords owned still reside.

▶ Tours available everyday except Mon. and Sat. Jan.-Mar.; everyday except Mon. Apr.-Dec. Grounds open Tues.-Sun. mid-May-Labor Day. Admission charged.

www.henryfordestate.org
(313) 593-5590

MICHIGAN

seasonal events

JANUARY
• Tip-Up-Town USA—Houghton Lake (*winter festival, fireworks, live entertainment, parades, ice sculptures, monster truck rides*)

FEBRUARY
• Winter Carnival—Houghton (*ice sculpture contest, sleigh rides, local food*)

MAY
• Tulip Time Festival—Holland (*live entertainment, regional food*)
• Highland Festival—Alma (*music, parade, dancing, regional food*)

JUNE
• Annual Lilac Festival—Mackinac Island (*hayrides, line dancing, live entertainment, garden tours*)

JULY
• Michigan ElvisFest—Ypsilanti (*classic car show, local food*)
• National Cherry Festival—Traverse City (*marching bands, carnival, pie contest, local food, sporting events*)
• U.S. Coast Guard Festival—Grand Haven (*parade, carnival, live entertainment, fireworks, children's activities*)

AUGUST
• Fish Sandwich Festival—Bayport (*regional culinary festival, live entertainment, arts and crafts, parade, classic car show*)
• Great Lakes Folk Festival—East Lansing (*live music, regional children's activities*)

OCTOBER
• Oktoberfest—Frankenmuth (*regional food and beer, dancing, live music*)
• Apple & BBQ Cook-off Festival— Silver Lake Sand Dunes (*dune buggy show, apple pie contest, entertainment*)

DECEMBER
• Dutch Winterfest—Holland (*parade, regional food, children's activities*)
• Holiday Balloon Fest—Battle Creek (*annual hot-air balloon launch*)

www.michigan.org

Minnesota

The Ice Age glaciers left a magnificent legacy of lakes, streams, valleys, hills, and rolling plains, an ideal land for touring and camping.

Grand Portage National Monument.
At 130 feet, these falls on the Pigeon River are Minnesota's highest (see page 173).

The exploits of Minnesota's Native Americans, French voyageurs, and fur trappers are recalled in scenic and historic places and in place-names throughout the state.

In the mining area one can descend almost half a mile underground to experience the unique world of the workers there. And at Pipestone National Monument one can visit the quarries of catlinite reserved for use by Native American in fashioning their traditional ceremonial pipes. Museums feature distinctive architecture; collections of tools, utensils, and equipment used by pioneers; and artifacts reaching far back into our past.

visit ➡→ **offthebeatenpathtrips.com**

1 ⮞ Zippel Bay State Park
CR-34, Williams
These 3,000 acres of wilderness parklands are situated along the shores of Lake of the Woods, a 950,000-acre body of water that forms part of the border between Minnesota and Canada. As early as 1700, the voyageurs—those French fur traders who plied the waters of the Northwest—traveled along this great waterway.

Zippel Bay, a reedy inlet running almost at right angles from the lake, borders the park on the west. It is a pleasant, quiet stretch of water with a small marina, a boat ramp, and a fish-cleaning station.

Along the lakeshore, reached from the park entrance by a straight gravel road, is the swimming beach—three miles of sand considered to be the finest in the state. The nearby picnic area, with tables and a shelter, is set in a mown meadow surrounded by woodlands. Sixty primitive campsites are available, located in remote areas of the park. Trails through woodlands of white birches are excellent for skiing and snowshoeing in winter.

Many visitors come just to pick blueberries in midsummer, when a plentiful crop borders the roadways, or for the excellent fishing. For others the anticipation of seeing a moose or black bear or the likelihood of hearing the forlorn call of the timber wolf is the

Voyageurs National Park. This watery wilderness is best explored by boat and on foot. When the bodies of water freeze in winter, snowmobiles come on the scene.

appeal. Other attractions are the white pelicans, which nest around the lake; the sandhill cranes; and the common loon, the state bird.

▶ Open year-round. Admission charged.

www.dnr.state.mn.us/state_parks/zippel_bay
(218) 783-6252

2 ⮞ Voyageurs National Park
3131 State Hwy. 53, International Falls
The trappers and traders who canoed the waters of this scenic wilderness in the 1700s would be surprised to know that their legacy is not in furs or dollars but in a 218,000-acre park named in their memory. Within the bounds of the park are countless streams and ponds and more than 30 lakes, interspersed by islands of bog, marsh, meadow, and forest, forming many hundreds of miles of waterways. The main way to see the entire area up close is by boat in the summer and snowmobile in the winter. The park plows a seven-mile ice road for vehicles. Fifty miles of hiking trails are maintained, of which $17^1/2$ miles are accessible only by water. There are also more than 120 campsites, 78 houseboat sites, and many day-use sites available.

Wildlife abounds here. Black bears are common, and the park is home to about 40 timber wolves. Beavers and white-tailed deer are also plentiful, and moose are sometimes seen. Among the birds that nest here are loons, eagles, and great blue herons.

From both Rainy Lake and Kabetogama Lake visitors centers park naturalists lead guided canoe trips, providing canoes, life jackets, and instructions. Tour-boat trips are also available on both lakes. Fishing is allowed throughout the park, and catches include black crappies, lake trout, muskellunge, northern pike, rock bass, and walleye. Several fine beaches offer excellent swimming.

During the winter snowmobiling, ice fishing, cross-country skiing, and snowshoeing are popular.

▶ Open year-round. Fee for boat rentals and guided trips. Free overnight-use permits required for overnight camping.

www.nps.gov/voya
(218) 283-6600

3 ▶ Grand Portage National Monument

Grand Portage

Long before Europeans arrived, Native Americans had been bypassing an unnavigable stretch of the Pigeon River by an overland route they called Great Carrying Place. French voyageurs, translating the title literally, named it Grand Portage. In 1778 the North West Company, formed by a group of Canadian traders, established its headquarters at the start of the trail on the shore of Lake Superior. At the time this was a crossroads for hundreds of fur trappers and traders. The headquarters was abandoned in

1803 and fell into disrepair. The general area became a Native American reservation in 1854.

In 1958 the Grand Portage Band of the Minnesota Chippewa tribe donated the site of the Grand Portage National Monument to the U.S. government. The monument now features a carefully re-created complex of North West Company buildings. The principal structure is the Great Hall, an impressive

log-and-post structure originally chinked with river clay and bear grease—and now with concrete. Also on the grounds are a kitchen fully equipped with period utensils, a fur press for packing furs into bundles, a warehouse with birch-bark canoes, and a cabin built in 1900 that is now a gift shop.

The site also has two trails: the original 8½-mile Grand Portage Trail, which cuts through the reservation to Fort Charlotte, where you will find primitive backpacking campsites, and the half-mile

Mount Rose Trail, which offers a view of Lake Superior.

▶ Open mid-May–mid-Oct. Admission charged.

www.nps.gov/grpo
(218) 475-0123

3 ▶ Grand Portage National Monument. A girl dons native dress during Grand Portage's Rendezvous Days and Pow Wow.

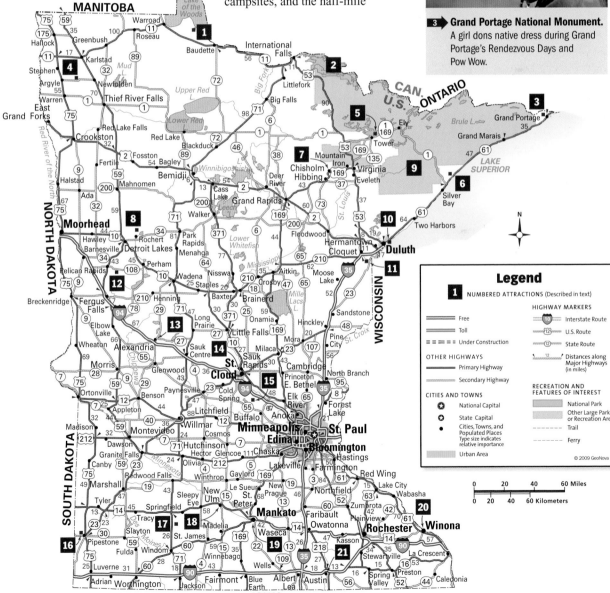

4 Old Mill State Park

33489 240th Ave. NW, Argyle

As you cross the seemingly endless open acres of the Red River valley's well-kept cropland, it is difficult to believe that the homesteaders who settled this region just over a century ago encountered prairies and riverine forests much like the ones found in this 406-acre park today.

Beavers, raccoons, deer, and an occasional moose may be seen, along with many native plants. Inviting paths, including a three-quarter-mile self-guiding nature trail, weave across the varied terrain. Many of these trails are groomed for snowmobiling and cross-country skiing in the winter. In addition, the park offers picnic and camping sites, a swimming pond, and winter ice-skating and sledding areas. Fishermen try for pike and bullheads.

The park's centerpiece, as the name suggests, is an old mill. Built in 1889, it is powered by an eight-horsepower steam engine, and grinding demonstrations are held on the last Sunday of August. A restored one-room log cabin, evoking the rugged life of the area's early homesteaders, may be seen nearby.

▶ Open year-round. Admission charged.

www.dnr.state.mn.us/state_parks/old_mill
(218) 437-8174

did you know ?

Soudan Underground Mine State Park is also home to the Soudan Underground laboratory, a high-energy physics lab run by the University of Minnesota. Visitors can take a 1½-hour tour of the laboratory, located on the lowest level of the mine.

7 ▶ **Minnesota Museum of Mining.** A locomotive in use until the 1950s was the first piece of mining equipment donated to the museum, which opened in 1954.

5 Soudan Underground Mine State Park

US-169, Soudan

The unusual centerpiece of this park is 2,341 feet underground and is reached by taking a three-minute elevator ("man cage") descent, a three-quarter-mile subterranean train ride, and a climb up a short flight of stairs. Visitors don hard hats and enter a "man cage" for the descent to the twenty-seventh and lowest level of the Soudan Iron Mine, sometimes called "the Cadillac of mines" because of its outstanding methods of operation and safety record in its 80-year history.

The rock here is ancient and stable, relatively dry, and does not produce toxic or explosive gases. The fine red dust that clings to some of the machinery on the surface is a silent reminder of the ore crusher, whose voice was a constant assurance that all was well when the mine was operating. The tunnel (called a drift), part of some 55 miles of underground access, is spacious, well lit, and a steady 50°F year-round. Fresh air circulates naturally from the surface, and guides make for an enjoyable and informative visit. Sturdy shoes and a sweater are recommended.

The visitors center offers exhibits explaining the area's geology and the mining process. In addition, various pieces of specialized mining machinery may be seen, including the giant ore crusher and the 500-horsepower air compressor that was used to operate the drilling equipment. It was last worked in the early 1960s.

The 1,300-acre park offers 5 miles of surface trails for hikers and about 50 miles of trails for cross-country skiing and snowmobiling. The park is home to timber wolves, deer, bats, and other creatures.

▶ Tours offered daily Memorial Day weekend–Sept. Additional group tours can be arranged off-season. Admission charged.

www.mdr.gov/soudan_underground_mine
(218) 753-2245

6 George H. Crosby–Manitou State Park

CR-7, Silver Bay

Dramatically highlighting the wild beauty of the rugged Manitou River valley is the rocky gorge shaped by ancient volcanic and glacial action and the river itself, tumbling through the forested landscape to Lake Superior.

At the cascades the river moves down through a series of branching waterfalls to a peat-dark pool. Along the edge, boulders, some convenient for sitting, show high-water marks indicating the water level during the spring melt. But even in August there is a quick, substantial flow between the conifer-shaded banks.

Twenty-three miles of wilderness trails follow the river and wind through the park's stands of birch, aspen, and hemlock. Some of the trails are difficult, but an easy quarter-mile path leads from the parking area to a picnic site beside Benson Lake in the center of the 3,400-acre park. The topographic trail map shows the relative steepness of the routes.

Along the river and by the lake, 21 primitive campsites have been cleared for backpackers. Water must be carried in or boiled, and fire rings are provided.

Moose come here to browse on the conifers, black bears are common, and timber wolves prey on the large population of white-tailed deer. Hikers often see the ruffed and spruce grouse. If you can get close enough, you can tell them apart by their markings. The tail of the spruce is dark, with a single band at the edge; that of the ruffed is striped white, brown, and black. Trout fishing is permitted in both stream and lake. Snow frequently stays from Nov.–Apr., and although the trails are rough, the campsites are open. Experienced skiers can enjoy 11 miles of cross-country trails.

▶ Open year-round.

www.dnr.state.mn.us
(218) 226-6365

7 Minnesota Museum of Mining

701 W. Lake St., Chisholm

When Minnesotans speak of "the range," they aren't referring to a string of mountains or to vast grasslands; they are talking about the Mesabi, Vermilion, and Cuyuna–some of the richest iron-ore ranges in the United States. Located in the heart of this area is a sprawling museum that rewards visitors with a vivid sense of the sheer magnitude and ruggedness of iron mining.

Fascinating exhibits of antique miners equipment, old photographs, and models of ore-processing operations are just the beginning. On the museum grounds visitors can tour a variety of heavy mining machines. One of these is a piercing machine that uses a high-velocity 5,000-degree flame to drill through rock. Dominating the area like some great mechanical dinosaur is a 1910 Atlantic steam shovel weighing 110 tons. But perhaps the awesome scale of iron mining is made clearest in a simple exhibit of ore truck tires, some 10 feet in diameter and weighing nearly three tons, each more costly than today's average automobile.

The most moving display is a life-size underground replica of a 150-foot turn-of-the-century mine drift. Visitors descend a short stairway to enter the miners daily world, where well-worn picks and drills, electric pit-mule carts, water pumps, columns of carefully placed support timbers, and wire-covered rescue stretchers make it easy to imagine the courage and determination of these early diggers of ore.

In the museum is a diorama of railroading by world-famous naturalist and artist Francis Lee Jaques.

▶ Open daily early May–Sept. Admission charged.

www.exploreminnesota.com
(218) 254-5543

8 Tamarac National Wildlife Refuge

35704 County Hwy. 26, Rochert

Crisscrossed with quiet roads and gently sloping hiking trails, just shy of 43,000 acres, these woodlands and wetlands offer the solitude of unspoiled nature. More than 20 lakes dot the refuge, their shores providing nesting sites favored by loons, herons, Canada geese, wood ducks, mallards, and teals. Bald eagles also nest here, and golden eagles sometimes may be seen during their fall migration. In all, more than 200 bird species have been observed within the refuge, along with deer, black bears, beavers, and moose.

Berry picking and mushrooming are allowed in the lower third of the refuge, where chokecherries, pin cherries, raspberries, and morel mushrooms are abundant. Fishermen are likely to catch northern pike, walleye, bluegills, and yellow perch, and boat-launching areas are provided. Nearly eight miles of trails are groomed for skiing in the winter.

Two of the most popular ways to enjoy the preserve are the Blackbird Auto Tour and the Old Indian Hiking Trail. The auto tour makes a 10-mile loop along refuge roads and passes many areas of geological and ecological interest. The hiking trail, about a one-mile loop, leaves Rte. 29 at the shore of Tamarac Lake and leads past an ancient Sioux burial ground to a camp area used as late as the 1930s by Native Americans gathering wild rice and sap for maple sugar. Harvesting the wild rice today is allowed only by special permit.

▶ Open daily year-round.

www.detroitlakes.com/tamaracrefuge
(218) 847-2641

9 Superior National Forest

North of Duluth

Established in 1909, this 3.85-million-acre national forest is an impressive natural resource. Rich in pine, spruce, aspen, birch, cedar, and tamarack, it harbors bald eagles, loons, and ospreys, moose and deer, black bear, and red fox.

Most notably, the forest is home to a large, stable population of more than 400 gray wolves. Within the dense woodland, explorers will also find evidence of sweeping sheets of ice dating back hundreds of millions of years. Over the eons glacial quarrying formed the forest's distinctive character, marked by huge boulders, polished bedrock outcroppings, deep eskers, and hundreds of lake basins. In addition, the forest contains more than 2,000 miles of lakes and streams, both cold and warm water, with walleye, pike, bass, and trout.

Canoeing, fishing, and wildlife viewing are the most popular pastimes here, but visitors also come to swim, bicycle ride, and rock hunt. Winters are ideal for cross-country skiing, sledding, and ice fishing. The forest hosts thousands of campsites.

▶ Open year-round. Fees charged for developed campgrounds and overnight use in the wilderness.

www.fs.fed.us/r9/superior
(218) 626-4300

9 Superior National Forest. This vast forest has three scenic byways to enjoy.

8 Tamarac National Wildlife Refuge. Although the refuge's birds and animals are protected, several of its lakes are open for fishing throughout the year.

10 Glensheen

3300 London Rd., Duluth

Among the welcome by-products of Minnesota's prosperous iron industry in the early 1900s are the stately homes built in the Duluth area. One such sumptuous manor house is Glensheen, the 39-room Jacobean-style home of millionaire attorney and iron-mine owner Chester Congdon, built from 1905–08 on the shore of Lake Superior. Named for the soft shimmer of the sun on a brook flowing through a small glen, the 7 1/2-acre estate includes a carriage house, boathouse, bowling green, and well-tended gardens.

Glensheen is noted for its hand-carved woodwork, elaborate ceiling plasterwork, and stained-glass windows. The entrance hall, oak-paneled in a 16th-century English pattern, is lighted by brass chandeliers incorporating the motif of the British lion. A red marble fireplace sets the color scheme of the mahogany-paneled drawing room, which is considered to be the most beautiful room in the house. The living room contains the "Little Museum," where mementos of the family's travels are displayed.

The reception room features a ceiling of gold leaf, and the billiard room has walls paneled of oak and "Japanese leather" (made of paper). For all the elegance and fine materials, an inviting sense of human scale is sustained throughout. A series of terraces with balustrades and a small pond lead from the house to the lakeshore.

Visitors are guided through the mansion but may tour the gardens and outbuildings on their own.

▶ Open daily mid-May–mid-Oct.; weekends mid-Oct.–mid-May; closed major winter holidays. Admission charged.

www.glensheen.org
(888) 454-4536; (218) 726-8910

11 Jay Cooke State Park

780 Hwy. 210, Carlton

The importance of railroads in the 19th century is easy to forget in this era of superhighways and jet planes. A reminder is the fact that this 8,818-acre park is named for Jay Cooke, who was instrumental in establishing Duluth as the eastern

10 **Glensheen.** This early 20th-century estate, the home of a Minnesota iron tycoon, calls to mind the grand manor houses of the English countryside.

11 **Jay Cooke State Park.** River water meets rock in this rugged park.

terminus of the Central Pacific Railroad's route to the West Coast. The park comprises the rugged countryside flanking both sides of the St. Louis River as it flows through massive rock formations toward Lake Superior. The hills, forested with hardwoods, harbor 46 species of animals, including timber wolves, black bears, and coyotes.

Fifty miles of trails wander through the woodlands and along the river. There are some easy hikes, but the Lost Lake and Silver Creek trails, traversing swamps, steep hills, and ridges are best left to the well-conditioned. Trout fishing is popular in Silver Creek.

The Grand Portage Trail, part of which lies within the park, was used by travelers 300 years ago to avoid an impassable section of the St. Louis River cutting through this area. Several trails are shared by hikers and horseback riders, and some lead to overlooks with fine views of the river valley. The Carlton Trail begins near the park nature center and crosses the river by means of a swinging bridge.

Modern campsites and group camps are located within walking distance to the river; backpacking sites are found in wilderness areas. Two picnic grounds, one by the river and the other on Oldenburg Point, are invitingly set among birch trees. In the springtime one should ask about the superb display of trilliums and other wildflowers.

In winter the park is popular with cross-country skiers as well as snowshoers.

▶ Open year-round. Admission charged.

www.dnr.state.mn.us
(218) 384-4610

12 Maplewood State Park

39721 Park Entrance Rd., Pelican Rapids

This exceptionally beautiful park—some 9,500 acres of hills, valleys, woodlands, and small lakes—lies between Minnesota's eastern forests and western prairies, and it has plants and animals native to each of the ecological zones.

Lida, the largest of the lakes, features a swimming beach and a picnic area nearby. Family campgrounds overlook Grass Lake, and smaller ponds in remote areas have primitive campsites. Miles of trails for hiking, horseback riding, skiing, and snowmobiling wander through the parklands; many lead to overlooks with superb views of the surrounding hills and valleys.

Two ramps are provided for boaters—at South Lake Lida and Beers Lake. Fishing is excellent at

did you know

Recent results of archaeological investigations strongly suggest that Native Americans inhabited the Maplewood State Park area some 6,000 years ago.

both, with walleye, northern pike, and panfish the likely catches.

Forty acres have been set aside as a demonstration woodland. Trees here are labeled with botanical notes and information as to their usefulness to man. Basswood, for instance, is good for beekeepers and cabinet- and toymakers. Paper birch, black cherry, sugar maple, and ironwood (including the largest such tree in Minnesota) are included. Experiments here show that shrubs and trees increase dramatically in size, number, and variety when deer and rabbits are excluded from the area.

▶ Open year-round.

www.dnr.state.mn.us/state_parks/
   maplewood
(218) 863-8383

13 Runestone Museum
206 Broadway, Alexandria
It's hard to miss the Runestone Museum. Just look for the 28-foot-tall fiberglass Viking with the spear and shield. "Big Ole," constructed for the 1965 New York World's Fair, symbolizes the Norse heritage of many of Minnesota's early settlers and is a fitting introduction to the Kensington Runestone, housed in the adjacent museum.

The Runestone—found in 1898 entangled in the roots of an aspen tree on the Olaf Ohman farm in Kensington—is a 200-pound slab of greywacke stone carved with runic symbols and dated 1392. Is it genuine or a hoax? That debate has raged almost since it was unearthed. Real or not, the stone has inspired a good deal of scientific study and a few modern pranks. The museum presents the case for and against in what a *New York Times* article termed "a well-balanced collection

of material devoted to the discovery and controversy," allowing visitors to reach their own conclusions.

The Runestone Museum also offers impressive exhibits devoted to Minnesota's Native American and pioneer history, including a log cabin, general store, one-room schoolhouse, and a replica of Fort Alexander, the military stockade built in 1862 to protect the early settlers.

▶ Open daily mid-May–mid-Oct.; Mon.–Sat. mid-Oct.–mid-May. Admission charged.

www.runestonemuseum.org
(320) 763-3160

14 Stearns History Museum
235 33rd Ave. S, St. Cloud
How many museums feature a city's best-known failure? The Stearns has a full exhibit devoted to Sam Pandolfo and his Pan Motor Company, which in the early 1900s promised to make St. Cloud the auto manufacturing capital of the country. Later, however, the company crumbled as its visionary founder, Pandolfo, was convicted of mail fraud and jailed. Something of a city planner, Pandolfo had built comfortable bungalows for his workers in Pan Town, which today remain in St. Cloud.

The Pan story is just one of the museum's entertaining, educational, and very family-friendly experiences. Exhibitions at the Stearns, located in Heritage Park, include a prairie environment with Ojibwe and Dakota summer lodges, a dairy barn, a granite quarry, and an intriguing collection that explores changing lifestyles by examining the clothing people wore. A whole gallery is devoted to kids' activities, including a child-size grocery store and a puppet theater, and

family historians can dig into the genealogical records in the well-equipped research center.

▶ Open daily except major holidays. Admission charged.

www.stearns-museum.org
(320) 253-8424; (866) 253-8424

15 Lake Maria State Park
11411 Clementa Ave. NW, Monticello
This hilly, forested land, with two lakes and numerous marshes and ponds, is a surviving 1,580-acre

15 ▶ Lake Maria State Park. The lake in this park is a favorite for anglers. Surrounding it are the remnants of an ancient forest, here glowing with autumn color.

fragment of the Big Woods, a mighty primeval forest that originally covered 3,000 square miles of south-central Minnesota. Glaciers advanced and receded here three times. The last incursion, during the Wisconsin Ice Age, which ended 10,000 years ago, deposited boulders and rocky debris, along with till and loam from the Lake Superior and Red River valley regions.

The landscape is a superb habitat for wildlife. Popular with

birders, it harbors more than 200 species, including goldfinches, meadowlarks, gulls, bald eagles, Cooper's hawks, and several species of owls. Blandings turtles, one of Minnesota's threatened species, also make their home here.

Lake Maria, fringed with tall reeds and water lilies and encircled by dense woods of maple, birch, and red oak, brings fishermen, who try for walleye, perch, sunfish, carp, bullhead, and bass. A boat ramp is provided.

A large, primitive group campground has a parking lot; several other primitive campsites must be reached by foot. Opposite a small wooded island in Lake Maria is a shady picnic ground.

The park has 6 miles of horseback riding trails and 14 miles of hiking and ski trails. Nature walks are conducted by the park's naturalist.

▶ Open year-round. Admission charged.

www.dnr.state.mn.us/state_parks/lake_maria
(763) 878-2325

16 Pipestone National Monument

36 N. Reservation Ave., Pipestone
For centuries tribal groups traveled to the pipestone quarries to obtain the soft red stone, known as catlinite, to make their ceremonial pipe bowls. Legend holds that at a time when the different tribes were at war with each other, the Great Spirit called them together here and fashioned a pipe from the stone. As he smoked the pipe, he told the tribes that this place belonged to them all, that they must make their ceremonial pipes of the stone, and that they must meet in this sacred place as friends.

Many tribes have occupied the area of the quarries, with the most recent being the Dakota Sioux. The 300-acre monument was established by Congress in 1937. The legislation contains a provision that guarantees the right of Native Americans to continue quarrying pipestone, even today.

The Circle Trail leads from the visitors center, past the quarries, through a tract of remnant tallgrass prairie. Signs identify the plants along the way. As you walk the trail, you can see the pipestone quarries, many showing recent quarrying activity. Visit the exhibit quarry where you can see an actual quarry from the bottom in which the floor and lower wall are pipestone. In the cultural center local carvers demonstrate how they work with pipestone. Many of their finished items are for sale in the visitors center gift shop.

▶ Open daily except major holidays. Admission charged.

www.nps.gov/pipe
(507) 825-5464

17 Jeffers Petroglyphs Historic Site

27160 CR-2, Comfrey
These enormous carvings of humans, animals, and ancient tools etched into the exposed rock of the Minnesota prairie were carved over a span of 5,000 years, produced between 3000 B.C. and A.D. 1750. The petroglyphs have served multiple functions, including depicting important historical events and sacred rituals.

Today the ancient artwork is preserved by the Minnesota Historical Society. In collaboration with the Native American community, the site directors work to respect the sacred nature of the glyphs while educating visitors about both Native American culture and the significance of the site—past and present.

A half-mile trail leads to the glyphs, which are best viewed at dusk. In the daytime interpreters are available to help visitors see the carvings. The visitors center features exhibits and a presentation about the site. Programs are offered on weekdays, ranging from learning to throw an atlatl to prairie scavenger hunts.

▶ Open daily Memorial Day-Labor Day; Fri.-Sun. in May and Sept.; by reservation Oct.-Apr. Admission charged.

www.mnhs.org/places/sites/jp/
(507) 628-5591

18 New Ulm

90 miles southwest of the Twin Cities
In 1854 a group of German immigrants landed in the heart of the scenic Minnesota River Valley and found the perfect spot for their new home. Named after the premier city in the settlers' homeland province, New Ulm continues to celebrate its German heritage.

Twelve blocks from downtown, the 102-foot-tall Hermann Monument stands as a glowing tribute to an ancient Teutonic hero who liberated Germany from Rome in A.D. 9. For $1 visitors can step inside and climb up to a railed outside lookout for stunning views of the valley from any one of its 10 windows. Nearby the New Ulm Glockenspiel plays like clockwork at noon,

16 ▶ **Pipestone National Monument.** The soft stone the Dakotas used to make ceremonial pipes gave this area its name. Shown here is Winnewassa Falls, on Pipestone Creek.

3 P.M., and 5 P.M. daily. During the holiday season a nativity scene replaces the clock's regular cast of diminutive moving characters.

Other sites of interest include the mansion that was home to John Lind—the first Swedish-born American to be governor of Minnesota—built in 1887 at a cost of $5,000 and placed on the *National Register of Historic Homes* nearly a century later; the childhood home of Wanda Gag—author of the classic children's book *Millions of Cats*—built in 1894; and Schell's Brewery.

▶ Many historic attractions are open year-round, free of charge.

www.newulm.com
(888) 463-9856, (507) 233-4300

19 R. D. Hubbard House

606 S. Broad St., Mankato
Rensselaer D. Hubbard, founder of the Hubbard Milling Company, built this elegant white brick two-story house in 1871, only 19 years after the town was first settled. Its handsome proportions, pillared porches, mansard roof of slate, and stained-glass windows set the style for local mansions yet to come. In 1890 he added a splendid carriage house next door. The buildings are now on the *National Register of Historic Places.*

The restored house has a notably rich interior, with carved cherry and oak woodwork and three unusual fireplaces (one of Brazilian white onyx and Italian black marble, another of Spanish marble, and a third of Georgia marble). Displayed in the rooms are 19th- and early 20th-century furniture, kitchen equipment, and other memorabilia from the early

Minnesota Marine Art Museum. Artistic expressions of life on sea, lake, and river run the gamut in this spacious museum's permanent collections and exhibits.

days of Mankato. Among the vehicles in the carriage house are a real Concord stagecoach and an 1895 Haynes-Apperson auto in perfect running condition.

▶ Open weekends May–mid-Sept.; group tours available year-round by prior arrangement. Admission charged.

(507) 345-5566

20 ▶ Minnesota Marine Art Museum

800 Riverview Dr., Winona
Opened in 2006, the Marine Art Museum is one of Minnesota's newest attractions, and a handsome one indeed. Located on a landscaped 6-acre site on the Mississippi River, the museum's modern complex was designed to recall a 19th-century Mississippi waterfront and harbor. In fair weather visitors can dine on a pier leading to the water's edge. Three galleries feature art and artifacts on maritime themes from the permanent and on-loan collections and special exhibits. Check out the exceptional marine paintings, folk-art collection, and upper Mississippi riverscapes of Prussian-born cartographer and photographer Henry Peter Bosse (1844–1903).

The inspiration for the Marine Art Museum came from the decom-

missioning of the dredge boat *William A. Thompson,* which plied the river for almost seven decades. The museum's founders worked with the U.S. Army Corps of Engineers to rescue and restore the 269-foot dredge.

▶ Open year-round Tues.–Sun. Closed major holidays. Admission charged.

www.minnesotamarineart.org
(866) 940-6626; (507) 474-6626

21 ▶ The SPAM Museum

1937 Spam Blvd., Austin, about 90 minutes south of Minneapolis
Since 1937 Hormel Foods has sold nearly 6 billion cans of SPAM, a mixture of cooked pork and ham, once a staple in American households. The museum, located right next door to the multinational food manufacturer, presents a nostalgic tribute to the all-American luncheon meat.

A treat for trivia buffs, it features 19 permanent exhibits, serving up facts of SPAM history and mania. Upon walking through the entrance, you see a towering wall of SPAM. Composed of 3,390 cans of SPAM, it rises to the lobby's ceiling. A video, SPAM Exam, challenges connoisseurs to test their product

knowledge. Promotions include SPAM spoofs (including the infamous Monty Python sketch) and recent corporate efforts to distinguish SPAM from the disparaging term for junk e-mail.

There's also a SPAM Cyber-Diner, a working radio station (K-SPAM), a display of advertising over the years, and a replica of a Hormel production line, where visitors can pack and label their own can of SPAM (fake, of course).

Visitors can take a quick drive to the eastern side of town, on 21st St. NE, for a stroll through the Jay C. Hormel Nature Center. This 507-acre expanse offers 10-plus miles of walking trails past restored and remnant prairie, hardwood forest, and wetlands. In addition, visitors can stop by the informative interpretive center, which features a touch-and-see exhibit and a live beehive.

▶ Open daily May–Labor Day; Tues.–Sun. the rest of the year. Closed major holidays.

www.spam.com
(507) 437-5100 Museum
(507) 437-7519 Nature Center

The SPAM Museum. Fun is on the menu at this shrine to SPAM.

seasonal events

FEBRUARY
• World of Wheels—St. Paul *(car show, vendors, autograph sessions)*

MARCH
• Giants Ridge Spring Carnival—Giants Ridge *(ski/snowboard competitions, music, costume contests)*

MAY
• Taste of Lakeville—Lakeville *(food and drink from local restaurants, wine and beer vendors)*

JUNE
• Minnesota Inventors Congress Invention & Idea Show—Redwood Falls
• Prairie Fest 2008—Long Prairie *(rides, fireworks, professional bull riding, demolition derby)*
• Annual Blackwater Barge Festival—Cohasset *(street dancing, barbecue, parade, live music, amateur baseball tournament, car show)*

AUGUST
• White Oak Rendezvous—Deer River *(replica 1798 Northwest Company Fur Post, camping facilities, period costumes, demonstrations)*

OCTOBER
• Big Island Rendezvous and Festival—Albert Lea *(historical re-enactment, live entertainment, Colonial crafts and cuisine)*
• Afton Apple Festival—Hastings *(hayrides, petting farm, straw mountain, corn maze, cider pressing)*
• Twin Cities Book Festival—Minneapolis *(author readings, panel discussions, book-making demonstrations, used and rare book sale)*
• Oktoberfest—New Ulm *(German fare, libations, music, crafts, horse-drawn trolley rides past the city's historic homes)*

DECEMBER
• Christmas in the Village—Montevideo *(food, gift items, entertainment, craftsmanship demonstrations)*

www.exploreminnesota.com

MINNESOTA

Mississippi

The history and culture of the Magnolia State was shaped in part by the mightiest of rivers and old King Cotton.

Tunica RiverPark. Sightseers on the *Tunica Queen* are treated to the best of both worlds: the luxury of an old-style riverboat and air-conditioned comfort (see right).

Plantation houses, river attractions, and a museum extolling cotton's impact on the world may distill the essence of Mississippi, but a tour of the state is further enriched by stops at other sites: a Clarksdale museum celebrating Delta blues musicians, the Oxford home of a Nobel prizewinning author, a small-town art museum exhibiting the works of Sargent, Whistler, and other American masters.

Scenic natural areas include an untamed forest at Clark Creek, a prairie wildlife preserve, a bird sanctuary, and two surprises in the heart of the Deep South: a petrified forest and a buffalo park.

visit ➾ **offthebeatenpathtrips.com**

1 Tunica RiverPark

1 River Park Dr., Tunica

At RiverPark you can sit in a rocking chair and gaze out over the mighty Mississippi. Or you can board the richly appointed *Tunica Queen* riverboat for a cruise. But the centerpiece of Tunica RiverPark is an award-winning glass-and-steel museum designed to suggest a boat's prow. Inside, four large aquariums house reptiles, catfish, gar, and more—all taken from the river and later released. Other exhibits include artifacts of the people who lived in the region during the Mississippian Period (A.D. 800–1600) and a full-scale replica of a tenant house destroyed by the great flood of 1927.

A 1.9-mile nature trail/boardwalk takes visitors through five riverbank ecosystems: cypress swamp, hardwood swamp, creek, seasonal marsh, bog meadow, and floodplain, each with a slightly different temperature and humidity.

▶ Open daily except Christmas.
Admission charged.
www.tunicariverpark.com
(866) 517-4837

2 J. P. Coleman State Park

13 miles north of Iuka, off State Hwy. 25

This park is a magnet for water sports enthusiasts of all stripes.

1 Tunica RiverPark. Viewing decks at the park afford sweeping panoramas of the Mississippi. In the museum visitors can view exhibits on river history and culture.

Though its 424 square miles are perched on a rocky bluff overlooking the Tennessee River, the action is at Pickwick Lake, with its vast body of water and some 490 miles of winding shoreline—the place to sail, water-ski, swim (lake, river, or pool), and fish (catch of choice: smallmouth bass). There's even a waterfall, a rarity in the state of Mississippi.

Campers and hikers take to the scenic wilderness along the riverbanks. The beauty of the park is evident at any time of year, but the hardwood trees are exquisite enough to appear on a calendar when they turn red and gold in autumn—a little bit of heaven for those visitors

exploring the park from its trails.

▶ Open daily except major winter holidays.
Fee for campsites.

http://mississippistateparks.
reserveamerica.com
(662) 423-6515

3 Rowan Oak

Old Taylor Rd., Oxford

Rowan Oak was the home of the famous American writer William Faulkner (1897– 1962). The scion of two old Southern families, he incorporated into his novels and short stories the myths, traditions, and memories of his locale. He was awarded the Nobel Prize for Literature in 1949 and two Pulitzer prizes, one in 1954 and the other in 1962.

A stately antebellum house with a columned portico, Rowan Oak is remarkable for its interior simplicity and for the sense it conveys of having been furnished by happenstance: Faulkner's work, not his home, was his object and his legacy.

To the left of the entrance is the library, in which the writer worked prior to 1952. His portrait as a young man hangs above two Chinese vases; copies of *Field and Stream* and a book about Switzerland lie on a small table beside a piece of abstract sculpture. To the right of the hall is a sitting room. The most interesting room is the one at the back of the house, where he worked for his last few years—on one wall is the outline of a novel written in his hand. Upstairs are four sparsely furnished bedrooms. The grounds, by contrast, are lush with magnolia and cypress trees and climbing rose vines.

▶ Open Tues.–Sun. except major holidays.

www.olemiss.edu/depts/u_museum/rowan_
 oak/interactive.html

(662) 234-3284

4 ▶ Tupelo Buffalo Park and Zoo

2272 N. Coley Rd., Tupelo
This is the ideal place to get to know the mighty buffalo. Home to the largest herd east of the Mississippi River, this park boasts more than 200 of the majestic creatures, including Gypsy the cougar, Bandit the black bear, the giraffes Tall Boy and Patches, and Ozzu the ball python. If you're lucky, you'll spot the rare white buffalo.

On the exciting Monster Bison Bus Tour, visitors get to ride right beside these gigantic beasts. The tour, which lasts about 35 minutes,

also provides visitors with striking views of Texas longhorn cattle.

After the tour visitors can stop at a petting zoo and play area. Or you can simply stay and watch the antics of the park's other residents, including beloved monkey Oliver and his son Opu! Before leaving the land of the buffalo, visitors might want to stop in the gift shop for a souvenir—or even a package of dried buffalo meat.

▶ Open year-round. Admission charged.

www.tupelobuffalopark.com
(662) 844-8709

5 ▶ Prairie Wildlife Preserve

3464 Balion Ferry Rd., West Point
Though the northern bobwhite quail population in the Southeast has been in decline, it has risen so high at this wildlife habitat management preserve that visitors are allowed to hunt the birds. The 6,000-acre scenic preserve works with the Wildlife and Fishers Department of Mississippi State University to spur the restoration of this species of quail across the state.

Non-hunters are drawn by the wildflower meadows and the superb bird-watching, while hikers and equestrians have more than 10 miles of trails to choose from. No camping facilities are available, but up to eight visitors can overnight at an authentic 1845 log cabin with three bedrooms, two full baths, and all of the modern amenities.

▶ Open daily. Fee for
 hunting packages.

www.prairiewildlife.com
(662) 425-5804

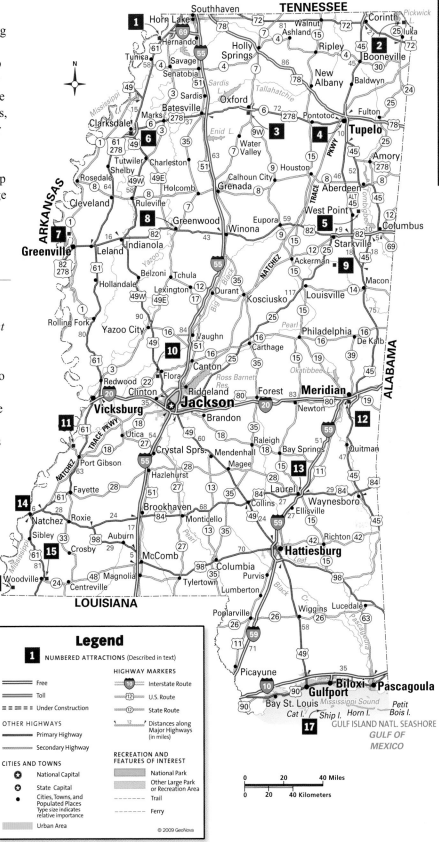

6 Delta Blues Museum

1 Blues Alley, Clarksdale
At this museum blues lovers can compare vintage Stella guitars (instruments favored by Delta musicians) and then "visit" one of Clarksville's favorite sons: Muddy Waters, embodied in a life-size statue capturing the spirit of the great bluesman. Another legendary local was John Lee Hooker, whose numerous guitars are displayed. Other featured stars include the pioneering blues singer Big Mama Thornton and harp master Charlie Musselwhite. During three local festivals held annually, classic blues waft from the stage at the museum, housed in a restored building dating back to the Jazz Age: the Yazoo & Mississippi Valley Railroad freight depot.

▶ Open daily except major holidays. Admission charged.

www.deltabluesmuseum.org
(662) 627-6820

7 Winterville Mounds

On Hwy. 1, Greenville
This is one of the ceremonial mound complexes built in prehistoric America by Native Americans of the Mississippian culture. Built about 1,000 years ago by an agricultural people who were the predecessors of the Choctaw, Chickasaw, and Tunica tribes, it was probably occupied for some 600 years before its populace was completely decimated by disease, drought, war, or famine.

The 40-acre park is said to contain 12 mounds, but only 8 are readily discerned. A flight of stairs leads to the top of the largest mound (about 55 feet high), where there is a roofless, windowless structure. The view is of pancake-flat Delta farmland, with a 360-degree horizon of woodland. One can see the pattern of other mounds, and to the east is an open space called the Sacred Plaza, where dances and other ceremonies were held.

A museum in the visitors center contains Native American artifacts, including arrowheads, celts, adzes, chunky stones and ball sticks, clay pipes, shell beads, and pots. A wall-length mural depicts Native Americans hunting and gathering food.

▶ Museum and grounds open daily.

www.mdah.state.ms.us
(662) 334-4684

8 Cottonlandia Museum

1608 Hwy. 82 W., Greenwood
Despite its name, this is far from being a one-crop museum. Cottonlandia offers a fascinating overview of the archaeological, natural, economic, historical, and social heritage of the Delta.

The museum's extensive collection of Native American artifacts includes some of the earliest arrow and spear points made on this continent; a few are of the type used about 10,000 B.C. to kill mastodons. You can also see examples of the earliest ceramics produced in the New World: small, fire-hardened clay balls made and used as a source of heat for cooking food by the people of the Poverty Point culture, which thrived in the lower Mississippi Valley some 3,000 years ago.

One of the most valuable—and exquisite—displays is the group of multicolored pottery effigy vessels, which depict a bobcat, deer, fish, opossum, and other creatures in a very naturalistic manner. The vessels date from sometime after A.D. 700.

The enormous and colorful collection of beads alone makes a visit to this museum worthwhile. Various methods of manufacturing beads are described, along with fashions in beads from prehistoric times. Cotton clothing on display includes World War II uniforms worn by GIs, WACs, and other

8 Cottonlandia Museum. WWII uniforms include those of a medical officer (center) and a naval captain (left), who at the time was the highest-ranking woman in the U.S. Navy.

members of the armed forces.

In 2004 the Leflore County Military History Exhibit opened, focusing on the effect of various wars on Greenwood and its citizens. On display are a working Blakely cannon, a scale model of Fort Pemberton, uniforms, veterans lists, victory posters, and artifacts from the wars.

Relics of King Cotton include a miniature Improved Eagle cotton gin, a John Deere tractor that retired mules from the cotton fields, an 1850 wooden harrow with hand-forged points made by slaves, and a boll weevil catcher.

A hands-on natural-science room and life-size diorama of a Mississippi swamp offer a break from the usual "no touch" rules of most museums.

A large collection of Mississippi artwork graphically displays the range of styles of native artists, from photography to abstract sculpture, watercolor to ceramics, and all things in between.

▶ Open weekdays and P.M. weekends except major holidays. Admission charged.

www.cottonlandia.org
(662) 453-0925

9 Noxubee National Wildlife Refuge

2970 Blufflake Rd., Brooksville
Surprisingly, only 3,000 of the more than 48,000 acres in the refuge are designated as a sanctuary. Anglers enjoy Loakfoma Lake and Bluff Lake and take good catches of largemouth bass, bluegills, and crappies from their waters.

For birders the best place is Canada Goose Overlook, an elevated walkway and viewing platform that juts out high above Bluff Lake. It's worthwhile to

9 Noxubee National Wildlife Refuge. The 48,000-acre refuge is home to American alligators, fish, and countless waterfowl species.

bring binoculars. From Nov.–Jan. tens of thousands of waterfowl, primarily wood ducks, green-winged teals, Canada geese, and American widgeons, visit the refuge. In late winter and early spring a variety of songbirds add their grace notes. Wood storks and wild turkeys may be seen, and occasionally the endangered red-cockaded woodpecker and the bald eagle. From this elevation one can see other wildlife as well, like white-tailed deer feeding in grassy meadows or the American alligator crawling about.

The refuge is crisscrossed with narrow gravel roads and seven hiking trails; a map may be obtained at refuge headquarters. Visitors entering the woods during the gun-hunting season in November and December are required to wear hunter orange.

▶ Open year-round.

www.fws.gov/noxubee
(662) 323-5548

10 Mississippi Petrified Forest

124 Forest Park Rd., Flora
Considering the comparatively short span of time allotted the human record, the scope of the geological record here is almost impossible to comprehend. The trees turned to stone (fossilized logs) in this small forest (the only petrified forest east of the Rockies and a National Natural Landmark) are some 36 million years old. The remains of living denizens of primeval forests, they were deposited here as driftwood and buried in and preserved by the sand and silt. Some are ancestors of maples, firs, and sequoia-like; others are unknown species. A smooth path traverses the lush woodland site of loblolly pines, sweet gums, elms, wild plums, and occasional clumps of yucca and pear cactus.

The most striking feature found here is a curiously anomalous section of deeply eroded red-and-pink cliffs, studded with extruding petrified logs, that resemble a miniature badlands. These exposed cliff walls are a fascinating cross section of natural history. The red sands in their lower parts were the river deposit in which the petrifaction process originally began.

Markers along the path are keyed to a descriptive leaflet available at the entrance to the site. The 40-minute walk terminates at a small but interesting museum devoted to petrified wood. The displays also include some vertebrate fossils and an array of gems and minerals.

▶ Open daily except major winter holidays. Admission charged.

www.mspetrifiedforest.com
(601) 879-8189

11 Grand Gulf Military Park

Port Gibson
The restored buildings here are reminders that this was once a thriving river port nurtured by the cotton boom and so prosperous that it was a candidate to become the state capital. But after a series of unfortunate events, including yellow fever, a major tornado, and shifting riverbeds, the prosperity of the city took a turn. Then in April 1863 Union naval forces attacked Grand Gulf, eventually forcing the Confederate troops established there to flee.

Today the park commemorates both the battle and Grand Gulf's heyday. The museum here has a detailed map of that battle and photos of the Union ironclads that were involved, along with swords, rifles, muskets, cannonballs, flags, and war-related documents.

On the handsome park grounds are a few hand-hewn log houses, a lovely Carpenter Gothic chapel, and an atmospheric graveyard overhung with Spanish moss. A paved road leads to the edge of the river, and a hilltop observation

12 Jimmie Rodgers Museum. A guitar was named for Rogers after the expert yodeler hit the big time with songs like *T for Texas* (1927).

tower provides an overview of this instrument of Grand Gulf's rise and fall.

▶ Open year-round.

www.grandgulfpark.state.ms.us
(601) 437-5911

12 Jimmie Rodgers Museum

1725 Jimmie Rogers Dr., Meridian
Jimmie Rodgers, "The Singing Brakeman," is honored here as the 1920s progenitor of country music.

Rodgers, who died in 1933, was indeed a brakeman, as well as a baggageman and switchman, during the era of the steam engine. The museum building resembles a train station, complete with an engine and caboose outside.

Rodgers's popularity is demonstrated by fan mail from as far away as Japan, honorary citizenship papers from the city of New Orleans, and first-day covers of the postage stamp acclaiming him as the Father of Country Music. Original recordings and sheet music of his songs are displayed, as well as his denim jacket and other belongings. In the spring Meridian sponsors a Jimmie Rodgers Memorial Festival.

▶ Open Tues.–Thurs. year-round except major holidays. Admission charged.

www.jimmierodgers.com
(601) 485-1808

13 ▶ Lauren Rogers Museum of Art

Fifth Ave. at 7th St., Laurel
The emphasis here is on 19th- and 20th-century painting, and this museum houses one of the most outstanding collections in the South. Seven elegant galleries invite one to linger with masterpieces by James McNeill Whistler, John Singer Sargent, Winslow Homer, and Mary Cassatt, among other notable artists. There is a rich collection of landscape paintings, from dramatic renderings of the American wilderness by Albert Bierstadt to Thomas Moran's grandiose sunset scene and the moody impressionism of George Inness's later works.

The museum also contains an excellent exhibit of Georgian silver. Highlights include a 1785 George III teapot by Hester Bateman, one of the few female silversmiths of her time; William Plummer's celebrated cake baskets; and plates by Paul Lamerie, acclaimed in the early 1700s as the finest of England's craftsmen of silver and gold.

Another of the museum's displays provides insight into the subtle relationship between art and archaeology. The Catherine Marshall Gardiner Native American Basket Collection features such superb craftsmanship that one set of miniature baskets is displayed under a magnifying glass.

The Georgian Revival building, with its golden oak hallways and elaborate ironwork, is itself an elegant tribute to the architecture of the Old South.

▶ Open Tues.-Sat. and P.M. Sun. year-round. Closed major holidays.

www.LRMA.org
(601) 649-6374

13 ▶ **Lauren Rogers Museum of Art.** The museum was established by a local founding family as a memorial to their son, Lauren Eastman Rogers, who died at age 21.

14 ▶ Historic Natchez

At the intersection of US Hwys. 61, 84, and 98, on the Mississippi River
Perched on the highest promontory north of the Gulf of Mexico, Natchez is the oldest civilized community on the Mississippi River. Originally settled by the Natchez tribe, it was claimed by the French in 1716, the British in 1763, the Spanish in 1779, and finally the Americans in 1798. In 1817 it was named the first capital of the new state of Mississippi.

During the early 19th century the city boomed as cotton was exported by steamboat. Today Natchez is known for its rustic beauty, sense of history, and Southern hospitality. Visitors can stroll scenic trails, try their luck at riverboat gambling, or take a nostalgic tour via trolley or horse-drawn carriage. The town is filled with antique shops and is home to the Old South Winery and numerous historic houses. One of the most impressive, Rosalie mansion, reflects the classic Federal style, enhanced by wide galleries and Doric columns. Its lovely garden borders a four-acre riverside park, which hosts the Great Mississippi River Balloon Race festival every October.

Nearby, Lansdowne Plantation invites travelers to experience the lifestyle of an elite antebellum home, surrounded by more than a hundred wooded acres. Built in 1853 and meticulously preserved—in fact, it has never been restored—Lansdowne includes original furnishings and décor.

From the plantation, visitors can head off on the Natchez Trace Pkwy. Over 440 miles long, this sweeping stretch commemorates the Old Natchez Trace, which evolved from a Natchez Native American trail into a post road and pioneer highway. Designated as a National Scenic Byway, it encompasses historic sites such as Emerald Mound, the second largest Native American ceremonial site in the United States. Winding across Mississippi, it tells the story of celebrated leaders, like Meriwether Lewis and Andrew Jackson, and notorious outlaws, like John Murrell and Samuel Mason. Along the way, the roadside features plenty of informative exhibits, interpretive markers, and self-guiding nature trails.

▶ Open year-round.

www.visitnatchez.com
(800) 647-6724
(800) 305-7417 Natchez Trace Parkway

15 ▶ Rosemont Plantation

On State Hwy. 24E, Woodville
Jefferson Davis grew up on this plantation, reached from the highway by a long, shady lane. Though best known as the president of the Confederate States of America during the Civil War, Davis had already made his mark as a soldier, congressman, senator, a founder of the Smithsonian Institution, and a U.S. Secretary of War.

The pastures and gardens of the plantation are bordered by hand-split rail fences, and the roses that gave the plantation its name still grow in profusion. Even in summer the grounds can be surprisingly cool, shaded by evergreen magnolias and immense live oaks festooned with Spanish moss. One can readily believe the roadside sign that reads: "Quiet, you are entering the early 19th century."

The inviting white manor house, built in 1810 by Jefferson Davis's father in the Federal "planter's cottage" style, has been well preserved. A porch with square pillars runs the width of the building, and a roof of multiple peaks rises high above the

did you know ❓

On the grounds of Rosemont Plantation is a little family cemetery, where Jefferson Davis's mother and relatives are buried.

first story. Dormer windows and white latticework add their appeal. At the end of the porch, the lattice supports a bush of tiny magenta roses. Among the furnishings of the Davis family are a whale-oil chandelier and a spinning wheel that belonged to Davis's mother.

Near the house are former slave quarters, an office, and a kitchen.

▶ Open Mon.-Fri. Mar.-mid-Dec. Admission charged.

www.rosemontplantation1810.com index.htm

(601) 888-6809

16 Clark Creek Natural Area

Off State Hwy. 24, four miles west of Woodville

Untamed forest, steep terrain, and wispy waterfalls await hikers here, along with a couple of world record-holding flowering trees: the

largest bigleaf snowbell *(Styrax grandiflorus)* and the largest Mexican plum *(Prunus Mexicana).* You'll also have to appreciate nature on foot, since no motorized vehicles are allowed.

Cleared trails and the occasional flight of wooden stairs are the only sign of human intervention here—no campsites, no amenities. (At the

edge of the forest, the white timber Pond General Store has old-time goods that make it a museum of sorts.) In some places inclines rise several hundred feet over the sandy creek bed, so you'll want to wear hiking shoes. Be sure to carry plenty of bottled water with you. Cell phone reception? No way.

▶ Open daily except major winter holidays. Admission charged.

http://mississippistateparks. reserveamerica.com

(601) 888-6040

17 Ship Island Excursions

Depart from Gulfport Yacht Harbor, where Hwys. 90 and 49 intersect

From a pier just beside the Marine Life Oceanarium, located at the Gulfport Small Harbor, the Ship Island Excursion ferry sets out on its one-hour, 12-nautical-mile trip through the Mississippi Sound to Ship Island, part of the Gulf Islands National Seashore. For most of the voyage, the shore is out of sight. Only

leaping dolphins and an occasional fleet of shrimp boats, their nets outstretched like wings, break the flat expanse of blue water.

The ferry lands at a pier to the right of which stands Fort Massachusetts, a grand brick structure with rows of arched passageways and waves of vault-ceilinged casemates that give the impression of walking through a Renaissance painting. Influenced by the French engineer Simone Bernard, the fort was begun in 1859 as part of a national coastal defense system. During construction, the fort was briefly occupied by Confederates, and then by Union forces in the Civil War. The fort is named for the Union ship *Massachusetts,* which was involved in a minor engagement here. Free tours of the fort are are conducted by National Park rangers.

The island is surrounded by high-quality white sand beaches, which are excellent for swimming, beachcombing, and bird-watching.

▶ Open year-round. Excursions run from Mar.-Oct. Fare charged for boat.

www.msshipisland.com

(228) 875-9057 Gulf Islands National Seashore

(228) 864-1014 Ship Island Excursions

17 **Ship Island Excursions.** Ferries take sightseers from Gulfport to Ship Island, where they can tour an elegantly designed 19th-century fort and stroll on the beach.

seasonal events

FEBRUARY
- Magnolia Mardi-Gras Parade and Festival—Magnolia *(parade, arts and crafts, carnival rides, food and games)*
- Oxford Film Festival—Oxford *(weekend celebration of filmmaking with film competitions and workshops)*

APRIL
- Old Tyme Bluegrass and Barbeque—Hernando *(lunch, Bluegrass entertainment, and a tour of the Desoto museum)*
- Ralph Morgan Rodeo—Meridian
- Annual Civil War Show—Vicksburg *(Civil War items on display for observation and sale)*

MAY
- Red, White, and "Blueberry" Festival—Ocean Springs *(blueberry pies and recipes, live music)*
- Raymond Country Fair—Raymond *(arts and crafts, food, and 5K and fun runs)*
- Classic Car and Fly-wheel Tractor Show—Olive Branch

JUNE
- Juneteenth Celebration—Columbus *(festival celebrating the Emancipation Proclamation with food, music, and fun)*

JULY
- Choctaw Indian Fair—Choctaw *(four days of Choctaw culture and spirit)*

AUGUST
- Watermelon Carnival—Water Valley *(arts and crafts, concessions, entertainment, watermelon eating, seed spitting, antique car show, and square dancing)*

NOVEMBER
- Native American Pow-Wow—Philadelphia *(more than 100 Native American tribes gather from across the U.S. and Canada)*
- Victorian Christmas Festival—Canton *(hundreds of twinkling lights, animation museum, old-fashioned rides in horse and buggies or miniature trains and fire trucks)*

www.visitmississippi.org

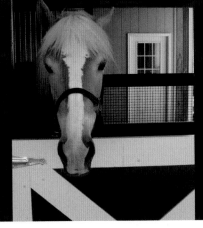

Missouri

The Show Me State has plenty to show off, from nature preserves to little-known but intriguing museums to numerous family-friendly attractions.

Jefferson Farm & Gardens. A Haflinger horse, a small draft horse breed from Austria, peers over a gate at an educational farm inspired by Thomas Jefferson (see page 188).

Native American treasures, a German schoolhouse, a river town dating from Missouri's days under the French flag . . . a diverse past is evident in this pleasant Midwestern state. Likewise, the historic figures honored here include Mark Twain, educator/scientist George Washington Carver, Gen. John J. Pershing, and even Winston Churchill.

Museums devote themselves to social and natural history, saddlebred horses, health and well-being, and more. The state's preserves and parks range from the tallgrass prairie to a wonderland of giant boulders, while marshlands and forests harbor waterfowl, pheasants, hawks, and mammals, including bison and elk.

visit ➡ **offthebeatenpathtrips.com**

1 Squaw Creek National Wildlife Refuge

US–159, Mound City
This sizable refuge—7,350 acres of marsh, pond, meadow, and wooded bluffs—provides a year-round haven for birds of many kinds.

Pheasants and hawks are best seen in January and February; a variety of waterfowl stop off in spring; May is the month for warblers; and in late summer the avocets and other shorebirds arrive. Come October legions of snow geese and ducks descend. In the winter months one of the largest concentrations of bald eagles in America—as many as 3,000 at peak—make this refuge a temporary home.

Squaw Creek also shelters white-tailed deer, minks, foxes, and Southern lemmings. Early in the morning, the wary coyote is often seen.

The extensive gravel roads and a number of different trails offer visitors a choice of driving, bicycling, or hiking. The Bluff Trail gives panoramic views of the ponds and marshes. In spring the area blushes with wildflowers, and the end of July finds the American lotus in flower.

▶ Open year-round.

www.fws.gov/midwest/squawcreek
(660) 442-3187

3 **Watkins Woolen Mill State Park and Historic Site.** The textile machines fell silent in 1898, but the mill remains the only one in America with its original machinery.

2 St. Joseph Museum

3406 Frederick Ave., St. Joseph
Known as the city "where Southern hospitality meets Western democracy," St. Joseph played a vital role in 19th-century westward expansion as a key stop for railroads and steamboats.

The St. Joseph Museum, established in 1927, is dedicated primarily to the preservation of diverse cultures, especially Native Americans. The museum has two interpretive sites. The Frederick Avenue site's extensive exhibits feature clothing, pottery, weapons, kachina dolls and archaeological artifacts from 10 cultural regions, including Pomo basketry and peyote fans.

The museum's second site, the 1879 Wyeth-Tootle Mansion, is located at 1100 Charles Street. Various mounted animals haunt the natural history section of the building, while the local history section devotes one room of the mansion to Jesse James, who was shot and killed in St. Joseph on April 3, 1882. The mansion illustrates the cultural, architectural, and economic history of 19th-century St. Joseph, with exterior features, such as a turret that makes the building resemble a castle. The interior highlights include oil-on-canvas

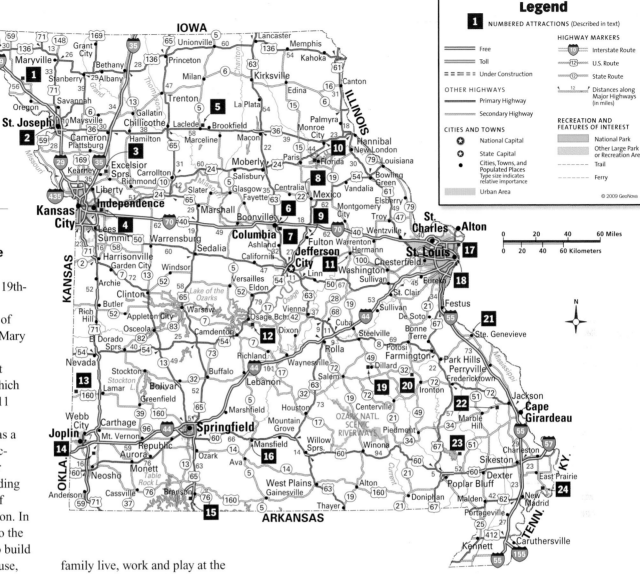

paintings on the first floor ceilings, stained-glass windows, and gorgeous walnut woodwork.

▶ Museum open daily. Mansion open Fri.-Sun. Admission charged.

www.stjosephmuseum.org
(800) 530-8866

---

3 ▶ Watkins Woolen Mill State Park and Historic Site

26600 Park Rd. N, Lawson

This interesting and attractive 19th-century complex includes the woolen mill and family home of Waltus Watkins and his wife, Mary Ann. Completed in 1854, the house has a simple but elegant brick façade and 20 rooms, which accommodated the family of 11 children.

Watkins's first venture was a cotton mill, which was unsuccessful, but he had a flair for farming and expanded a holding of 80 acres into a property of 3,600—the Bethany Plantation. In 1860 Watkins turned again to the textile business and began to build his woolen mill. Like the house, the mill was made from his own timber and bricks. Deer tracks made on the bricks before they dried can be seen in the floor of the storage shed. More than 50 textile machines were shipped in by railroad and steamboat and hauled the final 20 miles by oxen. The various hankers, pickers, twisters, and looms stand lean and elegant in silent tribute to a prosperous business that finally succumbed to new techniques of mass production at the turn of the century.

On weekends during the summer, visitors can watch an 1870s family live, work and play at the site's living history farm program.

Adjacent to the historic site is the park, which features a 100-acre lake, campsites with hookups, and trails.

▶ Open year-round except holidays. Admission charged for tours.

www.watkinsmill.org
(816) 580-3387

---

4 ▶ Burr Oak Woods Conservation Nature Center

1401 N.W. Park Rd., Blue Springs

This sprawling timber building is the jumping-off point for exploring 1,071 acres of woodlands, glades, and native grasses cut through by part of scenic Burr Oak Creek. But don't think you're in a state park: Conservation, not recreation, is the goal—no camping, no fishing, no horseback riding, and no filching of nuts, berries, or fruits! But you can hike and birdwatch to your heart's content. Five trails take you through forests of oak, ash, hickory, dogwood, and redbud, where you'll spot deer and wild turkeys along the way.

In the nature center a large solarium lets you watch birds (and the occasional raccoon) as they descend on bird feeders out back, and finned creatures of all sorts can be viewed at the 5,000-gallon aquarium.

▶ Conservation area open daily. Nature Center open year-round except holidays.

www.mdc.mo.gov/areas/cnc/burroak
(816) 228-3766

5 ⏵ Gen. John J. Pershing Boyhood Home State Historic Site

1100 Pershing Dr., Laclede

Graduated from West Point in 1886, Pershing underwent his baptism by fire against Geronimo's Apache tribe and completed his career as commander in chief of American forces in World War I.

Pershing's boyhood home is an unpretentious but attractive two-story white clapboard with restrained Gothic trim. While the furnishings are not all those of his family, they are of the period, and there are Pershing memorabilia throughout. Exhibit cases in the site's office display replicas of Pershing's many medals, including the Silver Star for gallantry.

Relocated on the site is the small school where Pershing taught for $30 a month before heading to West Point. The school has been transformed into a museum that features the many doorways that Pershing entered throughout his life. It features photos of his early campaigns and the bejeweled sword he received from the city of London in 1919. From an audiotape that outlines his life, you'll learn that his nickname, "Black Jack," was also a reference to his time commanding 10th (African American) Calvary, also known as the Buffalo Soldiers. A bronze statue of Pershing also stands on the grounds before a Wall of Honor inscribed with the names of several hundred war veterans.

▶ Open year-round. Admission charged.

www.mostateparks.com/pershingsite.htm
(660) 963-2525

6 ⏵ The YouZeum

608 E. Cherry St., Columbia

This museum takes the phrase "hours of family fun" to new

6 ⏵ **The YouZeum.** Phun Physiology, a 16-foot-tall audio-kinetic sculpture, is a working model of bodily systems.

levels—and even better, it's all about improving health and well-being. Interactive exhibits include the Fine Tune Body Shop, focused on body mechanics and maintenance; Snackster, a talking vending machine dispensing advice about food choices; and Body Fair, where you can test your balance, flexibility, grip strength, and other physical abilities. The 3-D film *All Systems Go!* zips through the human body to reveal how its systems function.

Young doctors-in-training can treat virtual patients in the ER exhibit, while the Healthy Baby exhibit offers young couples ways to keep a future bundle of joy safe and sound during pregnancy.

▶ Open daily except Tues.
  Admission charged.

www.youzeum.org
(573) 886-2006

7 ⏵ Jefferson Farm & Gardens

4800 New Haven Rd., Columbia

A project of the nonprofit Thomas Jefferson Agricultural Institute in

Columbia, this inviting 67-acre showplace enlightens young and old alike about the important role agriculture and horticulture play in our daily lives. On self-guided and guided tours visitors learn of corn, wheat, and other crops that changed history, the countless benefits of plants, and how food gets from farm to market. Agricultural and home gardening demonstrations are also part of the scene.

A paved path around the lake is lined with native plants, and a zig-zagged boardwalk offers a close-up view of aquatic plants and creatures. The Jefferson Garden is inspired by the third president's garden at Monticello, where he grew dozens of types of vegetables and rare plants.

▶ Call for hours. Admission charged.

www.jeffersonfarm.org
(573) 449-3518

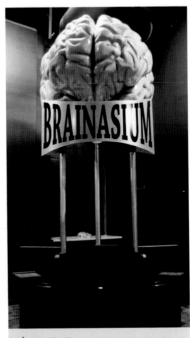

6 ⏵ **The YouZeum.** Fun games played on touch screens give the different parts of the brain a good workout.

8 ⏵ Audrain County Historical Society

501 S. Muldrow St., Mexico

Located within the 11-acre Robert S. Green Park, the historical society features two museums, a country school and church, and stables. Graceland Museum, an imposing mansion built in 1857, was bought in 1868 by Colby T. Quisenberry, who introduced Kentucky saddlebreds to the area, begetting Mexico's title as the Saddlebred Capital of the World.

The American Saddlebred Horse Museum adjoins Graceland and features trophies and other mementos of memorable horse Rex McDonald and famous trainer and equestrian Thomas Bass. Other exhibits include riding habits, the saddles of famous riders, and paintings of saddle horses by George Ford Morris.

The country church was reconstructed on the society's grounds in 1998 from the original 1889 structure. The one-room country school dates to 1903 and includes a slate blackboard and original desks and books.

▶ Open Tues.–Sun. year-round except holidays. Admission charged.

www.audrain.org
(573) 581-3910

9 ⏵ Winston Churchill Memorial and Library

501 Westminster Ave., Fulton

In 1946 Britain's former prime minister, Winston Churchill, accepted an invitation from his Missouri-born friend President Harry Truman to speak at Westminster College.

In that historic address Churchill described the Soviet grip on Eastern Europe: "From Stettin in the Baltic to Trieste in the

7 **Jefferson Farm & Gardens.** The Children's Barn, complete with hayloft, is home to horses, sheep, and other farm animals when they aren't grazing in the pasture.

Adriatic, an iron curtain has descended across the continent."

In the early 1960s the college decided to honor the great British leader by reconstructing on its grounds a London landmark destroyed in World War II. The structure was the church of St. Mary the Virgin, Aldermanbury, a 12th-century London church demolished by the great fire of London in 1666 and rebuilt by Christopher Wren in 1677. The church was knocked to the ground by German bombs in 1940.

Dismantling began in 1965. Seven thousand stones weighing a total of 700 tons were cleaned, numbered, and shipped to Fulton, with new stones hand cut as necessary. Wood carvings, plasterwork, windows, and brass chandeliers were all re-created from Wren's designs. A new organ was built in London, five new bronze bells were cast in Holland, windows were copied by a glass company in West Virginia, and a London wood carver matched the original pulpit.

Dedicated in 1969, the white church radiates an elegant simplic-ity. The interior is light and spacious, the decor rich but unobtrusive. A library and a museum in the undercroft relate the life and long public service of the prime minister.

▶ Open year-round except holidays. Admission charged.

www.churchillmemorial.org
(573) 592-5369

---

10 **Mark Twain Birthplace State Historic Site and State Park**
Off MO–107, Florida
Samuel Clemens was born November 30, 1835, in what he later described as "the almost invisible village of Florida, Monroe County, Missouri." On another occasion he noted: "Recently someone in Missouri sent me a picture of the house I was born in. Heretofore I always stated that it was a palace, but I shall be more guarded now." The small two-room plank cabin is modest, to say the least.

Moved to its present site in 1930, the house is now enclosed by museum. Here you will see first editions of his books and a manu-script copy of *The Adventures of Tom Sawyer.* Other displays offer a colorful view of Twain's adventurous life as a steamboat pilot, printer's apprentice, soldier, gold and silver prospector, laborer, newspaper reporter, and one of America's best-loved writers.

Just north of the birthplace site is Mark Twain State Park, a 2,775-acre expanse anchored by the sprawling Mark Twain Lake. Fishing, boating, and swimming are permitted. From the picnic area you can take a short, rugged path to the observation platforms on the sheer cliffs of Buzzard's Roost for excellent views of the surroundings.

▶ Museum open daily Apr.–Oct.; Wed.–Sun. Nov.–Mar.; admission charged. Park open year-round.

www.mostateparks.com/twainsite.htm
(573) 565-3449 Birthplace
(573) 565-3440 Park

---

11 **Museum at the German School**
312 Schiller St., Hermann
This building with its clock tower recalls an era when German immi-grants established a number of Midwestern towns like Hermann, founded in 1836. The bilingual school was built in 1871 and func-tioned as such until 1955. It now affords visitors a view of the clock mechanism and seven rooms of historical treasures.

The Legacy Room displays authentic German clothing and rare handmade textile printing blocks. The River Room showcases an exact replica of the steamer Pin Oak's (circa 1888) pilot house and its original seven-foot pilot wheel as well as other memorabilia from when Hermann was one of the busiest ports on the Missouri River.

▶ Open daily Tues.–Sun. Apr.–Oct. Admission charged.

www.historichermann.com
(573) 486-2017

9 **Winston Churchill Memorial and Library.** The London landmark church of St. Mary the Virgin, Aldermanbury, was reconstructed in Missouri stone by stone.

12 ► Lake of the Ozarks State Park

MO–134, Kaiser

Created in the 1930s after the damming of the Osage River, the Lake of the Ozarks is the largest state park in Missouri. The park's more than 17,000 acres embrace the Grand Glaize arm of the lake and the surrounding Osage River Hills. The landscape includes open woodlands, glades, caves, and bluffs eroded by the Grand Glaize Creek.

The park also offers 12 trails of varying lengths for horseback riders (a stable on Rte. 134 near the campground offers guided trail rides), hikers, mountain bikers, and backpackers.

The Trail of Four Winds features a scenic overlook of the valley, while the Woodland Trail tours the Patterson Hollow Wild Area, an untouched wilderness of old meadows and oak and sassafras woodland.

12 ► Lake of the Ozarks State Park. Angels' Showers, an unusual cave phenomenon, is a featured part of the Ozark Caverns tour.

The park also contains the Ozark Caverns cave system, which features unusual stalactite formations, and Angels' Showers, waterfalls descending from apparently solid rock. A guided one-hour tour covers $1^1/_2$ miles, where you may see sleeping bats, bear claw marks, and the same speleological wonders the first explorers did.

► Open year-round, cave closed mid-Oct-mid-Apr. Admission charged for cave tours.

www.mostateparks.com/lakeozark.htm
(573) 348-2694

13 ► Prairie State Park

128 N.W. 150th Ln., Liberal

Two hundred years ago one-third of Missouri—some 13 million acres—was prairie, a rolling expanse of tall grasses, wildflowers, and few trees. With settlement and farming there are now fewer than 65,000 acres. This nearly 4,000-acre park is the state's largest remaining preserve of tallgrass prairie landscape.

A number of trails traverse the open prairie and stream valley. You'll be struck by the spaciousness of the land and skyscape and the endless horizon with the sealike expanse of grass melting into the blue sky. It is easy to understand why the pioneers called their wagons prairie schooners. Striding freely along the mown path in the sweet-scented air, you'll also notice how this vast tableau is balanced by minute natural detail—petal, leaf, grass blade, and seedpod—calling for close scrutiny.

Bison and elk roam in some areas. For safety, stay in your car until you have learned at the nature center where the animals are on a given day. Naturalists conduct

13 ► Prairie State Park. Shooting stars dot the prairie in springtime.

interpretive programs year-round.

► Open year-round. Visitor center closed Mon., year-round and Sun. Nov.-Mar.

www.mostateparks.com/prairie.htm
(417) 843-6711

14 ► George Washington Carver National Monument

5646 Carver Rd., Diamond

Educator, scientist, and humanitarian, George Washington Carver was born a slave around 1864 on the 240-acre Moses Carver farm, located here. Shortly afterward he and his mother were kidnapped by bushwhackers and taken to Arkansas. The young child was found and returned to the Carvers, who reared him as their own. Though George left when he was about 12, the love of nature he gained on this site stood the future botanist in good stead.

On view in the museum are many tributes paid to this remarkable man: a model of the submarine named for him, stamps issued in his honor, a commemorative half-dollar, and a letter from Albert Einstein referring to him as "the great scientist."

Interactive exhibits include collections of his publications, photographs, and audio recordings. A $^3/_4$ mile Carver Trail includes the

birthplace site, Moses Carver's 1881 dwelling, and family cemetery.

► Open year-round except major holidays.

www.nps.gov/gwca
(417) 325-4151

15 ► Ralph Foster Museum

*College of the Ozarks
(near Branson)*

Ralph Foster, a pioneering radio broadcaster, was also a philanthropist whose donation of Native American artifacts to the history museum at this liberal arts college accounts for its name.

"Everything under the sun" aptly describes the thousands of items displayed here. A single glance may take in antique furniture, oyster plates, clocks, watches, international dolls, and a potpourri of other artifacts and improbable novelties. Take, for example, the original truck used on *The Beverly Hillbillies* television series, a gift from the show's producer.

The museum's first floor houses the Edwards Art Gallery, the Si Siman Country Music Room, and a kewpie doll exhibit from local artist Rose O'Neill. The second floor is dominated by an exhibit on firearms, while the third floor lightens things up with a nine-foot polar bear, a moose, and colorful birds, rocks, and minerals.

► Open Mon.-Sat. Feb.-Dec. except Thanksgiving week.

www.rfostermuseum.com
(417) 690-6411 Ext. 3407

16 ► Laura Ingalls Wilder Historic Home and Museum

3068 Hwy. A, Mansfield

This is a required visit for dedicated

MISSOURI

admirers of *The Little House on the Prairie* series. It was here that author Laura Ingalls Wilder penned her beloved books of rural America, published in some 40 languages.

Museum displays include foreign and domestic editions of her various books, press clippings, and worldwide fan mail, much of it from children. Among personal belongings are the 1889 lap desk Laura brought here by covered wagon from her home in De Smet, South Dakota, along with her sewing machine, samples of her needlework, her father Charles's famous fiddle, and several handwritten manuscripts.

Laura and her husband, Almanzo, moved to Mansfield in 1894 and into their house in 1897. Laura thought it best "to be happy with simple pleasures," and the small house—shown by guided tour only—is next door to the main museum.

Note the Currier and Ives prints and a Western Cottage organ in the drawing room, some throw pillows made by Laura, and several tables crafted by Almanzo, a carpenter. His workshop contains the tools of his trade as well as some leather and lasts for making shoes.

▶ Open Mar.–mid-Nov. except Easter. Farmhouse and museum tours Mon.-Fri. mid-Nov.–mid-Dec. Admission charged.

www.lauraingallswilderhome.com
(417) 924-3626

17 ▶ Old Chain of Rocks Bridge

10950 Riverview Dr., St. Louis
Opened to traffic in 1929, this marvel crosses one of the most historic and scenic sections of the Mississippi River, connecting Missouri to Illinois.

Once part of the fabled Route 66, the bridge is famed for a unique 22-degree turn at its midpoint. The bridge was closed in 1968 when a new structure was built to serve I-270. It sat abandoned and decaying until 1999, when it was restored and reopened, thanks to a preservation group.

Today the Old Chain of Rocks Bridge has a new life as a nature and recreation trail. There you'll see panoramic views of the St. Louis skyline, and the river views reveal the inspiration for the bridge's name: a collection of rocky shoals just to the south that create a water-

fall-like effect at low water levels.

Bald eagles are drawn to the open waters surrounding the rapids where fish, their primary food source, are easy prey. Visitors can watch the eagles hunt fish, ride ice floes, roost in trees along the shore, or soar majestically overhead.

▶ Open daily year-round.

www.trailnet.org/p_ocorb.php
(314) 416-9930

18 ▶ City Museum

701 N. 15th St., St. Louis
Call it eccentric, call it surreal. However you describe this museum housed in a former shoe factory, it's unlike anything you've ever seen. Case in point: Outside the museum stands MonstroCity, an all-ages jungle gym constructed from 4-foot-wide wrought-iron slinkies, airplane fuselages, a castle turret, and other flotsam and jetsam.

Indoor displays of architectural relics, vintage opera posters, and such are composed of the very stuff of the city. The offbeat reigns at The Museum of Mirth, Mystery, and Mayhem, celebrating the tawdry charms of the carnival midway and kitschy roadside attractions with exhibits that include the Elvis Channeler and "The Corn Dog Through the Ages." No less imaginative are Art City (where you can watch artists at work and create your own masterpiece), Circus Day (interactive circus entertainment), and the 13,500-square-foot aquarium.

▶ Open daily Apr.-Aug.; Wed.–Sun. Sept-Mar. Admission charged.

www.citymuseum.org
(314) 231-2489

18 ▶ City Museum. Built of "found objects" (some of them very large), MonstroCity is a jungle gym for the curious and sure-footed. This interactive installation reflects City Museum's mission to surprise and delight St. Louisans and tourists of all ages.

19 Dillard Mill State Historic Site

142 Dillard Mill Rd., Davisville
Situated by Huzzah Creek and surrounded by grassy bluffs, Dillard Mill is unusually picturesque and beautifully restored. During the heyday of water power in the late 1800s, Dillard was one of 20 mills within a 40-mile radius. At full summertime capacity it produced 25 196-pound barrels of flour a day in a 24-hour shift.

The mill closed for business in 1956, but the equipment is fully operational for daily tours. The roller mills, grain elevators, sifting machines, and original leather

drive belts are still impressive. The main drive wheel inside the mill has teeth of hard maple so that if anything goes wrong, the teeth break, not the wheel or belts. And the 24.2-horsepower Leffel turbine, which sits under water in the flume, runs on wooden bearings to avoid rust. The skills of the old millwrights and engineers are clearly in evidence.

The 132-acre site offers trails, picnic areas, and fishing in the clear Ozark creek. Spring and fall offer the best weather.

▶ Grounds open daily year-round; mill tours daily Mar.-Nov.; Thurs.-Sun. Dec.-Feb. Admission charged for mill.

**www.mostateparks.com/dillardmill.htm
(573) 244-3120**

20 Elephant Rocks State Park

Off MO–21, Graniteville
Elephants in the Ozarks? Ancient granite incarnations of the huge creatures abound at this geologic marvel. Giant boulders of red granite, dating back 1.5 billion years, populate the park with massive formations.

And this "population" is constantly—if gradually—changing, as the forces of nature continue to wear away existing rock forms while exposing new ones. The granite animals have been meticulously documented, with the park's patriarch, Dumbo, at 27 feet tall,

 Elephant Rocks State Park. A photographer sizes up a shot of a giant red granite boulder. The igneous rock in this park formed some 1.5 billion years ago.

35 feet long, and 17 feet wide, and tipping the scales at an estimated 680 tons.

The Braille Trail offers a quick and accessible route to the mammoth rocks. Featuring interpretive signage, this one-mile paved pathway is specially designed for those with visual or physical disabilities. The trail leads to the top of the granite outcrop, where explorers can wander through the maze of giant rocks at their leisure, or take a break at one of 30 picnic sites conveniently situated amid the red boulders.

Just outside the park is the state's oldest known commercial granite quarry, opened in 1869. The nearby town of Graniteville, once dominated by the quarry, still boasts original granite buildings, such as an impressive stone schoolhouse.

▶ Open year-round.

**www.mostateparks.com/elephantrock.htm
(573) 546-3454**

21 Ste. Genevieve

The oldest town west of the Mississippi, this charming community was settled by the French more than 250 years ago, when the area was still part of French-claimed Upper Louisiana. A walk through the streets reveals a rich architectural heritage, heavily accented by many old French-Creole buildings with walls constructed by logs set vertically, not horizontally.

Guided tours from the visitors center take in a number of historic buildings. One of the more prominent is the Guibourd-Valle House, built around 1784. In the attic take note of the handsomely pegged oak beams and fine Norman truss-

work. Another is the Bolduc House Museum, a strong example of the vertical log construction, first built in 1770 and reassembled in 1784 after a flood.

▶ Visitors center open year-round; houses generally open Apr.-Nov.

**www.ste-genevieve.com
(573) 885-7017**

22 Bollinger Mill State Historic Site

113 Bollinger Mill Rd., Burfordville
A picturesque scene from America's past is captured here. The four-story mill stands by a wide millpond and weir along the Whitewater River, and just beyond is one of Missouri's four covered bridges.

The present-day mill dates from 1867 and was built by Solomon Burford on the site—and atop the original foundation—where George F. Bollinger had first built a mill in 1800.

The 140-foot-long Howe truss bridge, originally built of yellow poplar, was begun in 1858, but completion was delayed by the Civil War. The bridge was restored in 1998 and is open to pedestrians only. Grounds and covered bridge open daily year-round.

▶ Mill open daily Mar.-Nov; Tues.-Sat. Dec.-Feb. Admission charged.

**www.mostateparks.com/bollinger.htm
(573) 243-4591**

did you know ?

George Washington Carver derived more than 300 products from the peanut, 100 from the sweet potato (including ersatz coffee, shoeblacking, and ink), and scores of products from Alabama clay.

23 Mingo National Wildlife Refuge

24279 MO–51, Puxico

The vast area of marsh, bottom-land forest, and river (21,592 acres) in the southeast corner of the state supports large numbers of wildlife but is maintained primarily as a feeding ground for migratory waterfowl on the Mississippi Flyway.

A gravel loop road skirting most of the refuge allows leisurely walking, horseback riding, and, in-season, driving. The diked waterways and the lovely Mingo River itself are open to canoeing, an ideal way to see this region. Motorboats are not allowed.

The mile-long Boardwalk Nature Trail loops through the woodland swamp, hung with vines and rich with sycamores, sweet gums, pin oaks, sugar maples, and some water tupelos and bald cypresses. The Bluff Overlook Trail, starting at the visitors center, is enchanting when spring wild-flowers bloom and affords splendid views across the marsh.

From late Sep. to mid-March, visitors are asked to stop at the center before venturing into the refuge. Limited picnic facilities are available.

▶ Refuge open daily year-round; admission charged. Visitors center open weekdays year-round; weekends Apr.–Jun. and Sept.–Nov.

www.fws.gov/midwest/mingo
(573) 222-3589

24 Big Oak Tree State Park

13640 MO–102, East Prairie

This 1,029-acre preserve is part of the virgin forest and swampland that once covered much of Missouri's Bootheel region.

The park, noted for state and national champion trees of dramatic size, was named for a bur oak that dated to about 1620. Felled in

24 Big Oak Tree State Park. Visitors survey the swampland scenery and wildlife from the park's boardwalk.

1954 after it died, it was 143 feet tall with a spread of 114 feet. Its sawn-off trunk stands at the head of a quarter-mile boardwalk that runs to a grassy swamp and passes some of the most magnificent trees in the forest.

The swamp was created by a series of earthquakes in 1811, and parts of it look like a giant bowling green planted with dead trees. The "green" is actually duckweed, and among the trees are some living bald cypresses. The loud plops you hear along the boardwalk may be slider turtles dropping into the water or perhaps a jumping buf-falofish, which can weigh as much as 20 pounds. The swamp is also home to the ruddy duck, the hooded merganser, and the harmless band-ed water snake.

The park is anchored by the 22-acre Big Oak Lake, which offers fishing in waters stocked with cat-fish, bass, and bluegill.

▶ Open year-round.

www.mostateparks.com/bigoak.htm
(573) 649-3149

22 Bollinger Mill State Historic Site. The 19th-century mill stands next to the Burfordville Covered Bridge—the oldest of four remaining covered bridges in Missouri.

MISSOURI

Montana

The Old West of story and song is recalled in the Big Sky State in a variety of ways, as are some of the more astonishing works of Mother Nature.

National Bison Range. Buffalo aren't the only animals making their home here. Pronghorn antelopes, shown above, are among the range's residents.

In Montana, museums are dedicated to the Native Americans who once dominated the plains, while a refuge protects a herd of bison descended from the millions that once thundered across this land. Earlier and now extinct residents—the dinosaurs—are the focus of a state-of-the-art natural history museum.

Here too is Little Bighorn, where the Sioux and Cheyenne won the battle that ultimately led to their defeat. Lewis and Clark left their mark in Montana, as did Charles M. Russell, the artist who captured the spirit of the Old West. Among the places where nature's beauty (and unpredictability) is on display are a massive "gate" to the West, a spectacularly scenic national forest and a rock avalanche and lake created by an earthquake that rocked the state in the mid-20th century.

visit ➤➤ **offthebeatenpathtrips.com**

1 ▶ The People's Center

53253 Hwy. 93 W, Pablo
The three layers of stone that form the exterior of this museum— owned and operated by the now-confederated Salish, Kootenai, and Pend d'Oreille—represent the nations who have lived in the Flathead region of western Montana for thousands of years. The exhibits inside tell the story of people with a rich history. In the center of the museum's main room stands a fully furnished buckskin tepee. An example of a tulle-reed Kootenai house that was easy to roll up and carry from place to place is also on display here.

Personal guides and recordings enlighten visitors as they view exhibits of native art, traditional clothing, tools, and other artifacts that paint a picture of daily life for Native Americans. Powwows and demonstrations by local tribal artists are also put on by the center.

▶ Open Mon.–Sat. Memorial Day to Labor Day, Mon.–Fri. off-season. Admission charged.

www.peoplescenter.net
(406) 883-5344

2 ▶ National Bison Range

On Rte. 212 in Moiese
An estimated 50 million bison once roamed the American prairies, but hunters reduced their

1 ▶ The People's Center. Among the exhibitions in this fascinating museum is a Kootenai tulle-reed tepee, which was easily rolled up and carried on long journeys.

numbers so drastically that by 1900 fewer than 100 were known to exist in the wild.

In 1908, with the help of President Theodore Roosevelt, the range was born: Some 18,500 fenced acres of high prairie, forest, and bottomlands in the Flathead Valley were dedicated to protect the bison. The first group on the range totaled 37, purchased with money raised by the American Bison Society. Today there are about 350 to 450 bison, the size of an average herd. Elk, deer, black bears, and more than 200 species of birds are just some of the wide

variety of wildlife that share the land here.

Two self-guiding auto tours provide a safe and leisurely way to see this untamed country, which is colored with wildflowers and flowering shrubs in late spring and rich with animal and bird life at all seasons. The shorter auto tour, the Buffalo Prairie Drive, takes only about 20 minutes.

The two-hour, 19-mile Red Sleep Mountain Scenic Drive (open mid-May into October) is in some places steep and winding, but its views range from mountains clad with ponderosa pine

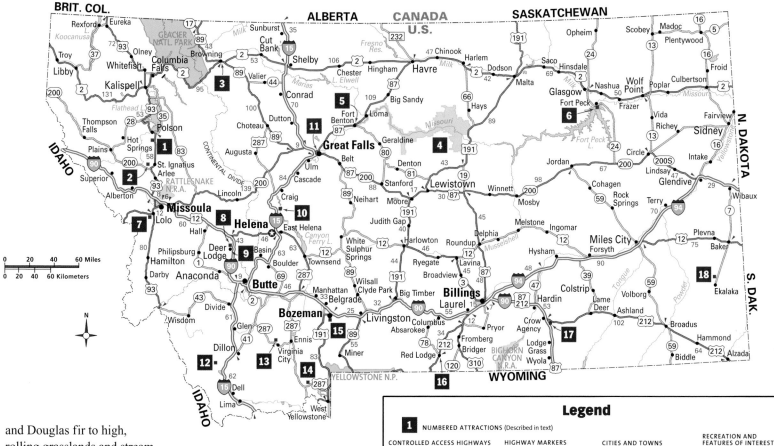

and Douglas fir to high, rolling grasslands and stream sides thick with alder, birch, and willow.

Golden eagles soar at the higher elevations, where mule deer and bighorn sheep range; pronghorn antelopes wander the high grasslands, and white-tailed deer and water birds frequent the marshy spots. Mission Creek, which is north of the range, is favored by migrating waterfowl in fall.

Fishing is allowed along stretches of the creek, and there are some scattered picnic spots.

▶ Open year-round. Admission charged.

www.visitmt.com
(406) 644-2211

3 ▶ Museum of the Plains Indian

On Rte. 2 in Browning
Managed by the U.S. Department of the Interior, this museum con-tains a superb collection of costumes, accessories, and dioramas that detail the lifestyles of 11 tribes of the northern plains before the arrival of white settlers in the 1800s.

Weapons, beadwork, ceremonial objects, toys, and other crafts are shown. The associated craft center also displays contemporary Native American work. Carved wood panels by the Blackfoot sculptor John Clarke can be enjoyed, as well as murals by artist Victor Pepion. During the summer there is a display of painted tepees.

▶ Open daily June–Sept.; Mon.–Fri. Oct.–May. Admission charged.

www.doi.gov/iacb/museum/museum _plains.html

(406) 338-2230

Legend

1 NUMBERED ATTRACTIONS (Described in text)

CONTROLLED ACCESS HIGHWAYS
— Free
— Toll
= = = = = Under Construction

OTHER HIGHWAYS
— Primary Highway
— Secondary Highway

HIGHWAY MARKERS
10 Interstate Route
12 U.S. Route
12 State Route
12 Distances along Major Highways (in miles)

CITIES AND TOWNS
⊗ National Capital
⊛ State Capital
• Cities, Towns, and Populated Places Type size indicates relative importance
Urban Area

RECREATION AND FEATURES OF INTEREST
National Park
Other Large Park or Recreation Area
— — — Trail
— — — Ferry

© 2009 GeoNova

3 ▶ **Museum of the Plains Indian.** In this display, clothing of the people of the 11 tribes of the northern plains ranges from the everyday to the ceremonial.

4 ▸ Upper Missouri River Breaks National Monument

Off Hwy. 191 near Lewistown
Declared a national monument by executive order of President Bill Clinton in January 2001, this awe-inspiring 377,346-acre site is composed of majestic cliffs of white sandstone overlooking the famous Upper Missouri River Breaks. Its impressive form was sculpted through the force of thousands of years of glaciers, volcanic activity, and erosion.

The area is home to herds of elk and bighorn sheep, as well as sage grouse, prairie dogs, and antelope. The cliff faces serve as perches for sparrow hawks, peregrine falcons, and golden eagles.

The centerpiece is the Upper Missouri National Wild and Scenic River. A ride down the 149-mile river is a trip back in time, passing by the vistas Lewis and Clark described as "scenes of visionary enchantment" on their 1805 expedition.

On a breathtaking voyage down the river by passenger boat or canoe, 21st-century explorers will see remnants of American Fur Company forts and other landmarks evoking the Western frontier, the lives of Native Americans, and the dreams of early homesteaders.

Back on land discover the Lewis and Clark National Historic Trail, the Nez Perce National Historic Trail, the Missouri Breaks National Back Country Byway, the Cow Creek Area of Critical Environmental Concern, and six wilderness study areas.
▸ Open year-round.

www.mt.blm.gov/ldo/um
(406) 622-4000

 Grant-Kohrs Ranch National Historic Site. A bright red wagon tells visitors they have arrived at the historic cattle ranch, still in operation after a century and a half.

5 ▸ Fort Benton

Off Hwy. 87, 40 miles NE of Great Falls
On the wooded banks of the Missouri River, this historic town was born more than 40 years before Montana became a state.

Fort Benton began as a fur and buffalo robe trading post in 1846. Spanning over 150 square feet, the actual fort was built with portholes in its bastion wall for both riflemen and cannons. After the decline of fur trading and prior to the arrival of the railroad, Fort Benton bustled as the travel hub for Western adventurers such as Lewis and Clark and Jim Bridger.

During the gold rush, 50 steamboats a season docked along its levee. Gradually the plains were claimed by ranchers and farmers, and Fort Benton settled down as a premier wheat-producing area. Today Fort Benton retains much of its "steamboat days" character, especially within its National Historic Landmark District along the river.

The steamboat levee is now a lovely park with great views of the Missouri. You'll see the remains of the old fort—still standing as the state's oldest building. In addition, the park features a museum devoted to the area's history.

Nearby is the Museum of the Northern Plains and Montana Agricultural Center complex, where you'll get a chance to explore a typical 1900s rural community. Most of the buildings such as a country church, bank, and drugstore have been accurately restored and furnished.

Fort Benton is also home to the Grand Union Hotel, Montana's oldest, opened in 1882 at the height of the town's steamboat-era prosperity and restored to its original splendor in 1999.
▸ Open year-round. Admission charged.

www.fortbenton.com
(406) 622-5316

6 ▸ Fort Peck Dam

Along Rte. 24 in Fort Peck
Among the world's largest earthfill dams, Fort Peck Dam is a major prototype for virtually all such dams now in existence. Begun in 1933 for flood control, improved navigation along the Missouri River, irrigation, and the creation of hydroelectric power, it was finished seven years later and is an astonishing colossus: 250.5 feet high, 3.96 miles long, and 0.96 of a mile wide at the base. The cutoff wall is 2 miles long and consists of 17,000 tons of steel sunk to a maximum depth of 163 feet.

During dam construction many fossils were excavated. You can examine some of these fossils, including the horn core of a 63-million-year-old triceratops, and see dinosaur displays, area wildlife exhibits, the dam's history and Montana's two largest aquariums at the Fort Peck Dam Interpretive Center and Museum next door.

Walled up behind the dam are the gleaming waters of Fort Peck Lake: 134 miles long and up to 16 miles wide. Its astounding 1,520-mile shoreline is surrounded by the million-acre Charles M. Russell National Wildlife Range. Fishing, boating, and swimming are allowed in the lake, and several public recreation areas offer boat-launch ramps, campgrounds, and picnic facilities.
▸ Center open year-round. Powerhouse tours offered daily Memorial Day–Labor Day.

www.corpslakes.us/fortpeck
(406) 526-3493

7 ▸ Travelers' Rest

¹/₂ mile west of Lolo on Hwy. 12
This campsite, used by Native Americans over thousands of years, was also the campsite of Lewis and Clark in 1805 and 1806. They called a nearby creek Travelers'

Rest. It is the only site on the Lewis & Clark Trail with enough physical evidence to prove the location of the explorers' encampments, as well as traces of mercury in the latrine area from a common medicine used at the time.

In the visitors center of this state park are replicas of objects found at the site after its discovery in 1998—among them a blue trading bead, a military button, and lead spilled when musket balls were being forged. With the aid of a self-guided brochure and trail markers, visitors walk a 0.6-mile trail pinpointing the location of the exploration party's campfire and other facilities.

▶ Open daily except major holidays. Admission charged, but free to Montana residents.

www.travelersrest.org
(406) 273-4253

8 ▶ Grant-Kohrs Ranch National Historic Site

Off Hwy. 90 in Deer Lodge
In the 1850s a Canadian fur trapper named Johnny Grant abandoned his traplines and started raising cattle in Montana. By 1866, when he sold his ranch to Conrad Kohrs, he had 2,000 cattle and the finest house in the state.

Kohrs became one of the great cattle barons of the American West. His wife, Augusta, made her frontier home a model of 19th-century elegance, importing the best furnishings from St. Louis and Chicago.

Now the Grant-Kohrs Ranch is maintained as a working ranch. The main house and its original furnishings are preserved intact, along with the bunkhouse, stables, barns, sheds, and workshops dat-

ing as far back as the 1860s. Park rangers conduct tours of the main house, provide guided wagon tours, and host a chuck wagon program; the 13 outbuildings are on a self-guiding tour.

▶ Open year-round except holidays.

www.nps.gov/grko
(406) 846-2070 Ext.250

9 ▶ Powell County Museum

1106 Main St., Deer Lodge
Deer Lodge is home to more museums than any other town in the Northwest. It boasts 22 acres of history and nostalgia in and around a complex that once was the Old Montana Territorial Prison.

Listed on the *National Register of Historic Places,* the towering structures alone are worth the trip. The Powell County Museum features photos of the area as it was, complemented by a collection of classic photo equipment, antique slot machines, and jukeboxes, along with 1920s household collectibles. Also on display are authentic mastodon bones, uncovered in a gravel quarry near town.

Nearby, the Frontier Montana Museum contains items actually used by cowboys, ranchers, and pioneers—including more than 300 handguns and rifles. Native American artifacts abound as well.

Also close by is Desert John's Saloon, which treats travelers to the most extensive collection of whiskey memorabilia in the United States. The saloon shelves are filled with whiskey bottles, shot glasses, and decanters, reflecting the names of popular bygone brands, like Old McBrayer and Samaritan Rye. Early brands are also colorfully promoted in the signs, trays, posters, and calendars

plastering the walls all the way up to the real tin ceiling.

Yesterday's Playthings houses the foremost collection of antique and collectible dolls in the state, while the Montana Auto Museum has 120 classic cars on display, all in mint condition.

▶ Open daily June-Sept; appointment only Oct.-May. Admission charged.

www.pcmaf.org/museums.htm
(406) 846-3111

10 ▶ Gates of the Mountains

Off Hwy. 15, about 12 miles north of Helena
Some 300 million years in the making, Meriwether Canyon, through which the Missouri flows, is spectacular to see. Limestone cliffs, intricately folded and studded with fossil remains from the ancient Mississippian sea, rise sheer above the river to 1,200 feet.

The "singular appearance" stunned Meriwether Lewis on the passage through here in 1805; it appeared the river had ended, until Lewis noted in his journal that the rocks opened up like "the Gateway to the Rocky Mountains."

The site can only be accessed by trail or boat. Cruises of the nearly six miles of gorge are available from Gates of the Mountains Landing. From the boat you can see ancient Native American pictographs and perhaps bighorn sheep, goats, and bald eagles. The boat stops at the Lewis and Clark campsite before its return run, where you can enjoy time off the boat swimming or bird-watching.

▶ Boat tours June-Sept. Fare charged.

www.gatesofthemountains.com
(406) 458-5241

10 ▶ Gates of the Mountains. On the Missouri, tourists pass one of the cliffs Meriwether Lewis described as one that opens up "like the Gateway to the Rocky Mountains."

11 C. M. Russell Museum

400 13th St. N, Great Falls

Charles M. "Charlie" Russell, "the cowboy artist" who came to Montana from Missouri in 1880 when he was 16, is honored at this authentic Western museum. Working as a rider and wrangler during the era of the great ranches, Russell made his first sketches to entertain his fellow cowboys. His first nationally famous painting was *Last of the Five Thousand*, showing a starving cow in the dreadful winter of 1886–87. From there he went on to become one of the most famous artists to draw and paint the West. Images of war parties, buffalo hunts, cowboys, and Native Americans demonstrate the wild beauty of the Old West.

In the museum are some of Russell's most famous paintings and sculptures, and some personal memorabilia, such as Russell's letters and sketches. The museum stands next to Russell's log Victorian home and studio—both of which are on the *National Register of Historic Places*.

▸ Open daily May–Sept.; Tues.–Sun. in Oct.–Apr. Admission charged.

www.cmrussell.org
(406) 727-8787

12 Bannack State Park

4200 Bannack Rd., Dillon

On July 28, 1862, gold was found in Grasshopper Creek, and the town of Bannack was born. Population surged to 3,000 in 1863, and Bannack became the Montana Territory's first capital in 1864.

Today Old Bannack is a ghost town, preserved as a state park but not restored. Along its dusty streets is a fascinating collection of over 50

11 ▸ C. M. Russell Museum. The studio of the famous Western artist was in his log-cabin home, built in 1903.

weathered buildings, all in their own way more descriptive of the frontier than perfect restorations would be. Most buildings can be explored, and brochures are available for a self-guiding tour.

There is also a replica of the gallows where Henry Plummer, sheriff of Bannack, and his deputies were hanged in 1864. He and his "road agents," who allegedly murdered more than 100 travelers, had for their secret identification a special password, "I am innocent."

Adjoining the town is a well-equipped campground in a grove of cottonwoods, where activities such as fishing, bird-watching, and bicycling can be enjoyed.

▸ Open year-round. Admission charged.

www.bannack.org
(406) 834-3413

13 Nevada City and Virginia City

On Hwy. 287 near W. Yellowstone

In 1863 the biggest gold strike in Montana's history took place at Alder Gulch. Within three years the deposits yielded some $30 million in gold, and Montana was declared a territory. Virginia City, a brand-new mining town at the

hub of an area where population boomed to more than 10,000, became the territorial capital in 1865.

Today Virginia City and nearby Nevada City, another frontier mining town, are owned by the state of Montana and are restored to look as they did in their heyday in the late 1800s. Along Nevada City's five streets are shops, a Chinese neighborhood, a music hall containing a notable collection of mechanical "music machines," and a hotel offering both Victorian rooms and restored miners' cabins.

A narrow-gauge railway line carries passengers along the 1 1/2-mile route between Nevada City and Virginia City, where tree-lined boardwalks lead you to authentically furnished stores and Montana's first newspaper office. The Fairweather Hotel is striking for its Victoriana.

▸ Open year-round. Nevada City guided walking tours Apr.–Sept. Admission charged.

www.virginiacitymt.com
(406) 843-5247

14 Madison Canyon Earthquake Area and Visitors Center

On Hwy. 191 in W. Yellowstone

This unusual site is a monument to a natural disaster that occurred on the night of August 17, 1959. In just 30 seconds 40 million cubic yards of rock and earth, an entire mountainside, broke loose from the south side of Madison River Canyon and, traveling at about 100 miles per hour, piled up 400 feet high against the canyon's northern wall.

The mile-long landslide was caused by an earthquake measuring 7.5 on the Richter scale. The earth had cracked open, dropping Hebgen Lake 100 feet and causing huge waves for hours. Behind the land-

slide a new lake, called Quake Lake, was formed. Twenty-eight people died, but 250 others, campers in the canyon, miraculously survived on the ridge now known as Refuge Point.

You can see the results of the quake from several sites and follow a hiking trail to a dolomite boulder that floated across the canyon. The visitors center explains the event with a slide show.

▸ Open Memorial Day–mid-Sept. Admission charged.

www.visitmt.com
(406) 823-6961

15 Museum of the Rockies

600 W. Kagy Blvd., Bozeman

Housed in a contemporary building at Montana State University, this research museum is a federal repository for dinosaur fossils. Its focus is reflected in the names of the exhibition rooms in the Siebel Hall Dinosaur Complex: Hall of Giants, Hallway of Growth and Behavior, and Hall of Horns and Teeth. Another clue is the "statue" out front: a 38-foot-long cast of a *Tyrannosaurus rex* known as Big Mike, whose fossilized original is on view.

The Martin Discovery Room for Children affords youngsters up to age 8 the opportunity to learn about paleontology through interactive exhibits, while the Taylor Planetarium whisks museum-goers back in time with in-house productions, such as *The Dinosaur Chronicles* and—beyond the paleontological realm—*Lewis & Clark and the High Frontier*.

▸ Open daily. Admission charged.

www.museumoftherockies.org
(406) 994-3466

16 ▶ Custer National Forest, Beartooth Ranger District

Red Lodge

The ecologically diverse Beartooth Mountain forest is a paradise for nature lovers. Bighorn sheep, mountain goats, bears, grouse, and wild turkeys live amid the towering conifers, while humans avail themselves of four National Recreation Trails: Wild Bill Lake, luring campers and trout fishers; Parkside, leading to picturesque Greenough Lake; Basin Lake, with 5- and 12-mile nature trails; and Silver Run, for cross-country skiers.

Winding through Custer, Gallatin, and Shoshone national forests is a road widely regarded as the most scenic in America: Beartooth National Scenic Byway, which switchbacks its way from Red Lodge to Cooke City and climbs to elevations as high as 11,000 feet. Numerous turnouts allow motorists to pause and gaze out over glacial canyons and craggy peaks.

▶ Open year-round. Fee for campsites.

www.fs.fed.us/r1/custer/recreation/
D2.shtml

(406) 657-6200

17 ▶ Little Bighorn Battlefield National Monument

Off Rte. 342 near Crow Agency

Few American military engagements are as infamous as the Battle of Little Bighorn.

During June 25–26, 1876, Col. George Armstrong Custer, hero of the Civil War and Plains Native American campaigns, and more than 200 of his troops were killed by Sioux and Cheyenne warriors under the command of Chief Crazy Horse and Chief Gall. News of Custer's disaster shocked the nation, and within months a strongly reinforced army destroyed the last remnants of Native American resistance in the Black Hills.

There are really two battlefields here. The larger contains the Custer National Cemetery and includes the site of Custer's "last stand" against the Lakota and Northern Cheyenne. The other battlefield is the Reno-Benteen area, where troops led by Maj. Marcus Reno and Capt. Frederick Benteen were surrounded.

A 4½-mile self-guiding trail connects the battlefields. At the visitors center is a scale model of the engagement and other excellent interpretive materials. The entire area is contained within the Crow Indian Reservation.

▶ Open year-round.

www.nps.gov/libi

(406) 638-3204

18 ▶ Medicine Rocks State Park

Off Rte. 7, 14 miles north of Ekalaka

Here is one of the strangest landscapes in Montana: The sandstone of a prehistoric riverbed has been eroded by wind and water into a gallery of surreal formations, rising 80 feet above the plain.

You will be dazzled by the arches, columns, caves, pinnacles, and flat-topped mountains up to 200 feet wide. Tan-colored by day, the bizarre formations are silvery and eerie in moonlight. Fossils of mammals that roamed this area 50 million years ago have been found, and there is evidence of human habitation dating back more than 11,000 years.

Theodore Roosevelt thought the Medicine Rocks "as fantastically beautiful a place as I have ever seen" and is said to have inscribed his initials on the soft stone. The rocks take their name from the Native American medicine men who performed ritual dances here before hunting expeditions.

The park has 12 primitive campgrounds, a six-mile guided nature trail, and a steep half-mile walk down to the badlands. Elevations here approach 3,500 feet, and the 320-acre expanse is home to mule deer, antelope, and sharp-tailed grouse.

▶ Open year-round, but may be inaccessible by car in winter.

www.fwp.state.mt.us

(406) 232-0900

seasonal events

JANUARY
- Frost Fever Winter Festival—Missoula *(a 5K run, snow football, ice skating, and other sporting activities)*
- Montana Winter Fair—Lewistown *(livestock show, fiddler's contest, art sale and swap, chocolate competition)*

MARCH
- Wine and Food Festival—Great Falls *(Over 100 samples of fine wine, beer, and other beverages)*
- Winterfest—Big Sky *(children's activities and races, cross-country ski events)*

MAY
- Annual Big Timber Bull-a-Rama—Big Timber *(bull riding competition)*

JUNE
- Annual Ghost Tour—Miles City *(walking tours through local historic districts)*
- Libby Logger Days—Libby *(traditional logging skill competitions)*

JULY
- Bannack Days—Bannack *(candlemaking, old-time dancing, pioneer craft demonstrations, live music)*
- Whitehall Frontier Days—Whitehall *(parade, barbecue, car show, horse pasture golfing, talent show)*
- Live History Day—Polson *(entertainment, traditional skill demonstrations, vintage vehicle rides)*
- Wolf Point Wild Horse Stampede—Wolf Point *(rodeo, parade, carnival rides, street dances, horse race)*

AUGUST
- Poplar Indian Days—Poplar *(powwow with dancing, food, crafts)*

SEPTEMBER
- Montana State Chokecherry Festival—Lewistown *(jams, jellies, and wines for tasting and judging, pancake breakfast, entertainment)*
- Beaverhead County Fair—Beaverhead *(rodeo, horse show, team roping, blacksmithing)*

www.visitmt.com

Nebraska

Native Americans, pioneers, and prehistoric animals have left their mark on the broad plains and sculptured landscapes of this state.

Toadstool Geological Park. Fossils, curious rock formations, and badlands scenery are the attractions at this park (see page 201).

At a Nebraska state park is a rock shelter where Native Americans lived for some 3,000 years, while a state historical park reveals the remains of incredible animals long vanished from the Earth. Fort Hartsuff, built to protect settlers, serves as a reminder of more recent history.

Visitors may also choose to travel a section of the Oregon Trail and see some of the natural features that both beguiled and guided the pioneers headed west. Other enticements on the windswept plains include a pioneer village, a community made famous by a Pulitzer prizewinning author, a grand old mansion, and peaceful, scenic recreation areas.

visit ➤➤ **offthebeatenpathtrips.com**

1 Wildcat Hills State Recreation Area

210615 Hwy. 71, Gering
The stealthy bobcats for which the area is named are seldom seen and are now few in number. But you will probably spot some elk and buffalo venturing near the fence in the enclosed game preserve. Wild turkeys are sometimes seen; falcons, eagles, and vultures often wheel overhead.

Although the area is just off Rte. 71, it is not heavily used, probably because there are no lakes and streams. This makes it an excellent choice for those seeking solitude and natural beauty.

In the recreation area there are several steep-walled canyons laced with about three miles of hiking trails. The trails cross two footbridges and lead to three shelters built of native stone in the early 1930s by the Civilian Conservation Corps.

Particularly inviting is the group shelter, with large picnic

2 Scotts Bluff National Monument. The pinnacle mountain known as Eagle Rock was a navigation point for the hardy wagoneers headed west on the Oregon Trail.

tables, two fireplaces, and a spectacular view down a canyon to the plain with the great monolith of Scotts Bluff far in the distance. Scatterings of ponderosa pine bring accents of green to the brown, arid ridges and canyon walls. Here, too, are mountain mahogany trees, rare in Nebraska, along with yucca, cactus, grasses, and wildflowers.

The nature center's split-level design takes advantage of the hilltop location, and the building's windows are deeply tinted so visitors can closely observe birds and other wildlife coming from the forest to

use the feeders. A dramatic 27-foot-tall artificial ponderosa pine tree extends from the lower level through an opening in the ceiling.

If you're pulling a trailer, leave it in the parking lot, at least until you explore the area. The roads are rough, and several are dead-end, with little or no room to turn a trailer around. Sledding and snow-tubing are popular here in winter.

▶ Open year-round. Admission charged.

www.ngpc.state.ne.us/parks
(308) 436-3777

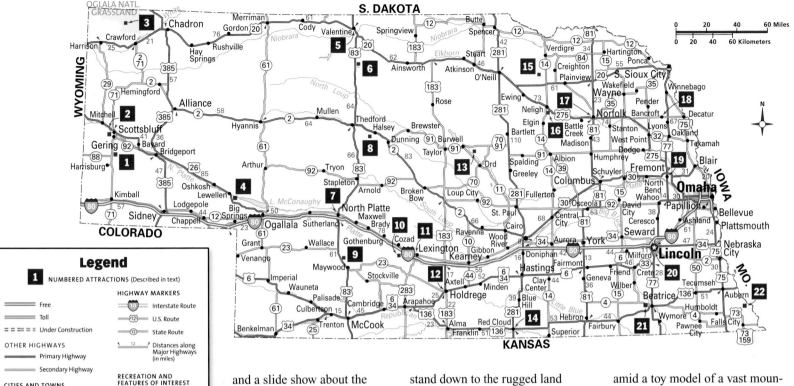

Legend

| **1** | NUMBERED ATTRACTIONS (Described in text) |

HIGHWAY MARKERS

══════	Free		Interstate Route
══════	Toll		U.S. Route
= = = =	Under Construction		State Route

OTHER HIGHWAYS

| ══════ | Primary Highway | 12 | Distances along Major Highways (in miles) |
| ══════ | Secondary Highway | | |

CITIES AND TOWNS

RECREATION AND FEATURES OF INTEREST

⊛	National Capital		National Park
✪	State Capital		Other Large Park or Recreation Area
•	Cities, Towns, and Populated Places Type size indicates relative importance	- - - -	Trail
		- - - -	Ferry
	Urban Area		

© 2009 GeoNova

---

2 Scotts Bluff National Monument

190276 Old Oregon Trail, Gering

This bluff takes its name from a trapper who met his end somewhere nearby about 1828. But long before that, the prominent landmark was known as "the hill that is hard to go around" by the Plains tribe and was a key guidepost for travelers heading west.

Much of the history here centers around Mitchell Pass, which proved to be a good route through these steep, eroded bluffs and became part of the Oregon Trail. Thousands of westward-bound travelers passed through here, resulting in a well-developed swale, an eroded remnant of the trail that can still be seen.

At the visitors center, exhibits and a slide show about the Oregon Trail tell the story of overland migration. In summer, living-history demonstrations bring the story alive.

The bluff's summit is accessible by vehicles (oversize vehicles are restricted due to tunnels with limited clearance), a free shuttle service, or by a 1½-mile hike gaining 400 feet in elevation. From the north overlook there's a spectacular view of the North Platte valley, with Chimney Rock on the horizon to the east and Laramie Peak to the west. Part of the legendary Oregon Trail can be seen from the south overlook.

Even more compelling than the view is the stark evidence of the power of erosion. By standing on the bluff's highest point and extending an imaginary line to the tops of the surrounding hills, you can establish the approximate level of the original nearly mile-high grassy plains that were once here.

Everything from where you stand down to the rugged land below has been slowly eroded and washed away to distant deltas, seas, and shorelines.

▶ Open year-round except major holidays. Admission charged.

www.nps.gov/scbl
(308) 436-9700

---

3 Toadstool Geological Park

20 miles northwest of Crawford

Toadstool Park is noted for unusual geological formations and valuable fossil deposits. It also contains the longest-known mammal trackway of the Oligocene epoch. This one-mile trail is featured in an interpretive kiosk and a self-guiding trail brochure.

Historically called Little Badlands, this remote unstaffed area is one of the most spectacular settings outside of Badlands National Park. Dramatic cliffs and gullies plunge among domes of clay some 100 feet high, creating the illusion that you are standing amid a toy model of a vast mountain range. Even more intriguing are the rock toadstools that give the park its name. Hard, rocky material was left balanced on slender columns when the soft clay beneath eroded more quickly.

These clay beds were deposited here by ancient rivers as many as 40 million years ago. The erosion that sculpted them has been going on for nearly a million years.

A mile-long hiking trail—showcasing eroded clay and sandstone formations—leads across the Badlands, where you have a good chance of seeing elk and hawks. The ground is loose and steep, so sturdy shoes are recommended. You can camp here, but be warned: It's rough and has few amenities.

▶ Open year-round but may be inaccessible in wet weather. Admission charged mid-May–mid-Nov.

www.fs.fed.us/wildflowers/regions/rocky
mountain/ToadstoolGeoPark/index.shtml
(308) 432-4475

4 Ash Hollow State Historical Park

Lewellen

Archaeological evidence indicates that the freshwater springs in this canyon have attracted visitors for some 8,000 years, including Plains tribes who used a rock shelter here for about 3,000 years and skeletal remains show that, even earlier, prehistoric mastodons and other mammals roamed these plains.

More precise are the records of the pioneers who sought this well-watered oasis with shady groves of ash trees as a place to rest, refresh their livestock, and repair their wagons and other trail-worn gear. The visitors center features exhibits describing prehistoric animals, early man, and Plains tribes. A restored schoolhouse, a trading-post site, and a nature trail are also located here. A short walk takes you to the rock shelter, and a steep paved path leads down to Ash Hollow Springs itself, reputed to have the best water on all the Overland Trail.

Wagon trains entered the hollow from Windlass Hill, about two miles to the south, and their tracks can still be seen. Another exhibition center there provides historic background on the challenge of the hill, and a covered wagon shows the size and weight of the equipment that had to be handled on this steep grade.

Apart from the historical interest of the site, the 1,000-acres-plus of upland prairie here are brightened by wildflowers in season. From late November until March, bald and golden eagles winter at nearby Lake McConaughy and frequently use the updrafts at Ash Hollow to reach their cruising altitude.

▶ Grounds open year-round; visitors center open Memorial Day-Labor Day. Admission charged.

www.ngpc.state.ne.us/parks
(308) 778-5651

---

5 Niobrara National Scenic River

146 S. Hall St. (Ranger Station), Valentine

The Niobrara River drains over 12,000 square miles of north-central Nebraska's Sand Hills, one of the largest windswept dune areas in the world. This is a grass-covered prairie expanse of rare natural beauty, of pine-scented rolling hills, flower-strewn prairies, tall sandstone cliffs, and tumbling waterfalls. Wildlife abounds. Deer, bison, elk, beaver, and mink roam the open prairie, while herons and kingfishers soar above the river before diving for fish.

Designated a National Scenic River by Congress, the Niobrara is ideal for boating. You can paddle along by canoe or kayak or float leisurely downstream in a tube or on a raft. Early morning and late evening are the best times to spot wildlife. Several hiking trails and a self-guided wildlife drive lead to glimpses of native animals.

▶ Open year-round.

www.nps.gov/niob
(402) 376-1901 Ranger Station

5 Niobrara National Scenic River. The Niobrara draws canoers, tubers, rafters, and kayakers from early spring through late fall. Hikers, too, find plenty to like.

6 Valentine National Wildlife Refuge

20 miles south of Valentine, off US-83

The rolling dunes that give the entire Sandhills region of north-central Nebraska its name were created by deposits of windblown sand from an ancient seabed to the west. Native grasses invaded the dunes, the water table rose, marshes and lakes were formed, and the grass became even more abundant.

The unusual environment was threatened by settlers who drained the marshes to obtain more cropland. But in 1935 this refuge of more than 70,000 acres was established to preserve a part of the Sandhills. In 1976 it was designated a National Natural Landmark.

Since the refuge was created primarily for the preservation of wildlife, anyone with an interest in nature will find it a fascinating place to visit. Trails for hiking lead to the more remote areas and to some of the lakes, nine of which are open to anglers. Among the animals occasionally seen are deer, coyotes, and badgers.

The most compelling attractions are the great flights of waterfowl that regularly take refuge here. In fall and spring up to 300,000 migrating ducks may inhabit the refuge. Most prevalent are teals, mallards, pintails, shovelers, and gadwalls; but many other species can be seen, including the trumpeter swan, once nearly extinct. Flocks of wild turkeys also may be spotted, and shorebirds are abundant.

▶ Open year-round.

http://valentine.fws.gov
(402) 376-3789

---

7 Lincoln County Historical Museum

2403 N. Buffalo Bill Ave., North Platte

To contemplate the small collection of restored frontier-era buildings on the museum grounds here is to sense the feeling of isolation and interdependence that the early settlers must have once had.

And here, too, is the urge to grow. The founders of the museum have continued in their quest to re-create a complete frontier town, just as their forebears worked to provide more amenities for their growing communities. Preserved structures include a depot, Pony Express building, army headquarters, log homestead, pioneer house, church, and schoolhouse.

In the museum building itself the displays recall many aspects of pioneer life on the plains. Weapons, Native American artifacts, tools, and barbed wire attest to the more demanding tasks, while gentler pursuits are represented by fashions, jewelry, musical instruments, and room settings. There are also replicas of a post office, doctor's office, barber and beauty shop, and telephone switchboard. The most unique re-creation is a World War II-era canteen that provided hospitality and entertainment for the men on passing troop trains.

Most of the objects were donated by local residents, which accounts for the aura of informal charm. The museum is likely to be crowded during Nebraskaland Days, the third week in June.

▶ Open Memorial Day-last Sun. in Sept. Admission charged.

http://npcanteen.net/lchm.html
(308) 534-5640

---

8 Bessey Ranger District, Nebraska National Forest

State Spur 86B, off Rte. 2, west of Halsey

Even native Nebraskans find it strange to come upon a huge, sprawling forest in the middle of the otherwise bleak Sandhills prairie; and indeed, these woods are unusual and have their own special beauty, for they were put here by humans.

9 ▶ **Dancing Leaf Earth Lodge.** The way of life of prehistoric Native Americans is revived in a reconstruction of a cottonwood timber lodge set in the rolling prairie hills.

The Nebraska National Forest was established by presidential proclamation in 1902 at the urging of Charles Bessey, a professor of botany at the University of Nebraska, who believed that forests could survive on the plains. In April 1903, 85 acres were planted. Today more than 20,000 acres flourish on the 90,000 acres.

At the Charles E. Bessey Tree Nursery, established to grow tree seedlings to transplant to forests in the Bessey district and to help build windbreaks on private land, more than 60 species of trees and shrubs can now be found.

The Bessey Recreation Complex offers campgrounds, a picnic area, canoeing in the Middle Loup River, and hiking trails. Backpack camping is generally allowed, and in winter the area is open for snowmobiling and cross-country skiing.

▶ Arboretum and recreation area open year-round. Fee charged for camping.

www.fs.fed.us/r2/nebraska/recreation/ by_unit/nnfbrd.shtml
(308) 533-2257

---

9 Dancing Leaf Earth Lodge

6100 E. Opal Springs Rd., Wellfleet

More than a thousand years ago Native Americans built earthen lodges for shelter and hunted and farmed along the Medicine Creek in Nebraska. Based on archaeological evidence from 800–1300 years ago, their way of life has been reconstructed in the Dancing Leaf Earth Lodge. The lodge inspires visitors to experience a way of life in communion with nature.

Set on 115 acres of rolling prairie hills, the Dancing Leaf Earth Lodge seems far from modern civilization. Its circular shape of

cottonwood timbers (whose leaves dance in the wind) has an opening at the top to let daylight in and smoke out. Music and storytelling events interpret ancient history.

Surrounding the lodge, scenic hiking trails wind past natural springs and Opal Lake. Canoes are available for exploring the lake. You can sign up for a buffalo-stew dinner followed by a "celestial happenings" sunset tour around the Medicine Wheel, a circle of stones aligned with the stars.

▶ Open year-round, Memorial Day-Labor Day. Admission charged.

www.dancingleaf.com
(308) 963-4233

---

10 Gallagher Canyon State Recreation Area

1 E. Park Dr. 25A, Cozad

This secluded camping and picnic area on a small lake is truly far off the beaten path. It is reached only by a labyrinthine but well-marked journey down winding backcountry roads.

Once you get there, you'll be on your own; the 400-acre park is unstaffed. The rustic facilities include shady picnic sites, a dirt boat-launching ramp, a swimming area, and a large, grassy campground. Fishing is permitted in the lake, which is part of the area's water supply. Many kinds of birds are attracted to the area by the abundance of wild berries and grapes. Orioles, cardinals, finches, magpies, and others may be seen flitting through the cover of the trees.

▶ Open year-round. Fee charged for camping.

www.ngpc.state.ne.us/parks
(308) 785-2685

12 **Nebraska Prairie Museum.**
Displays in this eclectic museum cover all the historical and cultural bases of the Cornhusker State.

11 Heartland Museum of Military Vehicles

606 Heartland Rd., Lexington
Conceived in 1986 by four friends with a shared passion for historic military vehicles—and who thrilled at driving their own vintage models in parades—this museum has developed into a place to honor America's other veterans of the battlefront.

It boasts a collection of more than 60 meticulously restored fighting machines, ready to roll at a moment's notice. Most vehicles have been acquired within a 150-mile radius of the museum. When tractors were in short supply in the 1940s and early 1950s, local farmers often relied on retired warriors—rugged jeeps, trucks, and half-tracks—to work their land.

The Heartland's dedicated staff has rescued many from rust and oblivion, returning them to mint condition. Beyond local treasures, the museum's collection features military ambulances, an M-60 tank, a U.S. Army Bradley Fighting Vehicle, and the rare Downed Airman Retriever, one of

the few remaining in the world. Since military vehicles commanded the skies as well as the road, the museum is also home to several "Huey" helicopters.

Visitors can touch and even sit in the formidable, fully operational vehicles. The museum's interpretive exhibits and its extensive reference library demonstrate how the collected machines were built, how they were used, and why those who wielded these weapons hope they will never have to be used again.

▶ Open year-round except major winter holidays. Donations encouraged.

www.heartlandmuseum.com
(308) 324-6329

12 Nebraska Prairie Museum

Hwy. 183, Holdrege
From Native American artifacts to the tools of homesteaders to unique World War II memorabilia, this expansive museum celebrates the vibrant history of the community and the state. Extensive collections of arrowheads, quilts, glassware,

household items, and vintage clothing, along with rooms decorated in period style, recall life as it was on the prairie.

A series of exhibits evokes a typical bygone town square, complete with a print shop, blacksmith, and general store. Visitors can walk around pioneering agricultural equipment and antique automobiles while contemplating the impact of technology on farmers and townsfolk. Other points of interest outside the main museum include a one-room schoolhouse, a classic farmhouse, a windmill, and an early Lutheran church.

In addition to its extensive prairie heritage, the museum stands out for its tribute to Camp Atlanta, a World War II POW camp for German prisoners, originally just five miles from the museum's present site. For years after their release, German prisoners told stories of their exceptional treatment at the camp, and many forged lifelong friendships with their former guards.

An authentic scale replica of the tower that stood at Camp Atlanta now serves as an interpretive center,

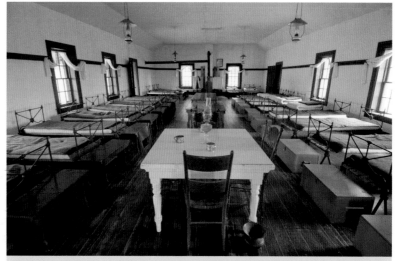

13 **Fort Hartsuff State Historical Park.** Nine of the original buildings at this army post still stand. Shown here is an authentically renovated and furnished barracks.

with items donated by U.S. military officers who worked at the prison, German soldiers confined there, and local people who got to know the POWs. Video interviews with former POWs and guards, as well as several books on the subject, are sold at the museum store.

▶ Open daily year-round except major holidays.

www.nebraskaprairie.org
(308) 995-5015

13 Fort Hartsuff State Historical Park

Fort Hartsuff Rd., north of Elyria
The frontier army post was established in 1874 to protect settlers and friendly Pawnees from hostile Sioux. Nine of the original main buildings still stand, stationed around a spacious parade ground.

With gravel and lime more readily available than lumber, most of the buildings were made of grout—which was scribed to give it the more fitting appearance of stone. Such symbolism was important; the soldiers organized an expedition to Long Pine Creek, some 70 miles to the north, to cut a 97-foot pine for a flagpole.

Times were hard when the fort was built, and the settlers were thankful for the construction work. Close ties with civilians continued, and the fort became the social center of the Loup Valley.

The garrison had only one major encounter, a battle in 1876 in which the Sioux were handily defeated. As more settlers moved in and the Sioux's power waned, so did the need for the fort. It was abandoned in 1881, and the grounds eventually became farmland; the ever solid buildings were left in place.

Now, after considerable restoration, the barracks, officers quarters,

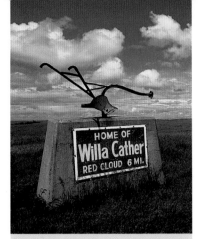

14 ▶ **Willa Cather Pioneer Memorial.** A road sign touts the town of Red Cloud as the home of the author of the famous novel *O Pioneers!*

and the other buildings look much as they did more than a century ago. It's especially convincing when living-history demonstrations are given, weekends from Memorial Day to Labor Day.

▶ Open year-round. Admission charged.

www.ngpc.state.ne.us/parks
(308) 346-4715

14 ▶ Willa Cather Pioneer Memorial and Educational Foundation

413 N. Webster St., Red Cloud
The Pulitzer prizewinning author lived in Red Cloud only from 1884 to 1890, when she left to attend the University of Nebraska. But she returned regularly to visit her parents and sometimes spent her summers there. Today the Willa Cather Foundation, based in the 1885 opera house where Cather gave her high school graduation address, gives guided tours of some of the historic buildings in the town that informed many of Cather's novels.

The people and places in this town appeared in six of her novels, including *One of Ours,* the 1923 Pulitzer prizewinner.

How specifically and accurately she wrote about the places she knew is demonstrated in the house rented by the Cathers from 1884 to 1904. Passages from her books are narrated while you view the rooms she described. The house itself, she wrote, had "everything a little on the slant."

The foundation publishes maps and brochures describing self-guiding driving and walking tours of the more than 190 sites—houses, streets, business and municipal buildings, monuments, churches, landscapes, farmsteads—in Red Cloud and around the region that have appeared under one guise or another in Cather's books. All these sites make up the Willa Cather Thematic District, which is the largest historic district in the United States dedicated to a single author.

▶ Open year-round except Sun. Oct.-Mar. and holidays. Admission charged for some tours.

www.willacather.org
(402) 746-2652

15 ▶ Ashfall Fossil Beds State Historical Park

86930 617th Ave., Royal
In the spring of 1971, heavy rains eroded part of a rural Nebraska cornfield. The farmer's bad luck proved to be a windfall for paleontologists: The exposed gully yielded the skull of a baby rhinoceros, preserved for some 12 million years beneath volcanic ash.

Since then, skeletons of hundreds of rhinos and other animals—including camels, cranes, turtles, and three-toed horses—have been uncovered. The onetime cornfield is now a 360-acre working excavation site that is open to curious observers. The park was named a National Natural Landmark in 2006.

A 17,500-square-foot structure, planned to open in 2009 will replace the 2,000-square-foot "Rhino Barn." It will provide decades of additional excavation of the intact, three-dimensionally pre-served fossil skeletons. The visitors center offers a fossil-preparatory laboratory where visitors will see what makes this excavation site so rare: the recovery of complete, intact skeletons that represent an entire rhino community.

On the grounds several short, easily accessible trails grant a closer look at the striking local geology. The park also offers opportunities for serious hiking, bird-watching, and picnicking.

▶ Open May-mid-Oct. Admission charged.

www.ashfall.unl.edu
(402) 893-2000

16 ▶ Neligh Mill Historical Site

N St. at Wylie Dr., Neligh
Of some 550 mills that have served Nebraska farmers over the years, this three-story brick mill, with branching annexes added at different times, is one of the few that remains with all of its machinery intact.

Construction on the building was started in 1873 by John D. Neligh, the town's founder. But it was another local luminary, W. C. Gallaway, who brought the mill to completion in 1874. In 1886 the original millstones were replaced with steel rollers.

The mill operated successfully with water power through World War I, but in 1920 a flood broke the millpond dam, and electricity had to be generated to keep the plant running.

Unlike many other local mills, this one survived the Great Depression and continued in the

flour business until 1959. It was sufficiently automated to produce 500 barrels of flour a day with a crew of 12 to 14 people per each 12-hour shift.

Although flour has not been ground here for a long time, one is reminded of the persistence of dust by the little piles of white stuff still visible in various places under the machines—tangible ghosts of a more prosperous past.

The warehouse and power-plant additions have exhibits relating to the mill's history. The old office, with its original furnishings, serves as a visitors center and bookstore, where you can buy your own copy of *The Neligh Mill Cookbook.*

▶ Open Tues.-Sun. Memorial Day-Labor Day; off-season Mon.-Fri. except state holidays. Admission charged.

www.nebraskahistory.org/sites/mill
(402) 887-4303

15 ▶ **Ashfall Fossil Beds State Historical Park.** A fossil bed in this park's Rhino Barn is a work site for paleontologists.

17 Elkhorn Valley Museum and Research Center

515 Queen City Blvd., Norfolk
Members of The Elkhorn Valley Historical Society wanted to preserve the memory and legacy of the people of their region. Their enthusiasm caught on, and thanks to the generosity of local residents, businesses, organizations, and grants, their dream of building a beautiful museum came true in 1997. It now proudly houses exhibits and a photograph collection that document the history of the region. A special gallery celebrates the television fame of a local Norfolk resident, Johnny Carson; a genealogy center contains valuable local data; and a library of 1,200 books on birding is available for research. Children learn by doing, and here they can have fun at the same time in the Children's Discovery Zone. Interactive exhibits are geared to children ages 2 to11.

▶ Open daily except holidays.
Admission charged.

www.elkhornvalleymuseum.org
(402) 371-3886

18 The John G. Neihardt Center

308 W. Elm St., Bancroft
The Nebraska poet, teacher, writer, and historian John G. Neihardt was posthumously designated the state's Poet Laureate in Perpetuity in 1982. This center, in his memory, has a research library largely dedicated to his life and works, illuminated by tape and slide presentations.

A major theme here relates less to the man himself than to his lifelong interest in the American Indians and his deep respect for their beliefs, best reflected in the Sacred Hoop Prayer Garden.

20 **International Quilt Study Center and Museum.** This museum celebrates quilting—part of Nebraska's heritage—with displays of quilts from around the world.

The hoop, prominent in Native American beliefs, is traditionally inscribed in the soil and represents the world. The world is divided by two roads. The east-west line marks the road of life experience, while the north-south line is the road of the spirit. From the center, where they cross, grows the tree of life, and each quarter of the circle has further symbolic meaning.

This concept is elegantly memorialized with a large prayer circle formed in the tiered brick floor of the circular exhibition gallery. The garden is also fashioned into a prayer circle and has signs explaining the symbolism.

Other displays illustrate highlights from Neihardt's remarkably productive writing career. First published at the age of 19, he wrote, lectured, and taught continually, compiling an impressive list of honors, including a special place of honor with the Lakota tribe. He was working on the second volume of his autobiography when he died in 1973 at age 92.

In striking contrast to the modern center with its curved, windowless brick walls is the humble one-room frame building which Dr. Neihardt used as a study to work from 1900 to 1920. It was built in 1888.

An old typewriter, kerosene lamp, potbellied stove, and comfortable rocker evoke thoughts of a homely, unhurried era that contrasts dramatically with the age of the word processor.

▶ Open daily Mar.–Nov.; Mon.–Fri. Dec.–Feb.
Donations encouraged.

www.neihardtcenter.org
(402) 648-3388

19 Louis E. May Museum

1643 N. Nye Ave., Fremont
When in 1874 Theron Nye, the first mayor of Fremont, chose the grandiose Italianate Revival style for his large new house, he was obviously out to make an impression.

Upon his death the big redbrick house was left to his son, Ray Nye, who chose to remodel, expand, and make it even more grand and imposing. Young Nye's taste ran to the classical, and he added a portico of two-story fluted white columns with Ionic capitals.

The structure—a 25-room mansion—is itself an architectural museum piece, and today it appropriately serves as the headquarters of the Dodge County Historical Society.

The museum, named for the benefactor who made its purchase possible, features changing displays of antiques, decorative arts, and historic photographs reflecting life from the late 19th and early 20th centuries.

The museum also includes a general store display, a one-room schoolhouse, a formal rose garden, and a Victorian garden with brick-lined paths. Outstanding details in the house itself include carved oak and mahogany paneling, stained-glass windows, decorative mantels, and some remarkable tile work in the master bathroom.

▶ Open Wed.–Sat. Apr.–Dec.; Sun. May–Aug.
Admission charged.

www.visitnebraska.org
(402) 721-4515

20 International Quilt Study Center and Museum

University of Nebraska-Lincoln, East Campus, 1523 N. 33rd St., Lincoln
The Quilt Study Center and Museum owns the largest known public collection of quilts from around the world. The center's goal is to collect and preserve historic and contemporary quilting traditions from all over the world and share their resources with the

19 **Louis E. May Museum.** The portico was a late addition to the mansion.

public. They have gathered quilts from 24 nations, showcased in frequently changing exhibitions built around cultural, historical, and artistic themes chosen to inform and inspire visitors of all ages and backgrounds.

You may study, admire, and imitate the prized quilts by viewing the collections in person and by browsing the collections in the virtual gallery or online. View quilts from the 1700s to the present.

▶ Open Tues.-Sun. Closed major holidays and when the university is closed. Admission charged.

www.quiltstudy.org
(402) 472-6549

21 Homestead National Monument of America

8523 W. State Hwy. 4, Beatrice
On May 20, 1862, President Abraham Lincoln signed the Homestead Act, enabling people to become landowners by paying $18 in fees and cultivating the land for at least five years. This National Park site pays tribute to one of the nation's most important laws. The gritty endurance of millions of Americans and immigrants spurred the westward spread of the country after the Civil War.

The Homestead Heritage Center offers a film and exhibits that explain homesteading history and examine the law's impact on immigrants, women, Native Americans, and African-Americans. The Education Center hosts traditional arts events demonstrations and special exhibits.

The park itself is located on the original homestead of Daniel Freeman, one of the first settlers to claim land under the provisions of the act. A tiny log cabin built in

1867 vividly evokes the homesteaders' daily life, and a farm implement exhibit explains changes in agricultural equipment.

A guide to the wildlife and plants you may see along the two miles of hiking trails is at the visitors center. A quarter-mile away stands a furnished one-room schoolhouse; ask at the visitors center for information.

Check ahead for the park's special events, all free of charge.

▶ Open year-round except holidays.

www.nps.gov/home
(402) 223-3514

22 Indian Cave State Park

Shubert
This magnificent area—3,000 acres of oak-clad hills and bluffs along the Missouri River—takes

did you know ?

In the 123 years of the Homestead Act's existence, 270 million acres of land have been distributed—that's 10 percent of the nation's land!

its name from a deep overhang of rock that provided Native Americans with a natural shelter. At the cave are large rocks incised with images of the hunt and the surroundings. Local residents call this area the Little Ozarks and come to see the lovely displays of redbud flowering in spring and the blazing colors of the hardwood forest in the fall. In fact, October tends to be the park's busiest month.

A scenic road and some 20 miles of trails for day walks and backpacking provide panoramic views. Horseback trail rides are also available. The Missouri River is the anglers delight. In winter 16 miles of trails are marked for cross-country skiing, and some steep hills provide excellent sledding. There are 274 campsites.

Also within the park are a reconstructed schoolhouse and general store, and the two graveyards that remain from the town of St. Deroin. The store and school are the site of living-history demonstrations given on weekends in summer and fall.

The unusual community of St. Deroin is a story unto itself. Established in the mid-1800s by Joseph Deroin, the town began as a small trading post and offered homes to orphans. These children were generally unaccepted and not considered citizens.

As people began to settle in the surrounding area, the post quickly grew into a small town, and it was named Deroin after its founder. "Saint," which Joseph purportedly was not, was added to the name of the town in a vain attempt to attract more settlers.

▶ Open year-round. Admission charged.

www.ngpc.state.ne.us/parks
(402) 883-2575

seasonal events

MAY
• Victorian Festival—Superior *(live entertainment, parade, children's activities, Victorian tea, tours)*

JUNE
• Limestone Independence Days—Weeping Water *(mine tours, tournaments, children's activities, donkey polo, fireworks)*

JUNE/JULY
• Shakespeare on the Green—Omaha *(theater productions, seminars, live music, performances)*

JULY
• Prairie Days—Tilden *(cow chip throw, street dance, parade, contests, antiques)*
• Omaha Riverfront Jazz and Blues Festival—Omaha *(live performances, food)*
• Meadowlark Music Festival—Lincoln *(classical music festival, statewide performances throughout summer)*

AUGUST
• Czech Festival—Wilber *(live music and entertainment, parade, arts-and-crafts exhibits, children's activities, sports events)*
• Nebraska Balloon and Wine Festival—Elkhorn *(wine tasting, hot-air balloon launches, live music, regional food, children's activities)*
• Hay Days—Atkinson *(children's theater, games, exhibits, antiques and crafts, tractor show, dance)*

SEPTEMBER
• River City Roundup—Omaha *(rodeo, live entertainment, children's activities, interactive exhibits, parade)*

NOVEMBER
• Nebraska Food Festival—Grand Island *(great variety of food, shopping, live presentations, raffle)*
• Cowboy Christmas—Fordyce *(arts and crafts, horse-and-buggy rides, children's activities, demonstrations)*

www.visitnebraska.org

NEBRASKA

Nevada

Ghostly tableaux of Nevada's boom-and-bust days are only a part of the picture in a land of beautiful desolation and multiple pleasures.

Rhyolite. The shell of Cook's Bank, which opened for business in 1908, is a ghostly reminder of the good old days in Nevada's last gold-rush town (see page 212).

Some of the mining camps and towns of Nevada have been spruced up, but more have gone to seed. All, however, are legacies of the wild and woolly prospecting era of the mid-19th century. The stage on which the drama played out is a vast desert with oases and intriguing plant life and landforms—a marshland attracting a million migrating waterfowl, gnarled pines that may be the oldest living things on the planet, and an unearthly "city" of rock spires.

Reminders of Nevada's earliest residents include a small-town museum's displays of Anasazi artifacts found in a pueblo unearthed when Hoover Dam was being constructed in the 1930s. Non-human denizens of the desert are seen in canyons and preserves—among them, red-tailed hawks, jackrabbits, wild burros, and the endangered desert tortoise.

visit ➡ **offthebeatenpathtrips.com**

1 Comstock History Center

20 Northeast St., Virginia City
Stuffing the rich history surrounding the Comstock Lode, one of the world's largest silver deposits, into one museum is no easy task—one reason the Comstock History Center in the boomtown of Virginia City presents a variety of temporary exhibitions.

The main permanent exhibit is the *Dayton,* locomotive #18 of the Virginia & Truckee Railroad, whose trains transported silver ore from Virginia City to Carson City. But visitors have also viewed artifacts retrieved from archaeology digs at historic saloon sites and noted artist Robert Cole Caples's haunting paintings of Virginia City. They've also pored over other Nevada phenomena—the state's wild horses, for example, captured in riveting photographs. Administered by the Nevada Department of Cultural Affairs, the museum has at times displayed the work of local artists.

▶ Open Thurs.-Sun. except federal and state holidays. Donations encouraged.

(775) 847-0419

2 Stillwater National Wildlife Refuge Complex

1000 Auction Rd., Fallon
Viewed from the road, Stillwater National Wildlife Refuge (NWR)

2 Stillwater National Wildlife Refuge Complex. An American white pelican swoops in for a landing on the marshlands of a refuge lying 60 miles east of Reno.

appears as a vast expanse of desert scrub. Yet a million-plus migrating waterfowl home in on the marshland that dates back for thousands of years—land wet enough for the American Bird Conservancy to have listed Stillwater as a Globally Important Bird Area. Native species include egrets, herons, and double-crested cormorants. Throw in long-billed dowichers, black-necked stilts, and other shorebirds and it's no wonder that countless binocular-wielding birders flock here.

Just to the northeast is the other open refuge in the complex: Fallon NWR. Anaho Island NWR, a sanctuary for colonial-

nesting waterbirds such as the white pelican, is closed to the public.

▶ Open daily.

www.fws.gov/stillwater
(775) 428-6452

3 ▶ Unionville

Off NV-400, 17 miles S. of Mill City

Perhaps 20 people still live along the main street of Unionville, which winds nearly three miles deep into Buena Vista Canyon. The road is flanked with ruined walls and foundations that recall earlier days of hope and, in the 1860s, a measure of prosperity.

The camp was settled in 1861 by silver miners of divided loyalties. Southern sympathizers named it Dixie, but when the Northern faction gained the upper hand, they changed it to Unionville. Mark Twain came to do some prospecting here, but he got involved in buying up shares in dozens of other mining operations and left after a week or two.

A fire in 1872 destroyed a number of buildings, and the mines were also slowing considerably by then. By 1880 Unionville was in a rapid decline.

There are a number of very well-preserved structures here, most notably a covered bridge and a schoolhouse built on a hill. And the Old Pioneer Garden Country Inn—built in 1861, meticulously restored, and operating today as a bed-and-breakfast—is a lodging oasis for travelers.

www.ghosttowns.com/states/nv/
unionville.html

(775) 538-7585 Old Pioneer Inn

3 ▶ Unionville. Today the Buena Vista school still stands proudly, complete with a stove, desks, and a handmade map of Africa.

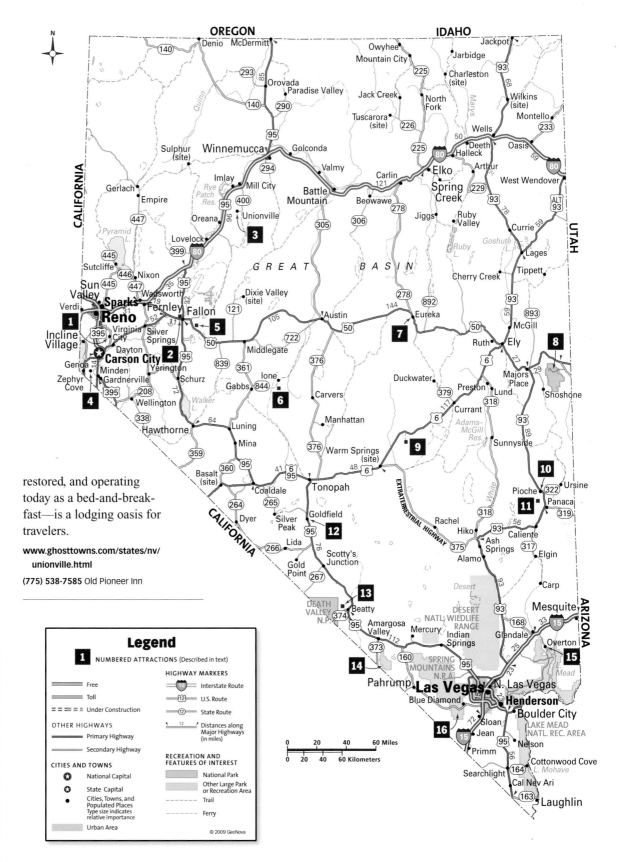

Legend

1 NUMBERED ATTRACTIONS (Described in text)

HIGHWAY MARKERS

Free
Toll
Under Construction

10 Interstate Route
12 U.S. Route
12 State Route
12 Distances along Major Highways (in miles)

OTHER HIGHWAYS

Primary Highway
Secondary Highway

CITIES AND TOWNS

✪ National Capital
✪ State Capital
• Cities, Towns, and Populated Places Type size indicates relative importance

Urban Area

RECREATION AND FEATURES OF INTEREST

National Park
Other Large Park or Recreation Area
Trail
Ferry

© 2009 GeoNova

Genoa

This attractive town has the charm of what in Nevada passes for antiquity: It was founded as a trading post and wagon-supply station in 1851 and contains the state's oldest saloon, the Genoa Bar, with its collection of electrified gas and kerosene chandeliers.

Two other buildings are worth a detour. The first is the Genoa Courthouse Museum, an elegant two-story brick building dating from 1865 (like the Genoa Bar, it is said to be the oldest building of its kind in Nevada). Washo Native American artifacts and other exhibits are on display, and you can wander through the old courtroom, the original jail cells, a period kitchen, and a blacksmith's shop.

Across the street is the Mormon Station Historic State Monument, which looks like a Wild West fort but is actually a reconstruction of the 1851 log-cabin trading post and its compound. The original burned in 1910; this replica (which houses a small museum devoted to pioneer life and Nevada history) was built in 1947.

▶ Museum and Mormon Station both open daily May–Oct. Admission charged.

www.genoanevada.org
(775) 782-4325 Museum
(775) 782-2590 Mormon Station

5 **Grimes Point and Hidden Cave**

Off US-50, 7 miles east of Fallon
Abundant echoes of the daily lives of ancient tribes of Native Americans are at the core of these linked archaeological treasures.

Prehistoric carvings and line drawings engraved on the stone surfaces of the self-guiding interpretive Grimes Petroglyph Trail form a timeline of development—from simple patterns that were begun at least 7,000 years ago to later, more pictorial images, such as lizards and deer.

A one-mile drive down a dirt road leads to Hidden Cave, which was first discovered in the 1920s by four schoolboys and is so named because of its well-concealed entrance.

Dust kicked up from centuries of bat droppings (guano) that littered the cave made exploration difficult at first, but by the late 1970s caches of artifacts as well as stratified deposits from the Ice Age waters of Lake Lahontan, now the Carson Desert, were unearthed. Basketry, unused dart shafts with points of shiny stone, and seeds and nuts perhaps reserved for meals indicate that the cave was used for storage.

Fallon's Churchill County Museum on Maine St. offers guided tours of the cave the second and fourth Saturday of every month. Plan to arrive between 9:00 and 9:30 A.M.

▶ Open year-round.

www.ccmuseum.org
www.recreation-areas.com/area/1198
(775) 423-3677 Museum

6 **Berlin-Ichthyosaur State Park**

23 miles east of Gabbs
The company town of Berlin, established in 1897, is now a classic ghost town. The wood shacks and the remains of the mill and gold mine look much as they did in 1910, when the town was virtually abandoned.

Some of the buildings have new roofs, but otherwise they show the effects of standing for some 90 years on the open hillside. Inside, a few remnants of furniture and utensils reinforce the reality that the miners essentially just picked up and moved on. A self-guiding tour is marked by signs that identify such sites as a miner's cabin, a boardinghouse, an assay office, and a stage station.

4 **Genoa.** The Genoa Bar and Saloon, opened in 1853 and now touted as "Nevada's oldest thirst parlor," was visited by the likes of Mark Twain and Teddy Roosevelt.

The ichthyosaur fossils are in Union Canyon in the heart of the Shoshone Mountains, a two-mile drive from Berlin. In the fossil shelter the remains of 11 of these huge "fish-lizards" (which became extinct 70 million years ago) are shown just as they were found.

Despite their resemblance to today's whales and porpoises, these predators were the largest animals of their time, ranging up to 50 feet in length. Their remains have turned up all over the world, but the ichthyosaurs here are among the largest ever excavated. If the shelter is closed, you can see these fossils through an observation window.

▶ Both sites open year-round, but call for weather conditions in the winter. Admission charged.

www.parks.nv.gov.bi.htm
(775) 964-2440

7 **Eureka**

Of the many Nevada mining towns whose fortunes have waxed and waned over the years, Eureka is today a small, quiet, well-preserved gem with a statewide reputation.

The people are friendly, and you can sense in them a pride in the restoration work they have lavished on such buildings as the handsome courthouse, the Sentinel Museum, and the Eureka Opera House.

The museum is located in what is possibly the oldest existing newspaper building in the state. On the ground floor you will find a complete press room from the 1800s, with posters that were printed by the Eureka *Sentinel* hanging prominently on the walls. The second floor has displays that include a schoolroom, mining room, parlor, barbershop, kitchen, and fraternal firehouse room.

Over at the Eureka Opera House you'll see the social center of the old town almost as it was when the structure was built in 1880. The elegantly appointed building was completely restored in 1993 and is busy today hosting conventions, business meetings, and a monthly performance.

A map of Eureka's attractions along the self-guiding walking tour is available at the courthouse and most other locations in town.

▶ Sentinel Museum open daily May–Oct.; Tues.–Sat. Nov.–Apr.; Opera House open Mon.–Fri. year-round.

www.co.eureka.nv.us
(775) 237-5010 Museum
(775) 237-6006 Opera House

8 Great Basin National Park

5 miles west of Baker on NV-488, by way of NV-487 and US-50
You know you're headed to one of the country's least visited national parks when you realize your car is almost the only one on the desert road that leads you there (US-50 is known as "the loneliest road in America"). And what do you see once you arrive? More desert. But don't be fooled: The park is not only alive with flora and fauna but is home to some of the oldest living plants on Earth. On Wheeler Peak (13,063 feet) a 12-mile scenic drive takes you to rocky glacial moraines on which grow Great Basin bristle-cone pines—small, gnarled trees that took root almost 5,000 years ago.

Down in Lexington Canyon the limestone Lexington Arch rises as high as a six-story building. Beneath the desert Lehman Caves is a cool refuge full of amazing sights. Sixty and ninety-minute cave tours are offered; the longest

 **Great Basin National Park.** A dead bristlecone pine of the type found only in the Great Basin lays bare the sculpture of a tree thousands of years old.

(and best) is the ninety-minute half-mile journey that winds past formations ranging from the expected stalactites and stalagmites to elegant, rippling drapery and rare shields—disk-shaped formations with streamers of flowstone.

Near the cave entrance is a picnic area, café, and visitors center. The center supplies information about the wealth of hiking, riding, and camping options in a vast park full of surprises.

▶ Open year-round except holidays. Café and gift shop open Apr.–Oct. Admission charged.

www.nps.gov/grba
(775) 234-7331

9 Lunar Crater Volcanic Field

Off US-6, 75 miles east of Tonopah
As close to a moonscape as most of us will ever get, Lunar Crater and the adjacent 100 square miles of volcanic terrain are very similar to features found on the moon. Indeed, before the 1969 moon shot, the area was used to test lunar-expedition equipment.

Thanks to the stable, dry climate at this national landmark, there's been little change since the volcanic activity that began some 2 million years ago and ended only a few millennia back—which in geologic terms is relatively recently.

It's a fascinatingly desolate place, dotted with saltbush and greasewood. But in the years when rainfall exceeds the four- to six-inch annual average, the wild-flower displays after the rainy season (about mid-May–early July) can be magnificent, particularly when globe mallow slashes the desert with scarlet.

Lunar Crater sets the scale for the field's formations. It's nearly three-quarters of a mile across and 400 feet deep. From the crater's rim you can see more than 20 extinct volcanoes in the nearby hills. The smaller Easy Chair Crater, four miles to the north, gets its name from its situation on the edge of a tall cinder cone—together the two formations look like an overstuffed chair.

Other features in the area include The Wall, a steep face of fused volcanic ash; Lunar Lake, a shallow lake in the midst of alkali mudflats; and Black Rock Lava Flow, a 1,900-acre basalt plateau.

There are no trails, but hiking is not difficult. Be on the alert for rattlesnakes, and avoid hazards like

abandoned mine shafts and unstable crater slopes. And remember to bring plenty of food and water and have enough gas for the trip. This is unforgiving land, and you are truly off the beaten path here.

▶ Open year-round.

(775) 482-7800

10 Pioche

Silver was found near Pioche as early as 1863, and after the mines opened in 1869, the settlement boomed. It also gained notoriety as a trigger-happy, lawless town, the toughest in the West. Local legend has it that not one of the first 70 entrants in its cemetery died of natural causes.

But this is no bust town. Pioche bills itself today as a "living ghost town," and it's a vibrant community that takes pride in its past. An annual heritage celebration is held in June and draws large crowds.

History is all around here, starting with the Million Dollar Courthouse, so named for its costly (some say corrupt) 60-year debt repayment on the initial 1871 construction costs of $26,400. Other reminders of days gone by are the Masonic Hall (1872), Thompson's Opera House (1873), and the exhibits in the Lincoln County Museum.

The town is a hub of a large high-desert mountain region with many outdoor recreational opportunities. Nearby, Eagle Valley Dam, Echo Canyon State Park, and Cathedral Gorge offer picnicking, camping, fishing, and boating.

▶ Courthouse open daily mid-May–Oct. Museum open year-round.

www.piochenevada.com
(775) 962-5544

11 Cathedral Gorge State Park

Panaca

The buff-colored, roughly hewn spires reaching heavenward from the Meadow Valley inspired the name of this state park.

The gorge is part of the Panaca Formation, created when the freshwater lake that had covered the land receded and erosion carved the montmorillonite clay into jagged pillars, gullies, and caves.

Nomadic tribes of Fremont, Anasazi, and Southern Paiute passed through from 10,000 B.C., hunting and gathering plants. Mormons founded the town of Panaca in 1864 after discovering water. Nearby Bullionville sprang up in 1869 when silver ore was found. In the 1920s open-air plays were performed against the otherworldly backdrop.

At an elevation of 4,800 feet, the park is home to a great variety of wildlife—like coyote, gophers, roadrunners, blackbirds, and nonpoisonous lizards and snakes. In the summer, however, the Great Basin rattlesnake stops for a visit.

11 Cathedral Gorge State Park.
Erosion carved a bentonite lake bed into an uneven mass of rock spires.

At the north end, where the park tapers sharply, Miller Point provides a panoramic view and can be reached by a road just north of the information center.

▶ Open year-round. Admission charged.

www.parks.nv.gov/cg.htm
(775) 728-4460

12 Goldfield

When Goldfield was going strong, the streets indeed seemed paved with gold. From its founding in 1902 until 1910, it was one of the most celebrated boomtowns in the country and the largest community in Nevada. A lot of people got rich quick.

Goldfield boasted banks, breweries, hospitals, newspapers, and the fanciest hotel in the West. Built in 1908, the Goldfield Hotel had a 22-karat gilt ceiling in the mahogany-paneled lobby, brass beds, and an electric elevator. But the gold began to run out after 1910, and a 1923 fire ravaged much of what was left of the town.

A monument on US-45 commemorates one of Goldfield's big claims to fame: a legendary 1906 title fight between Joe Gans and Oscar Nelson, won by Gans when Nelson was disqualified for a low blow—in the forty-second round. The fight is thought by many to be the longest in history.

Today the remnants of past glories are not so obvious, but with some patience and imagination, you can get a sense of what Goldfield used to be. Besides the hotel there is the courthouse, built in 1907, it is still well maintained. You can also belly up to the bar at the Santa Fe Saloon. Walking maps and other brochures can be obtained at the chamber of commerce.

15 Lost City Museum.
The collection at the museum ranges from Early Man to historic Pueblo and Paiute cultures. The pottery in the foreground (left) is Hopi.

▶ Open year-round.

www.geocities.com/
goldfieldhistoricnewsletter/
(775) 485-3560

13 Rhyolite and the Bottle House

When Rhyolite, one of Nevada's last great gold-rush towns, was founded in 1905, earlier Nevada mines were closing at a regular pace and thousands of prospectors started heading here for another fling with lady luck.

During the boom years the town, with a floating population of about 10,000, had its own stock exchange, three railroad depots, and a main street bustling with business and twinkling with electric lights. By 1911, however, it became evident that the quality and quantity of ore was less than expected. The miners and speculators began to leave as quickly as they had arrived.

The wishfully named Golden St. is now lined with the foundations and broken walls of once-

proud stone buildings, although the train depot has been restored.

One of the favorite stops is the Tom Kelly bottle house, with walls made of as many as 50,000 bottles set in clay. Most are Adolphus-Busch beer (known today as Budweiser) bottles, although there are also medicine bottles for good measure. When it was built in 1905, these no-deposit bottles provided a cheap alternative to lumber. Restored in 1925 for a movie setting, it is now maintained as a historic site.

▶ Open year-round.

www.rhyolite.org
www.rhyolitesite.com

14 Ash Meadows National Wildlife Refuge

22 miles west of Pahrump

The transparent one-inch-long Devil's Hole pupfish, an endangered species, spawns on a rock ledge in only one place.

You'll find that place here in a deep spring on a federally protected refuge in the Amargosa Valley of southern Nye County. Each of Ash Meadows's half-dozen geothermal pools claims its own variety of pupfish, and Point of Rocks is the best pupfish-viewing site.

Thousand-year-old "fossil" water comes to the surface in springs, providing rich and disparate environments. Carson Slough, an area of historic wetlands in the north and west, is in the midst of an ongoing restoration to help bring more wildlife here.

Desert oases, now very uncommon in other parts of the Southwest, can be found among the sagebrush and mesquite of this 24,000-acre former alfalfa and, later, cattle ranch. Sandy dunes populate the center.

Swimming is allowed only in the man-made Crystal Reservoir in order to protect the rest of the delicate ecosystem. Sport hunting is permitted for certain species, such as geese, quail, and jackrabbits.

▶ Open year-round.

http://desertcomplex.fws.gov/ashmeadows
(775) 372-5435

15 Lost City Museum

721 Moapa Valley Blvd., Overton
When Hoover Dam was built in the 1930s and vast Lake Mead was created, the construction came with a cost: the loss of historic Anasazi Native American sites. When one such treasure, Pueblo Grande de Nevada, was threatened, the National Park Service enlisted the Civilian Conservation Corps to excavate ancient artifacts. The CCC also helped to erect the adobe brick pueblo to house the trove—the Lost City Museum.

Built on the ruins of an actual pueblo, the museum displays tools and weapons made from bone, quartzite, chert, or obsidian;

turquoise pendants and beads; and an extraordinary collection of Anasazi pottery, known for its distinctive, highly stylized designs. Visitors who stroll the grounds of the three-acre site enjoy an intriguing array of desert plants, many of them labeled.

▶ Open daily except major winter holidays. Admission charged.

www.nevadaculture.org/docs/museums/
lost/lostcity.htm
(702) 397-2193

---

16 Red Rock Canyon

10 miles west of Las Vegas
With the glitter of Las Vegas in the distance, 8,000-foot cliffs rise out of Red Rock Canyon in the Mojave Desert.

The Spring Mountain Range and Aztec sandstone formations frame a scene of serenity that is home to 197,000 acres of unique geologic outcroppings, wild animals, and desert plants.

The passage of millennia can be seen in the petrified sand dunes and the canyon's most notable geologic feature, the Keystone Thrust Fault. Broad layers of gray limestone and red sandstone are visible where two of the Earth's plates collided with great force an estimated 65 million years ago.

Visitors will find waterfalls, sheltered ravines, scenic overlooks, and trails for both experienced and novice climbers. All areas at Red Rock are accessible from the highway. Late summer weather can be extremely hot.

Wild burros, whose ancestors were brought to the Southwest by gold and silver miners in the 1800s, roam freely in this National Conservation Area. They are best seen from a distance, as they have been known to kick and bite. The endangered desert tortoise is on view in its own habitat in the visitors center, and red-tailed hawks float on air currents over the Calico Basin.

▶ Open year-round. Admission charged.

www.redrockcanyonlv.org
(702) 515-5000

16 ▶ Red Rock Canyon. The collision of two tectonic plates resulted in a red sandstone and gray limestone natural feature known as the Keystone Thrust Fault.

NEVADA

New Hampshire

With its stretch of seashore, vast national forest, and hundreds of lakes and ponds, this is truly a state for all seasons.

Shelburne Birches. The people of Shelburne planted birch trees as a soldiers' memorial (see opposite page).

W here there's such a wealth of water-ways, a great forest, and a seashore, scenic beauty is expected. But there are also some man-made attractions. These include a castle built by a man who dreamed of beauty on every side, and made the dream come true. Beauty and grace were the concerns of a renowned sculptor whose studio and home are now on public view. President Franklin Pierce's homestead is here, as is the birthplace of Daniel Webster, the great orator and champion of national unity. And nature is all around, with majestic parks full of year-round pleasures, from great fishing to peerless cross-country ski trails.

visit ➡ **offthebeatenpathtrips.com**

1 Lake Francis State Park

439 River Rd., Pittsburg

The park is situated on an inlet of Lake Francis in the Connecticut Lakes region of the Great North Woods. From the park you can view the rapids of the Connecticut River. Wildlife is a major attraction here: More than 100 different species of birds have been sighted, including bald eagles, loons, and endangered woodpeckers. Moose and bears are occasionally seen.

The old logging roads that wind in and around the park are enjoyed by both hikers and bicyclists. For hikers there are several possibili-ties, starting with an easy trail that runs through the woods along the Connecticut River and leads from a campground to a covered bridge $1^1/_2$ miles away.

Another trail provides a three-mile hike up Magalloway Mountain. Although the last mile is quite steep, the spectacular view from the top makes the effort worth-while. On a clear day you can see Maine, Vermont, and Canada.

Fishing is good, and you can rent a boat or canoe nearby; the park has a public boat launch. Within a mile or so of the park are a swimming beach, a stable that rents horses, and riding trails.

▶ Open year-round. Camping mid-May-mid-Dec.; no water after mid-Oct. Admission charged.

Lake Francis State Park. The chilly waters of this 2,000-acre lake offer exceptional fishing, especially for trout of the brown, lake, and rainbow variety.

www.nhstateparks.com/francis.html
(603) 538-6965

2 Coleman State Park

Rte. 26, Little Diamond Pond Rd., Stewartstown

This small, remote park is in a beautiful, alpinelike setting on the shore of Little Diamond Pond, high in the White Mountains at the northern end of the Mt. Washington Valley. From it there is a beautiful view across the wooded slopes of Dixville Notch.

The park is isolated enough that bear and moose may be seen; sometimes moose come down to the pond in the evening to feed. Loons settle on the pond, and eagles and ospreys are occasionally spotted overhead.

The camping area here is the definition of basic: a large, grassy field with a scattering of fragrant balsam trees and hardwoods. There are no hookups for trailers, but each campsite has a fireplace with a grill, and during the camping season water comes in from an artesian well.

If you are lured by the prospect of catching rainbow trout or squaretail brook trout to grill over your campfire, you may want to bring a boat. A boat launch is located at a beach within the park; small boats are permitted, but speed is restricted. Boats can also be rented from the park or a privately owned outfit, which is a short way down the main road. Rainbow trout and lake trout are plentiful in the much deeper Big Diamond Pond, with spring and fall the best times for fishing. Little Diamond Pond is best in the spring, and rainbow trout are common here as well.

From Little Diamond Pond the road continues on to Big Diamond Pond a mile away, providing an enjoyable walk. For a more rigorous outing, you can hike the fairly steep, roughly half-mile trail from the campground up Sugar Hill. The park is on the Cohos Trail.

The park provides a good base for fall hunting, and in winter it is ideal for cross-country skiing, snowshoeing, and snowmobiling.

▶ Open year-round. Camping mid-May–mid-Dec.; no water after mid-Oct.

www.nhstateparks.com/coleman.html
(603) 237-5382; (603) 538-6707

3 Shelburne Birches Memorial Forest

Rte. 2, Shelburne
Flanking the highway for nearly one-fifth of a mile at Shelburne is a dense stand of paper birches, dazzlingly graceful throughout the year in their white bark, and especially ravishing in spring and autumn, when their leaves are in the first delicate flush of green or the last glory of gold and yellow.

Some of the trees growing here are giants—among the largest to be found in the eastern United States. This forest—a rare sight along the well-traveled highway—is a commemoration of Shelburne citizens who served in World War II, and it was established shortly after the war's conclusion.

▶ Open year-round.

www.shelburnenh.com
(603) 466-2262

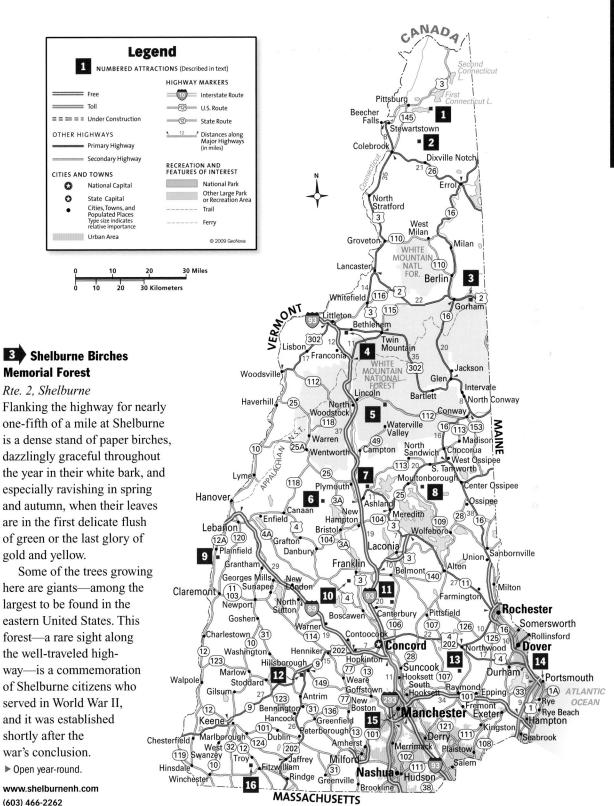

4 ▶ The Rocks Estate

4 Christmas Tree Ln., Bethlehem
A quintessential New Hampshire landscape spreads out across 1,400 acres of this former estate, now a forest reserve, in the heart of the White Mountains. Bear and moose ramble under white pines, while bobolinks fly and kestrels hunt overhead in the pristine mountain air. A famous giant pine towers over a meadow on the old estate, along with the Sleeping Astronomer, a rock formation resembling an old man lying on his back atop a mountain.

Take a tour of the Heritage Trail that has 13 homes on the *National Register of Historic Places,* or another along the nearby White Mountains Presidential Range, whose summits are named for U.S. presidents and other prominent Americans.

▶ Open daily.

www.therocks.org
(603) 444-6228

6 ▶ Sculptured Rocks Natural Area.
Mother Nature carved out a fanciful rock gallery near the town of Groton.

5 ▶ Greeley Ponds

Lincoln
There are two ways to access the excellent trails here. One entrance is off Livermore Rd., about two miles north of Rte. 49. The second entrance is off the Kancamagus Highway (Rte. 112), about nine miles east of I-93.

The two intersecting trails here run 2.1 miles and 5.4 miles. The shorter trail passes only one pond, although the second pond is just another half-mile more. It's fairly easy walking, with no extreme gradients. Log bridges span streams and swampy places, and the trails are clearly marked.

The only obstacles are the knotted tree roots that crisscross the path almost every step of the way. The forest here is a mixture of conifers and deciduous trees.

In winter these trails are a cross-country skiing paradise. The paths are well maintained, and routes are set up for novice and advanced skiers alike.

The Restricted Use Scenic Area (where fires and camping are not allowed) is more open than the rest of the forest, and as you enter it, you begin to glimpse the cliffs towering above you and realize that you have been walking up a wide valley. Near the first pond a steep trail leads to a peak on one of these ridges, Mount Osceola.

The ponds themselves are dark green and calm. As you approach the first, look for the mature hemlock growing atop a seven-foot-high boulder. The roots reach down the rock to the earth like muscular boa constrictors.

▶ Open year-round.

(603) 536-1310

7 ▶ Squam Lake.
The peaceful waters of Squaw Cove mirror the Sandwich Mountain range in the Squam Lakes region of east-central New Hampshire.

6 ▶ Sculptured Rocks Natural Area

Groton
At this intriguing stretch of the Cockermouth River, the stream has worn a chasm some 100 feet long and 30 feet deep. Its granite walls, striated in pale colors, have been carved and polished by the water into a fantasy of bowls, beaks, curves, and swirls. Adding to the scenery are ferns that have somehow established a precarious foothold in the rock.

The best viewing is from a bridge spanning the river. If you face downstream and look directly below, you can see the shape of a lion's head in the rock, with its nose at the stream and a round hole for the gape of the mouth.

Elsewhere you can see what appear to be toad and lizard heads, shell creatures with bulging eyes, and whatever else your imagination and the water level permit. The water is clean, pure, and very, very cold. The brave souls who can tolerate the water temperature can

jump from the cliffs, and there is even a small underwater tunnel to explore. The gorge is estimated to be about a million years old.

▶ Open year-round.

www.nhparks.state.nh.us

7 ▶ Squam Lakes Natural Science Center

23 Science Center Rd., Holderness
A lovingly tended place, the center introduces the visitor to a variety of natural environments.

An exhibit trail, which is open from May 1 to November 1, leads from the visitors center across rocky meadowland through which a small stream flows. The stream drains another ecological zone, an area of marsh, and finally flows into a trout pond. The attractive expanse of water, with white granite boulders at its edge, mirrors venerable white pines and paper birches on its dark surface.

Nearby are enclosures for bears, deer, owls, river otters, and bobcats.

In July and August naturalists enlighten visitors through spectacular live animal exhibits, natural science education programs, and lake cruises.

▶ Open May–Oct. Admission charged.

www.nhnature.org
(603) 968-7194

8 Castle in the Clouds

Rte. 171, Moultonborough
The castle was the dream of Thomas Gustave Plant, a multimillionaire whose objective was to have an environment in which he could behold nothing but beauty.

Purchasing 6,000 acres of woodland and sparing no expense, Plant built his mansion on a promontory with views of the island-studded lake below and the White Mountains in the distance. To achieve the perfection he required, Plant utilized the skills of vast numbers of European artists and craftsmen. The estate,

completed in 1914 at a cost of $7 million, was named Lucknow.

Miles of carriage roads and riding trails wind through quiet woods fragrant with pine to waterfalls, ponds, streams, and hilltops with breathtaking views of the surrounding countryside. There are garden walks and tours of the mansion, where the stained-glass windows depict some of the scenery. The best time to visit is from mid-Sept. to mid-Oct., when the autumn foliage is brilliant.

▶ Open weekends starting mid-May, daily June–mid-Oct. Admission charged.

www.castleintheclouds.org
(603) 476-5900

9 Saint-Gaudens National Historic Site

139 Saint Gaudens Rd., Cornish
This fine house—a large, elaborate structure set on high ground with distant views of the Vermont

hills—was once the home of one of America's most distinguished sculptors, Augustus Saint-Gaudens.

Originally a coach inn on the old stage road between Windsor and Meriden, it was bought by Saint-Gaudens in 1885 for a summer place, but from 1900 until his death in 1907 the estate served as his permanent home.

Here he combined his interests in gardening and the styles of the classical Greek and Roman periods to create a fairyland of porticoes, wide vistas, colonnades, and formal gardens. On the property are two studios, the Gallery and the Temple; the artist is buried in the latter. Many of Saint-Gaudens's most famous works are on display all around here.

Saint-Gaudens's father, an immigrant shoemaker, had encouraged his son's artistic interests; remembering this, the sculptor named the estate Aspet after his father's birthplace in France.

Saint-Gaudens was an inspirational teacher, and many young artists studied with him at Aspet. He encouraged students and apprentices to follow his personal inclination "to develop technique, and then to hide it."

▶ Park open year-round. Tours of Aspet offered late May–early Oct. Admission charged.

www.nps.gov/saga
(603) 675-2175

10 Daniel Webster Birthplace

Franklin, off Rte. 127
Daniel Webster was born here on January 18, 1782. The son of a poor farmer, he became one of America's preeminent statesmen.

Throughout his long career as lawyer, legislator, Cabinet member,

9 **Saint-Gaudens National Historic Site.** *The Golden Angel* is one of the sculptor's many works on display.

and presidential aspirant, he was renowned for his oratorical eloquence, powerful presence, and championship of national unity. For 40 years he was New England's most respected and influential spokesman, serving first as a representative for New Hampshire and then as a senator for Massachusetts. Webster, who died in 1852, was elected to the Senate Hall of Fame in 1957.

His birthplace, a small single-story building of dark gray clapboard with cedar shingles, is an essay on simplicity. The two-room interior is simple in the extreme, with wide-board floors, a brick fireplace, a bench, and a table. The house, in its modesty, is in telling contrast to the eminence that Daniel Webster later achieved.

The home serves as a snapshot of frontier life in the 1780s.

▶ Open weekends and holidays during summer. Admission charged.

www.nhstateparks.com/danielwebster.html
(603) 934-5057

8 **Castle in the Clouds.** Lucknow, the early 20th-century dream house built by shoe magnate Thomas Plant, overlooks island-studded Lake Winnipesaukee.

11 Canterbury Shaker Village

288 Shaker Rd., Canterbury

"Put your hands to work and hearts to God" was the essence of the Shaking Quakers way of life for 200 years, and the results of that philosophy are on display at this preserved community about a 20-minute drive north of Concord.

Visitors can take guided or self-guiding tours through 25 of the restored original 100 wood-frame buildings. The structures sit in austere relief on a hilltop surrounded by open fields and ponds. Nature trails through the rolling countryside lead to remains of old mills and dam sites.

Founded in 1792, the community had 300 people at its peak in the 1850s, living, working, and practicing celibacy and equality of the sexes. Shakers relinquished private property for the welfare of all, and in their utopian view of heaven on Earth, they worshipped, farmed, manufactured medicines, and created spare but finely made furniture and crafts.

Women came to the Sisters Shop for confessions and counsel. That is also where they perfected their needlecraft, called "fancy work," which was much in demand in the outside world.

The community creamery produced ice cream and butter for the village from its Guernsey cattle, and today there is a restaurant on site that serves the traditional food. Skilled craftspeople offer demonstrations in such arts as oval box making, broom making, and spinning and weaving.

▶ Open daily May–Oct., weekends only in Apr., Nov., and Dec. Admission charged.

www.shakers.org
(603) 783-9511

 Franklin Pierce Homestead. Outside and indoors, the elegant Pierce family home reflects the affluence of Franklin Pierce and his father, Benjamin, the builder of the house.

12 Franklin Pierce Homestead

Rte. 31N, Hillsborough

This white clapboard Georgian-style mansion was completed in 1804 by Benjamin Pierce, twice governor of New Hampshire, from 1827-1828 and from 1829-1830. That same year saw the birth of a son, Franklin, who later became the 14th president of the United States.

The Pierces were a sociable family, and many great men of the time, including Daniel Webster, visited them during Franklin's youth. Handsome, intelligent, and well liked, Franklin rose quickly in politics and left home in 1833 to serve as a Democratic congressman in Washington, D.C.; 20 years later he was inaugurated president.

Pierce's presidency was not a terribly memorable one; indeed, he is remembered today as the "Forgotten President." Unable to deal effectively with the issue of slavery, he lost his party's support and retired from politics in 1857.

The interior of the homestead at Hillsborough has been largely restored to its original appearance.

Of special interest is the elegant ballroom on the second floor, with hand-stenciled walls. Among the antique items in the barn is Franklin Pierce's fine old horse-drawn sleigh, decorated with painted flowers. The homestead is managed by the Hillsborough Historical Society.

▶ Open daily July–Aug.; open weekends late May–June, Sept.–mid-Oct. Admission charged.

www.historic-hillsborough-nh.org
(603) 478-3165

13 Pawtuckaway State Park

128 Mountain Rd., Nottingham

A rolling road through this varied park—5,500 acres of unspoiled nature—takes you to picnic grounds, a beach, and campsites on Pawtuckaway Lake. At the boundary of the park is Mount Pawtuckaway, with its granite cliffs.

The woodland here, primarily composed of oak, white pine, and birch, is especially interesting for the many large glacially deposited boulders that are scattered

throughout the area. The shores of the lake are also strewn with boulders.

Fishermen come for the bass and pickerel, while birders look for the blue herons, eagles, and Canada geese. In winter only the parking area is plowed. There are trails for cross-country skiing, snowshoeing, and snowmobiling.

▶ Open daily Memorial Day-Columbus Day and accessible for some winter activities; camping available mid-May-mid-Oct. Admission charged.

www.nhstateparks.com/paw.html
(603) 895-3031

14 Strawbery Banke Museum

14 Hancock St., Portsmouth

Sailing up the Piscataqua River in 1630, Capt. Walter Neal and his band of Englishmen spotted the wild strawberries ablaze on the western bank and decided it worthy enough to call home.

A London company had sent the men to develop a colony for trade, and with the wives' arrival, the community began to prosper. The name was changed from Strawbery Banke to Portsmouth because, it was said, "We are at the river's mouth, and our port is as good as any in the land."

Walk through centuries of this city's evolution in the restored homes and exhibit buildings of the waterfront neighborhood's historical museum, helped along by role players and regular activities.

Once a bustling port with sleek clipper ships built in its shipyards, the city has a rich history populated by sea captains, merchants, shopkeepers, revolutionaries, and waves of European immigrants. You will meet the children of the

Puddle Dock, playing ring toss and Jacob's ladder, as well as historical figures like Paul Revere and Daniel Webster. Jefferson Street's Herb Garden displays an assortment of remedies: angelica and flax, always dependable when warding off a witch; borage for courage; basil to repel flies; and Johnny-jump-ups, a one-time staple in love potions.

▶ Open daily May-Oct.; weekends only in Nov.; Mon.-Fri. in Dec. Closed major winter holidays. Admission charged.

www.strawberybanke.org
(603) 433-1100

---

15 ▶ **Currier Museum of Art**

150 Ash St., Manchester
A world-class collection of American, European, modern, and decorative works of art is housed in this 30,000-square-foot museum. Among the more than 11,000 creations on display are a 13th-century medieval tapestry, Impressionist-era paintings, and a gallery dedicated especially to New Hampshire artists, many with interpretive texts.

Also open to the public is the Zimmerman House. Designed by Frank Lloyd Wright and complete with its original furnishings, this "total work of art" is the only home Wright designed in New England that is open to visitors.

▶ Open daily except Tues.
Admission charged.

www.currier.org
(603) 669-6144

---

16 ▶ **Rhododendron State Park**

Rte. 119 W, Fitzwilliam
In the 2,700 rolling acres of this park is a 16-acre stand of

Rhododendron catawbiense and *Rhododendron maximum.* The stand of *R. maximum* is the largest to be found at such a northerly latitude. The shrubs, blooming in July, create a flowering canopy that runs as high as 15 feet.

The park's genesis dates to 1902, when Mary Lee Ware bought the land to preserve the rhododendrons from a proposed lumbering operation. The next year, she gave the land to the Appalachian Mountain Club, which donated it in turn to the state in 1946.

The rhododendron trail is easily walked in about an hour, and even when the shrubs are not in flower, it is a very pleasant excursion. Most of the woodland is open, and the higher parts of the trail offer an excellent overview of the carpet of rhododendrons.

Just off the path leading to the picnic area is the Wildflower Trail, where an interesting selection of wild plants has been planted and labeled. The Little Monadnock Mountain Trail also branches off this park; its one-mile hike offers a view of Mount Monadnock.

▶ Open mid-May-early Nov.
Admission charged.

www.nhparks.state.nh.us
(603) 532-8862

14 ▶ **Strawbery Banke Museum.** This 10-acre site is a living museum of New England architecture, gardens, and crafts. More than 40 structures line its paths.

seasonal events

APRIL
• 5 Colleges Book Sale—Lebanon *(35,000 gently used books, CDs, DVDs, for sale, sponsored by Wellesley, Mt. Holyoke, Simmons, Smith, and Vassar colleges)*

MAY
• Wildquack River Festival—Jackson *(rubber-duck race on the Wildcat River)*

JUNE
• A Taste of the North Country Festival—Littleton *(cooking demos, rides, fireworks, food from local restaurants)*
• Lupine Festival—Franconia Notch *(walking tours, wagon rides, arts and crafts, live music, photography contest)*

JULY
• Hopkins Center Big Apple Circus Show—Hanover

AUGUST
• Umbagog Wildlife Festival—Errol *(scavenger hunt, guided nature walks, wildlife photo contest, live music, crafts)*
• North Country Moose Festival—Pittsburg *(moose parade, hot-air balloon rides, auto show, moose calling contest, street fair)*
• Craftsmen's Fair—Newbury *(arts and crafts, demonstrations and workshops, sculpture, live music and storytelling, exhibits)*

SEPTEMBER
• Newmarket Heritage Festival—Newmarket *(presentations of multicultural music and dance, children's activities, boat tours, kayaking)*
• Winchester Pickle Festival—Winchester *(fair, parade, music)*
• Harvest Day—Canterbury *(games, storytelling, farm stands, animals, lectures)*

OCTOBER
• Milford Great Pumpkin Festival—Milford *(haunted trail, live music, pumpkin catapult, farmers market, walking tour, crafts)*

www.visitnh.gov

New Jersey

If you think "turnpike" when you hear "Jersey," it's time to seek out the many surprises to be found off that well-beaten path.

The Wetlands Institute. This non-profit was founded by the director of the World Wildlife Fund in 1972 to promote the appreciation of coastal ecosystems (see page 229).

New Jersey's natural resources made it an early leader in industry, as evidenced by the ironworks at Batsto, the glassworks at Wheaton, and the Delaware and Raritan Canal. Yet in a state associated with factories lies a wealth of wildernesses and historic sites to explore. It was here that George Washington made his dramatic escape from the British, was frustrated by a near victory at the Monmouth Battlefield, and saw his troops endure a bitter winter near Morristown.

Farming like that at the Howell Living History Farm produced the bountiful harvests that earned New Jersey the Garden State moniker, and efforts to protect nature and wildlife include a wetlands preserve/educational center, a much-visited but undeveloped barrier island off the coast, and a wildlife refuge named for a congressman who worked diligently to protect the natural environment.

visit ➡ **offthebeatenpathtrips.com**

1 Delaware Water Gap National Recreation Area

Exit 1 off of I-80

Winding through a deep, narrow rent in the Kittatinny Mountains, the Delaware River creates a vista that draws thousands of tourists annually. But just north of the water gap lies a seldom-visited recreation area of unspoiled beauty.

Flanking the Delaware River for some 35 miles as it flows between the Kittatinny Ridge in New Jersey and the Pocono Mountains in Pennsylvania, the largely wooded hills and vales around the Kittatinny Point visitors center include ponds, brooks, gorges, waterfalls, swimming beaches, and a variety of wildlife.

A blacktop road traverses the length of the recreation area on the New Jersey side, overlooking the river for part of its length. Heading north, the narrow lane threads through the fern-carpeted Worthington State Forest. The rural peace and quiet and lack of traffic hearken to earlier times.

Roadside trails lead to cool glens, swift brooks, and scenic points along the Delaware River, where on summer weekends several hundred canoes may be seen gliding downstream.

An ideal and well-marked picnic spot is found at Watergate, where the trees open on a large rolling meadow bordered on one

1 **Delaware Water Gap National Recreation Area.** Waterfall buffs are drawn to the water gap by the likes of Factory Falls, seen here on a fine autumn day.

side by a pond and on the other side by a brook shaded by trees. In summer the air is heady with the scent of mown grass drying in the sun; birds sing, and the brook ripples musically.

Maps and trail guides are available at the Kittatinny Point center.

▶ Park open year-round; Kittatinny Point visitors center open daily Memorial Day–Labor Day, then weekends through mid-Oct. Admission charged.

www.nps.gov/dewa
(908) 496-4458

2 Space Farms Zoo & Museum

218 Rte. 519, Sussex

Despite its name, you won't find spacecraft or alien creatures at Space Farms. Founded in 1927 by Ralph Space, this family-run attraction features one of the largest private collections of wild animals in the United States and an eclectic museum of curiosities and artifacts from rural America.

Zoo habitats offer thrilling close-up views of a remarkable variety of animals, including badgers, bears, bobcats, hyena, foxes, jaguars, lemurs, lions,

2 **Space Farms Zoo.** Left: Jersey is a long way from Australia, but Down Under's best-known marsupials make themselves at home at this family-run zoo. Right: Generations of Atlas African lions have been born and raised here.

tigers, wild ponies, and wolves. Buy a bag of animal crackers and you can hand-feed bison, deer, elk, goats, and llama. Be sure to peek into the snake exhibits to see hundreds of slithering serpents, including a 225-pound python!

Eleven museum buildings showcase a wide-ranging collection of Americana, including antique cars, farm equipment, dolls and toys, firearms, and Native American artifacts. Standouts include a complete miniature circus and a mid-1800s Prairie Schooner that a local pioneering family used on a 4,000-mile journey to Kansas.

▶ Open daily mid-Apr.–late Oct. Admission charged.

www.spacefarms.com
(973) 875-5800

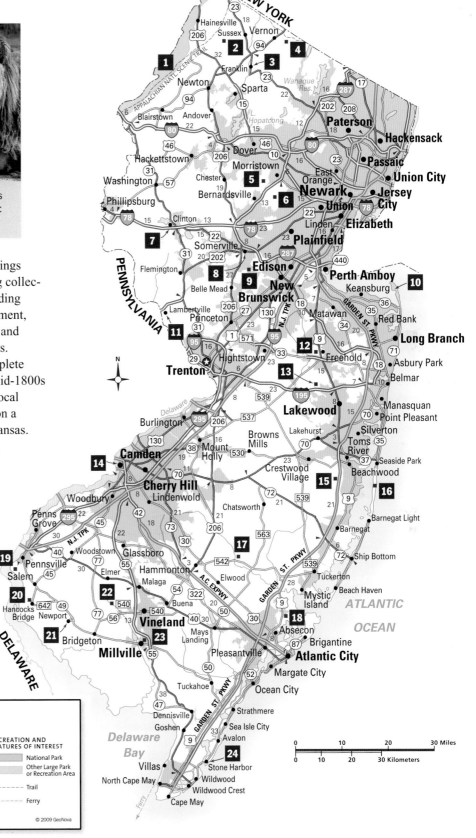

Legend

| | NUMBERED ATTRACTIONS (Described in text) |

CONTROLLED ACCESS HIGHWAYS
Free
Toll
Under Construction

OTHER HIGHWAYS
Primary Highway
Secondary Highway

HIGHWAY MARKERS
Interstate Route
U.S. Route
State Route
Distances along Major Highways (in miles)

CITIES AND TOWNS
National Capital
State Capital
Cities, Towns, and Populated Places Type size indicates relative importance
Urban Area

RECREATION AND FEATURES OF INTEREST
National Park
Other Large Park or Recreation Area
Trail
Ferry

© 2009 GeoNova

NEW JERSEY

3 Franklin Mineral Museum

32 Evans St., Franklin

Franklin is known as the fluorescent mineral capital of the world. From 1850 to 1954, the area was famous for its zinc mines. Within these rich zinc deposits an astounding number of minerals were discovered, including many not found anywhere else in the world. Franklin's Mine Hill produced a half billion dollars' worth of zinc, iron, and manganese over a period of 106 years.

The Franklin Mineral Museum is dedicated to preserving this fascinating history with exhibits on mineral science, geology, and local mining history. With a total of 6,317 specimens on display, including over 5,000 minerals, the museum is home to the largest, most comprehensive public display of minerals in the world. In addition, visitors can also view fossils, petrified wood, dinosaur footprints, and Native American artifacts.

The museum's most popular attraction is its fluorescent room, a dazzling 33-foot-long display of brilliantly colored fluorescent minerals. In addition, a life-size mine replica, constructed with timber, rails, and equipment from area mines, depicts the methods used to mine zinc ore.

Visitors inspired by the glowing nuggets inside can try their luck at one of three collecting areas on the property. In fact, amateur rockhounds scouring these mineral dumps are still discovering rare specimens!

▶ Open weekends in Mar.; daily Apr.–Nov. Admission charged.

www.franklinmineralmuseum.com
(973) 827-3481

4 Wawayanda State Park

885 Warwick Tpke., Hewitt

Spaciousness and excellent upkeep are the immediate impressions of this fine park, partly because of the manicured entrance grounds and the two miles of excellent road rolling from the park headquarters to the parking lot on Lake Wawayanda.

The 250-acre lake offers several islands, a swimming area with a sandy beach, and a shoreline edged with forests, coves, and cliffs. Picnic tables are located in the wooded areas nearby.

A short walk from the beach is a marina where canoes, rowboats, and live bait are available. Several species of trout and bass are caught in the lake. Ice fishing is a popular sport in winter.

More than 40 miles of hiking trails lead to small ponds, a swamp, and scenic overlooks. The park is an excellent place for riding, and horses are available from stables nearby. Bird-watching is another favorite recreation; lucky visitors might glimpse the endangered red-shouldered hawk.

A wide variety of topography is the signature here, from mountains to ravines to swamps to forests. Twenty miles of the Appalachian Trail traverses many of those settings. Camping (but no water) is available at three sites.

▶ Open year-round. Parking fee Memorial Day-Labor Day.

www.state.nj.us/dep/parksandforests/
parks/wawayanda
(973) 853-4462

5 Morristown National Historical Park

30 Washington Pl., Morristown

With the approach of winter in 1779, Gen. George Washington needed an encampment for the Continental Army from which he could keep close watch on the British in New York City.

Morristown was a strategic location, and Mrs. Jacob Ford, whose husband had died during one of the early campaigns, offered the use of her home and surrounding land.

The elegant Georgian-style frame mansion is furnished approximately as it was when it served as Washington's headquarters. Walking through the rooms, you can visualize the activity here, with George Washington and wife, Martha, Mrs. Ford and her four children, many servants and officers, and visitors such as the Marquis de Lafayette.

Guided tours of the house begin at the headquarters museum. There is also a film that attempts to capture the brutal conditions at the Jockey Hollow camp, where 10,000 ill-clad, starving soldiers endured one of the worst winters of the century.

Although it was a long ride by horse from headquarters, Jockey Hollow was chosen for the encampment because it had sufficient timber for firewood and the construction of nearly 1,200 huts. Today it is a serene 1,800-acre park populated with woodlands, brooks, and meadows.

From the entrance a pleasant road passes several reconstructed cabins and the parade ground. The park's 27 miles of trails are used for hiking, horseback riding, and cross-country skiing. Behind the Jockey Hollow visitors center are open fields, an old apple orchard,

3 ▶ **Franklin Mineral Museum.** Visitors can search through mine tailings for minerals at the 3.5-acre Buckwheat Dump, one of three collecting areas at the museum.

did you know

There are more mineral species found in Franklin than any other place on Earth. In fact, the 357 mineral species found here represent nearly a tenth of all presently known species. Some species discovered in Franklin are found nowhere else.

a re-creation of an 18th-century garden, and the sturdy Wick farm-house, where Washington aide Gen. Arthur St. Clair was head-quartered to watch over the camp.

Along with the tours and information available from the visitors centers, there are frequent special events and seminars that focus on the fascinating history here. The park is often heavily visited on spring and fall weekends and on Washington's birthday in late February.

▶ Open year-round except holidays. Admission charged.

www.nps.gov/morr
(973) 539-2016

6 Great Swamp National Wildlife Refuge

241 Pleasant Plains Rd., Basking Ridge
Established in 1960, the refuge has 7,800 acres of cattail marshes, grassland, and swamp woodlands; most of it has been designated a wilderness area, with more than 240 species of birds, both migratory and resident, that frequent the area.

The headquarters of the refuge supplies trail maps and brochures that list the wildflowers, mammals, birds, and reptiles found here season by season. Don't miss the Wildlife Observation Center, where a boardwalk crosses a small swamp to three wildlife observation blinds.

The swamp, marvelously beautiful, is covered by bright duckweed sprinkled in May with tiny yellow flowers and clumps of delicate purple iris. Here and there are open spots where turtles can be seen napping in the murky water. Peepholes in the blind offer an overlook of a larger swamp filled

5 **Morristown National Historical Park.** Smaller than the Ford Mansion where George Washington stayed, humble Wick House served as the quarters of Maj. Joseph Bloomfield of the Third New Jersey Regiment during the winter of 1776–1777.

with pond lilies. The croaks and peeps of frogs and calls of birds are the only sounds in this mysterious and fascinating place.

The best viewing times are early morning and late afternoon. Visitors should cover their arms and legs completely to protect them from this favorite habitat of mosquitoes and ticks.

▶ Open year-round.

http://greatswamp.fws.gov
(973) 425-1222

7 The Red Mill Museum Village

56 Main St., Clinton
The buildings comprising this picturesque 10-acre site are remindful of the life, work, and customs in the area from the early 1800s to the early 1900s.

The centerpiece is the old Red Mill on Spruce Run. Local enterprises such as this were indispensable in the days when transportation was slow and uncertain. Mills would grind

whatever might be profitable at the time. The Red Mill, which dates to about 1810, is a prime example of this versatility. The structure started as a woolen mill, and over the years it ground flaxseed (to make linseed oil), grains, plaster, and graphite. It even produced electricity and pumped water for the town.

Today it serves as a museum. On the top floor is a working model of a typical mill. The other three floors are devoted to room settings of tools and equipment, fixtures and furnishings, toys, and decorative objects illustrating the early-day life in this area.

Other attractions along Spruce Run are an old schoolhouse, a blacksmith shop, a general store and post office, a log cabin, and the stone crusher and kilns used to process limestone quarried from the cliffs that parallel the river.

▶ Open Tues.–Sun. Apr.–mid-Oct. Admission charged.

www.theredmill.org
(908) 735-4101

8 Wallace House

71 Somerset St., Somerville
The months Gen. George Washington spent in this house, from December 1778 to June 1779, must have been among the most pleasant in his years of service to the Continental Army.

He had endured the hardships and frustrations of the previous winter with his ill-equipped army at Valley Forge. Then at the Battle of Monmouth in June 1778, his troops had successfully harried the British as they retreated from Philadelphia (see site No. 12 for more). Now with the enemy engaged to the North and in the South and his own troops well established in the nearby Watchung Mountains, Washington was able to savor the mild winter weather and enjoy the chance to entertain in the finest house in the vicinity.

The eight-room house was built in the Georgian style for John Wallace, a Philadelphia merchant, but shortly after the Wallaces took residence, arrangements were made for its use as Washington's headquarters. On June 3, 1779, the army moved northward to the Hudson River, and life returned to normal for the Wallaces.

In 1897 the Revolutionary Memorial Society bought the place and in 1946 gave it to the state. The house has remained almost unchanged since the 18th century. It is furnished in a manner appropriate for a wealthy family of the era. The guided tours of the house provide an insight into the life and style of the times.

▶ Open Wed.–Sun. year-round.

www.state.nj.us/dep/parksandforests
(908) 725-1015

9 ▶ Delaware and Raritan Canal State Park

145 Mapleton Rd., Princeton
As early as 1676, William Penn is said to have considered building an inland waterway across the narrow "waist" of New Jersey to expedite the trip from Philadelphia to New York. More than 150 years were to pass, however, before work began on a canal connecting the Delaware River north of Bordentown and the Raritan River at New Brunswick.

This 44-mile waterway (7 feet deep and 75 feet wide) required 14 locks to complete its course. The water came from a feeder canal 22 miles farther up the Delaware. Largely dug by hand by Irish immigrants, these giant trenches exacted a high price: Scores of workers housed in labor camps died of cholera.

By way of the canal, which opened in the spring of 1834, the trip from Bordentown to New Brunswick took the better part of two days. The waterway remained in operation for nearly 100 years.

Since 1974 large sections of the canal have been set aside as a unique state park, which varies with its changing surroundings. With its 19-cent bridges, bridge-tender houses, cobblestone spillways, and stone-arched culverts the canal is a mecca for history lovers. Its trails are enjoyed by hikers, cyclists, horseback riders, and cross-country skiers.

Canoes can be rented near Bull's Island and at several towns along the canal, including Titusville, Kingston, and Griggstown.

▶ Open year-round. Camping only on Bull's Island.

www.state.nj.us/dep/parksandforests
(609) 924-5705

10 ▶ Sandy Hook Unit, Gateway National Recreation Area

Hartshone Dr., Highlands
For more than 200 years this sandspit in lower New York Bay has been identified with military defense and navigation. In Colonial times the shallows here were known as a graveyard for ships, and in 1764 a lighthouse was constructed to guide sailors through this thriving channel.

During the American Revolution the lighthouse was a crucial navigation tool for the British, who protected it from numerous attacks by the Continental rebels. Today the lighthouse, which was renovated in 2000, is part of the Sandy Hook Unit of the Gateway National Recreation Area, a unique park that covers portions of three New York City boroughs and this section of land in northern New Jersey.

Now maintained by the Coast Guard, this is the oldest working lighthouse in the country. Because ocean currents have deposited sand at the end of the peninsula, the octagonal structure is today about 1½ miles back from the edge of the point.

Of the many military defense systems that have been installed on the peninsula, the most colorful is Fort Hancock, which was built in the late 1800s and kept in use until the 1970s, when the last of the Nike missiles poised here were removed. You can explore the officers' houses and other buildings of this old army town. Also worth seeing are the 20-inch Rodman gun (1869) and the massive concrete mortar battery (1894).

But Sandy Hook has much more to offer. Its miles of ocean beach, dunes, and salt marsh invite exploration by pleasure seekers and nature lovers. Trails lead through the dunes and to a unique holly forest on the bay side. The best times to visit are summer weekdays and the off-season months, when crowds are small.

▶ Open year-round. Admission charged.

www.nps.gov/gate
(732) 872-5970

9 ▶ **Delaware and Raritan Canal State Park.** Now a National Recreational Trail, the canal and towpath lure canoers, fishers, joggers, bikers, and even horseback riders.

11 ▶ Howell Living History Farm

70 Woodens Ln., Lambertville
A visit to Howell Farm is a step back in time. Life passes on this 130-acre crop-and-livestock farm much as it did at the turn of the century. Farmhands in suspenders still plow, plant, and harvest using tools and techniques circa 1900.

A self-guiding tour takes visitors to 20 areas of interest, including an 1809 farmhouse, a chicken house, a hog shed, a sheep barn, an icehouse, and an 1840s barn.

Visitors are encouraged to lend a hand with typical farm chores such as milking cows, canning tomatoes, mixing feed, and collecting eggs. Saturdays feature events planned around the seasonal activities of the farm. During the corn harvest you can ride to the field in a horse-drawn wagon, help shuck and pick corn, return to the barnyard to help grind and sift cornmeal, and then sample homemade cornbread. Other events have included maple sugaring, ice harvesting, sheep shearing, honey harvesting, butter churning, hog slopping, evening barn dances, and old-time baseball games.

▶ Open Tues.-Sat. Feb.-Mar.; Tues.-Sun. Apr.-Nov. Donations encouraged. Fee for children's crafts.

www.howellfarm.org
(609) 737-3299

12 ▶ Monmouth Battlefield State Park

12 miles east of Exit 8 off NJ Tpke. on Rte. 33, Manalapan
The battle here on June 28, 1778, enhanced the morale of the Continental Army: For the first time, the Colonials engaged the British in open-field combat and stood them off.

Battleship *New Jersey*. Visitors to the U.S. Navy's largest and most decorated battleship, in service from 1942–1991, can tour everything from the captain's cabin and the crew mess to the post office and medical and dental facilities.

14 ▶ Battleship *New Jersey*

62 Battleship Pl., Camden
In service from 1942–1991, the Iowa-class battleship USS *New Jersey* saw action in WW2, Korea, Vietnam, and the Persian Gulf. Surviving kamikaze attacks and violent typhoons, the *Big J*, as it came to be called, is the largest and most decorated battleship in U.S. naval history. Now a floating museum, the battleship gives visitors the opportunity to learn about the ship's history and experience what life was like for a battleship sailor.

Self-guiding and volunteer-led tours take visitors to the many areas open to the public, including the bridge, the captain's cabin, berthing areas, the crew's mess, the Combat Engagement Center, the main gun turrets, and more. Visitors can sit in Admiral "Bull" Halsey's chair from which he commanded the U.S. Third Fleet, squeeze into sleeping bunks, and climb into one of the massive 16-inch gun turrets. Exhibits of artifacts from the ship's past and narratives from former crew members complete this memorable experience.

▶ Open Fri.–Mon. Jan.–Feb.; daily Mar.–Dec.; closed major holidays. Admission charged.

www.battleshipnewjersey.org
(866) 877-6262; (856) 966-1652

did you know ?

Iowa-class battleships, such as the Battleship *New Jersey*, were the largest U.S. battleships ever built—longer than three football fields and 11 stories high. To this day they are the fastest battleships ever launched.

Historians, however, consider the Battle of Monmouth a missed opportunity for a stunning American victory. At a critical point in the conflict, Gen. Charles Lee retreated instead of attacking as ordered, infuriating his commander, Gen. George Washington. The British, after a day of fighting, were able to retreat under cover of darkness and safely make their way north. Lee was court-martialed and found guilty of disobedience and misbehavior.

The visitors center displays artifacts recovered from the field and has a diorama that shows the sequence of the battle. The center also provides information on the historic Craig House, which can be reached by car or trails in the park.

A re-enactment of the battle takes place each year on the week-end closest to its anniversary. And if you can't make it for the summer fun, the park also offers winter activities.

▶ Open year-round.

www.state.nj.us/dep/parksandforests
(732) 462-9616

---

13 ▶ Turkey Swamp Park

200 Georgia Rd., Freehold
Long ago the nearby town of Adelphia was called Turkey, and the thickly forested, swampy lands and bogs surrounding it were known as Turkey Swamp. The name was adopted by this now roughly 2,100-acre park.

Several self-guiding nature trails around the 17-acre lake and bogs lead through the woodlands of oak and pitch pine, with their undergrowth of blueberry and pepperbush. The Fit-Trail, with 20 exercise stops along the 1¼-mile route, circles the entire park.

The park features a shelter—open in summer and enclosed and heated in winter—with a fireplace, picnic tables, and a kitchen. Family campgrounds are located in the woodlands; wilderness campgrounds in a remote section may be reserved by groups.

Canoes, rowboats, and paddleboats are available for rent, and there are playgrounds, picnic groves with grills, and fields for soccer and other sports.

▶ Open year-round; camping Apr.–Nov. Fees for camping and special facilities.

www.monmouthcountyparks.com
(732) 462-7286

15 ▶ Double Trouble State Park

Pinewald-Keswick Rd., Berkeley
This wilderness of woods and marsh in the Pine Barrens is a nature lover's delight at all times of the year, and on a gray day it has a misty, almost otherworldly aura that is especially appealing.

Originally a cranberry farm and packing plant the park's history actually goes back to the late 18th century, when a sawmill was built and a dam constructed for water power.

According to local lore, muskrats repeatedly gnawed through the dam, causing leaks that were announced with a cry of "Here's trouble" and quickly repaired. One day the owner found two gaps in the dam and shouted to his men: "Here's double trouble!" The park's name, at least, was born.

Then in the late 19th century, faced with a dwindling supply of timber, people in the area began to grow cranberries to augment their incomes. The land was sold to the state in 1965, but the sawmill and the cranberry-operation are still open for demonstrations.

Within the park's more than 8,000 acres are a general store, cranberry-packing house, one-room schoolhouse, migrants' cottage, and other early-day buildings, some of which are periodically being restored.

From the cranberry-processing plant a self-guiding nature trail about 1¼ miles long crosses Cedar Creek, winds around the bogs, and ends at the sawmill. The air is aromatic with cedar, and in season rhododendron, mountain laurel, sweet bay, and fragrant honeysuckle bloom beneath sassafras trees, pitch pines, and red maples. Plant-lovers might also find in this moist environment the insect-eating sundew.

Great blue herons, egrets, red-tailed hawks, and quails are seen here. Fishermen can expect pickerel and catfish. Cedar Creek is very popular with canoeists, and canoes can be rented nearby. The park is especially enjoyable in springtime and in autumn. Be sure to bring insect repellent in the summer.

▶ Open year-round.

www.state.nj.us/dep/parksandforests
(732) 341-6662

16 ▶ **Island Beach State Park.** This inviting park of more than 3,000 acres protects one of the few remaining undeveloped barrier islands on the North Atlantic coast.

17 ▶ **Wharton State Forest.** Fourteen of the 32 rooms in the Italianate-style Batsto Mansion, home to generations of ironmasters, are open to the public for tours.

16 ▶ Island Beach State Park

S. Central Ave., Seaside Park
On leaving New Jersey's heavily developed coast, you will find Island Beach State Park a pleasant surprise, with its 10 miles of undeveloped seashore.

The southern end of a long barrier beach, this area became an island in 1750, when raging seas broke through the narrow bar of land at Seaside Heights. The inlet was open until 1812, when another storm closed it.

In the 1950s, to preserve the fragile environment of dunes and grasses found here, the state purchased 2,694 acres for a park with a botanical preserve, a recreation zone, and a wildlife sanctuary; today the park boasts more than 3,000 acres. The nature center at the north end of the park offers guided walks and has exhibits of the shells, butterflies, and primitive maritime vegetation found all around the island.

A paved road lined with dunes and beach heather leads from the park entrance to the recreation zone (a marvelous stretch of white, sandy ocean beach) and continues to the wildlife sanctuary, which is also open to visitors. At the end of the road, the Barnegat Lighthouse can be seen 1½ miles in the distance.

The park is especially lovely in autumn, and the good weather can extend until Thanksgiving. The water stays warm, the beaches are empty of people but filled with shells, swarms of monarch butterflies cling to the branches of goldenrod, and the southbound birds are on the wing.

▶ Open year-round. Parking fee.

www.state.nj.us/dep/parksandforests
(732) 793-0506

17 ▶ Wharton State Forest

31 Batsto Rd., Hammonton
In this forest of more than 120,000

acres are the Batsto and Mullica rivers, Atsion Lake, several streams, nature trails, a long hiking trail, and a number of campgrounds.

The combination of iron ore from local bogs, plentiful forests, and waterways for transportation led to the growth of many small iron-manufacturing centers in southern New Jersey in the 18th century. These ironworks, including Batsto, made pig iron, water pipes, stoves, and firebacks. During the Revolutionary War and the War of 1812, Batsto produced munitions, camp kettles, and iron fastenings and fittings for artillery caissons, wagons, and ships.

When coal was discovered in Pennsylvania, factories with charcoal-burning furnaces found they could not compete. Batsto's ironworks closed in 1855, replaced by a glassmaking center that was active until 1867. Batsto would have disappeared, as did similar villages in the area, had it not been for Philadelphia industrialist Joseph Wharton, who bought the property in 1876 and redeveloped it into his "gentleman's farm."

The more than 30 buildings preserved here today include the mansion, general store, post office, sawmill, blacksmith shop, gristmill, and workers' houses.

The forest is mostly pines with cedar and mixed hardwoods. A nature area adjoins the village, and a section of the Batona Wilderness Trail is popular with hikers. Batsto and all of Wharton State Forest are part of the Pinelands National Reserve.

The visitors center features an exhibit on the history of Batsto and the New Jersey Pine Barrens, an auditorium for interpretive programs, and a museum store.

▶ Open year-round. Parking fee charged Memorial Day–Labor Day, on weekends at the village, and daily at the lake.

www.state.nj.us/dep/parksandforests
(609) 561-0024 Batsto Office
(609) 268-0444 Atsion Office

18 ▶ Edwin B. Forsythe National Wildlife Refuge

Great Creek Rd., Oceanville
Among the most effective conservationists are those who serve in Congress—where environmental

Birds are one of the main draws, since the refuge is a major stop on the Atlantic Flyway. The peak of northbound migration is mid-Mar.–mid-Nov. During the summer warblers, shorebirds, and wading birds are abundant. The southbound migration is from mid-Aug.–mid-Nov., with spectacular concentrations of ducks, geese, and brant in early November.

At the visitors center you can get a list of the more than 300 species observed here. Leaflets

19 ▶ Fort Mott State Park. At Battery Gregg, built at the fort in the 1890s, gunners guarded the underwater minefield laid at the entrance to the Delaware River.

concerns can be translated into law. It's fitting that one man who served that cause is remembered here.

The late congressman Edwin B. Forsythe worked diligently to protect the natural environment, and in 1984 the already established Brigantine and Barnegat Wildlife refuges were united and renamed in his honor. The area now includes more than 47,000 acres of bays, channels, salt marshes, barrier beaches, dunes, upland fields, woodlands, and abundant wildlife.

are also available for an eight-mile self-guiding auto tour; the suggested stops along the way include observation towers, a pool covered with water lilies, and other areas, where bald eagles, ospreys, and wood ducks may be seen.

For hikers the Akers Woodland Trail leads through a typical coastal woodland, while the Leeds Eco-Trail penetrates an estuarine environment where incoming tides mix with freshwater streams flowing seaward.

▶ Open year-round.

forsythe.fws.gov
(609) 652-1665

19 ▶ Fort Mott State Park

454 Fort Mott Rd., Pennsville
The strategic importance of the Delaware River was recognized as early as 1838, when the federal government purchased land here at Finns Point.

The first guns were installed in 1878. In 1895 strong American sympathy for the Cuban revolt against Spain led to the likelihood of a U.S. war with Spain. As a precaution, naval defense guns were placed here and Fort Mott was constructed. The fort never saw any action, because the brief conflict with Spain was confined to Cuba.

The garrison was gradually reduced and the guns removed; in 1951 the abandoned fort became a state park, where the plotting rooms, the ammunition and powder magazines, and the range-finder towers can still be seen.

But the attraction today is the peaceful setting in which one can savor the expanse of sky and see the oceangoing ships sailing the waters of the Delaware. In midstream on Pea Patch Island is Fort Delaware, the site of a Civil War prison camp (see Delaware site #5). In the national cemetery adjacent to the park is a memorial to Confederate soldiers and, in particular, to those prisoners who died at Fort Delaware. Another monument is dedicated to Union soldiers buried here.

▶ Open year-round.

www.state.nj.us/dep/parksandforests
(856) 935-3218

20 **Hancock House.** The brick design is one of many seen in area houses.

20 Hancock House

3 Front St., Hancock's Bridge
The Hancock House was built in 1734 by Judge William Hancock and his wife, Sarah, on land that had been in the Hancock family since 1675. The house was one of a number of handsome brick homes built around this time. Judge Hancock's home was attached to a simple structure erected a few years earlier.

The Hancock name has always been prominent here; the town of Hancock's Bridge was named for John Hancock, who helped the community grow by constructing a bridge across Aloes (now Alloway) Creek in 1708.

The exterior east and west walls of the two-story house show a decorative zigzag pattern made by using glazed blue and red clay bricks. The walls are a fine example of this patterned-end brickwork favored in this region. Near the top of the west wall the bricks form the initials WHS and the year 1734, which can be clearly seen. The interior has period furnishings.

During the Revolutionary War a tragic incident occurred in the house. About 30 Quakers, assigned to defend the drawbridge, were garrisoned here. The British had lost a battle at Quinton's Bridge on March 18, 1778, and were seeking revenge and a victory over the local militia.

Just before dawn three days later a force of 300 British troops and local Loyalists surprised the two sentries on duty at Hancock's Bridge and, without firing a shot, used their bayonets to massacre the guards and small garrison asleep in the house. Miraculously, some survived and their descendants come to pay their respects.

▶ Open Wed.–Sun. year-round.

www.state.nj.us/dep/parksandforests
(856) 935-4373

21 New Jersey Coastal Heritage Trail Route

From Perth Amboy south to Cape May and west along Delaware Bay to Delaware Memorial Bridge
Going to the shore takes on new meaning when you immerse yourself not just in surf, sun, and sand but in the natural and cultural heritage of the five coastal regions of New Jersey: Sandy Hook, Barnegat, Absecon, Cape May, and Delsea.

The nearly 300-mile Trail Route is meant for vehicular tourism, with markers along roadways indicating points of interest. Trail literature is available at local regional welcome centers.

You can find lighthouses, fishing villages, and cranberry bogs or learn about glassmaking. Eagles, ospreys, whales, and dolphins use the Jersey shore as a stopping-off point, as do other species for whom it is a seasonal refuge. Barrier islands, wetlands, tidal salt marshes, and dense maritime forests invite even closer inspection.

Visit the Nature Conservancy's Cape May Migratory Bird Refuge or explore the Pine Barrens at Double Trouble State Park (site #15) in the Barnegat Bay region. When you know what you're looking at, it makes the drive to the beach an event in itself.

▶ Open year-round.

www.nps.gov/neje
(856) 447-0103

22 Parvin State Park

701 Almond Rd., Pittsgrove
In this quiet retreat it is hard to imagine that it was once the site of a busy gristmill and sawmill. The Parvin family operated the mills, and the original millpond—created by damming Muddy Run—was given their name.

Although Parvin Lake and the smaller Thundergust Lake are major attractions, the eight miles of trails winding through the swamps, groves, thickets, and forest in this 1,952-acre preserve are of special interest to nature lovers. The woods include some 40 kinds of trees, 60 different shrubs, more than 200 flowering plants, and many ferns and mosses. Birders have spotted 123 species in the park, and deer, raccoons, squirrels, and other wildlife are all around.

The inviting picnic grounds and play areas on Thundergust Lake are sensibly separated. In summer a lifeguard is on duty at the swimming beach on Parvin Lake, boats and canoes are available for rent, and the fishing is considered worthy. This is a camper's delight as well, with 56 campsites and 15 cabins around the park.

▶ Open year-round. Admission charged Memorial Day–Labor Day.

www.state.nj.us/dep/parksandforests
(856) 358-8616

23 WheatonArts and Cultural Center

1501 Glasstown Rd., Millville
Southern New Jersey, with its abundant natural resources, including sand, soda ash, silica, wood, and excellent waterways, was the birthplace of the nation's glassmaking industry. America's first

22 **Parvin State Park.** Parvin Lake and its spillway were nonexistent until Muddy Run Creek was dammed. Today the lake is a magnet for anglers and boaters.

successful glassmaking factory was founded in 1739 by Caspar Wistar in Salem County. The country's oldest continually operated glass factory was located in Millville, and many of the country's foremost glass factories once operated in southern New Jersey.

The premier centerpiece of WheatonArts is one of the nation's first amphitheater-style hot-glass studios, where professional artists demonstrate a variety of glassmaking techniques.

The Museum of American Glass houses one of the world's most comprehensive collections of American glass—from the first glass bottles made in America to celebrated works by Dale Chihuly and other comtemporary artists.

 WheatonArts. Noted glass artists Dale Chihuly and Lino Tagliapietra crafted this unique vase.

The center also features artist demonstrations in its ceramic, woodcarving, and flameworking studios. (Flameworking uses a torch to melt glass for beads, marbles, and other items.) In addition, the Down Jersey Folklife Center preserves and

24 **The Wetlands Institute.** Visiting children can learn the basics of beach seining—casting fishing nets using a method that dates back to the ancient Phoenicians.

celebrates the many diverse cultural traditions of the area.

WheatonArts offers special exhibitions, workshops, performances, and several weekend festivals throughout the year.

▶ Open Tues.–Sun. Apr.–Dec.; Fri.–Sun. Jan.–Mar. Admission charged Apr.–Dec.

www.wheatonarts.org
(800) 998-4552

---

24 **The Wetlands Institute**
1075 Stone Harbor Blvd., Stone Harbor
The narrow strip of coastal wetlands that separates land from sea on southern New Jersey's Cape May Peninsula is a delight for bird-watchers and naturalists.

This people-friendly research center welcomes scientists, teachers, children, and families, and it is committed to preserving and encouraging understanding of the resources of the Atlantic Coast.

Species like the Louisiana heron and yellow-crowned and black-crowned night egrets find protection at the heronry, which is part of the 21-acre Stone Harbor

Bird Sanctuary. A mini-cam transmits live pictures of nesting osprey onto a television monitor in Marshview Hall for all to see.

The terrapin release program has won national attention: Terrapin babies, raised from eggs of mothers that have met an untimely death on the road, are re-introduced to the salt marsh. Horseshoe crabs, in residence here since before the dinosaurs, continue to lay billions of eggs, giving the migrating ruddy turnstones and red knots a solid meal before takeoff.

Three-hour kayaking tours of the coastal marsh ecosystem, salt marsh safaris, and Sunday morning bird walks can take you into a world full of surprises, such as a laughing gull from the world's largest colony or a glossy ibis picking its way out of the water on elegant, spindly legs. Many special events are held here throughout the year (see right).

▶ Open daily mid-May–mid-Oct.; Tues.–Sat. mid-Oct.–mid-May. Admission charged.

www.wetlandsinstitute.org
(609) 368-1211

seasonal events

FEBRUARY
• New Jersey Flower and Garden Show—Edison *(displays, marketplace, demonstrations, children's activities)*

MARCH
• Atlantique City—Atlantic City *(antiques, collectibles, appraisals, exhibits)*

MAY
• Jazz and Blues Festival—Red Bank *(dozens of concerts, arts and crafts, children's activities, food)*

• Shearing Festival—Valley Shephard Creamery, Long Valley *(shearing of 500 ewes, crafts, food, live music)*

JUNE
• New Jersey Seafood Festival—Belmar *(live entertainment, children's activities, arts and crafts)*

• Family Medieval and Fantasy Festival—Long Valley *(themed activities, demonstrations, live music, vendors)*

JULY
• New Jersey Festival of Ballooning—Readington *(mass balloon ascensions, concerts, fireworks, carnival)*

AUGUST
• Toms River Festival—Toms River *(pop music, fireworks, midway, food)*

SEPTEMBER
• Hoboken Italian Festival—Hoboken *(live entertainment, food, eating contests, procession, fireworks)*

• Cape May Food & Wine Festival—Cape May *(marketplace, tastings, seminars, culinary contests)*

• Wings 'n Water Wildlife Arts Festival—The Wetlands Institute, Stone Harbor *(folk music, carvers, crafts, guided walks)*

OCTOBER
• Festival of Fine Craft—Millville *(demonstrations, children's activities, live entertainment, food)*

• Cape May Wine Festival—Cape May *(wine tasting, food, crafts, entertainment)*

www.state.nj.us/travel

New Mexico

From its prehistory to the atomic age, ice caves to lava flows, arid deserts to snowcapped mountains—this is a land of incredible contrast.

Living Desert Zoo and Gardens State Park. The Chihuahuan Desert is the natural habitat for the kit fox, a nocturnal animal (see page 237).

In settings of superlative scenery is dramatic evidence of an ancient people who built intricate complexes, created communities connected by an extensive network of roads, and practiced sophisticated methods of agriculture.

Recent accomplishments, with untold implications for the future, are celebrated in museums dedicated to the atomic age and space exploration. The 19th century is recalled in a famous landform where pioneers literally left their mark, a historic army fort, a town that time forgot, and the mansion of a lucky miner.

Great sand dunes, sculpted monoliths, hiking trails and nature walks, a wildlife refuge, a treasure field for rockhounds, and a miniature world of carved wood further contribute to the contrast here.

visit ➤➤ **offthebeatenpathtrips.com**

1 Aztec Ruins National Monument

Ruins Rd., Aztec

Early explorers and scholars mistakenly believed these ruins had been built by the Aztecs in ancient times rather than by the ancestral Pueblo peoples that had actually inhabited the area. The centerpiece at Aztec Ruins is a 450-room structure built in the early 1100s, known today as West Ruin. In the central plaza of West Ruin lies the reconstructed great kiva, a circular semi-subterranean structure used for ceremonial purposes. In the surrounding fields are an elaborate complex of roads and buildings, including other kivas.

The first builders at the site emulated the building techniques and artistic traditions of the southern Chaco Canyon. Differences in masonry and architectural styles distinguish earlier constructions from later additions, which borrow from the northern Pueblo peoples of Mesa Verde.

An easy half-mile self-guiding trail leads through part of the ruins, allowing you to study the masonry and the interiors of the rooms. The ceilings here are original, and the green sandstone band running the length of the west wall is unique to this structure. The visitors center exhibits weaving, basketry, some fine pottery, and a 25-minute video with more background. The area

1 Aztec Ruins National Monument. Despite the name, it was the Pueblos who built a twelfth-century city on the edge of present-day Carson National Forest.

was named a World Heritage Site in 1987.

▶ Open daily year-round except holidays. Admission charged.

www.nps.gov/azru
(505) 334-6174

2 Chaco Culture National Historical Park

South of Nageezi

For anyone interested in architectural design or the history of Native Americans, Chaco Canyon is a place to stimulate the imagination. Evidence of a sophisticated culture existing here 800 to 1,100 years ago is overwhelming.

On a dozen major sites in the park, where ancestral Pueblo once lived and farmed, are the remains of their multistoried structures, believed to have been built as early as 850 and vacated by 1300. The most remarkable is Pueblo Bonito ("the beautiful village"), a stone

did you know

The Chacoan people did not just disappear. They migrated to join relatives along the Rio Grande, on the Hopi mesas, and around Zuni mountain. Their descendants still believe the spirits of their ancestors inhabit the canyon.

edifice covering nearly three acres. Its 660 or so rooms rise like steps to four or five stories.

A looping nine-mile road winds through the canyon with stops at each of the five major sites here, and each site in turn offers its own trail. The Casa Rinconada and Tsin Kletsin sites offer a magnificent view of the valley.

The campground lacks water, so stock up at the visitors center.

▶ Open year-round. Admission charged.

www.nps.gov/chcu

(505) 786-7014

■3▶ Bradbury Science Museum

15th St. and Central Ave.,
Los Alamos

The Los Alamos National Laboratory was built to support the Manhattan Project, which was responsible for designing and building the atomic bomb. The project's director, J. Robert Oppenheimer, chose the site for secrecy and scientific considerations, but also because he thought the ruggedly scenic country would appeal to his team of scientists.

The museum—named in honor of Norris E. Bradbury, the lab's long-serving second director—moved to its current location in downtown Los Alamos in 1993. Exhibits are divided into three main halls: history, technology, and national security. In the museum theater are regular films on scientific subjects.

Among the memorabilia on display is the 1939 letter from Albert Einstein to President Franklin D. Roosevelt suggesting the potential power of atomic fission and urging authorization for development.

Most of the museum is devoted to displays on geotechnology, solar

energy, nuclear reactor technology, and America's energy future. Various aspects of weapon design, testing, and deployment are also shown.

▶ Open year-round except holidays.

www.lanl.gov/museum

(505) 667-4444

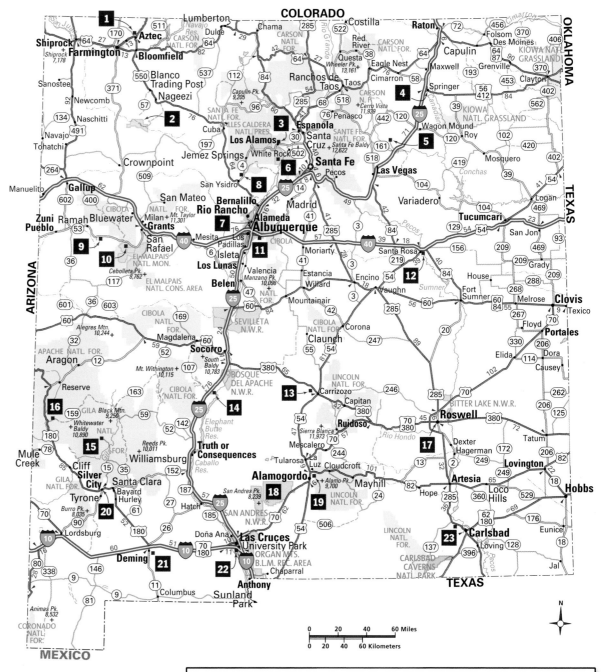

Legend

1 NUMBERED ATTRACTIONS (Described in text)

CONTROLLED ACCESS HIGHWAYS
— Free
— Toll
= = = = = Under Construction

OTHER HIGHWAYS
— Primary Highway
— Secondary Highway

HIGHWAY MARKERS
🔟 Interstate Route
12⃝ U.S. Route
12⃝ State Route
12 Distances along Major Highways (in miles)

CITIES AND TOWNS
★ National Capital
◉ State Capital
• Cities, Towns, and Populated Places Type size indicates relative importance
▨ Urban Area

RECREATION AND FEATURES OF INTEREST
▨ National Park
▨ Other Large Park or Recreation Area
---- Trail
---- Ferry

© 2009 GeoNova

4 Santa Fe Trail Interpretive Center and Museum

614 Maxwell Ave., Springer

The Santa Fe Trail, a 900-mile route across five states, brought a multitude of goods and people to the Western frontier. In 1821 trader William Becknell headed west and was advised by a company of Spanish dragoons to take his goods to Santa Fe. The newly independent Mexico was hungry for trade, and those willing to undertake the journey stood to make enormous profits. The trail grew rapidly, with traffic peaking in 1866 when 5,000 wagons traveled the route. However, the arrival of the railroad in New Mexico in 1879 put a halt to travel on the trail.

Today intrepid explorers can view the trail by driving the 480-mile Santa Fe Trail National Scenic Byway. At the end of the Cimarron Route, which winds its way from Clayton to Springer, lies the trail interpretive center. The center is housed in the former Colfax County Courthouse, built in 1881, with which it shares the Springer Museum. On exhibit are works of art, artifacts, and historic photos that pertain to the Santa Fe Trail. At the museum visitors can also see New Mexico's first and only electric chair, as well as a shoe owned by Robert Wadlow, the world's tallest man.

▶ Open Thurs.–Sat. year-round and Sun. in summer. Admission charged for museum.

www.nenewmexico.com
(575) 483-2998

5 Fort Union National Monument

Hwy. 161, Watrous

Fort Union has had three incarnations. The first fort, built in 1851, was a key station on the Santa Fe Trail. After the outbreak of the Civil War, a star-shaped earthen fortification was constructed in anticipation of a Confederate attack, which never came. The third and last installation was the largest in the Southwest upon its completion in 1867.

Troops stationed here waged several campaigns against the Native Americans of the Southern Plains. In 1879 the railroad replaced the Santa Fe Trail, and in 1891 the fort was finally abandoned.

Enough remains of the third fort to indicate how very extensive it once was. From the visitors center at the parking lot, a 1½-mile interpretive walk leads through Fort Union's two units: the Post, where the troops and their officers were garrisoned, and the Depot, where those who were responsible for supplies, transportation, and equipment were stationed.

Along the trail are photographs showing the fort when it was in use and recorded re-enactments of what dialogue among the men might have been like 150 years ago. The self-guiding trail also visits the site of the second fort. Exhibits in the visitors center relate to life at the fort and conflicts with the Native Americans.

▶ Open year-round except holidays. Admission charged.

www.nps.gov/foun
(505) 425-8025

6 Bandelier National Monument

Hwy. 4, Los Alamos

The road to Bandelier takes you through some of the most spectacular country in New Mexico, offering enormous vistas of mountains, mesas, cliffs, and canyons. The monument itself covers nearly 50 square miles, almost all of it undisturbed wilderness.

Some 70 miles of maintained hiking trails lead in and out of steep-walled canyons, bringing you to pueblo ruins, cave rooms hewn from rock cliffs, petroglyphs and pictographs, waterfalls, and scenic overlooks.

An easy self-guiding walk described in a pamphlet leads from the visitors center along the floor

6 Bandelier National Monument. A wooden ladder leads to a cavate, a space excavated from rock.

of Frijoles Canyon to the ancestral pueblo where the Anasazi people once farmed. A somewhat steep fork in the trail takes you to cave rooms and dramatic rock formations. From here one has a magnificent view of the valley and a stream lined with cottonwoods and box elder maples that turn a brilliant yellow in the autumn.

A popular summer activity is a bat walk, a tour of the bat cave at Long House, led by a park ranger. The Mexican freetail bats, seamlessly navigating the dark, are a unique, unexpected beauty. Also in the summer are one-hour night walks—silent pitch-black journeys

did you know ?

The ancestral Pueblo people lived in the area of Bandelier National Monument for approximately 400 years, between 1150 and 1550 B.C. Thousands of years before that, hunter-gatherer groups traversed the land in search of food.

6 Bandelier National Monument. A large cave room on Bandelier's 1.2-mile Main Loop Trail affords a splendid view of the snow-dusted slopes of Frijoles Canyon.

through the archaeological sites behind the visitors center.

A much longer, more demanding trail takes you down-canyon to two beautiful waterfalls and eventually to the Rio Grande as it courses through White Rock Canyon. The great variety of trees, shrubs, and flowering plants adds to the appeal of Bandelier. The monument is at an altitude of 6,500 feet, and the terrain is fairly rugged, so take it slow.

Permits are required (free at the visitors center) for backcountry hiking, horseback riding (bring your own steed), and cross-country skiing. Be advised, though, that there are strict no-fire regulations in the backcountry, and during peak fire season in the summer, access may be limited.

▶ Open year-round except holidays. Admission charged.

www.nps.gov/band
(505) 672-3861, ext. 517

7 The Anderson-Abruzzo Albuquerque International Balloon Museum

9201 Balloon Museum Dr. NE, Albuquerque
Named for the Albuquerque balloonists who made the first uninterrupted gas balloon flight across the Atlantic Ocean in 1978, this unusual museum is dedicated to preserving the history of ballooning. It also provides a vantage point from which to watch ballooning events or simply view the nearby Sandia Mountains.

The facility exhibits an extensive collection of ballooning equipment and memorabilia, including historic gondolas such as those used in the first transcontinental flight of North America and

7 ▶ **The Anderson-Abruzzo Albuquerque International Balloon Museum.** Known as America's ballooning capital, Albuquerque is a fitting home for this unique museum.

the first flight across the Pacific Ocean. Also displayed are a World War I observation balloon, navigation equipment, and a Victorian parachute. Exhibits detail the history and technical aspects of ballooning as well as the use of balloons for scientific, sporting, and military purposes. An interactive flight simulator is popular.

▶ Open Tues.–Sun. Admission charged except Sun. mornings and first Fri. of each month.

www.cabq.gov/balloon
(505) 768-6020

8 Pueblo of Jemez

Jemez Pueblo
The people of the Pueblo of Jemez have lived on the high mountain mesas and canyons of north-central New Mexico for a thousand years. They invite you to visit their ancestral tribal lands and experience their proud and rich culture, preserved throughout the centuries.

This is the last village of the Towa-speaking Pueblos, one of the mightiest of the Pueblo cultures when the Europeans arrived in 1851. Hemish ("the people") is

their original name, reconfigured by the Spanish into "Jemez." The Pueblo of Jemez is Walatowa, or "this is the place" in Towa.

Today this area, about an hour north of Albuquerque, is a window to the past as well as a living Pueblo town. A reconstructed traditional stone fieldhouse, once used as a hunting-and-farming base camp, is the cornerstone of the visitors center, which also offers photo exhibits, crafts, and oral histories. Feast days and ceremonial dances are held throughout the year.

This is also the gateway to the Jemez Mountain Trail, which meanders through the Santa Fe National Forest and the Valles Caldera National Preserve.

Fishing streams, hot springs, and trails weave through the magical geologic formations. The national forest area is managed through a unique partnership between the U.S. Forest Service and the people of Jemez.

▶ Open year-round.

www.jemezpueblo.org
(505) 834-7235

9 El Morro National Monument

Hwy. 53, Ramah
El Morro, or the "Inscription Rock," is the massive point of a sandstone mesa rising some 200 feet above the valley floor. A waterhole fed by rain and snowmelt at the base of the bluff has long attracted travelers passing through the desert.

Members of three civilizations—the Zuni tribe, Spanish soldiers and priests, and American settlers, soldiers, and adventurers—have left hundreds of inscriptions, from crude scratchings to elegant script, in the soft yellow stone. Indeed, El Morro is one of the great historical graffiti walls in America. The first inscription by an American is dated 1849.

A trail leads from the monument headquarters up the side of the mesa. Along the way are markers keyed to a self-guiding booklet, which identifies petroglyphs and translates Spanish inscriptions, including an eight-line poem elegantly incised in 1629.

Many inscriptions, however, are of the "Kilroy was here" variety, like the message of a passing official from the Santa Fe region, roughly translated as: "On the 25th of the month of June of this year 1709, passed by here on the way to Zuni—Ramon Garcia Jurado."

A steep climb continues to the windswept top, where there are two large Native American ruins and expansive views of the valley and the Zuni Mountain Range. And in case you're wondering, No, you cannot leave your mark here.

▶ Open year-round except holidays. Admission charged.

www.nps.gov/elmo
(505) 783-4226

10 ▶ **El Malpais National Monument.**
Lava tubes here became ice caves.

10 ▶ El Malpais National Monument

Ice Caves Rd. (Rte. 53)
The main attraction of El Malpais ("the badlands") is the stunning display of nature's extremes at the Bandera crater and ice caves.

The phenomena were promoted for nearly 100 years by the Candelaria family, but in 1987 most of this area was absorbed into the newly created El Malpais National Monument, managed by the U.S. Park Service and the Bureau of Land Management. However, the family continued to run its famous tours from its private ranch.

At a half-mile long and rising 150 feet, the dormant Bandera Volcano crater is a sight to behold. A trail runs the length of the crater and rises along with it. You're already at an altitude of 8,000 feet, so be sure to take it easy. At the top of the trail up here, you are on the Continental Divide.

When the volcano erupted some 10,000 years ago, molten rock coursed down the mountainside and created many lava tubes as it cooled. Sections of tubes collapsed by an earthquake have formed small caves; with a temperature that never exceeds 31°F, ice has slowly accumulated in them. You can reach one of the ice caves by a short, level trail across a lava field.

Oddly enough, this strange, moonlike area draws an abundance of hummingbirds, best seen in July, when flowers are in bloom.

▶ Open year-round except Sun., Mon., and holidays. Admission charged.

www.nps.gov/elma
(505) 783-4774

11 ▶ National Museum of Nuclear Science & History

601 Eubank Blvd. SE, Albuquerque
A visit to this museum is fascinating, terrifying, and unforgettable. Here one is brought face-to-face with the ultimate weapon.

An interactive exhibit called Energy Encounters allows visitors to learn about nuclear-reactor design and the impact of nuclear power generation on world energy issues. There's also a theater that shows two 50-minute documentaries—one on nuclear science, the other on the secret Manhattan Project, which led to the first atomic bomb.

On display in a separate section of the museum are aerodynamic containers in which atomic and nuclear warheads can be delivered—by land, sea, and air. Additional museum exhibits include cutting-edge uses of nuclear medicine and technologies associated with radiology.

Outside the museum are rockets, missiles, and a B-52 aircraft that was once used for testing nuclear weapons.

▶ Open daily year-round except holidays. Admission charged.

www.atomicmuseum.com
(505) 245-2137

12 ▶ Blue Hole

Off Rte. 66, Santa Rosa
The town of Santa Rosa, located on old Rte. 66, has an unexpected dimension that draws people from miles away. The otherwise unassuming town, also known as the City of Natural Lakes, contains Blue Hole, a crystal-clear artesian spring and popular scuba-diving site.

Once used as a fish hatchery, Blue Hole is bordered by trees, large rocks, and a low stone wall. The pool attracts divers due to a

12 ▶ **Blue Hole.** Once a fish hatchery, this artesian spring in a town called The City of Natural Lakes is the place for scuba diving in Santa Rosa, on famed Rte. 66.

year-round water temperature of 64°F and visibility of up to 80 feet in optimal conditions. The spring has a water flow of 3,000 gallons per minute, keeping the water constantly fresh. Below the surface of the bell-shaped spring, divers can investigate the algae-covered limestone walls, swim with the goldfish that inhabit the pond, or investigate the collection of golf balls and plastic toys left by divers.

Nearby is a dive center where visitors may refill their air tanks, rent equipment, or acquire the necessary diving permit. Permits may also be purchased at Santa Rosa City Hall during the week. In the pool, diving platforms are suspended at depths of 20 and 25 feet. The area is at an altitude of 4,600 feet, so divers are reminded to take the necessary precautions to avoid developing decompression sickness. Blue Hole is busier on weekends, especially during the winter months.

▶ Open year-round. Fee charged for diving permit, air refills, and equipment rentals.

www.santarosanm.org
(575) 472-3763 Santa Rosa Visitors Center

13 ▶ Valley of Fires Recreation Area

4 miles west of Carrizozo via US-380
Here you can see one of the youngest lava beds in the United States, the Carrizozo Malpais.

An estimated 5,500 years ago red-hot lava flowed for 44 miles from Little Black Peak. It was visible to the northeast, covering 125 square miles of valley floor, in some places to a depth of more than 150 feet. As it flowed, it began to cool and solidify.

The Malpais Trail leads into the park, a rugged 463-acre field of fissured black lava. Thick-soled shoes are recommended. A brochure describing the highlights on the trail is usually available near the trailhead. Along the loop trail, a very pleasant, easy, and dramatic walk, one sees a remarkable variety of shapes and textures, created by the cooling, moving lava.

For all the forbidding aspects of this landscape, many plants have established themselves in the lava crust. A number of animals—mice, snakes, and lizards—have also found the lava field a viable environment.

The Sierra Blanca Mountains to the south and east provide a superb backdrop. Hiking trails, interpretive displays, and camping sites are among the amenities. For best weather go in spring or summer, but the area is seldom crowded at any time of year.

▶ Open year-round. Admission charged.

www.blm.gov/nm/st/en/prog/recreation/ roswell/valley_of_fires.html

(575) 648-2241

---

14 ▶ Fort Craig National Historic Site

901 Hwy. 85S, Socorro
Built on the 1,200-mile trail from Mexico City to Santa Fe in 1854, this fort provided protection for travelers and settlers of the American frontier. During the Civil War, Fort Craig functioned as a Union Army Post and later saw the largest southwestern battle of the war. Although a Confederate victory, Union forces held the fort and destroyed many Confederate supply wagons; the eventual loss of the remaining wagons ended the Confederacy's western campaign. Troops stationed at the fort include New Mexico volunteers that were commanded by frontiersman Kit

15 ▶ Gila Cliff Dwellings National Monument. These Mogollon dwellings predated not only Columbus's voyages but also the Great Wall of China, built by the Ming dynasty.

Carson and Buffalo Soldiers. In the years after the war, before it was abandoned in 1885, the fort once again provided protection for the outlying areas, this time against raids by Native Americans.

Today, in addition to hiking trails and self-guiding tours, the fort holds living history re-enactments.

▶ Open year-round.

www.blm.gov/nm/st/en/prog/recreation/ socorro/fort_craig.html

(575) 835-0412

---

15 ▶ Gila Cliff Dwellings National Monument

Hwy. 527, 43 miles north of Silver City
Five natural caves high in the face of a cliff contain the ruins of dwellings built and occupied by the Mogollon peoples between the 13th and 14th centuries. A diligent farming people, they were also skillful weavers and artistic potters.

The ruins can be reached by a trail that climbs some 180 feet in its mile-long loop. A short flight of steps reaches up to the caves, which are very large, with arched ceilings. Gazing out from its cool,

dark recesses and seeing the West Fork of the Gila River as it flows past fields where crops once grew, one has a sense of having entered another era. Wandering through the rooms, one finds structural timbers dating back to the 1280s, as well as the remains of food stored centuries ago.

This is a popular site, but it is usually uncrowded except on weekends from Memorial Day– mid-Sept. The visitors center offers relevant information, exhibits, and an audiovisual presentation; guide booklets may be purchased. The Gila National Forest has picnic sites and campgrounds about a quarter-mile away. Be sure to carry water with you, and be advised: The trails are steep.

Because the Hwy. 15 approach out of Silver City is a severely winding road, cars with large trailers— or squeamish passengers—should take the Hwy. 35 alternate route, which is 25 miles longer but about the same driving time.

▶ Open year-round. Admission charged.

www.nps.gov/gicl
(575) 536-9461

---

16 ▶ The Catwalk and Mogollon

Catwalk: Hwy. 174
Glenwood: Hwy. 159
At separate times both Geronimo and Butch Cassidy used the hard-to-navigate boulder-strewn Whitewater Canyon as a hideout, but today its main attraction for visitors is the Catwalk.

The narrow metal walkway is firmly bolted into the canyon's steep walls. At the end of the trail, a vertiginous suspension bridge sways over the rushing waters of the Whitewater Creek.

The catwalk follows the route of a pipeline that was built to carry water to the gold-mining town of Graham in the 1890s. The town is gone, but the catwalk—with its dizzying views—remains.

The Catwalk was rebuilt in the 1930s as a recreation area for the Gila National Forest and strengthened again in the 1960s by the U.S. Forest Service. Expert climbers can continue up a dirt trail to a ridge 10,000 feet up in the Mogollon Mountains.

You can also drive or motorcycle to the town of Mogollon, once a gold rush–era boomtown that surged for about 20 years but now has a dwindling population. Almost deserted for most of the last century, it now has two small museums, some shops, and a bed-and-breakfast.

The road here is a breathtaking 8 1/2-mile ascent with no guardrails on the switchbacks. In the winter it is often impassable. Gouged out of the mountains, the old mines are easy to see, as are the deer, elk, and bison that live there.

▶ Open year-round.

www.mogollonenterprises.com
(575) 539-2481

17 International UFO Museum & Research Center

114 N. Main St., Roswell

A mysterious crash outside Roswell in July of 1947 was the impetus behind decades of cover-up theories and the fascination with the small New Mexico town that continues today. Officials initially reported that the object that had smashed into a local rancher's field was a flying saucer, but later it issued a second press release, stating that it was a weather balloon. Those that remember the incident have added new levels to the story, from other-worldly debris to alien autopsies.

The UFO Museum was established as a home for information regarding the town's extraterrestrial experience as well as other such phenomena across the world. The museum has perpetuated the region's fascination with aliens, keeping the story alive by educating visitors on the Roswell Incident. Exhibits at the museum also include information about crop circles, alien abductions, Area 51, and ancient visitors from space. Regardless of whether one is a true believer or simply curious, a visit to the museum is sure to be an educational and entertaining experience.

▶ Open year-round except major winter holidays. Admission charged.

www.roswellufomuseum.com
(575) 625-9495; (800) 822-3545

18 White Sands National Monument

15 miles southwest of Alamogordo, Hwy. 70

Ever changing and always beautiful, these vast, brilliantly white dunes trace their existence to the layers of gypsum in the surrounding mountains. Seasonal rains and

 **White Sands National Monument.** A sea of white sand, with 50-foot dunes for waves, spreads over south-central New Mexico for as far as the eye can see.

snow dissolve the gypsum and carry it to Lake Lucero, southwest of the dunes.

When the lake bed is dry, the wind grinds the gypsum crystals into tiny grains and deposits them in these undulating waves of sand. The dunes shift slowly to the northeast, and new dunes are formed behind them.

From the entrance a gypsum roadway leads for some eight miles into the sands. Numbered signs along the way are keyed to a pamphlet, available at the visitors center, which describes the area's remarkable geology, flora, and fauna.

Hiking and sand surfing are popular in the dunes. Hiking options range from a 1-mile self-guiding nature trail to a 4.6-mile (round-trip) backcountry trail. Picnic sites are provided, but water is available only at the visitors center, 8 miles away. The park advises visitors to call ahead, as testing at the nearby White Sands Missile Range occasionally closes area roads.

▶ Open year-round except Christmas. Admission charged.

www.nps.gov/whsa
(505) 479-6124

19 New Mexico Museum of Space History

Hwy. 2001, Alamogordo

Much of the development of rocketry in America took place in the New Mexico desert. Appropriately, this seemingly lunar landscape is the setting for a modern museum dedicated to those who introduced the Space Age.

Within the museum is the International Space Hall of Fame, where more than 130 key players from around the world are honored.

Inductees include Johannes Winkler, a German rocket pioneer; Robert Goddard, "the Father of Modern Rocketry"; test pilot Chuck Yeager, the first man to fly faster than the speed of sound; American and Soviet astronauts such as Neil Armstrong and Yuri Gagarin; Britain's William Congreve, who introduced a solid-propellant artillery rocket in 1805; and even newsman Walter Cronkite, an expert on space history.

Among the exhibits are satellites and capsules and a variety of rocket engines and guidance systems. Detailed history is the theme, with an emphasis on the long evolution of our understanding of the skies above us.

Other favorite attractions include a "physics playground," where visitors can explore the laws of aerodynamics; the sled that Dr. John Paul Stapp rode at 632 miles per hour; an IMAX theater; and a planetarium.

The Astronaut Memorial Garden on the grounds honors the heroes who died aboard *Apollo 1,* the *Challenger* shuttle, and the *Columbia* shuttle.

▶ Open year-round except major winter holidays. Admission charged.

www.nmspacemuseum.org
(575) 437-2840; (877) 333-6589

20 Silver City Museum

312 W. Broadway, Silver City

The eclectic charm of this little museum aptly recalls Silver City's rich and varied history.

The handsome Victorian house, with its square tower and mansard roof, was once the home of Henry B. Ailman, a young prospector who struck it rich in the 1870s. The building, listed on the *National Register of Historic Places,* is filled with furniture, clothing, household goods, and decorative objects typical of the era.

One room in particular evokes the heyday of the area's mining boom, with stylish mannequins in period attire and historic photographs that vividly recall impressions of the enormous profits and considerable dangers that surrounded silver mining.

The area's ranching heritage is represented by a fine display of cowpuncher's clothing and gear. Artifacts from Southwestern Native American tribes are also displayed, including an excellent collection of Casas Grandes pottery.

▶ Open Tues.–Sun. year-round.

www.silvercitymuseum.org

(575) 538-5921; (877) 777-7947

---

21 Rockhound State Park

Hwy. 141, 14 miles southeast of Deming

Unlike most national and state parks where removing natural objects is forbidden, visitors to this park are encouraged to prospect and take specimens.

The parkland, on a mountainside formed of volcanic rhyolite, is rich in semiprecious stones, primarily jasper, opal, blue agate, and psilomelane. Visitors can dig their own stones here and take away up to 15 pounds per visit.

You must bring your own equipment, but you can count on the park staff to provide helpful tips on methods and places for digging. A small exhibit in the visitors center displays many of the minerals found here. Summer is quite hot; the most comfortable season for digging is winter.

The 250-acre park is perched on a slope of the Little Florida Mountains, and it's a worthwhile destination just for the scenery. The campground and picnic area offer sweeping views of Deming and the valley below.

▶ Open daily year-round. Admission charged weekends, Apr.–Labor Day.

www.emnrd.state.nm.us/prd

(575) 546-6182

---

22 Mesilla

Hwy. 28

For scores of early Western towns, it was a disaster when the railroad laid its tracks elsewhere. Back in 1881 the railroad chose Las Cruces rather than its neighbor Mesilla.

But today this is considered by many to be a blessing, for the bypassed town has retained its tranquil charm and historic interest, unmarred by the rush of progress the trains brought to much of the rest of the country.

The first settlers arrived by wagon train in about 1847, during the Mexican-American War, when Mexican troops were stationed here. In 1854 the American flag was raised in Mesilla Plaza, and four years later the Butterfield Stage put the community on the map, despite continuing threats from the Apache.

Captured by Texans during the Civil War, Mesilla served briefly as the capital of the Confederate Territory of Arizona.

Famous and infamous visitors included Mexican revolutionary Francisco "Pancho" Villa and William Bonney, better known as Billy the Kid, who was once tried, convicted, and jailed here.

Mesilla, or "little tableland,"

22 ▶ **Mesilla.** A town the railroad passed by is now home to boutiques, galleries, and bed-and-breakfasts.

was declared a state monument in 1957. The visitors center is equipped with videos, brochures, menus, and photos dating to the late 1800s.

Around the plaza and elsewhere in the town are some old adobe buildings, many dating from the mid-19th century. Must-see highlights here are the twin-towered church of San Albino and Mesilla Plaza.

www.oldmesilla.org

(575) 524-3262 Ext. 117

---

23 Living Desert Zoo and Gardens State Park

Skyline Rd., Carlsbad

Set on a rise above the town, this park is a showcase for the native plants and animals of the Chihuahuan desert.

Paths bordered with hundreds of desert plants lead to the various buildings and enclosures. An amazing variety of cacti grow in a large greenhouse.

Enclosures flanking the park contain large animals. There is also a prairie-dog town, a bear den, a reptile house, and a nocturnal house. An aviary provides a close look at hawks, owls, roadrunners, and other desert birds. As you walk the trails, keep an eye out above for bobcats and mountain lions, part of an exhibit that showcases these animals in their natural habitat.

During the summer season here—from Apr.–Sept.—it is more comfortable to visit in the cool of morning or evening.

▶ Open year-round except Christmas. Admission charged.

www.emnrd.state.nm.us/prd/ livingdesert.htm

(575) 887-5516

seasonal events

JUNE
- Eastern Navajo Arts and Crafts Festival—Torreon/Star Lake Chapter *(traditional art, dancing)*

JULY
- Lavender in the Village Festival— Los Ranchose de Albuquerque *(bouquet picking, Village Growers Market, guided tours, live music)*
- Bat Flight Breakfast—Carlsbad Caverns National Park, White City *(outdoor breakfast at dawn; watch bats return to cave)*
- UFO Festival—Roswell *(live music, lectures, workshops, book signings)*

AUGUST
- Hatch Chile Festival—Hatch *(chile cook-off, tractor pulls, parade, live music)*
- Inter-Tribal Indian Ceremonial— Gallup *(dancing, ceremonial parades, rodeo, traditional arts and crafts)*

SEPTEMBER
- The Whole Enchilada Festival—Las Cruces *(world's largest enchilada, music)*

OCTOBER
- Farmington Renaissance Faire— Farmington
- Albuquerque International Balloon Fiesta—Albuquerque *(hot-air balloons, car show, competitions)*
- La Viña Harvest Festival—La Union *(wine tasting, grape stomping)*

NOVEMBER
- Dia de los Muertos—Las Cruces *(candlelight procession, displays of homemade altars, giant piñata)*
- Festival of the Cranes—Bosque del Apache National Wildlife Refuge, near Socorro *(tours, lectures, exhibits)*
- International Mariachi Conference—Las Cruces *(concerts, mariachi music, folkloric dance)*

DECEMBER
- Santa Fe Film Festival—Santa Fe *(revivals, retrospectives, independent productions)*

www.tournewmexico.org

New York

From Lake Ontario to Long Island, the Empire State is filled with grand enterprises, museums and historic houses, and quiet corners.

Boldt Castle. The Thousand Islands architectural oddity known as Alster Tower is one of the structures comprising the Boldt Castle complex (see page 242).

Upstate and downstate, New York has scores of out-of-the-way places to explore. Hidden gems are found from the Alleghenies to the Adirondacks. Explore small towns dating back hundreds of years. See the first water-powered mill and an early 20th-century aerodrome, both reborn. Observe birdlife at a national wildlife refuge near Niagara Falls and another within shouting distance of New York City. Walk what is considered to be America's oldest street in the town of New Paltz, and tour a castle that stands as a monument to the Gilded Age in the Thousand Islands. Even the nation's largest city has its hidden treasures—among them a one-of-a-kind museum of medieval rarities tucked away in a remote park.

visit ➤➤ offthebeatenpathtrips.com

1 Long Point State Park on Lake Chautauqua

4459 Rte. 430, Bemus Point
This pleasant day-use park is water-oriented, with an extensive marina, boat launch, a swimming beach with a bathhouse, and a large parking area for cars and boat trailers. Fishing is excellent for muskellunge, walleye, and perch.

The park has several trails: Some follow the scenic lakeshore, and one, flanked by fine old oak trees, goes out to the end of a long, narrow point projecting about a quarter mile into the lake.

▶ Open year-round. Per-vehicle fee May–Sept.

www.nysparks.com
(716) 386-2722

2 Rock City Park

505A Rock City Rd. (Rte. 165), Olean
Upon reaching this outlook high in the Allegheny Mountains (elevation 2,350 feet), one is at first riveted by the panoramic views. But the gigantic, dramatically shaped boulders found here are the featured attraction.

Estimated to be 500 million years old, the rocks, known as pudding stone, are a quartz conglomerate formed at the bottom of a prehistoric sea. During the uplifting of this mountain system, the rocks were exposed to the surface. When the shale beneath the pudding stone began to erode, the rocks toppled, creating the unusual forms seen today.

The trail, winding through Rock City, starts and ends near Signal Rock, once used by Native Americans for their signal fires. Walking single file, you squeeze through narrow passageways, pass beneath great overhanging boulders, and descend into crevasses carved out by extinct waterfalls. On the last leg of the trail, a stone stairway, said to have been built by the Native Americans, provides a way for visitors to climb to the top, which once served as a fortress.

▶ Open daily May–Oct. Admission charged.

www.rockcitypark.com
(716) 372-7790

3 Iroquois National Wildlife Refuge

1101 Casey Rd., Basom
One of the best-kept secrets of Western New York, this wildlife refuge is a nature lover's delight. Part of what the locals call the "Alabama Swamps," these 10,828 acres of wetlands, grasslands, and shrublands, are teeming with wildlife in all seasons.

Iroquois National Wildlife Refuge. The Onondaga Trail, named for one of the five original tribes of the Iroquois Federation, is an easily walked 1.2 miles.

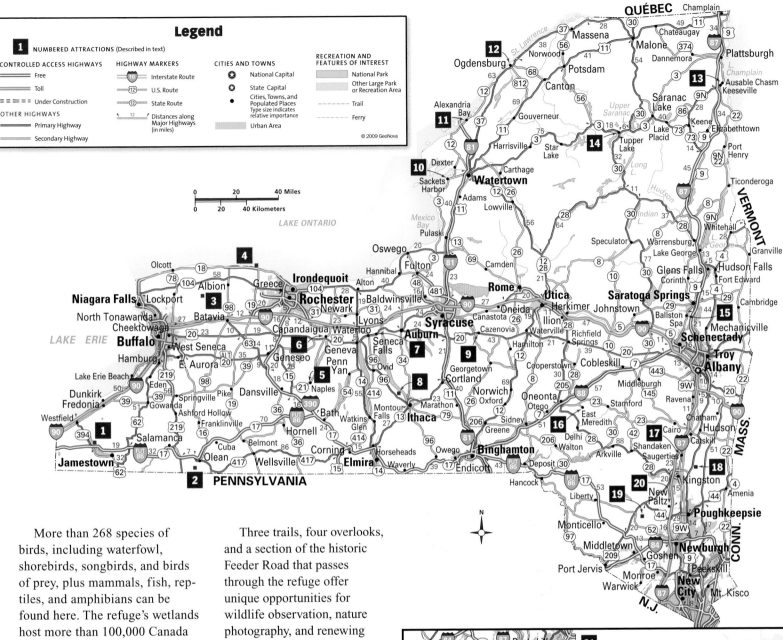

More than 268 species of birds, including waterfowl, shorebirds, songbirds, and birds of prey, plus mammals, fish, reptiles, and amphibians can be found here. The refuge's wetlands host more than 100,000 Canada geese and 20,000 ducks and swans annually, many en route to and from nesting grounds in Canada.

Three trails, four overlooks, and a section of the historic Feeder Road that passes through the refuge offer unique opportunities for wildlife observation, nature photography, and renewing your spiritual connection to the world of nature. Free nature programs are scheduled in spring and fall.

▶ Designated trails, overlooks, and fishing areas open year-round. Headquarters open daily except holidays; closed weekends in winter and summer.

www.fws.gov/northeast/iroquois

(585) 948-5445

did you know ?

The land that became the Iroquois National Wildlife Refuge in 1958 was purchased with funds raised entirely by the sale of Federal Duck Stamps.

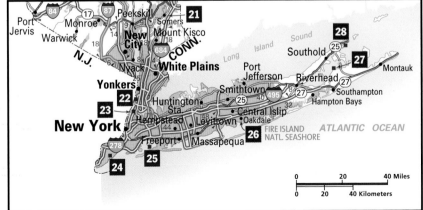

 Hamlin Beach State Park

1 Camp Rd., Hamlin

Stretching for three miles along the breeze-swept shore of Lake Ontario, this park is especially appealing in summertime. It has a mile of sandy beach, picnic tables, a ball field, walkways along the water's edge, campsites with electrical hookups, and a launching area for car-top boats.

The park's most unusual and interesting feature, however, is its Yanty Creek Nature Trail. Nearly a mile long, the trail leads through various ecological environments: deciduous woods, marshland, a coniferous woodlot, an old field returning to scrub and wood, and a pond. At frequent intervals the path is posted with interpretive signs describing what you can—or are likely to—see, hear, touch, and even smell.

Overlooking the Yanty Creek are four elevated platforms, where one can watch for wildlife and birds. In the springtime the pleasure of the walk is enhanced by the wild roses and dogwood blossoming beneath the oaks and white pines.

▶ Accessible year-round. Per-vehicle fee May–Sept.

www.nysparks.com
(585) 964-2462

 Naples Valley

Rte. 21, south of Canandaigua Lake

If you wander around the village of Naples in the Finger Lakes region of western New York, you'll notice a particular fondness for grapes and the color purple. Here, the fire hydrants are painted purple, and so are the police cars—and they even have grapes painted on the doors.

This is a place where 70,000 grape pies are sold every year, where a Grape Festival is held each September, and where two wineries open their doors to the public for tastings and tours.

The village itself is a picturesque throwback to the 1950s, with a single Main Street and offshoots fanning up into the glacier-created Bristol Hills. Surrounded by the Hi-Tor Wildlife Management Area, with its turkey, deer, and the occasional bear, the spot where Naples is set is so beautiful, even longtime

Naples Valley. Farmers markets in the Naples Valley, in the west of New York's Finger Lakes wine-growing region, give star billing to grapes fresh from the vine.

residents take the two-hour paddle-boat tour around the lake to enjoy the fall foliage.

Wizard of Clay Pottery, north on Rte. 20A, spirits away fallen leaves from the hills and incorporates them into its Bristol-leaf pottery glazes. Fifteen studios offer an array of creations, from wildlife sculptures to glass works to pottery.

Hiking trails in Ontario County Park at Gannett Hill connect to the extensive Finger Lakes Trail System, and Grimes Glen's 60-foot waterfall in the village is a restorative sight.

▶ Open year-round.

www.naplesvalleyny.com
(877) 386-4669

New York Wine & Culinary Center

800 S. Main St., Canandaigua

Located in the heart of the picture-perfect Finger Lakes region, the New York Wine & Culinary Center is a stimulating showcase for the wines, agricultural products, and culinary traditions of New York State. Opened in 2006, the center quickly became known for its innovative exhibitions, hands-on cooking classes, wine education classes, and inspiring culinary experiences.

An exhibit hall, paneled with recycled 100-year-old redwood wine barrels, highlights New York's unique agricultural heritage with engaging, interactive displays. A wine-tasting bar allows visitors to sample award-winning wines from all regions of the state. Upstairs the stellar Taste of NY restaurant serves seasonal dishes paired with fine New York wines and microbrewed beers.

New York Wine & Culinary Center. A state-of-the-art kitchen is the setting for hands-on classes and workshops.

The center also offers informative, entertaining culinary classes for people of all skill levels. A recent schedule included classes such as Personal Winemaking 101, New England Clam Bake, and a Knife Skills Workshop.

▶ Open year-round. Check the website below for hours. Fee for classes and wine tastings.

www.nywcc.com
(585) 394-7070

Women's Rights National Historical Park & National Women's Hall of Fame

136 and 76 Fall St., Seneca Falls

The same kind of rebellious zeal that motivated America's founding fathers to envision the Declaration of Independence also fired the passions of the 19th-century women who, chafing at their limited opportunities, went on to lead the women's rights movement.

"We hold these truths to be self-evident, that all men and women are created equal" is a line from their Declaration of Sentiments, presented at the first Women's

Rights Convention in July 1848 in this small mill town between Syracuse and Rochester. The 19th Amendment to the Constitution was not ratified until 1920, when women were granted basic rights —voting and property ownership among them—that we take for granted today.

The historical park focuses on sites in and around Seneca Falls, like the home of movement organizer Elizabeth Cady Stanton, and the Wesleyan Methodist Chapel, where the convention took place. There is a modern visitors center and a 100-foot-long waterwall engraved with the Declaration of Sentiments and its signers' names.

Stanton delivered her famous speech calling for women's suffrage not far from the building that now houses the National Women's Hall of Fame, conceived in 1969. Anthropologist Margaret Mead and astronaut Sally Ride are examples of the women whose lives are honored here with interactive displays and biographical information.

▶ Historical Park open year-round except major holidays. Hall of Fame open daily May–Sept.; Wed.–Sat. Oct.–Apr. Gallery closed in Jan. Admission charged.

www.nps.gov/wori
(315) 568-2991 Historical Park

www.greatwomen.org
(315) 568-8060 Hall of Fame

8 ▶ Taughannock Falls State Park

2221 Taughannock Rd., Trumansburg

Before the Continental Army marched through this area of the Finger Lakes in 1779, the Cayuga people, who lived in a village at Taughannock Falls and who were in the area for hundreds of years, decided to flee.

9 ▶ **Lorenzo State Historic Site.** In the mid-19th century the estate's gardens were redesigned to create a central path as an extension of the mansion's main hall.

During the 19th century settlers harnessed the power of Taughannock Creek to power mills and a gun factory, and in the 1870s a resort was developed in the area. As tourism here declined at the end of the century, the resort failed, and in 1925, on a tract of 64 acres, the state park was established. Today it includes almost 800 acres.

The falls, 33 feet higher than Niagara, plunge 215 feet into a natural amphitheater created by thousands of years of erosion and the effects of seasonal melting and freezing. They are named, according to legend, in memory of Chief Taughannock of the Lenape tribe, who was thrown over the cascade to his death after a disastrous battle with the Cayugas. Hiking trails lead along the north and south rims of the gorge and to the foot of the falls.

Taughannock Creek empties into Cayuga Lake, where there is a site for picnic grounds, a boat launch, and a swimming beach.

The park has campsites, cabins, a bathhouse, and a marina and in winter offers ice skating.

▶ Park open year-round; campsites open Apr.–mid-Oct. Admission charged.

www.nysparks.com
(607) 387-6739

9 ▶ Lorenzo State Historic Site

17 Rippleton Rd., Cazenovia

Sent to America in 1790 by Dutch investors to find land for development, John Lincklaen reached the rolling hills at the tip of Cazenovia Lake and stopped. "Situation superb, fine land," he wrote back. Authorized to proceed, he purchased 120,000 acres, laid out the village of Cazenovia (named for his company's manager), built roads and mills, and promoted the development of the region.

On a knoll overlooking the lake, Lincklaen built a magnificent Federal-style mansion in 1807 and named it Lorenzo, apparently after Lorenzo de' Medici. Formal and gracious, with a severe brick façade highlighted by delicately proportioned blind

arches, the house provided an appropriate setting for entertaining the notables of his time.

The property, which had been occupied by the Lincklaen/Ledyard families for 160 years, was purchased in 1968 by the state of New York as a historic site. On the surrounding grounds are formal gardens, groves of trees, paths, and a carriage house containing a wonderful collection of 19th-century horse-drawn vehicles. Check ahead for special events, which range from concerts to a horse-and-carriage race.

Allow time for a tour of Cazenovia. One of the most beautiful villages in the Northeast, it has a charming main street and hundreds of fine old houses, mostly 19th century and carefully maintained.

9 ▶ **Lorenzo State Historic Site.** The original furnishings remain in the elegant drawing room of Lorenzo.

▶ Open Tues.–Sun. mid-May–Oct. Grounds open year-round. Admission charged.

www.lorenzony.org
www.nysparks.com
(315) 655-3200

Sackets Harbor

1 mile from Rte. 3

This small lakeside village with its calm, relaxed air was not always so. During the War of 1812, the settlement, situated beside a bluff commanding access to the St. Lawrence River and blessed with a fine harbor, became an important naval base for the United States, which hoped to take Canada and expel the British. Soldiers, sailors, marines, and shipbuilders arrived here by the thousands; timber was cut, barracks flung up, a shipyard established, and a fleet built. Twice the British attacked, each time unsuccessfully, but the second assault, in May 1813, delayed the American effort to control the lake.

With the approach of winter in 1814, nearly 3,000 workers were engaged in constructing two vessels that would each carry 1,000 men. News of peace arrived before the ships were completed, and the young nation's largest shipbuilding venture was halted. Sackets Harbor, however, remained an active naval yard until the late 1800s.

The battlefield, a state historic site, is now a waterfront park offering views of Lake Ontario and a few reminders of the past. Nearby are officers quarters built in 1847 and the 1817 Union Hotel, now called the Seaway Trail Discovery Center, which houses exhibits about the War of 1812. Start your exploration of this picturesque harbor community and the War of 1812 at the Sacket Mansion, home to the village's visitors center and the headquarters of the New York State Heritage Area.

▶ Grounds open year-round.

www.sacketsharborny.com
(315) 646-2321

Boldt Castle

*Heart Island,
Alexandria Bay*

Situated on a five-acre island in the Thousand Island region, Boldt Castle is the most extravagant of the Gilded Age estates and the setting of a heartbreaking love story.

Designed in the style of a Rhineland castle, this 127-room turn-of-the-century stone mansion was built by hotel magnate George Boldt. Boldt conceived the castle as a testimonial to his beloved wife, Louise. Tragically, Louise died when the castle was only 80 percent complete. Devastated, Boldt halted all construction and never returned to the island again. For 75 years the castle fell into ruin.

Today, however, Boldt Castle is finally being restored according to Boldt's original vision. Visitors can take a self-guiding tour of the castle buildings and grounds and learn about the Boldt family's lifestyle, the restoration of Heart Island, and the history of the Thousand Island region.

did you know ?

The island on which Boldt Castle sits was originally named Hart Island, after a former owner. Ever the romantic, Henry Boldt changed the spelling to Heart Island and altered the shape of the island to more closely resemble a heart. Drawn by the aura of romance that still permeates Boldt Castle, over 700 couples have exchanged wedding vows on the grounds of Heart Island.

 Boldt Castle. The setting for a rare jewel of the Gilded Age is the Thousand Islands area of the St. Lawrence River.

▶ Open daily mid-May–mid-Oct. Admission charged. Fee for transportation to Heart Island by water taxi or tour boat.

www.boldtcastle.com
(800) 847-5263; (315) 482-9724

12 Frederic Remington Art Museum

303 Washington St., Ogdensburg

Housed in an 1809 white mansion, itself an architectural destination, the museum contains a most comprehensive collection of the artist's work.

Known as the foremost artist of the Old West, Frederic Remington was born in Canton, New York, in 1861 and spent most of his youth here in Ogdensburg, a town that claims him today as a native son. At 17 he attended Yale College School of Art for three semesters. With the exception of a few months at New York City's Art Students League, these classes were the only formal training he ever had—he was much more interested in boxing and football than in school. He soon headed west, where he gained inspiration to work as a Western illustrator and artist.

The museum's collection of 70 Remington oils includes *The Charge of the Rough Riders,* which stirringly depicts the famous battle in Cuba during the Spanish-American War. Seventeen bronzes (among them *The Bronco Buster*), 140 watercolors, and many pen-and-ink sketches are also on display in changing exhibits. You will see many of his personal belongings in the museum, including his rifles, Native American weapons, and a stuffed buffalo head.

Another collection that should not be missed is that of Remington's close friend, Sally James Farnham. It is the largest collection of her work for public viewing. Expanded in 1996, the museum now also houses a hands-on children's museum. Check hours for availability.

▶ Open daily May–Oct.; Wed.–Sun. Nov.–Apr. Admission charged.

www.fredericremington.org
(315) 393-2425

13 Ausable Chasm

Off Adirondack Northway, I–87, 12 miles south of Plattsburgh, on Rte. 9

This spectacular sandstone gorge has been an Adirondacks tourist attraction for 138 years. A geological wonder sculpted by the powerful current of the Ausable River over thousands of years, Ausable Chasm features breathtaking views of 150-foot cathedral-shaped cliffs, waterfalls, and strange rock formations, such as the Elephant's Head, Hyde's Cave, and the Broken Needle.

Visitors can explore the chasm along three miles of self-guiding walking trails and also by floating down the Ausable River in a raft or inner tube. On Friday and Saturday evenings visitors can explore the chasm after dark by lantern light. Be sure to carry drinking water with you. These two-hour guided tours start at dusk and include a campfire marshmallow roast.

▶ Open daily mid-May–mid-Oct.
Admission charged. Camping fee.

www.ausablechasm.com
(518) 834-7454 Welcome Center
(518) 834-9990 Campground

14 The Wild Center (Natural History Museum of the Adirondacks)

45 Museum Dr., Tupper Lake
This stunning state-of-the-art museum is devoted to helping people discover the science that shapes and sustains the unique natural world of the Adirondacks.

True to its name, The Wild Center lives and breathes with the sights, sounds, textures, and smells of this great expanse of wilderness. Re-created natural environments immerse visitors in an Adirondack marsh, give them a fish-eye view of a trout-filled river, and carry them to the summit of an alpine peak. On display are over 70 species of live animals, including back-flipping river otters, owls, walnut-size baby spotted turtles, and northern pike. Hands-on exhibits, high-tech multimedia displays, and a widescreen theater give visitors a naturalist's understanding of this fascinating world.

The Wild Center's collection rambles across 31 acres. In addition to the indoor exhibits, visitors can take a self-guiding or naturalist-led walk or snowshoe along several trails to view outdoor exhibits, a rare river oxbow marsh, a pond, open fields, and woodlands.

▶ Open daily late May–late Oct.; Fri. and Sat. early Nov.–late May; Closed major holidays. Admission charged.

www.wildcenter.org
(518) 359-7800

15 National Bottle Museum

76 Milton Ave., Ballston Spa
This museum preserves the history of bottle-making, which was one of our nation's first industries in the early 1700s. At that time there was an incredible demand for all types of glassware, from mineral water containers to whiskey flasks, sought after by hardworking, lonely men settling the Western frontier.

15 National Bottle Museum. Commercial products of the 19th century came in glass bottles of all sizes, shapes, and colors.

Collectors, potential collectors, and visitors with a more casual interest will be intrigued by the examples on display here. The pieces, mostly organized by kind, range from milk bottles and fruit jars to bitters bottles and soda bottles. One exhibit is a reconstructed pharmacy with bottles large and small, quaint and colorful, created for a remarkable variety of nostrums both herbal and alcoholic. Glassblowing tools and equipment are also on display.

In a newly purchased building across the street from the museum, a fully functional "Museum Glassworks" has been set up, which allows visitors to glimpse the mechanics of the industry in action. The museum also offers flameworking classes, allowing visitors to try glassblowing and other techniques themselves.

▶ Open daily June–Sept.; Mon.–Fri. Oct.–May. Admission charged.

www.nationalbottlemuseum.org
(518) 885-7589

14 The Wild Center (Natural History Museum of the Adirondacks). To meet the standards of the Leadership in Energy and Environmental Design (LEED) initiative, the museum—here mirrored in Tupper Lake—incorporated solar power and other "green" building requirements.

 Hanford Mills Museum

73 County Hwy. 12, East Meredith
Sixteen historic buildings preserved and restored here offer a vivid insight into the development of rural American industry and technology in the late 19th and early 20th centuries. The original water-powered mill, built on the banks of Kortright Creek in the 1840s, was first used to saw lumber. Later a gristmill was added.

In 1860 David Josiah Hanford purchased the property and created a multifaceted business, adding a supply store and a woodworking shop that produced everything from architectural trim to milk boxes and buggy parts. Around the turn of the century, Hanford's sons were among the first in the area to harness the flow of water to generate power for rural electrification.

Today this rich heritage can be appreciated in a fine collection of over 200 antique milling machines, including the 12-foot-wide, 10-foot-diameter 1926 Fitz waterwheel; shingle mills; barrel-top shapers; handhole cutters; and the eight-kilowatt dynamo that was used to produce electricity. A collection of early photographs provides a unique view of the social history of a rural area typical of the Northeast.

▶ Open Tues.-Sun. mid-May–mid-Oct. and on Memorial Day, Labor Day, and Columbus Day. Admission charged.

www.hanfordmills.org
(800) 295-4992

17 Opus 40 and The Quarryman's Museum

50 Fite Rd., Saugerties
One man's vision of paradise led to the monumental environmental structure and sculpture garden known as Opus 40, on the western shore of the Hudson River in Ulster County, 100 miles north of Manhattan. Harvey Fite took his inspiration from the Mayan Ruins in Honduras and spent almost 40 years of his life turning an abandoned bluestone quarry into a harmonious interplay of art, nature, and light in the shadow of the Catskill Mountains.

Flame, a female figure with her arms stretching toward the clouds, is one of the sculptures tucked into the six-plus-acre landscape. The centerpiece is a whorl of fitted stone that twists around fountains, pools, and trees, leading to a nine-ton monolith at the foot of Overlook Mountain. The sculptures can also be seen as a tribute to the industry that once thrived here, quarrying the bluestone and shipping it throughout the world.

Fite built the adjacent museum to house the traditional quarryman's tools he used in creating his magnum opus.

▶ Open Memorial Day–Columbus Day, Fri.–Sun., plus holiday Mon. Admission charged.

www.opus40.org
(845) 246-3400

18 Old Rhinebeck Aerodrome

9 Norton Rd., Red Hook
Equal parts history lesson and entertainment spectacle, this living museum re-creates the thrills and spirit of the golden years of flying, from 1900 to 1935. Housed in four large hangars, the museum's extensive collection of vintage aircraft, vehicles, and memorabilia vividly showcases the era of the Wright brothers, Charles Lindbergh, and the Red Baron.

On Saturdays and Sundays the old engines roar back to life as the aerodrome puts on two different air shows featuring World War 1 dogfights, acrobatic barnstorming antics, and even a bit of zany airborne theater. Pre-show fun includes a vintage fashion show and an old-time automobile parade. Visitors wanting to experience the feel and sounds of these classic machines up close can tour the flight line in a vintage automobile or take a 15-minute ride in an open-cockpit biplane over the scenic Hudson River.

▶ Open daily mid-May–late Oct.; air shows Sat. and Sun. mid-June–mid-Oct. Admission charged.

www.oldrhinebeck.org
(845) 752-3200

19 Sam's Point Preserve

400 Sam's Point Rd., Cragsmoor
Sam's Point Preserve, a 5,770-acre preserve owned by the Open Space Institute and New York State and managed by the Nature Conservancy, contains one of the world's best examples of a ridgetop dwarf pine barrens. It is also part of the 90,000-acre Northern Shawangunk Mountains, whose cliffs, summits, and plateaus form a unique landscape of extraordi-

16 ▶ Hanford Mills Museum. A father and his sons turned the original water-powered mill into a multifaceted business that operated until the 1960s. Today visitors, to what is now a museum, watch authentic demonstrations of historic milling operations.

nary ecological significance. Home to 35 natural communities with more than 1,400 species, including 57 rare and imperiled plants and animals, the northern Shawangunks are designated one of Earth's "Last Great Places" by the Nature Conservancy and represent one of the highest priorities for conservation in this part of the country.

The preserve offers expansive views that extend into five states, and 13 miles of trails are ideal for hiking, bird-watching, and cross-country skiing. The Ice Caves, a favorite destination for hikers, are a cool spot on a hot day. Formed along fractures in the bedrock and in a jumble of talus blocks that fell from the face of the cliff, the caves retain snow and ice in a naturally "refrigerated" environment into the summer. A new conservation center has maps and exhibits. Wear hiking boots and carry drinking water.

▶ Preserve open daily year-round. Ice Caves open late spring–late fall.

www.nature.org/samspoint
www.osiny.org
(845) 647-7989

20 Historic Huguenot Street

New Paltz

Even before King Louis XIV banned their religion (in 1685), many French Protestants, known as Huguenots, found refuge in neighboring countries. From 1660–1675 several Huguenot families arrived in the Hudson Valley. They bought land from the Native Americans, built log huts, and named their settlement after a previous refuge along the Rhine River. In the early 1700s they began to replace the huts with steep-roofed stone houses.

Seven of these quaint, medieval-looking dwellings remain on Huguenot Street, designated a National Historic Landmark with the claim of being "the oldest street in America with its original houses."

These were originally one-room structures, and the large family kitchens with enormous fireplaces and cupboards displaying pottery and old pewter are especially appealing. Also on Huguenot Street are the stone church, reconstructed in 1972 and rebuilt from its original 1717 plans, and the DuBois Fort (1705), used formerly as a home and meeting place and now as a visitors center.

▶ Grounds and programs available year-round. Visitors center and tours from May–Oct., closed Wed. Admission charged.

www.huguenotstreet.org
(845) 255-1660

21 Muscoot Farm and Elephant Hotel

Farm on Rte. 100, off Rte. 35; hotel at 335 Rte. 202, Somers

It's worth delving into the luxuriant greenery of northern Westchester County's countryside to find this living-history farm, originally owned by the inventor of "Mother Sill's Seasick Remedy." The elixir's success helped build Ferdinand T. Hopkins's fortune and enabled his family to live on Muscoot Farm for three generations.

Muscoot means "by the swamp" in a local Native American dialect. A red maple swamp, seven miles of woodland trails, and butterflies-in-residence are part of the farm's charm. The country gentleman's farming life, circa 1880 to 1950, is depicted in the original buildings. Barnyard animals and events such as a Victorian faerie woodland walk and seasonal hayrides appeal to young children.

The Federal-style Elephant Hotel houses the Somers Historical Society and Museum of the Early American Circus. It celebrates America's second elephant, Old Bet, brought here in 1805 by Hachaliah Bailey. The hotel was built by Bailey and later used as a meeting place for fellow menagerie owners. There is a wealth of circus information here, as well as local history. And be sure to view the display of Tom Thumb's suit.

▶ Muscoot Farm open daily. Elephant Hotel open Thurs. and the 2nd and 4th Sun. of the month. Donations accepted.

www.westchestergov.com
(914) 232-7118 Muscoot Farm

www.somershistoricalsoc.org
(914) 277-4977 Elephant Hotel

22 The Cloisters Museum and Gardens

Fort Tryon Park, New York

Don't think you can't venture off the beaten path in crowded New York City. Deep in a wooded park near Manhattan's northern tip

22 **The Cloisters Museum and Gardens.** Some of the capitals and columns of the Cuxa Cloister are from the original built in 12th-century France.

is The Cloisters Museum and Gardens, one of the city's most fascinating attractions.

A branch of the Metropolitan Museum of Art, The Cloisters Museum and Gardens is the country's only museum that is devoted exclusively to the art and architecture of medieval Europe. Surrounded by medieval gardens, five monastery-inspired buildings—with stone arches, columns and other elements from actual medieval structures—house a Romanesque chapel, statuary and crucifixes, a 12th-century apse brought from Spain, and hundreds of other rarities. Best known of these are the magnificent "Unicorn Tapestries" woven circa 1495–1505.

If the tranquil museum is an escape from the clamor of America's largest city, so is its location: a 66-acre park overlooking the shimmering Hudson River.

▶ Open Tues.–Sun. except major winter holidays. Admission charged.

www.metmuseum.org
212-923-3700

23 Museum of the City of New York

1220 Fifth Ave. at 103rd St., New York

The permanent and rotating exhibits in this unique museum, housed in a five-story neo-Georgian building across the street from Central Park, explore the past, present, and future of New York City. Exhibitions include Perform, spotlighting the history of New York theater and Broadway; New York Interiors, re-creating furnished rooms in the Dutch and English traditions; and Trade, depicting how the ports of the city led to its dominance in trade and commerce.

The extensive vintage toy collection, long beloved by New Yorkers, includes mechanical toy banks, board games, cast-iron vehicles, and more. The stars are the dollhouses, which present a picture of 19th-century New York home life in miniature.

▶ Open Tues.–Sun. Admission charged.

www.mcny.org
(212) 534-1672

24 Jacques Marchais Museum of Tibetan Art

338 Lighthouse Ave., Staten Island
Nestled into a hill on Staten Island, the Jacques Marchais Museum of Tibetan Art features Tibetan-style fieldstone buildings that resemble a Himalayan monastery. Terraced meditation gardens and a lotus pond add to the serenity of the place.

Inside the handcrafted walls, visitors can see a vast collection of rare and important Asian art. Jacques Marchais (1887-1948), an extraordinary American woman, created the center to share the artistic and cultural traditions of

23 Museum of the City of New York. Displays focus on the history and culture of the nation's largest city.

Tibet and the Himalayas with the world. Starting in the 1920s, Marchais amassed one of the nation's earliest and largest collections of high-quality Tibetan art, including sculptures, thangkas, ritual objects, furniture, textiles, and historic photographs.

Most of the rare objects are Tibetan Buddhist in nature. They were used in monasteries in Tibet and in neighboring countries within the sphere of Tibetan cultural influence; they are of significance to world cultural heritage and of sacred importance to the Tibetan population.

Ongoing programs include lectures and workshops, film screenings, musical performances, special events with Tibetan and Himalayan monks, art exhibitions, and classes in tai chi and meditation.

▶ Open Wed.–Sun. Admission charged.

www.tibetanmuseum.org
(718) 987-3500

25 Jamaica Bay National Wildlife Refuge

Cross Bay Blvd., Brood Channel
Perhaps the most singular feature of this watery wilderness is its contrast to the surrounding cityscape. In spring and fall thousands of birds swoop down to these wetlands for shelter and food, unfazed by the millions of people rumbling by in cars and the jets roaring overhead. In proximity humans and birds follow their own rhythms.

For city people the 9,155-acre refuge (which has five miles of paths) offers easy access to the natural world. Most visitors come during the migratory seasons, when many warblers, hawks, and waterfowl can be seen. Roughly 150 other feathered species are seen here.

But the summer and winter are also rewarding times to visit the refuge, not only for birding but for enjoying the scenery, the relative peace, and the pleasant illusion of being nowhere—but still within the sight of Manhattan's skyline.

The refuge is particularly lovely in wintertime, when crystals of ice form on the trees and grasses and the sense of solitude is heightened.

▶ Open daily Mar.–Dec. except major winter holidays; Wed.–Sun. Jan.–Feb.

www.nps.gov/gate
(718) 318-4340

26 Bayard Cutting Arboretum

440 Montauk Hwy., Great River
In the mid-1700s English gardening was revolutionized by the informal parklike landscape designed by Lancelot "Capability" Brown. One of his admirers a hundred years later was Frederick Law Olmsted, the landscape architect best known as the creator of New York City's Central Park.

When William Bayard Cutting established his arboretum in 1887, he employed Olmsted's firm to design it. The garden, much in the style of Capability Brown, is a magnificent 690-acre park of trees, rhododendrons, azaleas, wildflower plantings, small ponds, and wide lawns that sweep down to the Connetquot River.

The names of the five trails through the grounds indicate the special characteristics of each: Pinetum, Wildflower, Bird Watchers, Rhododendron, and Swamp Cypress. All are detailed on a map available at the arboretum center.

The estate, donated to the Long Island State Park and Recreation Commission by Mrs. William Bayard Cutting and her daughter, Mrs. Olivia James, includes the former Cutting home, which now serves as a center for the arboretum. The interior is noted for the ornate oak paneling, stained-glass windows, and handsome antique fireplaces. On

24 Jacques Marchais Museum of Tibetan Art. Collector Marchais (1887-1948) was an American enthralled by Tibetan art.

display are collections of mounted birds, Native American artifacts, and interesting plants. Near the entry is a spectacular specimen of a weeping European beech.

▶ Open Tues.–Sun. year-round, and Mon. holidays Apr.–Oct. Admission charged.

www.bayardcuttingarboretum.com
www.nysparks.com
(631) 581-1002

27▶ Morton National Wildlife Refuge

784 Noyack Rd., Sag Harbor
Long before the 17th century, when Europeans invaded eastern Long Island, this narrow strip of land between Little Peconic and Noyack bays was the home of the Montauk and Shinnecock Native Americans, who farmed and fished and traded with the Corchaugs, their relatives on the North Shore. The property was deeded in 1679 to John Jessup, who had come here from Massachusetts some 40 years earlier. Known as Jessup's Neck, the peninsula has 187 acres of woodlands, salt marshes, sandy shores, and a freshwater pond.

After almost 200 years of private ownership and use as farmland, the property was given by Mrs. Elizabeth Morton to the U.S. Fish and Wildlife Service in 1954; the land is now slowly reverting to its natural state.

The refuge is an important resting and feeding stop for birds on

their seasonal migrations. Since 1956, when the refuge was established, more than 200 species of waterfowl, songbirds, hawks, and waders have been observed. Black ducks, goldeneyes, and scaups are among those staying in the area all winter. An observation blind on the bank of the small pond is a great boon to bird-watchers.

A one-mile self-guiding nature trail leads through woods and past ponds and marshes to the beach. Guided tours and educational programs are available on request.

▶ Open year-round; partial beach closure Apr.–Aug. Admission charged.

www.fws.gov/northeast/longislandrefuges
(631) 286-0485

28▶ Orient Beach State Park

Long Island Expwy. (Rte. 495) east to end, then Rte. 25 east to Orient
That a state park exists here is due to the foresight of local farmers some 60 years ago. At that time, the land was owned by the Male Taxpayers of Orient, a farmers

organization with an interest in preserving this marshy peninsula as a barrier protecting their farms from the sea. In 1929 the organization donated the land to the state, hoping that the government would take over the burden of maintenance. The farmers plan worked, and in the early 1930s the park was established.

Today this 357-acre park is an inviting place for a family day trip. The five-mile-long peninsula in quiet Gardiner's Bay provides 10 miles of sand-and-pebble beach, a small portion of which is reserved for swimming. The lifeguards on duty and the gentle waters here make it suitable for children. The large picnic area is shaded by a grove of cedars. Fishing is allowed from the shore, but boats may not be launched. Flounder and snapper are the likely catch.

▶ Open daily year-round except Christmas. Swimming season late June–early Sept.

www.nysparks.com
(631) 323-2440

28▶ Orient Beach State Park. A playground on the beach strikes a nautical note, its equipment including a stylized tugboat and jungle gyms with cabana-style roofs.

seasonal events

FEBRUARY
- Winter Carnival and Ice Castle—Saranac Lake *(sporting activities, live entertainment, dances, fireworks, parades, children's activities)*

JULY
- Ironman USA Triathlon—Lake Placid *(sporting event)*
- Renaissance Festival—Sterling *(summerlong celebration)*

AUGUST
- Champ Day—Port Henry *(rides, children's activities, games, craft fair, all in celebration of Lake Champlain's mysterious monster)*
- Onion Festival—Elba *(carnival, pageant, local food)*
- Great New York State Fair—Syracuse *(carnival, live music, live entertainment, food, agriculture, history, arts and crafts)*
- International Celtic Festival—Hunter *(live music, dancing, regional food, vendors)*

SEPTEMBER
- Wine & Food Festival—Saratoga *(dining, dancing, decanting delights, expert presentations)*
- Revolutionary War Encampment—Fort Ticonderoga *(historical re-enactment, demonstrations, period food and crafts)*

OCTOBER
- The Great Jack O'Lantern Blaze—Croton-on-Hudson *(over 4,000 hand-carved pumpkins, large breathtaking displays, concessions)*
- World's Largest Garage Sale—Warrensburg *(flea market, arts and crafts, local food)*
- Pug Party and Parade—Chestertown *(dog show, costumes, parade)*

DECEMBER
- Corning Museum of Glass—Corning *(make your own glass holiday ornaments, glassblowing, holiday crafts, lunch with Santa)*

www.iloveny.com

North Carolina

The remarkable diversity of its out-of-the-way places is a cordial invitation to explore the byways of this pleasant state.

Snappy Lunch. *The Andy Griffith Show*'s TV hangout lives on in Griffith's hometown of Mount Airy, the inspiration for Mayberry (see page 250).

The deep, dramatic gorge that attracts river-runners, hikers, and fishermen contrasts sharply with the serenity of the farm where Carl Sandburg, the "people's poet," spent his last years.

State-owned settings have colorful displays of native wildflowers and flowering trees. Museums here are dedicated to such subjects as a pre-Revolutionary battle, two Civil War forts, gold mining, the good works of country doctors and a progressive governor, and a village that time almost forgot.

visit ➤➤ **offthebeatenpathtrips.com**

1 ➤ Nantahala Gorge

12 miles southwest of Bryson City

Carved by the Nantahala River, this eight-mile gorge takes its name from a Cherokee word meaning "land of the noonday sun." Indeed, the canyon here is so deep and narrow that only when the sun is directly overhead can its rays reach the bottom of the gorge.

The gorge burrows down some 1,800 feet at its deepest and is less than 100 yards wide at its narrowest. It is the centerpiece of the Nantahala National Forest, with easy access to the Appalachian

1 ➤ Nantahala Gorge. A Hwy. 64 lookout between Highlands and Cashiers affords a panoramic view of the forest, which is crossed by the Appalachian Trail.

1 ➤ Nantahala Gorge. Bridal Veil Falls spills lightly over weathered shale.

Trail, which crosses the eastern end of the gorge.

The river offers a variety of recreational opportunities. Water released from the Duke Power dam several miles upriver rushes down the gorge for about 12 hours on most days, creating an ideal run for whitewater rafting.

Rafts, canoes, and kayaks may be rented in the area, and the trip, while exhilarating, is not overly challenging for novices. Picnic areas are maintained, and the river is stocked with trout; fishing is better in the calm evening waters than in the daytime torrents.

▶ Open year-round.

www.greatsmokies.com
(800) 867-9246

2 ➤ Carl Sandburg Home National Historic Site

Little River Rd., Flat Rock

Named Connemara by previous owners, who likened its view of the distant Blue Ridge Mountains to that of a mountainous region in western Ireland, this was Carl Sandburg's last home. Though perhaps best known as a son of the Midwest, the poet and two-time

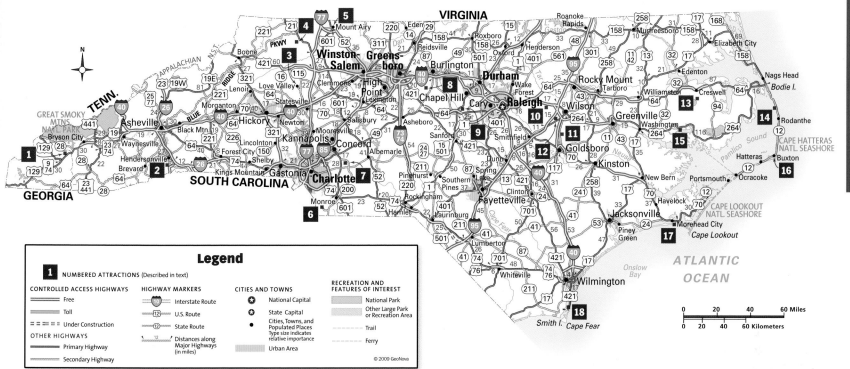

Pulitzer prizewinner lived here for 22 years until his death in 1967.

Large but unpretentious, the 1830s clapboard structure stands as a memorial to the man and his work, and its interior reflects his life at the height of his career. In the living room his guitar leans against a favorite easy chair, and magazines from the 1940s lie in untidy stacks on tables and across the floor. Over the fireplace is a framed photograph of Sandburg and his wife taken by his brother-in-law, Edward Steichen.

A large office contains a typewriter surrounded by piles of books and cardboard boxes filled with research material and notes. On his desk, giving the impression that he has left only momentarily, lies one of the green eyeshades he invariably used.

A self-guiding walk leads to the farm area, and trails cross the pastures and woodlands of the

260-acre park, leading up Glassy Mountain (about 2 1/2 miles round-trip), where bluebirds vie for attention with the wildflowers. A small, wooded picnic area is near the visitors center. Expect crowds in late spring and foliage season.

▶ Open year-round except Christmas. Admission charged.

www.nps.gov/carl
(828) 693-4178

2 ▶ **Carl Sandburg Home National Historic Site.** A house in the quiet countryside was ideal for both poet Sandburg and his wife, Lilian, who raised prizewinning dairy goats.

3 Love Valley

North of Statesville off I-40 and Rock Hill Church Rd.
Growing up, Charlotte native Andy Barker wanted two things in life: to live in a church-centered community and to be a cowboy. He got his wish in 1954 when he bought 300 acres on Fox Mountain and founded Love Valley—now a replica Wild West–style town that's become a popular destination for

horseback riders, hikers, and rodeo lovers. Open weekends only, Love Valley offers room and cabin rentals, campgrounds, meals, horse rentals, a tack shop and farrier—and Sunday worship services.

The town's 120 permanent residents are joined by hundreds of weekenders who own houses here.

Though cars aren't allowed in the actual town, horse-drawn vehicles will take you from the spacious parking area to your destination.

▶ Open Fri.–Sun. only.

www.townoflovevalley.com
(704) 592-7451

Legend

1 NUMBERED ATTRACTIONS (Described in text)

CONTROLLED ACCESS HIGHWAYS
Free
Toll
Under Construction

OTHER HIGHWAYS
Primary Highway
Secondary Highway

HIGHWAY MARKERS
Interstate Route
U.S. Route
State Route
Distances along Major Highways (in miles)

CITIES AND TOWNS
National Capital
State Capital
Cities, Towns, and Populated Places Type size indicates relative importance
Urban Area

RECREATION AND FEATURES OF INTEREST
National Park
Other Large Park or Recreation Area
Trail
Ferry

© 2009 GeoNova

4 ▶ **Stone Mountain State Park.** The smooth granite dome of Stone Mountain dominates the scenery at a park that attracts hikers, anglers, and nature lovers.

4 ▶ Stone Mountain State Park

3042 Frank Pkwy., Roaring Gap
Plunging waterfalls, granite outcroppings, narrow dirt roads, and trails twisting through catawba rhododendrons and mountain laurel populate this park's more than 14,100 acres.

Creeks stocked with trout—rainbows, browns, and "brookies"—make this a fisherman's paradise. In Bullhead Creek (a "fish for fun" stream where fly-fishermen may practice their techniques but must toss back their catch) rainbows as long as 26 inches have been hooked.

Trails lead to the 2,300-foot summit of rugged Stone Mountain, and you'll also find paths to Stone Mountain Falls, Cedar Rock, and Wolf Rock. Mountain climbers can choose from 13 different ascent routes, many of which are difficult and not recommended for beginners.

Throughout this densely forested area, lady's slippers, trilliums, bluets, and other wildflowers and ferns are often seen in settings that also frequently include feathered populations of red-tailed hawks, ruffed grouse, black vultures, wild turkeys, and owls. White-tailed deer, beavers, otters, minks, and foxes are occasionally glimpsed. Bears have also been reported but are extremely rare.

▶ Open year-round except Christmas. Fee for fishing.

www.ncparks.gov
(336) 957-8185

5 ▶ Mount Airy (a.k.a. Mayberry)

Mount Airy, birthplace of actor Andy Griffith and the likely inspiration for *The Andy Griffith Show,* is a trip down memory lane for fans of the 1960s TV series. You can head over to Wally's Fillin Station and tour Main St. in the Sheriff's squad car. Savor a pork-chop sandwich at The Snappy Lunch, which, like Floyd's barbershop, predates the show. See the bronze statue of Andy and Opie at the Andy Griffith Playhouse (site of the annual Old Time Fiddlers' Convention), and generally enjoy reminders of the popular series throughout the town.

Mount Airy and its environs have other claims to fame: The area was once inhabited by the mysterious Saura tribe of Native Americans and later was home to the original Siamese twins, Chang and Eng Bunker. These conjoined twins settled in nearby White Plains after retiring from P. T. Barnum's circus. Check out the local history at the Mount Airy Museum of Regional History. The town—officially a city since 1976—has much to enjoy year-round, including its picturesque setting in the Blue Ridge Mountains. Stop by the welcome center on E. Main St. for information, ideas of what to do, and maps.

www.visitmayberry.com
(800) 948-0949; (336) 786-6116

6 ▶ Museum of the Alphabet

JAARS Center, 7405 Jaars Rd., Waxhaw
For anyone who has ever wondered about the origins of writing, the Museum of the Alphabet has the answers. Inside its compact and unprepossessing building, visitors take a journey through the development of alphabets, from ancient Mesopotamia to modern times. Colorful multimedia displays and activities make for a highly entertaining as well as educational experience for all ages. Participate in activities such as writing your name with hieroglyph stamps.

7 ▶ **Reed Gold Mine State Historic Site.** Visitors of all ages can pan for gold at this historic lode, discovered in 1799 when a young boy spied a shiny rock.

Located about 30 miles south of Charlotte, the Museum was opened in 1990. It is a joint project of the Wycliffe Bible Translators, SIL (Summer Institute of Linguistics) International, and JAARS. Both are faith-based organizations that are engaged in the study, documentation, and translation of world languages.

If you have time for another stop, consider seeing the related Mexico-Cardenas Museum honoring Mexican president (1934–1940) Lazaro Cardenas del Rio, who encouraged and supported the work of SIL scholars studying the languages of Mexico's indigenous peoples. This museum's exhibits include folk art, native costumes and jewelry, and a 1938 Chevy sedan given to the young American linguists by President Cardenas.

▶ Both museums open Mon.-Sat. Closed major holidays.

www.jaars.org/museum/alphabet
(704) 843-6066

7 Reed Gold Mine State Historic Site

9621 Reed Mine Rd., Midland
In 1799 the young son of German immigrant John Reed found a shiny rock in Little Meadow Creek near his father's farm. Unable to identify its composition, the elder Reed used it as a

did you know ?

John Reed sold his 17-pound lucky find to an unscrupulous jeweler for $3.50—a fraction of its true value! However, despite this unfortunate sale, Reed later became a wealthy man due to his mining exploits.

8 **Alamance Battleground State Historic Site.** During the annual 18th-century Live-in & Militia Muster, re-enactors fire flintlock muskets and rifles. Their ancestors were among the first colonists to use armed resistance against the Crown.

doorstop until a jeweler offered him $3.50 for it in 1802; Reed sold it.

The shiny rock was a 17-pound chunk of gold—the first authenticated gold find in the United States. Reed soon established a mining company, and in 1831 he expanded the operation from placer mining (creek panning) to underground mining, an operation that continued under several ownerships until 1912.

Guided tours of the site today take you through a maze of mine shafts, restored to memorialize the nation's first gold rush.

A large building near the mine contains a restored 1895 stamp mill, used today to demonstrate how, with several crushing blows, gold can be extracted from quartz. At the panning area visitors are shown how to separate gold from

soil. Lucky panners may keep their strikes. Gold objects serving monetary and other purposes are displayed in old bank and office safes at the visitors center.

A self-guiding nature trail winds through the fields and forests of this 822-acre historic site. A picnic area is across the road from the main entrance.

▶ Open Tues.-Sat. year-round, but panning site open Apr.-Oct. Fee for panning.

www.nchistoricsites.org
(704) 721-4653

8 Alamance Battleground State Historic Site

5803 S. NC-62, Burlington
On May 16, 1771, more than two years before the Boston Tea Party, a brief revolt here ended in defeat for about 2,000 of the then-

colony's independent Western frontiersmen, who stood in armed rebellion against the royal governor and the colonial militia.

Known as Regulators, these men and their families had been voicing increasing dissatisfaction with the corruption of British rule for years. They began acting on their frustration early in 1771 by refusing to pay taxes. After warnings from the governor, a royal militia was sent to challenge the upstart Regulators.

For all of their justifiable anger, the poorly trained and ineffectively led frontiersmen were unable to prevail against the Crown. Their efforts, however, were not in vain. Their bold use of armed resistance became well known throughout the colonies, and it set the stage for the coming battle for independence.

Flags on the battlefield show where each side stood, and a bronze map explains the events that took place. A granite monument dedicated in 1880 commemorates the battle.

Another attraction on the grounds is the 1780 Allen House, an oak-and-ash log dwelling typical of those built by settlers of the era on this frontier. A clock with wooden gears, a walnut desk, and other original furnishings evoke the homespun comforts of the past. The visitors center displays weapons and uniforms of the time and presents a brief video show.

Expect crowds for the many special events that take place here during Colonial Living Week in mid-October.

▶ Open Mon.-Sat. year-round.

www.nchistoricsites.com/alamance
(336) 227-4785

9 Clyde Jones Haw River Critter Crossing

Bynum Hill Rd., Bynum

Once a mill town but now mostly residential, Bynum is home to folk artist Clyde Jones and his amazing critters, carved from local wood with a chain saw, decorated with found objects, and often painted in vibrant rainbow colors. You'll see examples of Jones's work throughout the village, but the real treat is his Critter Crossing near the Haw River. His small house, painted top to bottom with colorful murals, is surrounded by hundreds of whimsical critters.

Jones began sculpting in the early 1980s while recovering from a sawmill injury and took up painting a few years later. His pieces have been featured in galleries and museums nationally and internationally. He is known for giving away, rather than selling, his art, and at the Critter Crossing his menagerie is free for the looking.

While in town, check out the Bynum General Store, now a community center known for the live outdoor concerts it hosts during the summer.

www.chathamarts.org
(919) 542-0394 Chatham County Arts Council

10 The Country Doctor Museum

6629 Vance St., Bailey

In the rough-and-tumble environment of rural America's yesteryear, country doctors had to set bones, deliver babies, combat disease, and even prepare their own prescriptions. This museum demonstrates their multiple talents with a fine display of instruments, medical books, handwritten notes, and office equipment.

The collection is housed in a pair of connected 19th-century buildings once used by two North Carolina country doctors: Dr. Howard Franklin Freeman's office

11 **Governor Charles B. Aycock Birthplace.** Rustic original buildings at this site reflect the humble beginnings of the man known as North Carolina's "Education Governor."

dates to 1857, and Dr. Cornelius Henry Brantley's to 1887. In the front room is a vast wooden cabinet displaying apothecary jars and a large rolltop desk with cubbyholes for prescriptions and bills.

Civil War surgeons' amputation kits, a hinged leather artificial leg, turn-of-the-century obstetric instruments, and a model of a doctor's horse and buggy help to illustrate the history of medicine in the United States from about 1800 to the early 1900s.

One interesting exhibit shows the tools that were used to amputate the left arm of Confederate general Thomas "Stonewall" Jackson in 1863. Ironically, Jackson, who was shot accidentally by his own men, died eight days later, a devastating loss for the Confederates.

Walk across a small garden of medicinal plants to the Art of Nursing exhibit, showcasing uniforms and equipment of the trade spanning the last 200 years.

▶ Open Tues.–Sat. year-round. Admission charged.

www.countrydoctormuseum.org
(252) 235-4165

11 Governor Charles B. Aycock Birthplace

264 Governor Aycock Rd., Fremont

As governor of North Carolina from 1901–05, Charles B. Aycock improved the state's public education system; over 1,000 schools were built during his tenure.

The youngest of 10 children, Aycock was born in 1859 in the simple, unpainted frame house that is now the main attraction at this 19th-century farm complex. Among family furnishings on display are a pine chest, side table, and an assortment of frames. Two shed rooms flanking the front porch were used occasionally by travelers in need of lodging.

A restored kitchen in a separate building contains a large fireplace with many early pots and pans,

10 **The Country Doctor Museum.** The museum's collection of by-gone surgical implements, natural medicines, and books transports visitors to the nineteenth century.

along with a dining room. The original smokehouse, pantry, stable, and corn barn are still standing. An 1893 one-room schoolhouse was moved to the site and furnished with desks and blackboards, bringing to life rural education in the state at the turn of the 20th century.

Guided tours originate at the visitors center, where a small exhibit area displays Aycock's gold-headed cane, law books, and replicas of his law office and the parlor of his home in Raleigh. An audiovisual program describes Aycock's life and significant contributions to education.

Special events are scheduled throughout the year, and living-history demonstrations include candle dipping, spinning, and other home crafts.

▶ Open Mon.-Sat. year-round.

www.nchistoricsites.org
(919) 242-5581

12 ▶ Vollis Simpson's Whirligigs

Wiggins Mill Rd., Lucama
Anyone who has enjoyed a toy pinwheel spinning in the breeze will be blown away by the whirligigs of Windmill Farm—huge spinning, turning works of art and engineering created by Vollis Simpson, a machinist who once designed and made equipment to move houses and farm buildings. When he retired in the 1980s, Vollis began constructing wind-powered whirligigs, making use of his house-moving machinery and old industrial materials. More than 30 large-scale sculptural towers, a few mechanically powered but most driven by the wind, stand on his rural property. The whirligig structures emphasize motion and sound

12 ▶ Vollis Simpson's Whirligigs. Color and movement catch the visitor's eye.

as works of art, and each are covered by paint and reflectors, making them a spectacular sight both day and night.

His constructions have been exhibited by Atlanta's High Museum of Art, the Baltimore Visionary Art Museum, and the North Carolina Museum of Art in Raleigh. Four 40-foot whirligigs commissioned for the 1996 Olympics are now permanent fixtures in Atlanta.

The Lucama community, located about seven miles southwest of Wilson, is accessible from I-95 or Hwy. 301. Wilson, too, is worth a stop. The historic downtown area features whirligigs on its corners, and a park dedicated to Vollis Simpson will soon have a total of 12 whirligigs on display.

www.wilson-nc.com
(800) 497-7398 Wilson Visitors Bureau

13 ▶ Somerset Place State Historic Site and Pettigrew State Park

2252 Lake Shore Rd., Creswell
History and recreation blend nicely in this 17,873-acre park, part of which was once a coastal plantation named for the home county of its English owner, Josiah Collins.

His grandson built a handsome clapboard mansion on his ancestral land around 1830. The mansion's distinguishing features include marble fireplaces, wood-grain painted doors, and wide porches. A rare 1850 Wilson sewing machine and a toy stagecoach with beeswax horses are further reminders of the past. Close by are the kitchen, dairy, icehouse, and other clapboard outbuildings, and a formal garden adds to the gentrified feel here.

The park is named for the Confederate general James Pettigrew, who led the famous and deadly charge on Cemetery Ridge at the Battle of Gettysburg on July 3, 1863—a turning point in the Civil War.

Nine miles of trails penetrate the park's virgin forest of huge oaks, bald cypresses, poplars, and sweetgums, which shelter pileated woodpeckers, big-eared bats, and

did you know ?

Artifacts provide evidence of Native Americans in Pettigrew Park as early as 8,000 B.C. Over 30 dugout canoes have been found sunken in the lake—and the oldest is almost 4,400 years old.

black bears. A major attraction is Lake Phelps, second largest in the state and famous for the largemouth bass that entice anglers from near and far. Many ducks and geese can be seen on the lake in winter. The park has a picnic area, trailer and tent campsites, bicycle trails, scenic overlooks, a fishing pier, and a boat ramp.

▶ Park open year-round except Christmas; Somerset Place open daily Apr.-Oct., Tues.-Sun. Nov.-Mar.

www.ncparks.gov
(252) 797-4475 Pettigrew Park
(252) 797-4560 Somerset Place

13 ▶ Somerset Place State Historic Site. A plantation from 1785 to 1865, Somerset Place once covered up to 100,000 acres. The antebellum house was its centerpiece.

14 ▶ **Pea Island National Wildlife Refuge.** Ducks rest on a Pea Island pond at sunset. Herons, egrets, ibises, and other waterfowl can also be viewed at the refuge.

14 ▶ Pea Island National Wildlife Refuge

10 miles south of Nags Head
Each spring and fall geese, ducks, and other migratory birds use the Atlantic Flyway to get where they're going.

This sliver of an island—almost 13 miles long and no more than a mile across at its widest—is one of the Eastern Seaboard's finest vantage points to observe the migration. And beach lovers, fishermen, hikers, and photographers will also find much to enjoy here.

This complex of salt marshes and freshwater ponds supports otters, muskrats, nutrias, diamond-back terrapins, and loggerhead, sea, and snapping turtles. Ring-necked pheasants abound, while egrets, herons, and ibises are among the waterfowl and shorebirds that nest here. Peregrine falcons are often seen during spring and fall migrations, and more than 250 other bird species are occasionally observed.

A number of observation platforms facilitate sightings of all varieties, while ponds supporting ducks, geese, and swans are easily observed from the car.

Five access points to Atlantic beaches and one to Pamlico Sound along the western shore attract bathers. Anglers can cast for sea trout, channel bass, pompano, and bluefish.

▶ Open year-round.

http://peaisland.fws.gov
(252) 473-1131

15 ▶ Belhaven Memorial Museum

210 E. Main St., Belhaven
In the pantheon of pack rats, there must be a special place for Mrs. Mary Eva Blount Way (1869–1962). Beginning with a small button collection, a gift from her mother-in-law, "Miss Eva" amassed 30,000 buttons plus just about everything else that came her way—from cooking utensils, farm tools, and period clothing to a two-headed kitten, an eight-legged pig, and a dried flea wedding (bride and groom in full attire, visible under a magnifying glass). Friends and neighbors contributed oddities, and Miss Eva's odds and ends grew to more than 40,000 items, counting the buttons.

The collection filled her large house, expanded to her barn, and was finally moved in 1965 to its current home in the old Belhaven Town Hall, which is listed on the *National Register of Historic Places*. A remarkable repository of the stuff of daily life gathered over almost 80 years, the museum is often called a "granny's attic," assuming one's granny was an inveterate collector of the everyday and the exotic.

▶ Open daily except Wed.

www.beaufort-county.com/belhaven/
   museum/belhaven.htm
(252) 943-6817

16 ▶ Buxton Woods Coastal Reserve

Hatteras Island
Forests are rare on the Outer Banks, where wind and salt spray reign. But at Buxton the island

16 ▶ **Buxton Woods Coastal Reserve.** This wind-buffeted Outer Banks forest is home to wildlife of surprising diversity.

broadens to nearly four miles, and the distance from the ocean and higher elevations combines to create an example of ecological interdependence. Here in the 968-acre forest, stunted trees form a protective canopy over the undergrowth, and this low foliage in turn stabilizes the soil the trees need.

The three-quarter-mile loop of the self-guiding Buxton Woods Nature Trail offers an introduction to this symbiotic environment and its various inhabitants, many seldom found elsewhere on the islands.

Woodland songbirds and wetland egrets, herons, and grebes make the forest and adjoining marsh their home. Ospreys may be seen overhead, and in spring and fall the area is visited by migratory birds. Mammals, generally rare on the Outer Banks, live here, too, including raccoons, otters, minks, nutrias, and white-tailed deer.

▶ Open year-round.

www.nccoastalreserve.net
(252) 995-4474

17 ▶ Fort Macon State Park

NC-1190, Atlantic Beach
Since the early 1700s, when the pirate Blackbeard used Beaufort Inlet as a hideout, its importance has been recognized. After several unsuccessful attempts to fortify the island, construction of Fort Macon began in 1826.

But in the course of succeeding wars, the only action at this five-sided brick fort was on April 25, 1862, when it was shelled by Union forces after a long standoff and captured the next morning.

The fort, named for Nathaniel Macon, a North Carolina senator, is encircled by a moat that could be flooded with the tidewaters of

Fort Macon State Park. While the fort completed in 1834 was ingeniously designed and even boasted a moat, it would be the scene of only one military action.

Bogue Sound. From its impressive ramparts, which once overlooked the inlet, there are commanding views of the Beaufort region.

Circling the fort's inner grounds are quarters for the garrison, storerooms, and a kitchen. The commandant's quarters also have been restored, and there is a small museum.

In addition to the fort, the park offers a protected ocean swimming area, picnic grounds with grills, and hiking.

▶ Open year-round except Christmas.

www.ils.unc.edu/parkproject/visit/
foma/home.html

(252) 726-3775

18 Fort Fisher State Historic Site

*1610 S. Fort Fisher Blvd.,
Kure Beach*
Late in the Civil War the Union blockade of Southern ports prevented the South from receiving war supplies. In order to counter this, Confederate blockade runners made daring trips through fog

and moonless nights to get precious cargoes.

Fort Fisher was built to provide cover for the Confederate seamen entering Cape Fear River on their way to the Confederacy's major port in Wilmington. Extending for one mile along the Atlantic Coast and across a sand peninsula, this series of redoubts was the South's largest earthen seacoast fort. With a complement of 47 guns, it provided a mile of defense seaward as well as one-third mile inland.

Fort Fisher State Historic Site. The South's largest earthen fort could absorb the shock of heavy explosives. Today re-enactors replay Fort Fisher's Civil War battles.

Only a few mounds remain, preserved from the actions of erosion. Exhibits in a small museum detail events that took place here from December 1864 to January 1865, when the fort finally fell to a determined Union action that employed some 58 warships and 8,000 infantrymen.

A quarter-mile tour trail surrounds what remains of the fort today. Features along the route include wayside exhibits, a reconstructed palisade fence, and a partially restored gun emplacement.

The visitors center offers audio-visual programs and a permanent exhibit hall that displays an extensive collection of artifacts from the blockaders and the blockade runners. Also here is a large and impressive fiber-optic–powered map that shows the final battle for the fort in 1865.

▶ Fort open daily Apr.–Sept.; open Tues.–Sat. Oct.–Mar. Aquarium open year-round except holidays. Admission for aquarium.

www.nchistoricsites.org
(910) 458-5538 Fort
(910) 458-8257 Aquarium

seasonal events

JANUARY
- Fourth Friday—Fayetteville (exhibits, entertainment, refreshments, art displays)

MARCH
- Rumba on the Lumber—Lumberton (live music, kid's games, activities, food)
- Fremont Daffodil Festival—Fremont (food, crafts, entertainment)

APRIL
- Grifton Shad Festival—Grifton (fishing, storytelling contest, carnival rides, flea market, live entertainment, parade)

MAY
- Spring Daze—Thomasville (food, crafts, live music, plant sales)

JUNE
- National Hollerin' Contest—Spivey's Corner

JULY
- Underwater Bike Race—Beaufort

AUGUST
- Mineral, Gem, and Jewelry Festival—Spruce Pine (craft vendors, demonstrations, historic mining exhibits, food vendors)

SEPTEMBER
- Bugfest!—Raleigh (crafts, animal and insect exhibits, insect treats, roach races)
- Benson Mule Days—Benson (rodeo, parade, mule race, pulling contest, mule and horse rides, music, carnival rides)

OCTOBER
- Annual Woolly Worm Festival—Banner (caterpillar races, crafts, live entertainment, 10K "Woolly Worm Woad Wace")

NOVEMBER
- Hometown Holiday Celebration—Mebane (lights, decorations, carolers, carriage rides)

DECEMBER
- Window Wonderland—Franklin (refreshments, caroling, music)

www.visitnc.com

North Dakota

Here in the geographical center of North America are some fabulous landforms and bittersweet recollections of pioneer times.

Dakota the Edmontosaurus. A teenager found this mummified dinosaur that is now on display at the North Dakota Heritage Center in Bismarck (see page 260).

Dramatic sections of badlands terrain can be seen in different parks, and the pioneer era is memorialized by a museum of impressive early-day farm machinery and a reconstructed pioneer village with an extensive collection of memorabilia. The history of the inevitable and tragic conflict between the Native Americans, whose land this was, and the settlers, who claimed it as their own, is recalled in the forts and Native American villages.

Find peaceful retreats, such as an international garden, sanctuaries for game and waterfowl, and many good places to fish.

visit ➤→ offthebeatenpathtrips.com

1 International Peace Garden

Hwy. 281, north of Dunseith

This 2,300-acre wooded garden commemorates the heartening fact that the boundary between the United States and Canada is the longest undefended international border in the world. On a monument marking the line, the two nations pledge that "as long as men shall live, we will not take up arms against one another."

The garden, situated on land donated by North Dakota and the Canadian province of Manitoba and dedicated in 1932, was the inspiration of Henry Moore, a Canadian horticulturist. Moore's dream of a garden symbolizing the human yearning for peace is beautifully realized here amid the rolling foothills of the Turtle Mountains.

Two automobile tours, each 3½ miles long, have several stops for sightseeing and picnicking. The Canadian Natural Drive winds past Lake Stormon. At the start of the United States Cultural Drive is a 13-foot floral clock, which is one of the park's most photographed features. This drive also leads to the park's campground, International Music Camp, CCC Lodge, and the Legion Athletic Camp.

To enjoy the natural beauty more closely, one can take the 1½-mile Lake View Hiking Trail, where beavers may be seen at work. Another walk of the same length

1 International Peace Garden. This serene site on the North Dakota–Manitoba border commemorates the goodwill between the United States and Canada.

goes through the well-tended formal gardens marking the nations' boundary line in the center of the park, continuing on to the 120-foot Peace Tower. Also to be found on this walk is a September 11 peace memorial. Note that visitors need to have proper identification with them. U.S. citizens need their birth certificates or passports. Foreign visitors need their passports and any applicable visas.

▶ Open daily year-round. Admission charged.

www.peacegarden.com
(888) 432-6733

2 Missouri-Yellowstone Confluence Interpretive Center

15349 39th Ln. NW, Williston

Have you ever wondered what America looked like before it was plowed and planted, developed and populated? At the confluence interpretive center you can gaze over the point where the Missouri and Yellowstone rivers converge and see much of the same pristine vistas first beheld by Lewis, Clark, and their band of explorers in 1805.

In addition to the impressive view, the center, opened in 2003, features numerous artifacts and exhibits. Landscape paintings by

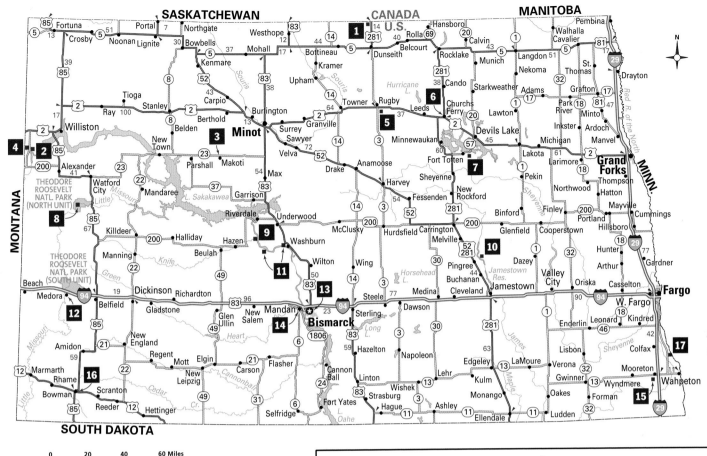

Philippe Regis de Trobriand, who commanded Fort Stevenson in the 1860s, and an eight-foot replica of a compass used by Lewis and Clark are displayed in the rotunda. The center also includes a petroleum exhibit with a core from North Dakota's first discovery well and early oil-and-gas drilling equipment. Admission to the center includes Fort Buford, a restored military barracks best known as the site of the surrender of Lakota Sioux chieftain Sitting Bull in 1881.

▶ Open daily mid-May–mid-Sept.; Wed.–Sun. mid-Sept.–mid-May. Closed major holidays.

www.nd.gov/hist/lewisclark/attractions_ mycic.html

(701) 572-9034

3 Makoti Threshers Museum

Makoti

The era when four-footed horsepower was first being replaced by four-wheeled machines has not been forgotten in the small agricultural community of Makoti. The Threshers Association boasts a remarkable museum of antique and classic threshers, farm tractors, and stationary engines. Housed in six buildings, this impressive collection includes a number of very rare pieces of farm equipment. Most of the machines are operational, and some have been lovingly restored.

You don't have to be a tractor buff to be fascinated by a 1909 Hart Parr, a 1917 Plow Boy, a 1920 Titain, and a wood-body thresher made by International Harvester in 1920. One prize exhibit is the massive 110-horsepower Case steam traction engine built in the early 1900s—about 14 feet high with iron rear wheels 7 feet in diameter.

The first weekend in October is the highlight of the year. That's when crowds of enthusiasts arrive for the annual Makoti Threshing Show, and the steam and gas tractors, antique cars, and trucks are paraded at the town's show-grounds by their owners. Also featured are a flea market and the John Deere Two-Cylinder Slow Race. Luncheon is served from the so-called cook cars that were hauled into the fields to feed farmhands.

▶ Open year-round by appointment. Admission free but donations encouraged.

www.makoti.net

(701) 726-5693 or (701) 726-5649 (weekends)

4 ▶ Fort Union Trading Post National Historic Site

Williston

On a typical busy spring day some 150 years ago, this fortified trading post on the banks of the upper Missouri River would have been surrounded by Native Americans grouped according to tribe, all eager to trade beaver and buffalo hides for guns, powder, beads, and blankets.

Fort Union was built by John Jacob Astor's American Fur Company in 1828 to buy and ship beaver pelts to the Eastern market. When silk top hats became more fashionable than ones made from beaver, the trade declined, supplanted by demand for buffalo robes.

As one of the most remote and luxurious large Western outposts of the period, the fort was visited by many prominent travelers and adventurers, including the artists John James Audubon and George Catlin, who traveled by steamboat 1,800 miles from St. Louis.

The fort was acquired by the U.S. Army and torn down in 1867. The National Park Service acquired the site in 1966 and began the excavations now open to visitors. Between 1985 and 1991 portions of walls, stone bastions, a Native American trade house, and Bourgeois House were reconstructed. The staff dress as trappers and traders and explain trade functions and tribunal relations of the years Fort Union operated.

▶ Open year-round, weather permitting.

www.nps.gov/fous
(701) 572-9083

5 ▶ Geographical Center Prairie Village and Museum

102 Hwy. 2 SE, Rugby

When you visit this 20-acre park, you are halfway "from sea to shin-

4 ▶ **Fort Union Trading Post National Historic Site.** What was perhaps the fanciest of all the Western outposts was built for fur traders and has now been reconstructed.

ing sea." Nearby is a cairn marking the exact geographical center of the North American continent. The Atlantic, Pacific, and Arctic oceans and the Gulf of Mexico are all about 1,500 miles away.

The village consists of 27 authentic North Dakota frontier homes, offices, a general store, livery stable, saloon, church, home-operated telephone exchange, and a stately windmill.

The town's main street transports you back to the region's tempestuous past as part of the Dakota Territory. In the extensive collections of frontier memorabilia are reminders of the conflicts between the Native Americans and the first settlers.

A fascinating railroad exhibit features an 1886 Great Northern Railroad depot and, on the other side of the tracks, a hobo jungle.

The museum houses a colorful array of frontier artifacts and old photographs and postcards.

▶ Open daily May–Sept. Admission charged.

www.prairievillagemuseum.com
(701) 776-6414

6 ▶ gardendwellers Farm

Orvis Ave. and 7th St. N, Churchs Ferry

In 2000 the town of Churchs Ferry all but disappeared, bought out by FEMA to prevent further damage caused by the unpredictable rise and fall of the aptly named Devil's Lake. Two years later Holly Mawby, a professional horticulturist, and her husband, Barry, decided to make lemonade from lemons, transforming a two-block section of the nearly deserted town into gardendwellers Farm—now the largest herb garden in the state and a learning center as well. Visitors are encouraged to drop by, enjoy the parklike gardens at their leisure, picnic, and relax in a family-friendly environment. Although there's a fee for guided tours, you can purchase instructions for self-guiding tours and activities for less than a dollar.

The farm's themed gardens include Medieval, Shakespeare, Bible, Floral Language, Children's, Bird and Butterfly, and the Churchs Ferry Garden of plantings from local residences. You'll also find a labyrinth of native prairie grasses, a vine-covered arbor, and two night

gardens with guided moonlight tours. Call for information about tours, classes, and special events. Easy access from Hwys. 2 and 281.

▶ Open daily May–Nov.

www.gardendwellersfarm.com
(701) 351-2520

7 ▶ Fort Totten State Historic Site and Sullys Hill National Game Preserve

Hwy. 20/57 S, Spirit Lake

In the summer of 1876, troopers of the U.S. 7th Cavalry rode from the fort into the pages of history. They joined a cavalry unit from Fort Abraham Lincoln, commanded by the flamboyant Lt. Col. George A. Custer, in a punitive expedition against American Indians led by chiefs Sitting Bull and Crazy Horse. The confrontation at the Little Bighorn region of Montana is recalled today as Custer's last stand.

Fort Totten is the best preserved of all forts west of the Mississippi built during the turbulent days of the Plains Indian wars, and Infantry Post looks much as it did on that fateful day more than a century ago. Restored officers' and enlisted men's quarters, the commanding officer's house, and other buildings still look out onto the broad square. A display of photos at the visitors center traces the history of the fort.

Almost next door is the Sullys Hill National Game Preserve, a 1,674-acre home for grazing herds of buffalo, elk, and white-tailed deer, a community of black-tailed prairie dogs, and birds. A four-mile auto tour leads to a scenic overlook and to Sullys Hill, where there is an observation tower and three Indian burial mounds. A short hiking trail and a 1¹/₂-mile ski trail are other attractions.

▶ Historic site open year-round. Fort Totten visitors center open daily mid-May–mid-Sept.; off-season by appointment only. An auto tour is available May–Oct., weather permitting.

www.nd.gov/hist/totten/totten.htm
(701) 766-4441

▶ Sullys Hill open May–Oct.
www.fws.gov/sullyshill
(701) 766-4272

8 Theodore Roosevelt National Park, North Unit

Watford City

In 1883 a young politician from New York came to the North Dakota badlands to hunt buffalo and was inspired by the beauty of the place. A few months after his return to New York, his wife and his mother died, both on the same day, whereupon he returned to this haunting wilderness for comfort and solace. Later, as president, Theodore Roosevelt championed the protection of public lands, and this, the only national park honoring an individual, is dedicated to his memory.

The badlands' configurations tell the history of this part of the continent. Some 60 million years ago runoff from the Rocky Mountains deposited the debris that forms the badlands' distinctive multicolored layers. Ash from volcanoes in the west added the layers of blue. Bolts of lightning ignited seams of soft coal, baking the sand and clay and adding red hues. In time swift-running streams cut through the layers, sculpting the terrain.

This moonlike landscape can be enjoyed along a 13-mile scenic drive or experienced on foot or

horseback along several well-marked trails that include 11-mile routes through the rugged back-country as well as a half-mile nature walk. Either way, the chances are good you will see some of the park's abundant wildlife. There is good canoeing when the water is high in the Little Missouri after the ice melts in early April.

▶ Open year-round. Admission charged.

www.nps.gov/thro
(701) 842-2333

9 Knife River Indian Villages National Historic Site

Stanton

Centuries before Lewis and Clark wintered nearby in 1804–05, Hidatsa, Arikara, and Mandan Native Americans established themselves productively along the Missouri River in this area of prairies and rich bottomland. They lived in round earthen lodges supported by wood frames. They were smart farmers and produced bountiful crops of corn, squash, tobacco, beans, and sunflowers, and they hunted buffalo, deer, and elk.

Hundreds of years ago the villagers traded with other Native American peoples, such as the Crow, Cheyenne, Arapaho, Cree, and Sioux. When European traders arrived, they quickly tied into this established system. Trade and prosperity increased until 1837, when a smallpox epidemic devastated the people living in the area.

In the present 1,765-acre park, the remnants of three Hidatsa villages can be explored. A walking path from the visitors center leads to two of the villages, and a separate path leads to the third.

A 15-minute video is offered in the visitors center, along with displays and artifacts. Summertime programs include daily tours of the earth lodge and other Ranger programs. Cross-country skiing is popular in winter.

▶ Open year-round except major holidays.

www.nps.gov/knri
(701) 745-3300

10 Arrowwood National Wildlife Refuge

Pingree

During the dawn of life in this region, glaciers created prairie potholes and shaped the gentle slopes that now provide a remarkably beneficial environment for a variety of wildlife.

Encompassing almost 16,000 acres on which 266 species of birds have been observed, this serene, uncrowded refuge also harbors a herd of about 300 deer, which are often seen along the 5¹/₂-mile self-guiding Auto Tour Route. Occasionally bison can be seen, too. Mourning doves, minks, and raccoons inhabit this route.

The 16-mile-long James River valley is an excellent site for observing white pelicans, Canada geese, and many duck species, including shovelers, canvasbacks, redheads, and coots. Boating and canoeing are permitted on selected waterways. In winter this peaceful place is ideal for cross-country skiing and ice fishing.

▶ Open daily mid-Mar.–mid-May.

www.fws.gov/arrowwood
(701) 285-3341 For refuge information and grouse-blind reservations

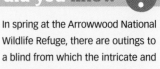

did you know **?**

In spring at the Arrowwood National Wildlife Refuge, there are outings to a blind from which the intricate and artistic mating dances of male sharp-tailed grouse may be seen at close range.

8 Theodore Roosevelt National Park, North Unit. The stone CCC Shelter at the park's River Bend Overlook was built by the Civilian Conservation Corps in 1937.

11 North Dakota Lewis & Clark Interpretive Center

Intersection of US-83 and ND Hwy. 200A on McLean County Hwy. 17 in Washburn

In 1804 captains Meriwether Lewis and William Clark settled into the long winter on the wild shores of the Upper Missouri River. For five frigid months until the spring thaw, as they prepared for their journey west to the Pacific Ocean, they mapped uncharted territory, recorded plants, and sketched animals they were seeing for the first time. Fort Mandan was the log compound they fashioned for shelter.

The interpretive center illuminates the explorers, expedition, and their relationships with the Native Americans. A guest can try on a buffalo robe or wear a cradle board like the one probably used by the Shoshone guide and interpreter Sakajawea to carry her infant. A complete collection of watercolorist Karl Bodmer's prints gives a reliable account of Native American cultures of that era.

▶ Open year-round. Admission charged.

www.lewisandclarktrail.com
(877) 462-8535

---

12 North Dakota Cowboy Hall of Fame

250 Main St., Medora

Cowboys, Native Americans, horses, cattle drives, ranching, and rodeos are the subjects celebrated at the North Dakota Cowboy Hall of Fame in Medora, at the gateway to Theodore Roosevelt National Park. Exhibits focus on Western cultural history, and a 5,000-square-foot patio gives visitors views of the Little Missouri River and the Badlands.

The small town of Medora, mostly reconstructed in Old West style, is full of history. Founded in 1883 by the Marquis de Mores, a wealthy French nobleman and entrepreneur, Medora was intended to be a meatpacking and shipping center. That venture failed, but the town had already attracted young Teddy Roosevelt, who came to

 North Dakota Cowboy Hall of Fame. Items that made the Great Plains unique during the settlement period are on display at the North Dakota Cowboy Hall of Fame.

hunt buffalo and fell in love with the land and the lifestyle. Roosevelt acquired two cattle ranches outside Medora and later called his Badlands experiences "the romance of my life." Roosevelt, by the way, was the first "Great Westerner" inducted into the North Dakota Hall of Fame.

▶ Open daily May–Sept.; Oct.–Apr. by appointment only. Admission charged.

www.northdakotacowboy.com
(701) 623-2000

---

13 Dakota the Edmontosaurus

North Dakota Heritage Center, 612 E. Boulevard Ave., Bismarck

In 1999 teenage Tyler Lyson found something unusual on his uncle's ranch, in the Hell Creek formation in the Dakota Badlands. Five years later Lyson began to investigate his find and realized it was very much out of the ordinary. Only four other significant mummified dinosaurs have been discovered worldwide, and this one was nearly intact, with fossilized skin and soft tissue.

In an international effort the specimen was unearthed in its surrounding stone and transported to California for CT scanning before being brought to the North Dakota Heritage Center. It dates to the late Cretaceous period, making it roughly 67 million years old. Its weight is an estimated 5 tons, and its length is about 30 feet.

▶ Open daily year-round.

www.nd.gov/hist/hcenter.htm
(701) 328-2666

---

14 Fort Abraham Lincoln State Park

Hwy. 1806, 7 miles south of Mandan

This wonderfully scenic park is rich in history. First called Fort McKeen,

the park was renamed for President Abraham Lincoln in 1872. But its grounds evoke another legendary figure: Gen. George Custer. From Fort Lincoln, Custer rode out with the 7th Cavalry to take on the Sioux tribe in the Battle of Little Bighorn. Several buildings from Custer's infantry post, including the house he called home before his "Last Stand," have been reconstructed.

The park also honors Native Americans—particularly the area's true pioneers, the Mandans. Complete with earth lodges, the On-A-Slant Indian Village captures the daily life and labors of the Mandan people. History buffs can learn more about the park's past in the visitors center.

From the park, avid walkers can pick up the Lewis and Clark Trail and choose from among the many inviting trails for hiking, biking, and horseback riding. The park also offers fishing, a playground, picnic areas, campsites, cabins, and breathtaking river views.

▶ Open daily year-round. Entrance fee.

www.ndparks.com/parks/FLSP.htm
(701) 667-6340

---

15 Bagg Bonanza Historical Farm

8025 169th St., Mooreton

Today's huge corporate farms are nothing new. Back in the 1870s, on the wheat-growing plains of North Dakota, "bonanza" farms of 30,000 acres and more—among the largest in the world—sprang up after the financial collapse of the Northern Pacific Railroad. Investors took land in place of worthless rail bonds and sold vast stretches to men like J. F. Downing, a Pennsylvania lawyer. Downing's nephew F. A. Bagg managed the 5,000-acre farm.

Bonanza farms initially thrived on mechanized equipment, modern methods, and large numbers of mostly itinerant laborers but soon foundered on declining profits. Thanks to the Bagg Bonanza Farm Historic Preservation Society, a restoration is under way. Completed buildings include the 25-room main house, bunkhouse, sheep barns, blacksmith shop, icehouse, laundry, machine sheds, and granaries. Listed on the *National Register of Historic Places,* it offers fascinating insights into the life of a 19th-century megafarm.

▶ Open Fri.–Sun. Memorial Day–Labor Day. Admission charged.

www.mnstate.edu/Heritage/BaggFarm
(701) 274-8989

---

16 Pioneer Trails Regional Museum

12 First Ave. NE, Bowman
The Pioneer Trails Regional Museum is known equally for its historical and its prehistorical research. Local history is highlighted in impressive exhibits illuminating the southwestern part of the state's original inhabitants, covering Native American culture and history before and after European settlement. Displays include those focused on territorial days and early statehood; ranching and homesteading; and transportation, communication, and the military.

15 Bagg Bonanza Historic Farm. The spacious main house, seen here from the side, was typical of the residences found on North Dakota's bonanza farms.

The museum also offers, through its paleontology department, day tours to active fossil dig sites in the Hell Creek Formation region (Tues.–Sat., June–July). It's hot and dusty, but both kids and adults love it. You'll need hats, sunglasses, plenty of sunscreen, and your own vehicle to drive to the dig. (For information, check the museum's website.)

If you're not up for a full day in the sun, take in the museum's collection of dinosaurs and other mammal, aquatic, and plant fossils.

▶ Open daily year-round. Closed major holidays. Admission charged.

www.ptrm.org
(701) 523-3600

---

17 Fort Abercrombie State Historic Site

Off Rte. 81, Abercrombie
This fort was established in 1858 to protect the northwestern frontier and guard the Montana gold fields. Four years later it withstood a six-week siege by Sioux Native Americans. Afterward the post was strengthened with log blockhouses and palisades. As the Native Americans were pushed farther west, the fort's importance diminished, and it was eventually abandoned in 1877.

The only surviving original building is a guardhouse. Three new blockhouses and a palisade have been reconstructed on the site, and signs indicate where officers quarters, storehouses, traders' posts, and other structures once stood.

An interpretive center has various exhibits and displays that showcase the oxcart trails of the later fur trade era, wagon trails, travel routes, and the military workings of Fort Abercrombie. Objects such as stone tomahawks, arrowheads, and padlocks found at the site are among the displayed items. Ceremonial ornaments and a thick buffalo robe also provide historical documentation of Native American daily life.

▶ Open Thurs.–Mon. mid-May–mid-Sept. Admission charged.

www.nd.gov/hist/abercrombie/
abercrombie.html
(701) 553-8513

Ohio

The Buckeye State has much to offer the traveler, from delights on Lake Erie's shores to the county with the world's largest Amish population.

Holmes County Amish Country. Amish men and women gather at meetinghouses and churches to cement bonds, preserve traditions, and worship (see page 266).

Art, pottery, and burial mounds confirm that advanced Hopewell peoples lived in Ohio some 2,000 years ago. How amazed these Native Americans would be to know that the first man to walk on the moon would be born near their tribal lands!

No less exciting in its time was the iron horse, now celebrated in a Conneaut museum that casts light on the relationship between the town and its railroad. The past is also recalled in the state's historic farms, glassworks, and museums—including a Dover house displaying the works of a wood-carver whose intricate detailing almost defies imagination.

visit ➤ offthebeatenpathtrips.com

1 Conneaut Railroad Historical Museum

363 Depot St., Conneaut

Trains have long been powerful symbols of freedom, high adventure, and expansion, and since the 1880s the economy of Conneaut has been linked to the Nickel Plate Rd. connecting Buffalo to Chicago with 523 miles of track. The railroad employed much of Conneaut's labor force, contributed substantially to the town's revenue, opened it to development, and became part of its folklore. That the bond between the railroad and the townspeople goes beyond economic factors is evident by the prodigious contributions of volunteer labor and donated money that went into the creation of this excellent museum.

Housed in the old New York Central Railroad depot, the museum overflows with railroad memorabilia. One eye-catcher is a 19th-century advertisement showing a train in mother-of-pearl inlay, with mountains painted in watercolors in the background. There are also timetables, a chart of hobo codes, railway bonds, and travel permits, including that of Abraham Lincoln, signed by his own hand in 1857 when he was chief attorney for the Illinois Central Railroad.

Workaday exhibits include carmakers' and inspectors' tools, telegraph equipment, a fully

2 Ashtabula County Covered Bridges. The 132-foot-long Olin Covered Bridge, built in 1873 and restored in 1994, spans the Ashtabula River in Plymouth Township.

equipped ticket office, and a working model of a boiler. There are also model trains, including an original cast-iron Lionel. Outside the depot, children and buffs will enjoy climbing into the cab of a handsome 100-foot-long Berkshire steam locomotive built in 1944.

▶ Open daily Memorial Day–Labor Day. Admission free but donations encouraged.

www.nrhs.com/chapters/conneaut.htm
(440) 599-7878

2 Ashtabula County Covered Bridges

Ashtabula County

On a day's driving trip through Ashtabula, discover covered bridges in Ohio's wine country. Located on Lake Erie, the county contains 17 historic covered bridges and 15 wineries.

Though the amount of covered bridges in the nation is declining, Ohio's number continues to rise, with the construction of the country's longest covered bridge, in Ashtabula. Because roofs protect the bridges, they are durable enough to survive the damaging effects of time and the elements. Many of the bridges throughout Ashtabula County have survived for more than a century needing only minimal repairs.

A self-guiding driving trail is the best way to see all of the bridges. Maps of the trail are available at the Ashtabula County Convention and Visitors Bureau in Austinburg.

▶ Open year-round.

www.visitashtabulacounty.com

(800) 337-6746

3 ▶ Holden Arboretum

9500 Speny Rd., Kirtland

This beautiful arboretum, established in 1931, is one of the largest in the country with 3,600 acres of land. Most of the land is designated as natural areas, with gardens occupying much of the remaining acreage. Thousands of plants thrive at Holden, including native wildflowers, gardens designed to attract butterflies, and a 20-acre rhododendron garden.

Guided tours are offered, or visitors can embark on a self-guiding tour of the natural areas and gardens, which are crisscrossed with over 20 miles of trails and walking paths. A lake and multiple small ponds attract waterfowl, and an observation blind attracts bird-watchers.

For children and teenagers, hands-on programs delve into environmental and science-related topics. On Friday mornings in the garden, presentations and walking tours with the experts are offered. The Corning Library offers further educational opportunities, ranging from field guides to rare books on botany.

▶ Open daily except major winter holidays. Admission charged.

www.holdenarb.org

(440) 946-4400

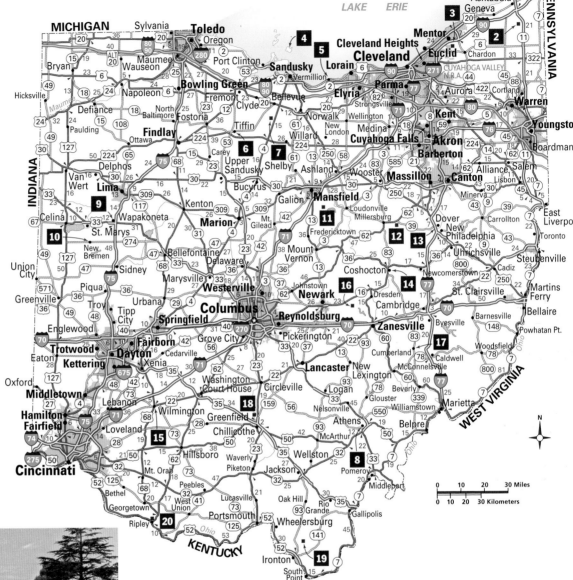

3 ▶ Holden Arboretum. Planned gardens and untamed natural areas await nature lovers and birders, who can choose from 20-plus miles of trails.

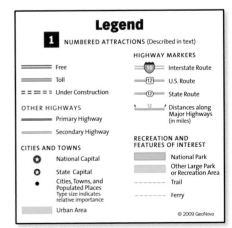

Legend

1 NUMBERED ATTRACTIONS (Described in text)

HIGHWAY MARKERS

Free		**10** Interstate Route
Toll		**12** U.S. Route
Under Construction		**12** State Route

OTHER HIGHWAYS

Primary Highway

Secondary Highway

⎯ 12 ⎯ Distances along Major Highways (in miles)

CITIES AND TOWNS

⊛ National Capital

⊛ State Capital

• Cities, Towns, and Populated Places Type size indicates relative importance

Urban Area

RECREATION AND FEATURES OF INTEREST

National Park

Other Large Park or Recreation Area

Trail

Ferry

© 2009 GeoNova

4 Kelleys Island

Take the ferry from Marblehead.

It is not known how long Kelleys Island was inhabited by people of the Erie or Cat nation before they were destroyed by the Iroquois in the late 1600s. But these first settlers are credited with leaving an enigmatic memorial: Inscription Rock, a large flat-topped slab of limestone covered with Native American pictographs of human-like creatures, birds and animals, and smoking pipes that have never been deciphered. The inscriptions, which have now been nearly obliterated by the elements, were copied by U.S. Army captain Seth Eastman in 1850; a reproduction of his work is placed at the site.

Kelleys Island was resettled in the early 1800s. By 1910 it had a population of more than 1,000 and a thriving economy based on limestone quarrying, agriculture, winemaking, and fishing. Today only about 375 people inhabit the island year-round. Ecotourism is the major industry, and fishing, boating, swimming, and dining facilities are plentiful.

Visitors can ferry their cars over from Marblehead but may prefer to rent bicycles or golf carts on the island to get about. About a 10-minute bike ride from town is Glacial Grooves. The limestone, scored to a depth of several inches by the tremendous force of a moving glacier, gives the appearance of smoothly rounded gray waves. Best times to visit are in spring through late fall.

▶ Open year-round. Accessible by ferry or boat spring-fall.

www.kelleysislandchamber.com
(419) 746-2360

www.ohiostateparks.org
(419) 797-4530

5 Inland Seas Maritime Museum

480 Main St., Vermilion

The Inland Seas Maritime Museum is operated by the Great Lakes Historical Society and overlooks Lake Erie from the shoreline of picturesque Vermilion. It is home to one of the nation's finest collections of Great Lakes maritime art. Original oil paintings, pen-and-ink drawings, watercolors, and mixed media are used to document the history of the Great Lakes, from steamers to lighthouses. The museum also maintains a collection of nautical artifacts, including ships' wheels, binnacle compasses, antique steam engines, and shipwright's tools. Of particular interest to many visitors are the original timbers from Commodore Perry's USS *Niagara,* a life ring and sounding board from the USS *Edmund Fitzgerald,* and the one-of-a-kind Second Order Fresnel Lighthouse Lens from Spectacle Reef in Lake Huron. Also available to the visitor is the actual pilothouse from the SS *Canopus,* with working whistles, bells, and ship-to-ship communications systems.

In 2001 the museum added a series of computer-based interactive exhibits. One can dive to eight various Great Lakes' shipwrecks using digitized video on a 42-inch plasma screen monitor or try to steer a freighter up the "crooked" Cuyahoga River. Children can build their own scale model of a 1,000-foot freighter or operate an engine-room telegraph.

▶ Open daily except major holidays. Admission charged.

www.inlandseas.org
(800) 893-1485

6 **Tiffin Glass Museum.** Glassware from the now-closed Tiffin factory is coveted by many a glass collector.

6 Tiffin Glass Museum

25 S. Washington St., Tiffin

Displaying nearly 100 years of glassware and memorabilia, this museum preserves both the work and the legacy created by the artisans of Tiffin's "Glass House."

The factory opened in 1889 as the A. J. Beatty & Son's Company, and it underwent a number of changes in leadership and production before it closed in 1984. The museum documents the company's many phases in a chronological display that comprises over 2,000 individual pieces. The exhibit shows the changing styles, techniques, and colors of glassware over the course of a century, illustrating the changing demands of buyers. Memorabilia and historical documents also make up a part of the collection.

The museum was established in 1998 due to the efforts of the Tiffin Glass Collectors Club. Members of the club also loaned many pieces to the museum for its comprehensive displays.

▶ Open Tues.-Sat. Donations encouraged.

www.tiffinglass.org
(419) 448-0200

4 **Kelleys Island.** Grooved rock outcrops on the island are unmistakable evidence of glaciers on the move during the last Ice Age, which ended around 8000 B.C.

7 Seneca Caverns

14248 Township Rd. 178, Bellevue
In 1872 two boys were out hunting when their dog chased a rabbit into a brush-filled pit. When the dog did not return, the boys began searching through the brush. Toward the bottom of the pit, they discovered a small hole with cool air streaming through it, and they could hear their dog barking below. As they dug to widen the opening, the limestone supporting them collapsed, and they tumbled some 10 or 12 feet down to the opening of a cave. The three companions climbed back out, and the caverns became a public phenomenon.

Unlike most caves, the Seneca Caverns were not formed by the dissolution of the bedrock, but by the collapse of the limestone into a subsurface void. Its physical aspect differs accordingly from the norm: Here one sees the bones of the Earth—the tumbled strata of Columbus limestone—in their raw condition, not smoothed by the flow of water or the action of ancient seas.

The path through the cave is a vigorous walk but not overly difficult. The largest chamber is some 250 feet long and 10 or 12 feet high. At one end is Pie Rock, so-called because it resembles a huge wedge of pie. Beyond it one descends to Ole Mist'ry River, whose waters are so clear that they seem to be a light mist at the bottom of the cavern.

The river's water level (which depends upon rainwater seeping down) determines how far one can descend. Twelve cave levels have been explored. The one-hour guided tour through seven rooms, or levels, ends on the seventh level 110 feet

9 Armstrong Air & Space Museum. A half-buried dome and outstretched wings housing galleries beckon visitors to a museum honoring the first man on the moon.

below the surface. On the return route one squeezes through the Needle's Eye and passes the Lock Stone, which is said to hold the jumbled and fractured strata in place; it's 150 feet long, 45 feet deep, and 60 feet wide and is estimated to weigh several hundred tons.

▶ Open daily Memorial Day–Labor Day; weekends only May, Sept., and mid-Oct. Admission charged.

www.senecacavernsohio.com
(419) 483-6711

8 The Dairy Barn Arts Center

Dairy Ln., Athens
This converted dairy barn, saved from destruction in 1977, now hosts a non-profit arts center and is listed on the *National Register of Historic Places*. The center seeks to support local artists and artisans through exhibitions and events, to nurture art appreciation, and to provide the community with access to art and

crafts from outside the region.

The 1914 dairy barn was scheduled to be razed in 1977 but was saved by local citizens with a dream of using it as an arts center. Artist Harriet Anderson and her husband, Ora, formed a Citizens Task Force Committee, which petitioned the governor until their campaign was successful—the building was rescued nine days before its scheduled demolition date.

This center offers a variety of exhibitions, from regional artwork to the renowned Quilt National, a juried exhibition of contemporary quilts from around the world in which quiltmakers hold fast to tradition while also exploring the newest materials and technologies. Also available are tours, classes, and educational programs.

▶ Open Tues.–Sun. Admission charged.

www.dairybarn.org
(740) 592-1981

9 Armstrong Air & Space Museum

500 S. Apollo Dr., Wapakoneta
"One small step for man, one giant leap for mankind," claimed the first man to set foot on the moon, astronaut Neil Armstrong. Armstrong's own first steps were taken in Wapakoneta, his childhood home, where this museum was established in his honor.

The museum building is a domed structure, half buried in a grassy mound, with two wings for galleries. The upper floor contains the Infinity Room, an 18-foot cube, where one walks between ingeniously positioned rows of mirrors that reflect each other, oneself, and moving lights in numerous planes. In the Astro Theater, pinpoints of revolving lights are thrown against the roof and walls. Both rooms seek to create a sense of being in infinite space. Also of note are the two landing simulators designed to test your skills and see if you have what it takes for space travel.

One of the most fascinating items found here is a genuine *Gemini VIII* spacecraft, with an open doorway that reveals the interior: This was the world's first docking satellite, flown by Armstrong and Maj. David Scott in March 1966. Another display includes the many honors bestowed upon the astronauts, including the Presidential Medal of Freedom. On display outside the museum is an F5D Skylancer, an airplane that Neil Armstrong flew as a test pilot.

▶ Open year-round. Closed Mon. and major holidays. Admission charged.

www.ohiohistory.org/places/armstron
(800) 860-0142; (419) 738-8811

10▶ The Bicycle Museum of America

7 W. Monroe St., New Bremen
High-wheelers, boneshakers, velocipedes, tandems, and more bits of bicycle esoterica than you knew existed are in this collection that was previously located in Chicago. Jim Dicke, whose grandfather worked at the Dayton Bicycle Company at the turn of the century, brought the group of multiwheeled wonders to Ohio.

When Leonardo da Vinci sketched the bicycle drive chain in the late 15th century, he couldn't have anticipated the infinite variety of vehicles that would ensue. Among those are the 1898 Chilion ladies' model, a wooden bike that didn't rust but did tend to splinter at inopportune moments; and the Schwinn Sting-Ray Orange Krate, circa late 1960s, which looks as though it were getting ready to burn rubber on the drag strip.

Some of the bicycles on display here were dedicated to popular entertainers: Crooner Cowboy Gene Autry, for example, had a Western model made in his honor in 1950, with a rodeo-brown finish, jeweled fenders, and a pony-head adornment. The Shelby Cycle Company produced a Donald Duck model in 1949 that intrigued many a baby in the boomer generation with its Donald eyes that flashed and a horn that squeaked "quack-quack."

▶ Open year-round. Closed Sun. Admission charged.

www.bicyclemuseum.com
(419) 629-9249

11▶ Malabar Farm

4050 Bromfield Rd., Lucas
In 1939 the Pulitzer-prizewinning author Louis Bromfield bought four neglected farms, built a large, comfortable, elegant home around one of the old farmhouses, and began to restore the fertility of his farmland. Since most of the money for the project came from the proceeds of a novel set on the Malabar Coast in India, he called the property Malabar Farm.

The "big house" is exceptionally attractive. The furnishings are predominantly French rural antiques, highlighted by such striking objects as an Italian marble fireplace surmounted by ceramic Chinese horses set against a huge mirrored wall in the living room; a Steinway grand piano beside the floating double staircase in the hallway; and in the Red Room paintings by Grandma Moses. An enormous curved desk with 28 drawers dominates the author's library despite the fact that it was too high for Bromfield to use comfortably.

The farm still supports a herd of beef cattle. You'll want to take the self-guiding tour of the barns, stables, meadows, and flower gardens. Be sure to allow enough time for kids to see the farm animals and touch those in the petting barn.

About half of the acreage here is under cultivation; the rest is woodland, where there are hiking trails and a campsite for horse riders.

▶ Open year-round. Admission charged.

www.malabarfarm.org
(419) 892-2784

12▶ Holmes County Amish Country

Holmes County
Gentle rolling hills and spectacular sunsets are the backdrop of this area that is home to the world's largest Amish population.

Although there are several groups of Amish, Holmes County is primarily made up of the Old Order Amish. This group maintains some of the most interesting and traditional customs; they do not use electricity or modern-day transportation, and they dress in traditional clothing.

The Amish and Mennonite Heritage Center in Berlin has been called the Sistine Chapel of the Amish and Mennonites due to its 10- by 265-foot cyclorama painting. The work of painter Heinz Gaugel, it traces the group's history from Zurich, Switzerland, from 1525 to the present day.

Since 1935 family-owned Heini's Cheese Chalet in Millersburg has produced all-natural cheeses from Amish Farm Milk. At the Chalet visitors can watch the cheese-making process through a 100-foot viewing corridor, stop at the Fudge Factory, or shop at the Lace Boutique for handmade Amish Heritage Lace. The 100,000-square-foot Amish Flea Market features Ohio-made crafts, antiques, primitive folk art, furniture, quilts, meats, cheeses, and much more.

▶ Fees charged for tours.

www.visitamishcountry.com
(303) 674-3975

13▶ Warthers

331 Karl Ave., Dover
Ernest Warther was quite different from other artists. Although his wood carvings of trains, locomotives, and an old steel mill were immensely valued during his lifetime (the Smithsonian called his *oeuvre* "priceless"), Warther never sold a single piece of his work because, he said, "My roof don't leak, and we ain't hungry. . ."

"Warthers" refers to the home the artist and his wife built in 1912, which now houses his remarkable collection of carvings in wood, bone, and ivory.

Inside is a working model of

10▶ The Bicycle Museum of America. A Schwinn Black Phantom from the 1950s is among the thousand-plus bikes exhibited at one time or another in this museum.

12 **Holmes County Amish Country.** Traditional clothing is a touchstone of the Old Order Amish way of life.

the American Sheet and Tinplate Company, where Warther worked from 1899 to 1923. It is made of walnut and ivory and re-creates in detail the floor of the factory— not only the machines but his friends there. His best friend, for instance, is shown eating rhubarb pie and a piece of Swiss cheese complete with holes. The model was done from memory nearly 30 years after he left the factory.

Many of the carvings are large. The eight-foot-long model of the Empire State Express is shown crossing a bridge, which is made of 4,000 individually cut ebony bricks, with strips of ivory for the mortar. Warther's favorite was the Lincoln funeral train. A keyhole in the funeral coach has an ivory key that fits it, and the body in its draped coffin can be seen through a window.

▶ Open daily except Sun. Jan–Feb and
   major holidays. Admission charged.

www.warthers.com
(330) 343-7513

14 Johnson-Humrickhouse Museum

300 N. Whitewoman St., Coshocton
The museum is located in Roscoe Village, a restoration of an 1800s canal town, and has five galleries. The Historic Ohio Gallery features a re-created pioneer home, 18th- and 19th-century tools and firearms (including Colt and Remington revolvers and the first rifle ever used by the U.S. military, the 1860 Spencer repeating carbine), and early advertising art (Coshocton is the birthplace of advertising art).

The American Indian Gallery displays an extensive collection of 19th-century basketry, prehistoric Southwest pottery, bead and quilt work, and Inuit garments and carvings.

The Golden Gallery has 18th- and 19th-century European and American decorative arts and textiles and a Victorian nook. Chinese and Japanese artifacts fill the Asian Gallery with such items as Samurai armor and swords,

exquisitely carved screens, embroidery, lacquerware, theater masks, carved jade, and porcelain. A fifth gallery hosts temporary exhibits.

Roscoe Village, a picturesque historic site, offers the opportunity to become acquainted with the canal era. In addition to exploring the small village with its attractive shops, you can walk along the towpath and take rides on a trolley and a canal boat.

▶ Open daily May–Oct., closed Mon.
   Nov.–Apr. Admission charged.

www.jhmuseum.org
(740) 622-8710

15 Rombach Place Museum

149 E. Locust St., Wilmington
This most pleasant and unpredictable museum of local history is listed on the *National Register of Historic Places* and furnished with handsome antiques. It was built in 1835 and was the home of Gen. James William Denver, commis-

13 **Warthers.** A working wood-and-ivory miniature of the steel factory where Ernest Warther worked, complete with fellow steelworkers, exemplifies the intricacy of his carvings.

sioner of Indian affairs under President Buchanan, governor of the Kansas Territory in the 1850s, and the man for whom the city of Denver, Colorado, was named.

The elegant house includes a collection of General Denver's memorabilia, such as his beaver top hat, his colonel's uniform, his personal library, and Native American relics.

The museum also houses artwork from local artists, as well as a collection of sculptures and paintings by Eli Harvey. Born in southwest Ohio, Harvey (1860–1957) was an internationally known Quaker artist, most famous for his animal sculptures, such as the lions at the Bronx Zoo in New York City and the bronze elk symbol of The Order of the Elks.

The early 19th-century photographs of Native Americans taken by Carl Moon, are another of the museum's specialties. Born in Wilmington, Ohio, in 1879, Moon became nationally renowned for visually recording the culture and traditions of Native Americans, particularly those in the Southwest. At the invitation of President Theodore Roosevelt, Moon's work was shown at the White House.

Visitors will also learn about Clinton County's history through textiles, Native American artifacts, medical equipment, fine china, furnishings, and a research library filled with many genealogical records.

▶ Open Wed.–Fri. Mar.–Dec. or by appointment. Admission charged.

www.clintoncountyhistory.org
(937) 382-4684

16 ▶ Blackhand Gorge State Nature Preserve

5213 Rock Haven Rd., Newark
About 10,000 years ago the runoff of melting glaciers carved a gorge here in the sandstone bedrock known as Blackhand conglomerate. The preserve follows the course of the Licking River through this gorge, and a number of trails and a paved bicycle path invite exploration of the terrain.

The bike path passes a buttonbush swamp and enters a woodland of sycamore, maple, sumac, and yellow poplar before opening up to dramatic views of cliffs towering above the woods, ferns, tree trunks, and roots delineating the weathered strata and fault lines. Across the gorge stands Blackhand Rock, a concave rock face above a bend and a wide pool in the river. The route is especially beautiful in July, when it is awash with phlox flowers and bergamot.

The bike path follows an old railroad bed that was originally used to carry sand from an adjacent quarry to the glassworks of Newark, the nearest sizable town. One footpath traverses the rim of the old quarry; a second footpath ascends to higher woodlands looping through ferny hemlock woods and then returning to the bicycle path.

▶ Open year-round.

www.dnr.state.oh.us
(740) 763-4411

17 ▶ The Wilds

1400 International Rd., Cumberland
A pastoral sight unfolds at twilight across the panorama of the wide-open range. The Southern white rhino grazes peacefully on the veldt. A sable antelope bounds across the savanna. Bactrian camel lope by, and a small herd of North American bison munches on prairie grasses. The animals are actually sharing almost 10,000 acres of land at a conservation center in Ohio. Endangered and threatened species from Asia, Africa, and North America have been brought together to live and prosper on this soil that has been reclaimed from strip mining.

Since the early 1970s the strip mining industry has replaced topsoil and replenished grasslands where the mining for coal took place. It is a "human-induced prairie" that affords these species a place to roam in their natural habitat. Wetlands are also being brought back to health so that the balance of interlocking ecological systems is restored.

At the Wilds visitors can savor the natural world via guided safaris. Conservation research and educational programs are key elements here, and work is ongoing in areas such as reproductive biology and animal husbandry.

▶ Open select days May–Oct. Call for schedule. Admission charged.

www.thewilds.org
(740) 638-5030

18 ▶ Hopewell Culture National Historical Park

CR-900, Chillicothe
The bountiful river valleys of south-central Ohio were home to a flourishing center of the Hopewell culture about 2,000 years ago. Known for their large geometric earthworks and elaborate artifacts crafted from exotic materials, the Hopewellian people prospered from 200 B.C. to A.D. 500.

Their mound construction was particularly extensive in the Scioto River-Paint Creek area. Five of the archaeological sites in this area are currently being preserved by the National Park Service.

16 ▶ **Blackhand Gorge State Nature Preserve.** The Licking River mirrors the sandstone walls of the gorge, which was carved by melting glaciers at the end of the last Ice Age.

Overlooking the banks of the Scioto River is Mound City, one of the most important sites of the Hopewell culture. The people built structures here that housed their political, economic, and social activities, including burial ceremonies. After a period of time, they razed each structure and constructed a mound over the location.

Today the park's visitors center, located at the site, establishes what is known of the Hopewell lifestyle and displays some of the artifacts found in excavations of these mounds. In some cases the quantity and types of objects, in particular the burial mounds, indicate the status and possibly the occupation of the deceased. Artifacts include shell beads, bear and shark teeth, pottery, ear spools of copper and silver, and a series of effigy pipes bearing the likenesses of animals and birds.

Beyond these parklike grounds is the Scioto River, which flows smooth, brown, and rapid. An interesting one-mile trail follows its banks, passing yet another earthwork. Along the way, plaques identify plants and shrubs once important to the Hopewell and other Native American populations.

▶ Grounds open daily from dawn to dusk; visitors center open daily except major winter holidays.

www.nps.gov/hocu
(740) 774-1126

19 ▶ Lake Vesuvius Recreation Area

Off Rte. 93, 6.5 miles north of Ironton
Set among the rolling hills and scenic woodlands of the Wayne National Forest, this is a place of tranquil beauty.

The recreation area takes its name from the Vesuvius Furnace, located in one of the picnic spots. This truncated giant, built in 1833, was one of the first iron-blast furnaces in the region, and it was one of the last to close, holding out against the prevailing economic winds until 1906. The structure has been partially restored by the U.S. Corps of Engineers. Though it lacks some of the ancillary buildings faithfully re-created at Buckeye Furnace, Vesuvius has the poignancy of a fallen hero.

Several loop trails, ranging from a half-mile walk to a 16-mile path for backpackers, skirt Lake Vesuvius and cross a varied terrain. The facility also offers a 31-mile horse trail, campsites, picnic grounds, a boat dock, and rental boats and canoes.

did you know ?

Ohio gave America its first hot dog, created by Harry M. Stevens in 1900.

Lake Vesuvius is ideal for canoeing and boating, and the sandy beach at Big Bend is inviting for swimmers.

▶ Open year-round.

www.fs.fed.us/r9/wayne
(740) 534-6500

20 Rankin House & Parker House

6152 Rankin Rd., 200 Front St., Ripley

A candle in the window of a house on a hill once signaled the all-clear to more than 2,000 runaway slaves looking for help from the Underground Railroad. The last leg on this part of the route to freedom was an arduous climb up 100 steps of an outside staircase that took people from the Ohio River to the home of Presbyterian minister John Rankin and his wife, Jean. As many as 12 people at one time could be hidden on this property in southern Ohio. Fugitive slaves were delivered to conductors like Rankin, who would help them get to the next depot in the network of stops. His home, with a commanding view of the river and a reconstructed staircase, contains memorabilia of his activities as an abolitionist.

John P. Parker, born into slavery in 1827, was able to buy his freedom at the age of 18 and went on to prosper in the iron-molding foundry business. He was among a small number of African Americans who became patent holders in the 19th century.

Parker returned to slave territory, risking his life to lead people to shelter in Ripley, often to the Rankin home. The Parker House, on Front St., is where many escapes from the borderlands of Kentucky were planned. Both houses are National Historic Landmarks.

▶ Open Tues.–Sun., May–mid-Dec. Off season by appointment. Admission charged.

www.johnparkerhouse.org
(937) 392-1627 Rankin House
(937) 392-4188 Parker House

OHIO

Oklahoma

From the wooded hills of the east to the lonely buttes on the High Plains of the west, history turns up in the Sooner State's nooks and crannies.

Woolaroc. A saddle once owned by William Frederick Cody, better known as Buffalo Bill, is among the 5,000 items displayed in the museum at Woolaroc (see page 272).

Native American culture is much in evidence in Oklahoma in various museums and on the riverbank where the Cheyenne battled General Custer. Reminders of the early days of the pioneers take the form of a heritage center commemorating the Chisholm Trail, a frontier drugstore, and the home of a 19th-century female painter who captured daily life on canvas. The lives of Will Rogers and Wild West showman Pawnee Bill are documented at a memorial and a historic ranch.

In the Quartz Mountains a trail lined with cedar, live oaks, prickly pear cactus, and yucca is a feast for the eyes. On the plains, travelers descend into caverns with walls of alabaster. And at the Grand Lake O' the Cherokees, pelicans alight as they pass through a state where the East meets the American West.

visit ➤ offthebeatenpathtrips.com

1 No Man's Land Historical Museum

Sewell St. and North E St., Goodwell, off Hwy. 54

Oklahoma's Panhandle, a 34- by 168-mile strip, was for many years unclaimed by any state or territory. In 1850 Texas, a pro-slave state, agreed not to extend its border north of latitude 36°30′. In 1854 the boundary of Kansas had been set at the 37th parallel, and thus the long, narrow area that remained became known as No Man's Land. The settlers here asked that Congress name it the Cimarron Territory. But Congress refused and in 1890 designated the area part of the Oklahoma Territory.

The museum, on the campus of Oklahoma Panhandle State University, has outstanding exhibits depicting the history of this region from prehistoric times to the tragic Dust Bowl days of the 1930s. The paleontology displays include mastodon and mammoth bones and teeth.

The William E. Baker Archaeological Collections, housed in the museum, documents man's existence in the area from paleo-times to the arrival of the Europeans. Included is evidence of the Basket Maker Native Americans and Antelope Creek people, the Plains Native Americans, and white pioneers. Over the main entrance to the

3 Washita Battlefield National Historic Site. The visitors center is close to the site where Custer attacked a Cheyenne village in 1868.

museum are the flags of Spain, France, Mexico, Texas, and the United States, all of which have flown over the territory.

▶ Open Tues.-Sat. except holidays.

www.opsu.edu
(580) 349-2670

2 Metcalfe Museum

4 miles south of OK–33 in Durham

Branding calves, riding horses, and doing household chores in the Oklahoma Territory didn't leave Augusta Corson Metcalfe much time for herself.

A pioneer woman who ran her farm and raised her son by herself

in the sagebrush-strewn red hills of the Upper Washita Valley in the late 19th century, when the Cheyenne and Arapaho lands were opened up to settlers, Metcalfe relaxed at night by recording the day's events in paintings and sketches, which eventually gained her renown as the Sagebrush Artist and entry into the National Cowgirl Hall of Fame.

Years later Howard Metcalfe, her son, donated their home for this museum, which stands on the Break O' Day Farm. Life on the high plains, from the rugged early frontier days to the Dust Bowl hardships of the 1930s, is depicted

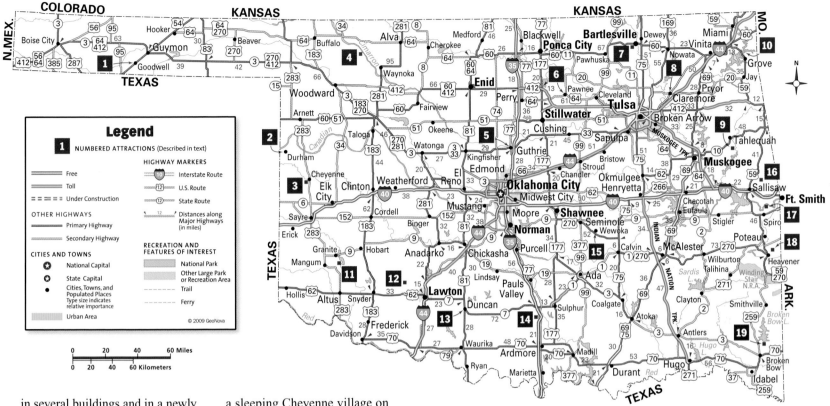

in several buildings and in a newly constructed gallery.

Also on view are items like the cook box her family brought across the plains, a spinning wheel, antique furniture, and farming tools. There is even a horse-drawn sorghum mill used in the making of syrup.

A pioneer-era general store has been re-created, and the Blue Goose Saloon is a remnant transported here from the territorial town of Hamburg that is no more.

▶ Open Tues.-Sat. Mar.-Nov.

http://metcalfemuseum.org/information.htm
(580) 655-4467

◼3 Washita Battlefield National Historic Site

Off OK–47, just west of Cheyenne
In the cold morning twilight of November 27, 1868, Lt. Col. George Armstrong Custer led his 7th Cavalry in a surprise attack on a sleeping Cheyenne village on the shore of the Washita River. The chief of the village was Black Kettle, an outstanding Native American statesman who just days before had gone to Fort Cobb attempting to negotiate the safety of his people. Figures vary concerning the number of Cheyennes slaughtered, but many women and children died. Black Kettle and his wife were killed while attempting to escape on their pony.

In 2007 the National Park Service opened a new visitors center, which features exhibits and a short film about the battle. There is a 1¹/₂-mile trail through the site, and rangers offer guided tours in the summer.

▶ Open year-round.

www.nps.gov/waba
(580) 497-2742

◼4 Alabaster Caverns State Park

Off OK–50, 6 miles south of Freedom
The feature here is a 2,300-foot-long cavern sectioned into chambers by spectacular formations of alabaster and glittering selenite crystals. Its formation began some 200 million years ago when a great inland sea receded, leaving huge deposits of gypsum. Underground streams slowly tunneled the rock, creating the series of chambers. Today a murmuring stream continues the ancient process of erosion.

The entrance to the cavern is in rugged Cedar Canyon. Short tours take visitors into chambers given such descriptive names as Gun Barrel Tunnel, Devil's Bathtub, Echo Dome, and Encampment Room. Bring comfortable walking shoes and a light jacket. For years the cavern was known as Bat Cave for the host of winged mammals that still reside here, hanging harmlessly from the rock ceiling by day, leaving by night to feed upon insects.

▶ Open year-round. Admission charged.

www.oklahomaparks.com
(580) 621-3381

did you know ❓

Within Alabaster Caverns State Park lies the largest natural gypsum cave in the world. The gypsum found here occurs mostly in various forms of the eponymous alabaster—including pink, white, and the rare black alabaster. Black alabaster can be found in only three places in the world: Italy, China, and Oklahoma.

5 **Oklahoma Frontier Drugstore Museum.** Museum director Mark Ekiss plays soda jerk for a day at the authentic old-time soda fountain.

5 Oklahoma Frontier Drugstore Museum

214 W. Oklahoma Ave., Guthrie
Step straight into the Oklahoma Territory's earliest days at the Oklahoma Frontier Drugstore Museum, housed in the 1890 Gaffney Building, the site of Oklahoma's first drugstore.

Patent medicines and period advertisements share space with such curiosities as a blue-and-white ceramic leech jar—a reminder that physicians once used leeches to rid the body of maladies. A period soda fountain in the museum serves up old-fashioned sundaes and phosphates, and an inviting apothecary garden on the building's west side scents the air with wild thyme, echinacea, and other medicinal herbs.

Explore the streets of Guthrie, whose 400-block downtown district is among the largest urban areas listed in the *National Register of Historic Places*.

▶ Open Tues.–Sat. Admission charged.

www.drugmusem.org
(405) 282-1895

6 Pawnee Bill Ranch

Off US–64, just west of Pawnee
Gordon William Lillie, pioneer rancher, Wild West showman, and successful businessman, chose Blue Hawk Peak, a hill in Pawnee Native American country, for the site of this handsome sandstone mansion. The sprawling two-story structure, built in 1910 of locally quarried stone, is maintained by the Oklahoma Historical Society.

Lillie had lived among the Pawnee, working as a teacher on the Pawnee agency. With his wife, May, an expert rider and sharpshooter, he formed the Pawnee Bill Wild West Show in 1888. For a quarter of a century, he toured the United States and many foreign countries—part of the time with the famous Buffalo Bill Cody. When his show finally closed in 1913, Lillie indulged his interests in the American bison and enlarged his herd to assure the preservation of these already endangered species.

His mansion today contains the original furnishings and treasures from his travels. The museum contains memorabilia of the family and prominent guests, a miniature replica of the Pawnee Bill Wild West Show, and a collection of Native American artifacts. A picnic area is located on the grounds, as well as a drive-through pasture where buffalo, longhorn cattle, and draft horses can be seen.

▶ Open daily Apr.–Sept.; Wed.–Sun. Oct.–Mar.

www.ok-history.mus.ok.us
(918) 762-2513

7 Woolaroc

On State Hwy. 123, 12 miles southwest of Bartlesville
This lovely 3,700-acre property in the rugged Osage hill country was acquired in the 1920s by Frank Phillips, cofounder of Phillips Petroleum Company, for a wildlife preserve and a family retreat. Now owned and managed by a foundation created by Phillips, Woolaroc (*woods*, *lakes*, and *rocks*) is open to the public. On the grounds are a world-renowned museum established by Phillips, the Native American Heritage Center, and the rustic but spacious lodge where the Phillipses entertained the nation's leaders and celebrities.

The museum, which portrays the story of man in the New World, contains 55,000 items from prehistoric times through the middle of the 20th century. Its displays of Native American blankets and Navajo and Plains jewelry are outstanding. A permanent exhibit of Western art (one of the world's finest) includes paintings, sculptures, and other works by Frank Tenney Johnson, Charles M. Russell, and Frederic Remington.

Next to the museum is the Native American Heritage Center, a longhouse with exhibits illustrating Native American culture and achievements. From the center the Enchanted Walkway leads to the $1^{1}/_{2}$-mile-long Thunderbird Canyon Nature Trail.

▶ Open Tues.–Sun. Memorial Day–Labor Day; Wed.–Sun. year-round. Admission charged.

www.woolaroc.org
(918) 336-0307

8 Will Rogers Memorial Museum

1720 W. Will Rogers Blvd., Claremore
"I never met a man I didn't like" is the saying usually associated with

7 **Woolaroc.** Woolaroc Museum celebrates the history and culture of various Native American tribes and the peoples who populated this land. Woolaroc was the name oil baron Frank Phillips created for his bucolic retreat in the Osage Hills, taking the letters from "woods," "lake," and "rock."

humorist and philosopher Will Rogers. Born in 1879, the man of Cherokee descent once remarked, "My forefathers didn't come over on the *Mayflower*, but they met the boat." Rogers had a remarkably varied and successful career. He was a trick roper, Ziegfeld Follies and vaudeville performer, and radio commentator. His witty, homespun remarks were published daily in 500 newspapers.

Rogers's movie career ultimately catapulted him to fame. The archives and nine galleries in this museum contain 15,000 photographs and 2,000 books about this man of the West and the world, whose spirit still permeates this part of northeastern Oklahoma. There are manuscripts, motion pictures, home movies, and a saddle collection. A sunken garden frames the Rogers family tomb. The museum is built on 20 acres Rogers had purchased in 1911 for his hoped-for retirement, but in 1935 he was killed in a plane crash with a fellow Oklahoman, pilot Wiley Post, over the Alaskan territory.

To get to Rogers's birthplace, take Rte. 88 out of Claremore to Dog Iron Ranch in Oologah, where newsreels run about Rogers's life and times.

▶ Open year-round. Donations accepted.

www.willrogers.com
(800) 324-9455

---

9 **Murrell Home and Nature Trail**

19479 E. Murrell Rd., Tahlequah
Vintage Americana and a state government's first attempt to provide self-guiding nature explorations for the handicapped combine at this unusual setting. The quiet, elegant atmosphere of the antebellum South

pervades a mansion built around 1845 by George Murrell at Park Hill, the cultural center of the Cherokee Nation after being displaced from Georgia in 1838–39.

Murrell, a longtime friend of the Cherokees, married a niece of the great chief John Ross in Tennessee in 1834, and after her death, her sister. He himself died in New Orleans in 1894.

Hunter's Home, so named because of Murrell's fondness for hunting, has high-ceilinged rooms, each with a fireplace. It is impressively furnished in antebellum style. Outbuildings on the 38-acre grounds include a springhouse, log cabin, and smokehouse. The three-quarter-mile nature trail, paved and wheelchair accessible, winds through dense stands of sycamore, Osage orange, willow, and hickory. Birders come especially for the flycatchers and vireos.

▶ Open Tues.–Sun. Mar.–Oct.;
  Wed.–Sat. Nov.–Mar.

www.okhistory.org/outreach/homes/geomurrell.html
(918) 456-2751

---

10 **Grand Lake O' the Cherokees**

I-44, Afton or Grand Lake exit
Flying in tight formation with air force–worthy precision, flocks of American white pelicans head annually to South America from Canada. But they know a good thing when they see it and always spend a six-week layover at Grand Lake in September. The gigantic reservoir was formed in 1940 by the building of the Pensacola Dam, the longest multiple-arch dam in the world, on the Grand River. There are 46,500 surface acres of water and 1,300 miles of shoreline here.

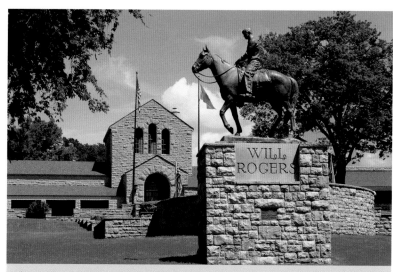

8 **Will Rogers Memorial Museum.** This storehouse of photos, manuscripts, and other memorabilia was built on land where Rogers planned to spend his retirement.

It's a migratory waterfowl haven, the mudflat areas having been seeded with Japanese millet in an effort to provide a food source for many types of birds, including buffleheads, shovelers, and cormorants. The lake wanders through 66 miles of the foothills of the Ozarks called Green Country. It's tucked into the corner where four states meet: Oklahoma, Kansas, Missouri, and Arkansas. Although fairs, flea markets, festivals, and rodeos occur throughout the seasons, people are often content to just look at the water here. Bass fishing is always popular, and sailboat enthusiasts can pick up prevailing winds for a pleasant ride across the lake.

▶ Open year-round.

www.grandlakefun.com
(866) 588-4726

---

11 **Quartz Mountain Nature Park**

State Hwy. 44A, Lone Wolf
Set in the lee of the rugged Quartz Mountains, whose enor-

mous red granite boulders seem to be tumbling down the hillsides, this park was once the winter campground of Kiowa and Comanche Native Americans. Today its 4,284 acres lure vacationers with a fine resort lodge, cabins, campsites, and picnic grounds along the shore of Lake Altus-Lugert, a large reservoir formed by a dam across the North Fork of the Red River. Fished for its bass, crappie, walleye, and catfish, the lake also offers excellent boating, canoeing, and swimming.

Native birds include hawks, cardinals, bluebirds, scissor-tailed flycatchers, wild turkeys, and roadrunners. The half-mile New Horizon hiking trail scales the park's namesake peak through live oak, yucca, prickly pear cactus, and stands of cedars. A golf course and a rugged backcountry area for off-road vehicles are additional attractions.

▶ Open year-round.

www.quartzmountain.org
(580) 563-2238

12 ▶ Wichita Mountains Wildlife Refuge

OK–49, north of Cache
Created in 1901 to protect endangered prairie animals, this 59,000-acre wildlife sanctuary is roamed by a buffalo herd maintained at around 600 head. Other protected species on the refuge include longhorn cattle, elk, and wild turkeys. A prairie-dog town may be seen east of the refuge headquarters.

Portions of the refuge are fenced off for the protection of wildlife and visitors, but much of it can be explored by car or on foot. Mount Scott rises 1,000 feet, and the drive is worth it for the views. Fifteen miles of hiking trails lead into remote regions, including the Charons Garden Wilderness, where backpack camping is allowed by permit. The challenging 900-foot ascent of Elk Mountain brings the hiker to a plateau with passageways and small caves among huge boulders.

▶ Open year-round.

http://wichitamountains.fws.gov
(580) 429-3222

13 ▶ Chisholm Trail Heritage Center

1000 N. Chisholm Trail Pkwy., Duncan
The trail through the center of the old Indian Territory, from Texas north to Kansas, was named for Jesse Chisholm, a part-Cherokee trader who opened up the famous route after the Civil War. With good grazing and plenty of water along the way, it was ideal for the great herds of Texas longhorns that were driven to a Kansas rail terminal for shipment east. The Chisholm Trail was used for about 20 years, from 1867 until the end of the 1880s, when the railroads reached Texas.

At the Chisholm Trail Heritage Center numerous exhibits explain how cowboys lived. Many of the exhibits are interactive, like the Steer Ropin' station, which gives kids a chance to practice their lasso skills. A film about the trail and a modern gallery of Western painting and sculpture round out the experience.

▶ Open daily except major holidays.

www.onthechisholmtrail.com
(580) 252-6692

13 ▶ Chisholm Trail Heritage Center. Sculptor Paul Moore's huge bronze commemorates the cattle drivers who traveled one of the Old West's most important trails.

15 ▶ Seminole Nation Museum. Commemorated here are the Seminoles, driven from their homes in the Florida Everglades to Oklahoma on the ill-famed Trail of Tears.

14 ▶ Turner Falls Park

Davis, off Rte. 77
Cascading over Honey Creek's 77-foot-high limestone rocks into a wide, natural plunge pool, these falls (named for Mazzepa Turner, who was a rancher and state representative of the early 1900s) are the centerpiece of a 6,000-acre park in the heart of the Arbuckle Mountains. The upward thrust of the terrain exposes many rock formations in nearly vertical positions so dramatically that the area is renowned as a geological window on the past. In spring the slopes and fields along the roadways turn a brilliant yellow as myriad black-eyed Susans begin to bloom.

A short walking trail to the bottom of the falls winds through Honey Creek Canyon, shaded by oak, poplar, cottonwood, locust, and walnut trees. Miles of more difficult hiking trails are also available, as are camping sites, cabins, and picnic grounds. Three natural caves are available to be explored.

▶ Open year-round. Day admission fee.

www.turnerfallspark.com
(580) 369-2988

15 ▶ Seminole Nation Museum

524 S. Wewoka Ave., Wewoka
"I fought in the Civil War and have seen men shot to pieces and slaughtered by the thousands," wrote a Georgia militia veteran, "but the Cherokee removal was the cruelest work I ever knew."

The tragic journey of the Seminole Native Americans in the 1830s, when the U.S. government mandated their removal from the farms of Florida's Everglades, led them to Wewoka on the Oklahoma prairie, the new capital of the Seminole Nation.

The museum chronicles the transition of the tribe from its southeastern roots to life in a new region. Displays range from a replica of a chuko—the traditional Seminole Everglades dwelling built of logs, palm leaves, and hides—to the reconstructed façade of the Wewoka Trading Post, the enterprise from which the new Native American capital grew. Historic photographs recall daily life in the 19th-century Indian Territory and the oil boom of the 1920s. An art gallery displays Native American art and artifacts. The museum also shows examples of the patchwork clothing for which the Seminoles are still famous.

▶ Open Mon.–Sat. Closed Jan. Donations accepted.

www.theseminolenationmuseum.org
(405) 257-5580

16 Sequoyah's Cabin

3 miles north of Sallisaw US-59, then 7 miles east on US-101

In 1829 George Guess, better known as Sequoyah, came to present-day Oklahoma and built a log cabin in what is now Sequoyah County. Today the restored cabin is enclosed in a museum.

Sequoyah invented the Cherokee alphabet—a syllabary of 86 characters. After it was adopted by the Cherokee Nation in 1821, it enabled the people to become literate in less than two years.

Another cabin built of logs, believed to have been hewn by Sequoyah, comprises an information center where his syllabary is demonstrated. Other displays include a Trail of Tears exhibit depicting the removal of the Cherokee Nation in 1838–39 from Georgia, North Carolina, and Tennessee.

▶ Open Tues.–Sun. except state holidays.

www.okhistory.org/outreach/homes/
    sequoyahcabin.html
(918) 775-2413

17 Spiro Mounds Archaeological Center

18154 1st. St., Spiro

One of the four greatest centers of the Mississippian Native American culture—and the most mysterious—flourished here at this wide bend in the Arkansas River from the 9th to the 15th century. The park includes 150 acres and 12 mounds.

In the 1930s the great Craig Mound, which contained more than 1,000 burials and a charnel house, was ruthlessly excavated and looted. Since then archaeologists have worked to restore it.

Among the rich grave goods taken from it were stone effigies, copper breastplates, textiles, pottery, wooden figurines, wooden masks with shell inlays, and delicate shell cups. Some of the artifacts were engraved with skulls, body parts, falcons, and the plumed serpent, the deity of earth and sky. Because of the strange symbolism of the mortuary art, some believe that for a time Spiro was a religious center where elaborate funerary practices were observed.

Many of the artifacts are displayed at the interpretive center. A two-mile-long trail winds among the mounds and passes a replica of a thatched-roof dwelling.

▶ Open Wed.–Sun. except state holidays.

www.okhistory.org/outreach/museums/
    spiromounds.html
(918) 962-2062

18 Heavener Runestone State Park

Runestone Rd., Heavener

Halfway up Poteau Mountain stands the Heavener Runestone, a 12-foot-high slab with eight Nordic runes (alphabet characters) representing a boundary marker for "Glome Valley." Some believe that the runestones were left by Viking explorers 500 years before Columbus arrived in the New World.

A hilly one-mile nature trail meanders through the 50-acre park. Hickory, dogwood, redbud, oak, cedar, and pine trees provide cover for raccoons, beavers, armadillos, and deer, as well as hawks, blue jays, quail, and brown thrashers.

16 Sequoyah's Cabin.
A bronze statue of Sequoyah sits on the grounds of the museum housing his cabin.

▶ Open year-round.

www.oklahomaparks.com
(918) 653-2241

19 Beavers Bend Resort

Hwy. 259A, 8 miles north of Broken Bow

Named for John Beavers, who once owned much of the land, this 3,482-acre park borders the Mountain Fork River deep in the Ouachita Mountains. Forested with pine and hardwood, along with mistletoe, dogwoods, and bald cypresses, the park is home to deer, small mammals, quail, wild turkeys, and many species of birds.

Forest Heritage Center, a rustic circular building, contains dioramas and other exhibits, including a slice of trunk from a 340-year-old bald cypress. A group of live Southern flying squirrels can be seen in the nature center.

In addition to the David L. Boren Hiking Trail, which extends for 26 miles, there are four nature trails. Broken Bow Lake and a nearby river are stocked with fish.

▶ Open year-round.

www.beaversbend.com
(580) 494-6300

seasonal events

APRIL
- Art in the Vineyard—Drumright *(art show with music, food, winery tours and wine tasting)*

MAY
- Mayfest—Tulsa *(fine- and performing-arts festival, children's activities)*

JUNE
- Rockets over Rhema—Tulsa/Broken Arrow *(music, giant inflatable games, car show, huge fireworks display)*

JULY
- Charlie Christian International Music Festival—Oklahoma City *(music of the world-renowned jazz-guitar legend, a native of the city)*

SEPTEMBER
- Choctaw Nation Labor Day Festival—Tuskahoma *(heritage exhibitions, intertribal powwow, concerts, buffalo tours, games, rides)*
- Fiestas de la Americas—Oklahoma City *(multicultural celebration, parade, singing, dancing, arts)*
- The Loose Caboose Antique and Craft Festival—Purcell *(antiques, collectibles, arts and crafts, music, wine tasting)*

OCTOBER
- Robbers' Cave Fall Festival—Wilburton *(arts and crafts, classic car show)*
- Grand Wine Country Fall Festival—Monkey Island *(wine, live jazz, art)*
- Oklahoma Flute Festival—Park Hill *(Native American music festival, workshops, demonstrations)*

NOVEMBER
- An Affair of the Heart—Tulsa *(one of the largest arts and crafts shows in the United States)*

DECEMBER
- Festivus for Rest of Us Party—Okema *(music, food, games that test feats of strength)*

www.travelok.com

Oregon

Wave-swept shores, green valleys, desert plains, and equally diverse historic sites await travelers to this Pacific Northwest wonderland.

John Day Fossil Beds National Monument. Prehistoric plants and animals left their mark in the layered mountains of rock near Kimberly (see page 279).

Along the Oregon coast are the sea stacks, promontories, dunes, and driftwood that grace countless picture postcards and calendars. Competing for attention are the state's verdant mountains and valleys, a paradise for hikers, campers, boaters, and birders.

In this nominal destination for the 19th-century wagoneers, travelers can walk in the footsteps of Lewis and Clark on a trail blazed to the sea, take a train ride through gold mine country, observe wildlife from sea lions to bighorn sheep, and find surprise after surprise on the topographically diverse land—a river that detours through a lava tube, the deepest river gorge in North America, and a canyon seemingly transported from the American Southwest.

visit ➤ (offthebeatenpathtrips.com)

1 Columbia River Maritime Museum

1792 Marine Dr., Astoria
For five miles its foghorn could cut through the heavy mist, heralding the way home for bone-tired sailors. The bright beacon of the lightship *Columbia* was a comforting sight for seamen approaching the mouth of the Columbia River, known for its danger to ships. The first lightship on the Pacific Coast began its tour of duty in 1892. The last *Columbia* lightship to be in active service was replaced in 1979 by an unmanned navigational buoy of heroic proportions, measuring 40 feet wide by 86 feet high. Both floating aids are now on display in this museum.

Two hundred years of Pacific Northwest maritime history are explored here, with the powerful waterway visible through the large windows of the wavelike structure. Interactive exhibits allow people to see what it's like to pilot a tugboat, engage in a Coast Guard rescue on the river bar, or go salmon fishing in Astoria. You can even clamber up to the bridge of a World War II naval destroyer, the USS *Knapp.*

▶ Open year-round; closed Thanksgiving and Christmas. Admission charged.

www.crmm.org
(503) 325-2323

1 ➤ **Columbia River Maritime Museum.** The museum sits on the banks of the mighty river whose maritime history it explores. Shown here is the Great Hall.

2 Fort to Sea Trail

Fort Clatsop National Memorial
After Lewis and Clark's Corps of Discovery built Fort Clatsop on the Oregon coast, they blazed a 6^1/2-mile trail to the windswept beaches—a trail that can be walked today. The path starts at the visitors center and gradually rises through Sitka spruce and hemlock forest to the top of a 400-foot-high ridge (the trail is classified as moderate to easy). You'll pass alders and skunk cabbage as the trail descends to pastureland, duneland, and finally, Sunset Beach. Look for the occasional bald eagle, but you're more likely to spot deer and Douglas squirrels, the pine squirrel native to the Pacific Northwest.

▶ Open daily.

www.forttosea.org
(503) 861-2471

▶3 Cape Meares State Park and Cape Meares National Wildlife Refuge

Off Three Capes Scenic Dr., Tillamook

In 1788 Capt. John Meares, exploring the coast, came upon this imposing headland and named it Cape Lookout. The coast was again surveyed in 1850, and a point 10 miles to the south was erroneously designated Cape Lookout. By 1857 the name had become so well known that the original site was renamed Cape Meares. The 40-foot octagonal lighthouse, perhaps built here by mistake, operated from 1890 to 1964.

The park and lighthouse sit atop Cape Meares, a 217-foot-high bluff with sheer cliffs dropping straight to the sea. A sturdy fence along the 250-yard path to the lighthouse protects visitors from a possibly fatal tumble.

Some 2½ miles of trail cross the 232-acre park. From the trail on the south side of the cape, you can view the Three Arches Wildlife Refuge, three islands of rock about 2½ miles to the south. With binoculars you may catch a glimpse of the sea lions inhabiting the marine refuge.

To find the Cape Meares Wildlife Refuge, take the Oregon Coast Trail east from the parking lot. On the way, you'll pass the Octopus Tree, a Sitka spruce that is striking for its enormous size and candelabra branching. Its six limbs extend horizontally from the trunk for 30 feet before turning upward. From early February through July, trilliums, skunk cabbage, lilies of the valley, and other wildflowers add color to the landscape. Tufted puffins and pelagic cormorants are among the numerous seabirds nesting on the

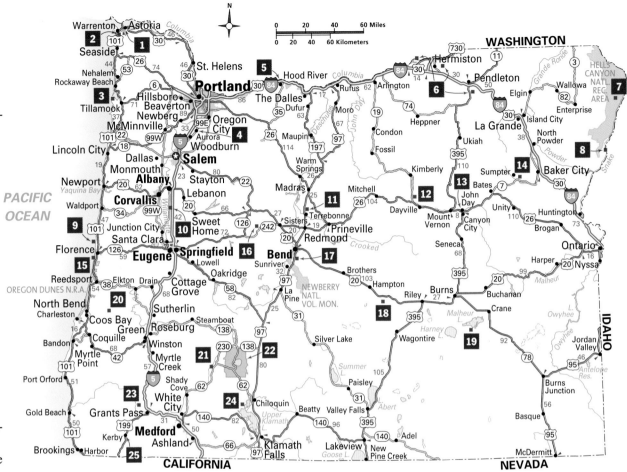

139-acre refuge, where black-tailed deer are also seen.

The Three Capes Scenic Drive, about 35 miles long, offers spectacular views of coast, dunes, and picturesque villages.

▶ Park open daily May–Oct.

www.oregonstateparks.org
(503) 842-4981

▶4 Aurora Colony Museum

Second and Liberty Sts., Aurora

Aurora was a utopian Christian colony founded on Oregon's Pudding River by Dr. William Keil, a charismatic Prussian who arrived in the United States in 1831. Though it thrived in the 1860s, the colony dissolved in 1883 after Keil's

death. Still 20 surviving buildings have been placed on the *National Register of Historic Places*.

The Aurora Colony Museum, housed in a former ox barn, is the anchor of a charming complex. Displays include a collection of colony quilts and an unusual wooden lathe used for turning wood. A small grassy courtyard out back is surrounded by buildings that include a restored log cabin; the Kraus House, a

Victorian complete with a rare "walking spinning wheel" upstairs; and a replica of a tie shed (where horses were tied and sheltered), with blacksmith and woodworking shops where the old trades are demonstrated today.

▶ Open Tues.–Sun. Closed Jan. Admission charged.

www.auroracolonymuseum.com
(503) 678-5754

Legend

1	NUMBERED ATTRACTIONS (Described in text)

CONTROLLED ACCESS HIGHWAYS
- Free
- Toll
- Under Construction

OTHER HIGHWAYS
- Primary Highway
- Secondary Highway

HIGHWAY MARKERS
- **10** Interstate Route
- **12** U.S. Route
- **12** State Route
- 12 Distances along Major Highways (in miles)

CITIES AND TOWNS
- ★ National Capital
- ◉ State Capital
- • Cities, Towns, and Populated Places Type size indicates relative importance
- Urban Area

RECREATION AND FEATURES OF INTEREST
- National Park
- Other Large Park or Recreation Area
- Trail
- Ferry

© 2009 GeoNova

5 **Historic Columbia River Highway State Trail.** An eye-popping view of mountain and river rewards eastbound motorists and bikers exiting the trail's Twin Tunnels.

5 Historic Columbia River Highway State Trail

East of Portland, between Troutdale and The Dalles

Called the king of roads, this expansive thoroughfare travels east-west through the Columbia River Gorge. Built between 1913 and 1922, this road was America's first scenic highway and was also the first modern highway in the Pacific Northwest. Running along the south side of the Columbia River, it was designed to be in harmony with nature. Since the mid-1980s more than 10 miles of abandoned highway have been restored as pedestrian and bicycle paths known as the Historic Columbia River Highway State Trail. You pass between two climate zones in the Twin Tunnels portion of the trail, between Hood River and Mosier. Leaving the car allows you to take a more leisurely look at the Ponderosa pine, moss-covered rocks, ferns, and wildflowers. The gorge itself is among the most awe-inspiring sights in the United States.

▶ Open year-round. Day-use admission charged per vehicle.

www.oregonstateparks.org/park_155.php
(800) 551-6949

6 Mid-Columbia River National Wildlife Refuge Complex

Burbank

Three of the eight refuges in this complex, all primarily sanctuaries for waterfowl, are located in Oregon. McKay Creek National Wildlife Refuge (NWR), south of Pendleton, is a serene, mirror-smooth lake. In spring and early summer the refuge attracts as many boaters, anglers, and water-skiers as it does birders out to spot blue herons, long-billed curlews, red-winged blackbirds, and other species. By August the lake shrinks to less than a fifth of its former size and sprouts vegetation for feeding wildlife.

Umatilla NWR, near Irrigon, is on the Pacific Flyway and serves as a wintering site for Arctic geese. Cold Springs NWR, near Hermiston in the desert of north-eastern Oregon, is an oasis for birds, western mule deer, and desert elk.

▶ Open daily.

www.fws.gov/mcriver
(509) 546-8300

7 Hat Point Overlook, Hells Canyon National Recreation Area

24 miles southeast of Imnaha, off Rte. 86 via one-lane dirt road

Hat Point Overlook is really only for those with four-wheel-drive vehicles. However, the trip is extremely rewarding because of the views of Hells Canyon, which is the deepest river gorge on the North American continent.

The 24-mile trip on a one-lane dirt road from Imnaha takes 1 1/2 hours, not counting stops, and goes from an altitude of approximately 1,700 feet to 6,982 feet. At Five Mile Viewpoint the road levels out and goes through pine forests and wildflower-filled meadows inhabited by a variety of wildlife.

Besides Hells Canyon, the view from the summit includes the Snake River, more than a mile below, and across the canyon in Idaho the craggy peaks of the Seven Devils Mountains. For an even more panoramic vista, visitors can climb the 100-foot tower, which is manned in summer.

A hiking trail begins in the picnic area and winds through meadows and down the cliff to the canyon far below. Campgrounds are provided for tents and light campers. No running water is available.

▶ Road open July-Nov.

www.fs.fed.us/hellscanyon
(541) 426-5546

8 Oxbow Dam, Hells Canyon National Recreation Area

70 miles east of Baker at junction of Oregon Rte. 86 and Idaho Rte. 71

When Hells Canyon Power Development Complex was completed in 1968, three dams spanned the Snake River Canyon—Oxbow, Brownlee, and Hells Canyon—their backwaters forming three man-made lakes and a recreation area 90 miles long.

10 **Thompson's Mills State Heritage Site.** In 1897 Martin Thompson bought and renamed Boston Mills, which had been destroyed by fire and rebuilt.

Oxbow is the center of the complex and the smallest of the three dams. It also has a fish hatchery, where steelheads can be seen from September through the end of April.

All three dam areas are popular with power-boaters, water-skiers, swimmers, and fishermen, who try for trout, bass, catfish, steelheads, and crappies. Here, too, are large populations of deer, elk, and bighorn sheep, as well as chukars, quails, Hungarian partridges, bald and golden eagles, cranes, geese, grouse, swans, and a variety of ducks and songbirds.

A scenic highlight of the entire recreation area is the 22-mile Hells Canyon Dr., which begins at Oxbow. Several miles of hiking trails and picnic areas are available.

▶ Park open year-round; hatchery open daily.

www.fs.fed.us/hellscanyon
(541) 426-5546

9 ▶ Sea Lion Caves

91560 Hwy 101, Florence
Both California sea lions and Steller's sea lions are found here. During fall and winter as many as 400 gather in the cave, their only permanent year-round home on the American mainland. In spring and summer they often bask on the rocky cliffs.

Entrance to the cave is by an elevator that descends 208 feet from the visitors center to the observation window. The 300-foot-wide cavern, about two acres in size with a dome 125 feet high, is believed to be the world's largest sea cave and a rookery for Brandt's cormorants, which usually arrive in April and stay until the middle of August. As many as 2,500 nests have been found on the cliffs. The

11 ▶ Smith Rock State Park. The park and the Crooked River Canyon therein stand in stark contrast to the forested mountain landscapes associated with Oregon.

view from the visitors center makes this a popular place for whale-watching.

▶ Open year-round except major winter holidays. Admission charged.

www.sealioncaves.com
(541) 547-3111

10 ▶ Thompson's Mills State Heritage Site

32655 Boston Mill Rd., Shedd
A five-story 19th-century grain mill is at the heart of this 20-acre heritage site in the Willamette Valley. Dating from 1863, this oldest water-powered mill in Oregon was a regular destination for rural families who came with their grain crops and left with bags of flour for the coming months. The mill also produced its own brands: Thompson's Best, Cream of the Valley, and Valley Rose.

On guided tours led by rangers, visitors view the Calapooia River (the still-operating mill's power

source), antique milling machinery, four silos, grain elevators, and a carpentry shop. They also pass the Queen Anne–style millkeeper's house, built in 1904.

▶ Open daily, weather permitting.

www.oregonstateparks.org/park_256.php
(541) 491-3611

11 ▶ Smith Rock State Park

9241 N.E. Crooked River Dr., Terrebonne
Smith Rock is known as one of the world's most popular rock-climbing destinations. The keynote here is color: 623 acres of spectacular sandstone formations—boulders, cliffs, crags, and pinnacles—in magnificent pale yellows, burnt reds, rich greens, and purples that change with the shifting sunlight. The Crooked River, a ribbon of blue, twists among them. Some speculate that the park was named for the man who discovered it, John Smith, a Kentuckian who

came to Oregon in the 1850s and rose to political prominence.

Picnic sites are scattered throughout the park. Several paved pathways lead from the parking lot to the river's edge and across a footbridge, where a network of trails spreads out among the formations.

▶ Open year-round. Day-use admission charged per vehicle.

www.oregonstateparks.org/park_51.php
(800) 551-6949

12 ▶ Sheep Rock Unit, John Day Fossil Beds National Monument

Intersection of Rtes. 19 and 26, Kimberly
Thirty million years ago sabertoothed cats pursued sheep-size horses amid vast forests here, while piglike entelodonts and rhinoceroses grazed the lush underbrush. You can see fossil evidence of these and other prehistoric plants and animals discovered in volcanic and sedimentary layers of a colorful near-desert landscape.

The place to closely examine hundreds of fossils is the Thomas Condon Paleontology Center, where you will find a working fossil laboratory and exhibits showcasing current research.

Hiking trails, most fairly easy, lead through spectacular "badlands" scenery, where fossils are still being found. (Collecting is prohibited without research permits.) The John Day River crosses the area and provides good fishing, mostly steelhead and smallmouth bass.

▶ Open daily year-round; Paleontology Center open daily.

www.nps.gov/joda/sheep-rock.htm
(541) 987-2333

13 Kam Wah Chung & Company Museum

116 N.W. Bridge St., John Day
Here is a 19th-century reminder of the days in American history when Chinese laborers outnumbered white miners and ranchers nearly three to one in eastern Oregon. Kam Wah Chung & Company, built in the 1860s as a trading post, was bought in 1887 by two young immigrants—Lung On, a merchant, and Ing Hay, an herbalist. They lived and worked there until the 1940s, having grasped the "Golden Flower of Opportunity," implied by the store's name.

Kam Wah Chung & Company became a center for the Chinese community: a general store, doctor's office, pharmacy, temple, gambling and opium den, and speakeasy. Today the tiny herbal dispensary is jammed with boxes, tins, and jars full of traditional remedies. The building's shrines are still hung with effigies, paper cutouts, and peacock feathers. Joss sticks and fortune sticks survive along with shriveled offerings of a variety of fruit.

And there's more: bootlegged whiskey bottles, fireworks, playing cards and dominoes, gold-mining pans, and scales. There are also pieces of handmade furniture built by members of the local Chinese community.

A visit to this well-preserved place of multifarious business evokes the history of Chinatowns in the West. Recently designated a National Historic Landmark, it is a worthwhile cultural and historical experience.

▶ Open Mon.-Sat. and P.M. Sun., May-Oct. Admission charged.

www.oregonstateparks.org/park_8
(541) 575-2800

14 **Sumpter Valley Railway.** Passengers in open-air cars pulled by a vintage locomotive take a trip back in time through Oregon's gold and timber country.

14 Sumpter Valley Railway

211 S.W. Austin, Bakercity
Travel back to the glory of eastern Oregon's turn-of-the-century lumber and mining industry aboard the open-air cars and original caboose of this restored narrow-gauge railway, driven by an authentic wood-burning Heisler locomotive.

The Sumpter Valley Railway Company, started in 1890 by lumber magnate David Eccles, was a highly prosperous operation by the time its tracks were extended to the Sumpter gold mines in 1896. However, during the 1930s business declined, and in 1947 the railroad, known as the Stump Dodger, ceased operation.

Since 1970 local volunteers have been restoring the track bed and offering rides through the picturesque countryside. Occasionally a run is attacked by "bandits," provided by volunteers, who add to the colorful illusion of the Old West. While you're waiting for the trip to begin, browse through the historic photographs and railroad memorabilia in the depot's museum or visit the engine cab, where the crew is happy to explain how the steam locomotive works.

▶ Open weekends Memorial Day–Sept. Admission charged.

www.svry.com
(541) 894-2268

15 Jessie M. Honeyman Memorial State Park

3 miles south of Florence
Oregon's second-largest overnight camp is a place for all seasons. Within the 522 acres that make up this park, there are sand dunes, ocean beaches, two freshwater lakes, and a forest of Douglas fir, spruce, and hemlock. The park design is a hallmark of the National Park Service and invokes harmony with nature, from the rustic buildings to the untouched landscape.

Cleawox Lake and Woahink Lake are perfect for summertime water activities. A swimming area, boat launching dock, and other offered activities make it easy to cool off in the water. Summer is also the season to enjoy berry picking, as the huckleberries and blackberries are ripe and ready. Autumn and winter brings, the Discovery Season, when you can access the sand dunes directly from reserved campsites, and flocks of geese and other birds populate the area. In the spring rhododendrons bloom and bring color to the landscape.

This park is a popular destination for day-use and campers. Campsites throughout the park are offered along with the always popular yurts, the tentlike domes that sleep up to five. Hiking trails range from short walks through the forest to longer treks over the dunes to the ocean.

▶ Open year-round, including the campground. Day-use fee charged per vehicle.

www.fws.gov/klamathbasinrefuges
(800) 551-6949

16 McKenzie Pass Lava Beds

Off Hwy. 242 between McKenzie Bridge and Sisters
Stretching for some 75 square miles on both sides of McKenzie Hwy. (Hwy. 242) are the jumbled lava beds that resulted from thousands of years of eruptions along the High Cascade volcanic chain. The half-mile Lava River Trail, which starts at the summit of the pass, has markers to explain lava

gutters, pressure ridges, cooling cracks, crevasses, and other formations. The markers also identify the fascinating dwarf trees—among them mountain hemlock, lodgepole pine, and Pacific silver fir.

Except for the Belknap Crater flows, which are rolling, graceful rivers of rock, the lava is a broken, jumbled mass of rocks, like ice breaking up on a river, the result of its surface cooling over molten turbulence. A 1.5-mile loop trail on the west end of Hwy. 242 leads to Proxy Falls. A 3.8-mile trail on the east end, quite steep in places, takes you from the highway at Windy Point to Black Crater.

The Dee Wright Observatory, at the crest between Proxy Falls and Black Crater, was built from lava rock during the Great Depression and completed in 1935. It remains one of the most popular attractions at the lava beds.

▶ Open July–mid-Oct.

http://gorp.away.com/gorp/activity/byway/
  or_mcken.htm

(541) 822-3381

High Desert Museum

59800 Hwy. 97S, Bend
Both the natural and cultural history of the high-desert region comes alive at this 135-acre indoor-outdoor museum. As visitors stroll on winding outdoor trails, they come up close to such high-desert wildlife as porcupines, otters, reptiles, eagles, falcons, and owls in their natural habitats.

Guests can also talk with staff dressed as historical figures from the high-desert past (stagecoach drivers, explorers, and a homesteader family at their 1880 mustang ranch cabin) and explore Native American exhibits as well

as western exhibits, like stagecoaches and Silver City, a re-created 1880s mine and town.

▶ Open year-round except major holidays. Admission charged.

www.highdesertmuseum.org
(541) 382-4754

18 Glass Butte Recreational Rockhound Area

Off US-20; at milepost 77 turn south
Serious rock hounds come from near and far to dig at Glass Butte. The Bureau of Land Management allows rock collecting for personal use only, and you can collect up to 250 pounds of rocks per year.

Formed by a volcanic eruption nearly 5 million years ago, the 6,400-foot mountain has some of the world's largest outcrops of obsidian—a black volcanic glass that forms when lava with a high silica content cools quickly.

Native Americans prized the brittle, easily chipped obsidian and turned this area into a virtual factory for axes, scrapers, chisels, and weapon points.

While ordinary jet-black obsidian is appealing and makes attractive jewelry, the material can also be streaked with gold, silver, and other colors or have an iridescent sheen. Even the rare fire obsidian is found here. Some 23,000 acres have been set aside for rockhounding, and in the valley chunks can be kicked up with a boot or found lying loose in the roadbed. However, anyone seeking the more valuable varieties should bring shovels, picks, and rock hammers along. No mechanical equipment is allowed.

The road to the site is rutted

17 ▶ **High Desert Museum.** Sunlight streams through floor-to-ceiling windows in one of the exhibition halls at this museum of natural and cultural history.

and rough and best avoided in the spring wet season. The area is primitive, with no facilities, although overnight camping is permitted. Camping or not, visitors should bring food and water.

▶ Open year-round.

www.fs.fed.us/r6/centraloregon/recreation/
  rockhounding/where–glass.shtml

(541) 416-6700

19 Malheur National Wildlife Refuge

Off Rte. 205, 32 miles south of Burns in Princeton
This 187,000-acre wetlands preserve, situated in desert uplands covered with sagebrush and juniper, encompasses two large, shallow lakes (Harney and Malheur) and a number of ponds, ditches, dikes, and canals. The refuge's permanent bulrush marshes and seasonally flooded meadows provide ideal habitats for both nesting and migrating birds. The best way to see it all is by car, starting at the refuge headquarters. Here the

George M. Benson Museum offers an impressive array of mounted birds, from common flickers to cranes and eagles, as well as tip sheets on current bird-watching hot spots.

Spring brings pintail ducks, sandhill cranes, tundra swans, and snow and Canadian geese, and fall draws mallards and warblers. Birds of prey spotted here include great horned owls and golden and bald eagles. Beavers and muskrats in the marshes and mule deer in the uplands are among the 58 mammal species seen.

Cross-country hiking is only allowed on designated trails. Flooding in the refuge's northern lowlands can limit access and may require detours. It's best to call first.

▶ Refuge, museum, and visitors center open daily year-round except weekends Nov.–Mar.; some roads may be impassable in spring and winter.

www.fws.gov/malheur
(541) 493-2612

Golden and Silver Falls State Park

Off Hwy. 101, 24 miles northeast of Coos Bay

The two falls, located at opposite ends of the 157-acre park, are about three-quarters of a mile apart. Golden Falls, named in honor of an early visitor, drops over a rounded ledge of lava. Silver Falls, named to complement its "sister," cascades from a basalt amphitheater over a series of boulders and divides into two streams that become Silver Creek.

A parking lot and picnic ground are halfway between the two falls. To reach Golden Falls, follow a half-mile path along the canyon through stands of evergreens; the trail offers a pleasant view of Glenn Creek. Silver Falls is reached by a quarter-mile path along the canyon floor among ferns and moss-draped trees.

The park, which has been left in its natural state, is notable for its grove of myrtles—rare and beautiful hardwood trees that flourish in southern Oregon. Chipmunks, porcupines, and black bears are found here, with elk and deer coming to forage in winter. Trout fishing in both Glenn and Silver creeks is excellent in early summer.

▶ Open year-round. Admission charged.

www.oregonstateparks.org
(800) 551-6949

21 Natural Bridge, Rogue River National Forest

55 miles north of Medford off Rte. 62

Natural Bridge is seen best during summertime periods of low water but is also a spectacular sight when the Rogue submerges it in swift whitewater rapids. The bridge is a large, intact lava tube that channels the river underground for about 200 feet before the waters resurface.

Its origins date back to the eruption of Mount Mazama, which formed Crater Lake nearly 7,000 years ago and sent lava flows raging across the surrounding countryside. As their surfaces cooled and hardened, tunnels formed underneath.

Natural Bridge campground has sites for tents and small trailers, each with a picnic table and grill. There are several hiking trails, including one to Woodruff Bridge, which is a favorite spot for catching rainbow trout. Wading in the waters is permitted, but avoid the opening near Natural Bridge; the slippery and smooth surface can be dangerous.

▶ Open Memorial Day–Labor Day.

www.fs.fed.us/r6/rogue
(541) 858-2200; (541) 560-3400

22 Crater Lake National Park

57 miles north of Klamath Falls, off Rte. 62

Crater Lake is the deepest (1,943 feet) and probably the bluest lake in the United States and is set like a sapphire in the bowl-shaped caldera of old Mount Mazama, a volcano that erupted and collapsed nearly 7,000 years ago.

Traces of past volcanic activity can be seen at The Pinnacles, reached by Sand Creek Highway, a seven-mile paved road passable from late summer until heavy snow. These pumice and scoria formations, 75 to 100 feet tall, rise like an army of obelisks from a 200-foot-deep canyon. Some 30 trails (ranging from less than a mile to 35 miles) crisscross the park.

Hikes up Watchman Peak and Mount Scott provide the best views of the lake. There are two campgrounds, at Mazama and at Lost Creek, both accessible by road from Rim Drive. And with a permit you can camp in the backcountry.

Crater Lake is particularly beautiful in winter and, despite an annual snowfall of 533 inches, easy to visit. The road is kept clear, and a ski trail circles the crater rim. On weekends from Thanksgiving to April, you can join snowshoe hikes led by a park ranger.

▶ Park and visitors center open year-round.

www.nps.gov/crla
(541) 594-3000

23 Indian Mary Park and Hellgate Canyon

11 miles north of Merlin on Merlin Galice Rd.

Indian Mary Park and Hellgate Canyon are side by side on Oregon's Rogue River. A portion of Indian Mary Park was once the smallest Native American reservation (40 acres) in the United States, granted by the government in 1855 to Umqua Joe, Mary's father, for warning white settlers of an impending massacre. The reservation is now a 65-acre park with exotic trees and shrubs planted among native ponderosa pine and Douglas fir. Spring brings extra touches of beauty, when the trees and shrubs, complemented by azaleas, lupines, and yellow monkey flowers, burst into bloom.

The park has shaded picnic grounds, playgrounds, and campsites with hookups. The river, which is wide and calm near the park, is popular with swimmers and fishermen. The Indian Joe Trail, a steep $3^1/2$-mile route, leads to a lookout from which you can see the grasslands and

did you know ?

Novelist Zane Grey, who owned a cabin on the river, wrote of Hellgate in several of his stories.

20 ▶ **Golden and Silver Falls State Park.** Torrential Silver Falls roils the waters of Silver Creek, whose calmer stretches lure trout fishermen in early summer.

 **Crater Lake National Park.** Summer boat tours allow visitors a close-up view of Wizard Island, a 760-foot-high cinder cone rising from the sapphire waters.

forested hills and of the Rogue River valley.

Hellgate Canyon, a jumble of sheer cliffs and overhanging rocks, is a favorite with rafters, kayakers, and tubers. An excursion boat, which departs from Hog Creek a mile above the canyon, also weaves through the chasm. Sandbars here attract gold panners as well as picnickers.

▶ Open year-round. Admission charged.

www.rogueweb.com/indianmary
(541) 474-5285 Indian Mary Park

www.southernoregon.com/merlin-galice/index.html
(503) 479-3735 Hellgate Canyon

24 ▶ Upper Klamath National Wildlife Refuge

Rocky Point, off Hwy. 140 W
There is only one way to tour this vast wetlands preserve: by boat. More than 14,000 acres of marsh and open water here provide food and nesting sites for some 250 species of birds. The small village of Rocky Point on the western edge of the refuge at Pelican Bay offers access to the marshes and a fine viewing spot on the shore.

From here you can follow a 9$^{1}/_{2}$-mile self-guiding canoe trail through the marshlands, a trip that provides a unique opportunity for watching bird life, particularly the pelicans, egrets, herons, and Canada geese. The best time for viewing these birds and other wildlife is at sunrise. Bald eagles and ospreys nest nearby and can occasionally be seen fishing the waters.

Both hunting and fishing are permitted in season on 5,700 acres of the refuge territory. Trout average four or five pounds. Yellow perch is another likely catch. Hunting is limited to geese, ducks, coots, and snipe.

The Forest Service maintains campgrounds near Rocky Point, and from Apr.–Nov., a few sports-men's resorts in the area offer marina facilities, cabins, and motorboat and canoe rentals.

▶ Refuge open year-round; campgrounds open year-round, depending on snow access.

www.fws.gov/klamathbasinrefuges
(530) 667-2231

25 ▶ Kerbyville Museum and History Center

24195 Redwood Hwy., Kerby
Following the discovery of gold on the banks of Josephine Creek in 1851, several towns, including Kerbyville (since shortened to Kerby) sprouted. Few of these towns remain, but the heirlooms, tools, and mementos of many of the people who once lived in them have been donated to the Kerbyville Museum.

In the main museum building you'll see a colorful facsimile of an old-time country store interior, Native American handiwork, a new military display featuring artifacts from the Civil War to the Vietnam War, and a collection of women's clothing illustrating that the apparel of a well-dressed lady could weigh as much as 100 pounds.

The complex also includes a quaint one-room log schoolhouse, a barn-size blacksmith's shop, farm equipment, and the 1871 Stith-Naucke House. A life-size replica of a Takelma pit house is also on display. The two-story building is furnished with charming Victoriana and other antiques that belonged to early Josephine County families.

▶ Open daily; call for winter hours. Admission charged.

www.u-s-history.com/or/k/kerbyvim.htm
(541) 592-5252

seasonal events

FEBRUARY
- Shakespeare Festival—Ashland *(various performances of Shakespeare)*

MARCH
- Wee Bit 'O Ireland—Happner *(parade, bowling competitions, music)*
- Airing of the Quilts Show—Milwaukie *(quilt displays, vendors)*

APRIL
- Spring in the Country—Canby *(annual bazaar featuring gifts, crafts, and home decor)*

JUNE
- Festival of the Arts—Lake Oswego *(art, special exhibits, food, music, crafts, family events)*
- Clackamas County Lavender Festival—Oregon City *(bluegrass music, lavender picking, wine tasting)*

SEPTEMBER
- Bend Oktoberfest—Bend *(traditional Bavarian food, music, games)*
- Mt. Hood Heritage Day—Mt. Hood *(museum open house, recreation club booths, silent auction, food)*
- Cider Squeeze—Eagle Creek *(folk music, food, vendors, games, horse-drawn carriage rides, cider pressing)*
- Grape Stomping Festival—Canby *(Bavarian music, brats and krauts, winery tours, grape-stomping contests)*

OCTOBER
- Colonial Harvest Days—Pleasant Hill *(live music, face painting, pumpkin launching, cow counting, hay rides)*
- Tribal Member Art Exhibit—Warm Springs *(art by local artists)*
- Potato Festival—Merrill *(music, agricultural exhibits, horseshoe contests)*

NOVEMBER
- Wagons Ho! Film Festival—Baker City *(films and discussions on the American West)*
- Starlight Parade—The Dalles *(chili feed, entertainment, parade of floats)*

www.traveloregon.com

OREGON

Pennsylvania

From east to west, the Keystone State is a treasure trove of history, culture, industry, agriculture, and remarkable landforms.

Buzzard Swamp Wildlife Area, Allegheny National Forest. A vast undisturbed marsh attracts thousands of waterfowl every spring and fall (see page 286).

From miles of hiking trails in the verdant Allegheny Mountains to a wolf sanctuary in a county made famous by the Amish, Pennsylvania invites exploration on its highways and byways. Not far from Hopewell Furnace, the birthplace of the American Industrial Revolution, a married couple crafts handmade cheeses on the family farm. Breathtaking views can be seen of the Grand Canyon of Pennsylvania, which was carved eons ago by what is now a creek, while the Delaware and Hudson Canal dates back a mere 150 years.

The lives of fascinating people are glimpsed within the walls of their grand residences—a Tudor mansion that grew from a trading post and the Southern plantation-style home of a Supreme Court Justice. And museums? They include those devoted to timepieces, antique tools, toy trains, Little League baseball, and the lives and work of a family of famous painters.

visit ➤ **offthebeatenpathtrips.com**

1 Pymatuning Reservoir

Accessible via US-6 or US-322, north of Jamestown

Once a great swamp, the reservoir was created when the Pymatuning dam was completed in 1934. It was intended to conserve water going into the swamp, impound floodwaters, and regulate the flow of water into the Beaver and Shenango rivers. The name Pymatuning came from the Iroquois and means "the crooked mouthed man's dwelling place," referring to someone's deceit.

The lake teems with activity in the summer, when warm-weather fishing is bountiful. The annual Winter Fun Days offer a whole range of winter sports, from ice fishing to cross-country skiing. Most of Pymatuning Reservoir is in northwestern Pennsylvania, but one-quarter of it rests in Ashtabula County, Ohio.

The spillway near Linesville is known as the place "where the ducks walk on the fish." So many carp congregate to catch stale bread thrown by visitors that the ducks have no room to swim, and it looks as though they're walking over the fish.

▶ Open year-round.

www.dcnr.state.pa.us/stateparks/parks/
pymatuning.aspx
(724) 932-3141

1 ▶ **Pymatuning Reservoir.** The Pymatuning Dam gatehouse and a bridge, both built of sandstone, date back to the opening of the reservoir in the mid-1930s.

2 Presque Isle State Park

301 Peninsula Dr., Ste. 1, Erie

Seven miles of pristine beach can be enjoyed in this 3,200-acre park on a peninsula jutting into Lake Erie. Fifteen miles of paved trail provide a great place for walking, biking, or in-line skating.

In addition to the swimming beaches, reached by a loop road, the park also has about 20 miles of hiking trails, some leading around inland ponds and a lagoon. Spring anglers bring in bass, walleye, steelhead, and perch. Birders come from all over the world for spring and fall migration.

In winter Presque Isle is a wonderland, with trees and ground mantled by sparkling white snow.

Cross-country ski trails abound, and ice fishing attracts hundreds of enthusiasts. Visitors will be thrilled by the incredible ice dunes that form. From the inland side of the peninsula, which hooks back toward the mainland to form Erie Harbor, the city of Erie serrates the horizon when the weather is clear.

▶ Open year-round.

www.dcnr.state.pa.us
(814) 833-7424

3 Baldwin-Reynolds House Museum

639 Terrace St., Meadville

Henry Baldwin, a U.S. Supreme Court justice from 1830 to 1844,

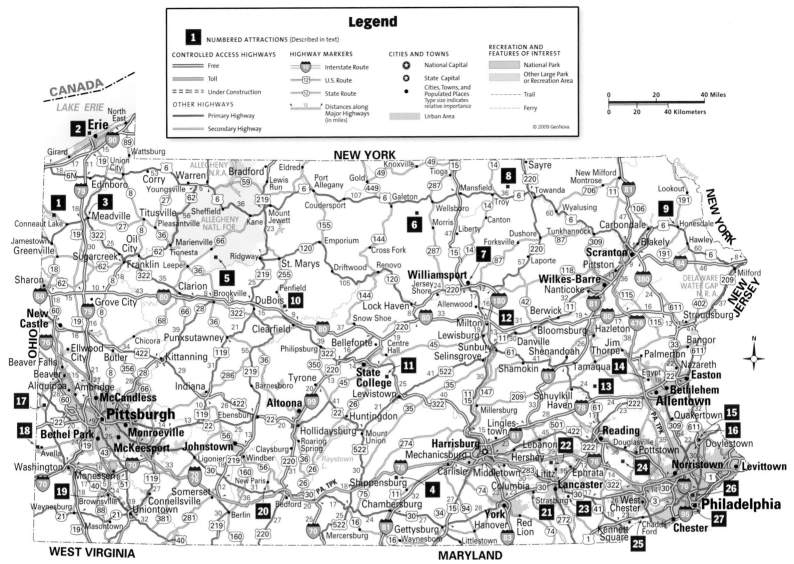

Legend

NUMBERED ATTRACTIONS (Described in text)

CONTROLLED ACCESS HIGHWAYS
- Free
- Toll
- Under Construction

OTHER HIGHWAYS
- Primary Highway
- Secondary Highway

HIGHWAY MARKERS
- 10 Interstate Route
- 12 U.S. Route
- 12 State Route
- 12 Distances along Major Highways (in miles)

CITIES AND TOWNS
- National Capital
- State Capital
- Cities, Towns, and Populated Places Type size indicates relative importance
- Urban Area

RECREATION AND FEATURES OF INTEREST
- National Park
- Other Large Park or Recreation Area
- Trail
- Ferry

© 2009 GeoNova

based the design of his stately three-story home on a Southern mansion. It sits on a gentle rise in the midst of landscaped grounds with a commanding view of French Creek, once the major trading route in the area. The pre–Civil War Southern culture and lifestyle are represented in this elegant frame structure.

After Baldwin's death in 1844, the house was bought by a relative, William Reynolds. Members of his family lived here until 1963.

The 19th-century kitchen and servants' lodgings are tucked away on the ground floor and in the basement. Massive rooms with high ceilings and arched doorways are given individual character with Italian marble floral designs and incredibly detailed cherry, ash, and walnut woodwork

The total effect is one of an opulence in which every conceivable personal whim is fulfilled. There are secret compartments in the library where important papers could be hidden, and specially designed false pillars that can be removed to reveal a small proscenium-style arch for family entertainment and performances.

The museum also contains a number of historical and antique displays, including a large collection of paperweights.

Next door to the Baldwin-Reynolds house is the Dr. J. Russell Mosier office, which was left intact after his death in 1938. It contains a pharmacy, a medical skeleton, and even the unopened mail received the day Dr. Mosier died.

▶ Open Wed.–Sun., mid-June–mid-Aug.; weekends only May and Sept.

www.baldwinreynolds.org
(814) 333-9882

 Presque Isle State Park. Bricks laid five layers thick helped the lighthouse weather fierce storms.

4 Otterbein Acres

10071 Otterbein Church Rd., Newburg

Don't expect a visitors center or anything remotely touristy at Otterbein Acres, an Amish farm 50 miles west of Harrisburg at the foot of Blue Mountain. The farm's bounty? Artisan cheeses made by owners John and Lena Fisher. On the edge of pastureland dotted with oaks and poplars, you can watch cheesemaking in action, from the milking of Jersey cows and dairy sheep to curd-cutting, milling, and molding. Outside the cheese shop you'll spy horses, hogs, and chickens, reminders that you've left the tourist track far behind.

You can taste (and buy) the finished product on the spot, be it Bandaged Cheddar (named for the muslin in which the cheese ages), Ewe's Dream (a Romano-style sheep's milk cheese), or any other of the Otterbein Acres cheeses limited to farmers markets and specialty cheese shops.

▶ Open Mon.–Sat. Apr.–Sept., but visitors should call ahead to confirm.

(717) 423-6689

5 Buzzard Swamp Wildlife Area, Allegheny National Forest

1 mile south of Marienville

Buzzard Swamp consists of 15 man-made ponds and just over 11 miles of hiking trails, with opportunities to see beaver, snapping turtles, turkeys, deer, bear, and other wildlife. The facility is maintained as a wildlife propagation area.

Buzzard Swamp is an important link in the Atlantic flyway and often has 20–25 species of waterfowl during spring migration. There is a resident population of Pennsylvania songbirds, but most of the species

are migratory. Early spring and early fall are the best times to visit.

The area provides a 1 1/2-mile self-guiding hiking trail called the Songbird Sojourn.

▶ Open year-round.

www.fs.fed.us/r9/forests/allegheny
(814) 723-5150

6 Leonard Harrison State Park and Colton Point State Park

10 miles west of Wellsboro, off Rte. 660

Occupying mountains on opposite sides of Pine Creek Gorge, each park offers breathtaking views of the Grand Canyon of Pennsylvania and the course of Pine Creek as it snakes its way between heavily forested ridges.

Although family camping facilities are available, both parks are largely in their natural state. Rhododendrons, azaleas, and wild laurel, which usually bloom in mid-June, abound. Both parks offer a variety of hiking trails. Those at Colton Point are somewhat more challenging.

6 ▶ **Leonard Harrison State Park.** The Grand Canyon of Pennsylvania is a favorite subject for photographers. Pine Creek streams its way through the gorge.

The popular Pine Creek Trail cuts through the floor of the canyon where a railroad once ran. The tracks were removed in 1988 to make way for a smooth, flat 62-mile biking and hiking trail that starts in Wellsboro Junction and runs to the Jersey Shore, while paralleling the beautiful Pine Creek the entire way. Cross-country skiers may enjoy it during the winter.

The great stands of pine for which the creek was named were logged off in the 19th century. The second-growth forest standing today includes black cherry, aspen, red oak, black birch, beech, white ash, shagbark hickory, sassafras, and sycamore. In autumn this diversity creates a broad palette of colors that dominate the landscape as far as the eye can see, making it a photographer's haven.

Mountain streams and creeks are stocked with trout and other freshwater fish. The best angling begins after mid-June, when the creek begins to dry up. Rafting should be enjoyed earlier. Both supervised and unsupervised white-water raft trips down Pine

Creek are arranged by a local concessionaire.

▶ Open year-round, but winter access is limited; camping mid-Apr.–mid-Oct.

www.dcnr.state.pa.us/stateparks/parks/leonardharrison.aspx

www.dcnr.state.pa.us/stateparks/parks/coltonpoint.aspx

(570) 724-3061

7 Peter J. McGovern Little League Museum

525 Rte. 15, Williamsport

Opened in 1982, the museum chronicles the development of Little League baseball—from the first three-team league that Carl Stotz started here in Williamsport in 1939 to the present-day organization, which has more than 7,000 teams in some 80 countries. Peter J. McGovern, the man for whom the museum is named, served from 1952 until his death in 1984 as the first full-time president of Little League.

The museum was created for baseball and softball fans of all ages. Here you will find pitching and hitting cages where prospective hurlers and hitters can study their styles with the aid of 60-second videotapes of themselves in action. Visitors can also time their sprints running between home plate and first base. Hands-on activities include displays about nutrition, drugs, and alcohol.

> **did you know** ❓
>
> The Peter J. McGovern Little League Museum Hall of Excellence has recognized 38 Little League graduates who have become outstanding citizens as adults, including a firefighter who perished on 9/11.

Here, too, are exhibits showing the evolution of Little League safety equipment, such as batting helmets, shin guards, and chest protectors. One exhibit includes mementos of current major league players who began as Little Leaguers. Any young player is likely to be inspired by the sight of his idol as a youngster wearing a Little League uniform.

Highlights of many past Little League World Championship games are shown on videotape. Team pictures of the winners dating back to 1947 are also on display.

The Hall of Excellence honors former Little Leaguers who have excelled in their field, including professional athletes, Olympians, educators, and actors.

Behind the museum is Lamade Stadium, where the annual Little League World Series is played. For ballplayers young and old the sight of the baseball diamond can conjure up stirring visions of what might have been–or what might yet come to pass.

▶ Open daily Memorial Day–Labor Day; closed Tues.–Wed. Labor Day–Memorial Day. Check ahead for schedule changes. Admission charged.

www.littleleague.org/museum
(570) 326-3607

---

8 ▶ Mount Pisgah State Park

West Burlington. Watch for signs on Rte. 6.
The 75-acre Stephen Foster Lake, named for the Pennsylvanian who wrote "Camptown Races," "Oh! Susanna," and other popular songs about the Old South, is the central feature of this 1,300-acre park. Stocked with bass, perch, crappie, bluegill, and bullhead, the lake offers good fishing, particularly in spring. Boats and canoes are for rent in the summer, or visitors can launch their own. The lake is restricted to electric motors only. In winter the frozen lake is popular for both ice fishing and skating.

Ten miles of trails pass through wooded acres, open farmland, and

7 ▶ Peter J. McGovern Little League Museum. Museum-goers find themselves immersed in the world of Little League from the moment they enter the lobby (above).

marshes. Since much of this countryside was once under cultivation, the effects of farming, such as fieldstone and stump fence rows, can be seen throughout the park.

The park sometimes sponsors maple syrup demonstrations in the spring. Visitors can see how sap is collected, boiled, and reboiled. Then everyone gets a free sample.

▶ Open year-round. Check ahead for maple syrup demonstrations.

www.dcnr.state.pa.us/stateparks/parks/mtpisgah.aspx
(570) 297-2734

---

9 ▶ Wayne County Historical Society Museum

810 Main St., Honesdale
In a superb 150-year-old brick building that was once the office of the Delaware and Hudson Canal Company, the Wayne County Historical Society Museum recalls the rich economic, geographical, and cultural history of the area.

When the eastern Pennsylvania anthracite mining industry started to prosper in the early 19th century, Honesdale became a focal point of commercial transport. Mined anthracite coal was taken to the town of Carbondale and then hauled to Honesdale by the Gravity Railroad, the first commercial locomotive to run on this track. From Honesdale the coal was shipped by boat through the 108 locks on the Delaware and Hudson Canal to the markets in New York.

The museum has an exhibit showing how the canal linked the county to New York City and beyond. The old photographs of bridge construction, relay designs, factories, and burgeoning towns show how challenging engineering problems were solved back then

8 ▶ Mount Pisgah State Park. The lake attracts picnickers and boaters in summer and ice skaters in winter.

and how the canals influenced the development of new communities.

Major industries of Wayne County are also explored. One room displays rotating exhibits, such as the work of craftsmen in the glass-cutting factories that once dotted the vicinity. Here, too, is a glassblower's typical work station, with several of the tools required to blow and shape glass.

A new wing features refurbished old favorites and photo displays. Connected to the museum by a glass hallway is the recently restored 19th-century Torrey Land Office that served Honesdale. On the streets of Honesdale one can still find many splendid early 19th-century buildings. Inquire at the museum about walking tours of the town.

▶ Hours vary; call or check the website. Admission charged.

www.waynehistorypa.org
(570) 253-3240

10 ▶ S. B. Elliott State Park

Off Hwy. 80 in Clearfield County
Formerly a climax forest of huge pines and hemlocks, this area was devastated by the logging industry by the turn of the century. In 1911, when the timber was gone, the conservationist Simon B. Elliott prompted the Pennsylvania legislature to establish a tree nursery here. During the Great Depression in the 1930s, the Civilian Conservation Corps built 20 cabins and other buildings as well as recreational and camping facilities.

Today there are eight hiking trails ranging from strolls to tough hikes through heavy foliage. All eight could be walked in one day.

Many of the mountain streams surrounding the park are stocked with trout, and an abundance of wildlife such as beavers, turkeys, foxes, squirrels, deer, and black bears can be seen.

▶ Open year-round; campground open mid-Apr.–Oct.

www.dcnr.state.pa.us/stateparks
(814) 765-0630

11 ▶ Penn Roosevelt State Park

Potters Mills. Head east on Rte. 322. When Rte. 322 changes to four lanes, turn right (south) onto Crowfield Rd. and go six miles.
This park was built in 1933 by one of the 12 African-American Civilian Conservation Corps work camps in Pennsylvania that constructed recreational facilities, trails, and forest roads during the Great Depression.

Picnic spots and rustic camping grounds are centered around a small spring-fed lake set within an 80,000-acre block of Rothrock State Forest. Although only five miles from the highway, the forest setting is so peaceful that the sound of a running stream can punctuate the stillness.

Penn Roosevelt Lake is not stocked, but occasionally you'll find brook trout from a nearby stream. Hiking trails within the forest are festooned with rhododendrons and laurel in season. Deer, turkeys, grouse, raccoons, and black bears are sometimes seen. One caution: Keep an eye out for the occasional copperhead snake or timber rattler.

13 ▶ **Hawk Mountain Sanctuary.** North Lookout is the prime viewing area when thousands of birds of prey migrate here in the autumn.

▶ Open year-round, but no winter road maintenance; camping mid-Apr.–mid-Dec.

www.dcnr.state.pa.us/stateparks/parks/pennroosevelt.aspx
(814) 667-1800

12 ▶ Clyde Peeling's Reptiland

18628 Rte. 15, Allenwood
The reptile is often feared or misunderstood. Reptiland owner Clyde Peeling dispels myths and increases understanding of reptiles and their amphibian cousins in an atmosphere that is both fun and educational. His specialized zoo, accredited by the American Zoo and Aquarium Association, offers five live shows each day. There are interactive games like "Lizard Wizard" and "Turtle Trivia" and daily feedings where you can observe natural behavior. Visitors are invited to touch harmless species. Snakes, turtles, frogs, lizards, and alligators populate the displays.

Special events during the year include October's "Flashlight Safari," a Halloween alternative where guests can observe the zoo's inhabitants at their most active. Also included are informative shows about animal poisons and the staggering variety in nature.

A multimedia show introduces beautiful but potentially deadly creatures to visitors. Just in case you're planning to venture out into the jungle again, remember: The Gaboon viper has two-inch fangs. A king cobra carries enough venom to slay an elephant. And if you're tempted to touch that beautiful, shimmering dart-poison frog from South America, don't. One of its species is the most poisonous on Earth, more than any snake or spider. Even touching its skin can be dangerous.

▶ Open year-round. Admission charged.

www.reptiland.com
(800) 737-8452

13 ▶ Hawk Mountain Sanctuary

Off Hwy. 78 in Kempton
Hawk Mountain is a favorite site for birders and is one of the few sanctuaries in the world set aside for migrating birds of prey. From this 1,500-foot ridge, one can view more than 200 species of birds that frequent the area, as well as 16 species of raptors—including eagles, ospreys, hawks, and falcons—on their journeys to their winter or summer ranges.

Hawk Mountain is named for the 18,000 raptors or so that soar past its lookouts between mid-Aug. and mid-Dec. each year. An eight-mile trail system leads visitors to many observation points, including the one-mile trek to North Lookout—the prime observation point for the fall migration.

12 ▶ **Clyde Peeling's Reptiland.** An Aldabra giant tortoise weighing in at nearly 350 pounds fascinates children of all ages. Aldabras are native to the Seychelles.

South Lookout is an easily accessible 100-yard stroll from the visitors center.

Deer, chipmunks, squirrels, and raccoons are plentiful here. After the mountain laurel blooms in early summer, nesting warblers and other songbirds take up residence on the tranquil mountain and fill the air with their gentle calls.

Don't forget to stop at the visitors center, which features a bookstore, the Wings of Wonder raptor gallery, and interpretive displays.

▶ Open year-round. Trail fee.

www.hawkmountain.org
(610) 756-6961

14 ▶ Troxell-Steckel House and Barn

Egypt

During the 18th and 19th centuries the Lehigh Valley was settled primarily by farmers from Germany. In 1756 the son of one of these immigrants, John Peter Troxell, built a medieval-style German farmhouse near what is now the town of Egypt. Fifteen years later the house and surrounding property were sold to Peter Steckel—thus the name.

The fieldstone farmhouse has been restored and furnished to suggest the lifestyle of the German settlers in the area. The home reflects the simple and rigorous lives of its inhabitants; a telling feature is a box built into a wall for the reverent storage of the family Bible.

The 18-acre property includes a small stream, an idyllic meadow, and a field that is still farmed. Beside the stream is a springhouse where dairy products were stored in the old days.

 Fonthill Park. Less interested in exteriors than in creating rooms he could ornament with tiles (right), Henry Mercer designed Fonthill from the inside out. His Moravian Pottery & Tile Works factory stands across the way in the park.

In the Swiss-style bank barn, built in 1875, each stall has its own exterior door; the animals were fed from a wooden platform above the stalls. Farming equipment and a collection of horse-drawn carriages and sleighs are displayed inside the barn.

▶ Open P.M. weekends, June–Oct. and by appointment. Admission charged.

www.lchs.museum/HistoricSites.htm
(610) 435-1074

15 ▶ The Mercer Museum

84 S. Pine St., Doylestown

Henry Mercer, a pioneering archaeologist and anthropologist born in 1856, saw that the essence of American culture was to be found in its tools and equipment. He collected 20,000 artifacts from the 18th and 19th centuries.

Mercer then designed and supervised the construction of a museum to accommodate the vast accumulation. The medieval-looking edifice was finished in 1916 according to specifications he carried in his head, without benefit of blueprints.

The exhibition hall is a gigantic barnlike room. Each of the six levels has a balcony-like corridor and small exhibit rooms. Each room contains tools and objects representing some 60 crafts and trades or facets of early American life with incredible completeness.

The museum, now a National Historic Landmark, has more than 40,000 items. Many of them—stagecoaches, sleighs, a whaleboat—are suspended from the walls and ceiling by iron rods set in the concrete.

Activities and games in the Imagination Gallery help families explore the museum's collections. And "Animals on the Loose" invites the youngest visitors on a participatory adventure in the museum. (See also site #16.)

▶ Open daily. Admission charged.

www.mercermuseum.org
(215) 345-0210

16 ▶ Fonthill Park

130 E. Swamp Rd., Doylestown

This astonishing four-story house—set on more than 60 acres of grounds now called Fonthill Park—was the vision of Doylestown native Henry Mercer, a world traveler, historian, archaeologist, and all-around Renaissance man who added ceramic tile-making to his repertoire. In 1908 he designed his

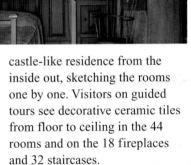

castle-like residence from the inside out, sketching the rooms one by one. Visitors on guided tours see decorative ceramic tiles from floor to ceiling in the 44 rooms and on the 18 fireplaces and 32 staircases.

Also in the park is Moravian Pottery & Tile Works, started in 1898 by Mercer. The tiles of this working history museum adorn buildings across the United States (the Pennsylvania State Capitol included) and the world. Now administered by Bucks County, the historic factory is open for tours. (See also site #15.)

▶ Open daily except major holidays. Admission charged.

www.fonthillmuseum.org
(215) 348-9461

17 Raccoon Creek State Park

3000 Rte.18, Hookstown

Although most of the land surrounding man-made Raccoon Lake is landscaped, much of the remaining 7,300-acre area is in its heavily forested natural state. In the fall the foliage of 42 different kinds of trees change color in a spectacularly vivid display of nature's diversity. Forty-one miles of trails await hikers, bicyclists, horseback riders, and cross-country skiers. The trail system includes a 20-mile loop for backpackers.

Hikers can follow the five miles of trail crisscrossing a 314-acre wildflower reserve where more than 500 species of flowering plants can be found. The peak blooming seasons are mid-Apr.–mid-May and Aug.–Oct. One of the other hiking trails includes a tour of the Frankfort Mineral Springs. During the 19th century the mineral water here was said to possess healing powers, and the springs were quite famous. The annual winter freeze forms tremendous ice sculptures that stand immobile until they melt in the spring.

The lake yields bluegills, sunfish, bullheads, brook and rainbow trout, walleye, crappies, largemouth and smallmouth bass, and yellow perch.

For visitors not solely concerned with recreational activities, the Wildflower Reserve Interpretive Center offers a wide variety of educational programs, including scheduled walks for bird-watchers, night hikes, snowshoe hikes, four self-guiding nature trails, and a Christmas bird count.

There are about 400 picnic tables throughout the park. All areas have grills, drinking water, and restrooms.

17 **Raccoon Creek State Park.** A calm Raccoon Lake awaits the arrival of fishermen, boaters, and swimmers. Visitors on land can hike or bike five miles of trail and admire hundreds of species of wildflowers and other flowering plants.

▶ Open year-round; camping mid-Apr.–mid-Oct.; modern cabins available year-round.

www.dcnr.state.pa.us/stateparks/parks/
raccooncreek.aspx

(724) 899-2200

18 Meadowcroft Rockshelter and Museum of Rural Life

40 Meadowcroft Rd., Avella

Fifteen thousand years ago western Pennsylvania was a land where humans hunted to survive. At this museum visitors can find out how archaeologists uncovered the earliest evidence of people living in North America and can check out a tool of their trade—a spear-thrower called an atlatl (at-LAT-tul).

Explore the re-created 19th-century village, with demonstrations of wool spinning and forging red-hot iron. Visitors can attend class in the schoolhouse or stroll across the covered bridge to a reconstructed 17th-century Native American village that provides a glimpse of life here before the Europeans arrived.

Other displays include the contents of a turn-of-the-century general store, horse-drawn vehicles, and farm tools. Racing fans will be interested in the Delvin Miller harness racing exhibit.

▶ Open Wed.–Sun. Memorial Day–Labor Day; weekends in May and Oct. Admission charged.

http://meadowcroft.pghhistory.org

(724) 587-3412

19 Nemacolin Castle

136 Front St., Brownsville

Named for the Native American leader Nemacolin, who established the first English trading route between Ohio and Maryland, Nemacolin Castle is an imposing brick edifice set on a hill with a commanding view of the Monongahela River. The early trading route connected with the river at present-day Brownsville. In 1806 it became part of Rte. 40, the country's first east-west national highway.

What is now the castle started as a simple trading post on the site of old Fort Burd, which guarded the trade route. As the post prospered, its owner, Jacob Bowman, gradually added onto the original stone structure, turning it into a Tudor-style castle with 22 rooms and a crenellated octagonal tower. The tower bedroom is especially memorable; a huge Victorian carved walnut bed is swallowed up by the room's sheer size. Next door the balcony gives a wonderful view of the entire town.

Most of the rooms contain original 19th-century furnishings. In the "bishop's bedroom" are a massive Victorian mahogany bed and a flawless mirror made in 1850. Marble fireplaces and delicate mahogany woodwork add to the air of 19th-century opulence.

Visitors are invited to picnic on the grounds outside the castle and contemplate the steady flow of the Monongahela River.

Open Tues.-Thurs. June-Aug.; weekends mid-Mar.-mid-Oct. Admission charged.

www.nemacolincastle.org
(724) 785-6882

20 Gravity Hill and Bedford Covered Bridges

Hill south of New Paris; bridges on roads throughout the county.
Gravity Hill in Bedford County would make Sir Isaac Newton's hair stand on end. The laws of gravity do not seem to apply here.

To find this unusual spot, take Rte. 96 one-half mile south of New Paris, cross a small metal bridge, and turn west onto Bethel Hollow Rd. Drive six-tenths of a mile and bear left at the "Y" in the road, staying on the main road. After 1 1/2 miles, bear right at the stop sign, drive two-tenths of a mile, and look for the letters "GH" spray-painted onto the road. Go about one-tenth of a mile and stop before the second "GH." Put the car in neutral and take your foot off the brake. You should now be rolling up the hill. If you need another thrill, proceed one-tenth of a mile past the second "GH." Look for the telephone pole painted "69." Stop beside the pole, and you'll defy gravity once more.

Some people speculate that what is occurring is no more than an optical illusion. Others insist that a gravity warp in the Earth causes what they're experiencing. Whatever the cause, it's definitely a natural funhouse.

Finally, if your head isn't spinning, you can drive through some of the county's 14 covered bridges, all built about 100 years ago. The romantic spans range from the 56-foot Palo Alto Bridge to the 136-foot Herline Bridge. A free booklet from the visitors bureau lists the locations of all the bridges, and another traces a 90-minute route through six bridges, a bison farm, and Gravity Hill.

Open year-round.

www.bedfordcounty.net
(800) 765-3331

20 **Gravity Hill.** There's more than meets the eye on this road, where your car will actually roll uphill.

21 National Watch and Clock Museum

514 Poplar St., Columbia
At this museum you're appropriately greeted by chiming bells as you walk through a time tunnel. The National Association of Watch and Clock Collectors manages the museum, which traces the history of time measurement—from a reproduction of the incredible non-mechanical Rhodes Antikytheron clock, circa 79 B.C., to the most sophisticated modern atomic clock.

Among the musical clocks played here are a 1770 Glune glass bell clock, an 1840 organ clock, and a one-of-a-kind animated monumental clock. The massive inner works of large tower clocks are contrasted with the delicate mechanisms of small pocket watches. On display also are clocks with Japanese characters, mantel clocks of various styles, mirror clocks, master-and-slave clocks, banjo clocks, a lantern clock, a Swiss water clock, and other novelty timepieces.

Many items are exhibited in glass cases so that the inner movements of wood, iron, and brass may be studied from all sides. Most of the clocks are originals.

Nearly all of the clocks and watches are in working condition. The museum is so filled with the various pitches and rhythms created by the precise mechanical measure of time that one is acutely aware of of each passing second. If you are in the museum at noon, you will hear the cacophony of chimes,

21 **National Watch and Clock Museum.** A watch made by Thomas Tompion in the 1690s is one of more than 12,000 timepieces on display.

rings, and gongs announcing the hour of 12. A 10-minute video presentation on the history of timekeeping in the new theater is well worth your time.

Open Tues.-Sun. Apr.-Dec. except major holidays. Open Tues.-Sat. Jan.-Mar. Admission charged.

www.nawcc.org
(717) 684-8261

19 **Nemacolin Castle.** As fur trader Jacob Bowman prospered, he built additions to his original stone trading post until it grew to a Tudor-style castle with 22 rooms.

22 The Wolf Sanctuary of Pennsylvania

465 Speedwell Forge Rd. E, Lititz
Since the 1980s this sanctuary has rescued and cared for abandoned pet wolves awaiting euthanasia. Timber wolves, buffalo wolves, and other species live out their lives on forested land in a historic pocket of Pennsylvania—the site of the Speedwell Forge, a 1750 ironworks that figured large in Lancaster County history. Here dozens of so-called Speedwell wolves are able to function as a pack, choose their mates, and raise their offspring.

On weekends guests are treated to coffee before heading out for guided visits with the wolves (weekday tours are by appointment). Visitors 16 years and older can also sign up for one of the monthly full moon tours—a popular choice for those wishing to commune with the wild by the light of the moon.

▶ Open weekends. Admission charged.

www.wolfsancpa.com
(717) 626-4617

23 Strasburg Rail Road, the Railroad Museum of Pennsylvania, and the National Toy Train Museum

Strasburg
The Strasburg Rail Road is the oldest short-line railroad in the United States. The steam-powered train runs through beautiful Pennsylvania Dutch farmland as it travels between Strasburg and Paradise, where it connects with Amtrak's main line between Philadelphia and Harrisburg.

The train features a parlor car, a lounge car, and a dining car, where you can have lunch or dinner. All cars are restored to look as they did in 1915. For railway enthusiasts especially, this is a bit of the real thing.

Across the street at the Railroad Museum of Pennsylvania, more than 100 historic locomotives and railroad cars are on display. Visitors can sit in the engineer's seat of a mammoth engine, board a real caboose, or check out the interactive education center.

Nearby, the National Toy Train Museum will appeal to anyone nostalgic for or curious about the era of the great steam locomotives and the wonderful toys they inspired.

The historical section of the Toy Train Museum has examples of all types of trains from 1880 to the present. Each era of development, including the standard-gauge classic period, is represented. Five complex operating layouts have push-button controls with which visitors can activate the trains and accessories.

▶ Strasburg Rail Road: call for schedule. Admission charged.

www.strasburgrailroad.com
(717) 687-7522

▶ Railroad Museum of Pennsylvania open daily Apr.-Oct.; closed Mon. Nov.-Mar. Admission charged.

www.rrmuseumpa.org
(717) 687-8628

▶ National Toy Train Museum open daily May-Oct.; weekends Apr., Nov., Dec. Admission charged.

www.nttmuseum.org
(717) 687-8976

24 Hopewell Big Woods

Northwestern Chester County and southwestern Berks County
The Hopewell Big Woods, a 100-square-mile expanse of woodlands and wetlands on rocky terrain, encompasses a state park beloved by boaters and hikers that surrounds an important historic site

24 **Hopewell Big Woods.** The metal-working shop at Hopewell Furnace National Historic Site is one of many buildings dating from Industrial Revolution days.

near the picturesque St. Peter's Village. French Creek State Park has two lakes for boaters, fishers, and swimmers and close to 40 miles of forested hiking trails. It is also a magnet for orienteers—cross-country runners who race with the aid of a map and compass.

Hopewell Furnace National Historic Site commemorates the birthplace of the American Industrial Revolution at an "iron plantation" that grew on the banks of French Creek from 1771. Exhibits at the restored complex and worker's village trace the process that turned out ton upon ton of iron, casting everything from cannons for the Continental Army to kettles for housewives.

www.hopewellbigwoods.org
(610) 582-8773

25 Brandywine River Museum

US-1, Chadds Ford
A 19th-century gristmill overlooking the Brandywine River has been handsomely renovated with a circular wing to make a spacious and airy three-story museum with informal galleries for the display of paintings and sculptures.

Major works of art from three generations of the Wyeth family are featured, including paintings by N. C. Wyeth, his son Andrew, and his grandson Jamie. The renowned commercial illustrations of N. C. Wyeth and Howard Pyle, the father of modern American illustration, and works by Pyle's students are also shown.

Much of the museum is devoted to the art of the Brandywine region and to the still life and landscape painters and sculptors associated with the "Brandywine Tradition."

The collected works represent more than 100 years of activity, and the tradition continues.

Part of each floor serves as a lobby where visitors can rest and enjoy the enchanting views of the Brandywine countryside through floor-to-ceiling windows, which flood the area with sunshine. The effect helps provide an understanding of the source of inspiration for this celebrated school of painting, with its emphasis on natural light.

The Brandywine River Museum is named for the adjacent river. Visitors are encouraged to picnic on its banks, enjoy the wildflower gardens and nature trail, and discover for themselves the beguiling character of a place that has influenced so many artists.

▶ Open daily except Christmas. Admission charged.

www.brandywinemuseum.org
(610) 388-2700

26 Laurel Hill Cemetery

3822 Ridge Ave., Philadelphia
Set on 78 acres and affording a sweeping view of Schuylkill River, Laurel Hill Cemetery was designed in the 1830s as an estate garden— a merging of art with nature. Its founders pictured the tranquil tract not only as a burial ground but also as a place for the living. True to their vision, the cemetery attracted strollers, picnickers, and sightseers in horse-drawn carriages.

A century and a half later tourists, nature lovers, watercolorists, cyclists, joggers, and dog-walkers frequent the beautifully landscaped cemetery, which was named a National Historic Landmark in 1998. In the background marble and granite obelisks are transposed with elaborate

26 **Laurel Hill Cemetery.** The monuments here make an impressive, if unlikely, backdrop for picnickers, joggers, and others who frequent the riverside cemetery for recreation.

gravestones and mausoleums in revivalist styles ranging from Egyptian to Gothic to Classic.
▶ Open daily.

www.theundergroundmuseum.org
(215) 228-8200

27 The Mütter Museum of the College of Physicians

19 S. 22nd St., Philadelphia
If you are interested in the history of medicine and medical anomalies, this is the place to go. In 1859 Thomas Dent Mütter, a professor of surgery, donated his teaching collection of more than 1,000 objects to display pathological anatomy. The museum now has more than 25,000 objects, including human specimens, models, and medical instruments.

Inside the National Historic Landmark building is an elegant 19th-century-style gallery with its original wood exhibit cases. Among the exhibits is the Hyrtal Skull Collection, which presents 139 skulls from Central and Eastern Europe. The connected livers of conjoined twins Chang and Eng (the original Siamese twins,

1811–1874) are shown, along with a plaster cast of their torsos. You can also explore the Dr. Chevalier Jackson collection of 2,000 objects swallowed or inhaled and then safely removed. They range from safety pins to dental material.

Other interesting and uncommon displays are slices of the head; the tallest skeleton in North America; and a portion of tissue from the thorax of Lincoln assassin John Wilkes Booth. Make sure to see the tumor of President Grover Cleveland—taken from his jaw in a secret operation in 1893.
▶ Open year-round. Admission charged.

www.muttermuseum.org
(215) 563-3737

did you know ?

Quaker John Jay Smith founded Laurel Hill Cemetery after he deemed it impossible to find a resting place for his daughter. At the time Philadelphia was suffering from crowding, disease, and scarcity of public space.

seasonal events

FEBRUARY
• Groundhog Day Festival— Punxsutawney *(family entertainment, live music, groundhog appearance)*

MARCH
• Philadelphia Flower Show— Philadelphia *(vendors, workshops, lectures, food)*

MAY
• Blair County Arts Festival—Altoona *(juried art exhibits, entertainment, arts and crafts, canoe races, food)*

JULY
• Tour de Toona—Altoona *(annual bicycle race)*
• Wings over Pittsburgh—Pittsburgh *(demonstrations, fly-bys, performances, activities)*

AUGUST
• Pocono Garlic Festival—Shawnee on Delaware *(entertainment, food, garlic education and braiding, vendors)*

SEPTEMBER
• Mushroom Festival—Kennett Square *(5K run/walk, crafts, contests, food, souvenirs)*
• Thunder in the Valley Motorcycle Rally—Johnstown *(food vendors, demo rides, manufacturer displays, live music, children's activities)*

OCTOBER
• Hartslog Day—Alexandria *(homemade crafts and gifts, vendors, barbecue, children's activities)*
• Autumnfest—Champion *(crafts, food, family entertainment, outdoor concerts)*

NOVEMBER
• Poe Evermore—Manheim *(tribute to Edgar Allan Poe, including bizarre characters from his stories of mystery and mayhem)*

DECEMBER
• Holiday Lights on the Lake— Altoona *(lights, ice sculptures, animated displays, contests, hot chocolate)*

www.visitpa.com

Rhode Island

The seashore and bustling Narragansett Bay define Rhode Island, but our smallest state offers plenty of inland discoveries as well.

Green Animals Topiary Garden. Children and adults alike take delight in this garden's "living" animals (see page 296).

One of our most densely populated states, Rhode Island also recognizes the importance of nature and wildlife, as evidenced by bird sanctuaries and an Audubon environmental education center. Playful topiary animals hold court on the grounds of an estate, and the changing seasons are celebrated with a succession of harvest festivals. Speaking of harvests, the colorful history of food is charted at a museum devoted to the culinary arts.

visit ➡️ offthebeatenpathtrips.com

1 George Washington Management Area

2185 Putnam Pike, Chepachet
Land for the camping area in this 4,000-acre park was donated to the state in 1933 to honor the bicentennial of our first president's birth. There are 45 camp sites near the tip of Bowdish Lake, where a sandy beach invites swimmers and fishermen. A launching ramp may be used by boats with motors under 10 horsepower. The picnic ground on Peck Pond, at the other side of the management area, also has a sandy beach and a supervised swimming area.

Access to the more remote regions is provided by the Walkabout Trail, an easy eight-mile loop with several cutoffs allowing shorter hikes. The trail was built in 1965 with the help of Australian sailors.

Winter is one of the best seasons here. Many snow-covered gravel roads, accessible from the campground, are open for snowmobiling; in the area around Peck Pond, four trails ranging from three-quarters of a mile to more than four miles in length are groomed for cross-country skiing.

▶ Open year-round. Camping mid-Apr.–mid-Oct. Fee charged.

www.riparks.com/georgewashcamp.htm
(401) 568-2013

2 **The Museum of Work and Culture.** This museum pays tribute to the French-Canadian immigrants who flocked to the textile mills of Woonsocket in the late 1800s.

2 The Museum of Work and Culture

42 S. Main St., Woonsocket
In the heart of Woonsocket's historic Market Square, an interactive museum celebrates New England's French-Canadian immigrants. Maintained by the Rhode Island Historical Society, it tells the story of those who left their farms for a new world of factories—a story of hardship and resilience.

Housed in a converted textile mill, the museum traces the dramatic rise of the Independent Textile Union and opens a window into the everyday life of a close-knit community determined to preserve its language, customs, and faith.

Filled with hundreds of photographs, and many interactive audio presentations, the museum has nine walk-through exhibits dating from 1870 through 1934. Visitors can tour a rural Quebec farmhouse and follow the course of a typical day in Woonsocket. From the textile mill shop floor to the front porch of a tenement, from a parochial school to the union hall, visitors will experience the struggles and dreams of working-class immigrants.

▶ Open Tues.–Sun. year-round. Admission charged.

www.rihs.org
(401) 769-9675

3 Culinary Arts Museum

315 Harborside Blvd., Providence

The Culinary Arts Museum of Johnson & Wales University is *the* place for a journey into cooking history from olden days to modern times. The collection of more than 500,000 items includes utensils dating back to ancient Egypt, Greece, and China; kitchen gadgets and equipment; an extensive collection of cookstoves; and thousands of cookbooks—the oldest dating to the early 1500s.

Visitors can step into a colonial tavern and a classic 1926 art-deco diner. Equally interesting is the presidential exhibit of items and writings that serve to reveal the formal and informal relationships of America's leaders with food and dining. Don't miss the museum's tribute to the world's greatest chefs.

▶ Open Tues.–Sun. Closed major holidays and during school breaks. Admission charged.

www.culinary.org
(401) 598-2805

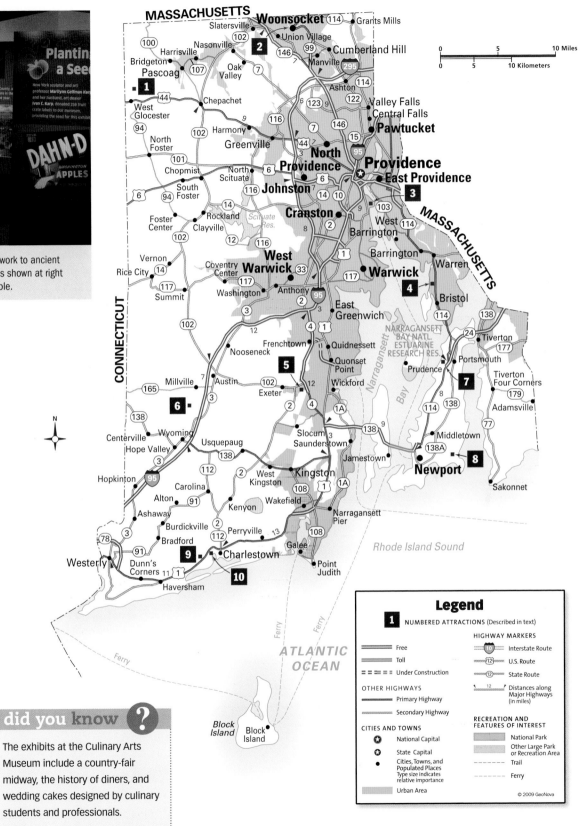

did you know ?

The exhibits at the Culinary Arts Museum include a country-fair midway, the history of diners, and wedding cakes designed by culinary students and professionals.

The Audubon Society of Rhode Island's Environmental Education Center

1401 Hope St. (Rte. 114), Bristol
Surrounded by a 28-acre wildlife refuge on the scenic Narragansett Bay, the society's 10,300-square-foot state-of-the-art Environmental Education Center is home to the state's largest aquarium. For hands-on experiences it features tide-pool touch tanks teeming with marine life. The center's showpiece is an authentically detailed life-size 33-foot model of a typical 3,200-pound North Atlantic right whale. Look inside its body for up-close views of a whale's heart, tongue, ribs, spine, baleen, and blubber. Other exhibits reflect the diversity of Rhode Island's native habitat. A boardwalk leads visitors through freshwater wetlands and a salt marsh to the shore of Narragansett Bay, where you can see frogs, turtles, shorebirds, ducks, and maybe even a seal or two in the winter.

The Audubon Society of Rhode Island protects nearly 9,500 acres of wildlife habitat containing an extensive trail system for nature enthusiasts of all ages to enjoy. Visit their website for a map of Audubon refuges throughout the state and a complete calendar of events.

▶ Open daily year-round. Admission charged.

www.asri.org
(401) 245-7500

Lafayette State Trout Hatchery

424 Hatchery Rd., North Kingstown
Also known as Goose Nest Spring Hatchery, this complex, founded in 1922, is one of the oldest hatcheries in the country. It consists of about 20 raceways, each about 100 feet long, and buildings in which tanks containing fingerling trout may be seen. The hatchery's capacity of about a million trout helps to stock Rhode Island's streams for the enjoyment of an estimated 40,000 fishermen. The place, charming in appearance, is fascinating to see. Since the fish are accustomed to being fed by humans, they rise to the surface as one approaches the edge of the cement raceways.

▶ Open year-round. Free admission.

(401) 294-4662

Tomaquag Indian Memorial Museum

390 Summit Rd., Exeter
Situated amid the Arcadia Management Area, this large white house contains several cabinets containing Native American artifacts from various North American tribes, with a focus on those of the Northeast. In addition to stone tools and leather strapwork by Plains tribes, weavings by Navajos, and baskets by northwestern tribes, the collection features ash splint basketwork of the Mohegans, Scaticooks, and local Narragansetts.

The museum serves as a focal point for four annual festivals of thanksgiving associated with the harvesting of important crops: maple sugar in March, strawberries in June, string beans in July, and cranberries in October. In addition, the Nickomo Festival is celebrated in early December with an exchange of gifts.

These gatherings offer seasonal foods and Native American dances, led by local Narragansetts, in which visitors are encouraged to participate.

▶ Open seasonally and by appointment. Donation requested.

www.tomaquagmuseum.com
(401) 539-7213; (401) 491-9063

Green Animals Topiary Garden

380 Cory's Ln., Portsmouth
Thomas E. Brayton, a Massachusetts manufacturer, purchased this seven-acre estate in 1877 and summered here until his death in 1939.

Exquisite evidence of Brayton's interest in topiary may be seen today as one wanders through the gardens. But it was his daughter, the late Alice Brayton, an amateur horticulturist, who helped bring these 80 forms to their present perfection, putting them in a class with the nation's best examples of topiary.

Among the animal shapes are a lion, a peacock, a camel, a giraffe, a horse and rider, and an elephant. A fat bear is especially appealing. Elsewhere, perennial, biennial, and annual flower beds, as well as plantings of ferns, shrubs, and fruit trees, create a subtle blend of scent and sight.

From the clapboard main house there is a lovely view of Narragansett Bay. Inside, a small toy collection is displayed, including an impressive exhibit of toy soldiers.

▶ Open daily mid-May–mid-Oct. Admission charged.

www.newportmansions.org
(401) 847-1000; (401) 683-1267

Norman Bird Sanctuary

583 Third Beach Rd., Middletown
George Norman was a late 19th-century Newport, Rhode Island merchant who made a fortune in waterworks and utilities. His daughter, Mabel, donated the land for this nature center in 1949. More than seven miles of walking trails weave through the 325-acre site, where birders and nature lovers can look for many common and some unusual species.

Each trail has its own appeal. The three ridge trails provide hik-

 Audubon Society Environmental Education Center. An exhibit hall guide readies schoolchildren for their exploration of the center's tidepool touch tanks.

7 ▶ **Green Animals Topiary Garden.** An elephant and a giraffe are among the dozens of animals in this botanical menagerie, the oldest topiary garden in the United States.

ers with breathtaking views of Rhode Island Sound. Other trails wind through meadows, woods, and shady glades. In addition to the hiking trails, the sanctuary offers public programs, educational weekend programs, vacation camps, and other activities.

The sanctuary's 19th-century barn highlights Rhode Island's natural history with a variety of wildlife and ecosystem exhibits. Visitors to the sanctuary can experience different habitats—forest, field, ridge, and beach—all with an historical perspective that goes back to the area's Native Americans and leads up to modern times.

▶ Open year-round. Admission charged.

www.normanbirdsanctuary.org
(401) 846-2577

---

9 ▶ Audubon Kimball Wildlife Refuge

180 Sanctuary Rd., Charlestown
The land for this 29-acre woodland sanctuary was bequeathed by William Hammond Kimball, a summer resident of the area, to the Audubon Society of Rhode Island

in 1924. Two years later Everett and Mary Southwick became caretakers. Today's well-tended trails and the garden memorializing past benefactors reflect this naturalist couple's lifelong devotion to the development of the refuge.

Situated on a glacial moraine deposited some 12,000 years ago, the sanctuary invites contemplation of a glacier's irresistible force. One trail leads past several bowl-shaped kettle holes carved as the giant ice sheets receded. Indeed, Toupoyesett Pond here is really a large kettle hole deep enough to reveal the water table. In May and June starflowers, Canada mayflowers, and pink lady's slippers are in bloom along the quiet trails, and the memorial garden is occasionally visited by ruby-throated hummingbirds. Adjacent to Burlingame State Park, the refuge hosts migrating warblers and a variety of resident songbirds. The refuge offers a number of nature programs throughout the year.

▶ Open year-round.

www.asri.org
(401) 949-5454

10 ▶ The Fantastic Umbrella Factory

4820 Old Post Rd., Charlestown
The Fantastic Umbrella Factory is not really an umbrella factory at all. It's an offbeat assemblage of stores that sell everything from blown glass to natural foods to Halloween costumes. There are umbrellas for sale, too, but they're not the main focus here.

What is the main attraction at this place, founded in 1968, is a farmstead that dates from at least the 19th century. Out in back a menagerie includes guinea hens, sheep, emus, and chickens. There's a main store and international bazaar, with trinkets galore.

The Umbrella Factory Gardens are known for their moss baskets. While they custom-plant your basket, you can drink a smoothie, check out the art gallery, or find some antiques or incense at one of the many stores there.

▶ Open year-round.

(401) 364-6616

9 ▶ **Audubon Kimball Wildlife Refuge.** Watchaug Pond is one of the stops on the nature trails of the sanctuary, which is set on a glacial moraine.

seasonal events

FEBRUARY
• Rhode Island Spring Flower and Garden Show—Providence *(horticulture show, vendors, demonstrations, lectures)*

MAY
• Waterfire—Providence *(citywide art event, sculpture, music, selected Saturdays May through October)*

JUNE
• Festival of Historic Houses—Providence *(house and garden tours)*
• Great Chowder Cook-Off—Newport *(seafood festival, live music, games and entertainment)*

JULY
• Providence Sound Session—Providence *(live music, theater, parade)*
• Wickford Art Festival—Wickford *(original art, live entertainment, regional food)*
• Blessing of the Fleet—Narragansett *(boat parade, seafood festival, road race)*

AUGUST
• Newport Folk Festival—Newport *(live folk and country music, craft market)*
• JVC Jazz Festival—Newport *(world-renowned jazz performers, craft market)*
• Charlestown Seafood Festival—Charlestown *(seafood, amusement rides, games, car show)*

SEPTEMBER
• Pawtucket Arts Festival—Pawtucket *(live music, theater, dance, original art, antiques show)*
• Fall Carnivorous Plant Show—Providence *(over 300 kinds of carnivorous plants on display)*

OCTOBER
• Scituate Art Festival—Scituate *(arts and crafts, antiques, regional food, live music)*
• Autumnfest—Woonsocket *(parade, carnival rides, regional food, arts and crafts, live entertainment, games)*

www.visitrhodeisland.com

South Carolina

Storied towns, houses grand and humble, and a gracious sense of the past are among the enticements awaiting visitors to the Palmetto State.

Town of Abbeville. The Burt-Stark Mansion was the site of the final Confederate Council of War meeting. It was here, in May 1865, that the Confederacy realized their cause was lost (see page 299).

The thread of cotton weaves through two centuries of South Carolina life, and the state's antebellum mansions built with profits from the cotton trade attest to its importance. Early enterprise also lives on at a gristmill and a hand-dug canal.

Reminders of the Revolutionary and Civil wars are found in a land settled by French Huguenots and the English in the second half of the 17th century, while the natural world is on dramatic display in vast preserves set aside for local wildlife—and, in yet another context, an extraordinary collection of mounted African animals.

visit ➡ **offthebeatenpathtrips.com**

1 Hagood Mill

138 Hagood Mill Rd., Pickens
Benjamin Hagood was an entrepreneur who sought to capitalize on the traffic generated by the gristmill he built in 1825. On the same site, he also operated a tannery and a general store. Rebuilt in 1845, the mill stands as solid evidence of the fine workmanship that went into the two-story clapboard structure, with its heavy beams securely held in place by wooden pegs.

The mill was active for more than 100 years. Old-timers in the area recall that as late as the 1960s, crowds of farmers still gathered here to have their corn ground.

A descendant of Ben Hagood's donated the mill to Pickens County in 1972, and it was subsequently completely restored. The mill is situated beside a narrow creek spanned by a wooden footbridge in a quiet setting of oaks and mountain laurel. The huge wheel is still turned by water from a mountain stream that is carried to the mill via a wooden sluice. On special occasions the sluice is opened, the wheel begins to turn, and with a great, rumbling racket of wooden cogs and gears, the mill again confirms the ingenuity of its builders.
▶ Open year-round Wed.–Sat.

www.co.pickens.sc.us/culturalcommission
(864) 898-5963; (864) 898-2936

1 Hagood Mill. Once a hub of Pickens County, this 19th-century gristmill returned to action after a lull from the early 1960s to 1992, when it was fully restored.

2 Museum of York County

4621 Mount Gallant Rd., Rock Hill
This fine museum of natural history, technology, and the arts imaginatively presents aspects of the larger world as well as the universe. On display in the Stans African Halls is the Southeast's largest collection of more than 200 full-mounted African animals; the North American Hall features large animals; and the Hometown Habitats exhibit displays of plants and animals special to the Carolina Piedmont. There are also several galleries of changing exhibitions in history, science, natural history, and art.

On weekends explore the cosmos in the state-of-the-art Settlemyre Planetarium. Afterward take a stroll on the 0.7-mile nature trail and explore the native trees, shrubs, and wildflowers.
▶ Open daily year-round. Admission charged.

www.chmuseums.org
(803) 329-2121

---

did you know ?

The Museum of York County is home to the Vernon Grant Gallery, which is devoted to the creator of the Rice Krispies' characters Snap! Crackle! and Pop!

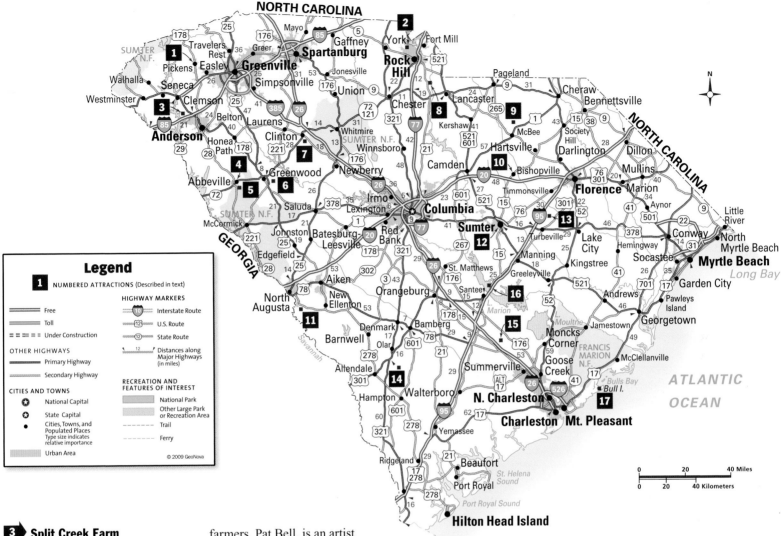

SOUTH CAROLINA

3 ▶ Split Creek Farm

3806 Centerville Rd., Anderson
Located in the scenic foothills of
South Carolina's Blue Ridge
Mountains, this dairy goat farm
specializes in Grade A organic
goat cheeses, unique goat-milk
fudge, and goat-milk soap. The
farmers here take pride in their
products—and also great care of
each of the 350 Nubian goats in
their herd. Every hardworking
animal receives plenty of personal
attention daily, and the extra care
pays off. The cheese made from
their milk wins national goat-cheese
competitions, and the farm's
healthy goats have topped records
in quantities of milk produced.
Coincidentally, one of the resident

farmers, Pat Bell, is an artist
whose work has won regional
fame. She combines traditional
craft techniques in unique ways
and transforms timeworn items
into collectibles. Her work is also
on display at the farm. Visitors can
sample the farm's wares and purchase both the goat-milk products
and the folk-art objects.

▶ Farm shop open daily year-round.
Reservations required for tours. Admission
charged.

www.splitcreek.com
(864) 287- 3921

4 ▶ Town of Abbeville

86 miles west of Columbia on SC-72
Before the American Civil War this

town was the epitome of the gracious and leisurely lifestyle of the
Old South. It was the birthplace of
the Confederacy when South
Carolina's leaders drafted and read
their defiant papers on the site now
known as Secession Hill, thus
launching South Carolina as the
first state to break away from the
Union.

Abbeville later became the
deathbed of the Confederacy, when
President Jefferson Davis held his
last War Cabinet meeting in the
front parlor of the home of his
friend Armistead Burt. At this
meeting he officially acknowledged
the dissolution of the Confederate

government, sadly admitting,
"All is indeed lost."

The historic district boasts
300 buildings and has retained its
19th-century charm. The historic
Burt-Stark Mansion on 400 N.
Main St., which was renowned for
its Old South hospitality, has
antique furniture, fine china, crystal, silverware, and rugs on
display. The home of John C.
Calhoun, vice president under
President Andrew Jackson and
notable states rights activist, is
also located here.

www.visitabbevillesc.com
(864) 366-4600

5 ▶ Parsons Mountain Lake Recreation Area

Edgefield. From Abbeville go south on Rte. 28 for 2.1 miles. Turn left onto Rte. SI-251 and drive 1.5 miles to entrance on right.

A quiet lake is the centerpiece of this fine wooded tract devoted to tent and trailer camping, picnicking, hiking, riding, and fishing. A large picnic grove flanks a supervised swimming area on the lakeshore, and a boat ramp invites fishermen to try for crappie, catfish, bass, and other species common to the region.

From the top of a nearby 80-foot tower, one has a panoramic view of the mixed pine and hardwood forests of the Carolina piedmont. In the woods are deer and small mammals and a variety of birds to observe. Indian paintbrush and lady's slipper are among the wildflowers that brighten the woodland trails.

▶ Open Apr.–mid-Dec. Admission charged.

www.fs.fed.us/r8/fms/forest/recreation/pm.shtml

(803) 637-5396

6 ▶ Emerald Farm

409 Emerald Farm Rd., Greenwood

Spanning nearly 75 pristine acres, this unique dairy farm is a treat for novelty as well as nature enthusiasts. Fans of lush green pasture will find it here in abundance, along with hay barns, smokehouses, fruit trees, herb gardens, and an array of animals—sheep, cows, horses, chickens, and productive honeybees, along with Saanen dairy goats.

But they won't find a nibble of cheese. This working farm puts its goat milk to work to create exquisite soaps. All natural, each

8 ▶ **Landsford Canal State Park.** In this historic park the swift-running Catawba River is graced by one of the largest-known stands of rocky shoals spider lilies.

bar of soap is made completely by hand in the on-site soap factory. The farm also serves up homemade food, emphasizing healthy, satisfying fare for people with special nutritional needs and challenges, from lactose intolerance to diabetes.

Beyond its eclectic homemade products, Emerald Farm boasts its very own train station and airplane hangar—in miniature forms. The main depot features a large and meticulously detailed railroad layout, complete with miles of tracks and fast-moving whistling trains, while the hangar features an extensive selection of model plane kits and remote-control airplanes.

Visitors can arrange for guided tours of the dairy farm and soap factory. For those eager to rest awhile after exploring and shopping, the grounds offer grassy spots for picnicking, a pavilion overlooking a pond, and plenty of meandering paths.

▶ Open Mon.–Sat. year-round.

www.emeraldfarm.com

(864) 223-2247; (888) 747-9246

7 ▶ Musgrove Mill State Historic Site

398 State Park Rd., Clinton

Frontier militiamen leaning toward the American colonists' cause played a pivotal role in the Revolutionary War battle they fought at Musgrove Mill in the Piedmont woods near Clinton in 1780. This preserved historic site offers interpretive reconstructions of their bloody struggle.

Outnumbered and armed only with farmer's rifles against a cohort of Tory Loyalists to the British Crown and hordes of British Army Regulars, with grit and determination they routed the enemy and turned the tide for the Americans in the struggle for independence.

The site contains nearly 2½ miles of trails that interpret the battle as

well as the British camp that was located on the Musgrove property. These trails also offer views of the Enoree River, Cedar Shoals Creek, and Horseshoe Falls, where legend has it that the owner's daughter Mary Musgrove once hid an American soldier from the British.

▶ Open daily year-round.

www.southcarolinaparks.com

(864) 938-0100

8 ▶ Landsford Canal State Park

2051 Park Dr., Catawba

Had the 19th-century canal promoters known how quickly the railroads would develop, many of them would probably never have started the laborious process of digging. The Landsford Canal is a case in point. Starting in 1820 with picks and shovels, the Irish laborers took three years to create a two-mile stretch of navigable water. The canal was used primarily to bring cotton from the backcountry to the market at Charleston. After a few years the railroad put the canal out of business.

Landsford is the best-preserved complete canal in the state, and its remarkably well-preserved 200-foot section of locks built of cut stone blocks is an example of the fine masonry work required for the early-day canals. Note in particular the precise stonework on the arched bridge at the end of the locks.

A peaceful pine-shaded area with tables and grills beside the Catawba River provides a pleasant place to picnic, and the 1½-mile towpath suggests an after-lunch stroll.

▶ Open daily year-round. Admission charged.

www.southcarolinaparks.com

(803) 789-5800

9 Carolina Sandhills National Wildlife Refuge

Off Rte. 1, between McBee and Patrick

With American wildlife habitats dwindling due to human activities, the 450 national wildlife preserves in the country have become key to sustaining the natural scene. The Carolina Sandhills Refuge is of particular interest because of its long history.

Eighty-five million years ago winds from the nearby Atlantic Ocean created sandhills from eroded sand washed down from the Appalachian Mountains. Later, European settlers, in their struggle to survive, cut the timber and over-worked the land. Poor farming practices depleted the soil. In 1939 the federal government bought 46,000 acres of these eroded lands and established a wildlife refuge.

Now restored to its natural state, with a forest of longleaf and a diverse understory of grasses and shrubs, the land once again supports its original inhabitants. Beavers, deer, bobcats, rare woodpeckers, owls, and wild turkeys are among the 42 species of mammals and 190 species of birds observed here.

A nine-mile drive, hiking trails, observation towers and platforms, wildflower displays, and a photo blind provide access to the wildlife. Picnic tables are found at the Lake Bee Recreation Area.

▶ Open year-round.

www.fws.gov/carolinasandhills/
(843) 335-8401

10 South Carolina Cotton Trail

Stretching from Bishopville, off I-20, to Bennettsville, off I-95

Much more than the premier crop, cotton shaped the fabric of Southern culture and life for hundreds of years. Spanning eight towns rich in history and character, this sweeping trail traces its thread of influence.

The trail begins at Bishopville, home to the South Carolina Cotton Museum. Capturing the toil and spirit of tenant farmers, it features a life-size replica of a farmhouse, with original furnishings from "shotgun houses." Nearby is a working cotton gin.

Hartsville features beautifully restored houses, including one seized by the Yankees during the Civil War. Transformed into enemy

10 ▶ South Carolina Cotton Trail. At the South Carolina Cotton Museum the backdrop for a bale scale is a depiction of the shipping docks of 19th-century Charleston.

11 ▶ Redcliffe Plantation. An on-site ranger shows touring schoolchildren how to work a cup-and-ball, a toy for youngsters who grew up in the plantation house.

headquarters for two days, the Jacob Kelly House now hosts living-history demonstrations.

Society Hill claims the state's only working commercial rice plantation: the Carolina Plantation. It is also home to lending libraries built in 1822.

One of South Carolina's oldest and loveliest towns, Cheraw, is named for the Cheraw tribe. Its attractions include Old St. David's Anglican Church, built in 1770—and the last "state" church decreed by King George III.

Bennettsville was once famous for its rich, fertile soil. Along with a local history museum and stunning antebellum homes, it boasts a unique church, the Evans Metropolitan AME Zion Church, founded in 1867 by African Americans recently freed from slavery.

The towns of Chesterfield, Clio, and Darlington are also on the trail.

▶ Call for hours; some admission fees.

www.sccottontrail.org
(888) 427-8720

11 Redcliffe Plantation State Historic Site

181 Redcliffe Rd., Beech Island

Before the Civil War started, South

Carolina's outspoken senator James Henry Hammond famously declared, "Cotton is King!" in a fiery speech in the halls of the U.S. Senate. A successful cotton planta-tion owner, Hammond completed his family's Greek Revival man-sion in 1859. Interpreter-led programs on this picturesque 369-acre estate help visitors experience gracious and elegant Southern living on a 19th-century antebellum plantation. Magnolias, now almost a century-and-a-half old, still line a long entranceway that cuts across the expansive front lawn. The view from the top floor of the house is of the Savannah River below and the city of Augusta in the distance. Visitors can relax in the breezes that sweep across the wide veranda and tour the garden, aromatic with heirloom plants. Tours also focus on the site's African-American history, including a visit to the preserved slave quarters, also on the grounds.

▶ Park and museum open year-round Thurs.-Mon. Admission charged for mansion tours.

www.southcarolinaparks.com
(803) 827-1473

12 Sumter County Museum

122 N. Washington St., Sumter
The Sumter County Museum is represented by structures dating from an 1812 one-room cabin to the new Heritage Education Center. Relocated from the Pinewood area, the Weeks Cabin was lived in for more than 150 years by several families, including slaves, freedmen, and tenant farmers.

Other structures include exhibits on farming life, the railroads, and transportation. The turn-of-the-century barn holds a carriage and a classic surrey, complete with fringe on top. A pole barn contains an array of farm equipment used when mules were the primary mode of power in the South.

The handsomely furnished Williams-Brice House (c.1916) includes period rooms; an exhibit on Gen. Thomas Sumter, the "Always Coca-Cola" exhibit, with several examples of Coke memorabilia; and rotating exhibits on topics ranging from World War II to quilts. The gardens surrounding the house are beautiful year-round.

Along with the Carolina Backcountry Exhibit that portrays life as it was on a farm from 1750 to 1850, it's worth seeing the brand-new 10,500-square-foot Heritage Education Center that features the Witherspoons of Coldstream Plantation Collection.

▶ Open Tues.–Sat. year-round. Closed holidays.

www.sumtercountymuseum.org
(803) 775-0908

13 Woods Bay State Natural Area

11020 Woods Bay Rd., Olanta
Carolina Bays—some of the wide, swampy, and marshy depressions scattered along the mid-Atlantic coastal plain—are ecological natural wonders. In the 1,500-acre Woods Bay State Natural Area, visitors can marvel at the splendor and diversity of its marshlands, sandhills, an oak-hickory forest, and a shrub bog. The area is home to more than 75 species of mammals, reptiles, and amphibians. Over 150 bird species come and go with the changing seasons.

A 500-foot boardwalk leads visitors easily into a cypress-tupelo swamp. The more adventuresome can paddle their way along a one-mile canoe trail amid towering trees to get an up-close glimpse of the diversity of fauna and flora, where silent alligators cruise the murky waters and noisy carpenter frogs call out to their mates. Unusual carnivorous plants can also be spotted along the route.

▶ Open daily year-round.

www.southcarolinaparks.com/
park-finder/state-park/216.aspx
(843) 659-4445

14 Rivers Bridge State Historic Site

325 State Park Rd., Ehrhardt
This is the only Civil War battle site in South Carolina that has been preserved. It was here in February 1865 that a force of Confederate artillery, cavalry, and infantry under Gen. Lafayette McLaws fought in vain to stop Gen. William T. Sherman on his devastating march from Savannah north to Virginia. Outnumbered and outflanked, the Confederates were only able to delay Sherman for two days before he went on to burn Columbia.

Years later the bodies of the Confederate soldiers who died here were brought back for reburial

14 **Rivers Bridge State Historic Site.** At the Memorial Grounds are the graves of rebel soldiers who fought in vain to keep Gen. Sherman from burning the state's capital city.

did you know ❓

Rivers Bridge was the site of the only significant resistance that Sherman's army faced between Savannah and Columbia.

and a monument was erected. Donations and purchases of land adjoining this hallowed ground brought the total acreage to 390, and in 1945 it was acquired by the state for a park.

A trail follows the progression of the battle and leads visitors past the preserved Confederate earthworks. Beneath trees draped with Spanish moss, the trail becomes aglow in April with the colorful blossoms of wisteria, dogwoods, and azaleas. Hikers may see pileated woodpeckers, which are among the more unusual birds in this area.

▶ Park open Thurs.–Mon. year-round.

www.southcarolinaparks.com
(803) 267-3675

15 The Francis Beidler Forest in Four Holes Swamp

336 Sanctuary Rd. (Beidler Forest Entrance Rd.), Harleyville
Ancient groves of bald cypresses taller than a 10-story building and up to 1,000 years old; virgin stands

12 **Sumter County Museum.** Four times a year costumed guides at the Carolina Backcountry Homestead demonstrate farming skills of the early 1800s.

of loblolly pine and tupelo gum trees; alligators, cottonmouths, and fish-eating spiders hiding in a maze of swamp waters—all these contribute to the somber and mysterious majesty of this primeval sanctuary.

The forest preserve within the swamp was named for Francis Beidler, a remarkable lumberman and conservationist. In 1960 the National Audubon Society acquired 3,415 acres from the Beidler family for a sanctuary. Today it encompasses more than 16,000 acres.

The swamp is a flooded forest and, by its nature, difficult to penetrate. Some sense of the inner character of this ecosystem is provided by the 1³/4-mile-long boardwalk with its informative signs along the way. In season experienced canoeists can take a half-day trip with a naturalist guide to reach the interior of the swamp.

Exhibits in the visitors center help people understand and appreciate the wildlife that abounds here.

▶ Open Tues.-Sun. year-round.
   Admission charged.

www.beidlerforest.com
(843) 462-2150

---

16 Santee National Wildlife Refuge

2125 Fort Watson Rd., Summerton
Four separate units, all flanked by Lake Marion, make up this 15,095-acre tract, where a vast array of bird, mammal, fish, reptile, and amphibian species thrive in a protected environment. The visitors center, on a cove called Scott's Lake, has a diorama, an aquarium, and other displays that help to acquaint nature lovers with some of the wildlife indigenous to the reserve, including American bald eagles, ospreys, river otters, striped bass, and alligators.

Across Scott's Lake is the site of Fort Watson, which was recaptured from the British in 1781 by Gen. Francis "The Swamp Fox" Marion. It stands on the site of a Santee Native American ceremonial and burial ground.

17 ▶ **Cape Romain National Wildlife Refuge.**
Loggerhead sea turtles, an endangered species, benefit from this refuge's intensive nest-protection and relocation program.

This general area is ideal for hiking, bicycling, and fishing— Lake Marion is known for its trophy catfish, striped bass, crappie, and bream. Each unit in the refuge has its own boat ramp. Birders can obtain a free printed checklist of the 293 species observed here. Among the permanent residents are pied-billed grebes, little blue herons, painted buntings, blue-winged teals, and Cooper's hawks. The many winged visitors include American woodcocks, barred owls, and rock doves.

▶ Open year-round; visitors center open
   Tues.-Fri. and first three Sat. each month.

www.fws.gov/santee
(803) 478-2217

17 Cape Romain National Wildlife Refuge

5821 Hwy. 17N, Awendaw
Except for changes brought about by erosion, this area is virtually as it was in the days of the Sewee tribe, who fished and hunted here.

Most of the refuge's 20-mile stretch of coast, barrier reef, salt marshes, and open water are inaccessible by land. Its remoteness makes this a most likely environment for the preservation of such endangered species as loggerhead turtles that nest here. The bird list available at the Sewee Visitor and Environmental Education Center includes 262 species, plus 76 that are considered rare. The greatest population here is during the spring and fall migrations and in the winter.

White-tailed deer are frequently seen. Southern fox squirrels are plentiful, and raccoons, though nocturnal, may be seen during the day. If you are lucky, you may spot a playful family of river otters or dolphins cruising the creeks and bays. Alligators are common and should be given a wide berth. Also keep an eye out for cottonmouths and copperheads, the poisonous snakes in the area.

Bull Island (named for an early settler) is the focal point for visitors. A two-mile trail, with informative plaques, leads through a lush forest. A fine beach, fishing, and excellent birding are other attractions on the island. Surf fishermen try for channel bass. Access to Bull Island is by ferry from Garris Landing.

▶ Refuge open year-round.

www.fws.gov/caperomain
(843) 928-3368; (843) 928-3264

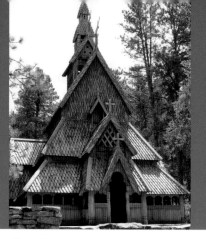

South Dakota

Welcoming parks and forbidding landscapes merge here with memories of trappers, traders, homesteaders, and the steadfast native peoples.

Chapel in the Hills. This striking church on the outskirts of Rapid City was built from the blueprints of the most famous stavkirke, or stave church, in Norway (see page 307).

South Dakota's natural wonders range all the way from the treeless Badlands to the dense forests of the Black Hills. The state's human history and achievements are no less a contrast: a museum centered around an archaeological excavation vs. a Benedictine abbey; an interpretive center devoted to the role of the buffalo vs. a museum of rare musical instruments; a small prairie town made famous by a series of books and a TV dramatization vs. a Norwegian church copied exactly from one in the old country. Also here are vivid reminders of the indigenous Sioux and the homesteaders who settled the prairie.

visit ➡ offthebeatenpathtrips.com

1 **Petrified Wood Park and Museum.** The park's buildings and cone-shaped pyramids are made from petrified wood and fossils. The museum, shown above, houses a collection of historical artifacts and antiques from the area.

1 Petrified Wood Park and Museum

500 Main Ave., Lemmon

Long ago tropical swamps covered the region around Lemmon. Gradual climatic and chemical changes and the passage of time turned the remnants of that distant era—trees, grasses, plants, and marine and animal life—into stone. In the 1930s O. S. Quammen, an amateur geologist, collected some of the best specimens of the petrified material for an unusual but artistic outdoor display.

The small park is studded with cone-shaped pyramids and piles of "cannonballs." A fairy-tale castle, built with more than 300 tons of petrified material, including tree trunks more than 30 feet tall, is especially intriguing.

Teeth marks, petrified snakes, and fossilized marine life are eerily recognizable in many surfaces. The castle contains the fossils of enormous animals, while a circular museum built of petrified logs and slabs of petrified grass houses pioneer artifacts. The multiplicity of forms and the incredible range of colors make this a fascinating place to visit.

▶ Park open year-round; museum open mid-May–mid-Sept.

www.lemmonsd.com/petrified
(605) 374-5716

2 Klein Museum

1820 W. Grand Crossing, Hwy. 12, Mobridge

This museum, with its excellent collection of Native American and early pioneer artifacts, was the inspiration of Jake Klein, an early South Dakota homesteader, and a room displays his family's heirlooms. You can explore the old-time offices of a doctor, dentist, and barber, and see a trapper's shack and a general store. Among the Native American exhibits are a pictograph, quill items, parfleche bags, and beaded work.

In addition there are three 1920 restored buildings—a house, a school, and a post office—as well as a re-created log cabin with a farm toy collection and a scale model of turn-of-the-century farm machinery. Many outstanding photos reflect Mobridge in the early 1900s and the life of the area's Plains Native Americans.

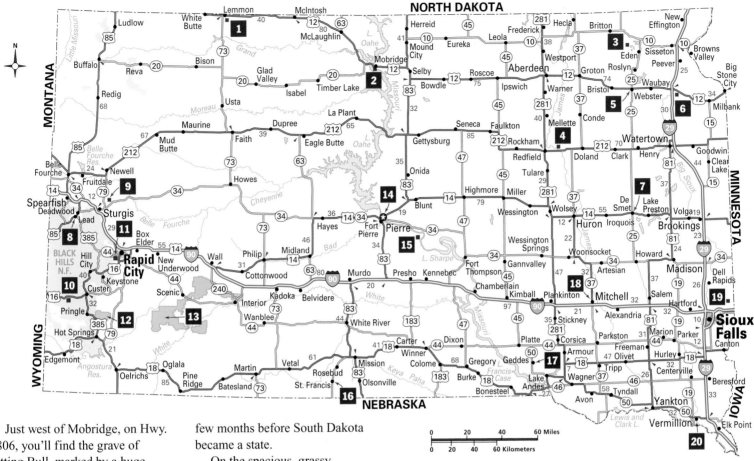

NORTH DAKOTA

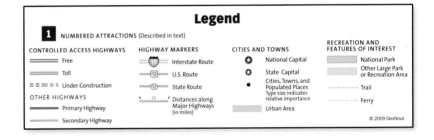

Legend

NUMBERED ATTRACTIONS (Described in text)

CONTROLLED ACCESS HIGHWAYS
— Free
— Toll
= = = Under Construction

OTHER HIGHWAYS
— Primary Highway
— Secondary Highway

HIGHWAY MARKERS
🔟 Interstate Route
⑫ U.S. Route
⑫ State Route
12 Distances along Major Highways (in miles)

CITIES AND TOWNS
✪ National Capital
⊛ State Capital
• Cities, Towns, and Populated Places Type size indicates relative importance
▨ Urban Area

RECREATION AND FEATURES OF INTEREST
National Park
Other Large Park or Recreation Area
--- Trail
--- Ferry

© 2009 GeoNova

Just west of Mobridge, on Hwy. 1806, you'll find the grave of Sitting Bull, marked by a huge stone sculpture of this Hunkpapa medicine man and leader. Nearby, overlooking Lake Oahe, is a monument to Sacajawea, the young Shoshone woman who in 1804–06 served as a guide and interpreter for Lewis and Clark on their expedition to the Pacific Coast.

▶ Museum open daily except Tues. Apr.–Oct. Admission charged.

www.mobridge.org
(605) 845-7243

---

❸ ▶ Fort Sisseton State Park

11907 434th Ave., Lake City
The establishment of Fort Sisseton in 1864 followed the Sioux rebellion against broken treaties and the influx of settlers on their lands. In service for 25 years, the fort was finally closed in June 1889, just a

few months before South Dakota became a state.

On the spacious, grassy grounds dotted with shade trees are 15 buildings, including officers quarters, a stable, and a library-schoolhouse. The visitors center and museum are housed in the North Barracks, designed as living quarters for 200 soldiers. Picnic areas and camping facilities are available.

▶ Park open year-round; visitors center open daily June–Aug. Admission charged.

www.sdgfp.info/parks
(605) 448-5474

---

❹ ▶ Fisher Grove State Park

17290 Fishers Ln., Frankfort
Along the banks of the winding James River, this pleasant grove is a welcome oasis in the midst of the seemingly endless prairies, its cottonwoods, willows, and

box elders fringing the riverbanks and sheltering the picnic and camping grounds.

The 360-acre park honors Frank I. Fisher, an early settler who in 1878 purchased 80 acres of land here along the James for 40 cents an acre with the intention of establishing a settlement. Shortly afterward, however, the railroad bypassed the area, and the few buildings that had been constructed were torn down and

used for firewood. A three-quarter-mile nature trail winds through the park and leads to the location of the original settlement. An 1884 schoolhouse, fully restored, serves as the visitors center. A boat ramp is provided for canoeists and kayakers.

▶ Open year-round. Admission charged.

www.sdgfp.info/parks
(605) 472-1212

---

5 The Museum of Wildlife, Science & Industry

760 W. Hwy. 12, Webster

One thing you might not expect to find on the plains of South Dakota is an extremely large replica of the shoe of Mother Goose. The Shoe House is one of 24 structures, 12 of which are historic, that comprise this museum intended to preserve both the heritage and culture of the northeastern part of the state.

The big shoe contains more than 9,000 shoes that Mildred Fiksdal O'Neill began accumulating in high school—from her father's snowshoes to moccasins used to carry messages during World War II.

Another interesting item here is the one-cell Grenville Jail, notable for not being bolted to the floor, which was moved here in 1988. Men held for minor infractions would lift the cell but never managed to walk it out of the building.

Two other buildings that were moved here to add interest to the museum were the Kozy Korner Kafé and the general store, both originally located in Butler, circa 1940.

Another building, dedicated to pioneer women, contains a Norwegian-style bedroom and a loom. Native American stone tools, a sleigh and buggy, vintage farming vehicles, and early printing presses also give a flavor of what life was once like here.

▶ Open daily mid-May–Oct.
  Donations encouraged.

www.sdmuseum.org
(605) 345-4751

6 Blue Cloud Abbey

12 miles west of Milbank off Hwy. 12, Marvin

The doors are never locked at this quiet, peaceful abbey, a Benedictine monastery founded in 1950. Guests are welcome to come here for rest and contemplation and, with reservations, may stay the night or longer. The monks have vowed to live by the rule of St. Benedict, written by the saint in the 6th century and emphasizing the importance of prayer and work.

The monks labored for 17 years in building the abbey. Today they are involved in making candles, keeping bees (honey is sold at the abbey), and tending the gardens that provide much of their food. In a workshop open to visitors, they create ornate and colorful vestments for churches of many different denominations throughout the world.

On the outside wall of the monastery is an excellent mosaic of the Virgin Mary. Contemporary stained glass enhances the church's sanctuary, and current artwork hangs in the lower lounge. Everyone is welcome at the abbey church, and the monks are known throughout the region for their hospitality.

The home cooking and caring atmosphere provided here make even a short visit a pleasant and memorable one.

▶ Open year-round.

www.bluecloud.org
(605) 398-9208

7 De Smet

105 Olivet Ave., De Smet

This is the Little Town on the Prairie made famous by Laura Ingalls Wilder in the Little House books describing her childhood here in the 1880s. For a self-guiding map of the town locating the places she wrote about, go to the Laura Ingalls Wilder Memorial Society, next to the Surveyor's House.

The map leads you to 16 restored places and sites, including the Loftus store, the church that "Pa helped build," the home where Laura and Almanzo Ingalls lived, and the family homestead.

The society gives guided tours of the Surveyor's House, where the family lived for the first winter on the Dakota prairie, and the Ingalls House, built by Laura's father, furnished with many original pieces.

▶ Open year-round. Tours weekdays year-round, and Sat. May–Sept.; daily Jun.–Aug. Admission charged.

www.liwms.com
(800) 880-3383

De Smet. Laura Ingalls Wilder's depiction of her life in the "little house on the prairie" won the hearts of two generations of readers and television viewers.

8 George S. Mickelson Trail

Deadwood to Edgemont

Calamity Jane and Wild Bill Hickok. Steam trains chugging through the landscape. Our notions of the Black Hills of South Dakota have long been intertwined with Western myth and legend.

Now a 109-mile trail that traverses the whole length of the Black Hills can be used by hikers, bicyclists, horseback riders, snowshoers, and cross-country skiers.

Following the tracks of the abandoned Burlington Northern Railroad, this "jewel" of the state park system takes you from Deadwood to Edgemont, through hard rock tunnels and across trestle bridges. Some portions of the trail are considered to be strenuous, but the grade is never more than 4 percent. The crushed limestone surface and wide path offer comfortable travel and spectacular scenery through the heart of the Black Hills.

▶ Open year-round. Admission charged.

www.mickelsontrail.com
(605) 584-3896

9 Bear Butte State Park

Hwy. 70, 6 miles NE of Sturgis

The centerpiece of this park is a solitary cone-shaped mountain that rises 1,200 feet above the plains.

Named Bear Mountain by the Sioux, it was regarded as a holy place by both the Sioux and the Cheyennes. Red Cloud, Sitting Bull, and other Native American leaders paid visits here. A Native American conference was held at Bear Butte in 1857 to discuss the encroachment of white settlers and gold prospectors in the region.

For more than a century the mountain has also drawn geologists from far and wide. It is a famous example of a laccolith—a volcano that never erupted, formed millions of years ago by a great upheaval of molten rock.

For hikers a national recreation trail leads from the parking lot to the summit. Camping and boating facilities are found at Bear Butte Lake, just across the highway.

▶ Open daily year-round.

www.sdgfp.info/parks
(605) 347-5240

10 Jewel Cave National Monument

US-16, 13 miles west of Custer
The dazzlingly beautiful cave filled with jewel-like calcite crystals is the star attraction in this 1,275-acre park. Located in Hell Canyon, it was discovered in 1900 and declared a national monument in

1908. Visitors to the cave have a choice of four tours. The popular 80-minute-long Scenic Tour follows a paved half-mile route, with aluminum stairways and handrails, and is illuminated to show the diverse cave formations. The easy, 20-minute Discovery Tour shows visitors one large room in the cave, accessed by an elevator and a staircase. The nearly two-hour, more difficult Lantern Tour is unpaved, with ladderlike steps and no lighting (visitors carry lanterns). Reservations are required for the Spelunking Tour, part of which is covered on hands and knees.

To avoid long waits, arrive early or visit early or late in the season. Wear low-heeled walking shoes and a sweater, because it's chilly.

▶ Monument and visitors center open daily year-round. Discovery and Scenic Tours year-round, Candlelight and Spelunking Tours summer only. Admission charged for cave.

www.nps.gov/jeca
(605) 673-2288

did you know ❓

Jewel Cave is the second-longest cave system in the world with more than 143 miles of passageways that have been found by explorers.

11 Chapel in the Hills

3788 Chapel Ln., Rapid City
The unusual multiroofed timber building seen in the woods at the foot of the Black Hills is a Norwegian stavkirke (stave church). It is an exact replica of the Borgund Stavkirke, the best-preserved example in Norway (the Norwegian government provided the original blueprints for its Rapid City twin). The gabled roofs, growing smaller as they ascend, are these churches' most eye-catching feature.

The tranquillity of the church and its hilly grounds is as much of a draw as the architecture, as a stroll on the Prayer/Meditation Walk winding behind the church will attest. Also on the grounds are a log cabin built by a Black Hills prospector, and the gift shop is housed in a stabbur—a Norwegian wooden building with a grass roof.

▶ Open May–Sept.

www.chapel-in-the-hills.org
(605) 342-8281

12 Wind Cave National Park

US-385, 12 miles north of Hot Springs
The cave here, named for the strong barometric winds found at the entrance, contains more than

130 miles of chambers and passageways. It is famous for the excellent examples of boxwork, a strange, honeycomb-like formation of calcite, and for other decorative deposits, such as frostwork, flowstone, popcorn, and delicate helictite bushes.

Cave tours of varying difficulty and length are offered throughout the year. Wear good walking shoes and a jacket. Reservations are recommended for the special Candlelight Tour, which ventures through unpaved and unlighted parts of the cave, and they are required for the strenuous four-hour Wild Cave tour.

The 28,000-acre park is a wildlife refuge, with 36 miles of hiking trails that offer access to great stretches of mixed-grass prairie interspersed with hardwood and ponderosa pine forest. One might see buffalo, elk, pronghorn antelope, coyotes, mule deer, badgers, and prairie dogs.

The park has a campground and amphitheater, three self-guiding nature trails, and a picnic area.

▶ Park open year-round. No cave tours on major winter holidays. Admission charged for tours.

www.nps.gov/wica
(605) 745-4600

8 George S. Mickelson Trail. Cyclists and hikers from far and wide flock to this well-groomed, 114-mile trail, famous for its beauty, numerous access points, and gentle grade.

13 Badlands National Park

Interior

One can imagine the dismay with which pioneers eyed this 50-mile stretch of seeming moonscape that appears so abruptly on the grassy plain. The cliffs, gorges, soaring spires, knife-edged ridges, flat-topped mesas, and fossil-filled canyons—carved and etched by millions of years of rain, wind, and frost—stand as a classic example of the effects of erosion.

Most visitors to the Badlands simply drive the scenic 30-mile loop along Hwy. 240. But for those willing to venture off this well-worn path, there are many little-known spots to enjoy. The park encompasses nearly a quarter-million acres, and some 64,000 acres of the most spectacular landscape are a roadless wilderness area open only to hikers, back-packers, and horseback riders.

During the summer the Ben Reifel Visitor Center, at the eastern end of the park, schedules several ranger-guided nature walks, evening slide lectures, and stargazing programs. The White River Visitor Center is located in the south unit of the park, which includes part of the Pine Ridge Indian Reservation.

▶ Park open year-round; Ben Reifel Visitor Center open daily except major holidays; White River Visitor Center open June–mid-Sept. Admission charged.

www.nps.gov/badl
(605) 433-5361

14 South Dakota Cultural Heritage Center

900 Governors Dr., Pierre
South Dakota history, from the time of its early Native American cultures up through World War II, comes alive in this splendid

13 **Badlands National Park.** Children and adults alike are intrigued by the barrenness and desolate beauty of this rocky, moonlike landscape sculpted by erosion.

underground museum. Among the displays are those of a Sioux in traditional dress, a walk-through tepee, and a magnificent stream-lined wooden-stick carving of a galloping horse (circa 1875). The carving was included in a Native American art show sent to England in 1976.

An exhibit of special historic interest is the Verendrye Plate, a lead plate that was placed on a bluff overlooking the Missouri River by a French expedition in 1743, claiming this area for France and found in 1913.

Other displays show how the lives of South Dakota's people have been affected by such change as the fur trade, the gold rush, and the coming of the railroad.

▶ Open daily year-round except major holidays. Admission charged.

www.sdhistory.org
(605) 773-3458

15 Buffalo Interpretive Center

29349 Hwy. 1806, Lower Brule
This state-of-the-art interpretive center stands on a buffalo range edged by the Missouri River in central South Dakota. The building itself is striking; inspired by early Sioux culture, it is said to resemble a medicine pipe from a distance. At the entrance to the circular exhibition hall stands a buffalo-hide tepee. Nearby is a 70-by-20-foot tepee-studded mural depicting Brule Sioux community life. A long corridor is hung with artwork depicting the integral role the buffalo played in Native American life. Large glass windows look out on the pastureland where buffalo graze. Visitors are also able to view the animals from the fence outside.

▶ Open May-Dec. Admission charged.

http://lewisandclarktrail.com/section2/sdcities/pierre/buffalo.htm
(605) 223-2260

16 Buechel Memorial Lakota Museum

350 S. Oak St., St. Francis
The small but fascinating museum is part of St. Francis Mission on the Rosebud Indian Reservation. The museum was established as a memorial to Father Eugene Buechel, a Jesuit missionary who spent a great deal of his life among the Lakota, or Sioux, and died in 1954. In addition to collecting and preserving the artifacts of their culture, he helped to preserve their language, writing three books and compiling 30,000 entries of Dakota words that formed the basis for a dictionary.

The museum's collection includes elaborate tribal robes, headdresses, jewelry, tools, hunting knives, bows and arrows and other weapons, musical instruments, horse gear, and games. Some of the pieces date back to the 1850s.

▶ Open weekdays Memorial Day–Labor Day.

www.sfmission.org/museum
(605) 747-2361

17 Papineau Trading Post

Main St., Geddes
The trading post, a 20-by-30-foot log cabin, was built in 1857 by Cuthbert Ducharme, a French-Canadian fur trader, on the banks of the Missouri River a few miles from Geddes. The original log structure was relocated to this small turn-of-the-century railroad town when the first site was flooded.

Soldiers, cowboys, boatmen, and westward-bound travelers stopped at the post for supplies, including liquor. Legend has it that Ducharme, who was nicknamed Papineau (meaning pap water, or whiskey), poured the whiskey into a dishpan and tied a tin cup to it, allowing his customers to help themselves—a full cup for 25 cents. Ducharme was also known for his skill at handling a gun, and the records of the U.S. Army Corps of Engineers state that the original Ducharme cemetery contained 27 graves, 14 of which were unidentified. Several of the tombstones have been removed to the trading post in Geddes; they are considered fine examples of 19th-century mortuary art.

This historic post contains the accoutrements of a fur trader's life in the second half of the 19th century: traps, knives, guns, a kerosene lamp, dishes, pots, a table, rawhide chairs, and a liquor barrel, plus Native American relics.

▶ Open daily May–Sept.

Donations encouraged.

(605) 337-2501

18 Prehistoric Indian Museum

Two miles north of Mitchell
One of three "archeodomes" in the world, this museum includes an archaeological dig on the shores of Lake Mitchell. Visitors can view an excavation pit revealing the foundations of two Mandan lodges. At times it is possible to watch the archaeologists at work. While the archeodome is a research facility/museum complete with a laboratory, darkroom, and computer classroom, it's

14 **South Dakota Cultural Heritage Center.** The Medora-Deadwood Stagecoach, better known by its nickname of "Kitty," carried travelers between the two Old West towns it was named for. The trip covered about 215 miles and took 36 hours to complete.

hardly "all archaeology, all the time" at this complex. Events, including Native American musical performances beside the lakeshore, are regularly scheduled in the spring and summer.

The Boehnen Museum is the site's other main building. Here you can walk through a reconstructed lodge, see a model of the thousand-year-old village as it might have looked in its prime, and marvel at the pottery, tools, and spear points of the era.

▶ Open daily May–Sept.; Mon.–Fri. Oct.–Apr.

Admission charged.

www.mitchellindianvillage.org
605-996-5473

19 Palisades State Park

25495 485th Ave., Garretson
This strikingly beautiful park of gorges, vertical cliffs, and dramatic rock formations borders both sides of Split Rock Creek.

The massive layers of quartzite

in the cliffs are interspersed with beds of pipestone, or catlinite, a soft red stone held sacred by Native Americans.

The creek, which has several rapids and quiet pools, provides excellent swimming, fishing, and canoeing. The 111-acre park has a tree-shaded campground and two picnic areas overlooking the picturesque stream. Hiking trails follow its course, wandering along 80-foot-high cliffs, which are very popular with rock climbers.

▶ Open year-round. Admission charged.

www.sdgfp.info/parks
(605) 594-3824

20 The National Music Museum

414 E. Clark St., Vermillion
Professor Arne B. Larson gathered more than 2,500 musical instruments from around the world and donated them to the university in 1979. Today the museum houses over 14,000 instruments, including a rare Stradivari guitar.

There are also some marvelous oddities, such as a zither in the shape of a crocodile, a trombone whose bell is a dragon's head, and an ancient harp so elegantly arched that one wonders how it could be plucked. These instruments, both ancient and modern, are valued not only for documenting the history of music in various cultures of the world but also for revealing the imagination and superb craftsmanship of those who created them.

▶ Open daily year-round except major holidays.

Donations encouraged.

www.usd.edu/smm
(605) 677-5306

seasonal events

FEBRUARY
• Mardi Gras—Deadwood (*Cajun cuisine, nighttime parade of lights, crowning of Mardi Gras King and Queen, over 50,000 sets of beads*)

JUNE
• Czech Days—Tabor (*dancing, live music, regional food, carnival, parade*)
• Fort Sisseton Historical Festival—Lake City (*historical re-enactments, demonstrations, live music*)
• Wild Bill Days—Deadwood (*historical re-enactments, live music, contests*)
• Festival Of Presidents—Rapid City (*patriotic festival, live music, parades, arts and crafts, regional food*)

JULY
• Red Cloud Indian Art Show—Pine Ridge (*summer-long fine arts and crafts show*)
• Fourth of July Celebration—Springfield (*frog-hopping contest, dancing, live music, fireworks*)
• River City Racin'—Chamberlain (*boat race, children's activities, live music, local food*)

AUGUST
• Potato Days—Clark (*harvest festival, arts and crafts, tractor parade, regional food, sporting events*)

SEPTEMBER
• Mickelson Trail Trek—Custer (*bike riding event*)
• Western Heritage Festival—Hill City (*historical re-enactments, live music, regional food, parade*)
• Buffalo Roundup—Custer State Park (*1,500 buffalo, annual roundup with cowboys and cowgirls*)

OCTOBER
• Pumpkin Fest—Webster (*harvest festival, regional food, baking contest, quilt show, parade*)
• Black Hills Pow-Wow—Rapid City (*live music and dancing, arts and crafts, sporting events*)

www.travelsd.com

Tennessee

The "three states of Tennessee"—West, Middle, and East—are full of surprises, one being a passion for preserving historic small towns.

Mule Day Festival. Mules are the stars at this popular festival, held every April in the Middle Tennessee town of Columbia (see Seasonal Events, page 317).

Diverse Tennessee communities to visit include a treasure trove of Victorian architecture, a gentlemanly but naive experiment in colonization, and the oldest town west of the Appalachians. Here, too, is a reconstruction of a Native American village abandoned five centuries ago.

See the home and locomotive of the immortal Casey Jones in West Tennessee and ride the rails on the old L&N Railroad in East Tennessee. Tour a famous whiskey distillery (where you'll be treated to an excellent drink of lemonade), browse a million-dollar collection of unusual teapots, and entertain yourself royally at the ranch of a country music legend.

visit ➤ offthebeatenpathtrips.com

1 Reelfoot Lake State Resort Park

3120 State Rte. 213, Tiptonville
A cataclysmic earthquake on February 7, 1812—perhaps the most violent ever to strike the continental United States—caused an enormous area of land to sink as much as 10 feet. Water from the Mississippi River entered this depression, creating a 14-mile-long lake. Much of the lake's charm and strangeness is imparted by the venerable bald cypress trees that fringe its margins. They rise tall and ghostly from the dark water and in spring and summer canopy the shoreline with delicate, fresh green foliage.

The shallow 15,000 acres of water are dotted with islands. The park includes a narrow strip around most of the shore, where campgrounds, picnic and day-use areas, and boat launches are available. From May through Sept., a cruise boat leaves from a jetty near the visitors center every morning for a three-hour cruise, stopping at Caney Island, where visitors can walk a nature trail and see Native American mounds. In mid-summer the American lotus blooms abundantly in parts of the lake; when that happens, the cruise boat stops to let people pick the flowers.

A sanctuary for wildlife, Reelfoot Lake is a resting place for a

1 Reelfoot Lake State Resort Park. Adapted to swamps, deciduous bald cypress trees have needlelike leaves and can grow up to 100 to 120 feet tall.

large number of migrating waterfowl and therefore a favorite with birders. Between Jan. 2 and the first weekend in March, the park conducts daily bus tours to look for wintering bald eagles. The tours depart from the Reelfoot Lake State Airpark Inn in the morning and take about two hours. Reservations are required.

Known as the Turtle Capital of the World, the lake features thousands of sliders, stinkpots, and mud-and-map turtles. The visitors center, located in Tiptonville, has a small museum of natural and local history.

▶ Park open year-round. Fee charged for tours and cruises.

http://state.tn.us/environment/parks

(731) 253-8003
(731) 253-7756 For bald eagle tours.

2 Teapot Museum

309 College St., Trenton

Although known locally as the Teapot Museum, this exhibition's official title is The World's Largest Collection of Rare Porcelain Veilleuse. A *veilleuse-théière* is hardly an ordinary teapot; it is also a night-light. The earliest *veilleuses* were food warmers, with a vessel in which a candle or oil was burned with a bowl above, on a stand. Eventually a teapot replaced the bowl. In 19th-century Europe these simple utensils for brewing tea and providing a night-light became works of art.

This unique 19th-century collection—valued at more than $1 million— was donated to Trenton by Dr. Frederick C. Freed, a local citizen. The town gave it a home in the local municipal hall. Housed in glass-fronted cases, the 525 teapots— several from Napoleon's own collection—are decorated in varying degrees of sophistication and charming naiveté, with palm trees, Romeos and Juliets, birds, dogs, horses, flowers, vines, mermaids, cathedrals, and castles.

2 Teapot Museum. Everyday ceramic teapots are nowhere in sight in this collection, assembled over the decades by a local physician.

Seeing these ornamental objects, you can easily envision one glowing and flickering on a bedside table, offering comfort in an era before electricity.

▶ Open year-round.

www.teapotcollection.com
(731) 855-2013

3 Mindfield/West Tennessee Delta Heritage Center

Brownsville

At first glance Brownsville, in the heart of cotton country east of Memphis, might seem like other Delta towns with interesting historic districts. But what's that gray metal structure rising above the downtown? A tall building going up? A power plant? Something from the set of a film? Not even close. Mindfield is, in the words of a longtime Brownsville resident, "a man's life in steel." It's the ongoing work of Brownsville native Billy Tripp, and even in the world of visionary folk art, not easy to classify. The construction, which Tripp began in 1988, includes a salvaged water tank, a fire tower, and an embellished Harley-Davidson named Sylvia. It is the largest work of art in the state; some elements top 100 feet in height. It reminds some of the Watts Tower in Los Angeles, but Mindfield is a uniquely personal ever-changing vision.

While in Brownsville, stop by the West Tennessee Delta Heritage Center. The music room pays tribute to jazz, blues, and rock greats who were born or lived in the area, including Tina Turner, Yank Rachell, Hammie Nixon, and Sleepy John Estes. Next time you hear the song "Delta Dawn" and Tanya Tucker sings, *"All the folks in Brownsville think she's crazy,"* you'll know exactly where the town is located.

▶ Mindfield open daily year-round. Heritage Center open Mon.–Fri. year-round.

www.tnvacation.com/vendors/west_tennessee_delta_heritage_center

(731) 779-9000

Legend

1 NUMBERED ATTRACTIONS (Described in text)

HIGHWAY MARKERS

Free	Interstate Route
Toll	U.S. Route
Under Construction	State Route

OTHER HIGHWAYS

Primary Highway

Secondary Highway

12 Distances along Major Highways (in miles)

CITIES AND TOWNS

National Capital

State Capital

Cities, Towns, and Populated Places Type size indicates relative importance

Urban Area

RECREATION AND FEATURES OF INTEREST

National Park

Other Large Park or Recreation Area

Trail

Ferry

© 2009 GeoNova

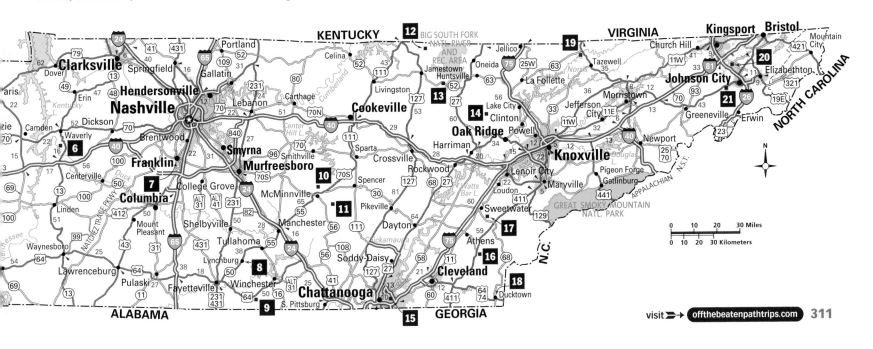

4 C.H. Nash Museum at Chucalissa

1987 Indian Village Dr., Memphis

Named for its founding director, the archaeological museum devoted to Native Americans preserves a site that was occupied, abandoned, and reoccupied numerous times between A.D. 1000 and 1550. Artifacts unearthed during excavations cast light on daily life in a Mississippian village of 800 to 1,000 people—

 C.H. Nash Museum at Chucalissa. Painted hands and unique designs were the signatures of Chucalissan pottery.

how they farmed, dressed and ornamented themselves, and even treated illnesses with native plants. Also displayed are a range of stone tools and hunting weapons.

Visitors to the archaeology lab are actually allowed to pick up and examine pottery pieces and other items from a representative sampling of artifacts. The museum is unusual in another respect as well: Native Americans have acted as the primary interpreters for decades, and their service is honored with displays of individual photographs and profiles.

Displays fast forward to the present at the Choctaw Heritage Exhibit, featuring the basketry, ceramics, and handmade clothing items of contemporary Choctaw artisans. Outdoors in the arboretum, visitors learn how the early inhabitants of Chucalissa used indigenous trees and plants to make housing materials, weaponry, everyday items, and herbal medicines.

Chucalissa lies on the southern edge of Memphis just outside the boundary of T. O. Fuller State Park. Here travelers seeking nature and recreation will find picnic grounds, sports fields, a swimming pool, and six miles of trails winding through woods inhabited by deer and wild turkeys. Birdwatchers can spot numerous treedwelling species and waterfowl on the shores of adjacent Lake McKellar.

▶ Museum open daily except Mon. Dec.-Mar. Admission charged.
Park open year-round.

http://cas.memphis.edu/chucalissa
(901) 785-3160

5 Casey Jones Home and Railroad Museum

Jackson

The legendary railroad engineer and hero of the song "The Ballad of Casey Jones" died in the wreck of the *Cannonball Express* the night of April 30, 1900, in Vaughan, Mississippi. His train had rounded a bend and come upon a freight train; Casey heroically stayed at the throttle in order to save the lives of his passengers.

His house, now located in Casey Jones Village, is as it was at the time of his death: a simple white one-story clapboard structure with green shutters and wraparound porch. Two rooms are devoted to memorabilia and railroad history, including a model of the fatal accident scene complete with miniature trains and watch Casey wore, marking the time of the accident at 3:52 A.M. There are tributes to Wallace Saunders, the engine wiper who wrote the song, and Sim Webb, Casey's friend, who kept the legend alive.

There are also some lovely period touches—a lead tub, marble sink, straight-edge razor and strap, and a bottle of Nash's Laxative Syrup in the bathroom; a coal stove, and a churn and dasher in the kitchen. Expanded exhibits and a theater to view the Casey Jones story will be featured in a train station, set to open in 2009.

Outside the house is a replica of Illinois Central Railroad engine No. 382, the train in which Jones died. You can climb into the cab, lean out the window, and ring the bell just like Casey.

▶ Open daily. Admission charged.

www.caseyjones.com
(731) 668-1222

6 Loretta Lynn's Ranch

44 Hurricane Mills Rd., Hurricane Mills

Loretta Lynn, one of country music's best-known divas, is also a good businesswoman. One of her most popular ventures is Loretta Lynn's Ranch (originally Dude Ranch), about an hour's drive west of Nashville. The place offers a variety of things to do, much of it related to Loretta's life and career; the large Coal Miner's Daughter Museum and the antebellum-style house where she lived for many years are musts for fans. You'll find a replica of the Butcher's Hollow house, where Loretta grew up, as well as a simulated coal mine. At the Grist Mill Museum visitors will be able to view Lynn's extensive doll collection, and a Wild West town offers plenty of shopping, dining, and entertainment.

RV grounds, cabin rentals, and tent camping are available, but if you want to feel like a star, you could reserve Loretta's deluxe tour bus (featured in the movie of her life) for the night. There are also frequent special events, such as concerts, trail rides, cross-country racing, and the Loretta Lynn Amateur National Motorcross Championship.

▶ Open Mar.-Oct. Admission charged.

www.lorettalynn.com/ranch
(931) 296-7700

7 Franklin

South of Nashville

The town of Franklin is a treasure of Victorian architecture surrounded by neatly trimmed lawns and sheltered by the venerable maples lining its quiet streets. A 15-block section of the downtown area is listed on the *National Register of Historic Places*.

6 ▶ **Loretta Lynn's Ranch.** The Coal Miner's Daughter Museum is only one of the many attractions surrounding the country music great's former home.

Most of the homes are privately owned, but the exteriors can be enjoyed from the car or on a leisurely stroll. One of the few open to the public—and also one of the best—is the Carter House, built in 1830 by Fountain Branch Carter.

His son, Capt. Tod Carter, was mortally wounded in the fierce battle that was waged on the grounds and is now commemorated in a museum and tour. The rooms are appointed with family heirlooms and furnishings. Outbuildings of the same era include a smokehouse, toolshed, family kitchen, and slave cabin. The farm office, with 207 bullet holes, is the most gunshot-riddled building of the Civil War.

Information for self-guiding walking tours of the historic district is available at the Franklin Chamber of Commerce in the city hall building on the town square.

▶ Admission charged for house tours.

www.visitwilliamson.com
(615) 791-7554

8 ▶ Jack Daniel's Distillery

182 Lynchburg Hwy., Lynchburg
Here's your chance for a spirited tour of one of America's most famous distilleries. From the moment you enter, the air is permeated by the pungent aroma of Tennessee sour mash whiskey.

A brief introductory slide show explains the reasons for the distillery's location: the ready availability of good spring water, high-quality grain, and ample supplies of maple, from which the charcoal for filtering is made. This all-important material gives the whiskey its unique flavor.

You'll pass through a warehouse, one of almost 70, where the whiskey is aged in white oak barrels, made locally and used just once. Each warehouse holds 20,160 of the 55-gallon barrels (worth about $500 million in U.S. taxes alone). In turn you'll see all the operations required for the production of this heady concoction.

Along the way, you'll visit the original company offices, which serve as a museum, and see the safe that led to the demise of Jack Daniel: Unable to open the safe, he kicked it in a fit of rage, broke a toe, and developed a fatal case of blood poisoning.

On a happier note: At the end of the one-hour tour, complimentary coffee and lemonade are served.

▶ Open daily except major holidays.

www.jackdaniels.com
(931) 759-6180

9 ▶ Falls Mill

134 Falls Mill Rd., Belvidere
A good mill site must have a dependable flow of water for the raceway, a solid streamside foundation for the building, and easy road access to a nearby trading area. When these conditions are met, the turning wheels can be adapted to serve a variety of needs, as has been demonstrated here.

Beginning operation in 1873, Falls Mill produced cotton thread and wool for home spinning. In 1906 it became a cotton gin, and after World War II the structure served as a woodworking shop. In 1969 the mill was restored and, with equipment purchased from nearby mills that had closed, it was converted to a gristmill.

The first floor of the building has the grain milling equipment and an antique printing press. On the second floor there are a textile exhibit and a country store with a working player piano.

▶ Open daily except Wed. and major holidays. Admission charged.

www.fallsmill.com
(931) 469-7161

8 ▶ **Jack Daniel's Distillery.** A museum at the distillery pays homage to Tennessee whiskey, a spirit frequently confused with the bourbon made in neighboring Kentucky.

10 Falcon Rest Mansion

2645 Faulkner Springs Rd., McMinnville

Southern gentleman and clever entrepreneur Clay Faulkner sweet-talked his wife, Mary, into letting him build her "the finest mansion in the region" in 1896. The only stipulation was that it had to be next to his woolen mill, 2 1/2 miles outside of town. The promise of electric lights, central heating, and indoor plumbing convinced his wife that living next to the factory wasn't such a bad idea after all, and the Victorian dream of the man whose mill made Gorilla Pants ("so strong even a gorilla couldn't tear them apart") became a reality.

The home, a 10,000-square-foot all-brick tribute to the elegance of the Gay '90s era, has meticulous woodwork, gracious rooms filled with antiques, statuary, and music boxes; and a sweeping staircase.

After a period in which the large house was turned into a hospital, an enterprising couple bought Falcon Rest at auction. Today the well-loved home that reigns as Tennessee's "premier Victorian mansion," halfway between Nashville and Chattanooga, offers guided tours and a Victorian Tea Room for lunch. The faint chuckle that lingers in the air might even belong to Clay Faulkner's ghost, who occasionally visits for old times' sake.

▶ Open year-round. Admission charged.

www.falconrest.com
(931) 668-4444

11 Cumberland Caverns

1437 Cumberland Caverns Rd., McMinnville

Three hundred feet below the surface of the ground, these remarkable caverns were formed some 500 million years ago by the erosive action of the prehistoric Gulf of Mexico, which then extended this far north.

A stream flows through the entrance gallery into a crystal-clear pool swarming with blind white crayfish. From the center of this pool rises a 4-million-year-old flowstone (formed by a conjunction of a stalactite and a stalagmite) named Moby Dick. Covering the ceilings is a wide and leaflike stalactite mass referred to as curtains. When lightly tapped, they produce the bell-like tone of a pipe organ.

Equally mysterious caverns follow: the Graveyard, the Popcorn Bowl, and the largest of the tour, the truly cavernous Hall of the Mountain King—600 feet long, 140 feet high, and enhanced with curious formations called the Pagodas and the Chessmen. As you proceed through this enormous space—the largest cave in Tennessee—the sensation of being at the bottom of the Grand Canyon gives way to the impression of climbing through an archaic Italian hill town.

▶ Open daily except major winter holidays. Admission charged.

www.cumberlandcaverns.com
(931) 668-4396

12 Pickett State Rustic Park

4605 Pickett Park Hwy., Jamestown

Rolling hills and deep valleys, sparkling waterfalls, and natural bridges and caves are but some of the discoveries to be made in this 17,372-acre wilderness nestled in the Cumberland Plateau. The park also includes some excellent runs for white-water canoeing.

The sinuous shoreline of a dark green lake, the centerpiece of Pickett, rewards boaters and hikers alike with an ever-changing view. The road to the lake sweeps past lightly wooded bluffs and dales set discreetly with cabins and campsites. The park is laced by a network of nine marked hiking trails. One of the most pleasing and accessible is the Lake View Trail, which is true to its name. Reaching this trail is a delight—first by a swinging bridge (which really swings), then a path winding above the laurel, dogwoods, and magnolias fringing the lake.

Another scenic excursion is the Natural Bridge Trail. For a distance of about 1 1/2 miles, the path wends upward through a forest of evergreens and hardwoods to higher altitudes and panoramic views before descending toward its terminus at Natural Bridge.

▶ Open year-round.

http://state.tn.us/environment/parks

10 **Falcon Rest Mansion.** An oak-and-chestnut "half-tester" canopy bed, one of many antiques piquing visitors' interest, dominates a bedroom in the mansion.

13 Rugby

The 19th century bred a number of attempts at utopian living. Rugby, one of the more curious and colorful, was a British colony founded by Thomas Hughes, a social reformer, writer, and the author of *Tom Brown's Schooldays.*

In the model community he hoped to provide the younger sons of the English upper classes an opportunity to lead useful lives in endeavors considered beneath them in England, where the law of primogeniture denied inheritance to all but the eldest son.

Named after the school Hughes had attended in England, Rugby was plagued by problems from its very beginnings in 1880. Some

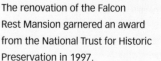

did you know ?

The renovation of the Falcon Rest Mansion garnered an award from the National Trust for Historic Preservation in 1997.

13 ▶ **Rugby.** The Rugby Pilgrimage is held in the fall every other year.

of its members were ill-equipped to wrest a living from the wilderness of the Cumberland Plateau. Although Hughes's colony was fraying at the edges by 1893, it attracted attention in America and Europe.

Today the village, with its charming Victorian air and architecture, comes as a surprise in the rural countryside. Twenty of the town's almost 70 original buildings have been preserved, and others have been reconstructed.

Four of the most important of the original structures are open for guided tours. These include the Thomas Hughes Library, the oldest, completely preserved public library in America; Christ Church, built in the Carpenter Gothic style; and Kingstone Lisle, which contains many of Hughes's belongings. Enjoy year-round workshops, concerts, and events, as well as lovely river gorge trails built by the colonists in the 1880s.

▶ Open year-round except winter holidays.
  Admission charged.

www.historicrugby.org
(866) 253-9207

14 ▶ Frozen Head State Park and Natural Area

964 Flat Fork Rd., Wartburg
This is an out-and-out backcountry wilderness area for hikers and serious backpackers, with development confined to the trail system and one picnic area.

The region is crisscrossed by 20 blazed trails of varying difficulty, some of which are described on a trail map available at the headquarters. It is a 3 1/2-mile hike to the Frozen Head fire tower at an elevation of 3,324 feet. From the tower there's a fabulous view of the Cumberland Plateau and the Tennessee River valley.

The area is renowned for its wildflowers and flowering trees and is especially popular in April, when they begin to bloom. August is the time for the Folk Life Festival, with its dancing, arts, and crafts. There are over 80 miles of foot trails that meander throughout the natural area, passing by waterfalls, rock shelters, and giant mountaintop cap rocks.

▶ Open year-round.

http://state.tn.us/environment/parks
(423) 346-3318

15 ▶ Tennessee Valley Railroad and Museum

Grand Junction Station,
4119 Cromwell Rd., Chattanooga
This fine preservation of our colorful railroad history includes steam and diesel locomotives, Pullman cars, day coaches, mail cars, and all the other rolling stock that once made train travel such an exciting adventure.

In Office Car 98, the Eden Isle, you'll discover how executives traveled in the heyday of the steam trains. Built in 1917 for the presi-

dent of the Baltimore & Ohio Railroad, it contains the original mahogany paneling, a sitting room, three bedrooms, a dining room with elegant glass-fronted cabinets, and a kitchen. A museum car contains such intriguing items as semaphore signals, pressure gauges, and lanterns.

One of the museum's major attractions is a six-mile round-trip on the Missionary Ridge Local, departing from Grand Junction Station six times daily. On arrival at East Chattanooga Station, you'll find yourself in an exact copy of an old small-town Southern railroad station.

The North Pole Limited runs from Grand Junction Station on evenings in November and December.

▶ Museum open daily Apr.–Oct.; weekends in Nov. Admission charged.

www.tvrail.com
(423) 894-8028

16 ▶ **Hiwassee River Rails Adventure.** Half-day excursions on vintage trains take passengers alongside (and over) the wild Hiwassee River and into Cherokee National Forest.

16 ▶ Hiwassee River Rail Adventure

727 Tennessee Ave., Etowah
Where can today's family experience the romance of the rails? In East Tennessee you can head to Etowah and hop a vintage train for an exciting half-day round-trip excursion along and over the

Hiwassee River and into scenic Cherokee National Forest. Rails served this area from the late 1800s, and the town of Etowah was founded by the L&N Railroad as the major depot. But after passenger and freight service ended, starting in the 1960s, the Old Line was abandoned until the Tennessee Overhill Association and the Tennessee Valley Railroad Museum joined forces to preserve the line and rescue the tradition.

Their Adventure excursion includes the amazing Great Hiwassee Loop—climbing up Bald Mountain to a point where the track spirals over itself, so you'll be riding 62 feet above the rails you just traveled! A full-day trip includes the Loop plus a stopover in the historic mining town of Copperhill.

Trips begin and end at Etowah's restored L&N Depot and Museum, where a shuttle takes you to your train in short order. Trip schedules vary; check the online calendar or call for dates and times. Advance reservations are recommended.

▶ Open Apr.–Dec. Admission charged.

www.tvrail.com
(423) 894-8028 Tennessee Valley Railroad Museum

17 Lost Sea

140 Lost Sea Rd., Sweetwater

Although not exactly a sea, the underground lake in this cave system is said to be America's largest. The lake itself was not discovered until 1905, but the caverns were known in pioneer times as a source of red clay, which when mixed with buttermilk produced a durable red paint.

During the Civil War the Confederate Army mined the cave for saltpeter for use in gunpowder. Some of their mining tools are on display, as well as moonshine equipment.

Descending to the lake on the Commercial Tour, you pass through a number of surreal chambers. There is the 600-foot-long Keel Room, where they made the paint. The Baby Grand Canyon is so rifted it resembles a miniature canyon. The Sand Room was used by settlers to store food. (The cave has a steady temperature of 58°F and is largely free of insects.) If you take the longer, Wild Tour, you'll also visit the Cat Chamber, where the remains of a Pleistocene jaguar were found.

There are glass-bottom boat trips on the lake, which occupies 4½ acres. So perfectly do the still, clear waters reflect the ceiling that at first glance there seems to be no lake at all.

The lake has been stocked with trout. Regularly fed in an environment free of predators (and fishermen), many reach old age and great size.

▶ Open daily except Christmas. Admission charged.

www.thelostsea.com
(423) 337-6616

17 Lost Sea. Boat tours allow visitors a leisurely view of the largest underground lake in the country.

18 Ducktown

Copperhill. In Ducktown follow signs to the Burra Burra Mine and the adjacent museum.

Picture this: From the edge of the museum parking lot, you look down upon a desertlike area of red earth, undulating and rifted, with scant and scrubby vegetation that extends into the distance. In the foreground of this landscape, far below you, is a chasm filled by a deep green lake.

The colors in this stark landscape, from soft pastels to glowing reds and copper tones, constantly change with the seasons and time of day. The barren beauty of the 56-square-mile area has prompted comparison with the Dakota Badlands. But this is Tennessee's Copper Basin, and the vista is man-made.

Full-time copper mining began in 1851, and the early settlement grew into Ducktown, named for Chief Duck, a Cherokee. Over the years a number of mines have flourished, and the creation of this surreal scene may be claimed

jointly by timber stripping, erosion, sulphur dioxide fumes, and subterranean blasting done 20 years ago to crumple the network of exhausted mines. The green lake is said to be 4,100 feet deep.

The Ducktown Basin Museum is located on the historic Burra Burra mine site where 300 acres of land have been set aside as a memorial to the devastation of the Copper Basin. After you finish your visit to the museum, you can drive a short distance to inspect the massive machinery used for mining. The museum proper displays items of local history.

▶ Site and museum open year-round. Admission charged for museum.

www.tnvacation.com/cities-towns/ducktown
(423) 496-3846

19 Abraham Lincoln Library and Museum

Lincoln Memorial University, Harrogate

In 1863 President Abraham Lincoln expressed to Gen. Oliver Otis Howard (founder of Howard University) the hope that after the Civil War, Howard would "do something for these people who have been shut out from the world all these years." He was referring to the loyal mountain youth of East Tennessee.

Howard carried through, founding Lincoln Memorial University in 1897. The museum, opened in 1977, is now among the top five devoted to the great president. It houses more than 30,000 objects, over 6,000 rare books, including regimental histories, and 2,000 pamphlets and is still growing. The museum is remarkable in melding the dark and light sides of Lincoln's life and the period of history he helped to shape.

Arranged thematically, the exhibits trace the various periods and undertakings of Lincoln's life, from his days as a rail splitter to the fateful night in Ford's Theatre. Among the many personal objects to be seen are a photograph of Lincoln's father, Thomas; the

20 Gray Fossil Site and Museum. Here a late Miocene period rhinoceros is being assembled on-site from bones discovered by accident in the East Tennessee mountains.

carriage belonging to Lincoln's Secretary of State, William H. Seward; and the silver-topped cane Lincoln carried the night he was shot.

▶ Open daily except major holidays and when the university is closed. Admission charged.

www.lmunet.edu/museum
(423) 869-6235

20 Gray Fossil Site and Museum

1212 Suncrest Dr., Gray
One of the most significant fossil finds of recent years, the Gray site was uncovered in 2000 during excavation for a highway in upper East Tennessee. The black clay differed from anything workers had seen in the region, and state geologists were called in. What emerged was an entire ecosystem, centered on a large watering hole some 4.5–7 million years old and rich in fossilized plants and animals of the late Miocene period. More than 60 types found so far include several new species, and fossils range from fish and turtles to extinct saber-toothed cats, tapirs, camels, shovel-tusked elephants, short-faced bears, and alligators.

The Gray Site Natural History Museum (adjacent to the site) is base camp for East Tennessee State University's paleontology department. You can observe working labs where fossils are assembled and prepared, see fossil exhibits and graphic representations of the ancient environment, and hear what it might have sounded like when the site teemed with life. Tours of the dig site include fossil hunting.

▶ Open daily. Charge for site tours.

21 ▶ Jonesborough Historic District. The oldest town west of the Appalachians became the portal to the Southwest in the days before the Louisiana Purchase of 1803.

www.grayfossilmuseum.com
(866) 202-6223

21 Jonesborough Historic District

Jonesborough
The oldest American town west of the Appalachians, Jonesborough was established in 1779 and later became the portal to the Southwest prior to the Louisiana Purchase in 1803. The picturesque community, filled with restaurants, unique shops, and bed-and-breakfasts, is the first town in Tennessee listed on the *National Register of Historic Places* and is intent on preserving its 200-year-old legacy of history and architecture.

Daily guided tours of historic Jonesborough, the central part of the town, begin in the visitors center at the History Museum, where the community's development is charted by displays featuring pioneer tools and building techniques, early trades, commerce, transportation, religion, education, and recreation.

One can enjoy the rich variety of architectural styles, with Victorian homes predominating on and near Main St. Among other highlights are the Chester Inn, the town's oldest commercial building (1797), and the Christopher Taylor House, a two-story log house where President Andrew Jackson once lived as a young lawyer. You'll pass the Mail Pouch building, formerly a saloon, and the Salt House, where salt was rationed to the townspeople during the Civil War. Also to be seen are some very fine pre–Civil War churches.

Jonesborough is home to the annual National Storytelling Festival, which draws some 10,000 visitors.

▶ Museum open year-round.

www.jonesboroughtn.org
(877) 913-1612

did you know ❓

Jonesborough was once the capital of Franklin, a short-lived state that was never recognized by Congress.

seasonal events

JANUARY
● Appalachia Fest—Pigeon Forge (*celebration of traditional mountain music*)

APRIL
● Cornbread Festival—South Pittsburg (*arts and crafts, children's activities, classic car show, beauty pageant, live entertainment, historic tour*)
● Mule Day Festival—Columbia (*mule and horse shows, arts and crafts, flea market, parade, square dance*)
● Riverfest Celebration—Clarksville (*live music, interactive entertainment, children's activities, live entertainment*)

MAY
● Strawberry Festival—Humboldt (*live entertainment, street dance, parade, beauty pageants*)

JUNE
● Secret City Festival—Oak Ridge (*arts and crafts, live entertainment, WWII living-history demonstrations, tours, children's activities*)

OCTOBER
● Spooky Days—Chattanooga (*storytelling, art activities, cider, s'mores*)
● Heritage Festival—Ames Plantation, Grand Junction (*live entertainment, demonstrations, living-history displays, antique auction*)
● Franklin Wine Festival—Franklin (*over 300 wines from around the country, food tastings, live entertainment*)
● Witches Wynd—Kingsport (*spooky atmosphere, storytellers relate chilling tales of the past*)

NOVEMBER
● Winter Magic Kickoff and Chili Cookoff—Gatlinburg (*over 3 million Winter Magic lights, sample chilis from local restaurants*)

DECEMBER
● Carols in the City—Cleveland (*Christmas-tree lighting, Santa Claus, caroling*)

www.tnvacation.com

TENNESSEE

Texas

The oil wells and cowboys that once defined Texas remain, as does the great diversity of the only state whose residents lived under six flags.

Brenham/Washington. An ox team does duty at Barrington Living History Farm near Washington-on-the-Brazos, where the Texas Declaration of Independence was signed in 1836 (see page 325).

In the Lone Star State the mountain ranges and scrubby deserts of West Texas give way to the fertile plains of the interior and the piney woods of the East. On this stage played out a drama documented in a petroleum museum in Midland, a vast cattle ranch on the bend of the Rio Grande, and a historic river port near the Arkansas border. Much earlier, the first residents left behind a pre-Columbian flint quarry in the Panhandle and a Mexican-border cave dwelling whose walls bear 4,000-year-old pictographs.

Wildlife lovers can visit the winter habitat of the endangered whooping crane on the Gulf Coast, while live-music fans can dance the night away at a historic dance hall in the Hill Country. Among the state's unexpected pleasures are a beautiful small canyon near Austin, a Brenham convent where the sisters raise miniature horses, and, in Brownsville, one of the country's finest zoos.

visit ➔ offthebeatenpathtrips.com

1 Panhandle-Plains Historical Museum

At West Texas A&M University, 2503 Fourth Ave., Canyon

The long and varied history of the northernmost section of Texas is captured in this well-conceived museum. One panoramic presentation, in chronological order, covers Paleozoic fossils, the culture of early man, the coming of the conquistadors, the Native American–frontier era, ranching, the petroleum boom, and modern industry.

Ranch life in the Panhandle is represented by saddles, branding irons, guns, and a chuck wagon with the aroma of coffee on the campfire. In the Pioneer Village are reconstructions of buildings that were once essential to frontier towns; all are authentically equipped and furnished.

"People of the Plains" tells the story of human occupation of the southern Great Plains over the past 14,000 years. This state-of-the-art exhibit compares the various ways different cultures have solved their needs for water, food, shelter, trade, and transportation—from prehistoric creatures to modern-day cowboys.

A century-long parade of fashion (1850–1950) is presented in a series of realistic settings. These displays change, as do those in the center's art galleries. One building is devoted to buggies, sleighs, wagons, and automobiles. Also on the grounds is the headquarters of the T-Anchor Ranch, the oldest original structure in the Panhandle.

1 Panhandle-Plains Historical Museum. An authentic chuck wagon complete with the aroma of fresh-brewed coffee harks back to early ranch life in the Panhandle.

▶ Open daily except winter holidays. Admission charged.

www.panhandleplains.org
(806) 651-2244

2 Alibates Flint Quarries National Monument

On Hwy. 136, about 6 miles south of Fritch. Watch for signs to Bates Canyon and the quarries.

To walk along the bluff here is to walk in the footsteps of the prehistoric people who first came to this place some 12,000 years ago in search of stone that was hard enough to kill the mammoths and buffalo upon which their subsistence depended. The Paleo-Indians, who discovered Alibates flint, used it for spear points, arrowheads, knives and scrapers, axes and awls, and other necessities. It was the only wealth they knew.

Flint is usually a solid color, but here it is rainbow-hued in infinite variations and patterns. The craftsmanship shown in the ancient articles made of this material is usually so superior to that of objects made of ordinary flint that the early artisans must have been responding to its beauty.

The quarries are shallow pits in the ground from 5 to 25 feet across, not much to see—except that they are the source of some of the oldest evidence we have of human technology in the continental United States. The only access to the site is by a two-hour guided walking tour from the information station at spectacular Bates Canyon on Lake Meredith. Tours are by reservation only.

You'll need sturdy shoes and a hat for protection from the hot sun. There's no water, so a canteen is a good idea.

▶ Open year-round except holidays. Reservations required.

www.nps.gov/alfl
(806) 857-3151

2 Alibates Flint Quarries National Monument. Paleo-Indians chipped flint into spear points here.

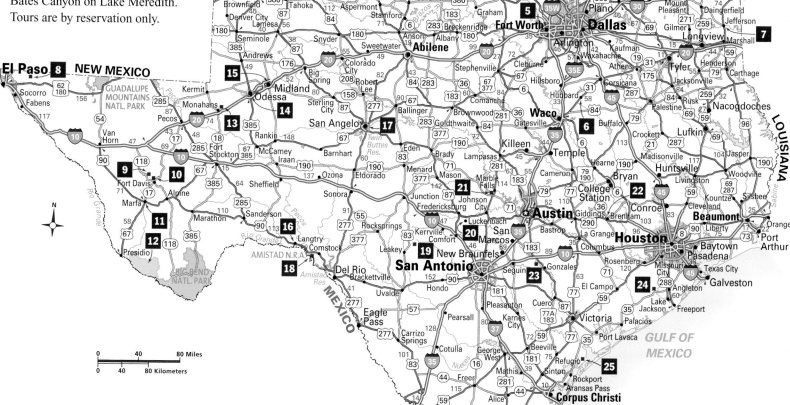

© 2009 GeoNova

3 Palo Duro Canyon State Park

Twelve miles east of Canyon on Hwy. 217

Calling Palo Duro Canyon "The Grand Canyon of Texas" is no idle boast: This multicolored world of rock is the second-largest canyon in the United States. Artist Georgia O'Keeffe, who lived for a time in the Panhandle town of Canyon, described Palo Duro as "filled with dramatic light and color," and the thousands who visit this scenic state park each year would agree.

Horseback riders, mountain bikers, campers, and picnickers descend on the canyon for relaxation or adventure. Longhorn cattle graze on the rim, the jumping-off point for a dramatic eight-mile drive to the canyon floor. The signature rock formation, the Lighthouse, towers above the nearly 30,000 acres of dry washes, side canyons, honey mesquite and soapberry trees, and riverbeds shaded by cottonwoods.

Bursting on the scene from June–mid-Aug. is the musical costume drama *Texas*. Staged in the Pioneer Amphitheater on the canyon floor, the extravaganza traces the struggles and triumphs of Texas Panhandle settlers of the nineteenth century.

▶ Open year-round. Admission charged.

www.palodurocanyon.com
(806) 488-2227

4 Grapevine

Northwest of Dallas

Wild mustang grapes spilled over the black-land prairie in 1844, when this settlement, one of the oldest in North Texas, started its life under the Lone Star Flag. Statehood was just around the

3 **Palo Duro Canyon State Park.** The landmark formation at the nation's second-largest canyon is aptly known as the Lighthouse.

corner. Although it's in one of the busiest corridors in Texas, Grapevine holds on to its history with a tenacious grip. Main St. itself is a historic district, preserved by descendants of the original settlers. At the Heritage Center artisans demonstrate and teach 150-year-old techniques. The Historical Museum fits nicely into an old railroad depot that dates from 1901.

The Tarantula, a refurbished 1896 steam locomotive with open-air patio cars, heads daily from the Cotton Belt Depot to Fort Worth's historic Stockyard Station. Willie Nelson, Brenda Lee, and the Judds made country-western history when they graced the stage at the Palace Theatre, which is the home of the Grapevine Opry.

▶ Open year-round.

www.grapevinetexasusa.com
(800) 457-6338

5 The National Cowgirl Museum and Hall of Fame

1720 Gendy St., Fort Worth

Golden girls of the golden West, all trailblazers in their own way, have a new building in which their achievements are honored. Almost 200 women, including U.S. Supreme Court Justice Sandra Day O'Connor, who is as comfortable in a saddle as she is on the bench, are in the Hall of Fame. Each year four to six women get the nod to enter the hall.

Bona fide ranch women, as well as more famous entertainers, rodeo competitors, artists, and writers, get their due here. Dale Evans and her stuntwoman, Alice Van Springsteen, are in the hall. The first pioneer woman to cross the Rockies, Narcissa Prentiss Whitman, and eight-time world-champion cowgirl Tad Lucas all possess the grit and spirit that make a true cowgirl.

The museum began in a library basement in Hereford and has made the move to Fort Worth's Western Heritage Center in the Cultural

District. Housed in a 33,000-square-foot building, the word "Cowgirls" is emblazoned across one side and an impressive rotunda contains the women's stories.

You'll find interactive exhibits, with listening stations telling about how committed a cowgirl has to be. And for wannabe cowgirls and their sidekicks wanting to experience a simulated wild ride in a Wild West show, a bronco is raring to go.

▶ Open daily year-round except winter holidays. Admission charged.

www.cowgirl.net
(817) 336-4475

6 Blackland Prairie Scenic Farm Roads

North of Hubbard

A 46-mile drive on farm roads of the fertile Blackland Prairie shows north-central Texas at its most scenic. From Hubbard, on TX-31, drive a mile north on US-171 and turn west on hilly FM-2114 (FM stands for farm-to-market). Take in

4 **Grapevine.** A wine-tasting room housed in a pretty 1890s cottage features Homestead wines, produced north of Grapevine in the fertile Red River Valley.

the lovely views on your way to tiny Penelope, then turn north onto FM-308 to pass through the hamlets of Malone and Irene to Mertens, on TX-22.

Beneath a huge sky studded with Texas-size clouds, farmhouses and rustic barns dot the gently rolling land. Cattle graze beside silver ponds shaded by oaks, elms, and mesquite, and the late-summer fields form an eye-popping patchwork of spent golden cornstalks, rust-colored milo, and emerald sorghum hay.

Before setting out, drive by the Victorian houses in the northwest section of Hubbard, then head to the history museum at Historic Hubbard High School, boasting a world-class doll collection.

www.hubbardtexas.net
(254) 576-2576 Hubbard City Hall

7 Jefferson

Junction of Hwy. 59 and Hwy. 49
In the 1840s steamboat captain William Perry moved to Jefferson from New England and saw potential in Big Cypress Creek, a tributary of the Red River. The captain oversaw its dredging, and soon steamboats from Shreveport and New Orleans were transporting cotton downstream and returning with manufactured goods. By the 1870s the inland port's volume of commerce was second only to that of the Gulf Coast city of Galveston.

In 1873 the new Texas and Pacific Railroad bypassed Jefferson. But what was a blow economically was a boon to historic preservation. Today the Excelsior House Hotel (built in the 1850s by Captain Perry) is the grand dame of area hotels and is a popular spot for breakfast. Another

5 ▶ **The National Cowgirl Museum and Hall of Fame.** Twelve murals in the rotunda showcase the lives of some of the most noted women of the American West. Among the Hall of Fame inductees is former Supreme Court Justice Sandra Day O'Connor.

architectural jewel is the House of the Seasons, whose murals and cupola are the star attractions; each of the cupola's four windows has glass reflecting a different season.

Hour-long boat tours of the Turning Basin, where the sternwheelers loaded and unloaded cargo, include narrations on the town's history and the diverse wildlife and vegetation of the bayou.

www.jefferson-texas.com
(888) 467-3529

8 Hueco Tanks State Historic Site

32 miles east of El Paso on Ranch Rd. 2775
Four massive granite hills rising from the floor of the Chihuahuan Desert are at the core of this intriguing 360-acre site—a world of rock labyrinths, alcoves, overhangs, and the huecos (hollows) that fill with water after a rain and are the source of the area's name. Not surprisingly, rock climbers and boulderers from far and wide converge on the park, sharing

company with hikers, campers, and birders attracted by an exceptional variety of avian species. Another natural curiosity is the tiny fairy shrimp, a branchiopod whose eggs can live in the huecos for more than a decade and then hatch a day or two after the hollows fill with rainwater.

From the first millennium A.D. to prehistoric times, Hueco Tanks was home to the Jornada Mongollon people, who left behind perhaps the most fascinating gallery of rock art in the American Southwest. The pictographs include human, animal, and mythological figures; geometric designs; and more than 200 paintings of faces, or "masks."

▶ Open year-round. Admission charged.

www.tpwd.state.tx.us/park/hueco/hueco.htm
(915) 857-1135

9 McDonald Observatory

Off TX-118, 14 miles northwest of Fort Davis
Almost 7,000 feet high, 160 miles away from the nearest major city,

and with two out of every three nights crisp, cloudless, and clear, Mount Locke and its neighbor Mount Fowlkes are perfect locations for studying the stars. So when a wealthy banker left the University of Texas a large part of his fortune in 1926 with instructions to build a telescope, this is where they built it.

Since then, the university has continued to develop this scientific site, adding more powerful telescopes as the technology has become available, making it one of the country's most important stations for astronomical research. The newest addition, the massive Hobby-Eberly telescope, began operations in 1999 and remains the world's fourth largest optical telescope.

The McDonald Observatory differs from many other research institutions, though, in the emphasis it puts on public outreach and education. Every year thousands of visitors—experienced amateur astronomers and interested novices alike—participate in the programs offered by the observatory, from daytime tours and live solar monitoring to the evening "star parties." Held three times a week, these are tours of the universe as seen through the observatory's smaller instruments and are equally fascinating for both children and adults.

For those interested in the full experience, the observatory schedules occasional "special viewing nights" for three of the larger telescopes. These nighttime events include dinner and usually sell out months in advance.

▶ Open daily except winter holidays.

http://mcdonaldobservatory.org
(432) 426-3640

10 ⏵ Fort Davis National Historic Site

101 Lt. Flipper Dr., Fort Davis

For nearly 30 years both infantry and cavalry troops from this frontier outpost protected mail and stagecoaches, freighters, emigrants, and travelers along the San Antonio–El Paso Rd., fending off Apache, Kiowa, and Comanche raiders. The Apache leader, Victorio, surrendered in 1880, signaling an end to the Native American wars in western Texas. The U.S. Army abandoned the fort in 1891.

The restored fort, now a unit of the National Park Service, stands with its face toward an open plain and its back against the cliffs of the majestic Davis Mountains. Fort Davis housed some 500 people in buildings that included living quarters, storehouses, a hospital, bakery, chapel, and guardhouse. Four all-black regiments were posted here after the Civil War, an important part of African-American history in the military.

The fort is considered one of the most intact surviving examples of a post–Civil War frontier military post in the Southwest. Of the 24 structures that have been restored on the outside, five have had their interiors restored and are refurnished. During periods of high visitation, costumed interpreters give tours.

A former enlisted men's barracks houses a visitors center, museum, and an auditorium, where a short video shows the fort's history. And an 1875 sound program plays at 11 A.M., 2 P.M., and 4 P.M.

▶ Open daily except major holidays. Admission charged.

www.nps.gov/foda
(432) 426-3224

11 ⏵ Marfa

Junction of Hwy. 90 and Hwy. 67

It could be said that outsiders put the West Texas village of Marfa on the map twice in 20 years: first in the mid-1950s, when Rock Hudson, Elizabeth Taylor, and James Dean called the Paisano Hotel home during filming of the now-classic movie *Giant;* second, when world-renowned minimalist sculptor Donald Judd moved to town in the mid '70s and converted Fort D. A. Russell into an arts center to again put the spotlight on Marfa. Today the Paisano Hotel (now listed on the *National Register of Historic Places*), the pastel 1886 courthouse, and assorted adobe buildings rub shoulders with art galleries and upscale restaurants. Still, Marfa's dusty high-desert soul remains.

Judd drew international attention to Marfa with the Chinati Foundation, a non-profit contemporary art museum exhibiting his own spare installations and works by Claes Oldenburg and others.

10 ⏵ Fort Davis National Historic Site. A row of Victorian porches in the men's housing section contrasts starkly with the rugged and rocky terrain of West Texas.

www.marfacc.com
432-729-4942 Marfa Chamber of Commerce

12 ⏵ Big Bend Ranch State Park

East of Presidio on Hwy. 170 and Hwy. 169

Big Bend National Park's little brother is anything but small. At 300,000 square acres, Big Bend Ranch is the Lone Star State's largest state park. At the same time, its remoteness makes it the least visited—a blessing for anyone seeking to get away from it all.

Visitors who take State Hwy. 169 into the heart of the park are hit with one breathtaking vista after another. Canyons, waterfalls, and the Solitario—the enormous collapsed caldera of an extinct volcano—are set in the Chisos mountains. Hikers have more than 60 trails to choose from, canoers can paddle Colorado and Close canyons, and overnighters can either pitch a tent or enjoy full-service lodging at the Saucedo ranch-house complex.

With its juniper woodlands at high elevations and cactus-studded desert grasslands below, the park is home to 300 species of birds, 30 kinds of snakes, and a wide variety of interesting mammals.

▶ Open year-round. Admission charged.

www.tpwd.state.tx.us/spdest/findadest/ parks/big_bend_ranch
(432) 358-4444

13 ⏵ Monahans Sandhill State Park

Monahans

Undulating dunes rise to heights of 70 feet above a table-flat landscape, remnants of a sea that was here in the Permian period some 280 million years ago. Part of a vast dune field extending for several hundred miles into New Mexico, most of the 3,840-acre park is now stabilized by vegetation; many dunes, however, are still active—they are shaped and reshaped by the incessant winds.

An interpretive center displays local natural history, including the flora and fauna of the area, and an interactive exhibit features the variety of wildlife found here.

A self-guiding trail begins at the interpretive center. Among the highlights of this short walk are sand sagebrush, mesquite, and the useful prairie yucca. Native Americans used yucca fibers for rope, the roots for soap, and other parts of the plant for food.

Scaled quail, Harris's hawks, cactus wrens, and other desert birds are often seen year-round, and many migratory birds stop off. The park's field checklist includes some 80 species. Trailer sites and picnic spots are located among the dunes.

▶ Open year-round.

www.tpwd.state.tx.us/park/monahans
(432) 943-2092

14 ▶ The Presidential Museum

4919 E. University, Odessa

Not long after President John F. Kennedy's assassination in November 1963, a group of Odessa citizens decided to dedicate a new museum to those who have held the nation's highest office. In the Hall of the Presidents there are portraits of each chief executive, along with personal memorabilia.

Exhibits show the evolution of ideas, techniques, and materials that have been used in campaigning for office, including banners, buttons, posters, and bumper stickers that feature the names and faces of winners—as well as losers all but forgotten today.

The important breakthrough of radio and television campaigning is documented. Another advance, not as obvious but important, too, was the advent of campaign buttons made of celluloid. With this new material it was possible to show the candidates' likenesses in color instead of black and white. An interesting curiosity was the use in 1896 of "soap babies": baby-shaped cakes of soap colored either silver or gold as reminders of an important monetary question.

America's first ladies are represented by a collection of exquisite dolls, each in her inauguration ball gown, with matching accessories and in the hairstyle worn on that memorable occasion.

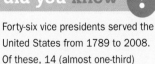

did you know ?

Forty-six vice presidents served the United States from 1789 to 2008. Of these, 14 (almost one-third) became president of the nation: 5 were elected, 8 were sworn into office after the death of a president, and 1 after a president resigned.

14 ▶ The Presidential Museum. Portraits and personal memorabilia of every U.S. president are exhibited here. Other displays document the evolution of presidential campaigns, from the first campaign buttons and giveaways to radio and TV commercials.

▶ Open Tues.–Sat. year-round except major holidays. Admission charged.

www.presidentialmuseum.org
(432) 363-7737

15 ▶ The Petroleum Museum

Exit 136 off I-205, Midland

This extraordinarily creative and surprising museum will fascinate people of all ages—whether or not they have an interest in the subject of oil. Exhibits move, talk, and invite participation. The persons in old photos recount in local accents anecdotes from their lives. A spin of a dial allows you to win or lose a theoretical fortune in oil wells. A fascinating film takes you on a plane ride looking for leaks in a pipeline, while a full-size plane above, suspended from the ceiling, sways along with the film.

Highlights in one of the museum's three wings are the rooms that re-create the boomtown experience of the 1920s, and an enormous walkthrough replica of the Permian Basin Sea, with nearly 200,000 realistic models of coral, fish, and other marine creatures—all of which bear upon the geology of petroleum deposits. More than 200 million years of time and unimaginable pressure within the Earth converted the materials in reefs like this one to the oil and natural gas we use today.

Displays in another wing feature the human history of the area and include branding irons, barbed wire, windmills, and tepees. Historical paintings by Tom Lovell are complemented by audiotapes. The North Wing shows an oil-well blowout that no visitor will ever forget. Outside the museum, in the Oil Patch Exhibit, you'll find the world's largest collection of antique oil-drilling equipment. A new museum wing features seven of the Jim Hall Chaparral race cars and the history behind them.

▶ Open daily except winter holidays. Admission charged.

www.petroleummuseum.org
(432) 683-4403

16 ▶ Judge Roy Bean Center

Torres Ave., Langtry

In the last decades of the 19th century, this part of Texas was still very much the Wild West, and law enforcement was a continuing problem. A former Pony Express rider and saloon keeper named Roy Bean was appointed justice of the peace and became known as the "Law West of the Pecos" (the Pecos River is about 10 miles distant).

Where Bean dispensed his quick version of justice along with hard liquor in his combination courtroom, billiard hall, and saloon, the modern visitors center now dispenses travel information and features dioramas with earphones.

Listeners hear about the life and times of the hard-bitten judge, including such colorful stories as that of the world championship Maher-Fitzsimmons prizefight he staged on an island in the Rio Grande in defiance of the governmental authorities in the United States, Texas, and Mexico.

Behind the visitors center is the restored courtroom-saloon, with its potbellied stove, antique bottles, and photographs of Bruno, the judge's pet bear. The saloon is named the Jersey Lilly for the English actress Lillie Langtry, whom Bean greatly admired. (She was called the Jersey Lily after her birthplace, and the misspelling of Lily is a sign painter's error.)

Actually, the town was probably called Langtry after a railroad worker of that name, but Bean convinced the actress that it had been named for her, and she accepted his invitation to visit in 1904. The judge died, however, months before she arrived. The visitors center also has a five-acre garden with more than 100 species of cacti and other native plants.

▶ Open daily year-round except major holidays.

www.traveltex.com
(432) 291-3340

17 Fort Concho National Historic Landmark

630 S. Oakes St., San Angelo
Established by the U.S. Army in December 1867, Fort Concho started as a tent city and later developed into a large military post, serving the vast territory of West Texas until 1889. Hundreds of soldiers, infantry, and cavalry—white and black (including the famed African-American Buffalo soldiers)—called Fort Concho home for 22 years.

The army built and staffed a wide range of forts west of the Mississippi after the Civil War to protect settlers from Native American attack and to guard mail, stage, and railroad building lines, as well as to serve as a general police force in a wide-open region. Often the army found itself in the middle of competing interests among settlers, Native American tribes, buffalo hunters, and government/business interests back East.

Today the fort prospers as a National Historic Landmark owned and operated by the city of San Angelo, with 40 acres and 24 original, rebuilt, and restored structures. Tours show up to 10 of those buildings, including the visitors center, artillery exhibit, soldiers barracks, headquarters, hospital, chapel, and an officers quarters. The fort has special events, displays, and living-history festivals all year.

▶ Open daily year-round. Admission charged.

www.fortconcho.com
(325) 481-2646

18 Seminole Canyon State Park and Historic Site

Off US-90, 9 miles west of Comstock
Water can erode rock into spectacular formations, and paradoxically, its effect may be most dramatic where it is scarce, as in this rugged area. Near the park a high bridge offers a magnificent view of the Pecos River Canyon, and visitors to the park can join a guided tour to explore Seminole Canyon itself. The streambed will most likely be dry, but the effect of its flow of water through the ages is evident in the width of the canyon and in the polished surface of its limestone.

Some of the oldest works of mankind are also in evidence here. Fate Bell Shelter is one of the oldest cave dwellings, housing layer upon layer of large, colorful pictographs that were painted on the rock walls 4,000 years ago. They depict animals, people, and some mysterious figures that may never be identified.

Exhibits at the visitors center, where the guided hikes begin, include a realistic life-size representation of a family living in a rock shelter; another reproduces pictographs painted in other caves.

Other displays depict local sheep- and goat-ranching and history of the early railroad. Visitors can enjoy the desert area, especially attractive in spring, and a gentle three-mile walk to an overlook above the Rio Grande. The 2,173-acre park has a picnic area overlooking Seminole Canyon.

▶ Open daily year-round. Canyon tours Wed.–Sun. Admission charged.

www.tpwd.state.tx.us
(432) 292-4464

20 ▶ **Luckenbach.** The empty dance hall, dating all the way back to 1850, awaits the dancers and music lovers who flock nightly to this isolated Hill Country hamlet.

19 Lost Maples State Natural Area

Five miles north of Vanderpool on Ranch Rd. 187
When glaciers advanced over North America during the last Ice Age and later retreated, the Uvalde bigtooth maple kept its foothold in the canyons at the western edge of the geological region known as the Edwards Plateau. Today a canyon carved by the Sabinal River is home to the so-called Lost Maples, which every autumn change the Texas Hill Country's muted greens to a blaze of red and gold.

The moist, cool microclimate in this 2,200-acre park makes it a paradise for birders, hikers, and campers at any time of year. Endangered golden-cheeked warblers and black-caped vireos might be glimpsed on the 10 1/2 miles of wooded trails, and campers can choose from primitive and serviced campsites. Leaf-peepers typically stick to the popular 0.8-mile Maple Trail.

Visitors can fish in the spring-fed ponds, and anyone and everyone can splash about in the river or one of the park's many swimming holes.

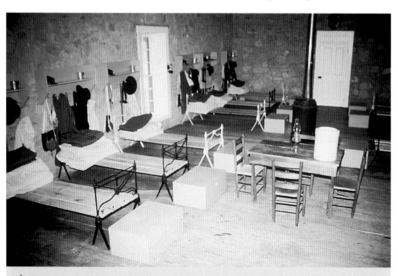

17 ▶ **Fort Concho National Historic Landmark.** When the fort was occupied, as many as 50 soldiers bunked in this barracks, now authentically restored.

► Open year-round. Admission charged.

www.tpwd.state.tx.us/spdest/findadest/
parks/lost_maples

(830) 966-3413

20 Luckenbach

*Seventeen miles south of
Fredericksburg on Ranch Rd. 1376*
The proverbial spot in the road,
Luckenbach is as much a state of
mind as a town. Known for its
association with country singing
stars Waylon Jennings and Willie
Nelson, it distills the heart and soul
of the Austin/Texas Hill Country
vibe. The town motto? "Everybody
is somebody in Luckenbach."

The barnlike dance hall, dating
from 1850, is action central. Live
music is on tap nightly at what has
been called the best dance hall in
the state. The general store and
post office building is as rustic and
atmospheric as they come. And
aside from a barbecue-and-burgers
joint and the Snail Creek Hat
Company, that's about it. And
that's how the handful of residents
and the stream of music-loving
visitors like it.

Then there's the scenery. To
drive to Luckenbach is to appreciate the beauty of the Hill Country's
stony green rivers, cedar-flecked
slopes, gnarled oaks, and multicolored native wildflowers.

www.luckenbachtexas.com
(830) 997-3224

21 Westcave Preserve

*West of Bee Cave, on Hamilton
Pool Rd., west of Austin*
A 600-year-old bald cypress tree
with Spanish moss hanging from
its branches like wispy tentacles
stands sentinel over this fragile 30-
acre nature preserve in Travis
County. Neighboring tall trees
form a canopy that keeps moisture
in and blocks out the sun.

The 35- to 125-foot sheer limestone walls of the canyon are a
natural barrier to destructive
intruders. Almost hidden along the
banks of the Pedernales River, this
place of profound beauty has been
kept safe through the combined
efforts of nature and man. A foundation has been set up to preserve
the site and to educate future generations who will protect the land.

After centuries of erosion, a
large limestone shelf collapsed into
a streambed more than 100,000
years ago, creating the canyon. A
spring-fed waterfall courses down
40 feet, nurturing the moss and
maidenhair ferns that feed off the
canyon walls.

Guided tours take place four
times a day on weekends down to
the canyon's semitropical bottom,
where wild orchids grow in a cool
emerald green grotto one-third of a
mile down. It is a world away from
the arid grassland at the top, with
its cactus and ash juniper trees.

The tours leave from an educational center, opened in 2003,
whose exhibits explain the natural
processes that created and sustain
the wonderland in the valley.

► Open weekends year-round.

www.westcave.org
(830) 825-3442

22 Brenham/Washington

TX-105, Washington County
For two small towns on a state
highway, Brenham and
Washington are chock-full of
Texas history and surprising dis-
coveries. A good time to visit is
April, when bluebonnets blanket
the hillsides and fields on State
Hwy. 105.

Speaking of flowers, you can
literally "stop and smell the roses"
at Brenham's Antique Rose
Emporium; unlike modern hybrid
varieties, the roses of old are full
of fragrance. Amid the shops of
Brenham's historic Main Street
district is the Brenham Heritage
Museum, with a nineteenth-century
steam fire engine sitting outside.
But the hottest spot in town is
also the "coldest": Blue Bell
Creameries has been churning out
Texas's favorite ice cream there
since 1907.

22 Brenham/Washington. The roses
at the Antique Rose Emporium are
coveted heirloom varieties.

Driving northeast to Washington,
stop at the Monastery of St. Clare
Miniature Horse Farm, where
Franciscan Poor Clare nuns
support themselves by raising
miniature horses and selling their
handmade ceramics.

In Washington, Washington-on-
the-Brazos State Historic Site
boasts a replica of Independence
Hall, the site of Texas's declaration
of independence from Mexico on
March 2, 1836. The centerpiece of
the Barrington Living History
Farm is the family home of Anson
Jones, the last president of the
Republic of Texas.

www.brenhamtexas.com
(979) 836-3695

22 Brenham/Washington. A sister greets one of her diminutive charges at the Monastery
of St. Clare Miniature Horse Farm.

23 Palmetto State Park

78 Park Rd. 11S., Gonzales

In this part of Texas, where the land is flat or gently rolling and the horizon is expansive, this park comes as a delightful surprise, with its unusual mixture of natural environments and its 550 species of Eastern and Western plants, including the dwarf palmetto.

The two-mile scenic roadway from the park entrance to the San Marcos River climbs a small hill above a rich green pasture dotted with cattle and interspersed with woodland, in striking contrast to the sculptural forms of the cactus nearby. From the hilltop the road continues through a natural arcade of pecan, elm, and oak to the trails, campsites, and picnic grounds built on the banks of the river, which flows through the 270-acre park.

Birding is best in winter; more than 240 species have been spotted, including kingfishers, cardinals, red-shouldered hawks, and the caracara, or Mexican eagle. One of the hiking trails is gravel-surfaced and easy to walk. Swimming, tubing, and boating are enjoyed in the river, and fishermen appreciate the small oxbow lake for its bass, crappie, and catfish. The park is a checkpoint on the Texas Water Safari, a 419-mile canoe race held in July.

▶ Open year-round. Admission charged.

www.tpwd.state.tx.us
(830) 672-3266

24 Varner-Hogg State Historic Park

1702 N. 13th St., West Columbia

The aura of grace, charm, peace, and quiet that one encounters on this former plantation is surely a reflection of its long and productive past as part of Texas and Southern culture. In 1824 Martin Varner was one of 300 applicants granted land when Texas was still a province of Mexico. He built a cabin, worked the land, and raised stock for about 10 years before heading on to the less populated parts of northeast Texas.

Under a succession of subsequent owners, this remained a working plantation until 1901, when James Stephen Hogg, a former governor of the state, bought the place to use as a country estate. His belief that there was oil on the land was substantiated in 1917, nine years after his death.

In 1920 the main house was remodeled by Hogg's eldest son, William, and refurbished by his daughter Ima. In 1957 the plantation was deeded to the state by Miss Hogg and named for its first and last owners. The house is furnished in the style of prosperous planters of the mid-19th century.

▶ Open Tues.–Sun. year-round. Admission charged.

www.thc.state.tx.us
(979) 345-4656

25 Aransas National Wildlife Refuge

FM-2040, Austwell

At this preserve on San Antonio Bay, the plants, the birds, and the other Gulf Coast wildlife are protected from the incursion and depredation of mankind. Fittingly enough, the refuge has played a major role in the saving of the whooping crane, a magnificent bird that hunters had reduced to near extinction. Only 15 were here in 1940. By 1985 there were 69 adults and 14 young (a record number) on the refuge and from 150 to 180 in America. A platform with mounted telescopes provides an overview of the otherworldly waterscape and distant grassy islands.

The 54,829 acres are none too many for their purpose. Up to 350 species of birds winter here, and

there are deer, javelinas, wild hogs, raccoons, armadillos, alligators, and turtles, while frogs thrive in the lakes and sloughs. Live oak, red bay, and hackberry are the dominant trees along the 16 miles of roadway through the preserve.

On the well-marked nature trails be sure to wear sturdy shoes and keep an eye out for rattlesnakes.

There are excellent wildlife displays at the visitors center, with weekend films of the various forms of wildlife on the refuge. Whooping cranes linger from Nov.–Mar. It is hot in summer, and mosquitoes are abundant. Insect repellent is recommended.

▶ Open year-round.

www.fws.gov/southwest/refuges/texas/aransas
(361) 286-3559

26 Padre Island National Seashore

Park Rd. 22, Corpus Christi

Looking at the hard sand beach and grass-covered dunes of the 67-mile-

23 **Palmetto State Park.** One of the park's oft-visited places is the group picnic pavilion, a 1930s stone structure equipped with picnic tables and a kitchen.

26 ▶ **Padre Island National Seashore.** Any footprints seen in the most isolated reaches of this barrier island are more likely to have been left by waterfowl than by beachgoers.

long island, one might think that this is a stable environment. But as on all barrier islands, the scene is ever changing. And this, of course, is part of the attraction.

Also ever changing (but annually consistent) is the great variety of birds seen here in their season. Winter residents include sandhill cranes, snow geese, and redhead and pintail ducks, while in spring falcons and a variety of songbirds return from their winter sojourn to the south. Great blue herons, gulls, terns, and brown and white pelicans may be seen year-round. All in all, from 350 to 400 species have been sighted.

The northern part of the island, around Malaquite Beach, is sometimes crowded. Swimming is good here, but there are no lifeguards on duty. Ordinary passenger automobiles can go several miles farther on the beach, but south of that point a four-wheel-drive vehicle is required. Beachcombing and fishing are popular, and there are some good shell beaches between 10 and 20 miles south of the ranger station. Glass, nails, and the stinging purple jellyfish (Portuguese man-of-war) make bare feet inadvisable.

▶ Open year-round. Admission charged.

www.nps.gov/pais
(361) 949-8173

27 Gladys Porter Zoo

500 Ringgold St., Brownsville
One of the most delightful open-plan zoos in the country sits on the border with Mexico. A 31-acre preserve built on an old channel of the Rio Grande, the Gladys Porter Zoo is home to 1,600-plus animals from 464 species (47 of them endangered), all living in the open air amid tropical and semi-tropical plants and flowing waterways.

The four sections—Tropical America, Indo-Australia, Asia, and Africa—acquaint zoo-goers with a world of wildlife. Separate sections spotlight bears, California sea lions, and Komodo dragons. Small World allows children to interact with domesticated animals.

Visitors can't get enough of the three generations of gorillas who live on their own small island. Another star attraction is Macaw Canyon, where three species of macaws make their home in a replica of the kind of canyon found in their Mexican habitat. The Free Flight Aviary is the place to see dozens of species of birds, including many that the zookeepers call "our free-loaders"—great kiskadees, gallinules, and others that drop in from the wild.

▶ Open year round. Admission charged.

www.gpz.org
(956) 546-7181

27 ▶ **Gladys Porter Zoo.** Caribbean flamingos reside in the zoo's Tropical America section, one of six showcasing the world's fauna and flora. The ring-tailed lemurs at right perch on a tree limb in the Africa section, home to a number of rare species.

seasonal events

MARCH
- North Texas Irish Festival—Dallas (*Celtic music festival, workshops, arts and crafts, regional food*)

JUNE
- Texas Blueberry Festival—Nacogdoches (*blueberry picking, cooking contests, live music, car show, arts and crafts*)
- Bay Jammin' Concert and Cinema Series—Corpus Christi (*summer-long outdoor concerts and outdoor movies*)
- Texas Folklife Festival—San Antonio (*crafts, food, folkways, music from the state's more than 40 different cultures*)

JULY
- Great Texas Balloon Race—Longview (*balloon flights, demonstrations, live music, arts and crafts, children's activities*)

AUGUST
- Texas International Fishing Tournament—South Padre Island (*week-long fishing tournament, contests, games*)
- Hotter'n Hell Hundred—Wichita Falls (*bike racing and endurance event, road and mountain biking, consumer show, food and entertainment*)
- Marfa Lights Festival—Marfa (*live entertainment, arts and crafts, local food, street dance, sporting events*)

SEPTEMBER
- Austin City Limits Music Festival—Austin (*massive pop, rock, country, and world music festival*)
- Grapefest—Grapevine (*wine tastings, grape stomp, auction, carnival, local food, children's activities*)

OCTOBER
- State Fair of Texas—Dallas (*three-week fair, live music, agricultural displays, parades, light show, arts and crafts, food, sporting events*)

www.traveltx.com

Utah

Rock is sculpted into fantastic shapes in a state boasting five major national parks and more than a few hidden corners.

Goblin Valley State Park. Eerie formations in Utah's Castle Valley were dubbed goblins after their discovery. Years later they were protected by a state park (see page 332).

Red rock fantasies and a many-hued petrified forest . . . a sparkling mountain lake and lush marshes harboring waterfowl . . . ski trails and scenic drives. Travelers in Utah discover one pleasure after another. In fact, the Beehive State may offer more wonderment per square mile than any other in the Lower 48.

Take in the stunning view from Dead Horse Point and see the fossilized bones of the giant reptiles that once ruled the land at Dinosaur National Monument. Gaze in awe at the ruins of six 10,000-year-old pueblos at Hovenweep and walk the streets of Spring City, a beautifully preserved 19th-century pioneer town. At your leisure take advantage of the state's inviting places to picnic, boat, fish, swim, hike, or observe winged creatures of many species.

visit ➤ **offthebeatenpathtrips.com**

1 ▶ Bear Lake State Park

1030 N. Bear Lake Blvd., Garden City

There are two separate areas in this lakeside park, each of them offering access to the turquoise waters of Bear Lake, which covers 112 square miles and is surrounded by exquisite mountain scenery.

Sailing, powerboating, and fishing are the main attractions at the state marina in the northern section. On the south shore near Laketown, at Rendezvous Beach, the emphasis is on swimming, although here, too, boats may be rented or trailered in. Four campgrounds—Willow, Cottonwood, Birch, and Big Creek—are attractively situated along the shore.

Fishermen hook cutthroat trout here and mackinaws that can weigh up to 30 pounds. Ice fishing for smelt—like ciscoes—is popular in winter. Sandhill cranes are common in the park's meadows and wetlands from late May–early June.

▶ Open year-round. Admission charged.

www.stateparks.utah.gov
(435) 946-3343

2 ▶ Spiral Jetty

15 miles southwest of Golden Spike National Historic Site, off Rte. 83. Directions available at the Golden Spike NHS Visitors Center.

1 ▶ Bear Lake State Park. Sailboats are a common sight at the northern portion of Bear Lake, high in the Rocky Mountains. The marina has more than 300 boat slips.

Conceived by American sculptor and visionary Robert Smithson, *Spiral Jetty* successfully intertwines landscape and sculpture. This earthwork—built of mud, salt crystals, basalt rocks, earth, and water—projects into the otherworldly pink-tinged waters of the northern Great Salt Lake and forms a massive counterclockwise coil 15 feet wide and 1,500 feet long. Completed in 1970 *Spiral Jetty* is considered an icon of late 20th-century art and has been an inspiration to generations of contemporary artists.

This monumental sculpture has been underwater for much of its existence, but it re-emerged in 2002. *Sprial Jetty* is accessible only by dirt roads through an isolated area and four-wheel-drive vehicles are recommended. The nearest visitor facilities are located at the Golden Spike National Historic Site, 15 miles away. *Spiral Jetty* is in the collection of the Dia Art Foundation.

▶ Golden Spike NHS Visitors Center is open daily except major holidays.

www.spiraljetty.org
(212) 989-5566 Dia Art Foundation

3 Bear River Migratory Bird Refuge

Exit 363 off I-15, 15 miles west of Brigham City

Countless waterfowl and other birds find their way annually to this 74,000-acre refuge in northern Utah, an expanse of lush marshes at the mouth of the river, where it flows into the Great Salt Lake, making it a paradise for anyone with a passion for sighting and studying birds.

A mosaic of diverse brackish and freshwater habitats, the marshes nonetheless form the largest freshwater component of the Great Salt Lake ecosystem. Surrounded by the arid desertlike terrain of Utah, the wetlands provide an unexpected oasis for waterfowl; they are a critical habitat for the thousands of migrating birds that ply their way along both the Pacific and Central flyways.

Congress established the sanctuary in 1928 as a feeding and breeding ground for migratory fowl. The refuge has since been designated as a Western Hemisphere Shoreline Reserve Network Site, and it received the National Audubon Society accolade of Important Bird Area. Tours are available, and a wildlife center offers a wetland diorama and other exhibits.

▶ Open year-round Mon.–Sat. except national holidays.

www.fws.gov/bearriver
(435) 734-6425

Spiral Jetty. Salt crystals that formed on the jetty throw the artwork into clear relief.

4 Mirror Lake Scenic Byway

SR-150, near Kamas

If you have ever had the need to "get away from it all," Mirror Lake Scenic Byway provides a splendid escape route. Starting at Kamas, a leisurely drive along this 78-mile road heads east through the backcountry wilderness of the Uinta-Wasatch-Cache National Forest high atop the Uinta Mountain range. Traversing pine-covered high-altitude terrain, it climbs to an elevation of 10,682 feet at Bald Mountain Pass before descending past the tranquil waters of Mirror Lake and finally continuing on to Evanston.

Convenient "picture spots" along the way afford views of spectacular alpine meadows, jagged rugged peaks, and cascading waterfalls. Interpretive centers introduce the visitor to the local fauna and the rich array of mountain flora. If you decide to stay awhile, hotel and camping accommodations are available year-round. The high-altitude cross-country skiing trails along the mountain ridge are especially inviting during the winter months.

www.utah.com/byways/mirror_lake.htm
(801) 466-6411

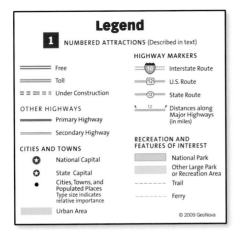

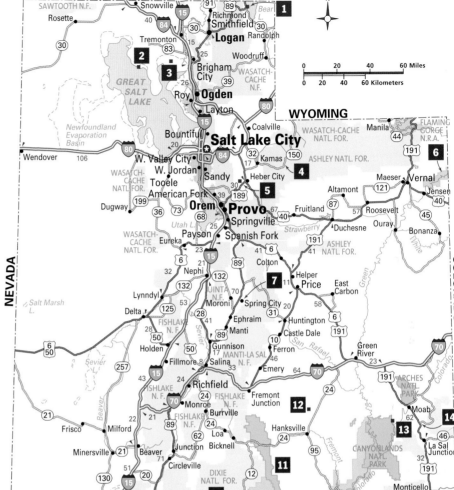

8 **Kolob Canyons, Zion National Park.** Sagebrush, the endless sky, and towering rock formations on the far horizon paint an unforgettable picture for travelers.

5 Soldier Hollow
Olympic Venue

Soldier Hollow Ln., Midway

During the 2002 Olympic winter games, Soldier Hollow hosted 38 events in all, including cross-country, biathlon, Nordic combined, and paralympics. Athletes and officials proclaimed this one of the best-designed Nordic ski courses in the world because spectators rarely lost sight of competitors.

The 31-kilometer track now hosts a variety of activities and special events in an area that is typically 15 degrees cooler than temperatures in Salt Lake City. Now that the Olympics are history, this 600-acre corner of northern Utah's 23,000-acre Wasatch Mountain State Park has embarked on an ambitious plan to become a year-round travel destination as well as Olympic training ground.

One new summer offering for tourists is the biathlon, which is essentially a combination of Nordic skiing and target shooting. The event evolves into either a run-and-shoot or mountain bike-and-shoot exercise. Other summer activities include an in-line skate-and-shoot, wheelchair-and-shoot, and a world-class golf course.

For the winter Soldier Hollow hosts Nordic skiing, snowshoeing, and tubing. A fully equipped shop rents cross-country skis, boots, and poles. A separate 700-foot tubing hill is also available.

www.soldierhollow.com
(435) 654-2002

6 Dinosaur National Monument

Quarry Area, off SR-149, 7 miles north of Jensen, UT; Canyon Area, US-40, 2 miles east of Dinosaur, CO.

Dinosaur National Monument is a legacy of rivers, past and present. Here, preserved in the sands of an ancient river, is a time capsule from the world of dinosaurs. This land has revealed many secrets of the past, but there is much more to Dinosaur than dinosaurs.

The Canyon Area, for example, preserves the canyons of the Green and Yampa rivers, rich with human history and geological features that are easily viewed from the 31-mile Harpers Corner Scenic Drive.

At the Quarry Area visitors can take an 11-mile auto tour and see petroglyphs and great views of the Green River. This drive with dramatic canyon scenery has brought as much fame to Dinosaur as its fossils have. More remote areas can be explored along several rugged, unpaved roads and by backpacking and river trips (permits required).

▶ Visitors center open year-round except winter holidays; Canyon Area Visitor Center open seasonally.

www.nps.gov/dino
(435) 781-7700

7 Spring City

While many communities claim that they have been saved by being astride the interstate highway system, the fact that I-15 bypasses Sanpete Valley has actually saved what has been described as the best concentration of houses, structures, and cultural elements reflecting 19th-century Mormon Utah in the state.

One of many small towns along "Heritage" Hwy. 89, Spring City is in the heart of what is called Little Denmark after the Scandianavian pioneers who setled here. The town, which is listed on the *National Register of Historic Places,* is now home to a growing community of artists and craftspeople attracted by the historic architecture and mountain scenery. If you want to see the inside of some of the remarkable buildings, come for Spring City Heritage Days and Home Tour the Saturday before Memorial Day.

www.springcitycorp.com
(435) 462-2244 City Hall
(435) 462-2211 Tours

8 Kolob Canyons, Zion National Park

Exit 40 off I-15, Springdale

Spectacular geological formations and a wide variety of environments make Kolob Canyons a place of exceptional beauty and interest. Within this less-used section of Zion National Park are the park's

6 **Dinosaur National Monument.** At the visitors center, an *Allosaurus* skeleton stands near murals depicting dinosaurs as they appeared 100 million years ago.

highest peak, 8,726-foot Horse Ranch Mountain, and the world's longest freestanding natural span, the Kolob Arch.

A five-mile paved auto route into the five Finger Canyons of the Kolob is marked by 14 numbered stops keyed to an accompanying pamphlet available at the visitors center. The road winds between canyon walls of reddish Navajo sandstone sculpted by 13 million years of geological upheaval and erosion into the numerous buttes, arches, and ridges we see today.

Part of the road follows Hurricane Fault, a 200-mile-long fracture in the Earth's crust, which elevated the land to the east nearly a mile. The change in altitude from valley to clifftop creates temperature differences averaging between 10° and 15°F. As a result, three distinct ecological zones can be observed in the canyons, from the valley's semiarid juniper woodland to the lush forests of aspen, fir, and pine crowning Timber Top Mountain.

A strenuous hiking trail, requiring eight hours for a round-trip, leads from the canyon road to

Kolob Arch. Backcountry camping is allowed with a permit.

▶ Open year-round.

www.nps.gov/zion
(435) 772-3256

---

9 **Coral Pink Sand Dunes State Park**

South of Mount Carmel Junction
You will hear the sound of revving motors here, because the 2,000 acres of rolling dunes in this 3,730-acre park attract dirt bike and dune buggy enthusiasts from far and wide. The sand is extremely fine, and off-road vehicles should have paddle-type tires.

The coral-pink dunes are beautiful, especially just before sundown, when they come alive with shifting shadows. Backpackers will find the campground here an excellent staging point for challenging, unmarked hikes through butte and mesa country. Be wary, however; rattlesnakes, black widow spiders, and scorpions thrive in this desert climate.

A 256-acre conservation area prohibits motorized vehicles in order to protect the coral-pink beetle, found nowhere else in the world. Birders are likely to see scrub jays and hummingbirds.

▶ Park and campground open year-round. Admission charged.

www.stateparks.utah.gov
(435) 648-2800

---

10 **Escalante Petrified Forest State Park**

Off SR-12, Escalante
The petrified forest in this 1,350-acre park is among the most remarkable in the country. In the Late Jurassic Period millions of

years ago, the area was a vast plain occasionally flooded by streams powerful enough to transport whole fallen trees. The trees grew heavier as they became water-logged and eventually sank to the river bottoms, where they were covered with gravel and silt. Over the ages water percolated through the soil, and as the wood cells dissolved, they were replaced by silica as well as oxides of iron and manganese. The results can be seen in the startling reds, yellows, purples, and other colors in the petrified logs scattered throughout the park.

Hikers enjoy the moderately difficult Petrified Forest Trail and the more strenuous Trail of Sleeping Rainbow, which wind their way through the ancient forest. The Wide Hollow reservoir offers opportunities for swimming, boating, and fishing.

▶ Open year-round. Admission charged.

www.stateparks.utah.gov
(435) 826-4466

---

11 **Capitol Reef National Park**

SR-24, 10 miles east of Torrey
Magnificent canyon landscapes, well-maintained hiking trails, and a 25-mile scenic drive make this desert park a backcountry enthusiast's delight. The primary feature of its rugged wilderness is a 100-mile-long ridge, or "reef," created by a buckling of the Earth's crust as it was thrust upward by subterranean pressure.

Millennia of erosion and other geological forces have carved a stunning gallery of canyons, arches, towers, and buttes. One particularly striking dome, which is reminiscent of the U.S. Capitol in Washington, inspired the reef's name.

On the canyons' sandstone walls, one can still see the glyphs carved by the Fremont People, who inhabited the area from A.D. 800 to 1200. Later the Paiute Native Americans lived here, and in the 1880s Mormon settlers planted orchards that were so successful their community eventually came to be called Fruita. Today the Mormons' 1896 school-house can be toured, and the orchards, about a mile from the visitors center, are maintained by

park personnel and are open to visitors in season.

A gravel road, following the path of a pioneer wagon trail, provides a scenic drive through the canyons into Capitol Gorge. A guidebook is available at the visitors center. Hiking trails also abound; bring plenty of water and insect repellent.

▶ Open year-round; visitors center closed winter holidays. Admission charged.

www.nps.gov/care
(435) 425-3791

12 Goblin Valley State Park

Hwy. 24, 24 miles south of 1-70

Thousands of phantasmagoric sandstone creatures in the eerie landscape of Goblin Valley State Park dare children of all ages to come venture among them. Scores of these eroded creatures even greet visitors at the entrance.

Time, wind, and water have conspired to sculpt orange-brown hard-rock boulders atop soft sandy layers into these "goblins." Their wildly contorted shapes sprang into being wherever the underlying sandstone layers eroded more quickly. First discovered by cowboys searching for stray cattle, the goblins were publicized by Arthur Chaffin in the 1950s. His publicity attracted visitors to the valley despite its remoteness. To protect the fantastical creatures from vandals, Utah declared the whole area a state park in 1964.

Its desert beauty can be explored on hikes between goblins, following three marked trails. For an extra-eerie adventure join one of the park naturalists for a night-time walk among the goblins.

▶ Open daily year-round. Admission charged.

www.stateparks.utah.gov
(435) 564-3633

13 Dead Horse Point State Park

SR-313, Moab

Toward the end of the last century, packs of wild mustangs roamed the mesas around what is now

called Dead Horse Point, a stone promontory surrounded by high cliffs overlooking the Colorado River, 2,000 feet below.

Cowboys fenced the narrow neck of land leading onto the promontory to use it as a natural corral for the mustangs. Once they had selected the best horses for personal use or sale, the gate was opened and the unwanted culls were allowed to find their way off the point and onto open range. One group never made it; according to legend, those broomtails died of thirst within distant view of the Colorado River.

Dead Horse Point is just one of the breathtaking overlooks in this 5,200-acre state park. Paved and primitive trails radiate outward from the visitors center to six points overlooking the river and the heavily eroded cliff walls, with their towering spires and steep bluffs.

The park offers self-guiding hikes and, in summer, rock climbers and hang gliders occasionally pursue their sports along the precipice.

▶ Open year-round. Admission charged.

www.stateparks.utah.gov
(435) 259-2614; (800) 322-3770

14 La Sal Mountain Scenic Loop

6 miles south of Moab

Looming above the Moab Valley, the snowcapped La Sal Mountains were named by 18th-century Spanish explorers in the region. These dramatic mountains stand in sharp contrast to the fiery red sandstone rocks spread across the landscape and offer cool retreat from high summer temperatures or endless backcountry snow adventures in the winter.

The La Sal Loop climbs from the desert environment of Spanish Valley up to alpine meadows beneath 12,700-foot peaks. The 60-mile-long road is paved except for a few sections of gravel. The

steep climb, much of it over narrow switchbacks, is slow-going and should not be attempted by cars towing trailers or recreational vehicles.

The high-country road is closed by snow in the winter, but during the rest of the year, it offers panoramic views of the Colorado Plateau and the Blue and Henry Mountains off in the distance.

The loop leaves Hwy. 191 six miles south of Moab and climbs the west side of the La Sals before descending through Castle Valley, which you can follow along the Colorado River back to Moab.

▶ Scenic drive generally accessible May–Oct.

www.discovermoab.com/byways.htm
(800) 635-6622

15 Natural Bridges National Monument

SR-275, 30 miles west of Blanding

The three huge sandstone bridges

13 ▶ Dead Horse Point State Park. From Dead Horse Point the view of the Colorado River winding through red rock mesas is as breathtaking as any in the West. Trails starting at the visitors center lead to five additional overlooks in this 5,200-acre park.

15 ▶ **Natural Bridges National Monument.** Owachomo Bridge takes its Hopi name from the large sandstone formation at left—owachomo, meaning "rock mound."

here were first named by prospectors who explored the area in the 1880s. They were given Hopi Native American names by President William Howard Taft in 1909 shortly after the site was designated a national monument. The oldest bridge is called Owachomo ("rock mound"); the longest is Sipapu ("the place of emergence"); and the youngest is Kachina, named for the masked divinities of the Hopi religion.

All three bridges were formed by the erosive action of streams as they flowed through the switchback bends of a canyon. A nine-mile loop road links the starting points of the short trails to the three bridges and provides access to overlooks offering splendid views of the surrounding canyon scenery.

For those seeking longer hikes, nearly six miles of trail traverse the canyons' floors and connect the bridges. The terrain here, however, may be hazardous, and hikers should be alert for flash flooding.

The monument site was recently designated the first International Dark Sky Preserve because of having the darkest skies in the lower 48 states.

▶ Open year-round, but some trails may be closed in winter. Visitors center closed major winter holidays. Admission charged.

www.nps.gov/nabr
(435) 692-1234

16 ▶ **Goosenecks State Park**

SR-316 W. off Rte. 261, north of Mexican Hat
The dramatic beauty of Utah's precipitous landscape is epitomized by the view from this 10-acre park set atop a towering mesa. From an overlook four "gooseneck" bends can be seen in the muddy San Juan River as it wends 1,000 feet below.

These bends, for which the park is named, are important examples of a geological phenomenon known as an entrenched meander: a curving streambed that by gradual water erosion or land upheaval is cut deep below the surface of the valley. Here the meanders have worn so deep that they have exposed layers of sandstone, shale, and limestone dating back more than 300 million years.

The mesa's vegetation has evolved to derive maximum

moisture from the arid land. The Indian ricegrass, and other sandy lowland plants provide cover and food that is too sparse to support much indigenous animal life, but birders will find the overlook rewarding, and it's an excellent place to stop for a picnic.

▶ Open year-round.

www.stateparks.utah.gov
(435) 678-2238

17 ▶ **Hovenweep National Monument**

30 miles east of SR-191, between Blanding and Bluff
Spread out over a 20-mile expanse of high mesas and down in shallow canyons along the Utah–Colorado border are the ruins of six prehistoric Puebloan-era villages. The Hovenweep Natonal Monument has been established as a monument site to ensure the area's preservation.

Hovenweep is the Ute/Paiute word for "deserted valley." Atop the mesas and along the canyon floors are examples of the finest ancient stone-architectural achievements in the Southwest. Dating from more than 10,000 years ago, towers and buildings are perched on canyon rims and balanced on boulders, attesting to the skill of the long-ago artisans who migrated over the area while gathering food and hunting game. Interpretive trails highlight their skill and legacy and let you roam in their world of the past.

▶ Open daily year-round; visitors center closed major winter holidays. Admission charged.

www.nps.gov/hove
(970) 562-4282

UTAH

Vermont

The fall color, white church steeples, maple syrup, cheese, and great skiing might well be enough—but there's more.

Billings Farm and Museum. Dairy cows are the star attraction at Billings Farm (see page 338).

Among the surprises along the byways of the Green Mountain State are two attractions dedicated to the spirit: one is a shrine where healing is said to take place, the other a church built in the round to (perhaps) keep the devil from lurking in corners. More earthly concerns are recalled in a cheese factory and marble exhibit. Here are the homestead of a man who had a great idea for education and the boyhood home of our thirtieth president. Art is acknowledged in a petroglyph site and a display of works by a famous grandmother.

visit ➤➤ **offthebeatenpathtrips.com**

1 St. Anne's Shrine

92 St. Anne's Rd., Isle La Motte

Vermont's oldest white settlement was founded here at the water's edge in 1666, when a French officer, Capt. Pierre La Motte, built Fort St. Anne as a bastion against the Mohawk tribe. The fort was needed for only a short time, but soon afterward Jesuit priests built the first Christian chapel on the site in the woods.

Within the small cruciform chapel is a simple wooden altar with the figures of St. Anne and the Virgin Mary. To the left another altar is dedicated to St. Anne; on the walls near it hang abandoned crutches and plaster casts, evidence of the healings that are said to have taken place here. A rustic grotto near the chapel shelters a figure of the Virgin Mary. Also close by is an A-frame shrine that houses a marble statue of St. Anne. On the hill behind the chapel are other shrines, which are dedicated to saints Anthony and Francis.

In a grove of pine trees on the site of the old stockade is the Gethsemane Garden, where the stations of the cross are inscribed on copper tablets. Beyond the Gethsemane Garden stands a granite statue of Samuel de Champlain, in a canoe with a Native American companion, marking the site of his landfall at Isle La Motte in 1609. Because of the crowds attracted to

1 St. Anne's Shrine. Champlain, the French explorer, founded Quebec City in 1608—the year before he first set foot on Isle La Motte, in the lake now bearing his name.

the shrine on weekends and holidays, it is best to visit on weekdays. Dock facilities are available for those who come by boat.

▶ Open mid-May–mid-Oct.

www.saintannesshrine.org
(802) 928-3362

2 Missisquoi National Wildlife Refuge

29 Tabor Rd., Swanton

The Native American name *Missisquoi,* which means an area of "much waterfowl" and "much grass," well describes this place. Vast numbers of migratory waterfowl traveling the Atlantic Flyway stop to feed and rest here on some 6,600 acres of marsh, open water, and woodland. The best time to observe them—black ducks, mallards, wood ducks, Canada geese, and many other species— is early fall, mid-Sept.–early Oct. The nearly 200 species of birds that are observed here include osprey, bald eagles, and black terns.

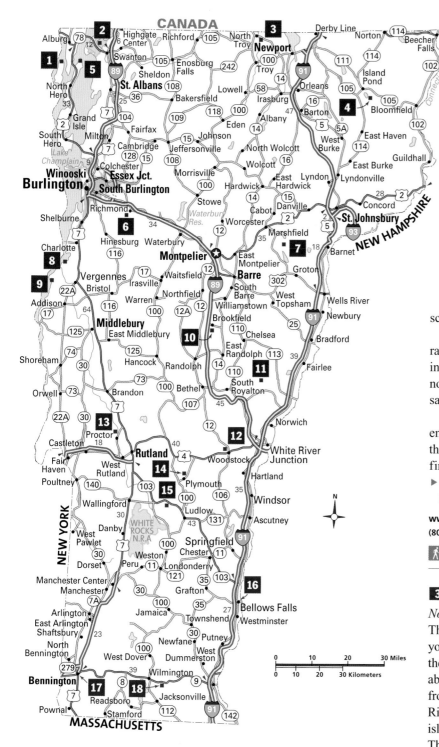

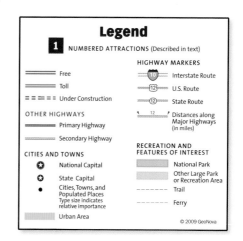

Legend

1 NUMBERED ATTRACTIONS (Described in text)

HIGHWAY MARKERS

- Free
- Toll
- Under Construction

OTHER HIGHWAYS
- Primary Highway
- Secondary Highway

CITIES AND TOWNS
- ⊛ National Capital
- ⊙ State Capital
- • Cities, Towns, and Populated Places
  Type size indicates relative importance
- Urban Area

- 10 Interstate Route
- 12 U.S. Route
- 12 State Route
- 1 12 Distances along Major Highways (in miles)

RECREATION AND FEATURES OF INTEREST
- National Park
- Other Large Park or Recreation Area
- - - - Trail
- — — Ferry

© 2009 GeoNova

The Black Creek and Maquam Creek nature trails, together about 1½ miles in length, are easily walked. They follow the course of two woodland creeks, where points of interest are numbered and described in the trail guide along the way, and include muskrat burrows and duck "loafing sites." Beavers are abundant here, along with signs of their activities— felled birch trees, wood chips, scent mounds, runs, and lodges.

White-tailed deer, red fox, raccoon, otter, and mink are also in residence; among the fish are northern pike, walleye, bass, salmon, and carp.

Kayaking and canoeing enthusiasts will want to paddle the 11-mile loop that starts and finishes on the Missisquoi River.

▶ Open year-round, but trails may be flooded in spring.

www.fws.gov/northeast/missisquoi
(802) 868-4781

3 Big Falls

North Troy. River Rd., off Rte. 105
The first pull-off on the left after you see the falls gives access to the best viewing spots, which are above the waterfall. Just upstream from the falls, the Missisquoi River divides around a rocky island topped by small conifers. The scene is elegant enough to have been designed by a Japanese gardener. Below this the river plunges, boils, fumes, and roars into a narrow chasm perhaps 60 feet deep and then continues wide and placid between banks

set with hemlock and juniper.

There are no facilities for tourists here, but the falls may be seen at any time of the year. In wet weather they should be approached with extreme caution: The granite underfoot can be very slippery. The height and plunge of the falls could cause dizziness, and the spectacle is so attractive as to tempt the unwary viewer beyond a safe foothold.

www.newenglandwaterfalls.com
(802) 525-4386

4 Brighton State Park

102 State Park Rd., Island Pond
The park is small but charmingly situated on the shore of Island Pond Lake. Adjacent to the white sandy beach are picnic tables and a bathhouse, fine views of the conifer-clad island from which the lake takes its name, and the surrounding hills.

The town of Island Pond, which would seem at home in the Swiss Alps, is attractively situated at the far end of the lake and adds to the appeal of the setting. It was the site of the first international railroad junction in the United States.

▶ Open Memorial Day–Columbus Day; accessible year-round.

www.vtstateparks.com/htm/ brighton.cfm

(802) 723-4360

5 ▶ North Hero State Park

3803 Lakeview Dr., North Hero
Heroes from Vermont who fought in the Revolutionary War gave their name to the island this park is named for in Lake Champlain, the sixth-largest lake in the country. Not too far from the bustling university town of Burlington, which is the home of the University of Vermont, the peaceful, spacious campgrounds consist of three loops containing 99 wooded tent/trailer sites and 18 lean-tos, nestled in a heavily wooded forest over 399 acres, 13 miles from the Canadian border.

The level of the lake fluctuates from 95 to 100 feet above sea level, and about one-third of the park lies below 100 feet, so a fair portion of the park becomes seasonally flooded.

Chain pickerel and northern pike spawn in the flooded portions, map turtles nest on the beach, and white-tailed deer, poised to run, noiselessly observe the human activities. Ruffled grouse, American woodcock, and a whole variety of migratory waterfowl like wood ducks and mallards are common here.

Nearby attractions on the interconnected islands include the 1665 French settlement, St. Anne's Shrine in Isle La Motte, and a state-of-the-art hatchery, the Grand Isle State Fish Culture Station. Jedediah Hyde's log cabin, also in Grand Isle, is thought to be one of the oldest in the United States.

▶ Open Memorial Day–Labor Day. Admission charged.

www.vtstateparks.com/htm/ northhero.cfm

(800) 252-2363; (802) 372-8727 summer

7 ▶ Groton State Forest. Almost logged to extinction in the late 19th century, the forest on the Vermont–New Hampshire border now covers 25,000 acres and sustains wildlife, including moose, black bear, mink, otters, and countless species of woodland birds.

6 ▶ Old Round Church

25 Round Church Rd., Richmond
From the time it was built in 1813, this remarkable 16-sided two-story frame building has attracted comment. The reason for its shape is not certain. Local lore says it was to keep the devil from lurking in corners or to prevent an enemy from hiding around a corner. Another suggestion is that 16 men each built a side and a 17th added the belfry. A page from the account book of William Rhodes, the master builder, lists 17 workers in addition to himself. But the most likely explanation is that it was modeled after a round church in Claremont, New Hampshire, where Rhodes's parents lived.

The Old Round Church was built to serve as both a house of worship and a town hall. Five denominations cooperated to raise money for its construction by selling pews. Regular church services ceased around 1880, but town meetings were held here until 1973, when the church was declared structurally unsafe.

It was restored by the Richmond Historical Society and is a National Historic Landmark. Of special interest are the box pews, the hand-wrought hinges, and the hand-painted wood graining on both the pulpit and the horseshoe-shaped balcony.

▶ Open daily mid-June–Labor Day and weekends during late spring and fall foliage season.

www.oldroundchurch.com
(802) 434-3654

7 ▶ Groton State Forest

West of Groton and Peacham
The nine recreation areas in this beautiful forest offer opportunities for a variety of outdoor activities throughout the summer and in winter as well. The forest, a mix of hemlocks, birches, maples, and other hardwoods, is threaded with trails for hiking, snowmobiling, and nature study. In several of the areas, inviting campsites can be found.

The Boulder Beach State Park is on Lake Groton, the largest body of water in the forest. Here the dense woods, which elsewhere come right down to the edge of the lake, have given way to a pleasant sandy beach studded with large boulders deposited by a glacier thousands of years ago. On your way to the beach, look for a massive boulder with a large paper birch growing from the top. A brisk bubbling stream runs alongside.

Dedicated trout fishermen may want to seek out Seyon Pond in the Seyon Ranch State Park, where fly casting is permitted only from boats and canoes. From Groton go west on Rte. 32 for three miles. Turn right on Seyon Pond Rd. and go three miles to the park entrance.

► Boulder Beach area open early June–Labor Day; accessible year-round. Seyon area open early May–Oct.

www.vtfpr.org/lands/vtna.cfm
(802) 241-3670

8 ► Kingsland Bay State Park

787 Kingsland State Park Rd., Ferrisburgh

This exceptionally pretty park is set on an inlet on the east shore of Lake Champlain, a place of quiet green water and gray pebble beaches strewn with small boulders and bleached driftwood. Ledges of granite, clothed in juniper and arborvitae, project into the lake from miniature headlands; far beyond are the peaks of the Adirondacks.

The road into the park, running along and above the shore, is fringed on the lakeside by wild grape, white pine, bittersweet, and arborvitae; on the other side lie open meadows. The road leads to a picnic area where there are tables and charcoal grills. There is also a beach where boats can be launched.

► Open Memorial Day–Columbus Day; accessible year-round.

www.vtstateparks.com/htm/kingsland.cfm
(800) 658-1622 summer
(802) 877-3445 year-round

9 ► Button Bay State Park

5 Button Bay State Park Rd., Vergennes

Button Bay, a wide inlet on the east shore of southern Lake Champlain, is approached across an alluvial plain that becomes a patchwork of vivid green meadows and cultivated fields in the spring. On the western side of the lake are the undulating foothills of the Adirondacks. At a distance to the east rise the Green Mountains—which from here take on a lovely shade of blue.

The 253-acre park wraps around the shore of Button Bay, which is relatively open, with conifer woods to the north and south. There are well-arranged tent and trailer sites and several lean-tos, as well as a picnic area and boat-launching sites. Nature trails and a small nature museum add to the park's appeal.

► Open Memorial Day–Columbus Day.

www.vtstateparks.com/htm/buttonbay.cfm
(802) 475-2377

10 ► Floating Bridge

Hwy. 65, Brookfield

Brookfield is a charming village of white clapboard houses and trimmed lawns nestled beside the waters of Sunset Lake. In 1820 Luther Adams built a floating bridge across the lake, and back then people, animals, carts, and cars crossed the water—a journey of about 100 yards—by this curious means.

The present bridge, built in 1978 by the Vermont Agency of Transportation, is the seventh at the site. Made of pressure-treated timber, the bridge is supported by 380 floating polyethylene drums filled with polyurethane foam. At each end is a hinged ramp, and at these points the water can be as much as five inches deep. Driving across the bridge is no longer permitted, but the area is a popular spot for fishing and swimming.

www.central-vt.com/web/floating/index.html
(802) 222-4619

11 ► The Justin Smith Morrill Homestead

Strafford

On July 2, 1862, President Lincoln signed the Morrill Act, a measure

that contributed mightily to the cause of higher education by granting public lands to the states to help finance colleges offering courses in "agriculture and the mechanic arts." Representative and, later, senator, Justin Morrill worked on his far-reaching legislation here in the house he designed and built from 1848–51. A wood cottage painted rosy pink to simulate stone and adorned about its windows, porches, and gables with Carpenter Gothic trim, it seems as visionary as the schools that Morrill proposed.

The land rises to fields and woods behind the house, and not far up the hill are several farm buildings, also pink. From the hillside may be seen the Strafford Town House, erected in 1799 as a meetinghouse for local officials and as a place of worship for all denominations.

The furnishings of the Morrill homestead include pieces from Morrill's Washington home as well as family memorabilia. Among the intriguing features of the house are the screens on the parlor and dining-room windows. They have romantic landscapes hand-painted on the outside to keep people from looking in while allowing those inside to see out.

► Open weekends Memorial Day–Columbus Day. Admission charged.

www.morrillhomestead.org
(802) 765-4484

8 ► Kingsland Bay State Park. Beauty isn't the only lure for visitors to the Lake Champlain shoreline: The area's average summer temperatures top out at 68°–70°F.

12 Billings Farm and Museum

Rte. 12N & River Rd., Woodstock

This working farm harks back to the late 19th century. The lives of Vermont farm families of 1890 are portrayed in exhibits of dairying, planting and harvesting, ice cutting, and maple sugaring. Explore the Farm House, horse barn, calf nursery, and dairy barn. Get comfortable with the livestock through interactive activities, programs and events.

The progressive dairy farm, which remains a working dairy to this day, was started by conservationist, lawyer, and railroad magnate Frederick Billings. Billings and his farm manager selectively bred the herd for optimum production and planted over 10,000 trees to restore the forest cover.

Billings's granddaughter, the late Mary French Rockefeller, and her husband, Laurance Rockefeller, established the farm and museum to interpret Vermont's rural life and agricultural history and to ensure the continuation of the dairy industry.

▶ Open early May–late Oct.; weekends Nov.–Feb. including major holiday weekends. Admission charged.

www.billingsfarm.org
(802) 457-2355

13 Vermont Marble Exhibit

Proctor

There are extensive deposits of marble in Vermont's Green

did you know ?

One of the Billings's cows returned from the 1893 Chicago World's Fair with the title "Champion Heifer of the World."

Mountains, and most of the stone quarried there is processed in the village of Proctor, the largest center for such work in North America. The Vermont Marble Exhibit, which is also the largest of its kind, documents every aspect of this remarkable stone and many of the ways in which it is used. An 11-minute movie details the history of the Vermont Marble Company.

Among the displays are walls of marble of different kinds from all over the world: Peru, golden vein, Carolina rose, Andes black, and many others—as varied, intriguing, and beautiful as their names. Exhibits include tabletops, baths, flooring, and a complete series of relief busts of the presidents of the United States. Other exhibits explore the geology of marble and quarrying and production methods.

12 **Billings Farm and Museum.** Winter visitors to this historic (and still operating) dairy farm enjoy a horse-powered sleigh ride over snow-covered fields.

▶ Open daily mid-May–early Oct.

www.vermont-marble.com
(802) 459-2300

14 Calvin Coolidge State Historic Site

3780 Rte. 100A, Plymouth

In the early hours before dawn, on August 3, 1923, Vice President Coolidge, who was vacationing at his boyhood home in Plymouth, was awakened when a courier brought word that President Warren G. Harding had suddenly died. By the light of a kerosene lamp in the sitting room, Coolidge was sworn into office as the new president by his father, a notary public.

During his five years as chief executive, Coolidge returned here for vacations. Content with the simplicity of the house and its air of peacefulness, it was not until 1932 that he installed electricity and other modern amenities. He was buried, as he requested, in the cemetery nearby in 1933.

The small white farmhouse stands in a spacious meadow at the edge of Plymouth village. Lovely period gardens complete the simple ambience. Nearby is a handsome large barn that houses a Farmers Museum. The homestead, barn, and church that Coolidge attended now constitute a National Historic Landmark.

▶ Open daily late May–mid-Oct. Admission charged.

www.historicvermont.org/coolidge
(802) 672-3773

15 Crowley Cheese Factory

14 Crowley Ln., Healdville

At the country's oldest cheese factory, Colby cheddar cheese is still made by hand, just as it was a hundred years ago. Visitors can see the curds being cut and raked in the big vats, then handworked and formed in hand-cranked presses. The tools, techniques, and product haven't changed.

The factory was built by Winfield Crowley in 1882, when his business outgrew the farm kitchen where he had by then been making cheese for almost 60 years. The establishment today is still redolent of the less hurried, more peaceful time when it got its start. A collection of old cheesemaking tools—curd knives, a cheese press, and a centrifuge—is on display. You can sample the product or buy it at the gift shop, along with candy, maple syrup, jams, and baked goods. Crowley is one of many cheese factories found on the Vermont Cheese Trail.

▶ Factory open Mon.-Fri.; shop open daily.

www.vtcheese.com/cheesetrail.htm
www.crowleycheese.com
(802) 259-2340

16 ▶ Bellows Falls

Bellows Falls is a historic community along the Connecticut River Byway that harkens back to a simpler time. This quaint picturesque town has breathtaking scenery, tranquil countryside and an entire district that is on the *National Register of Historic Places,* with about 200 historic buildings. A descriptive pamphlet takes visitors on a self-guiding walking tour past 27 of them; the homes are not open to the public.

Due to its location by the falls, Bellows Falls has served as an important crossroads for travel and commerce, with bragging rights to one of the nation's first canals, the first bridge (in 1785) to cross the Connecticut River in Vermont.

www.bellowsfalls.org
www.linkvermont.com/townsvill/
   upperconnecticutrivervalley/index.htm

17 ▶ Grandma Moses Gallery and Schoolhouse

75 Main St., Bennington
Grandma Moses began to paint in oils in her 70s. Although she had no technical training, her farm scenes and rural landscapes had a cheerful, naive quality that soon won her acclaim as a "primitive." She completed more than 1,500 works before her death in 1961 at the age of 101. The museum has the largest public collection of plates and tiles and the tilt-top pine table she used as an easel.

14 ▶ Calvin Coolidge State Historic Site. Considered one of the best-preserved presidential sites, the homestead remains just as it was when Coolidge took the oath of office here.

Adjoining the gallery is the schoolhouse Grandma Moses attended as a girl in Eagle Bridge, New York. Built in 1834, the schoolhouse was moved to Bennington in 1972 and now serves as a museum. The main part of the room re-creates the appearance of the old schoolhouse, with church pews (instead of benches) and antique desks.

The Grandma Moses Gallery and Schoolhouse are part of the well-known Bennington Museum, which has fine collections of pottery, glass, furniture, paintings, uniforms, and firearms on display.

▶ Open daily in Sept. and Oct.; closed Wed. Nov.-Aug. and major holidays. Admission charged.

www.benningtonmuseum.com
(802) 447-1571

18 ▶ Molly Stark State Park

705 Rte. 9E, Wilmington
Situated in a beautiful valley on the west side of Mount Olga, this small park has several appealing

features. The local roads are favored by cyclists, and in winter the countryside is inviting for skiers and snowshoers. In addition, the forest of hardwoods and pines harbors deer, raccoons, Cooper's hawks, and other wildlife. The park's campsites are in the woods around a clearing with apple trees.

Perhaps the main attraction is the trail leading from the campground to the summit of Mount Olga. About three-quarters of a mile long, it is easy to follow, although it is somewhat steep near the summit. Your reward for going to the top of the fire tower is a 360-degree view of wooded hills and valleys with an occasional barn roof glinting in the sun. On a clear day you can see New York, Vermont, New Hampshire, Massachusetts, and Connecticut.

▶ Open for camping Memorial Day- Columbus Day.

www.vtstateparks.com/htm/mollystark.cfm
(802) 464-5460

seasonal events

JANUARY
• Stowe Winter Carnival—Stowe

APRIL
• Vermont Maple Syrup Festival— St. Albans

JUNE
• Vermont Dairy Festival—Sheldon
• Vermont Solstice Festival—Norwich

JULY
• Middlebury Festival on the Green— Middlebury
• Pownal Valley Fair—Pownal *(crafts, antique tractor pull, fireworks, music)*

AUGUST
• Deerfield Valley Farmer's Day— Wilmington *(competitions, agricultural exhibits, cattle judging, kid's rides, live entertainment)*

SEPTEMBER
• Turnbridge World's Fair—Turnbridge *(vendors, entertainment, livestock shows)*
• Cheese & Harvest Festival—Plymouth Notch *(cheese sampling, wagon rides, craft demonstrations, activities)*

OCTOBER
• Pumpkin Carving Festival— Manchester
• Annual Harvest Bazaar—Burlington *(homemade food, crafts, antiques)*
• Apple Pie Festival—Cabot *(pie sales, cider, crafts, entertainment)*
• Quechee Balloon Festival— Quechee *(hot-air balloons, crafts, kid's activities, entertainment)*

NOVEMBER
• Southern Vermont Fiber Event— Battleboro *(vendors, various fiber crafts and items, food)*
• IndieCon—Burlington *(live music, films, workshops, discussions)*

DECEMBER
• Wassail Weekend—Woodstock *(lights, period dances, carriage rides)*

www.vermontvacation.com

Virginia

From the Tidewater to the Blue Ridge, the pastoral landscapes of the Old Dominion bespeak the state's historic past.

George Washington's Distillery & Gristmill. An interpreter in period dress demonstrates how flour was made in Washington's water-powered mill in the 18th century (see page 341).

From Patrick Henry's tomb to Booker T. Washington's birthplace to the Richmond neighborhood where Edgar Allan Poe lived and wrote, Virginia is steeped in American history. History is also on view at a Native American village and an Appalachian cultural center. Inviting nature sites are a Mount Solon park named for its towering rock sentinels and, despite its name, the vast forested wetlands known as the Great Dismal Swamp. Unexpected stops along the way include a museum celebrating fishing and fishermen, another housing vintage train cars and automobiles of all stripes, and a copper shop where ornamental objects are crafted as in the distant past.

visit ➡➡ **offthebeatenpathtrips.com**

1 Museum of the Shenandoah Valley

901 Amherst St., Winchester
Framed by the Blue Ridge and Allegheny mountains, the Shenandoah Valley is renowned for its magnificent vistas. Now the history, art, and culture of this region is represented at a site that includes the museum, the 18th-century Glen Burnie Historic House, home to descendants of Col. James Wood, founder of the city of Winchester, and six acres of beautifully landscaped gardens.

A stately brick Georgian dating back to 1794, Glen Burnie is shown as it was when Julian Wood Glass, Jr. (1910-1992), Col. Wood's last descendant, lived in the home with furniture, paintings, and other items from the region. Some date back to Glen Burnie's first residents. The largest single collection of portraits by Edward Caledon Bruce is displayed here along with the impressive collection of art and antiques Glass acquired for his ancestral home.

Outside, visitors can wander or follow an audio tour of the grand gardens graced with sculpture, fountains, and flowers, especially hundreds of rose bushes.

The museum tells the story of the Shenandoah Valley through films, oral histories, furniture, ceramics, fraktur, silver, textiles, and folk art. One documentary is devoted to a presentation of the Civil War. The Julian Wood Glass Jr. Gallery displays its namesake's fine and decorative arts, including paintings by Thomas Gainsborough. The R. Lee Taylor Miniatures Gallery shows miniature houses and rooms collected by Taylor, the late curator of the Glen Burnie gardens. Another gallery presents changing exhibitions on a variety of topics.

1 ▶ Museum of the Shenandoah Valley. Dating to 1794 and located on the only working farm remaining in Winchester city limits, the Museum of the Shenandoah Valley's Glen Burnie Historic House is furnished with an impressive collection of fine art and antiques.

▶ Museum open Tues.-Sun. year-round; house and gardens Tues.-Sun. Mar.-Nov. Admission charged.

www.shenandoahmuseum.org
(540) 662-1473

2 George Washington's Distillery & Gristmill

Rte. 235, 3 miles south of Mount Vernon

These impressive reconstructions give us a unique view of the private life and interests of our first president. Based on archaeological investigations and plans and papers found among his personal effects, the gristmill and distillery are detailed replicas of those built by George Washington.

Always a clever entrepreneur, the future president was sensitive to northern Virginia's agricultural transition from tobacco to wheat, and in 1770 he decided to abandon an old gristmill at the Mount Vernon estate and build a new stone one to capitalize on the region's changing economy. Some three decades later, his Scottish farm manager encouraged him to build a whiskey distillery next to the mill. By 1799, Washington's distillery was the largest in America, producing 11,000 gallons of corn and rye whiskey annually.

Visitors touring the gristmill and the distillery watch demonstrations of 18th-century milling and spirit-making on equipment ranging from a 16-foot waterwheel to copper stills, mash tubs, and a boiler. The distillery also features a video and a museum exhibit about the history of whiskey in America.

The picture is made all the more intriguing by the thought that this busy enterprise was a product of the same insight, determination, and stamina with which our first president helped to forge a new nation.

▶ Open daily Apr.–Oct.. Admission charged.

www.mountvernon.org
(703) 780-2000

did you know ❓

George Washington's distillery is the only known re-created 18th-century distillery in America.

3 The Museum of Culpeper History

803 S. Main St., Culpeper

This state-of-the-art facility contains collections ranging from 215-million-year-old dinosaur tracks to 21st-century technology. But it also focuses on an event of great importance to American history.

The museum, established in 1975 as the "Culpeper Calvary Museum," has a large gallery dedicated to the Civil War in the surrounding region. A large interactive topographical map illuminates all the battles in the area. Commemorated in the gallery is the 1862 Battle of Brandy Station, which took place five miles from town. With 19,000 mounted soldiers, it remains the biggest cavalry encounter ever fought in the Western Hemisphere.

Along with the Civil War gallery, where firearms and other items of warfare are displayed, the museum highlights the heritage of the region. Native American tools, memorabilia from the American Revolution, WWI, and WWII, and local artwork and decorative items are on view on rotating schedules.

▶ Open daily year-round except Jan.

www.culpepermuseum.com
(540) 829-1749

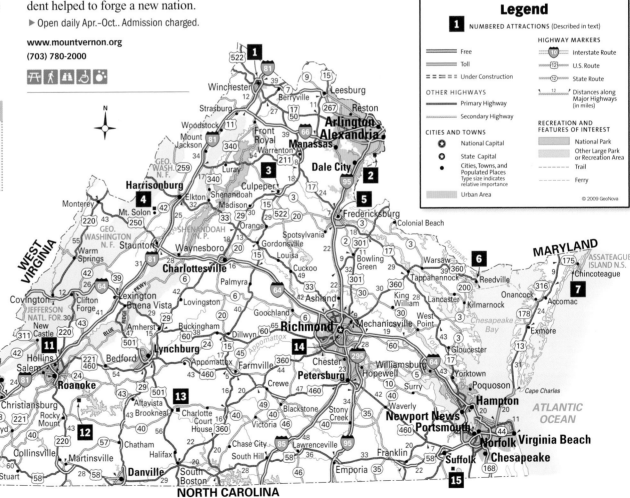

4 **Natural Chimneys Regional Park.** When an ocean covering the Shenandoah Valley dried up over the ages and wind and rain went to work, towers of rock were left intact near present-day Mount Solon. Today they stand guard at a recreation area.

4 Natural Chimneys Regional Park

94 Natural Chimneys Ln., Mount Solon

Soaring above the surrounding plain, the chimneys are a strange remnant of a time, centuries ago, when an ocean covered the Shenandoah Valley, leaving behind these rocks etched by the forces of nature.

It takes little imagination to see in these weathered, highly textured formations such shapes as turrets, gargoyles, distant cities, or perhaps menacing fortifications. Small junipers growing among the rocks help to create a curiously deceptive scale.

Since 1821, on the third Saturday of August a jousting tournament has been held on the plains below the chimneys. Modern-day knights on galloping horses try to spear three steel rings hanging from crossbars suspended over the 75-yard course in the meadow known as the National Jousting Hall of Fame.

Self-guiding nature and biking trails wander through the fields and woodlands. The park also has 145 tree-shaded campsites with electric and water hook-up, a swimming pool, picnic areas, and a children's playground.

▶ Open year-round. Admission charged.

www.uvrpa.org/naturalchimneys.htm
(888) 430-2267

5 The Copper Shop

1707B Princess Anne St., Fredericksburg

Owned and run by coppersmith Allen H. Green III, the shop offers a fascinating look at how in early America, simple tools and materials were used to create objects both beautiful and useful. It is one of the few places in the country where one can still see swell-bodied weathervanes and other copper objects being made.

The work is done entirely by hand, from making the pattern to cutting the copper sheets and hammering them to shape on hard sandbags. Traditional designs are used for many of the objects, and most are made to order.

One of the specialties of the shop is the Fredericksburg Lamp, an elegantly designed candleholder with a slim hurricane chimney created by Mr. Green's father in 1976. It comes with or without a reflector in six different versions, including a patio lamp, a chandelier, and a table lamp. The Island Sconce, fashioned by Allen III, is also an impressive feature of this collection of copperware.

▶ Open year-round.

www.thefredericksburglamp.com
(540) 371-4455

6 Reedville Fishermen's Museum

504 Main St., Reedville

Overlooking a generous creek, this museum celebrates the maritime heritage of a proud historic town that remains one of the nation's most active fishing ports. In addition to tracing the birth, rise, and influence of the local menhaden fishing industry, specializing in catch used for bait, it honors the men who have mined the waters of

5 **The Copper Shop.** Copper objects are made the old-fashioned way at this workshop in Fredericksburg.

the Chesapeake Bay for centuries.

The main building features intricate models of Chesapeake Bay workboats; authentic tools used by the area's watermen to harvest crabs, oysters, and wide-ranging fish; and detailed dioramas illuminating the trade, its practices, and its impact, from the earliest Native American fishermen to today's dedicated purveyors.

Next door, the William Walker House—the oldest house still standing in Reedville, built in 1875—has been meticulously restored and appointed in the style of a typical waterman's home at the turn of the century. The museum also offers educational programs and rotating exhibits, including a summer tribute to skipjacks—distinctive sailboats known for their seasonal races on the bay. Amateur and vicarious fishermen will delight in the gift shop, stocked with books of regional interest, crafts made by local artisans, prints, maps, and children's toys.

For a final treat, a walk on the museum's deck offers views of the shimmering creek, still fished for its menhaden by modern fleets.

▶ Open daily late Apr.–Oct.; Fri.-Sun. Nov.–late Dec.; Sat.-Sun. mid-Mar.–late Apr. Admission charged.

www.rfmuseum.org/index.html
(800) 453-6529

7 Chincoteague Island

Visitors Center, 6733 Maddox Blvd.

Virginia's only resort island, Chincoteague is best known as the gateway to the Chincoteague Wildlife Refuge on Assateague Island and as home of the annual wild pony roundup immortalized in Marguerite Henry's *Misty* stories. Named from a Native American word meaning "beautiful land across the water," Chincoteague today combines up-to-date amenities with natural beauty, so visitors can find plenty of activities, including eco-touring, or just relax in peace.

Popular island attractions include the Oyster & Maritime Museum and Refuge Waterfowl Museum, located next to each other on Maddox Boulevard. At the Chincoteague Pony Centre, you can meet and ride Chincoteague ponies. Not far away, on Hwy. 175, the NASA Visitor Center at Wallops Flight Facility has space exhibits that are surefire kid pleasers. Plus, the Wildlife Refuge is just minutes away by car or on foot.

▶ Chamber of Commerce Visitors Center open Mon.-Sat.

www.chincoteaguechamber.com
(757) 336-6161

8 ▶ Historic Abingdon

Convention & Visitors Bureau,
35 Cummings St.
Abingdon, named for Martha Washington's ancestral home, was incorporated during the Revolutionary War, and the town's history

9 ▶ Historic Crab Orchard Museum & Pioneer Park. Appalachian culture from centuries ago to the present is spotlighted at this museum.

is an all-American tale. Attractions include a tavern in continuous operation since the late 1700s, and almost two centuries of legends and lore—including several reported ghosts—associated with the elegant Martha Washington Inn.

History and modernity meet congenially in the homes, churches, businesses, and galleries that line Main Street's shady brick sidewalks. A stop at the Barter Theater, named for its Depression-era practice of trading tickets for local farm produce, is a must. Internationally known for nurturing talents such as Gregory Peck, Patricia Neal,

and Kevin Spacey, the Barter stages productions year-round.

A town on Virginia's Heritage Music Trail, the Crooked Road, Abingdon hosts the Virginia Highlands Festival, a celebration of traditional music and arts, every August.

▶ Abingdon Visitors Bureau open daily.

www.abingdon.com
(800) 435-3440

9 ▶ Historic Crab Orchard Museum & Pioneer Park

3663 Crab Orchard Rd., Tazewell
How did our forefathers survive the wilderness before modern conveniences were dreamed of? The nonprofit Crab Orchard Museum and Pioneer Park dusts off history to re-create the past. The park comprises 15 original structures (the earliest, a cabin built in 1802) that were moved to the site, carefully reconstructed, and furnished with equally authentic artifacts. These homes, barns, and village shops paint an intriguing portrait of real life on the frontier. Even the vegetable and herb gardens grow varieties specific to settlement days.

The museum offers numerous exhibits about the history, geology, and wildlife of this Appalachian region, including the Native Americans who preceded the first Europeans. Special attention is paid to the crucial role pioneer women played in settlement and farm life.

▶ Tues.-Sat. year-round. Open Sun. Memorial Day-Labor Day only. Admission charged.

www.craborchardmuseum.com
(276) 988-6755

10 ▶ Wolf Creek Indian Village and Museum

6394 N. Scenic Hwy., Bastian
In a tree-sheltered valley below the breathtaking mountains of southwest Virginia, archaeologists uncovered evidence of a thriving settlement of about 100 Native Americans, dating back to the year 1215. Where they came from or where they went is unknown, but they left behind a story you can experience in this museum.

The re-created village offers a trip back into a distant culture with opportunities for hands-on exploration. Dressed in the fashion of the day, interpretive guides demonstrate skills of industry, artistry, and survival needed at that time. Nearby, a more traditional museum showcases artifacts from the excavation site plus artifacts and art from various Native American groups.

Before returning to modern civilization, visitors can explore the pristine nature trails surrounding the village.

▶ Open Tues.-Sat. year-round. Admission charged.

www.indianvillage.org
(276) 688-3438

6 ▶ Reedville Fisherman's Museum. Volunteers helped to restore the museum's vintage skipjack—the Claud W. Somers, which dredged for oysters in the Chesapeake Bay.

11 Virginia Museum of Transportation

303 Norfolk Ave. SW, Roanoke
From vintage locomotives to an official post-office bus, this museum celebrates the history and development of vehicles that have kept people and businesses moving in Virginia and throughout the world. Its impressive collection of rail and road veterans includes a Norfolk & Western Class J

11 ▶ **Virginia Museum of Transportation.** A sleek J Class 611 locomotive and a 1962 Studebaker Lark taxi are among the exhibits in a museum dedicated to the vehicles that plied Virginia's rails and roads.

Locomotive, a 1942 Ford/American LaFrance Fire Engine, a DC Transit Company Streetcar— retired in 1945—and a classic Model T Ford.

In addition to celebrated trains, trucks, and cars, the museum offers an array of exhibits exploring the impact of the transportation industry on the region. Highlights include a continually expanding documentary honoring the contributions of African-Americans to the Norfolk & Western Railroad, from 1930 to 1970, and an exhibit

called "Working the High Iron," displaying photographs of the men and women who worked for Norfolk & Western over the years.

Visitors can also peruse many vehicle-related photographs, including rare shots of early wagons, carriages, and airplanes in the Roanoke Valley; an eclectic assortment of railroad artifacts; and some early automotive ads.

Classic car enthusiasts can catch up on the progress of the museum's developing automobile gallery. Kids and lifelong fans will delight in the huge model-train layout, with four tiers of track, swift-moving trains, and viewing levels to accommodate all sizes.

▶ Open daily Memorial Day–Labor Day. Tues.- Sun. Sept.–May. Closed major holidays. Admission charged.

www.vmt.org
(540) 342-5670

12 Booker T. Washington National Monument

Rte. 122, Hardy, between Bedford and Rocky Mount, 25 miles SE of Roanoke
Burroughs Plantation, where Booker T. Washington was born in 1856, was a poor, small 19th-century farm with master and slave working side by side. When Booker was nine years old, the Civil War ended and liberation came; Booker, his siblings, and his mother were able to move to West Virginia. He became a teacher, writer, and orator, and founded the Tuskegee Institute in Alabama in 1881 as well as fostered hundreds of other schools for African-American education.

The plantation has been reconstructed, and once again it has the character and appearance that it had when Booker was a child. None of the original buildings remain, but

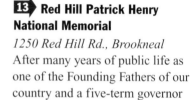

the same chinked log construction has been used in the restoration. Racks of drying leaves hang in the tobacco barn; chickens and turkeys wander around freely; Tamsworth, a historic breed of hogs, occupy the pen.

A quarter-mile walking trail winds through the grounds where you can experience the sights, sounds, and smells of the plantation. At the visitors center you will find a printed guide to the trail that

gives highlights of Washington's life and career.

Jack-O-Lantern Branch Trail, named for the small stream that flows through the fields and forests surrounding the plantation, is a 1 1/2-mile walk. A detailed guide to this path is also available at the visitors center.

▶ Open daily except major winter holidays.

www.nps.gov/bowa
(540) 721-2094

13 Red Hill Patrick Henry National Memorial

1250 Red Hill Rd., Brookneal
After many years of public life as one of the Founding Fathers of our country and a five-term governor of Virginia, Patrick Henry bought Red Hill Plantation in 1794 and retired there to continue his practice of law. He died five years later and was buried in a small cemetery on the grounds beside his second wife, Dorothy.

The plantation is now restored and includes a complex of several buildings, featuring the main house, a 1 1/2-story structure rebuilt on its old foundations; the kitchen; the carriage house; and the office where Patrick Henry practiced law.

Dominating the entire scene is an Osage orange tree. With an 85-foot spread and a height of 60 feet, it is said to be the largest and oldest Osage orange in the country. The American Forestry Hall of Fame lists it as both the Virginia champion and national champion of its kind.

At the visitors center a collection of Patrick Henry memorabilia is displayed including his flute, cuff links, salt dishes, an ivory letter opener, wineglasses, his house

 Red Hill Patrick Henry National Memorial. Patrick Henry spent the last years of his life at bucolic Red Hill Plantation in Charlotte County. The five-term Virginia governor who uttered, "Give me liberty, or give me death!" was also laid to rest here.

keys, his law office desk, his telescope, and several letters written in his hand. A guide to a walking trail is available at the visitors center.

▶ Open daily except Mon. in winter and major winter holidays. Admission charged.

www.redhill.org
(800) 514-7463

14 The Edgar Allan Poe Museum

1916 E. Main St., Richmond
A building known as the Old Stone House, dating from the 1730s, is one of five houses devoted to the memorabilia, the life, and the times of author Edgar Allan Poe. Behind the stone house is the small, wall-enclosed Enchanted Garden inspired by two of Poe's poems, "To One in Paradise" and "To Helen." The garden is planted with evergreens, rhododendrons, and ivy-bordered lawns, with wrought-iron benches. Altogether, the atmosphere of the Poe Museum seems imbued with the spirit of its subject.

The museum's most elaborate display is a large painted clay model of Richmond as it was in the first half of the 19th century.

Museum guides point out the places where Poe lived and worked.

Also on display are Poe's walking stick, a pair of boot hooks, and his wife's trinket box and mirror—suitable mementos, perhaps, of a man whose life was that of a wanderer and whose temperament was insuperably romantic.

The collection contains a number of photographs and drawings of Poe and his circle of friends and includes a strange, ethereal sketch of his wife, Virginia. First editions of his works and manuscripts are on display, along with drafts of some of his famous poems.

▶ Open Tues.–Sun. major winter holidays. Admission charged.

www.poemuseum.org
(804) 648-5523

15 Great Dismal Swamp National Wildlife Refuge

Suffolk
The 111,000 acres of heavily forested wetlands and extensive waterways of the refuge spill over from Virginia into North Carolina, providing habitats for black bears, bobcats, otters, white-tailed deer, and hundreds of bird species.

Birding is best during spring migration from April to June, when the greatest diversity of species (particularly warblers) occurs.

Lake Drummond, a 3,100-acre, natural lake in the heart of the swamp, is fed by many creeks whose mirrorlike black waters are colored and purified by tannic acid from the bark of trees and other vegetation. Remnants of a great cypress forest can be seen in the many "knees" encircling the lake.

To enter the swamp by water, you can launch your boat at the public ramp on U.S. Route 17 at Dismal Swamp Canal. There is a 25-horsepower motor limit.

An interpretive three-quarter-mile-long boardwalk trail starts just beyond the parking lot. Fishing, permitted only in Lake Drummond, is best in spring, when the sunfish, catfish, and crappie are plentiful.

▶ Open year-round. Portions of the refuge may be closed in the fall during the white-tailed-deer hunt.

www.fws.gov/northeast/greatdismalswamp
(757) 986-3705

14 **The Edgar Allan Poe Museum.** A bust of the famous novelist and poet peers out over the museum.

seasonal events

MARCH
- Daffodil Festival—Gloucester *(entertainment, live music, local and regional artwork, food court, children's games)*
- Virginia Festival of the Book—Charlottesville *(readings, panel discussions, hands-on events)*

APRIL
- Shenandoah Apple Blossom Festival—Winchester *(parade, carnival, fireworks display, concessions)*

JUNE
- Strawberry Jubilee—Bluemont *(strawberry picking, contests, live music, food)*
- Magic in the Mountains—Clifton Forge *(crafts, antiques, entertainment, concessions, carnival games)*

JULY
- The Virginia Highlands Festival—Abingdon *(entertainment, antique market, juried art, writers, lecturers)*
- Fourth at the Fort—Fort Monroe *(live music, games, rides, children's activities, military exhibits, concessions, fireworks)*

AUGUST
- Old Fiddlers Convention—Galax *(competitions, performances)*

SEPTEMBER
- Civil War Weekend—Winchester *(re-enactors portray the life of the average soldier)*
- Alexandria Festival of the Arts—Alexandria *(more than 200 artists display and sell a variety of artwork)*
- Bristol Rhythm and Roots Reunion—Bristol *(national, regional, and local music and entertainment)*
- Corn Maze Days—Ararat *(corn and hay mazes, pumpkin launching, produce sales, food)*

NOVEMBER
- Virginia Gourd Festival—Middletown *(silent auction, live music, food)*

www.virginia.org

Washington

From the heights of Mount Rainier to the fields of the Columbia River Plateau, the 42nd state is a treasury of historic sites and scenic wonders.

Sunrise, Mount Rainier National Park.
The highest point travelers can reach on Mount Rainier—once known to the local Native Americans as Tahoma, or "great mountain"—is the Sunrise area (see page 350).

The San Juan Islands and a mountain lake in the Cascades, a lush green rain forest in Queets Valley and a petrified forest located on the edge of the dry eastern plains—paints Washington as a seductive study in contrasts. Wildlife lovers on the seacoast and in remote areas may spot everything from whales and Olympic marmots to rare gyrfalcons and snowy owls.

The history of human habitation of the Evergreen State is preserved in a museum housing thousands of Makah Native American artifacts frozen in time by a mudslide in the 1500s and in Stellacoom, the oldest incorporated town in the state. Washington also has its share of surprises, including a palatial art museum in the proverbial "middle of nowhere" and hiking trails and campsites at Mount St. Helens, the volcano whose eruption rocked the state in 1980.

visit ➡  **offthebeatenpathtrips.com**

1 Orcas Island

Accessible by ferry from Anacortes
Looking for grand scenery, rustic adventure, and places to shop and dine in style? Orcas could be your island paradise. Eastsound, the main township, is brimming with boutique shopping, galleries, eateries, entertainment, and welcoming folks. For island history visit the local museum, a unique facility constructed of original homestead cabins from the late 1800s.

The 5,000-plus-acre Moran State Park offers a full menu for outdoors lovers: five freshwater lakes for fishing, swimming, and boating; hiking, biking, and horse trails; picnicking, camping, and a wealth of wildlife to observe. Head up Mount Constitution for breathtaking panoramic views of land and sea.

Orcas, the largest of the San Juan Islands off Washington's west coast, is accessible by ferry and boat or seaplane and airplane, but day trips are a realistic option.

▶ Moran State Park open year-round.

www.parks.wa.gov
www.visitsanjuans.com
(888) 468-3701 San Juan Islands Visitors Bureau

1 **Orcas Island.** An orca, or killer whale, breaches the waters off Orcas Island. The orca belongs to one of the three Southern Resident whale pods that frequent the San Juan Islands off the northern Washington coast from April to October.

2 Gardner Cave, Crawford State Park

12 miles north of Metaline
Shortly beyond the collapsed sink-hole that serves as the entrance to this 2,000-foot-long cavern, you will find a glistening world of flowstone, dripstone formations, and gours, which are dishlike basins in the cave floor. Their names—Christmas Tree, Queen's Throne, and Fried Eggs—aptly suggest the strange shapes and effects created by rainwater laden with carbon dioxide as it slowly dripped through the 500-million-year-old metaline limestone here. Perhaps the most striking feature is a speleothem, a floor-to-ceiling column of calcite that formed here by the union of a stalactite and a stalagmite.

About 500 feet of the cave is equipped with lighted stairways and walkways and may be viewed on guided tours conducted by the park staff. Wear warm clothing, since the cave temperature remains at about 40°F, and bring a flashlight to peer into darker corners.

To reach the cave, which is the featured attraction of the 49-acre park, you follow a 200-yard paved walkway up a small hill from the parking lot. The walk serves as a nature trail, with plaques identifying the flora.

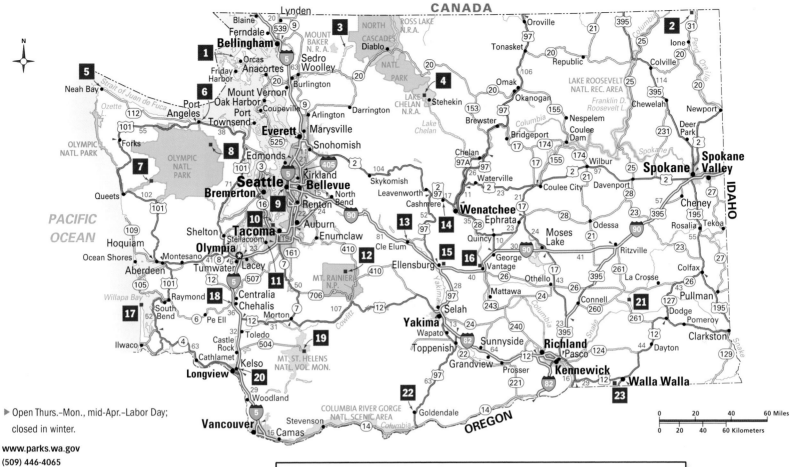

CANADA

PACIFIC OCEAN

OREGON

IDAHO

▶ Open Thurs.–Mon., mid-Apr.–Labor Day; closed in winter.

www.parks.wa.gov
(509) 446-4065

Legend

▶ 3 Baker Lake

15 miles north of Concrete, on Baker Lake Rd.

Here is the essence of the Pacific Northwest: a land of dense, dark green aromatic forests, snow-capped mountains, large lakes lying in wooded valleys, and high-

▶ **3 Baker Lake.** Sockeye salmon are plentiful at man-made Baker Lake.

land lakes fed by glacial streams. Although Baker Lake and Lake Shannon are man-made (created by power-company dams), they sit beautifully and naturally at the base of majestic Mount Baker. At nine-mile-long Baker Lake, which is the more accessible, boating and fishing are the main activities; prior to July 5 each year it is plentifully stocked with rainbow trout. Baker Lake is also one of the state's best sources of sockeye salmon.

Hikes range from short strolls to treks requiring several days into rugged backcountry and up the slopes of Mount Baker. Along the area's eastern edge you can reach vast wilderness areas of North Cascades National Park.

For an introduction to the region's plant life, take the Shadow of the Sentinels nature trail (near the main entrance highway), which has interpretive signs along the way. Some of the Douglas firs you will see along the trail are more

than 600 years old. At the mouth of Swift Creek, near the north end of Baker Lake, agates and jaspers can be found. Several campgrounds are maintained along the access road. The area is heavily visited on summer weekends.

▶ Access road open year-round, but check in winter for snow closings.

www.fs.fed.us/r6/mbs/about/mbrd.shtml
(360) 856-5700 Ext. 515

4 Stehekin Valley and Rainbow Falls

Accessible from Chelan

Stehekin is a Native American term for "the way through," and it aptly describes the narrow fjord-like valley in which 50-mile-long Lake Chelan lies, providing a way through the almost impenetrable mountain barrier of the North Cascades.

At the upper end of the lake is the quiet, isolated village of Stehekin; settled in 1885, it has fewer than 100 residents. Even today there are no roads to Stehekin, but it can be reached by a delightful four-hour cruise from Chelan on a diesel-powered boat. Floatplane trips are also available. A shuttle bus runs up the valley from the village to campsites, trailheads, and Rainbow Falls, which plunge 312 feet.

Stehekin is a popular starting point for backpacking into the North Cascades; horses and bikes can be rented here, and there are numerous trails to explore.

Spring and fall are the best times to visit; summers are often crowded. Lodging is limited, and reservations are recommended.

▶ Boat operates year-round. Daily mid-Mar.–mid-Oct.; Mon., Wed., Fri. mid-Oct.–mid-Mar. Cruise fee charged.

www.stehekin.biz
www.ladyofthelake.com (for cruise info)
(800) 536-0745

5 Neah Bay

US-101 to SR-112

Famous for its scenery and salmon, Neah Bay also has one of the finest museums of Native American culture in the United States. The $2 million Makah Cultural and Research Center

4 ▶ **Stehekin Valley and Rainbow Falls.** This tiny and isolated village, accessible only by boat or floatplane, looks out over 50-mile-long Lake Chelan.

houses the best of more than 55,000 archaeological items from the remains of Ozette, a nearby Makah Indian village that was buried and preserved by mudslides about 500 years ago. The exhibits—totem poles, seagoing canoes, a wealth of exquisitely crafted artifacts, clothes, household articles, and a reconstruction of a tribal longhouse—give a complete picture of an ancient and highly developed lifestyle.

Cape Flattery, the most northwestern point in the lower 48 states, is a comfortable half-hour hike from Neah Bay through dense forest on a cedar-planked boardwalk and groomed earthen trail with observation decks. The Cape is noted for its rugged headlands and crashing surf.

At the lookout from the end of the trail, you can see the rugged coastline, Tatoosh Island, and the Cape Flattery Lighthouse, which is unmanned. Koitlah Point and Hobuck Beach, each a short drive from Neah Bay, also offer stunning

scenery. Whale-watching is popular, and birding is excellent here.

▶ Open daily year-round except major holidays. Admission charged.

www.northolympic.com/makah
(800) 942-4042

6 Olympic Coast Discovery Center

111 E. Railroad, Port Angeles

In 1994, following a series of devastating oil spills, a 3,300-square-mile segment on the western edge of the Olympic Peninsula was designated a federal marine sanctuary under the aegis of NOAA (National Oceanic and Atmospheric Administration). NOAA's duty is to protect, conserve, and study the rich biological, geological, and historical diversity of the Olympic Coast National Marine Sanctuary, which attracts more than 3.5 million visitors annually, as well as scientists and researchers.

Numerous activities are avail-

able, from hiking, camping, and viewing awesome wildlife and birds to cold-water ocean diving (for advanced, experienced divers only). But it is strongly advised that sanctuary visitors start at NOAA's Olympic Coast Discovery Center, located on the Port Angeles waterfront. Here you'll find all the information you need to plan an exciting, safe, and environmentally sensitive adventure in the wild.

▶ Open daily June–Aug.

www.olympiccoast.noaa.gov
(360) 457-6622

7 Queets Valley Rain Forest, Olympic National Park

The cooling of moisture-laden ocean air as it is driven upward by mountain slopes is responsible for the unusually heavy annual precipitation—about 145 inches—in this remote part of the Olympic National Park. The result is a temperate rain forest that grows with almost tropical intensity. Sitka spruces and Western hemlocks are the dominant trees, along with Douglas firs and Western red cedars. Club moss hangs everywhere in festoons, and licorice fern grows in the shade of big-leaf maples. There is scarcely a square inch of soil that does not support vegetation of some kind. A landslide destroyed a significant portion of the main road in 2005, but the park service has restored access through a series of forest roads.

The most famous inhabitants here are the noble Roosevelt elk, frequently seen in meadows along a three-mile loop trail. You might also glimpse black-tailed deer or a pileated woodpecker.

Trout and salmon fishing is good, and visitors can see salmon spawning in the fall and winter.

Float trips are popular from Apr.–June. Be careful of submerged logs and overhanging boughs, however. There are launching places for boats, canoes, and rafts along the access road and at the campsite.

▶ Park and campground open year-round; call for conditions. Camping fee.

www.nps.gov/olym
(360) 565-3130

8 Deer Park Campground, Olympic National Park

18 miles south of US-101 on Deer Park Rd., Port Angeles
Among firs and pines at the end of a steep, tortuous dirt road, Deer Park has 14 primitive campsites near the summit of 6,007-foot Blue Mountain. A one-mile hike climbs from the camping area to the summit, where there are superb views of the Olympic Range, the Strait of Juan de Fuca, Vancouver Island, and the Cascade Mountains. Other trails, steep and arduous in places, lead through valleys and meadows where one is likely to see Columbia black-tailed deer, for which the area is named, as well as Olympic marmots endemic to these mountains. Piper's bellflowers, Flett's violets, and a species of astragalus, all unique to the Olympic mountains, bloom here in the summer, as well as swaths of Indian paintbrush, lupines, and avalanche lilies.

In this fragile environment campfires and wood gathering are prohibited. A ranger station is staffed here during the summer.

▶ Road and campground open as snow permits, generally late June-Oct. Campground fee.

www.nps.gov/olym
(360) 565-3130

9 Olympic Sculpture Park

2901 Western Ave., Seattle
This park, opened in 2007, began with the bold notion to reclaim and transform a distressed stretch of waterfront. The nine-acre site, once a petroleum depot, was wasteland until the Seattle Art Museum and the Trust for Public Land purchased it. Now a lush green swath overlooking Puget Sound, the park reconnects the downtown with its natural environment.

Prominently featured are sculptures by some of the foremost names of modern art, including Alexander Calder, Richard Serra, Louise Nevelson, and Tony Smith. The landscaping itself is sculptural; environments representing distinct regional ecosystems shift from forest to meadow to shoreline. Visitors are free to stroll the unique 2,500-foot walkway or veer off for closer looks at the art. Operated by the museum, the park also hosts temporary exhibits, special outdoor performances, and other public events.

▶ Open year-round.

www.seattleartmuseum.org
(206) 654-3100

10 Fort Nisqually Living History Museum, Point Defiance Park

5400 N. Pearl St. #11, Tacoma
In the deep wilderness, where beaver trapping was a lucrative business and the arm of the law was remote, the British Hudson's Bay Company built forts to trade with the Puget Sound Native Americans and safeguard its money and stock of furs. Such was the case of Fort Nisqually, a lonely post on Puget Sound.

At the restored fort visitors travel back in time to the year 1855, experiencing life in Washington Territory during the fur-trade era. Two original buildings are on the site: the 1850 Granary (the oldest standing structure in Washington State) and the 1855 Factor's House. Other buildings, such as the Men's Dwelling House and the Large Storehouse, are authentic reconstructions.

Volunteers and staff in period clothing engage visitors by using mid-19th-century language and demonstrating old-time crafts. There's a new interpretive center and education building. Special events are held throughout the year.

▶ Fort open daily Memorial Day-Labor Day; Wed.-Sun. the rest of the year. Admission charged.

www.fortnisqually.org
(253) 591-5339

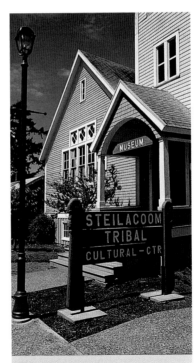

11 Steilacoom. The Native American heritage of the Chambers Creek area is celebrated in this Tribal Cultural Center and Museum.

11 Steilacoom

Pierce County, on the shores of Puget Sound
Founded by a sea captain and officially established in 1854, Steilacoom has the distinction of being the oldest incorporated town in the state of Washington. Just strolling its streets is a trip back to the past; the small town has 32 buildings and landmarks named to the *National Register of Historic Places*. Lovely historic homes abound, including the Nathaniel Orr Home and Pioneer Orchard, decorated with original furnishings and artifacts. Now under renovation is the Bair Drug & Hardware Store, established in 1895. It will display patent medicines, hardware relics, and an early town post office, along with a 1906-vintage soda fountain to serve up old-fashioned milkshakes and sundaes in style.

Steilacoom Historical Museum focuses on the years from 1860 to 1900, with fascinating artifacts of local pioneer life. Features include original volumes from Washington Territory's first library, a blacksmith shop, a Victorian parlor, and a barbershop with a unique collection of shaving mugs.

A few blocks away, in a former church on Main St., the Steilacoom Tribal Cultural Center and Museum celebrates the area's Native American legacy. Exhibits trace the history of the Steilacoom tribe, with a collection of items ranging from hunting tools to clothing made from cedar bark.

▶ Open year-round. Admission charged.

www.steilacoom.org/museum
(253) 584-4133 Historical Museum

www.steilacoomtribe.com
(253) 584-6308 Tribal Cultural Center & Museum

12 Sunrise, Mount Rainier National Park

State Hwy. 410, east of Enumclaw
Among America's most ravishing sights is the 14,410-foot volcanic peak of Mount Rainier, with its 25 glaciers reaching down like fingers to subalpine meadows carpeted in summer with wildflowers.

The Sunrise area, at an elevation of 6,400 feet, is the highest point you can reach in the park by car. It is an excellent place to admire this majestic mountain and to explore a region where a variety of plants and animals manage to survive in extremely marginal circumstances. The 15-mile paved access road to Sunrise offers breathtaking mountain scenery.

Hiking trails lead through subalpine firs and Alaska cedars. At the timberline are gnarled whitebark pines and Engleman spruce, some of which may have taken 75 years to reach a height of 18 inches. Mount Rainier's famous meadows of wildflowers bloom in two stages on the eastern slope.

There are no overnight accommodations at Sunrise; the nearest campsites can be found at White River Campground.

▶ Open July–Labor Day; confirm ahead. Admission charged.

www.nps.gov/mora
(360) 569-2211

13 Cle Elum Historic Telephone Museum

221 E. 1st St., Cle Elum
On April 5, 1901, when store owner Theron Stafford made the first phone call in Cle Elum, he had some 10 numbers to choose from. In 1966, when the dial system was installed—completing the transition to dial phones in the towns served by Pacific Northwest Bell—he would have been able to reach 96 million in the United States alone.

To commemorate this extraordinary development, the Pacific Northwest Bell Telephone Company gave the original telephone exchange building to the Cle Elum Historical Society, along with historic equipment ranging from an 1894 model with a crank to the designs of today.

The museum, however, is not solely devoted to the telephone. A collection of photographs from newspapers and other sources depicts the life and times of this small coal-mining town. One oddity is a camera owned by Etta Place, who, along with Butch Cassidy and the Sundance Kid, tried to rob a nearby bank.

▶ Open weekends Memorial Day–Labor Day.

www.nkcmuseums.org
(509) 674-2770

14 Cashmere Pioneer Village and Museum

600 Cotlets Way, Cashmere
This museum and pioneer village traces life as it has been lived in this area for more than 9,000 years.

Touring the museum, one marvels at the ingenuity of the Native Americans. Visitors learn, for example, that 5,000 years ago they practiced a form of brain surgery using fermented herbs similar to penicillin. No less impressive are the tiny beads carefully drilled with primitive stone tools, the basketry, and the fine leather and feather work.

The Hudson's Bay Company display gives a vivid view of what went on in the fur business here in the early 1800s. You not only see an assortment of trade goods but also learn the rates of exchange: a one-foot-high metal bucket, for instance, bought a one-foot-high stack of fur pelts.

There are 20 authentic log cabins,

14 Cashmere Pioneer Village and Museum. The village's name was changed from Mission after a local judge visited India and found the scenery in Cashmere similar to that back home.

all over 120 years old, in the village. Each is amazingly complete, down to the stacks of period-labeled canned goods on the shelves of the general store and the books and inkwells in the schoolhouse.

Many buildings have fascinating stories. The jailhouse was originally designed as a home by an escaped convict. The waterwheel used for irrigation, incorporating the drive shaft of an old Columbia River paddle steamer, is a nationally recognized symbol of the pioneers' ingenuity. There is so much to see here that you may wish to bring a lunch; a picnic area overlooks the village and a river. To avoid crowds, visit in Apr., May, or Oct.

▶ Open daily Mar.–mid-Oct.; Fri.–Sun. Nov.–mid-Dec. Admission charged.

www.visitcashmere.com/pionvilandmu.html
(509) 782-3230

15 Olmstead Place State Park

N. Ferguson Rd., Ellensburg
Samuel and Sarah Olmstead, attracted by the grasslands and rich soil of the Kittitas Valley, arrived here in 1875, built a 40- by 30-foot cabin, and began farming a 160-acre homestead. Their family lived here for two generations, including the year 1878, when the cabin was used as a fort in the Nez Perce War.

Today this historical park offers an intriguing opportunity to see how a Kittitas Valley family farm developed from the 1870s through the 1950s. Touring the four rooms of the original cabin, you'll see the saddles, crockery, cookware, china, storage chests, organ, stove, and desk that were the stuff of the family's daily life.

A house built in 1908 is more elegantly appointed, with wrought-iron lamps, carved desks, and a

16 **Ginkgo Petrified Forest State Park.** Ancient peoples etched a number of petroglyphs into the stone "walls" of the forest.

library furnished with a red plush velvet love seat. The renovated red barn—originally used for grain storage—now houses hands-on farm activities and exhibits.

The three-quarter-mile Altapes Creek Trail leads along the tree-lined creek to the picturesque Seaton schoolhouse, a small log cabin built more than 100 years ago. Altapes is a Kittitas word meaning "most beautiful creek in the valley."

▶ Open year-round for day use. Guided tours of historic buildings on weekends Memorial Day–Labor Day and by appointment all year.

www.parks.wa.gov
(509) 925-1943

16 Ginkgo Petrified Forest State Park

Exit 136 off I-90, Vantage
Specimens from one of the world's most spectacularly varied fossil forests can be seen here on a 7,470-acre site that encompasses prehistoric swamp and lake beds repeatedly inundated by lava. Felled trees from the dense forests

of the Miocene Epoch—not just the ginkgo for which the park is named, but some 200 other species—were preserved beneath the solidified basalt, gradually turning to brilliantly colored stone as mineral deposits replaced their cell structure. Ice Age erosion brought them to light again.

Now cross-sections of the fossilized logs can be seen in the park's Heritage Area Interpretive Center, along with an array of intelligently planned explanatory exhibits. The area also contains a number of delicate Native American carvings incised in black basalt. You can see logs in their original setting by taking either of the hikes through the Natural Area, the first a three-quarter-mile interpretive trail, the second a 2$\frac{1}{2}$-mile trek.

It's a good idea to make your camping headquarters at Wana-pum Recreation Area, which is located within the park three miles south of Vantage on the shore of the Columbia River.

▶ Park open daily Apr.–Oct.; weekends and holidays only Nov.–Mar. Camping fee. Interpretive center open daily, Memorial Day–Labor Day.

www.parks.wa.gov
(509) 856-2700

17 Leadbetter Point, Willapa National Wildlife Refuge

Stackpole Rd., Oysterville
The three-mile-long refuge at the tip of Long Beach Peninsula is a world of mudflats, sand dunes, saltmarshes, and oyster beds—a home or way station for more than 200 species of birds, especially during the migratory seasons. Virtually every kind of shorebird in Oregon and Washington congre-

gates here at some time during the year. Black brants by the thou-sands stop on their way north from Mexico in April and May, and scores of sooty shearwaters en route to New Zealand drop by in August. In January the point is a good place to glimpse such rarities as gyrfalcons and snowy owls.

On the ocean side of the point, you may see seals sunning them-selves. In summer the 500-acre Salicornia salt marsh, which has never been dredged, produces a

depot, built in 1912 and spanning about a block in length, this charming museum evokes pioneer life in Lewis County, the first official county in Washington State. Four galleries provide a trip back in time, starting with displays celebrating the region's original settlers, the Cowlitz and Chehalis tribes. Visitors are also invited to step inside a blacksmith shop and a vintage secondhand store, as well as ponder typical farming, logging, and mining tools.

18 **Lewis County Historical Museum.** Objects from southwest Washington's earliest days are on view in a 1912 train depot.

rich display of grindelia, jaumea, asters, and other wildflowers. The refuge is accessible only by foot trails from the parking lot. Mosquitoes are numerous, and repellent is recommended.

▶ Open year-round.

www.fws.gov/willapa
(360) 484-3482

18 Lewis County Historical Museum

Off I-5, Chehalis
Tucked inside a classic brick train

Child-friendly attractions include a bygone mercantile store and the Home Sweet Home house, stocked with old-time dress-up clothes and pretend cooking utensils. Grown-ups can arrange for a guided tour of the museum or sign up for one of the periodic classes offered in pioneering crafts and skills, like soap-making.

▶ Open year-round Tues.–Sat.; Tues.– Sun. in summer. Closed major holidays. Admission charged.

www.lewiscountymuseum.org
(360) 748-0831

19 Mount St. Helens National Volcanic Monument

Exit 49 off I-5, Castle Rock

On May 18, 1980, when a massive explosion tore the top off Mount St. Helens, residents of the northwest received a ringing reminder that the huge, majestic mountains that surround them are actually active volcanoes. The eruption displaced nearly a cubic mile of the mountain, launching rock and ash 14 miles into the air, decimating hundreds of square miles of forest, and killing 57 people. In the wake of the disaster, this national monument was established to preserve the site for scientific study and to provide the curious with opportunities to explore.

Today there are two main visitors centers. The Silver Lake center, just east of Castle Rock, offers exhibits and interpretive programs that help explain the history and geology of the mountain. The Johnston Ridge Observatory, in the heart of the monument at the end of Rte. 504 and just 5^{1}/$_{2}$ miles from the crater of the volcano, provides spectacular views of the mountain and the areas affected by

the eruption. A short trail provides additional vantages and informative displays about the eruption and the forest's slow regeneration, and naturalists are often on hand to supplement that information.

A warren of forest service roads circles the monument, providing access to campgrounds, trails, and additional viewpoints, including Windy Ridge, which overlooks Spirit Lake, choked with thousands of dead trees washed down from the mountainside. Call for current conditions, because these roads may be closed by snow or landslides.

▶ Silver Lake open daily year-round; Johnston Ridge open mid-May–mid-Oct.

www.fs.fed.us/gpnf/mshnvm
(360) 449-7800

20 Cowlitz County Historical Museum

405 Allen St., Kelso

This well-organized museum chronicles the main themes of 19th- and 20th-century life in the Pacific Northwest. Canoe anchors, arrowheads, and carrying

21 **Palouse Falls State Park.** The sun sets on Palouse Falls, also viewable from the floor of the canyon.

baskets reflect the Native Americans' mode of survival in this abundant land. The hardships of pioneers on their overland journey and the struggles of early settlers are recalled by displays of early-day tools and equipment, as well as an 1884 cramped but sturdy log cabin lived in by a Toutle River settler.

The all-important logging industry is also portrayed. The rapid changes in lifestyles of the Northwest are depicted in the colorful tableaux of a general store, with a stereoscopic viewer on the premises, a steamboat dock, and a railroad depot.

▶ Open Tues.–Sun. Closed major holidays.

www.co.cowlitz.wa.us/museum
(360) 577-3119

21 Palouse Falls State Park

Southeast of Washtucna

The grace, beauty, and power of Palouse Falls as it drops 200 feet into a horseshoe-shaped basin create one of Washington's most spectacular sights. From the park viewpoint you can photograph the awesome surge of water and the rainbows created by its sunstruck mist. Surefooted visitors hike 250

feet down to the basin for a water-level view (or to try for catfish, which spawn in the canyon pools). Others walk the path that meanders around the bluffs above the falls for a bird's-eye view. Below the falls the wild waters of the Palouse rush through its natural canyon, which extends for eight miles, and then wind among rolling bluffs to empty into the Snake River.

The falls and canyon have a long history. Twenty thousand years ago a glacial lake spread from northern Idaho to northwestern Montana, covering more than 3,000 square miles. As the climate warmed, the ice dam burst, and a tremendous flood of water and debris roared down the Snake and Columbia rivers, rearranging the landscape as it went.

▶ Open year-round. Camping fee. Closed to camping late Sept.–mid-Mar.

www.parks.wa.gov
(360) 902-8844

22 Maryhill Museum of Art

35 Maryhill Museum Dr., Goldendale

The palatial stone mansion set high on a remote spot overlooking the Columbia River, surrounded by 26 acres of parklike gardens, was built by the multimillionaire Samuel Hill, the son-in-law of railroad magnate James J. Hill—an international peace promoter, world traveler, and friend of royalty. Sam Hill, of Quaker parentage, had intended to start a Quaker agricultural community here with Maryhill as his residence. The colony did not materialize, and he was persuaded by Loie Fuller, an avant-garde dancer, to turn the building into a museum.

The centerpiece of the museum

19 **Mount St. Helens National Volcanic Monument.** A heavy snowfall blankets a volcano covered with deep layers of ash after it blew its top in the spring of 1980.

22 ▶ Maryhill Museum of Art. Permanent and rotating exhibits at this secluded mansion range from Rodin sculptures to the works of notable artists of today.

is Sam Hill's collection of "Rodin's Rodins"—bronzes, plasters, and sketches that the famous sculptor kept in his studio for reference. Among them is a plaster cast of a reduced version of "The Thinker."

Other displays include 19th-century American and European paintings, weaponry, icons, Native American baskets, antique chess sets, 1940s French fashion mannequins, and the Queen Marie Room, where you'll find her throne, a coronation gown, and many of her personal belongings. There is also an outdoor sculpture garden.

Maryhill is as much a curiosity as it is a museum of fine art. Nothing really quite prepares you for this imposing structure—filled

with priceless art and artifacts—literally in the middle of nowhere. An eccentric added attraction is a concrete model of England's Stonehenge, visible from the highway leading to Maryhill.

▶ Museum open daily mid-Mar.–mid-Nov. Admission charged.

www.maryhillmuseum.org
(509) 773-3733

23 ▶ Whitman Mission National Historic Site

Off US-12, 6 miles west of Walla Walla

This pastoral setting of open fields with a millpond, a memorial obelisk, a reconstructed covered wagon, some ruins, and a gravesite is the scene of a tragic conflict of cultures that took place in 1847.

Marcus and Narcissa Whitman, along with their companions, Henry and Eliza Spalding, came west in 1836 to convert Native Americans to Christianity. The mission that they built here at Waiilatpu soon became an important way station for thousands of other immigrants. Whitman's efforts at conversion,

however, achieved far less success: The Cayuse didn't want to give up their centuries-old spiritual and religious beliefs. Their tenuous trust of settlers collapsed when an epidemic of measles killed half the tribe. Believing they were being poisoned, a band of desperate Cayuses attacked the mission on November 29, 1847, killing the Whitmans and 11 others and taking 50 captives, who later were ransomed. About 250 members of the Cayuse village died as well. The immigrant's punitive campaign against the Cayuses drove them from their land and into the mountains.

The visitors center at this 98-acre site displays implements belonging to the Whitmans and some beautiful Cayuse garments, including a feathered headdress, a beaded leather shirt, and dresses ornamented with shells. In summer craft demonstrations are presented.

▶ Open year-round except major winter holidays. Admission charged.

www.nps.gov/whmi
(509) 522-6360

23 ▶ Whitman Mission National Historic Site. Pioneers used this covered wagon on the Oregon Trail.

WASHINGTON

West Virginia

Deep in the forested hills and valleys, visitors have gratifying encounters with nature and the vibrant history of a hard-won land.

West Virginia State Farm Museum. The classroom at the 1870 Mission Ridge School was typical of the rural one-room schools of the 19th century (see page 355).

Mountains, great forests, and a vast, mossy bog where orchids and swamp plants grow accent the dramatic natural scene in West Virginia. The abundant game that made this rugged land a favorite hunting ground for many Native American tribes is still appreciated and has been protected in a wildlife center and fish hatchery. The demanding life of the early pioneers is depicted in an excellent farm museum, and the prehistoric Adena people, the first inhabitants of this land, left behind invaluable treasures for us to explore 2,000 years later.

visit ➤➤ **offthebeatenpathtrips.com**

1 Grave Creek Mound Archaeological Complex

801 Jefferson Ave., Moundsville
The largest conical mound in the Americas, Grave Creek Mound rises impressively to a height of 69 feet from a base 295 feet in diameter. It contains an estimated 60,000 tons of earth from the encircling moat and the nearby borrow pits. At an average load of 40 pounds per basket, the construction required 3 million basketfuls.

Built about 2,000 years ago by Native Americans of the Adena culture, the structure was discovered in the early 1800s by white settlers. Its first excavation, in 1838, revealed two burial chambers containing human remains, ornaments, tools fashioned of bone, stone, and shell, and a small tablet of sandstone inscribed with signs that have been interpreted as a kind of pre-Columbian writing.

On climbing the spiral path to the top and looking down upon the Ohio River and the surrounding hills, one can't help wondering what inspired the mound builders to create their massive works. The mound provokes a perplexed melancholy over a mystery that may never be solved and a people lost forever.

Adjacent to the mound is the Delf Norona Museum, which contains artifacts and other displays dealing with the mound, the

 North Bend State Park. Recreation seekers can rent boats and fish from piers at the park's placid 305-acre lake, created when the Hughes River was dammed.

Adena, and associated cultures in the vicinity.

▶ Open daily year-round except major holidays.

www.wvculture.org/sites/gravecreek.html
(304) 843-4128

2 North Bend State Park

Cairo
Named for the horseshoe curve of the north fork of the Huges River, this beautiful 1,405-acre park supplies the wonderment of exploring a high plateau. The central area lies on a bluff at the horseshoe curve. A scenic trail skirts the rim of the escarpment, sometimes descending into and climbing out of miniature valleys

that run down to the river's edge. Other trails through the woodlands lead to a variety of overlooks and rock formations.

Featured in the park is the 72-mile North Bend Rail Trail, which is designed for hiking, mountain biking, and horseback riding. And the newly added Cokeley Recreation Area provides five miles of multi-use non-motorized trails, along with a lake stocked with fish, boat rentals, boat and canoe launches, and two accessible fishing platforms.

▶ Open year-round.

www.northbendsp.com
(304) 643-2931

4 ▶ West Virginia State Farm Museum

Just off Rte. 62, 4 miles north of Point Pleasant

This memorial to America's early-day farmers and pioneers takes one back to the time when do-it-yourself was a way of life. Broom making, quilting, and other such demonstrations provide you with a sense of actually being part of the 19th century. In early autumn you can see the steam engine and belt-driven threshing machine in action and buy the cider, apple butter, and molasses made here.

Among the 31 buildings housed on the farm's 50 acres are an 1805 log cabin, a one-room schoolhouse, an operating blacksmith's shop, a country store that is stocked with nostalgic items, and a replica of a Lutheran church built in 1815. Also included is the historic log home built in 1800 by Abner McCoy, which was recently moved and reconstructed to be added to the museum's collection. The church, a simple log cabin, has a safety balcony for women and children and a musket rack by the entrance—reminders of the conflicts between the Native Americans and the encroaching white settlers.

Also found here are fascinating collections of household and farm equipment of the 1800s, barnyard animals, and a museum with a taxidermic collection of birds and animals. With advance notice groups can arrange to purchase a special "pioneer" lunch here.

▶ Open Tues.–Sun. Apr.–mid-Nov. Donations encouraged.

www.wvfarmmuseum.org
(304) 675-5737

Belle Boyd House. The Corning Room museum displays clothing from the years 1860 to 1920.

3 ▶ Belle Boyd House

126 E. Race St., Martinsburg

Regional historians will tell you that Belle Boyd, a colorful Confederate spy, possessed such charm and persuasiveness that she convinced Abraham Lincoln in a letter to pardon an imprisoned traitor—a man from whom she'd wheedled Union military secrets and whom she later married.

The Library of Congress has that letter, but the museum in the redbrick house that Belle's father built in 1853 maintains a trove of material about her, including dramatic pictures and a letter to a cousin describing her own considerable beauty. Herbs that were used to treat wounded Civil War soldiers grow outside, and fashions of Belle's time are on display. Tribute is also paid here to Martinsburg's Hack Wilson, the baseball great.

▶ Closed Wed., Sun., and major holidays mid-Apr.–Dec.

www.bchs.org
(304) 267-4713

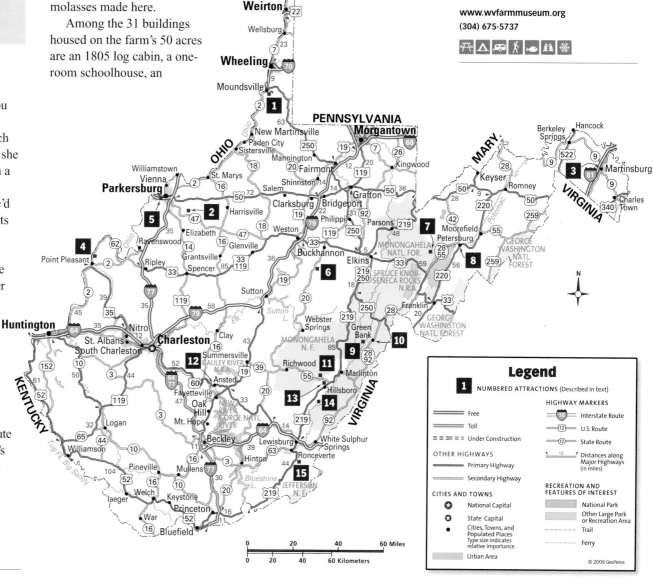

Legend

1 NUMBERED ATTRACTIONS (Described in text)

HIGHWAY MARKERS

Free
Toll
Under Construction

OTHER HIGHWAYS
Primary Highway
Secondary Highway

CITIES AND TOWNS
National Capital
State Capital
Cities, Towns, and Populated Places Type size indicates relative importance
Urban Area

10 Interstate Route
12 U.S. Route
12 State Route
12 Distances along Major Highways (in miles)

RECREATION AND FEATURES OF INTEREST
National Park
Other Large Park or Recreation Area
Trail
Ferry

© 2009 GeoNova

5 ▶ Blennerhassett Island Historical State Park

In the Ohio River, 2 miles west of Parkersburg

A scenic 20-minute ride on a vintage 19th-century riverboat is the perfect way to begin a day at this quaint, tranquil island—and about the only way to get there. Stern-wheelers depart from the docks of downtown Parkersburg, just outside a museum devoted to the island's colorful, turbulent history.

On the island, visitors can tour the Blennerhassett mansion, catch a narrated horse-drawn carriage ride, stroll along tree-shaded paths, or enjoy a picnic.

Originally built in 1800, the mansion was the proud homestead of Harman Blennerhassett, a

Blennerhassett Island Historical State Park. An air of luxury surrounds the mansion of Harman and Margaret Blennerhasset, reconstructed after it burned to the ground.

wealthy Irish aristocrat. Six years later he was forced to flee the island due to charges of complicity in a treason plot with the famous U.S. politician Aaron Burr. In 1811 the magnificent mansion burned to the ground. More than 160 years later archaeologists unearthed its foundations and inspired its glorious rebuilding. Today docents in

period costumes conduct tours.

Harman Blennerhassett was not the island's only notable resident. It was once claimed by Native American tribes. Then during the 1760s the celebrated Delaware Native American chief Nemacolin made his home here, before the white settlers came in the 1780s. In its pioneer heyday Blennerhassett was visited by such legendary figures as Walt Whitman, Henry Clay, and Johnny Appleseed.

▶ Museum open year-round; island reachable only when stern-wheelers run, from early May–late Oct. Separate admission fees for each.

www.blennerhassettislandstatepark.com
(304) 420-4800

6 ▶ West Virginia State Wildlife Center

On Rte. 20S, French Creek

At this well-kept parklike zoo you can see the wild animals and birds that once were—and mostly still are—native to West Virginia. The 329-acre farm was started in 1923 to protect diminishing wildlife and to pen-raise animals and game

birds for release into the countryside. That program was halted, and now the place is devoted to education and recreation. Native wildlife wander freely in the fenced natural habitats.

The most spectacular of the creatures to be seen are the mountain lion of formidable size, black bears, elks, river otters, and bison. Among the more engaging specimens are white-tailed deer, coyotes, raccoons, and showy ring-necked pheasants. Wild turkeys, foxes, timber wolves, opossums, and other species are also at home here. A newly completed fisher exhibit provides a close-up view of the shy animals, and a special display of Jack the black bear will please past visitors. In addition, the wildlife center maintains a stocked trout pond open to fishing, and a spacious picnic area.

▶ Open year-round. Admission charged Apr.–Oct.

www.wvdnr.gov/wildlife/wildlifecenter.shtm
(304) 924-6211

West Virginia State Wildlife Center. Baby foxes, or kits, are among the residents here.

7 ▶ Dolly Sods

Forest Rds. 75 and 19, between Canaan Valley and Petersburg

Stunning vistas await you on the 32,000 acres that hug a ridge of the eastern Continental Divide. In fall visitors see leaves ablaze with color. In spring, mountain laurels in full flower abound. Visitors also find the ultimate getaway here: camping on more than 10,000 acres of wilderness and the peace that comes with being immersed in nature.

Once dense forest, the vast acres of the Sods were clear-cut by loggers in the 1880s and then scorched deeply by fire—set off by sparks from steam locomotives. Since then the forest has regrown, and cranberry, huckleberry, and blueberry bushes thrive amid the rock formations. In summer at Bear Rocks, a bountiful berry harvest is yours for the picking.

▶ Open year-round. Fee for camping.

www.fs.fed.us/r9/mnf/sp/dolly_scenic.html
(304) 257-4488

Dolly Sods. Rock formations in the forest serve as natural overlooks.

8 ▶ Petersburg Trout Hatchery

Off Rte. 220, Petersburg
Regardless of whether you prefer trout in a stream or on a dinner plate, it is fascinating to see how the demand for that prized fish is met. At this hatchery (one of many in the state) 1 million trout, rainbow and golden, are hatched every year for introduction into West Virginia's streams.

The golden trout were bred selectively in Petersburg from a gift of 10,000 rainbow fry that was given to the hatchery in 1949.

8 ▶ Petersburg Trout Hatchery. The golden rainbow trout bred here are released into streams.

They were then introduced on a large scale into West Virginia's rivers in 1963. The golden trout are a shining gold color, with red-striped sides and tails.

The fish are kept in four large, dark pools constantly aerated by fountains, side sprays, and a stream flowing through. However, only one of the ponds is dedicated to holding and rearing the trout that will become the brood fish.

The trout can be seen swimming in shoals, darting, or resting at times. Younger trout—which are 1 1/2 to 2 inches long—are kept in two raceways, each holding some 100,000 of the fish.

The trout to be released in streams are transported in stocking trucks through which water is constantly circulated. About 90 percent of the fish will be caught by appreciative anglers enjoying a day out on the water.

Perhaps the best time to visit the hatchery is mid-Aug.–early Oct., when spawning and hatching occur.

▶ Open year-round.

(304) 257-4014

9 ▶ Cass Scenic Railroad State Park

State Rte. 66
An old coal-fueled steam locomotive pulls riders on the Cass railroad up a steep incline—rising 11 feet for every 100 feet traveled at its steepest—to Bald Knob for spectacular mountain views. It's the same locomotive that West Virginia Pulp and Paper used here more than a century ago to transport lumber to a mill.

Today visitors can be transported back in time to an era when steam-driven locomotives were a part of everyday life. They can also take a free tour of the company town or shop and walk the wooden sidewalks on their own. Lodging is available at some 20 houses where loggers and their families once lived. Visitors can also stay overnight in 1920s-era cabooses. Restorations have been carried out with a modest bow to modern comforts and convenience.

▶ Open year-round; trains run from late May-late Oct.

www.cassrailroad.com
(800) 225-5982

10 ▶ The National Radio Astronomy Observatory. The surrounding mountains shield one of the world's largest fully steerable radio telescopes from unwelcome radio interference.

10 ▶ The National Radio Astronomy Observatory

Rte. 92, Green Bank
The radio dish antennas of this observatory loom from the valley floor to tune in to distant galaxies, quasars, and pulsars. Founded in 1956, NARO is operated by a consortium of universities. The observatory also maintains a research facility in New Mexico. It chose this secluded valley, which is part of the National Radio Quiet Zone, because the surrounding hills provide a shield from harmful radio interference.

The site is home to one of the most advanced astronomical instruments on Earth, the Robert C. Byrd Green Bank Telescope (GBT). The GBT is the world's largest fully steerable radio telescope and the largest moving structure on land. At 485 feet in height, it is taller than the Statue of Liberty. Other equipment here includes a 140-foot equatorially mounted telescope, and the interferometer, which makes use of three telescopes together.

The center also has several historical telescopes and antennas, including an exact replica of the Jansky telescope.

Learning of the mind-boggling work that goes on here and seeing the sci-fi landscape and equipment, you can't help but get a thrilling and yet eerie awareness of remote worlds. A 30-minute narrated bus tour of the site, following a 15-minute movie on radio astronomy, is provided. The science center also offers fascinating hands-on exhibits, a cafe, and a gift shop. Tours are available year-round.

▶ Open daily June-Aug.; Wed.-Sun. Sept.-May.

www.gb.nrao.edu
(304) 456-2150

did you know ?

Physicist Karl Jansky's study of the Milky Way in 1930–32 led to the recognition that radio signals are produced by natural processes in space.

11 ▶ Cranberry Glades Botanical Area

Take Forest Rd. 102, off Rte. 39/55, 23 miles east of Richwood

One walks in wonder here in an open, treeless basin completely out of character with the dense surrounding forest of evergreens and hardwoods.

The major theory about how this intriguing island of botanical nonconformity came to be is that the deep layers of sphagnum moss developed over the centuries in shallow basins that were created by the shifting sedimentation of the local streams. There, plants able to tolerate the extremely acid conditions eventually became established.

The glades are here to be enjoyed. In the botanical area, which encompasses 750 acres, a half-mile-long loop boardwalk with interpretive signs gives you a close view of two of the bogs, with their cranberry vines, thickets of chokeberry, wild raisin, speckled alder, spongy mosses, grasses, sedges, and flowers. Among the latter are swamp candle, orchids, trilliums, monkshood, swamp buttercups, jewelweed, and the carnivorous sundew.

The adjacent 35,864-acre Cranberry Wilderness Area (which is within a black-bear sanctuary) offers more than 70 miles of trails varying in length from 1 1/2 to 13 1/2 miles, along with primitive campsites for backpackers. Adjoining the wilderness area and the Cranberry Glades are many more acres of land and trails suitable for hiking and other recreational activities. The Cranberry Mountain Nature Center provides information on these areas. Accessible year-round, weather permitting.

13 ▶ Pearl S. Buck Birthplace.
The house is furnished much as it was when the Pulitzer prizewinning author of *The Good Earth* was born here in 1892.

▶ Nature center open Thurs.–Mon. May–Oct.

www.fs.fed.us/r9/mnf/sp/
cranberry_glades.html
(304) 653-4826

12 ▶ Contentment Museum

Rte. 60, Ansted

The antebellum house, restored one-room schoolhouse, and small museum that make up this complex provide an insight into the quiet rural life of 19th-century West Virginia.

The house, built about 1830 with a white-columned veranda across the front, was named Contentment by the wife of the ex–Confederate officer who acquired the property in 1872. One can easily imagine the serenity the couple found in this setting. Among the modestly elegant antique furnishings, one particularly charming piece is the fainting sofa, popular generations ago, when ladies were expected to be creatures of delicate sensibilities.

The schoolhouse, with its benches and desks with inkwells, evokes the days of blue-back spellers and *McGuffey's Readers*.

Among the museum displays are moonshiners' copper stills, confiscated by the revenuers, an 1880s wedding gown, a quaint Godey trunk, old pictures of the mining camps, Civil War memorabilia, and American and Native American artifacts.

▶ Open Wed.–Sun., June–Sept. Admission charged.

www.museumsofwv.org
(304) 658-5695

13 ▶ Pearl S. Buck Birthplace

Rte. 219, Hillsboro

Pearl Comfort Sydenstricker, who is better known under her married name, was born here on a small farm in 1892. The writer, who won acclaim in the 1930s for her novel about China, *The Good Earth*, became the first American woman to receive both the Pulitzer Prize (in fiction) and the Nobel Prize (in literature).

A National Literary Landmark, the gracious white-frame homestead, built after the Civil War by her mother's family, the Stultings, is furnished approximately as it was in 1892. Much of the furniture was built by Mrs. Buck's grandfa-

ther. The memorabilia displayed includes photos of the author during her years in China and the Bible that her father, a missionary, had transcribed into Chinese.

On the property is the Stulting barn, which has been restored and contains an assortment of farm implements of the same period. The Sydenstricker house, in which Pearl Buck's father was born, has been relocated here as part of this interesting historical farm complex.

▶ Open Mon.–Sat. May–Oct.

www.pearlsbuckbirthplace.com
(304) 653-4430

14 ▶ Beartown State Park

Rte. 219, 7 miles southwest of Hillsboro

Except for the boardwalk, this area of unusual rock formations is entirely the creation of nature. The rock is Droop sandstone, which tends to break up into huge blocks along nearly vertical planes. As the result of erosion, these blocks have shifted downward, causing deep fissures of varying width and sheer cliffs.

Some of the cracks are two to three feet wide with flat floors, suggesting streets running between buildings. Colonies of black bears are said to have lived among these rocks because they contained many cavelike openings—hence the name.

To see this fascinating place, one goes by a sturdily railed boardwalk over torrents of fallen rock and deep, mossy straight-walled crevasses. Tall, feathery hemlocks grow from towering wedges of rock as though from the prows of ships; the roots of the trees are sometimes high above you, sometimes below, and often crawling down the sides of the rock like writhing snakes. In accompaniment to this grandeur, windsong fills the air in the trees and crevasses and among the boulders.

The boardwalk crosses miniature canyons and valleys in the rock, their sides occasionally blushed with patches of pale red, yellow, and orange and streaked with mineral deposits. The boardwalk continues through rock walls pocked with skull-like depressions and erosion holes and worn into soft pleats, folds, and bony skeletal formations.

The walkway loops back to the parking lot, where you can have a refreshing drink of water from a hand-pumped fountain. The half-mile walk has interpretive signs. The best time to visit the park is in the autumn, when the crowds are not as large.

▶ Foot travel welcome year-round; gate opened only by request Nov.–Apr.

www.beartownstatepark.com
(304) 653-4254

15 ▶ Organ Cave

South of Lewisburg on Rte. 63
This national natural landmark is distinguished for its geological and archaeological features, its historical significance, and its impressive length (45 miles) and depth (486 feet). For centuries, long before it began to offer tours to stagecoach riders in 1822, explorers were mesmerized by its massive passageways, with more than 200 passages remaining to be mapped.

Throughout, stunning limestone sculptures, formed from the bones of prehistoric animals and forces of water, date back hundreds of millions of years and continue to evolve today. The name Organ Cave was inspired by the largest, and arguably most awesome, of all the calcite formations, evoking a grand church organ.

In addition to its astounding natural architecture, the cave contains the largest collection of saltpeter vats in the United States, mined during the Civil War for making gunpowder. The cave also served the spiritual needs of sol-

15 ▶ Organ Cave. Passageways in this cave that have yet to be explored number around 200.

diers: Religious services for over 1,000 of Gen. Robert E. Lee's men were held in the shelter of its huge underground entranceway.

Visitors can sign up for a variety of specialized guided tours, including an easy two-mile walking tour. For those ready to climb and crawl, extended exploring expeditions, ranging from 2–18 hours, lead you deep underground and bring you face-to-face with such wonders as a trio of breathtaking waterfalls that cascade over a 90-foot drop, or a rare growth of gypsum flowers, or bustling communities of bats. On the first August weekend Organ Cave resounds with gospel singing, showcasing talented voices from surrounding counties.

▶ Open daily year-round. Admission charged. Additional fees for specialized tours.

www.organcave.com
(304) 645-7600

14 ▶ Beartown State Park. Some cracks in the behemoths of Droop sandstone are large enough to have accommodated hibernating bears—hence the park's name.

seasonal events

FEBRUARY
• Fasnacht Festival—Helvetica (*parade with masked participants, square dancing, bonfire*)

MARCH
• George Washington's Bathtub Celebration—Berkeley Springs (*historical events, dollar sales*)

MAY
• Vandalia Gathering—East Charleston (*fiddles, banjo players, storytellers, clogging, crafts, food*)

JUNE
• Smoke on the Water Chili Cook-Off—Charleston (*80–100 chili variations to sample*)
• FestivALL—Charleston (*celebration of the arts, including theater, film, and dance, food, entertainment*)

SEPTEMBER
• Treasure Mountain Festival—Franklin (*homemade crafts, heritage demonstrations, food, natural treasures*)
• Swinefest—Huntington (*carnival rides, dunking booth, eating contests, live auction, food vendors, motorcycle and car show*)
• Paw Paw Festival—Paw Paw (*musical entertainment, fireworks*)
• Pilot Club of Hunting Antique Show—Huntington (*antique show and sale*)

OCTOBER
• October Sky Festival—Coalwood (*scale model rocket from NASA, vendors, book signing, music, food, tour of the original rocket site*)

NOVEMBER
• Mountaineer Week—Morgantown (*football game, Appalachian dance, food, music, quilt and craft shows*)
• Festival of Trees—Martinsburg (*decorated trees, live auction*)
• Yuletide in the Park—Hurricane (*animated displays, horse-drawn wagon rides, caroling, hayrides*)

www.westvirginia.com

Wisconsin

The Badger State has no shortage of variety—in the splendid parks and wildlife areas, in the arts and architecture, and in historic places.

Mid-Continent Railway Museum. A parlor car from the Chicago & North Western Railroad is on display at this museum in North Freedom (see page 365).

The hardworking pioneers who laid the foundation for a prosperous state are honored here. A logging museum, an old wayside inn, and the re-creation of a typical small town—Stonefield—throw light on a vigorous past.

Nature lovers will find great birding, hiking in a blessedly quiet wilderness, and two refuges harboring waterfowl. Other attractions include folk art cast in concrete, art inspired by nature, and the estate named Villa Louis—Victorian furnishings and 19th- and 20th-century art all under one roof.

visit ➡ **offthebeatenpathtrips.com**

1 Amnicon Falls State Park

Superior

The Amnicon River, which courses through this pleasant park, has a dramatic series of waterfalls and cascades. And surprisingly the water rushing over them is root-beer brown—a color imparted by tannic acid from vegetation. But the waterfalls are more than a scenic attraction. They also make it possible to see the park's other interesting feature, a geological fault line running through the area.

The Douglas Fault, visible at the foot of the Upper Falls, was created about 500 million years ago when a deep layer of volcanic basalt rock began to push its way through the thick sandstone bed on which the park rests. Today at the falls the river flows through a channel in an upthrust cliff of dark basalt before tumbling into a plunge pool and proceeding on to red sandstone cliffs even more eroded and smoothed by the water. Just below the falls a 12-foot-wide zone of brownish red rocks and pebbles (fault breccia) marks the point where the basalt and sandstone ground against each other.

A covered bridge leading to a charming pine-covered island in the river offers excellent views of the falls. The river can be followed on trails that extend along its bank and circle the island. Swimming in the river is a great adventure.

1 Amnicon Falls State Park. Tannic acid leached from the vegetation in this northwest Wisconsin park gives water rushing over the falls the look of foamy root beer.

However, jumping or diving off the cliffs isn't allowed. During the long Wisconsin winter the park provides a tranquil setting for snowshoers.

▶ Open year-round. Admission charged.

www.dnr.state.wi.us
(715) 398-3000

2 Madeline Island Museum

2.5 miles from the city of Bayfield, on northern Wisconsin's Apostle Islands

Just a short ferry ride from the mainland takes visitors to enchanting Madeline Island on Lake Superior. Since 1693, the date marking its first foreign visitors, the island has attracted dreamers and schemers.

Built on a partnership between

did you know ?

The Madeline Island Museum is filled with rare artifacts from the United States Lighthouse Establishment. For example, an 1862 French-made Fresnel lens that once beamed a guiding light from the Raspberry Island lighthouse tower is on display here.

French fortune-seekers and the Ojibwe people, the island's fur trade flourished for 150 years. Over the centuries Madeline also has attracted fishermen, loggers, missionaries, and beginning in the 1890s, summer residents.

In 1955 Leo and Bella Capser, a couple who had been longtime summer residents, embarked on a mission to provide the island with a special place to ensure the preservation of its colorful history.

Rallying other residents— seasonal and year-round—they amassed a collection and pieced together a complex from part of a surviving American Fur Company building, the former town jail, a memorial to a drowned seaman, and an old barn. On June 15, 1958, the Capsers proudly opened the museum to the public.

Now managed by the Wisconsin Historical Society and substantially expanded with the addition of a modern exhibit hall, the museum tells the island's unique story— from its prehistoric beginnings to the present day.

The museum also features objects that reflect the life and spirit of the Ojibwe people.

Visitors to the island can enjoy seasonal activities such as fishing, swimming, snowshoeing, bicycling, camping, concerts and more.

▶ Open daily Memorial Day–early Oct. Admission charged.

www.madelineislandmuseum.org
(715) 747-2415

2 **Madeline Island Museum.** Artifacts from the fur trade and the early logging industry are on display at this local-history museum.

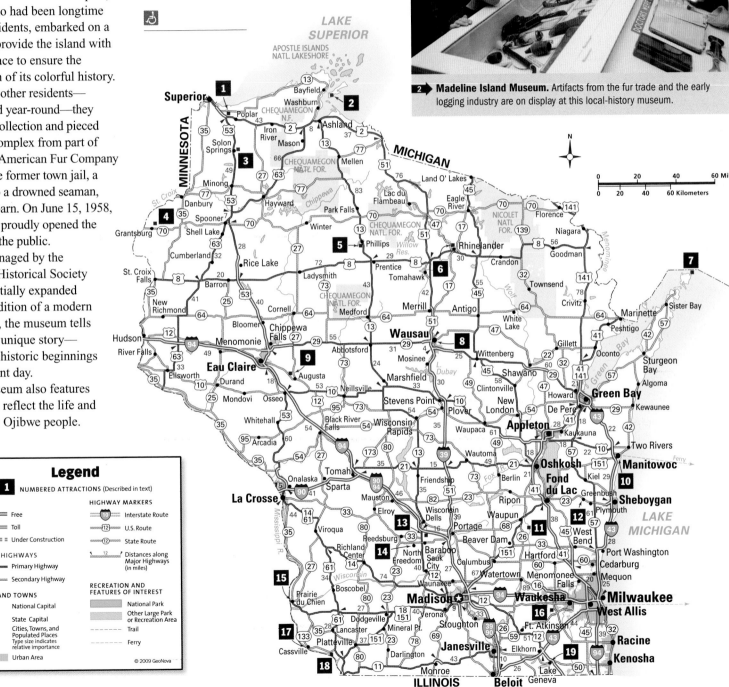

Legend

1 NUMBERED ATTRACTIONS (Described in text)

HIGHWAY MARKERS

Free
Toll
Under Construction

OTHER HIGHWAYS
Primary Highway
Secondary Highway

CITIES AND TOWNS
⊕ National Capital
✪ State Capital
• Cities, Towns, and Populated Places Type size indicates relative importance
Urban Area

Interstate Route
U.S. Route
State Route
Distances along Major Highways (in miles)

RECREATION AND FEATURES OF INTEREST
National Park
Other Large Park or Recreation Area
Trail
Ferry

© 2009 GeoNova

3 ▶ Lucius Woods County Park

US-53, Solon Springs

Tucked compactly between U.S. Hwy. 53 and St. Croix Lake, this park has only 41 acres. But it is enjoyable to visit for its pleasant swimming beach and its tall stands of ancient red and white pines—and in winter for its variety of winter sports.

The beach is a small half-moon of sand nestled in the wooded shoreline of the invitingly spacious lake. A picnic area and a play-ground are nearby. The lake also offers fishing and boating.

The white pines with their deeply furrowed bark, and the red pines with their scaly plates of ruddy bark, are best seen along the hiking trail that follows the creek through the grounds.

An amphitheater is the summer home to a local symphony and serves as the stage for summer music shows, ranging from jazz to country and western.

Winter activities center on ice fishing. Cross-country skiing is also permitted, but trails are not cleared.

▶ Open mid-May–Sept. Fees charged for music shows.

www.douglascountywi.org
(715) 378-2219

4 ▶ Crex Meadows Wildlife Area

102 E. Crex Ave., Grantsburg

Uncommonly beautiful and richly endowed with wildlife, this nature preserve ranks among the most appealing in the country. Its open landscape encompasses 30,000 acres of grassy meadows, prairie and heathlike terrain, open pools and lakes, bogs, and marshes. There are small stands of scrubby oak and willow as well.

Sandhill cranes, white-tailed deer, and trumpeter swans are common sights, and one might see a black bear wandering in the marsh grass. More than 150 species of birds nest here, and some 275 species have been observed. Crex Meadows is a major stopover site for songbirds and waterfowl. Spring and fall are the best viewing times. The wildlife area is also home to a wolf pack called the Crex pack.

Gravel roads provide excellent access, but they are not suitable for bicycles with narrow racing tires. There are four hiking trails, two of which are handicapped accessible. In winter cross-country skiers have free run of the ungroomed trails, and snowmobilers can swoosh along a 15-mile groomed trail. To avoid disturbing birds during their crucial nesting period, camping is permitted only from Sept.–Dec. A wildlife education and visitors center features displays and dioramas of the brush prairie and wetlands.

▶ Open year-round. Camping only in fall.

www.crexmeadows.org
(715) 463-2739

5 ▶ Wisconsin Concrete Park

Hwy. 13, Phillips

Fred Smith and his amazing colorful concrete sculptures are a part of the lore and legend of this part of Wisconsin. A lumberman, Smith retired at the age of 64 in 1950 and immediately began to make his folk-art sculptures—an impulse that, he said, "just comes to me naturally." By the time a stroke disabled him 15 years later, he had created more than 200 figures. He refused to sell to collectors, choosing to leave his work "for the American people."

Smith's farm is now a public

5 ▶ Wisconsin Concrete Park. Figures made of concrete and adorned with broken glass were the stock in trade of Fred Smith, who turned to folk sculpture when he retired.

park, and his artistic endeavor preserved there is a strange but delightful collection of concrete figures: giant Native Americans, folk heroes, scenes from movies and history, life-size deer, bears, and other animals, and local characters whom Smith knew, such as Mabel the Milker milking a cow. Some pieces incorporate real buggies and wagons. His last work portrayed a beer wagon drawn by a team of eight Clydesdale horses.

Smith applied his concrete over a frame of wood and chicken wire and then embedded bits of glass and other materials in the surface for decoration. The resulting figures are storybook primitives with a rigid straight-armed stance. The effect is at once outrageous, touching, funny, and charming.

4 ▶ Crex Meadows Wildlife Area. Sandhill cranes and hundreds of other bird species nest in the marshes, meadows, and ponds of this 30,000-acre preserve.

▶ Open year-round but partly inaccessible when snow is deep. Admission free but donations encouraged.

www.friendsoffredsmith.org
(800) 269-4505; (715) 339-6371

6 Rhinelander Logging Museum

Off Business US-8 in Pioneer Park, Rhinelander
In the 1870s the town of Rhinelander was established as a supply center for the logging camps that were clearing the last of northern Wisconsin's virgin wilderness. This museum, with its reconstructed log cookhouse and bunkhouse, re-creates a logging camp of that era.

In the authentically furnished cookhouse are a period stove, sink, cookware, and long tables. Here, too, is the horn used to call the men to dinner.

The rest of the museum displays ox yokes, pulleys, saws, axes, peavies, pike poles, and the spiked shoes lumbermen wore when they were floating logs downstream.

The exhibits continue outdoors under tall pines, with a combination blacksmith's and carpenter's shop, a boat shed, and a rural schoolhouse. Most notable, however, is the collection of heavy equipment, which includes vintage fire engines, locomotives, log-hauling equipment, a water truck used to ice roads for log sleds, and boom sticks—the huge chain-linked logs used to raft pulpwood across Lake Superior.

The 500 Line Depot was built in 1892 and moved to the museum complex. The depot has been restored to its original design and paint scheme. In the basement you'll find a model railroad display

8 **Leigh Yawkey Woodson Art Museum.** Blooming crabapple trees set off *The Rites of Spring*, a bronze by the renowned Swedish-born sculptor Kent Ullberg.

of the trains operating in the area in the 1920s–40s.

▶ Open daily Memorial Day–Labor Day. Donations accepted.

www.rhinelanderchamber.com
(715) 369-5004

7 Rock Island State Park

Lake Michigan
No cars, no bikes, no wheeled vehicles of any kind: That's the rule for visitors to Rock Island, a 912-acre piece of wilderness off the tip of the Door Peninsula in Lake Michigan. Forty primitive campsites, 10 miles of hiking trails, and 5,000 feet of beach lure back-to-basics backpackers and daytrippers who find few, if any, amenities.

Besides communing with nature, visitors can explore the Pottawatomie Lighthouse, the oldest lighthouse in Wisconsin

(originally constructed in 1836 and rebuilt in 1858) and as picturesque as you would expect. Scandinavian-themed exhibits are found at Viking Hall and the Viking Boathouse, built not by Norse explorers but by Iceland-born inventor Chester H. Thordarson as part of his large estate. (Before Rock Island became a state park, it was owned by Thordarson, who began buying up land in 1910.)

Rock Island is accessible only by a ferry leaving from Washington Island—which in turn is accessible only by a ferry from the town of Northport.

▶ Open year-round. Fees charged for campsites.

www.dnr.state.wi.us/org/land/parks/ specific/rockisland
(920) 847-2235

8 Leigh Yawkey Woodson Art Museum

Franklin and 12th Sts., Wausau
Artwork inspired by nature is the specialty of this museum, which is housed in a gabled brick residence resembling a comfortable country house and large modern galleries that offer a striking contrast to the home's more intimate spaces.

Visitors strolling through the beautifully landscaped 1 1/2-acre sculpture garden and surrounding gardens and grounds will discover nearly two dozen sculptures invitingly placed for viewing.

An autumn tradition is the flagship exhibition, *Birds in Art*, which presents more than 125 all-new paintings and sculptures annually by artists from around the world. The museum's interest in avian art extends to its permanent collection of more than 4,000 works, encompassing historic graphics by John James Audubon, Alexander Wilson, and John Gould; masterworks by Martin Johnson Heade, Jasper Cropsey, and Frank Benson; and contemporary interpretations by Robert Bateman, Ray Harris-Ching, and Lars Jonsson.

In keeping with the wishes of the three daughters of Leigh Yawkey Woodson, who established the museum as a memorial to their mother, 10 to 12 changing exhibitions each year explore a broad spectrum of art. Check the museum's schedule for these shows and the diverse educational programs.

A decorative arts collection includes Royal Worcester porcelain and contemporary studio glass.

▶ Open Tues.-Fri. and weekends except major holidays.

www.lywam.org
(715) 845-7010

9 Dells Mill

Off Rte. 27, 3 miles north of Augusta

Today Wisconsin is famed as the dairy state, but during the second half of the 19th century, the chief agricultural product was wheat, and it was an important part of the nation's breadbasket. Dells Mill, which opened in 1864, was one of hundreds of gristmills that sprang up to grind the grain into flour and feed.

Rising high above a rocky streambed (terrain called dells in Wisconsin), the mill is an impressive five-story structure built by German millwrights with hand-hewn pine timbers secured with pegs of oak. The well-preserved mill is still capable of doing a good day's work, but it is now primarily a museum reflecting country life in bygone days. The exhibits include plows, scythes, harnesses, a ropemaking machine, sleighs, buggies, a reconstructed prairie schooner, and Civil War artifacts.

The most intriguing exhibit, however, is the mill itself, with its old overshot waterwheel, its drive shaft and cogged wheels with hard maple teeth, its grain bins, and its complexities of beams, pipes, and more than a half mile of leather belts that drive the roller mills.

▶ Open daily May-Oct. Admission charged.

www.dellsmill.com
(715) 286-2714

10 Rahr-West Art Museum

610 N. Eighth St., Manitowoc

Consistent with its two-part name, this museum has a split personality. The original building, given by the Rahr family, is a shingled Queen Anne–style mansion built by Joseph Vilas in 1891. It is filled with authentic Victorian furnishings and 19th-century art, including works by such noted painters as Rembrandt Peale, Adolphe Bouguereau, and George Paxton. The mansion also has collections of contemporary porcelain, antique dolls, and most notably, rare Chinese ivories.

In striking contrast the museum's sleek, modern exhibition wing, a gift of John and Ruth West, is home to a collection of 20th-century art with more than 150 canvases. Most of the painters are Americans, ranging from abstractionists such as Frank Stella, Joseph Raphael, and Sam Francis to more representational artists, such as Neil Welliver, Milton Avery, and Jane Freilicher. The new wing also devotes a large space to traveling exhibits.

▶ Open daily except major holidays.

www.rahrwestartmuseum.org
(920) 683-4501

---

did you know ?

On September 6, 1962, a piece of the Russian satellite *Sputnik IV* crash-landed in the middle of Manitowoc's North 8th St., right in front of the Rahr-West Art Museum.

---

11 Horicon National Wildlife Refuge

W4279 Headquarters Rd., Mayville

Millions of waterfowl migrate along the great Mississippi Flyway, and this federal wildlife preserve of 21,000 acres and an adjoining state wildlife area with 11,000 acres was established primarily to provide them with a refuge. Careful management has turned this into one of the nation's greatest areas for wildfowl—and for people who enjoy seeing them.

The marsh is best known for the big black-necked Canada geese that touch down here by the hundreds of thousands in the fall—and unfortunately attract thousands of viewers. But at other times of the year, the marsh is a quiet refuge for the visitor as well as for the plentiful wildlife.

In the spring northbound geese and ducks stage a smaller migratory show. And during the summer the marsh teems with nesting egrets, blue-winged teals, coots, great blue herons, mallards, wood ducks, and redheads. An occasional white-tailed deer and red fox may be seen as well.

Six miles of interconnecting trails wind through the marsh and along the impoundments around the edges. They traverse a beautifully austere landscape of lush reeds and rough marshlands mingled with clear lakes, sparse pockets of brush, and small stands of trees. Some areas can be seen by car along perimeter roads. Fishing is allowed on designated areas from the banks of the lakes and ditches. Northerns, bullheads, and crappies are likely catches.

▶ Most areas open and accessible year-round.

www.fws.gov/midwest/horicon
(920) 387-2658

12 Wade House Historic Site

Off State Hwy. 23, W7824 Center St., Greenbush

This attractive Greek Revival inn, built in 1850 by Sylvanus Wade, is the centerpiece of a group of preserved buildings here that give an intriguing insight into life and travel in 19th-century America.

Wade, an optimistic entrepreneur from the East, built the inn in the Wisconsin wilderness to cater to travelers making the bone-rattling stagecoach journey along the plank road between Sheboygan and Fond du Lac. Tours of the Wade House by costumed interpreters reveal stories of life within

12 ▶ **Wade House Historic Site.** The Herrling Sawmill is one of the buildings at innkeeper Sylvanus Wade's compound, a stop for 19th-century travelers.

13 **International Crane Foundation.** Whooping cranes are the rarest of the world's 15 crane species. Shown here are an adult pair with their youngest in ICF's wetland exhibit.

the 27-room inn, which is authentically furnished in period décor. Amazingly, 60 percent of the inn's original furnishings remain intact.

Nearby is a blacksmith shop where a smithy plies his trade, once integral to 19th-century plank road travel and commerce. The Herrling Sawmill, authentically reconstructed in 2001 and outfitted with 19th-century machinery, sits on the same spot by the Mullet River where German immigrant Theodore Herrling and his family operated a sawmill for more than six decades. It still draws power from the river to operate an up-and-down muley type saw—one of the few working reproductions of its kind in the country.

Also located on the site is the Wesley Jung Carriage Museum, which has an outstanding collection of nearly 100 antique horse-drawn vehicles—the largest of its kind in Wisconsin. It is particularly notable for the vehicles manufactured in the small Jung Carriage Factory in nearby Sheboygan and everyday work vehicles, such as a butcher's wagon and a coal wagon that were once

commonplace in America. The cost of admission includes horse-drawn wagon transportation on the site.

▶ Open daily mid-May-mid-Oct.
Admission charged.

www.wadehouse.org
(920) 526-3271

13 International Crane Foundation

Northeast of Baraboo on Shady Lane Rd.
The only place in the world to see every species of crane (15 in all) is the International Crane Foundation (ICF), set in the tall-grass prairie and wetlands north of Baraboo. The ICF, best known for its work to restore a migrating population of whooping cranes in the eastern United States, is a nonprofit organization working in 30-plus countries to protect cranes and the ecosystems on which they depend.

Amid the crane breeding facilities and education buildings on the 225-acre site are opportunities for viewing the cranes, ranging from *Anthropoides paradisea* (blue

crane) to *Grus nigricollis* (black-necked crane). Nature trails wind through the restored prairie landscape, and a short introductory film in the visitors center spotlights the world of cranes and their habitats. Guided tours are offered daily between Memorial Day and Labor Day, though only on weekends in Apr.–May and Sept.–Oct.

▶ Open daily mid-Apr.-Oct.
Admission charged.

www.savingcranes.org
(608) 356-9462

14 Mid-Continent Railway Museum

W. Walnut St. in North Freedom
Commemorating the Golden Age of Railroading, this outdoor living museum features a large collection of vintage trains and equipment, plus its own classic operating railroad. Just stepping onto the grounds recalls a bygone way of life.

Authentic turn-of-the-century structures stand beside new buildings based on old design plans. The museum's signature depot was orig-

inally built in 1894 by the Chicago & North Western Railway—in a town three miles away. The antique depot, among several attractions, was painstakingly transported to the museum site for restoration and permanent residence.

Spanning the years 1880 to 1916, the museum's collection reflects a time when steam locomotives ruled—moving 90 percent of the nation's passengers. In addition to more than a dozen steam locomotives, it includes 38 passenger cars and 31 freight cars, both wooden and steel; 21 cabooses; and an assortment of service equipment, from snowplows to crane-wreckers.

Visitors can climb aboard the famed iron horses for a nostalgic ride. Each day, authentic diesel-powered locomotives make runs around the museum's miles of restored rolling track.

▶ Open daily mid-May-Labor Day; weekends Sept.-Oct., one weekend in Nov. and Feb. Admission charged.

www.midcontinent.org
(608) 522-4261; (800) 930-1385

14 **Mid-Continent Railway Museum.** Engine No. 49 was a steam locomotive for the Kewaunee, Green Bay & Western Railroad, which ran the rails from 1890 to 1969.

15 ▶ Villa Louis

521 N. Villa Louis Rd., Prairie du Chien, 62 miles south of La Crosse

Built in 1870 by H. Louis Dousman, a prosperous frontier entrepreneur, and impeccably appointed by his wife, Nina, this stately hilltop estate is now one of the most authentically restored Victorian homes in the United States.

Under the auspices of the Wisconsin Historical Society, it has been painstakingly and strikingly re-created in the style Mrs. Dousman selected for her 1885 redecoration: British Arts and Crafts.

Atypical for a Midwestern home, even for a mansion of its time, the furnishings feature ornate brass filigree, hand-wrought faux grain woodwork, and lush fabrics. Throughout the magnificent home visitors will also find priceless family heirlooms, collectibles, and artwork.

While distinguished for its Victorian splendor, this expansive country estate also enjoyed a brief heyday as a hub for harness racing. Passionate about the popular sport, Dousman transformed his homestead into a breeding ground and finishing school for thoroughbred trotters called the Artesian Stock Farm. Hailed for its elegant setting and enviable stable of 75 trophy winners, the racing enterprise flourished until 1886, ending with Dousman's sudden death. The estate was renamed Villa Louis in his honor.

Each September, Villa Louis celebrates the memory of the Artesian Stock Farm when it opens its grounds to the Midwest's largest and most classically stylish competitive carriage driving event.

The mansion also hosts popular Victorian cooking workshops, tours by lamplight, and a historic

15 ▶ Villa Louis. The front hall of this estate is a veritable museum of Victoriana. The hilltop house is said to be the most authentically restored Victorian house in the nation.

battle re-enactment: In its premansion days the estate's sprawling lawn had served as Wisconsin's sole battlefield in the War of 1812.

▶ Open daily May–Oct. Admission charged.

www.wisconsinhistory.org/villalouis
(608) 326-2721

16 ▶ Ten Chimneys

Genesee Depot, 6 miles south of I–94

No acting team ever shone brighter on Broadway than Wisconsin-born Alfred Lunt and his British wife, Lynn Fontanne. From the 1920s they charmed audiences with their wit and naturalistic dialogue when stilted stage speech was the norm. Lunt and Fontanne were so influential they rated a U.S. postage stamp, issued posthumously in 1999.

When not in New York or touring, Lunt and Fontanne retreated to Ten Chimneys, their three-story 18-room house set on 60 bucolic acres in southeast Wisconsin. Lunt designed the colorful mural-filled

mansion to reflect his Swedish heritage. In what is now a National Historic Landmark, visitors eye furniture once lounged on by Katharine Hepburn, Noël Coward, Laurence Olivier, and other stage and screen greats. Books, collections, and objets d'art remain where the couple left them.

In the separate Program Center the permanent exhibit—Alfred Lunt and Lynn Fontanne: A Life on the Stage—is complemented by an entertainment-world exhibition that changes year by year. Public programs in this "home for the arts" include workshops, lectures, and student outreach.

▶ Open May–mid-Nov. Admission charged.

www.tenchimneys.org
(262) 968-4161

17 ▶ Stonefield

Cassville, off Hwy. 133 on CR-VV

Centered around a classic village square with bandstand and apple

trees, Stonefield re-creates the small-town Wisconsin of nearly a century ago. The 30-odd mostly clapboard structures are constructed in a turn-of-the-century style, and most are filled with authentic period furnishings.

The law office has leather volumes and wooden file cabinets; the doctor's office boasts an examination table and surgical tools. The butcher shop has a marble counter and scales, while the ladies' hat shop is an oasis of feathers, lace, and satin. The goods in the Farmers' Store include corsets and chewing tobacco.

A wonderful array of patent medicines and toiletries line the drugstore's shelves. The cheese factory, newspaper printing shop, cigar factory, and photography studio all display period equipment. Other buildings include a train station, bank, church, creamery, stables, school, firehouse, and saloon. There is even a furniture-undertaker's shop (a common combination at the time) with cabinetmaking tools in front.

16 ▶ Ten Chimneys. Theater legends Alfred Lunt and Lynn Fontanne (inset) lived well in their manse.

A visit to the village should include the adjoining State Agricultural Museum—formed by the walls of a former sheep barn—which has displays devoted to the settlement of Wisconsin and the evolution of agriculture here. Especially interesting are the beautifully crafted scale models of reaping machines complete with horses and humans.

The ticket to the village also admits the visitor to another Stonefield, the mansion that gave its name to the village. The restored brick structure, which stands just across the highway in the Nelson Dewey State Park, was the home of Wisconsin's first elected governor.

The 756-acre park, which is open year-round, offers quiet beauty, camping sites, nature trails, and excellent bird-watching. More than 85 species nest here in summer. The overlook on the bluffs above the village provides fine views of the Mississippi meandering through a wide valley.

▶ Open daily late May–Aug., weekends Sept.–mid-Oct. Admission charged.

http://stonefield.wisconsinhistory.org
(608) 725-5210

18 National Brewery Museum/Potosi Brewing Company

209 S. Main St., Potosi
Beer lovers and history buffs alike will enjoy browsing the National Brewery Museum, memorializing breweries of days past and housing collections of "brewiana"—antique equipment, beer signs, coasters, novelty beer steins, and other artifacts—donated by members of the American Brewiana Association. But that's not all

you'll find at the Potosi Brewing Company, which operated from 1852 to 1972 and whose imposing buildings have been restored.

The Polosi Brewery Transportation Museum traces the history of the company through various modes of transportation (riverboats, rail cars, carriages). Elsewhere in the brewery, a glass wall allows you to peer into "the cave"—a 75-foot space dug into the hillside the brewery sits next to, where ice hauled

 Stonefield. In this re-created town, get a taste of village life in Wisconsin at the turn of the 20th century. More than 30 clapboard buildings can be explored.

from the adjacent Mississippi River refrigerated the beer. A glass floor reveals the flowing spring water that was used in brewing.

A new, elaborately carved bar boasts columns shaped like beer bottles and relief carvings of all of the company's beer labels. And in the beer garden you can sample the four beers (plus root beer for the kids), all currently brewed on the premises.

▶ Open daily year-round. Admission charged.

www.potosibrewery.com
(608) 763-4002

19 Black Point Estate

Geneva Lake
Perched on a bluff on Geneva Lake's south shore, the grand Black Point estate was built in 1888 by Chicago beer magnate Conrad Seipp as a summer retreat. The most distinctive feature of the pale yellow Queen Anne–style house is its tall, elaborate crow's nest.

A house tour gives you a look at the life of a prosperous Victorian clan. The library, original furniture, and linens are on view, and a restored dollhouse delights visitors of all ages.

A stop at Black Point estate is part of a narrated Lake Geneva Cruise Line tour that acquaints visitors with the area's history as a favorite retreat for wealthy families at the height of the Gilded Age. Boats depart the Riviera Docks in the town of Lake Geneva twice daily in the summer and once daily in the fall.

▶ Open mid-May–Oct. Admission charged.

www.blackpointpreserve.org
(800) 248-1888

seasonal events

FEBRUARY
- Klondike Days Family Celebration—Eagle River *(living-history demonstrations, chain-saw carving competition, craft show, dog and horse weight-pulls)*
- Hot-Air Affair—Hudson *(hot-air balloon launches, parade, arts and crafts, children's activities, live music, fireworks)*

JUNE
- Strawberry Festival—Cedarburg *(live music, hayrides, "Strawberry Bob," pancake breakfast, contests, crafts)*
- Fyr Bal Festival—Ephraim *(live music, traditional Scandinavian dancers and singers, community fish boil, chieftain ceremony, children's activities, tours, crafts, fireworks)*
- Prairie Village Rendezvous—Prairie du Chien *(historical re-enactments, demonstrations)*

JULY
- Lumberjack World Championships—Hayward

AUGUST
- National Mustard Day—Mount Horeb *(live music, games, free hot dogs)*
- Sweet Corn Festival—Sun Prairie *(live entertainment, children's activities, petting zoo, midway, craft show, parade)*
- Wilhelm Tell Festival—New Glarus *("Wilhelm Tell" performance, traditional Swiss campfire, family campout, art fair, live entertainment)*
- Wisconsin State Cow Chip Throw—Prairie du Sac

SEPTEMBER
- Cranberry Festival—Warrens *(cranberry marsh tours, contests, live entertainment)*

OCTOBER
- Kornstalk Karnival—Manitowish Waters *(concessions, raffles, costume parade, games)*
- Oktoberfest—St. Germain *(craft show, beer garden, hayrides, German music)*

http://tourism.state.wi.us

Wyoming

The history of this sparsely populated state revolves around native peoples, trappers, pioneers, cowboys, and prospectors—all embodiments of the Old West.

Fort Bridger State Historic Site. A young girl dresses for the occasion at the Fort Bridger Rendezvous, held annually on the first weekend of September (see page 372).

In a state where the population of the largest city is well under 100,000, remoteness comes as no surprise. Ghost towns and lonely roads befit Wyoming's identification with the early West and its compelling cast of characters. Telling the story are historic sites and museums paying homage to Native Americans, fur traders known as mountain men, miners who stayed while the digging held out, and a famous Wild West showman.

Nature and recreation can be enjoyed at a state park with the world's largest hot springs, Devils Tower (our first national monument), and a small park with a huge natural bridge over a stream as its centerpiece. Wildlife ranges from wild horses running free in a refuge in northern Wyoming to elks, antelopes, badgers, and bald eagles living amid unearthly rock formations near the southern border.

visit ➤ **offthebeatenpathtrips.com**

1 Buffalo Bill Historical Center

720 Sheridan Ave., Cody
Dubbed "the Smithsonian of the West" by author James Michener, this place is famous for celebrating America's frontier heritage. Inspired by its flagship Buffalo Bill Museum, established in 1927, the 237,000-square-foot complex has expanded its focus through the decades to house the Whitney Gallery of Western Art, the Plains Indian Museum, and the Cody Firearms Museum.

The latest addition is the state-of-the-art Draper Museum, showcasing the biological and geological wonders of the Greater Yellowstone ecosystem. Using cutting-edge technology, this museum leads visitors down an interactive trail through the sights, sounds, and sensations of the West's natural world. Visitors get to delve into exhibits such as ranching, logging, and oil development.

▶ Open daily Apr.-Oct.; Tues.-Sun. Nov.-Mar. Admission charged.

www.bbhc.org
(307) 587-4771

2 Bighorn Medicine Wheel

Off Alt. Rte. 14, east of Lovell
In 1776, when the Crow Indians first occupied this mountain on the western edge of Bighorn National

1 Buffalo Bill Historical Center. Exhibits reach beyond the Wild West showman to include a Plains Native American museum and displays of western art and Cody firearms.

Forest, they discovered the great Medicine Wheel, a circle of limestone slabs and boulders with a circumference of 245 feet, 28 spoke-like lines of stone, and a round pile of stones about 2 feet high that served as the hub.

Its origin and purpose remain a mystery. Speculation is that a sun-worshipping people built the wheel. The hub supposedly symbolizes the sun, and the spokes indicate the 28 days of the lunar month. Radioactive carbon dating of wood found inside a rock pile conducted by the University of Wyoming puts the construction of the wheel at 1760, but it may be quite a bit older.

The wheel is reached by a steep 1½-mile dirt road offering glori-ous views of surrounding mountains and valleys.

▶ Entrance Rd. Hwy. 14 open June-Sept.

www.codywyomingnet.com/attractions/medicine_wheel.php
(307) 674-2600

3 Pryor Mountain Wild Horse Range and Red Gulch Dinosaur Tracksite

Big Horn County, near Lovell and near Greybull, respectively
Just up the road from Yellowstone National Park, Big Horn County has hundreds of miles of trails tranversing habitats ranging from deserts to subalpine meadows. At the Pryor Mountain Wild Horse Range visitors might spy as many

3 **Pryor Mountain Wild Horse Range.** The mustangs' ancestors came over with European explorers.

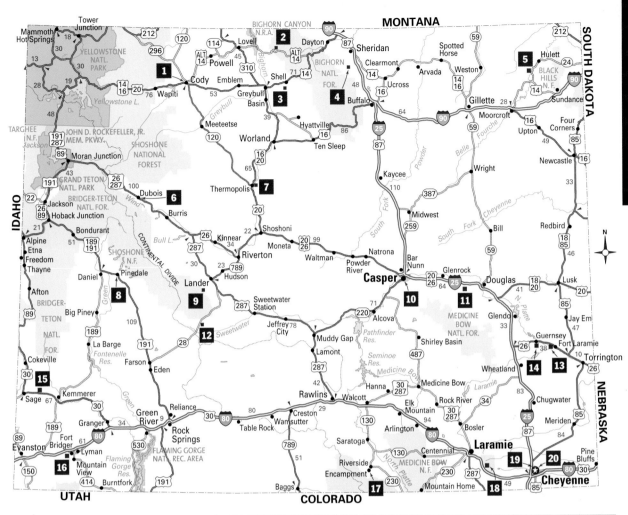

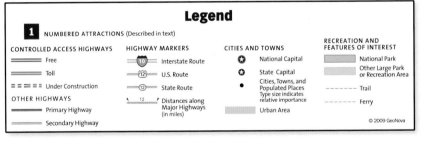

as 180 wild mustangs on a 31,000-acre sweep of land. First prized by Native Americans, the distinctive horses are direct descendants of breeds cultivated in ancient Spain, Portugal, and Africa.

Nearby at Red Gulch, covering 40 acres of publicly guarded ground, visitors can trace the footsteps of dinosaurs dating back some 160 million years to the Middle Jurassic period. Until 1997, when the prehistoric footprints were uncovered, most scientists viewed Big Horn County as the former home of a huge ocean, inhabited exclusively by sea creatures. Yet, as the tracks of gigantic mammals attest, the area was once covered by soft mud. Over the eons the mud hardened, leaving whole footprints preserved beneath. Today visitors can easily spot over 100 footprints and other fossil traces and are permitted to take home petrified wood and plant fossils they find but must leave any animal vertebrae for the local experts to study.

▶ Open year-round.

www.pryormustangs.org
(307) 548-7552 Pryor Mountain

www.blm.gov./wy
(307) 347-5100 Red Gulch

4 ▶ **Bradford Brinton Memorial & Museum**

Big Horn
Lives well lived can be glimpsed at the gracious ranch house now known as the Bradford Brinton Memorial & Museum. Bradford Brinton (1880–1936) made a fortune in the family farm implement business (he later headed a threshing machine company), fought in World War I, and had an eye for art. In 1923 he bought the Quarter Circle A Ranch and extensively remodeled the house, which is situated in the beautiful Little Goose Creek Valley.

Brinton's sister Helen established the memorial and museum in 1960. Today the house is filled with the family's fine art and furnishings. Original works by John James Audubon, George Bellows, Hans Kleiber, Frederic Remington, Charles M. Russell, and other noted artists form the collection's centerpiece. One of the highlights is Remington's *Fight on the Little Bighorn,* which vividly captures Custer's Last Stand. Rare books and historic documents are also on display, and the Reception Gallery houses the Brintons' impressive collection of Native American art.

▶ Open Memorial Day–Labor Day. Admission charged.

www.bbmandm.org
(307) 672-3173

Legend

1 NUMBERED ATTRACTIONS (Described in text)

CONTROLLED ACCESS HIGHWAYS
Free
Toll
Under Construction

OTHER HIGHWAYS
Primary Highway
Secondary Highway

HIGHWAY MARKERS
10 Interstate Route
121 U.S. Route
12 State Route
12 Distances along Major Highways (in miles)

CITIES AND TOWNS
National Capital
State Capital
Cities, Towns, and Populated Places Type size indicates relative importance
Urban Area

RECREATION AND FEATURES OF INTEREST
National Park
Other Large Park or Recreation Area
Trail
Ferry

© 2009 GeoNova

0   20   40   60 Miles
0   20   40   60 Kilometers

5 Devils Tower National Monument

Off Rte. 24 in Devils Tower

About 60 million years ago, molten magma from the Earth's core forced its way upward into the softer sedimentary rock here. The magma cooled underground and formed a huge stock of hard igneous stone. Slowly the sedimentary rock eroded away by the Belle Fourche River, exposing the stock. Known as Devils Tower, it rises abruptly from its base and looms 1,267 feet above the river. The tower formed into a network of 4-, 5-, and 6-sided columns, each 8 to 15 feet in diameter, separated by the thermal gradient cracks, as the entire mass began to cool. In 1906 the imposing formation was designated the nation's first national monument. Each year expert climbers edge their way to the top, a domed area of 1½ acres.

The surrounding park offers hiking trails and campsites. Birding is quite good, since the park is located at the juncture of wooded mountains and plains. More than 100 bird species have been sighted here, including bald and golden eagles and prairie falcons. White-tailed and mule deer inhabit the woodlands, and inquisitive prairie dogs pop up from their town near the park entrance to pose for photographers.

▶ Park open year-round; campground open mid-Apr.–Oct. Admission charged.

www.nps.gov/deto
(307) 467-5283

6 National Bighorn Sheep Interpretive Center

Dubois

If any animal deserves a museum of its own, it's the rare and majestic bighorn sheep. Two centuries ago these mountain dwellers numbered more than 2 million in North America—but, like the buffalo, they dwindled to only a few thousand before making a comeback and dodging extinction.

The sheep take their name from the large, curved horns of the rams—the horns that in turn gave their name to rivers, creeks, and towns in the Rocky Mountain West. Everything you ever wanted to know about the animals can be found here.

Sheep Mountain, the central exhibit, takes you into the bighorn's unique habitat of alpine plants and rocky terrain. Hands-on exhibits acquaint you with bighorn adaptations, dominance battles, predator-prey relationships, and more. Guided tours of the sheep's winter range give you an up-close view of these fascinating animals that once roamed the Rocky Mountains by the thousands.

▶ Open Memorial Day–Labor Day. Tours Nov.–Mar. Admission charged.

www.bighorn.org
(307) 455-3420

5 ▶ **Devils Tower National Monument.** This eons-old tower of solidified molten rock was the first natural wonder to be designated a National Monument.

7 Hot Springs State Park

Thermopolis

The world's largest hot springs...a herd of wild bison...eye-popping flower gardens...a rejuvenating soak in a mineral bath. What's not to like at Hot Springs State Park?

Daily some 3.6 million gallons of hot spring water flow over colorful rock terraces along the Wind River (the name for the Bighorn River in these parts). The State Bathhouse is where you can soak for free, while families prefer the two commercial baths equipped with water slides, tanning decks, and spa facilities.

You can gaze down on the steaming terraces from the Swinging Bridge (a suspension bridge) or set out on 6.2 miles of hiking trails to take in the surrounding landscape. The bison pasture affords views of these fabled American animals called the Monarch of the Plains.

In the town of Thermopolis ("Hot City"), the Hot Springs Country Museum and Cultural Center boasts the cherrywood bar from the old Hole-in-the-Wall Saloon, said to be a favorite hangout for Butch Cassidy and the Sundance Kid.

▶ Park and bathhouses open year-round. Admission charged at private facilities.

http://wyoparks.state.wy.us
(307) 864-2176

8 Museum of the Mountain Man

Pinedale

The romantic era of the fur trapper lives on in this museum, located in the heart of Rocky Mountain rendezvous country. (A rendezvous was a business gathering of fur trappers and traders at a predetermined place.) These mountain men came from all walks of life and were among the first to explore the West. One of the best-known trappers was Jim Bridger, who eventually became a scout for the U.S. Army and established Fort Bridger in Wyoming Territory. Another who gained fame was the trapper, scout, and buffalo hunter Christopher (Kit) Carson.

A monument to the fur trade and the men who opened the West, the Museum of the Mountain Man offers exhibits from a mountain man camp to Jim Bridger's rifle to a reproduction of the fully furnished tepee of Chief American Horse (1800–1876). The buffalo-hide tepee—the only one on display outside the Smithsonian—lets visitors glimpse an Ogala-Sioux chief's way of life. Items in the tepee include furnishings, buffalo rugs and robes, headdresses, parfleches (rawhide bags), bows and arrows, and a hand-painted drum.

▶ Open May–Oct.

www.museumofthemountainman.com
(307) 367-4101

9 Sinks Canyon State Park

3079 Sinks Canyon Rd., Lander
This ecologically diverse park takes its name from its most noted natural phenomenon. The Popo Agie River "sinks" here into a limestone cave, proceeds underground for half a mile, and then resurfaces into a pool known as The Rise. The area around The Rise contains two strikingly different ecosystems, reflecting the amount of sunlight received on the canyon's slopes. The shadier north-facing slope is a forest of Douglas fir, limber pine, and aspen, while the arid south-facing slope supports juniper and sagebrush.

Black bears, beavers, moose, and bighorn sheep range the hillsides, and the river abounds with trout. A nature trail can be walked easily in an hour. The park road is part of a 60-mile loop through scenic mountain backcountry between Lander and South Pass City.
▶ Park open year-round, weather permitting; visitors center open Memorial Day–Labor Day.
http://wyoparks.state.wy.us/parks/sinkscanyon
(307) 332-3077

10 National Historic Trails Interpretive Center

101 N. Poplar, Casper
Here visitors can literally walk in the paths of the American pioneers. Many sections of westward trails forged more than 150 years ago are open to foot traffic, enhanced only with historic markers.

Operated by a unique partnership among the Bureau of Land Management, the National Historic Trails Center Foundation, and the city of Casper, the 27,000-square-foot interpretive center captures the stories of the Oregon, Mormon, California, and Pony Express trails in the 1800s and explores the everyday life of local Native Americans.

State-of-the-art interactive exhibits follow arduous journeys across the desert in wagons and on horseback. Highlights include the westward mission of religious freedom embraced by some 70,000 members of the Church of Latter-day Saints and the frenzied California Gold Rush years.
▶ Open daily Apr.–Oct.; Tues.–Sat. Nov.–Mar. Closed major holidays. Admission charged.
www.blm.gov/wy/st/en/NHTIC.html
(307) 261-7700

11 Ayres Natural Bridge

12 miles west of Douglas
Exit 151 on Interstate 25 takes you to a small county park with a great big centerpiece: Ayres Natural Bridge, a 100-foot-long, 50-foot-high expanse of red rock looming over tranquil LaPrele Creek. The bridge is named for Alva Ayres, the 19th-century homesteader on whose land it lay and whose son donated it to Converse County. The bridge is one of only three natural bridges in the world with a trout stream running underneath. Wagoneers traveling west often rested in this spot, which sits only a mile or so from the Oregon Trail.

Set in the grassy foothills studded with box elders of Laramie Peak, and surrounded by red-rock cliffs, the diminutive park (just shy of 20 square acres) attracts bird-watchers, campers, flyfishers partial to rainbow and brown trout, and visitors in search of unspoiled scenery.
▶ Open Apr.–Oct.
www.jackalope.org
(307) 358-3532

12 South Pass City State Historic Site

125 S. Pass Main, South Pass City
Gold was discovered here in 1867, and within a year 28 mines were established. The area's population boomed. But five years later no one had yet hit a mother lode; discouraged miners moved on to more promising locations, and the town rapidly declined.

Now restored, South Pass City is a living ghost town with a handful of residents. Its bustling past is visible in 30 or so buildings that were once of vital importance, such as the 1868 Sherlock Hotel, the South Pass Hotel, and the Miner's Exchange Saloon. Giving authenticity to the scene, a few optimistic prospectors still work the mines.
▶ Visitors center open daily mid-May–Sept. Admission charged.
www.southpasscity.com
(307) 332-3684

13 Fort Laramie National Historic Site

965 Grey Rocks Rd., Fort Laramie
In 1834, two fur traders, William Sublette and Robert Campbell, established a trading post here near the confluence of the Laramie and North Platte rivers. The U.S. government bought it in 1849 and turned it into a military fort. In 1938 it became a national historic site.

Several of the buildings have been restored, including the commandant's home, the surgeon's quarters, the bakery, the guardhouse, the store, and "Old Bedlam," Wyoming's oldest surviving military structure, which provided housing for the post's officers. Park staff in 1800s period clothing demonstrate cannon firing, baking, and other fort activities. Displays in a small museum include 19th-century U.S. Army uniforms and weapons. Park rangers conduct tours in summer.
▶ Open daily except major holidays.
www.nps.gov/fola
(307) 837-2221

6 National Bighorn Sheep Interpretive Center. A diorama of North American wild sheep acquaints visitors with the five species of the *Ovis* genus.

14 Register Cliff/ Oregon Trail Ruts

S. Wyoming Ave., 3 miles south of junction with Rte. 26, Guernsey

The pioneers who traveled west on the Oregon Trail left their mark on a soft sandstone cliff rising 100 feet from the North Platte River valley. Wagoneers who camped on the riverbanks etched their names into the cliff and the date they passed through, sometimes noting their hometowns back East. Many of the inscriptions on what is today called Register Cliff were made during the peak years of travel on the trail—the 1840s and 1850s. As far back as 1829, journeying fur trappers and traders also carved their names into the rock. A plaque at the base of the cliff tells visitors more about this roster of people headed for a new life.

In nearby Guernsey State Park is the Oregon Trail Ruts State Historic Site. Here you'll see deep ruts gouged into the sandstone outcrops by untold numbers of wagon wheels, more reminders of the parade of pioneers along the North Platte River.

14 Register Cliff/Oregon Trail Ruts.
History is gouged into the earth at the trail ruts site near Guernsey.

▶ Open year-round.

http://wyoparks.state.wy.us
(307) 864-2176

15 Fossil Butte National Monument

15 miles west of Kemmerer on Hwy. 30

Tectonic forces warped the land 50 million years ago creating a lake where ancestors of many modern mammals, birds, fish, and reptiles flourished in a subtropical climate. When these creatures died, their remains were protected by layers of sediment. Later, under pressure, the sediment turned to limestone, preserving the animals' fossilized skeletons in almost perfect condition.

At the visitors center of this 8,198-acre monument, fossils of fish including gar, paddlefish, and herring are exhibited, along with rare fossils of stingrays, a 13-foot crocodile, boas, birds, and bats. There are video presentations as well as a Junior/Senior Ranger program available year-round; Ranger programs are only offered in the summer.

On Fridays and Saturdays between Memorial Day and Labor Day, visitors can assist staff with the digging of fossils at a small research quarry. Two moderately strenuous trails (1 1/2 and 2 1/2 miles) and interpretive signs help visitors explore the monument and understand its geology, paleontology, and ecology.

An auto route winds for 2 1/2 miles through native sagebrush and grasslands to a picnic area in an aspen grove.

You may have cows for company in this open range country, and you may see a few mule deer. In winter the monument may be explored on cross-country skis or snowshoes, but there are no groomed trails. Fossil Butte is one of the least visited national parks and is a good place to find solitude.

▶ Park and visitors center open daily except major winter holidays.

www.nps.gov/fobu/expanded/gen.htm
(307) 877-4455

16 Fort Bridger State Historic Site

Fort Bridger, Ext. 34 on I-80

Jim Bridger, justly famous beaver trapper, trader, and guide, established a trading post here in 1843 with his partner Louis Vasquez and supplied the needs of wagon trains on the Oregon Trail. Twelve years later the Mormons said they bought the post as a resting place for their people emigrating westward, but after a dispute with the U.S. government, they burned the post before retreating to Salt Lake City. U.S. troops arrived in 1857 and built what was to remain an important fort until 1890, putting up 29 buildings.

Today visitors can see the stables, which were used by the Pony Express, and the sutler's complex (post store), stocked with goods from the 1880s. Army uniforms, buffalo robes, and the evidence of a poker party are shown in the officers quarters. The Commanding Officers Quarters have been restored with period furnishings, including a moose-horn chair.

▶ Open daily May-Oct.; weekends only Oct.-mid-Nov. and mid-Mar.-May. Admission charged.

http://wyoparks.state.wy.us
(307) 782-3842

17 Grand Encampment Museum

Intersection of Rtes. 70 and 230 in Encampment

The discovery of a copper lode in 1897 brought affluence to the ranch town of Grand Encampment. However, the prosperity lasted only 11 years—the mines were closed in 1908, when the owners were accused of fraud.

The aura of the mining community has been re-created at this museum complex—a cluster of 14 weather-beaten buildings. On a guided tour you can inspect an 1870s stagecoach station, a saloon, and a general store equipped with a huge coffee grinder and a brass cash register. The Doc Culleton Interpretive Center displays a variety of artifacts, old-time photographs, and the Oldman research center. Also of interest is the Mosley folding bathtub and a two-story outhouse designed for use when deep snow and drifts buried the lower unit.

▶ Open Memorial Day-Labor Day. Mon.-Sun. Donations accepted.

www.grandencampmentmuseum.org
(307) 327-5308

18 Vedauwoo

Medicine Bow–Routt National Forest

In the Laramie Range rock formations in the 10-square-mile area known as Vedauwoo (Arapaho for "land of the earthborn spirit" and pronounced vee-dah-voo) aren't just any old rocks. Some 70 million years ago geologic uplift left a fold that ran from southeast Wyoming into northern Colorado, and Mother Nature later sculpted its exposed granite into strange shapes with nooks and crannies to spare. Today the formations are a

Vedauwoo. This curious formation is one of many in the Vedauwoo area, a destination for rock climbers and boulderers from far and wide.

dream come true for fans of rock climbing and bouldering.

The Arapaho and Cheyenne who lived in what is now Medicine Bow-Routt National Forest believed the rocks at Vedauwoo were piled up by playful spirits. But you need not be a climber to be enthralled by strangely configured rocks with names like the Coke Bottle, the Rat Brain, Hassler's Hatbox, and University of Mars.

When hiking the area's nature trails through pine and aspen forests, keep an eye out for elk, pronghorn antelopes, badgers, wild turkeys, bald eagles, and assorted other wildlife.

▶ Open May-Oct.

www.fs.fed.us/r2/mbr
(307) 745-2307

19 Cheyenne Frontier Days Old West Museum

Cheyenne
The mission of the Cheyenne Frontier Days Old West Museum is to preserve the history of America's most famous rodeo: the Frontier Days ridin' and ropin' extravaganza that was first held in 1897 and gained the moniker of "The Daddy

of 'em All." Permanent exhibitions include one of the nation's most extensive collections of horse-drawn carriages and wagons, while rotating exhibits always delight. For example, Hawaiians Take Cheyenne! was a 2008 exhibition that celebrated the 1908 Frontier Days Rodeo when a group of Hawaiian paniolo (cowboys) took top awards and caused a sensation in Wyoming and Waimea alike.

Visitors can experience the action by viewing films of exciting rodeos from days past in a large section of the old grandstands, and by dialing into an audio tour on their cell phones. Children can explore an interactive gallery.

When the Frontier Days festival rolls around (held annually during the last full week of July), one of the most outstanding Western Art shows in the world hangs in the museum for public viewing. And there's parkland aplenty—Frontier Park lies right out the museum's doors, and Lions Park is across the street.

▶ Open daily year-round.
  Admission charged.

www.oldwestmuseum.org
(307) 778-7290

20 Wyoming State Museum

Barrett Building, 2301 Central Ave., Cheyenne
Cheyenne was founded in 1867 as a major depot along the Transcontinental Railway, and less than a year later the Territory of Wyoming was created by Congress. The museum itself was started in 1895, just five years after Wyoming was granted statehood.

Remodeled in the late 1990s, the museum's new exhibits encompass a wide range of subjects, including wildlife, mining, dinosaurs, art, Native Americans, ranching, agriculture, the military, state traditions, and noted state citizens, both famous and infamous. The Hands-on History Room offers interactive exhibits.

Cheyenne Frontier Days Old West Museum. The museum is famous for its collection of carriages.

The museum also hosts several temporary exhibits throughout the year.

▶ Open Mon.-Sat. year-round. Closed state and federal holidays.

http://wyomuseum.state.wy.us
(307) 777-7022

seasonal events

JANUARY
• Sierra Madre Winter Carnival—Encampment *(sled races, snow sculpture contest, snowmobile race, other winter activities)*

FEBRUARY
• Mid-Winter Broncs and Bulls—Torrington *(bronco-and-bull riding competition)*

MAY
• Rocky Mountain Leather Trade Show—Sheridan *(annual trade show with over 100 leather suppliers, manufacturers, and dealers)*

JUNE
• Wings Over Carbon County Birding Festival—Saratoga
• Lovell Mustang Days—Lovell *(parade, rodeo, barbecue, music)*
• Jackson Hole Film Festival—Jackson Hole *(shows winners of annual Wyoming Short Film Contest)*

JULY
• Platte Valley Festival of the Arts—Saratoga *(juried art show and invitational craft show, musical performances, cowboy poetry, barbecue, artist quick-draw, auction)*
• Frontier Days—Cheyenne *(biggest rodeo in the West, featuring bull riding, barrel racing, and team roping)*

AUGUST
• Northern Arapaho Pow Wow—Fort Washakie *(concessions, arts and crafts, dance competitions, drum contests)*

SEPTEMBER
• Buffalo Bill Art Show—Cody *(art show and sale with a Western theme)*

NOVEMBER
• Parade of Lights—Worland *(lights, music, chili, and Christmas spirit)*

DECEMBER
• Annual New Year's Dance—Evanston *(family-oriented dancing, music, fireworks)*

www.wyomingtourism.org

Acknowledgments

Alabama—Marilyn Jones Stamps, Alabama Tourism Department; Brittney L. McAlister-Hughes, Naturalist, DeSoto State Park; David Odom, Park Superintendent, Cheaha State Park

Alaska—Mia Costello, Senior Account Manager, Bernholz & Graham, Inc.; Alex Lindeman, Information Specialist, Denali National Park & Preserve; John Wilber, Chief Ranger, Susitna/Denali Ranger Districts, Alaska State Parks, Mat-Su/Copper Basin Area; Smitty Parratt, Chief of Interpretation, Wrangell-St. Elias National Park and Preserve; Sandra Snell-Dobert, Chief of Interpretation/Education, Klondike Gold Rush National Historical Park; Allison Banks, Environmental Protection Specialist, Glacier Bay National Park and Preserve

Arizona—Kiva Couchon, Arizona Office of Tourism Communications Manager; James Dryer, Archaeologist, Navajo National Monument; Anne Worthington, Superintendent, Hubbell Trading Post NHS; Carol Kruse, Interpretive Specialist, Wupatki National Monument; Ed Cummins, Chief Ranger, Montezuma Castle & Tuzigoot National Monuments; Hallie Larsen, Park Ranger, Petrified Forest National Park; John Boeck, Tonto Natural Bridge State Park; Rick Elder, Boyce Thompson Arboretum State Park; Dave Winchester, Park Ranger, Casa Grande Ruis National Monument; Andy L. Fisher Chief of Interpretation Organ Pipe Cactus National Monument

Arkansas—Kerry Ann Kraus, Travel Writer, Arkansas Dept. of Parks & Tourism; Casey Crocker, Arkansas Dept. of Parks & Tourism, Photography; Walt Reding, Assistant Superintendent, Withrow Springs State Park; Mark A. Ballard, Superintendent II, Jacksonport State Park; Marlon Mowdy, Park Superintendent, Hampson Archeological Museum State Park; Lee Howard, Park Superintendent, Lake Ouachita State Park; Kimberly Garland, Crater of Diamonds State Park

California—Amelia Neufeld, Media Relations Manager, Visit California; Roy Stearns, Deputy Director for Communications, California State Parks; Dave Kruse, Superintendent, Lava Beds National Monument; Lynn Cullivan, San Francisco Maritime National Historical Park

Colorado—Caitlin Sullivan, Senior Account Executive, MMG Mardiks; Patty Hill, Visitor Services, Sylvan Lake State Park; Michelle Wheatley, Park Ranger Supervisor/Education Coordinator, Colorado National Monument; Sally Bellacqua, Park Photographer, Colorado National Monument; Patrick Myers, Park Ranger, Visitor Services/Interpretation/Education, Great Sand Dunes National Park and Preserve; Rick Wallner, Chief of Interpretation, Bent's Old Fort National Historic Site; Alexa Roberts, Superintendent, Bent's Old Fort NHS and Southeast Colorado Group

Connecticut—Maria Castro, M. Silver Associates Inc.; Melinda Testori, Connecticut Commission on Culture & Tourism; Nicole Chalfant, Gillette Castle State Park

Delaware—Adam I. Berger, Marketing Coordinator, Delaware Economic Development Office, Delaware Tourism Office; Arthur K. Angelo, Assistant Superintendent/Park Ranger, White Clay Creek State Park; William Koth, Park Interpreter, Trap Pond State Park

Florida—Kerri L. Post, Vice President of New Product Development, VISIT FLORIDA®; Patrick W. Hartsfield, PSS, Grayton Beach; Mitzi Nelson, Information Specialist, Stephen Foster Folk Culture Center State Park; Laura Henning, Supervisory Park Ranger of Visitor Services, Canaveral National Seashore; Chris Kimball, Park Services Specialist, Collier Seminole State Park; Gary Bremen, Park Ranger, Biscayne National Park; Christi Carmichael, Flamingo Interpretation, Everglades National Park

Georgia—Stefanie Paupeck, Communications Specialist, Georgia Department of Economic Development; Joshua McKinley, Interpretive Ranger, Cloudland Canyon State Park

Hawaii—Karl Nakagawa, Media Information Specialist, Travel and Tourism, McNeil Wilson Communications, Inc.; Melissa Malahoff-Kamei, Senior Account Executive, McNeil Wilson Communications, Inc./Travel and Tourism; Kelii Brown, Director of Public Relations/Promotions, Maui Visitors Bureau (Maui/Molokai/Lanai); Jessica Ferracane, President, Irondog Communications LLC, Representing the Big Island Visitors Bureau; Mari Takamura, Stryker Weiner & Yokota Public Relations, Inc.; Martha Yent, Interpretive Program, Division of State Parks, Dept. of Land and Natural Resources; Jennifer L. Cerny, Chief of Cultural Resources/Cultural Anthropologist, Kalaupapa National Historical Park

Idaho—Diane Norton, Idaho Division of Tourism Development; Ted Stout, Chief of Interpretation, Craters of the Moon National Monument and Preserve; Bryan W. Cross, Park Manager, Bruneau Dunes State Park; Raechel Driscoll, Park Interpreter, Bruneau Dunes State Park

Indiana—Curt Brantingham, Public Relations Manager, Indiana Office of Tourism Development; Howard Luehrs, Naturalist Interpreter, Chain O'Lakes State Park; Sam Arthur, Interpretive Naturalist, Raccoon State Recreation Area\Historic Mansfield Roller Mill; Pamela A. Nolan, Park Ranger, George Rogers Clark NHP; Bett Etenohan, Interpretive Naturalist, Falls of the Ohio State Park; Mike Capps, Chief Ranger, Lincoln Boyhood National Memorial

Iowa—Jessica O'Riley, Communications Manager, Iowa Tourism Office; Larry Zirkelbach, Park Ranger, Maquoketa Caves State Park;

Kansas—Richard Smalley, Marketing Manager, Travel and Tourism Division, Kansas Department of Commerce; Felix Revello, Fort Larned National Historic Site

Kentucky—Marge Bateman, Media Coordinator, Communications Branch, Kentucky Department of Tourism; Rebecca Clark, Naturalist/Recreation Supervisor, Pennyrile State Resort Park; Sheila Rush, Director, Old Mulkey Meetinghouse State Historic Site

Louisiana—Jeff Richard, Louisiana Office of Tourism

Maine—Rose Whitehouse, Account Coordinator/Office Manager, Nancy Marshall Communications; Wanda Moran, Information Park Ranger, Acadia National Park

Maryland—Connie Yingling, Public Relations Coordinator, Maryland Office of Tourism Development; Ranger Kenny Hartman, Herrington Manor State Park

Massachusetts—Amy Gallagher, Account Supervisor, Mullen; Renee Weihn, Acting Supervisor II, Department of Conservation & Recreation; Marianne Peak, Superintendent, Adams National Historical Park

Michigan—Kirsten Borgstrom, Media Relations Manager, Travel Michigan; Gregg L. Bruff, Chief of Heritage Education, Visitor Services and Cultural Resources Management Pictured Rocks National Lakeshore; Dusty Shultz, Superintendent, Sleeping Bear Dunes National Lakeshore

Minnesota—Chuck Lennon, Golf/Travel Media Relations, Explore Minnesota Tourism; Gary Hoeft, Assistant Park Manager, Tettegouche, Temperance River and George H. Crosby-Manitou State Parks; Glen H. Livermont, Superintendent, Pipestone National Monument

Mississippi—Cheryl K. Eley, Publications/Inquiry MDA, Division of Tourism

Missouri—Lori Simms, Communications Director, Missouri Division of Tourism; Jennie Sieg, Public Information Specialist, Division of State Parks, Missouri Department of Natural Resources; Walt Busch, Elephant Rocks State Park; Cyndi A. Cogbill, Interpretive Resource Specialist III, C.I.G., Prairie State Park

Montana—Donnie Sexton, Media Relations / Staff Photographer, Travel Montana; Susan Buhr, Travel Montana; John Phillips, Interpretive Specialist, Bannack State Park; Ken Woody, Little Bighorn Battlefield National Monument

Nebraska—Lindsey Walsh, Account Director, Snitily Car; Jodi Paus, Art Director, Snitily Carr; John Kuehnert, Park Ranger, Scotts Bluff National Monument; Marci Mitchell, Administrative Support Assistant, National Park Service, Scotts Bluff National Monument; Mark Engler, Superintendent, Homestead National Monument of America

Nevada—Angela M. Froelich, Assistant to Media Relations, Travel Nevada

New Hampshire—Betty A. Gagne, Customer Service Assistant, Department of Resources and Economic Development, Division of Travel and Tourism Development; Stacy L. Bell, Department of Resources and Economic Development, Division of Travel and Tourism Development; Gary Richardson, Park Ranger, Coleman State Park; Colleen Mainville, Greeley Ponds

New Jersey—Jennifer Szczepanski, Public Information Assistant, Department of State, Division of Travel and Tourism; John R. Wright, Chief of Visitor Services, Delaware Water Gap National Recreation Area; Jude M. Pfister, D.Litt., Chief of Cultural Resources, Morristown NHP

New Mexico—Mike Stauffer, Communications Director, New Mexico Tourism Department; George D. Herring, Park Ranger, Interpretation Aztec Ruins National Monument; Russ Bodnar, Chief of Interpretation, Chaco Culture National Historical Park; Steve Riley, Superintendent, Gila Cliff Dwellings National Monument

New York—Ed Muhl, Director Tourism Operations, NYS Division of Tourism; John Williams, Photographer, New York State Parks, Long Island Region; Lee Werst, Chief of Interpretation, Women's Rights National Historical Park

North Carolina—Jennifer Francioni, Public Relations Representative, North Carolina Department of Commerce, Division of Tourism, Film and Sports Development; Paul Branch, Fort Macon State Park

North Dakota—Kim Schmidt, Public & Media Relations Director, North Dakota Department of Commerce–Tourism Division; Scooter Pursley at North Dakota Tourism Division; Judie Chrobak-Cox, Acting Chief of Interpretation, South Unit District Interpreter, Theodore Roosevelt National Park; Brian K. McCutchen, Superintendent, Knife River Indian Villages National Historic Site; Stacy High, Administrative Assistant, Fort Abraham Lincoln State Park

Ohio—Jessica Wagner, Public Relations Coordinator, Ohio Tourism Division; Karen Beckman, Assistant Manager, Lake Erie Islands State Park; Dean Alexander, Hopewell Culture National Historical Park

Oklahoma—Lindsay Vidrine, PR Director, Travel & Tourism Division, Oklahoma Tourism & Recreation Department

Oregon—Linea Carlson, Public Relations Coordinator, Travel Oregon; Frank Howard, Oregon Parks and Recreation Department

Pennsylvania—Melissa Orwan, Account Executive, Tierney Agency

Rhode Island—Joseph Blanchette, Communications Specialist, Rhode Island Tourism

South Carolina—Marc Rapport, Media Relations Manager Public Relations & Information, S.C. Department of Parks, Recreation & Tourism; Trampas Alderman, Manager, Rivers Bridge State Historic Site, SC Department of Parks, Recreation, and Tourism

South Dakota—Nick Fosheim, Media and Public Relations Intern, South Dakota Office of Tourism; Katherine Bogue, Fort Sisseton State Park; Connie Wolf, Administrative Assistant, Badlands National Park

Tennessee—Tara Leurs, News Bureau Editor, Tennessee Department of Tourist Development ; George Hatton, Pickett State Rustic Park

Texas—Nate Gieryn, Travel Research Specialist, Office of the Governor, Economic Development & Tourism State of Texas; Debra Bustos, Tourism Marketing Specialist, Office of the Governor, Economic Development & Tourism; Chuck Hunt, Superintendent, Fort Davis National Historic Site; Glen Korth, Park Manager, Monahans Sandhills State Park; John Moore, Park Specialist, Palmetto State Park

Utah—Clayton Scrivner, Media Relations, Utah Office of Tourism; Jonathan Hunt, Bear Lake State Park; Bruce Strom, Park Manager Wasatch, Mountain State Park; Brant Porter, Assistant Chief of Interpretation, Dinosaur National Monument, National Park Service; Alison Cebula, Park Naturalist, Escalante Petrified Forest State Park; Michael Franklin, Park Manager, Coral Pink Sand Dunes State Park; Steve Bridgehouse, Natural Bridges National Monument

Vermont—Christiane Skinner, Tourism Specialist, State of Vermont Department of Tourism & Marketing; Rochelle Skinner, Vermont State Parks, Department of Forests, Parks & Recreation

Virginia—Danielle Emerson, Public Relations, Virginia Tourism Corporation; Betsy Haynes, Park Ranger, Booker T. Washington National Monument

Washington—Kristin Jacobsen, Public Relations & Special Events Manager, Washington Tourism; Patti Wood, Interpretive Media Specialist, Mount Rainier National Park

West Virginia—Tricia Sizemore, Public Information Specialist, Department of Commerce, Communications; Michael A. Smith, Superintenden, Droop Mountain Battlefield and Beartown State Parks

Wisconsin—Lisa Marshall, Communications Coordinator, Wisconsin Department of Tourism; William H. Eldred, Ranger/Property Manager, Amnicon Falls State Park

Wyoming—Lori Hogan, Sr. Communications Specialist, Visit Wyoming

Photo Credits

Photo Credits continued

Dodson **193** *Both* Missouri Department of Natural Resources **194-198** Donnie Sexton/Travel Montana **199** Museum of the Rockies/Rob Outlaw**200** *Left* R. Neibel, Nebraska DED; *Right* NPS Photo **202** M. Forsberg, Nebraska DED **203** R. Neibel, Nebraska DED **204** *Top* Dan Christensen Photography; *Bottom* R. Neibel, Nebraska DED **205** *Top* M. Forsberg, Nebraska DED; *Bottom* R. Neibel, Nebraska DED **206** *Top* Aaron/Esto; *Bottom* Richard Rader Photography **207** NPS Photo **208** *Left* Nevada Commission on Tourism; *Right* Janet Schmidt **209-210** Nevada Commission on Tourism **211** iStock/Dave Rock **212** *Top* Lost City Museum Collection; *Bottom* Nevada Commission on Tourism **213** Nevada Commission on Tourism **214** *Left* Androscoggin Valley Camber of Commerce; *Right* New Hampshire Division of Parks & Recreation/Ellen Edersheim **216** *Top* iStock/Ken Brooks; *Bottom* New Hampshire Division of Parks & Recreation/Ellen Edersheim **217** *Top* NHDTTD; *Bottom* Excelsiorgarphics **218** Frank Gannon **219** Ralph Morang **220** *Left* Wetlands Institute; *Right* iStock/Tang's NatureLight Photography **221** *Both* K. Talasco **222** FMM/DLongo **223** NPS Photo **224** NJ DEP, Division of Parks & Forestry **225** Battleship New Jersey Museum and Memorial **226** *Top* NJ DEP, Division of Parks & Forestry; *Bottom* Shutterstock/Andrew F. Kazmierski **227-228** NJ DEP, Division of Parks & Forestry **229** *Top* Wetlands Institute; *Bottom* Courtesy of Wheaton Arts and Cultural Center **230** *Both* New Mexico Tourism Department **232** *Both* Sally King/NPS Photo **233** International Balloon Museum **234** *Both* New Mexico Tourism Department **235** NPS Photo **236-237** New Mexico Tourism Department **238** *Left* Shutterstock/artconcept; *Right* USFWS **240** *Left* VisitFingerLakes.com; *Right* Randall Tagg Photography **241** *Both* www.waltercolleyimages.com **242** Courtesy of the Thousand Islands Bridge Authority **243** *Top* National Bottle Museum; *Bottom* The Wild Center **244** Darren McGee, New York State Department of Economic Development **245** *Top* Courtesy of Metropolitan Museum of Art; *Bottom* Old Rhinebeck Aerodrome **246** *Top* Harry Zernike; *Bottom* The Jacques Marchais Museum of Tibetan Art **247** New York State Parks, Long Island Region **248** *Left* Bill Russ/North Carolina Department of Commerce. Division of Tourism, Film & Sports Development; *Middle* Shutterstock/Jill Lang; *Bottom* Shutterstock/Phil Anthony **249** NPS Photo, courtesy of Carl Sandburg Home NHS **250** *Top* N.C. Division of Parks and Recreation; *Bottom* Reed Gold Mine **251** North Carolina Department of Cultural Resources **252** *Top* Gov. Charles B. Aycock Birthplace State Historic Site; *Bottom* Bill Russ/North Carolina Department of Commerce. Division of Tourism, Film & Sports Development **253** *Both* Bill Russ/North Carolina Department of Commerce. Division of Tourism, Film & Sports Development **254** *Top* Shutterstock/Newton Page; *Bottom* North Carolina Department of Commerce **255** *Both* Bill Russ/North Carolina Department of Commerce. Division of Tourism, Film & Sports Development **256** *Left* North Dakota Tourism/David Lee; *Right* North Dakota Tourism/Ren Davis **258** North Dakota Tourism/Gene Kellogg **259** NPS Photo **260** North Dakota Tourism/Brian Payne **261** North Dakota Tourism/Bruce Wendt **262** *Both* Ohio Tourism Division **263** The Holden Arboretum **264** *Both* Ohio Tourism Division **265** Ohio Historical Society **266** The Bicycle Museum of America **267** *Top* Ohio Tourism Division; *Bottom* Warthers **268-269** Ohio Tourism Division **270** *Left* Woolaroc Museum, Bartlesville Oklahoma; *Right* Robert Spude/NPS Photo **272** *Top* Nell Thalasinos; *Bottom* Woolaroc Museum, Bartlesville Oklahoma **273** Will Rogers Memorial Museum **274** *Top* Steve Boots; *Bottom* Chisholm Trail Heritage Center **275** Jerry Dobbs **276** *Left* John Day Fossil Beds; *Right* Michael Mathers **278** *Both* Courtesy of Oregon Parks and Recreation Department **279** Shutterstock/zschnepf **280** Sumpter Valley Railway **281** High Desert Museum **282** Courtesy of Oregon Parks and Recreation Department **283** iStock/Mike Norton **284** *Left* U.S. Forest Service; *Right* DCNR **285** VisitErie.com **286** DCNR **287** *Top* Endless Mountains Visitors Bureau; *Bottom* Little League Baseball, Incorporated **288** *Top* Shawn P. Carey; *Bottom* Clyde Peeling's Reptiland **289** *Top* Bucks County Historical Society; *Bottom* Jack Carnell **290** DCNR **291** *Left* DCNR; *Top* Bedford County Conference and Visitors Bureau; *Right* National Watch & Clock Museum **292** Shutterstock/Zack

Frank **293** Courtesy of Friends of Laurel Hill Cemetery **294** *Left* The Preservation Society of Newport County; *Right* RI Historical Society **295** Culinary Arts Museum **296** Audubon Society Education Center **297** *Top* The Preservation Society of Newport County; *Bottom* Barbara Money/Audubon Society **298** *Left* S.C. Department of Parks, Recreation & Tourism; *Right* Perry Baker/SCPRT **300** Perry Baker/SCPRT **301** *Top* Perry Baker/SCPRT; *Bottom* South Carolina Cotton Museum, Inc. **302** *Top* Perry Baker/SCPRT; *Bottom* Sumter County Museum **303** Shutterstock/Joe White **304** *Left* Chapel in the Hills; *Right* LaQuita Shockley Owner of the Dakota Herald **306-307** Courtesy of South Dakota Office of Tourism **308** iStock/Jody Dingle **309** South Dakota State Historical Society **310-311** Courtesy of Tennessee Department of Tourist Development **312** *Left* Chucalissa Museum; *Right* Courtesy of Tennessee Department of Tourist Development **313** Courtesy of Tennessee Department of Tourist Development **314** Historic Falcon Manor/Dennis Keim **315** *Top* Courtesy of Tennessee Department of Tourist Development; *Bottom* Steve Freer **316-317** Courtesy of Tennessee Department of Tourist Development **318** *Left* Courtesy of Barrington Farm; *Right* Panhandle Plains Historic Museum **319** NPS Photo **320** *Top* Shutterstock/Mike Norton; *Bottom* Courtesy of Texas Visitors Bureau **321** Rhonda Hole/Cowgirl Hall of Fame **322** iStock/Dave Hughes Photography **323** The Presidential Museum **324** *Top* Courtesy of Luckenbach Texas, Inc.; *Bottom* Fort Concho **325** *Top* Courtesy of Antique Rose Emporium; *Bottom* Courtesy of St. Clare's Miniature Horse Farm **326** *Top* Shutterstock/Paul S. Wolf; *Bottom* Palmetto State Park **327** *Top* Shutterstock/James Beach; *Bottom (both)* Gladys Porter Zoo **328** *Left* iStock/Dess; *Right* Utah Office of Tourism/Frank Jensen **329** Utah Office of Tourism/Steve Greenwood **330** *Top* NPS Photo; *Bottom* Utah Office of Tourism/Steve Greenwood **331** *Left* iStock/ValuePix; *Right* iStock/Tonda **332** Shutterstock/Natalia Bratslavsky **333** Shutterstock/Alexey Stiop **334** *Left* Billings Farm & Museum; *Right* State of Vermont, Department of Tourism & Marketing **336** Vermont Department of Forest, Parks & Recreation **337** Karen Pike/State of Vermont, Department of Tourism & Marketing **338** Billings Farm & Museum **339** State of Vermont, Department of Tourism & Marketing **340** *Left* Bob Creamer/Mount Vernon Ladies' Association; *Right* Ron Blunt/courtesy Museum of the Shenandoah Valley **342** *Top* Virginia Department of Tourism; *Bottom* Allen Green/The Copper Shop **343** *Top* Crab Orchard Museum; *Bottom* Marianne Miller **344** *Both* Kathy Thompson **345** *Top* The Patrick Henry Memorial Foundation; *Bottom* Poe Museum **346** *Left* Washington State Tourism/Levy Sheckler; *Right* iStock/twphotos **347** iStock/Robert Koopmans **348** Courtesy of Michelle West-Loomis **349** Tacoma Pierce County Visitors Bureau **350** Washington State Tourism/LevySheckler **351** *Left* Washington State Parks; *Right* Lewis County Convention & Visitor Bureau/Sandy Baltazar **352** *Top* Shutterstock/Chris Mullins; *Bottom* iStock/Beisea **352** *Top* Mary Hill Museum; *Bottom* Whitman Mission **354** *Both* Steve J. Shaluta/West Virginia Department of Commerce **355** Berkeley County Historical Society **356** *Top* WVDNR West Virginia State Wildlife Center/Jack Mills; *Left* Blennerhassett Island Historical State Park; *Bottom* David Ede **357** *Left* Tom Oldham; *Right* NRAO/AUI **358-359** Steve J. Shaluta/West Virginia Department of Commerce **360** *Left* Mid-Continent Railway Museum; *Right* Wisconsin Department of Tourism/Bob Queen **361** RJ & Linda Miller Photography/Courtesy of Wisconsin Historical Society **362** *Top* Wisconsin Department of Tourism/Bob Queen; *Bottom* Crex Meadows Wildlife Area **363** Woodson Art Museum **364** RJ & Linda Miller Photography/Courtesy of Wisconsin Historical Society **365** *Top* International Crane Foundation; *Bottom* Mid-Continent Railway Museum **366** *Top* Courtesy of Wisconsin Historical Society; *Bottom* Courtesy of Ten Chimneys **367** RJ & Linda Miller Photography/Courtesy of Wisconsin Historical Society **368** *Left* Wyoming State Parks & Cultural Resources; *Right* Marke Gocke **369** Wyoming Travel & Tourism **370** Fred Pflughoft **371** Tom Laycock **372** Fred Pflughoft **373** *Top* Fred Pflughoft; *Bottom* Wyoming Travel & Tourism

Index

INDEX

INDEX

By ILENE COOPER

Illustrated by GABI SWIATKOWSKA

Abrams Books for Young Readers
New York

THE GOLDEN RULE

DO UNTO OTHERS
AS YOU WOULD
HAVE THEM
DO UNTO YOU

A boy and his grandfather stood on a city sidewalk looking up at the words printed on a billboard.

"Grandpa, what does that say?" the boy asked.

"**DO UNTO OTHERS AS YOU WOULD HAVE THEM DO UNTO YOU.** People all over the world call those words the Golden Rule."

"What does it mean?" The boy wanted to know. "And why is it golden?"

"It means this: Treat people the way you would like to be treated. It's golden because it's so valuable, and a way of living your life that's so simple, it shines."

Grandfather led the boy to another billboard, farther down the sidewalk. "Some people put the Golden Rule another way:

DO NOTHING TO OTHER PEOPLE THAT YOU WOULD NOT LIKE HAVING DONE TO YOU.

"Either way," he said, "it's a very good rule."

"Who's it for?" the boy asked.

"You, me. Anyone can practice the Golden Rule."

"A rule that's the same for children and grown-ups?"

"Same rule."

"There aren't too many rules like that."

"Very few."

"And it's for people everywhere?"

"Everywhere."

"Whatever their religion, people find the idea of the Golden Rule in their holy books," Grandfather said.

CHRISTIANITY SAYS:
You should love your neighbor as you love yourself.

JUDAISM SAYS:
What is hateful to you, do not do to your fellow humans.

ISLAM SAYS:
Hurt no one so that no one may hurt you.

HINDUISM SAYS:
This is the sum of duty: to do nothing to others which would cause them pain.

BUDDHISM SAYS:
Do not do to others what would hurt you.

THE SHAWNEE TRIBE SAYS:
Do not kill or injure your neighbor, for it is not he or she that you injure; you injure yourself.

The boy and his grandfather sat on a park bench.

"So, Grandpa, how can I start to practice the Golden Rule?"

"You begin by using your imagination."

"My imagination?"

"You imagine how someone else feels. For instance, a new child who is joining your class. How do you think that boy or girl is feeling?"

"New kids always look scared."

"Would you be scared if it was you?"

"Oh, yes."

"What would make you feel better?"

"If . . . if someone smiled at me."

"So to practice the Golden Rule, you would . . ."

"Smile at the new kid?"

"YOU'VE GOT IT! I bet you can think of other ways you'd like to be treated. And ways you wouldn't want to be treated. How do you feel when you're teased? Or bullied?"

"Sad."

"Yes."

"Mad."

"Yes."

"Small. I feel small."

"Sad, mad, small. Do you like feeling like that?"

"No."

"Neither does anyone else."

The boy thought for a moment about the Golden Rule. "I see. There are lots of things I can do. I should tell the truth because I don't like being lied to. I want people to listen to me, so I should listen to other people. When I'm sick, or when I'm tired, sometimes I need help. So I should offer my help to those who need it." "You're getting the idea." Grandfather nodded.

The boy looked at his grandfather. "Practicing the Golden Rule seems like it can be hard."

"I said it was simple. I didn't say it would always be easy."

"Grandpa," the boy said, "the Golden Rule is a very big thing, isn't it?"

"Very big. And very small. And very old. It's been around for thousands of years."

"Thousands of years? Well then, I don't think everyone is practicing the way they should. Otherwise, there wouldn't be so many problems. Between people. Between countries."

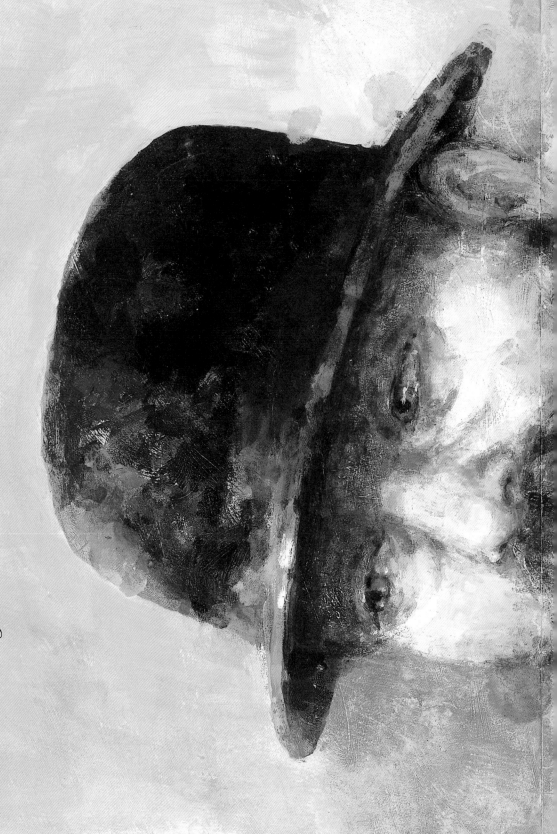

"You're right, my boy. I wonder how things would change if everyone lived by the Golden Rule."

"I think people would be nicer. Kinder. They'd act better toward their families and friends, and even strangers."

"What if countries lived by the Golden Rule?" Grandfather asked.

"Well, then people wouldn't want to hurt each other, because they don't like being hurt. Maybe there wouldn't be wars."

"That would be wonderful, wouldn't it?"

"Wonderful, Grandpa."

"But you can't make everyone in the world practice the Golden Rule. There's only one person you can ask to do that."

"Me?"

IT BEGINS WITH YOU.

"YOU. YOU."

For John, who makes it easy
to follow the Golden Rule
— I. C.

For my Smoogli and Żakoloogooms and Moi
— G. S.

Library of Congress Cataloging-in-Publication Data:

Cooper, Ilene.
The golden rule / by Ilene Cooper; illustrated by Gabi
Swiatkowska.

p. cm.

Summary: Grandfather explains that the Golden Rule is a simple
statement on how to live that can be practiced by people of all ages
and faiths, then helps his grandson figure out how to apply the rule
to his own life.

ISBN 13: 978-0-8109-0960-1
ISBN 10: 0-8109-0960-X
[1. Golden rule—Fiction. 2. Conduct of life—Fiction.]
I. Swiatkowska, Gabi, ill. II. Title.

PZ7.C7856Col 2007
[E]—dc22
2006013333

Text copyright © 2007 Ilene Cooper
Illustrations copyright © 2007 Gabi Swiatkowska

Book design by Chad W. Beckerman
Production manager: Alexis Mentor

Published in 2007 by Abrams Books for Young Readers,
an imprint of Harry N. Abrams, Inc.

Printed and bound in China
10 9 8 7 6 5 4 3 2

HNA
harry n. abrams, inc.
a subsidiary of La Martinière Groupe
115 West 18th Street
New York, NY 10011
www.hnabooks.com

AUTHOR'S NOTE

In a world where it sometimes seems there is more that divides people than unites them, it is heartening that the Golden Rule is an underlying moral principle found in almost every religion and culture. The Golden Rule appears in different forms in various holy books, and translations sometimes state the rules in different ways. In some cases I have chosen to simplify the language to make the statements more understandable to children. Here are the original forms of the Golden Rule and where they are found.

CHRISTIANITY (KING JAMES BIBLE):

Matthew 19:19: Thou shalt love thy neighbor as thyself.

Luke 6:31: And as ye would that men should do to you, do ye also to them likewise.

JUDAISM:

Leviticus 19:18: Thou shalt love thy neighbor as thyself.

Talmud, Sabbat 31a (attributed to the rabbi Hillel the Elder): What is hateful to you, do not to your fellow man. This is the law: all the rest is commentary.

BUDDHISM:

Udana-Varga 5:18: Hurt not others in ways that you yourself would find hurtful.

ISLAM:

Muhammad, the Farewell Sermon: Hurt no one so that no one may hurt you.

Sunnah: No one of you is a believer until he desires for his brother that which he desires for himself.

HINDUISM:

Mahabharata 5:15:17: Do naught unto others which would cause you pain if done to you.

(The Hindu belief in karma also has a deep connection to the Golden Rule.)

SHAWNEE NATIVE AMERICANS:

Preserved by Thomas Wildcat Alford: Do not kill or injure your neighbor, for it is not him that you injure; you injure yourself. But do good to him; therefore, add to his days of happiness as you add to your own.

Forms of the Golden Rule are also found among the ancient Egyptians and Romans; in Jainism, Shintoism, Sikhism, Sufism, and humanism; and in the Bahá'í faith. It is my hope that introducing children to the Golden Rule—and discussing its meaning and implications—will give them an early understanding of how to treat and take care of one another.

ARTIST'S NOTE

The Golden Rule is a remarkably conceptual book. Religion tends to dwell in the place of personal philosophy and way of life. It stays close to one's heart. Not an easy subject to broach, especially while making it "safe" for one to look at others' beliefs and appreciate their different opinions and views.

I believe the text successfully unites the many versions of a single truth, so I wanted the art to bring its own layer, complementing the text but not defining it. The imagery for each religion is inspired directly by the original art I associate with that faith. I decided to keep the spreads rich in visual patterns offering a rather loose connection to the text, which, I believe, allows the space for readers' own thoughts and interpretations.

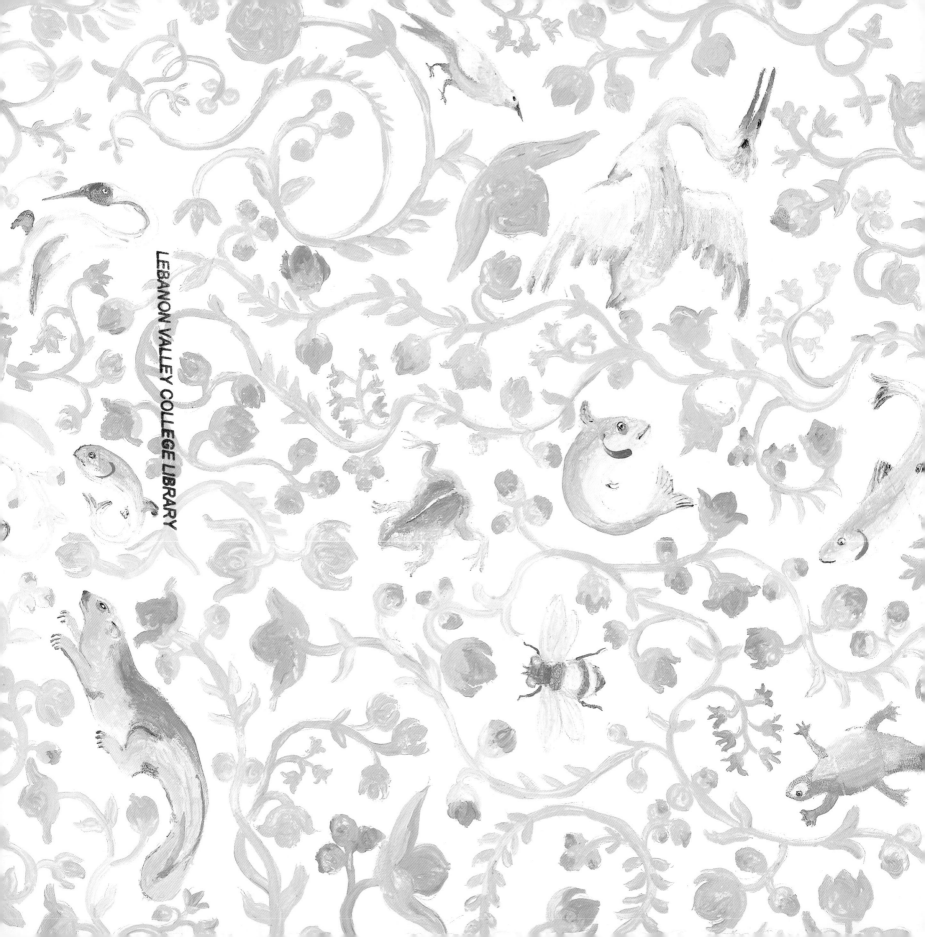